Fading Victory

Fading Victory

THE DIARY OF
Admiral Matome Ugaki

1941–1945

·

Foreword by Gordon W. Prange

Masataka Chihaya, Translator

with Donald M. Goldstein and Katherine V. Dillon

UNIVERSITY OF PITTSBURGH PRESS

Published by the University of Pittsburgh Press, Pittsburgh, Pa. 15260
Copyright © 1991, University of Pittsburgh Press
Eurospan, London
Manufactured in the United States of America

Library of Congress Cataloging-in-Publication Data

Ugaki, Matome, 1890–1945.
  [Sensōroku. English]
    Fading victory: the diary of Admiral Matome Ugaki, 1941–1945 / Masataka
Chihaya, translator; foreword by Gordon Prange, Donald M. Goldstein and
Catherine V. Dillon, editors.
       p. cm.
    Translation of: Sensōroku.
    Includes bibliographical references and index.
    ISBN 0-8229-3665-8.—ISBN 0-8229-5429-X (pbk.)
    1. Ugaki, Matome, 1890–1945—Diaries. 2. World War, 1939–1945—Naval
operations, Japanese. 3. World War, 1939–1945—Personal narratives, Japanese.
4. Admirals—Japan—Diaries. 5. Japan. Kaigun—Biography. I. Prange, Gordon William, 1910–. II. Goldstein, Donald M. III. Dillon, Catherine. IV. Title.
D777.U3513 1991
940.54'5952'092—dc20
                                                                    90-12904
                                                                    CIP

A CIP catalogue record for this book is available from the British Library.

CONTENTS

Contents

LIST OF ABBREVIATIONS

AA	antiaircraft
ACS	assistant chief of staff
AF	air force
AKA	attack cargo ship
AKD	converted destroyer transport
AM	minesweeper
AP	transport
APD	destroyer transport
AV	seaplane tender
B-17	army four-engine heavy bomber, *Flying Fortress*
B-24	army four-engine heavy bomber, *Liberator*
B-25	army two-engine medium bomber, *Mitchell*
B-26	army two-engine medium bomber, *Marauder*
B-29	army four-engine heavy bomber, *Superfortress*
BB	battleship
Brig. Gen.	brigadier general
CA	heavy cruiser
C.A.P.	combat air patrol
Capt.	captain
Cardiv	carrier division
Cdg.	commanding
CG	commanding general
CinC	commander in chief
CL	light cruiser
CM	minelayer
cm	centimeter
Cmdr.	commander (rank)
CNO	chief of naval operations
Co.	company

CO	commanding officer
Col.	colonel
Crudiv	cruiser division
C/S	chief of staff
CV	aircraft carrier
CVE	escort aircraft carrier
CVL	light aircraft carrier
DD	destroyer
DE	destroyer escort
DM	destroyer minelayer
DT	destroyer transport
Ens.	ensign
F4O	navy fighter, *Corsair*
F4F	navy one-engine fighter, *Wildcat*
F6F	navy one-engine fighter, *Hellcat*
GS	General Staff
H.I.H.	His Imperial Highness
H.I.M.	His Imperial Majesty
H.M.A.S.	His Majesty Australian ship
H.M.S.	His Majesty's ship
H.N.M.S.	Her Netherlands Majesty's ship
IJN	Imperial Japanese Navy
IJND	Imperial Japanese Navy Directive
IJNO	Imperial Japanese Navy Order
Inf.	infantry
kg	kilogram
km	kilometer
LCI	landing craft, infantry
LCI(G)	landing craft, infantry, gunboat
LCS	landing craft, support
LCS(L)	landing craft, support, large
LCT(L)	landing craft, tank, large
LSM	landing ship, medium
LSM(R)	landing ship, medium, rocket
LST	landing ship, tank
Lt. Col.	lieutenant colonel
Lt. Gen.	lieuenant general
Maj. Gen.	major general

NGS	Naval General Staff
P-38	army two-engine fighter, *Lightning*
P-39	army one-engine fighter, *Aircobra*
P-40	army one-engine fighter, *Warhawk*
P-51	army one-engine fighter, *Mustang*
PBY	navy two-engine patrol bomber, *Catalina*
PGS	mine disposal vessel
PT	motor torpedo boat
RADM	rear admiral
RAF	Royal Air Force
Rgt.	regiment
RN	Royal Navy
RNN	Royal Netherlands Navy
SBD	navy one-engine dive bomber, *Dauntless*
Sublt.	Sublieutenant
TF	task force
TG	task group
Transdiv	transport division
USA	United States Army
USMC	United States Marine Corps
USN	United States Navy
USS	United States ship
VADM	vice admiral
VCS	vice chief of staff
VLR	very long range
WO	warrant officer
YMS	motor minesweeper
WP	patrol vessel

FOREWORD

The diary of Vice Admiral Matome Ugaki is the best documentation of the last days of Japan's road to war in the Pacific and her conflict with the United States from the hand of any Japanese public official in any branch of the government. Thorough, revealing, frank, and analytical, his account follows events closely, with lengthy entries covering virtually every day of the war. In fact, the original manuscript in Japanese fills fifteen volumes.

Ugaki was well qualified to keep such a record, for his career in the Imperial Navy had been long and distinguished. Born on 15 February 1890, in Seto-machio, Okayama Prefecture, to Zengo and Chiku Ugaki, he entered the Naval Cadet School at Etajima on 11 September 1909 and graduated on 17 July 1912. He had the usual training of every Japanese naval officer—sea duty complemented with experience as a staff officer ashore. In 1922, he was already a student at the Naval Staff College in Tokyo and graduated in 1923. Then he served on the Naval General Staff, studied in Germany, and returned to teach in the Naval Staff College. He later became captain of the battleship *Hyuga* and was promoted to rear admiral on 15 November 1938.

On 10 August 1941, he was appointed chief of staff of the Combined Fleet. He served Admiral Isoroku Yamamoto in that capacity until both were shot down over Bougainville Island on 18 April 1943, resulting in the death of Yamamoto and the serious wounding of Ugaki. On 22 May 1943, he was attached to the Naval General Staff for hospitalization and recuperation.

Ugaki again went to sea on 25 February 1944, in command of the First Battleship Division, which included the superbattleships *Yamato* and *Musashi*. After much action, this division was disbanded and he returned to Tokyo on 15 November 1944, pending reassignment. Then, on 19 February 1945, he was entrusted with command of the Fifth Air Fleet on Kyushu. From this southern outpost on the Japanese homeland, Ugaki organized the famous Special Attack Corps (*Tokkotai*) and directed the final effort to stem the rising American tide in the Pacific.

The Ugaki diary gives the reader intimate glimpses of the Imperial Navy at war. One follows the admiral to a conference in the Combined Fleet or a meeting with his own staff officers. One stands beside him aboard *Yamato,* when the admiral prepared a personal, on-the-spot description of the sinking of her sister ship, *Musashi,* in the Battle of Leyte Gulf, or during an hour of last-ditch operational planning in a dirty bunker on Kyushu where Ugaki organized and directed the suicide attacks against U.S. forces on Okinawa.

Not only is the diary full of strategy, tactics, planning, combat operations, military thinking, and domestic politics, but also contains critical and historically valuable postmortems of Japan's conduct of the war, plus interesting appraisals of the Americans, their methods, decisions, weaknesses, strengths, and virtues. Germany, Italy, Britain, the Netherlands, Australia, the Soviet Union, and China—the touchstone of Japanese policy—all come within the range of Ugaki's probing and skillful brush.

The admiral was a vigorous representative of the profession he served dutifully for almost thirty-five years. Secure in his belief in and devotion to Japanese destiny, policies, thought, and tradition, Ugaki was a patriot to the core. He was also a man of iron will, burning pride, and fierce determination. Convinced of the rightness of Japan's cause, and passionately loyal to his emperor and country, Ugaki was willing to die for either or both. His multiplex character, the soul-searching pressures of the war, and the natural churning of his reflective mind caused him to record many philosophical reflections on life and death. He loved life, lived it fully but did not fear death.

One can clearly follow the changing contours of Ugaki's thinking through the course of his diary. At the outset, one sees him as a proud, arrogant, and boastful antagonist glorying in Japan's spectacular triumphs as she rode the crest of early victories. He is electrified by his country's daring plunge to glory, convinced of her ultimate victory, and ever grateful to a beneficent providence that has guided Japan for ages eternal. The Greater East Asia Co-Prosperity Sphere would be established and the haughty Anglo-Saxons taught a bitter lesson.

Gradually, another phase of Ugaki's war career emerges. He tasted the full bitterness of defeat in June 1942 when the Americans sank the carriers *Akagi, Kaga, Hiryu,* and *Soryu* in the crucial Battle of Midway. In April 1943 Ugaki was shot down while on an inspection tour of the Solomons area front. Though he miraculously survived, he lost his beloved commander in chief, Admiral Yamamoto, symbol of Japan's destiny at sea and the bold architect of her daring attack against Pearl Harbor.

One sees Ugaki taking stock of the situation, coming to grips with harsh realities that refuse to be rationalized away. As he tries to figure out what has gone wrong with Japan's grandiose plan of war, his thoughts race up one channel of his troubled mind, hurriedly backtrack, and go scurrying down another. Facing the undeniable fact of America's growing strength and the certainty of Japan's ebbing tide is for Ugaki a slow, difficult process. Still grimly determined and defiantly buoyant, he does not want to believe what is happening to his country. He is at a loss to fathom the phenomenon and helpless to prevent it.

The spectacular victories of American forces in 1944 and 1945 bring Ugaki to the last stages of his diary. During much of this period he commanded the First Battleship Division. He was on hand in the battle of the Philippine Sea in June 1944 when Japan lost her last reserves of naval aviation. He also fought through the entire battle of Leyte Gulf when the United States gained a strategic foothold in the Philippines in late October and reduced the Japanese Navy to a "fishpond fleet." From February 1945, as commander of the Fifth Air Fleet, Ugaki lived through the terrible days of the B-29 raids, Iwo Jima, Okinawa, and the atom bomb.

Throughout all this, the reader comes to know Ugaki the man as well as Ugaki the admiral. His diary gives a clear picture of his daily life, with personal insights into a fully realized human being who could enjoy with zest the loveliness of spring, a sunset at sea, or meeting an old friend on leave. One sees Ugaki praying to his ancestral gods, composing a few lines of poetry, and caring faithfully for the members of his family. Always he spices his diary with frankly expressed prejudices and ideas.

By the summer of 1945, Ugaki is torn between the two major aspects of his own personality. The pragmatic professional sailor sees all too clearly that Japan's position is hopeless, while the patriot—the almost mystical patriot—wants Japan to fight to the last man, and he tries to inject into his entries notes of hope and courage. Finally came the "hateful news" of Japan's surrender, and the emperor's broadcast on 15 August 1945.

The loss of the war was the end of Ugaki's world. He could not bear to see the holy soil of Japan and her proud people under enemy occupation. Nor could he allow himself to go on living after he had sent so many brave young men to certain death. The least he could do was follow in their footsteps and die in the spirit of the Special Attack Corps. So, on 15 August 1945, he decided on a suicide mission against U.S. forces on Okinawa. Although his friends tried to dissuade him, he would not reconsider his decision. As he was not a pilot, he called for volunteers to take him on his last mission. About a dozen young men vied for the honor.

During Ugaki's last hour on Japanese soil he composed his final entry. Because the diary contained highly personal and secret matters, he entrusted it to the secretary of his "classmate association," so that it might "never fall into enemy hands."

Before enplaning, Ugaki stripped his uniform of all insignia. He addressed his corpsmen and spoke to his immediate staff. Taking with him only his binoculars and the small sword Yamamoto had given him, Ugaki boarded the dive bomber *Comet* for his final flight.

Gordon W. Prange
University of Maryland
College Park, Maryland

PREFACE

During his tour of duty in General Douglas MacArthur's headquarters in Tokyo, Gordon W. Prange became acquainted with Admiral Matome Ugaki's diary and was enthusiastic about it, not only as a unique source document but for its intrinsic interest. He secured the English-language rights and found the diary invaluable in preparing his books about Pearl Harbor and Midway. Recognizing the potential value of the diary to students of World War II and fans of naval history, he hoped and planned to see it published in English. Indeed, he believed that no one could write about and fully understand the Pacific war without having access to the Ugaki diary. In anticipation, he prepared a foreword for an English-language version and, with very minor changes, it is the foreword published here.

Until the publication of this volume, Ugaki's diaries had not been available to the English-speaking public, having been previously accessible only to those well-versed in Japanese. Kyodo of Tokyo published it in that language under the title *Senso roku: Ugaki Matome nikki* (*Seaweeds of War: The Diary of Matome Ugaki*) in 1953.

Fading Victory is the seventh of the manuscripts we have published from the Prange files. The previous six were *At Dawn We Slept, Miracle at Midway, Target Tokyo: The Story of the Sorge Spy Ring, Pearl Harbor: Verdict of History, December 7, 1941: The Day the Japanese Attacked Pearl Harbor,* and *God's Samurai*. While Prange was not the author of *Fading Victory*, publication in English would not have been possible without him.

Our portion of this project has been confined to consolidation, explanatory interpolations, and refinement of the English translation. The latter presented a special problem: No one could fault Chihaya on either vocabulary, grammar, or elegance; however, Japanese is one of the most difficult of all languages to render into English. As a result, what may be a perfect technical translation may strike the English-speaking reader as a bit unpolished. We have tried to avoid this while at the same time keeping to Ugaki's own style. Lay readers may find his style somewhat stiff and formal; however, those with experience in the armed forces will recognize it as "militaryese," if we may coin a word. An American admiral of comparable position and education who kept an equally detailed diary would have used much the same manner of writing.

Ugaki began each day's entry by recording the weather. We have left these entries in place because they are more than examples of meticulous notekeeping. The weather played a very important role in the type of naval and air engagements that concerned Ugaki.

Regardless of where he was actually located, Ugaki dated his entries in Tokyo time. Thus, for example, the Pearl Harbor attack is dated 8 December. We have given all times in the twenty-four-hour system, which is in use throughout the military, and which avoids any possible confusion between A.M. and P.M. Many geographical names have changed since 1941; however, we have retained the names in effect in Ugaki's time.

The text is divided into twelve parts preceded by brief comments that touch upon section highlights and, where necessary, give some background.

The main body of the diary is in standard print. Minor explanations, such as full names in place of surnames, are placed in brackets.

Bracketed paragraphs represent instances where the diary was condensed due to Ugaki's discussion of routine events. The enormous size of the diary made full publication of such inconsequential events impractical. Nothing of historical importance has been deleted; we have consolidated, not omitted. Eventually, the full text in its manuscript form will be available for examination in the Prange collection at the University of Maryland.

Bracketed italicized material represent major interpolations that help to place Ugaki's narrative in historical perspective.

The diary was originally translated by Lieutenant Commander (Baron) Masamitsu Takasaki, IJN Reserve. The version which Prange used was almost entirely the work of Masataka Chihaya, former commander, IJN. Chihaya's translation begins with 1 January 1942. Shinobu Higashi, a Nisei employed by Associated Press, translated the 1941 portion.

Chihaya was eminently suited to translate Ugaki's diary: he served throughout the Pacific war, knew many of the individuals mentioned in the diary, is thoroughly acquainted with naval terminology and material, and has an excellent command of English. He corrected our original draft, gave us much-needed encouragement, and undertook the tedious task of checking the proper names. In addition, he wrote the epilogue based on material available to him in Japan. In a very real sense, this is his book.

We believe Ugaki would approve our dedicating this translation of his diary to the memory of those on both sides who lost their lives in the Pacific war.

Donald M. Goldstein, Ph.D.
University of Pittsburgh
Pittsburgh, Pennsylvania

Katherine V. Dillon
CWO, USAF (Ret.)
Arlington, Virginia

Fading Victory

I

Now Our Combined
Fleet Forces Are Deploying

Preface through 7 December 1941

T HE PREFACE *with which Ugaki begins his journal reveals that he had no doubt this would be a "war diary." Obviously he believed that the march of events over the past four years could reach only one destination. His attitude toward Japan's policies was by no means one of unquestioning acceptance; yet his duty as an officer gave him no choice but to follow once the course had been set. For example, he had opposed the Tripartite Pact, understanding that it would lead to trouble with the United States; however, once it was signed, he attended the celebration so as not to divorce himself from his country's policy. He also understood the good sense of having at least a temporary rapprochement with the Soviet Union, despite his dislike of that country. In this he came up against "the unwilling army."*

This was inevitable, for it was at the root of the interservice antagonism that surfaces occasionally throughout the diary. In brief, the navy's strategy was predicated upon conflict with the United States and Great Britain, and hopefully to command the Pacific and the Asiatic seas; the army visualized war with the Soviet Union and eventual exploitation of the Asian landmass.

Meanwhile, relations with the United States were rapidly reaching stalemate. The day Ugaki selected to begin the main body of his diary is significant of that fact, for on 16 October 1941, the Konoye Cabinet fell and Japan's government came into the hands of General Tojo.

In the following entries we follow the Combined Fleet and its chief of staff as they prepare for war with the United States, Great Britain, and the Netherlands. We see the top brass absorbed in war plans, coordinating with the army in the massive Southern Operation, and engaged in fleet training. We catch glimpses of the preparations for the Pearl Harbor attack, and throughout watch the Combined Fleet command and staff anxiously following political developments at home and the progress of the talks in Washington between Secretary of State Cordell Hull and Japanese Ambassador Admiral Kichisaburo Nomura.

3

The Hull Note of 26 November disappointed Ugaki, who considered it an insult; now all Japan could do was "make short work of the United States."

If he entertained any doubts that Japan could indeed beat the United States "into fits," Ugaki did not confide then to his diary in this period. On the contrary, he genuinely believed in the coming war as being necessary to Japan's continued existence as a nation. He was enthusiastic about the Pearl Harbor operation, considerably less so about the First Air Fleet's commander in chief and chief of staff. At this stage of his life, Ugaki was very much the samurai—by no means unintelligent but almost blusteringly convinced of his own ability and valor—and was ready, even eager, to die for his country.

A theme which weaves through the rest of the entries already appears in the diary—Ugaki's fascination with suicide. He expressed admiration and praise for the crews of the midget submarines that were to engage in the Pearl Harbor attack and whom no one expected to return. He paid no such tribute to the naval airmen who would also be risking their lives in American territory but who, presumably, hoped to live through the engagement to fight again.

In this as in other sections, Ugaki had to balance candor against security and on the whole did very well. The diary sheds some light on a few controversial points. While Ugaki didn't attend briefings before the throne, he makes it clear that the upper echelon in Tokyo kept the emperor au courant of events. Ugaki did not record in his diary what he thought of Hirohito's reported words and actions. He had an almost superstitious reverence for his emperor and would never dream of questioning, much less criticizing, anything issuing from the throne.

As to the Pearl Harbor attack, Ugaki's entries leave no doubt that the task force maintained radio silence on its voyage to Hawaii. And Imperial Order No. 12, authorizing the navy "to use arms after 0000 8 December" was opened by naval general staff direction on December 2 (Japanese time), whereupon Ugaki issued the famous message: "Climb Mt. Niitaka 1208."

Regrettably, from a historical point of view, Ugaki did not give a more complete, well-rounded picture of the personality and work patterns of that remarkable man, Admiral Yamamoto. Yet Ugaki was uniquely placed to do so, for as Yamamoto's chief of staff he was quartered on the same ship, frequented the same bridge, and was in almost minute-by-minute contact with the admiral. Obviously Ugaki both liked and respected his chief, and what he did set down on paper is revealing and interesting. The two admirals would experience both glory and grief together in the days following this period of preparation.

Preface. [*Here Ugaki begins his diary.*] Four years have passed since the Chinese Incident [*as the Japanese called their war with China*] started,[1] but we have a long way to go before we can reach our goal. Changes in the development of the situation during these few years, especially the outbreak of the second European war in the northern part of Europe, our empire's entrance into the Axis alliance, together with the China Incident—these events are both nominally and virtually international and worldwide, and the latter two are inseparable from the former. Did the persons responsible for starting the incident ever dream or realize that it would eventually develop into the present state? We can't be proud of human wisdom. However, for two and a half years, holding the important office of chief of the First Bureau, Naval General Staff,² I have tried my best to solve the problems of the incident, but in vain.

I was also, however, one of those responsible for consenting, against my will, to the Tripartite Alliance of Germany, Italy, and Japan last November [sic].³ I put in an appearance at the official residence of the minister of foreign affairs where they drank in celebration of the signing which had been done in Berlin, although I usually refrained from appearing at gatherings of that sort. Before I joined the party, I said to one of my fellow staff officers, Captain [Takeji] Ohno, and to Captain [Tasuku] Nakazawa, "I decided to go today because I want to clarify the Naval General Staff's responsibility, in the capacity of one of those concerned with it, though I don't know whether this will turn out to be a victory cup or a bitter dose for the future empire."

A year has passed since then, and relations between the United States and Japan have become more serious. The China Incident, the Tripartite Alliance, and the occupation of northern French Indochina (last year) form the remote causes; the immediate one is the occupation of southern French Indochina, which took place at the middle of this year.⁴ I am one of those who enforced the decision for the latter at the council in the imperial presence last year. On reflection, I should blame myself first before I accuse others.

As for the problems of the Tripartite Alliance, I had already presupposed that the alliance would lead the relationship of Japan with the United States to its present condition. Accordingly, I opposed it twice at the liaison meetings between the Naval General Staff and the Navy Ministry. Both the minister of the navy [Admiral Koishiro Oikawa] and the director of the Bureau of Naval Affairs [Rear Admiral Takasumi Oka] approved of it. The vice chief of the General Staff [Vice Admiral Nobutake Kondo] never said a word, though he should have spoken up on such an occasion. The vice minister [of the navy, Vice Admiral Teijiro] Toyoda assumed a cautious attitude toward it. Finally, the minister said very simply, in a frank and conciliatory manner, "How about giving general approval to it at this point?"

Then I answered, "If you are going to do it, there is nothing for me to do but follow you. But, in case the United States should enter the war, it's absolutely necessary for Japan to act independently and autonomously." And, once it was agreed upon, the Naval General Staff determined to set about preparations to dispatch fleets against the United States, instead of waiting until the treaty was concluded, and arranged to emphasize the urgency of naval war preparations at the coming council in the imperial presence with regard to the treaty. Thanks to the minister's considerable efforts at this point, various preparations made fair process. Our navy had been deadlocked on account of shortages of material, but on the strength of this situation could promote its preparations, fortunately or unfortunately. This meant that one of the hidden objectives of the treaty from the naval point of view, or rather what I wished, was obtained.

At the same time, there is a problem with Soviet Russia. The object of the German-Japanese Alliance, demanding our toil and care in the first part of 1941, was settlement of our Russian problems; so the alliance may be considered an extension of the Joint Defense Agreement. I had cherished the idea that Japan should ally with Russia. I brought it before a meeting, but the result was an unpleasant waste of time with the unwilling army. But this ended with the resignation of the Baron [Kiichiro] Hiranuma Cabinet, which declared, "Too uncanny complications." [*This odd phrase* (fukuzatsu-kaiki) *was an expression in vogue in Japan's journalistic world at the time.*][5]

What was done last year makes the United States (England) our opponent(s); this seems to conform to the empire's objective. Germany has already concluded a Non-Aggression Treaty with Russia. From these circumstances comes my belief that one of our main objectives should be to join hands with Russia, believing [Heinrich] Stahmer's statement that he would take the initiative in mediating the trouble between Japan and Russia because of the above-mentioned treaty. This meant that our empire would be stuck in the mud in case Russia should become our enemy besides America, England, Holland, and China. In order to avert the worst such situation, I tried to persuade people into making common cause with Russia, even though I don't like Russia very much. The situation was urgent. [Foreign Minister Yosuke] Matsuoka's going to Europe, which caused such diverse opinions in our country, finally came about last March. At the beginning of April, the Russo-Japanese Diplomatic Adjustment Treaty was effected between those two countries, to my relief. On 10 April I was newly appointed commander of the Eighth Heavy Cruiser Division [*Tone* and *Chikuma*], being relived of my post at the Naval General Staff.

But on 22 June Germany declared war against Russia! What a cynical world we live in! It seems [Adolf] Hitler can make fools of people.

Though we have been stressing that the unexpected can happen by crying "Wolf! Wolf!" for several years in order to maintain and heighten the morale of our country, nation, and army, to be ready for an emergency and to face strong enemies, yet people have become accustomed to it, to my regret. But now big wolves, several huge ones at that, are lurking around us.

The Nomura-Hull talks had started already, beginning last March or April. [*Admiral Kichisaburo Nomura was Ambassador to the United States; Cordell Hull was U.S. Secretary of State.*] Since our occupation of southern French Indochina, the attitude of the United States had turned firm and positive, and it cut off our way of obtaining oil by freezing our funds. Trade with the United States was discontinued.⁶ Seeing these unfavorable changes, [Prime Minister Prince Fumimaro] Konoye took a step forward and sent a message to the president of the United States [Franklin D. Roosevelt], proposing that they hold a Pacific conference to arrange diplomatic adjustments between the two countries. After fifty days, an answer to that came on 2 October, after much meandering, because of the president's policy of delay. Of course, what it stated was discouraging to us Japanese.⁷ The most important and impassable barriers are the request for evacuation of our forces from China, and the United States's attitude of not recognizing our superior position in the western Pacific, including China.

As I see it, the army insists on no more discussion about this matter, and the government and the navy want to negotiate again. It won't be possible for us to continue the parley, even if we hope to, until [the Americans] meet our minimum demands which were agreed upon at the council in the imperial presence. Rain—or storm? A final situation—the most serious one, as we had expected—is gradually approaching. This war will be the greatest on record, and a matter of vital importance to the welfare of our empire. With due reverence, I imagine the matter is causing His Imperial Majesty a good deal of concern.

Once the cabinet decision is made, our Combined Fleet will proceed to its post with the mission of placing the empire in a position of perfect security, overcoming our outnumbering enemy with the utmost efforts of our numerically inferior officers and men. This mission is by no means usual. Though the way to our victory is not an easy one to follow, yet there is nothing that cannot be obtained when preparedness for ultimate victory is secured, a far-sighted scheme worked out in detail, both officers and men remain faithful to the emperor with one mind, and everything is done with dauntless resolution.

This is one of the paragraphs that I drew up myself for the commander in chief's address of instruction the other day.

I know there are enough reasons to justify the outbreak of war when war breaks out, but some circumlocution is necessary until it's finally decided. This also applied in the case of the Russo-Japanese War which caused uproarious disputes at home before its opening, and began "after ten years of our hard struggles against fortune." [*Translator's note: from the military point of view.*] This time, by June 1939, the consensus was reached the war would be inevitable, but the actual opening of the war came the next February. When we think about it, arms are the most serious matter for the state. This is especially true this time, because the situation is quite unlike the Russo-Japanese War. Since we have long followed the principal policy of avoiding trouble with the United States and not fighting with her, it won't be easy to reverse this policy. Certain steps will be necessary to get there, and I think the process by which matters are moving toward that end has already been appearing.

Unless I take up my pen beginning with this introduction, the following diary won't hang together. It's true that I don't know any cardinal state secrets, now that I'm serving at sea far from the center of government, but I'm sure it will be necessary to record frankly in my diary about matters of official business that won't appear on official records, my opinions, my impressions, my speeches and actions, and my private matters, without regard to distinction, as they come into my mind day by day. This will be of some use to someone else in the future, because of my past guilt in bringing events to the state they're in today, and because of my present post as chief of staff of the Combined Fleet that carries the burden of the welfare of the state. Accordingly, it will be appropriate to give this diary the name "Wastebasket of War" or, rather, "Seaweeds of War."

Thursday, 16 October 1941. Fine, Off Murozumi, on board *Nagato* [flagship of the Combined Fleet]. Each group of the Combined Fleet, except the First Fleet and the First Battleship Division, headed for its training spot on the 14th of this month. Murozumi is isolated, as it will be. The units are perfectly at home with each other in training day and night, "enemy" planes and submarines attacking the leviathan at anchor, in accordance with the Second Special Training Plan.

At 1830 the radio announced that the third Konoye Cabinet resigned en bloc. The main reason he gave up was broadcast as being that his cabinet colleagues cannot be of one mind in deciding important national policy. Of course, that means the problems with the United States. And no doubt it is due to the answer from the United States on the 2nd. [*Ugaki referred to* the "oral statement" that Hull gave Nomura in reply to Japan's proposals of 6, 23, and 27 September 1941.] I feel it rather too late to expect Konoye to succeed. Concessions have to be made in the adjustment of diplomatic relations. In this case, concessions would have to be beyond the minimum decided at the council in the imperial presence.[8] If that were done, the result would be that the China Incident, which has cost 150,000 souls and more than fifteen billion yen in war costs, will be all for nothing, and the idea of establishing the Greater East Asia Co-prosperity Sphere must be given up as a fruitless dream. Konoye, who has been responsible for them from the beginning, will not be able to find it in his heart to do so. Will he then choose to open a war? This needs a prompt decision. Rather strenuous opposition can be expected among the cabinet ministers. It is a deadlock. I realize that the only alternative left for him was to abandon the cabinet.

Is no one else among our politicians but Konoye capable of being premier now? I think there should be, and is. But in fact a man of ability worthy of such an important responsibility usually turns up in some more remote position. After sticking in such mire as this, probably no one will be willing to wear his mantle.

Konoye is "a lord who wears long sleeves at court" [*i.e., an easy-going, leisurely man*]. He used to abandon anything once he lost interest in it. Of course, this time will be no exception. At the Diet session last year in the presence of His Imperial Majesty, he gave many assurances of his readiness which sounded soothing to our ears, but I wondered whether he had a sincere love for the state and sufficient patriotism to do his bit unselfishly. Still, today's crisis is too much for a dilettante. I would rather admire Konoye if he were to reform his cabinet with the purpose of purging the moderate faction. But I doubt if he can do this on his own responsibility. Then who will succeed him? A navy man? Or army? And can he win the war? Or will it come about after another political change? One way or another, we have no time to lose. After the cabinet is formed, much time will be required before our great plan can be framed. During that period, their [the Western allies] war preparations will climb hand over hand, while we shall fall into poverty by inches, expending the oil on hand. A day's delay costs us that much disadvantage. The conclusion is to place our state under a military administration, if need be, at one bound.

[On Friday, 17 October 1941, the fleet was so busy training at sea that it neglected to celebrate Harvest Thanksgiving Day, for which Ugaki had "no words to apologize." As they practiced firing, he reflected that soon they would be shooting in earnest.]

I ordered one of the staff to put down what was broadcast. Reportedly the Council of Chief Vassals who had served as premier was held at court in the morning. It came over the air at night that His Majesty asked [War Minister] Lieutenant General [Hideki] Tojo to form a new cabinet. The official residence of the war minister was fixed up for the Cabinet Organization headquarters.⁹ It went so far as to report the names of several visitors already. "Tojo should be prime minister!" I felt a slight resistance, but he is a man of excellent caliber. He will do the job, I am sure.

Without hesitation, in spite of the shortage of talent, this same man was plucked out of the domain of the army, which has been urging war. He has a deep understanding of the present situation and has merely changed his post. If we don't go to war, this selection could be a way to put down the army. If we decide to open war, he will be the man to dare to do so. Will he retire from active service, like [former Premier] Admiral [Mitsumasa] Yonai,¹⁰ when a military administration is rejected, or will a particular exception be made to allow him to remain on active service?

It was also reported that His Majesty sent for the navy minister, Admiral Oikawa, and honored him with gracious words. Well, what can they be? Should the navy cooperate with all our efforts with the cabinet whose premier is a lieutenant general? However, I imagine Admiral Oikawa will not remain in the new cabinet. Then who will assume the post of navy minister and meet this difficult situation? I can't but feel uneasy. But the present circumstances are much easier to go through than the ones at the time of cabinet changes in the past. Anyone will do, if he expresses his definite opinions as the minister and fully realizes the circumstances the navy is now facing.

It is easily imagined that our boss [Yamamoto] would have been made navy minister had he been commander in chief of, say, Yokosuka Naval Station at this juncture. Be that as it may, it would be a bit difficult to take him away from the Combined Fleet just at the threshold of war. If it could have been possible, he should have been sitting in the chair at Yokosuka a little earlier. When my thoughts reach this point, who will it be? [Admiral Shigetaro] Shimada? Or [Admiral] Soemu Toyoda? The former has just returned from China and is supposed to be commander in chief of the Combined Fleet in the immediate future, [*probably a slip on Ugaki's part. Shimada became commander of the Yokosuka Naval Station before his appointment as navy minister*] while the army will not welcome the latter (there is reason enough for this conjecture) and we too are somewhat dissatisfied with him. Well, what am I to think? Indeed, to build character is one of the most important national aims, and it cannot be done in a day or two. When I think of it, I cannot help respecting General Kazunari [Issei] Ugaki for his constant diligence and hard work as well as his uncommon viewpoint, though people criticize him as ambitious. [*The army had blocked*

General Ugaki, a distant relation of the admiral, from forming a cabinet in 1937. He was foreign minister from 26 May to 29 October 1938.][11]

[On 18 October Ugaki turned his thoughts from the cabinet crisis to the "extraordinary grand festival of Yasukuni Shrine," where some fifteen thousand spirits of those fallen in battle were to be enshrined that day. He mused that if he could be so honored some day, he would be content. Then he returned to politics:]

The radio reported that the organization of the new cabinet is making fair progress. The men who either come up or are sent for are not outstanding. I wonder if the upcoming new cabinet will be just an ordinary transition one. And Shimada's name appears. Then it was reported that the organization will be completed in the morning, and in the afternoon the ceremony of installation by His Majesty will take place.

[That morning the training exercise ended, so Yamamoto and his staff had lunch at a tourist hotel at Murozumi. Ugaki recorded that the dinner was "substantial, but the waitresses were hopeless." He added almost casually that he had sent Captain Kameto Kuroshima, the senior staff officer, "to Tokyo to make arrangements with regard to operations."]

[*To be specific, Kuroshima flew to Tokyo to persuade the Naval General Staff to (1) include the Pearl Harbor attack (Operation Hawaii) in Japan's war plan and (2) to commit the First Air Fleet's six CVs to the mission.*][12]

["Having had a nice recreation," the officers returned to the ships early the afternoon of Sunday, 19 October. Once more Ugaki's thoughts turned to politics:]

The personnel of the new cabinet are:

Premier, Home, War	Tojo, Hideki
Finance	Kaya, Okinobu
Foreign, Colonization	Togo, Shigenori
Navy	Shimada, Shigetaro
Justice*	Iwamura, Michimori
Education*	Hashida, Kunihiko
Agriculture*	Ino, Sekiya
Commerce, Industry	Kishi, Nobusuke
Communications, Railway	Terashima [VADM Ken]
Welfare	Koizumi, Chikahiko
Planning Board	Suzuki, [Lt. Gen.] Teiichi

[*Ugaki's asterisks. These were holdovers from the Konoye Cabinet.*]

I don't feel that anything is novel. Is this as it should be? Is it too much to expect a little more? It was good that the organization was finished in twenty hours under the present circumstances. Can this cabinet work its way to war? If it fails, some admiral will form a cabinet. Vice Admiral Noboru Hirata was appointed commander in chief of Yokosuka Naval Station, being succeeded by Vice Admiral [Jisaburo] Ozawa in his former post. This settled the problem of the seniority of the commander in chief of the Southern Expeditionary Fleet and that of the Second Fleet. I suppose the director of the personnel bureau [of the Navy Ministry, Rear Admiral Giichi] Nakahara, must have been much relieved.

Monday, 20 October 1941. Partly cloudy. Inspection at Saeki Bay. Sailed out at 0500, before daybreak. The commander in chief bantered me, "You got up this morning at the time you went to bed last night, eh?" Entered Saeki Bay after various exercises at sea.

The chiefs of staff of the Sixth Fleet [Rear Admiral Hisashi Mito] and First Air Fleet [Rear Admiral Ryunosuke Kusaka] and the skipper of *Yamato* [Captain Hidenori] Miyazato, visited our ship. Chief of Staff Kusaka told us of the arrangements made at Tokyo concerning the "AMO" Operation [the Pearl Harbor attack]. The previous conference held at Tokyo with the Naval General Staff would have settled the issue if he had been as enthusiastic then as he was this time, but he was rather troublesome as he reversed his previous opinion. [*Kusaka had opposed the Pearl Harbor attack as unsound strategy.*] The senior staff officer must have had a worrisome time.

For the first time I have seen a really huge ship [the superbattleship *Yamato*] navigating. Magnificent indeed! I am more than satisfied that this ship will add great power to the fleet. We must train her so that she can display her strength as soon as possible.

[The next morning, 21 October, the fleet practiced "assault training of submarines and planes." Ugaki was very much disgruntled when two submarines, *I-7* and *I-66*, collided, both suffering damage.]

Wednesday, 22 October 1941. Fine today, too. Newspapers came after two days' delay in delivery, but I found that matters hadn't changed much. It seemed for a while that the formation of the Tojo Cabinet threw the United States into an uproar, but now they appear to have regained their former calmness. I came across some articles which showed an attitude of continuing the American-Japanese parley. In my opinion, if they [the Americans] take this into serious consideration, they must fully realize how foolish it would be to fight with us. But when some in the United States have an idea Japan in sixty or ninety days, continuing the negotiations is out of the question. To beat such guys into fits will be good for our empire, and in order to do that it will be advantageous not to dilly-dally. Even General Tojo (promoted at his inauguration to premier) will not be able to firm up his resolution at once to do that, I suspect. One always experiences difficulties; that is the way of the world.

[Experimental firing, using a "wireless control glider," proved very unsatisfactory, and Ugaki was disgusted. "Why and for what purpose" had the fleet received "such mere trash"? He turned to the more satisfactory area of Pearl Harbor planning:]

Towards evening the senior staff officer came back. It was a great success that he could have made them agree with us in the arrangements for AMO Operation. I heard that the commander in chief had already made up his mind to step down if this agreement had not been reached. I judge his resolution was mentioned in his talk with the commander in chief of the First Air Fleet who pressed him for an immediate answer the other day.

[*Yamamoto had indeed authorized Kuroshima to tell the Naval General Staff that he would resign with all his staff if the Pearl Harbor plan was not accepted. Whereupon the Naval General Staff acceded to his wishes.*][13]

That request was too hasty, wasn't it? How contradictory the air fleet is! In view of the fact that the air fleet had evaded the plan at first, the fleet should have suggested others for the job after it proved that it can't control its subordinates. It's asking too much to demand a prompt answer. That man [Vice Admiral Chuichi] Nagumo [commander in chief, First Air Fleet] not only has words with others but is given to bluffing when drunk. He is not fully prepared yet to advance in the face of death and gain results two or three times as great as his cost by jumping into the jaws of death with his men as well as himself. One could see this clearly when in his blank dismay he was not able to speak a word at the time of the outbreak of the China Incident, in spite of his important post of chief of the Second Section, Naval General Staff. If the commander in chief [Nagumo] and chief of staff [Kusaka] stoutly oppose this operation, and feel that they cannot carry it out, they should resign their posts. I expressed this to the commander in chief [Yamamoto] and he also said he thought so. But today I have been arranging so as not to take such an undesirable course by any means. With Vice Admiral Ozawa just sent to be commander in chief of the Southern Fleet, it can be said that the matter came to a happy end because the navy had no other adequate candidate [to replace Nagumo]. Such problems are always a source of worry, but that's why we are in the navy! I hope he [Nagumo] performs his mission well.[14]

[Major] Prince Mikasa [brother of the emperor] became engaged to Miss Yuri Takagi.

[On Thursday, 23 October, the glider experiments continued. That afternoon Rear Admiral Naosaburo Irifune and Lieutenant Commander Takeshi Naito, who had spent several months in Germany, briefed the staff about German war operations. Ugaki thought Hitler's "skill in his air operations, especially in long-distance sea flights," left something to be desired. "Notwithstanding this, he is displaying the enormous power of his air corps in the overwhelming number of planes and his forestalling operations." This led Ugaki to some uneasy reflections:]

When can we vie for superiority with foreigners? So far as the naval air arm is concerned, everyone can be free from anxiety, but the Army air and the civilian air are very unreliable. Moreover, our capacity to produce planes and replenish air crews are two causes of anxiety, but fear often exaggerates danger. In war, both parties have the same sort of defects. It's essential that we not underestimate the enemy too much. We would like to see the operation go on smoothly after learning that the enemy strength was not so powerful as previously thought.

[Ugaki had a more immediate problem: A little disagreement arose concerning how to handle the submarine collision of the 21st. Ugaki wanted it "hushed up," but Yamamoto "was firm in his opinion that it should be brought into the open." This worried Ugaki, for there would "often be such cases in the future," and he feared morale would suffer if the navy had to operate under the prospect of reprimand "by this minister and that every time."

The next day, Friday, 24 October, the decision was reconsidered and Ugaki wrote to the director of military affairs asking for guidelines. He gave this to the communications staff officer, Commander Yujiro Wada, to hand carry to Tokyo.

Ugaki had been in touch with those concerned in the accident, and Yamamoto visited the scene in person. Ugaki remarked, "With such solicitude as his, we can willingly die for the sake of our superiors."

Saturday, 25 October, was a day of social activities for Ugaki. He had no luck shooting or fishing, but visited with Vice Admiral Shira Takasu, commander in chief of the First Fleet. He tried to see Rear Admiral Tadashige Daigo, but he was out. Later he met with three of his Eta Jima classmates, Captains Ryujiro Tanaki, Shiku Yoshimura, and Hanku Sasaki.

The next day, Sunday, 26 October, Ugaki and his fellow officers returned on board ship.]

Monday, 27 October 1941. Wind became slightly weaker, but cold. Have not heard much lately about the diplomatic relations between the United States and Japan; in my judgment opinions to deliberate further began to prevail recently. In England, too, press comments on this matter give the impression that they take it to be a bad policy to open a war in the East. Learned that the president, [Frank] Knox, secretary of the navy, and

[Admiral Harold R.] Stark, chief of naval operations, would broadcast today on the occasion of the Memorial Day of the U.S. Navy. Have they or have they not enough pluck and are they prepared to refer to the Pacific and Eastern problems?

This, however, is only one side of things. I want our navy to make our viewpoints definite, say at some liaison meeting which may be held without delay at this time just after the change of cabinet.

[*A liaison conference consisted of a core membership of the premier, foreign minister, ministers of war and the navy, chiefs of the army and naval general staffs. Others functioned as assistants and as secretariat.*][15]

They say an extra session of the Diet will be called the coming 15th of November. They [Diet members] will not only discuss military expenses or a supplementary budget, but should help our state to have a firm resolution by taking the nation fully into its confidence. From my point of view, Premier Tojo should do it and this is the very moment to do it. Prompt action is most necessary (as the premier said) under the present situation.

[Here Ugaki quoted a paragraph written by Nansha Saigo, probably at the time he demanded the invasion of Korea in 1877. The gist was that the only way to handle diplomatic relations was from a strong stance.[16]

The next morning, Tuesday, 28 October, a research meeting was held concerning the First Battleship Division. Ugaki had to admit a "deterioration of fighting power" due to extensive personnel shuffles. Again the international situation claimed his attention:]

The broadcast by President Roosevelt yesterday served to inspire the nation's enthusiasm for war, yet he never referred to the Pacific problem, as I had expected. Was this due to diplomatic delicacy or a conciliatory attitude toward Japan?

I was told that secret telegrams sent by Chief of Naval Operations Stark to his fleets or naval stations amount to sixteen since the 24th; that's record-breaking. Does he have any confidence at all to fight, or not? We are simply burning to have a call, but, according to the communications staff officer who has just returned from Tokyo, such words had been picked up as "I'll clean the slate and start over again." Is this true or not? Will he [Tojo] throw into the wastebasket the decision made at the last council in His Majesty's presence—he who is now prime and war minister, and has been war minister? Though I know it is the government that carries out policy, yet should the national policy that has once been decided be changed so easily?

Wednesday, 29 October 1941. Autumnal clear sky, became warm. The bay lies lonely with the First and Second Battleship Divisions, others having moved out for training. The chief of the first section, Naval General Staff, [Captain Sadatoshi] Tomioka came with staff officer [Commander Yugi] Yamamoto [in charge of liaison with the army], bringing down operational principles and the Central Agreement (a draft members of the headquarters deliberated over from 1500 to 1930. We had our say at great length and conferred to our heart's content. The important point that [Vice Admiral Shigeru] Fukudome, chief of the First Bureau of the Naval General Staff, said in his letter brought with them is as follows:

> At the inauguration of the Tojo Cabinet, His Majesty gave the message to the effect that he should clean the slate and reexamine the national policy. Since the 23rd, liaison meetings have been held continuously. Perhaps by the 24th we can reach some conclusion. Of course, the peaceful development of the situation has been the fundamental and common principle to be discussed. But since the situation has developed into what it is now, a confident policy is not easy to find, though anticipatory policy appears as it does. It is not to be presupposed what conclusion might be reached because the Premier has not yet expressed a word of his own policy. But I desire you who are in the active service to prepare wholeheartedly, expecting the worst.
>
> The American-Japanese parley has not been interrupted, yet it does not progress. There have not been any diplomatic activities between Japan and England, Siam, or Germany and Italy.
>
> The political situation cannot be judged to be definitely fixed by the conclusion of the liaison meeting. Moves that will be seen in those couple of days are the most important to observe.

Who would dare draw back, reducing our demands, under the present situation? There is no alternative just before a war is going to break out. Procrastination means falling into the enemy's trap. If we negotiate the matter with the intention of opening war against him, after preparing for war, he might give in. That is the only alternative left for us. If he does not concede, this means use of military power. But if we anticipate a scarcity of materials on our side in the future, we can never initiate war against him. It is not uncommon in life that a way to survive is found at the last moment after desperate efforts.

The following who have been designated staff of the new Southern Area Army came down to Saeki to greet the commander in chief and put up there. I suddenly thought of inviting them to a restaurant to let them and

our staff understand each other. I left the ship at 1940 and came back
at 2330.

Asst. Chief of Staff	Lt. Gen. [Shigemasa] Aoki, 25th Class
	Maj. Gen. Sakaguchi, 25th Class (not joined)
Senior Staff	Col. [Motoyoshi] Ishii
Air Operations	Col. Tanii*
	Lt. Col. [Okikatsu] Arao**

* and ** [*Ugaki's note*]: I know them very well from when I was at Naval
General Staff headquarters, Arao being a student at that time.

[In the morning of Thursday, 30 October, the above officers and
Nagumo came aboard *Nagato* to discuss the projected operations. As
usual, Ugaki was rather antagonistic toward Nagumo:]

Commander in Chief Nagumo seems to be extremely anxious about his
special assigned mission. I know it is natural that he should be, yet I hope
he will not fall into nervous prostration beforehand. Life and death are
according to the will of heaven. If only he can obtain a glorious result in
the coming fight, he may rest in peace. Once a task is given us, I will do my
best to accomplish it with the help of God, regarding that task as one of
the most glorious of honors. Nothing will worry me. No one can fight it
out to the last, fearing this and worrying about that. If there is any prospect and estimate of getting a result of more than sixty percent, one should
go ahead valiantly and decidedly, after making preparations in case anything goes wrong. They urge us to give them a prompt answer as to the
decision on X-Day, but I wonder how the atmosphere at Tokyo is? I think
it will take much more time until the opening of war, after putting any
reasonable intermediate policy into practice, however cleanly Premier
Tojo might clean the slate. He would not agree with that evacuation
proposal at this junction, in spite of his insistence during his post in the
former cabinet. Can he do anything suitable now? For he was the man
most responsible for the disagreement on political opinions in the former
cabinet.

Friday, 31 October 1941. Fine. Sailed out at 0730. The Twenty-fourth
advanced training was enforced off Tosa-oki on all the forces of the Combined Fleet. From morning till noon and from noon till evening every
phase of tactical training was practiced, up until the fifth course. Very busy
indeed for one day! Fundamental as the training exercises are, they are still
done as efficiently as possible. At night, night battles in the clear moonlight. Our "opponents" did not surround us easily, because we had an

intense will to beat the "enemy," but at last we allowed them to do so for the sake of training.

[On Saturday, 1 November, a "fine, windy" day, training continued at sea. Ugaki evaluated it as "pretty good" in spite of the high seas. He was more enthusiastic over night battle training, which the Japanese considered a specialty—"it was really a rare and grand sight." That afternoon Yamamoto received a significant message, as Ugaki recorded.]

At 1600 a telegram from the minister marked "urgent and confidential" came to the commander in chief requesting him "to come up to the official residence of the minister by noon of 3 November, evading others' notice." What does this telegram mean? Today is already the 1st of November. It is high time for the cabinet council to come to some conclusion. To my question, "Was it decided?" the commander in chief answered, "They are summoning me because they could not reach a conclusion." Which way will it be decided?

[Yamamoto asked Ugaki's views on a question he thought the navy minister might ask, that is: "How long can the navy postpone action in case the negotiations continue?"]

I gave it further consideration From the viewpoint of the Combined Fleet, December 8 will be the best, in view of completion of preparations, day of the week, and age of the moon. But even if it is delayed a little, I don't say we can't manage. But the conclusion is that to put it off until next June would be the worst case.

Could there be any other purpose in sending for the commander in chief? At present, I don't think it has any relation to the political situation, but if it should have, the idea of Admiral Yamamoto becoming premier and minister of the navy is surely against his ill. While I was pondering those things in my mind, the night battle training ended at 2145. While heading north, we had a short rest on the way.

[*A cabinet crisis was narrowly averted on 1 November 1941, but we have found no indication that anyone considered taking Yamamoto away from the Combined Fleet.*][17]

Sunday, 2 November 1941. Very fine, ideal, autumn weather. Arrived at Saeki Bay anchorage at 0500. The moon was not full, but just before we anchored it hung on the edge of the mountain, as if to suggest it had finished its day's task. The commander of the Twenty-fourth Squadron [Raider], Rear Admiral Moriji Takeda, paid his respects to me.

I had a talk with our commander in chief over last night's affairs and the negotiations between Japan and the United States. He left the ship at 1020, by sea reconnaissance plane from Saeki to Kure, and thence by express train for Tokyo.

[That afternoon Ugaki inspected *Hokoku Maru,* a converted cruiser, flagship of the Twenty-fourth Squadron. This had been a cargo passenger ship intended for the South America run. Ugaki noted that its capacity of four hundred passengers would allow her to pick up crews of enemy merchant ships after she had sunk them. But the international situation soon demanded his attention.]

An urgent telegram came from the chief of the First Bureau, Naval General Staff, this evening, asking us whether or not we have any objection to negotiations toward reaching an Army-Navy Central Agreement being held at Tokyo from the 8th to the 10th of this month. Sent an answer at once that we have no objection. Judging from this telegram, they have already made up their minds.[18]

Monday, 3 November 1941. Partly cloudy. Amid this ever-pressing situation, our full-dressed ships welcomed the birthday of Emperor Meiji today. The autumn sky was serenely high, and my reflections deep. Oh, this sacred age of Showa! When I reflect upon the great achievements of past heroes and the sacred virtue of the emperor with his great and glorious works, they inspire me with fresh courage. Can we who have received the gift of life in this age of Showa idle away our time without conquering this national peril and expanding the Imperial work, thus placing the state in a position of perfect security?

[Ugaki treated himself to a brief spell of fishing on this day. His catch was meager, but he was satisfied. As often in moments of emotion, either turbulent or tranquil, Ugaki turned to poetry, and wrote a few lines expressing his "perfect beatitude" while fishing in the sun. Soon duty called him back.]

At 2000 received a telegram from the commander in chief, who has been in Tokyo, that he would arrive at Kure sometime tomorrow afternoon. According to the message, he will finish the conference at the ministers' official residence this afternoon, so he will leave Tokyo a day early; this is evidence that the final decision has been reached. At the same time, received information from the chief of the First Bureau confirming that the conference with the army will be held from the 8th to the 10th. Everything is O.K.

> You die,
> You all die for the sake of the land.
> I, too, will die.[19]

Tuesday, 4 November 1941. Cloudy and then fine. Special Combined Fleet training [a dress rehearsal for Operation Hawaii]. Masses of planes attacked the ships at anchor. Much progress was noted in their skill in attacking ships at anchor.

The press comments on the stiff attitude toward the United States are the same in tenor. It is high time to carry on active propaganda. They should stir up high-spirited public opinion by ringing bells and banging drums to prepare the people, while we call for grave reflection on the part of the United States, then study American reaction. Then we should lower our pitch to make it appear to the United States that we are ready to submit. Nothing is more important than the political and strategical moves during this month. Anyway, I hope they will be managed successfully.

[That afternoon target practice was held for land-based bombers of the Twenty-First Air Flotilla, not effective enough to suit Ugaki. That evening's night firing practice was little better.]

Forty-five minutes after we entered the harbor, the commander in chief [Yamamoto] came back to the ship. He told me as follows:

> After the installation of the Tojo Cabinet, His Majesty's message was received through the Lord Keeper of the Privy Seal, saying that the foreign policy shall be reexamined, cleaning the slate. To bring this about, meetings were held twelve times to discuss the seven articles; and at last the way we should take was decided on the 4th. That is, negotiations with the U.S. shall be continued, modifying our demands to some degree. At the same time, the army and navy will continue our strategic war preparations. The final decision will be made by 0000 hours, 1 December. In case we open war, its outbreak will be some day at the beginning of December (the navy intends to establish X-Day as 8 December). By the way, in a day or two, a council in the presence of His Majesty will be held, as a result of his inquiry to the councilors of the army and navy. The commander in chief agreed with the idea that every operational force in deployment movements will immediately turn back when such order is given before 1 December. It was concluded that the army-navy agreement and others will be effected on the 8th or 10th.

Furthermore, the minister asked him [Yamamoto] for his opinion about the necessity of changes in personnel of the Combined Fleet. He answered that he did not desire any such changes, since a change of even a couple of brass hats is considered to have no little influence over the morale of the whole fleet. Anyway, since the Combined Fleet has made up its mind to fight and prepare for war, he asked that the navy minister consider how to meet promptly the Combined Fleet's operational requirements.

He further told me that the commanders in chief of naval stations and secondary naval stations would be assembled around the 6th. In a word, though negotiations will be continued, our operational preparations will be advanced more rapidly and fully to be prepared for diplomatic failure, and the time for deciding war or peace was definitely established.

[For the rest of the day Ugaki reflected that the economic problems involved, even "the alliance problem," could be settled somehow, but how could Tojo deal with the question of evacuating French Indochina?]

Wednesday, 5 November 1941. Ideal autumn day. Had a succession of business last night. Direction telegrams to the fleet amount to an unusual quantity.

All the staff are desperately studying the Combined Fleet's operational order and the army-navy agreement. Both seem rather roughly planned because the drafters were too easily satisfied with themselves. But they wouldn't welcome my poking my nose into it. I must supply the staff with some officer who is accurate in writing and keen in thinking, as one of the operational staff. A proper one is hard to find and obtain. An air pilot is the most suitable for the job, but will not be assigned to such a post, much to my regret. Put on winter clothes last night, but today I perspired; rechanged into my spring suit.

[Ugaki tasted a new dish for the first time—salted *matatabi*—which he found "a little bitter." He also recorded that his dental work had been finished. "But the alveolar purulence is not completely cured."]

Thursday, 6 November 1941. Fine. Changing my mind, I decided to leave here for Tokyo today, as the weather will not be suitable for flying tomorrow. Left the ship at 0800 with staff officers, including the commander in chief. Leaving Saeki, we arrived at Oita by train.

At that time in the morning, there was dense fog on the sea. Amid the fog, planes belonging to the B Force were vigorously attacking Saeki Air Field with much-improved skill, showing us bystanders their promise of future success in actual battle.[20]

We boarded a passenger plane which had been sent from Tokyo for us. We arrived at Yokosuka Air Corps as early as 1510, with favorable wind through the autumnal sky. After a short pause, I let everyone act as he pleased instead of as a group. I got to my home at dusk. All my family were surprised at my unexpected appearance. They all complained of the shortage of food and the scarcity of necessities, but I didn't notice that anyone had lost weight! After the death of my Tomoko [*his late wife*], they have been experiencing considerable hardships; nevertheless, they are getting along, and they will have to keep on somehow.

Friday, 7 November 1941. Fine. Appeared at the navy ministry. Exchanged civilities with my fellows. The atmosphere of every department and section seemed to be very cheerful and aggressive, with active, lively business under way. One can fully realize that people's on-the-job efficiency depends entirely upon their mood.

The chief of the Naval General Staff, Admiral [Osami] Nagano, again told me that he tried to discuss the Tripartite Alliance separately from the present issue, but in vain. But it is no use to talk about the alliance problem. It wasn't the German-Japanese alliance but the Manchurian incident that brought about the present situation. The chief warned me not to have a "slip 'twixt the cup and the lip," citing as an example the ships *Hatsuse* and *Yashima,* which sank by carelessly touching mines. I welcomed his well-intentioned advice. I also met the vice minister, vice chief, and the director of military affairs. I asked the director many questions. Then I called the staffs together at the First Council Chamber and made final amendents to the Combined Fleet's operational order.

The following are Imperial Japanese Naval Order No. 1 and Imperial Japanese Naval Directive No. 1, which were sent and received by us just before we left the ship yesterday:

IJNO No. 1

With an Imperial Order, the chief of the Naval General Staff orders the commander in chief of the Combined Fleet, Admiral Yamamoto, as follows:

1. The Japanese empire expects to open war against the United States, England and Holland at the beginning of December for the sake of its self-existence and self-defense and has decided to prepare for operations in every department.

2. The commander in chief of the Combined Fleet will effect necessary operational preparations.

3. In regard to details, the chief of the Naval General Staff will direct you.

[IJND No. 1-1 spelled out operational activities to implement the above. Operational Order No. 2 set the day to commence war as 8 December 1941.

[On Saturday, 8 November, representatives of the Combined Fleet, the Second Fleet, and the Southern Army discussed the operational agreement. Ugaki spent the morning of Sunday, 9 November, at home, tending to his potted plants. That afternoon he want to the Military Staff College to hear junior staff officers discuss the arrangements made.

[The army-navy agreement was signed at 1130 on Monday, 10 November. Ugaki listed some of the major brass present. The next day, Tuesday, 11 November, the Combined Fleet party returned to *Nagato* by way of Yokosuka Air Base. On Sunday, 12 November, Ugaki had to catch up business which had accumulated during his absence. "All day I sensed a constant stirring."]

Thursday, 13 November 1941. Rainy but cleared up later. We left the ship at 0900 for Iwakune Air Corps to make arrangements for Combined Fleet operations. All the commanders in chief of the fleets, their chiefs of staff and senior staff officers, as well as the commander in chief of the Combined Fleet gathered together. The commander in chief of the Fourth Fleet [Vice Admiral Shigeoshi] Inouye, appeared in the meeting for the first time in that capacity.

Admiral Yamamoto's opening address was extraordinarily wonderful, as it should be for the supreme commander at the start of a major expedition. Then followed the chief of staff's explanation, with various advice and suggestions.

We were entertained with dishes of *surume* and *kachiguri* [Surume *(dried cuttlefish) and* Kachiguri *(walnuts) were customary food when drinking to success in advance of battle*], praying for our success in war. At 1300, we had our picture taken in the rain at the entrance hall, and each member autographed a sheet of paper around the signatures of the commander and chief of staff. These will be the best of souvenirs.

At about 1430 I finished my explanation, followed by the Southern Army's operational discussions. Everything was over at 1800.

We left the corps by cars. We had a meeting at the Fukagawa Restaurant. All the officers who engaged in the council met there. We had plenty of *sake* but not good food. Over fifteen girls attended, but their performance was less than inspired. The countryside is still the countryside! Left there at 2100 for the ship.

[On Friday, 14 November, discussions relating to the army-navy agreement were held. Ugaki had little to do but make himself agreeable to the attendees. That afternoon he crossed swords briefly with the chief engineering officer of the fleet, Captain Goro Yakamura, who was sulking because he was not invited to the previous day's operational discussions. Then Ugaki turned his thoughts to Washington and the Neutrality Act.]

At its session yesterday, the United States Congress approved amending the Neutrality Act, including abolition of the article prohibiting arming of merchant marine ships and the articles prohibiting their entry into belligerent waters, which the president will sign. The president's message in the House of Representatives overcame stout opposition. This approval will have a great influence upon Japan, for American aid to England will become more and more active and positive, with the result that the latter will transfer her spare forces in the Atlantic to Pacific waters. England's naval strength in the Far East (including the eastern coast of Africa) already amounts to four battleships, two CVs, and other craft. After the outbreak of war, reinforcements certainly will be sent from the Mediterranean Sea in view of the Italian navy's weakness. Consequently, our Southern Operation must seriously be reconsidered. On this point I have already given some suggestions to the commander in chief of the Second Fleet.

Saturday, 15 November 1941. Indian summer. In spite of the world facing a great storm, what a fine day it is today!

Today His Majesty called the Seventy-seventh Extraordinary Session [of the Diet]. What is to be discussed and the general atmosphere of the session will prove very significant.

[Ugaki recorded that the armed forces had demanded an "extraordinary war expenditure" of 3,800,000,000 yen. But he realized that when the war was fully joined, military expenses would be "incomparably above such a sum" and could only be met by government bonds.

[More to Ugaki's taste were the graduation ceremonies at Eta Jima, the Naval Engineering Academy, and the Naval Paymasters' School. He was pleased with the idea of new midshipmen who entered port that evening aboard battleship *Haruna*.

[That evening the Twenty-fourth Squadron left port for its mission of destroying commercial shipping. This was a task after Ugaki's own heart. "Of course, if unsuccessful they will die with the ship they are in, but to hunt for passing game on the wide sea, far from land, taking them by surprise, is surely thrilling. If I were ordered to do that, I'd have perfect confidence in hitting the bull's eye through my elusive movements."

[On Sunday, 16 November, final consultations on the army-navy agreement were held at Iwakuni. To signify the importance of this event, the vice chief of the Naval General Staff, Vice Admiral Seiichi Ito, flew from Tokyo "to extend greetings." Ugaki's thoughts winged to Tokyo.]

The opening ceremony of the Diet was held in the presence of His Majesty. Ambassador [Saburo] Kurusu arrived at Washington by clipper yesterday across the Pacific Ocean, in the capacity of special envoy. After arranging with Ambassador Nomura, he will start the final parley at last.

Monday, 17 November 1941. Very fine. At 0700, left Iwakuni for Saeki Bay on board the battleship. On our way we met many vessels going in and out of Kure Naval Station, which seems a busy strategical port at present.

At 1340 arrived at Saeki. Left ship at 1500 for the flagship *Akagi*, which was going to sail out on a very important mission at midnight today, leading the task force, to say farewell to the crews.

[*This mission was to rendezvous with other ships at Hitokappu Bay in the Kuriles, thence to embark upon the Pearl Harbor attack.*]The commander in chief, Admiral Yamamoto, gave an address on the flight deck to every class of commanders and staff officers, especially to the flying officers. What came from his heart went to their hearts. I saw on their faces unshakable loyalty, determined resolution, even a degree of ferocity. But they were all self-composed. We cannot but expect some damage to us, yet I pray that by the grace of heaven they will succeed in their objective.

[*Although Ugaki did not record Yamamoto's remarks, many who heard them recalled the gist very well. He warned the Pearl Harbor task force that Japan was facing the strongest, most resourceful foe in her history. They hoped for surprise, but must consider the possibility that the Americans might be prepared for any contingency, and they might have to fight their way in.*][21]

Just after our arrival at the ship, the commander in chief of the First Air Fleet [Nagumo] came aboard with his staff, and we drank to their success. In his parting, Chief of Staff Kusaka said to me, "Perhaps I may be thick-skinned by nature. I don't have any profound feelings, though people say we are going to do an enormously big thing." I answered him, "That's enough, isn't it?" It's natural that there should be a little difference between admirals and staff officers in their sentiments; anyway, you can't take anything too seriously. When you do your best, God will surely protect you, then you have nothing to complain about, even if you die. Whichever route we may take, we arrive at the same point because we aim at the same end. Thus we can find calm resignation.

[After this, Ugaki briefed and talked with the skippers of *Nagato* and *Mutsu*. Then he had a few favorable remarks about the addresses of Premier Tojo and Foreign Minister Togo before the House of Peers.

[Not much happened on Tuesday, 18 November. The First Battleship Division conducted firing exercises at sea from 0745 to 2100.]

Wednesday, 19 November 1941. Fine. It has cleared up agreeably in spite of a shower at midnight. Left port at 0845. Through Nuwajima Channel entered Hashira Jima Anchorage. At sunset moored to central buoy.

I haven't read the newspapers or listened to the radio for several days. Starboard the helm, or port?

On our way northward out of Saeki Bay, we saw a queer-shaped submarine with no mark or number heading south. It proved to be the flagship of the First Submarine Division, *I-22*, which had a midget sub on it. This morning about five of them were to be gathered together off

Tosa. They were all to head east with a distance of ten miles between each of them. The surprise attack on X-Day will be an entirely unexpected storm.

[*These five midget submarines were scheduled to participate in the Pearl Harbor attack. They were lost with all hands except for Ensign Kazuo Saka-maki, who was captured.²² Ugaki had a special regard for these men.*]

No one can predict what results they will bring about. Young lieutenants were seen on their decks smiling. They expect never to return alive; they are ready to die at the scene of battle. Their preparedness is admirable. Our old "death-defying spirit" never changes. We can rely fully upon them.

[*To Japanese of the day,* kesshitai no seishin (*death-defying spirit*) *was closely connected to* tokko-seishin (*the special or suicide attack spirit*).]

Thursday, 20 November 1941. Fine, later cloudy. Rear Admiral [Setsuzo] Yoshitomi, commander of the Fourth Submarine Squadron, came to the ship to say farewell, with the commanders and staff officers under his command. The squadron will leave here this afternoon. At 1100, the Seventh Division and the Third Destroyer Squadron stayed temporarily around *Nagato*. In the afternoon the commanders of both squadrons came to the ship to say good-bye. At 1530 and 1600, they respectively headed for the prearranged points of operation. The commander of the Seventh Heavy Cruiser Division, Rear Admiral [Takeo] Kurita, who is supposed to meet the most dangerous situation, was the most calm. He is most trustworthy. That might be because of his many experiences, having already engaged in two battles—the occupations of northern and southern French Indochina.

At 1600, Chief of the First Bureau of the Naval General Staff Fukudome came to the ship via Iwakuni by plane with Captain [Shigenori] Kami. [*Kami was in charge of war and operational plans in the Operations Section of the Naval General Staff.*] The reason they came here was so that we could speak frankly with them concerning the naval order and the naval directive to be issued dated tomorrow and the events contingent upon them both in the future.

He told me that Hull thinks the principle of worldwide equal opportunity is not necessary and hopes to get rid of it. And the Tripartite Alliance has caused much debate. After the arrival of Ambassador Kurusu, the parley will proceed along the B Plan; that is to say, the present situation of French Indochina will revert to the time before invasion. To keep the United States out of the China Incident will make reconciliation with us more difficult. His attitude is very strong because of their underestimation of our national power and ignorance of our resolution. The only alternative left for us is to strike them vehemently, if they can't understand us.

Newspapers write in a high-flown style about the Diet, but I was told it is in a very low mood. How unreliable it [the Diet] is!

We left the ship by the commander in chief's boat with them, including Senior Staff Officer Kuroshima, for much was left to talk about with them, and I wanted to entertain them. After much difficulty in the pitch dark, sometimes going aground the pier, we arrived at Iwakuni Air Corps at last.

[On Friday, 21 November, the Combined Fleet entertained their guests from Tokyo with sukiyaki, and Ugaki scrounged five pounds of beef for them to take back with them, "for the purpose of curing the malnutrition of the staff at the command center in Tokyo!"

[In the afternoon Ugaki presided over mourning services for the officers and men who had died in the line of duty and "who used to belong to the First Battleship Division, First Fleet, and its attached forces." These numbered sixty-eight.]

Imperial Japanese Naval Order No. 5 was issued to the commander of the Combined Fleet, dated the 21st of this month, authorizing the dispatch of forces to the operational points and also the use of arms for the purpose of self-defense. Accordingly, an order, "Second Battle Disposition for the Opening of War," was issued to the Combined Fleet at 0000 this morning. I saw with my own eyes that everything was going without a hitch today, according to plan. It's to be hoped that the "First Battle Position for the Opening of War" won't come back. If our demands should be met in diplomatic negotiations, we'll never be unwilling to withdraw, but such a possibility is lessening step by step, much to our regret. The Extraordinary Session of the Diet closed today as scheduled, and the closing ceremony was held.

Saturday, 22 November 1941. Cloudy. Attended the research meeting for the first class training. At the meeting I had much to ask and much to say about the results of training. Rear Admiral [Shoji] Nishimura, commander of the Fourth Destroyer Squadron, came to the ship to say farewell. He said that his squadron will head for Mako (at Formosa), through Terashima Channel after negotiations with the Third Fleet. His squadron will support the landing at the northern part of the Philippines. There is no small probability of a sea battle. I pray for his success and that of his squadron in the coming battle.

Three staff officers went to Kure Naval Station to make arrangements.

Incoming documents became very few these days and telegrams for some requisitions became rare. This is clear evidence that each of the forces has already deployed for their tasks apart from everyday routine. Up until the 20th, formal parleys were held three times, and informal once in Washington. What will be their effect?

Sunday, 23 November 1941. Rain. Rain began to fall in the morning and in the afternoon to pour vehemently. It also grew chill. Those who sailed for the north [the Pearl Harbor task force] may have been feeling very cold this morning. At 0915, Harvest Festival was held, with the ceremony of worship facing east.[23]

[Ugaki admitted, however, that the rice crop of Japan proper for the year was considerably less than the previous one. On board ship there was plenty to eat, but the government should "manage so that people can carry on without worrying about rice." He turned to the discussions in Washington.]

Radio news just reported that there was an off-the-record negotiation at Hull's official residence, lasting as long as three hours. It was also reported that the nature of the parley was of as general a character as ever, but the United States has already talked with the representatives of five countries. The United States might have come to an understanding, albeit an informal one, with those representatives, for this one is a little later than the five-country parley.

If the United States knew anything about the resolution of our empire, she might not keep quiet, and we can't lose any time. It is absolutely necessary for the United States to ascertain the intentions of England, Australia, and Holland, not to say of China, and secure their understanding, before she can reach a compromise. That is clear, judging from the insistence of the United States recently. The sooner the better for her, though she might not know our deadline is 0000 1 December.

[Ugaki was sure that England did not want to fight in the Orient, and that Holland would not want to lose the Netherlands East Indies on top of what the Dutch homeland was suffering.]

The representative of Chiang Kai-shek, Dr. Hu Shih, in the United States is very active, but he will be forced to let the matter drop if the United States will make up her mind not to interfere in the China Incident. The long and the short of it is entirely dependent upon the attitude of the United States toward us, since we will not change our minds. If she abandons the idea that, being the watchdog of the world, she can have her way in everything, she will be spared much. If she doesn't understand that, it can't be helped. Hull may have been cudgeling his brains. As he's clever, he might avoid war politely. But as for us, everything will be O.K. if our position is accepted and our demands met completely. Nothing else will do. How will these three principles which Tojo enunciated publicly be settled? A hook-and-crook policy should be discarded. If war is not to be opened now, we must assume that war will be postponed for at least several years.

Now our Combined Fleet forces are deploying in preparation for war. Everything is advancing in profound secrecy, taking advantage of the poor preparations for war of the United States, England, and Holland. From the viewpoint of naval operations, this is the most advantageous occasion for us. If not now, when can we undertake such operational movements with sure confidence of success? But war is a serious affair of state. We have suffered a great loss in four years of war against China, owing to scarce materials, though it has been a sacred enterprise. Weak minds will faint to hear that we are going to take on a war bigger than this by far. Those who have bullish feelings say anything can be done once begun. However, no sure measures exist to surrender to the United States. Here, then, I repeat—war is a serious affair of state.

On the other hand, it seems to me there will never again occur a better chance to push him down than this occasion.

What is to be, will be. We have to let the situation run its course; that's the way of the world, and I must live resignedly in this world without any peevishness.

Let me give up such trivial thoughts and go to bed.

Monday, 24 November 1941. Cloudy. I took to trying to stare down a colored operational map on the wall. Whichever way I look, enemy forces were drawn in red pencil. The Pacific is so wide! Well, where shall I begin? It is by no means easy to start when I think of the various cases that are supposed to happen, though the way to begin has been defined, and the fleets have deployed so as to meet the opening of war. We can get full marks if everything goes as planned, but it is more important to adapt ourselves adroitly to altered circumstances. Up to this point the prearrangements have been like tilting at windmills, as it were; that is my constant fear. A plan is a plan, but the responsibility of carrying it into practice lies with us who have to do it. This task of ours is what I worry about.

If we could consider our work done, with nothing to do but show off our strength before the enemy, the war would not be worth worrying about. But every imaginable change will happen, just as the aspect of a chessboard will fluctuate according to a move of a chessman of enemy or of friend. However many planes are gathered on the flight deck, they can't take off if the weather doesn't permit. The ocean is so wide that even if a few mines were laid and some subs deployed, they might not be able to intercept enemy ships blessed with ignorance. We mustn't be slaves to mere volume. Numbers and volume are limitless, taking quality into no account. Then we mustn't feel reassured at seeing such and such things before our eyes. There surely are many sore spots to be touched in one's own planning. The coming war, which isn't based upon a reasonable estimate of strength, can't be waged if we're devoured by such anxieties that come against us in battalions. Audacity and adaptability to changing situations are what counts. And to fight a desperate fight to the last.

[That afternoon Admiral Kondo, commander in chief of the Second Fleet, visited *Nagato* with his staff to say good-bye. Rear Admiral Ruitaro Fujita, commander of the Eleventh Division (float planes) came a little later to bid adieu. Then Yamamoto and his staff returned the Second Fleet's call.

[On Tuesday, 25 November, the Combined Fleet's top brass went to Kure, where they visited Admiral Soemu Toyoda and the commander of the Ninth Light Cruiser Division, Rear Admiral Fukuji Kishi. Upon return to ship, Ugaki inspected *Yamato*.

["Favored by happy weather" on Wednesday, 26 November, Ugaki went for a walk and that evening practiced penmanship with his brush-pen in case anyone asked for his autograph. He had an impromptu drinking party with Captain Morisada Tonaki of the Naval General Staff, and Kuroshima and Captain Yasuji Watanabe, the Combined Fleet's staff planning officer.]

The parley between Japan and America has advanced considerably further; I don't know the result, though. That other [Pearl Harbor] force must have left port from the north [Hitokappu Bay] today. It will encounter much hardship on the way. I pray for its success.

[On Thursday, 27 November, Ugaki wrote two poems on the general subjects of loyalty and remembrance. Then he called upon Rear Admiral Mitsuharu Matsuyama, Kure's commander, and spoke with Captain Yoshitake Miwa, the Combined Fleet's operational staff officer, who had just returned from Tokyo. Ugaki noted that the Japanese-American parley was "at a deadlock. It is more than clear that it will break up."

[*It so happened that on this day, 26 November, in Washington, Hull presented his famous Ten Point note to Nomura and Kurusu.*][24]

Friday, 28 November 1941. Cloudy but cleared up later. On the 26th, it was reported, Hull had an interview with Ambassador Kurusu. The former handed a document to the latter, in which was stated what the United States wanted to say to Japan. Will we not lose our prestige entirely if we agree with this man who brandishes his Four Principles, demanding that we entirely withdraw our troops from China and French Indochina, but not ceasing his aid to Chiang, and requesting us to destroy the Tripartite Pact? No measures remain but to go ahead. If we have determined to do so once, it isn't good policy to continue diplomacy with such friction. Even now it's a little late for that.

[*Hull's Four Principles,*[25] *presented to Nomura on April 16, 1941, were: (1) respect for the territorial integrity and sovereignty of each and all nations; (2) support of the principle of noninterference in the internal affairs of other countries; (3) support of the principle of equality, including equality of commercial opportunity; and (4) nondisturbance of the status quo in the Pacific except as the status quo may be altered by peaceful means.*]

[At the urging of many of his colleagues, Ugaki attended a party that afternoon where "everybody was merry in their cups" and Ugaki decided he had best leave instead of moving on to the next gathering.]

Saturday, 29 November 1941. Fine. Left port at 1000. Everything is O.K., just as usual.

1245 arrived at the Hashira Jima anchorage.

Prior to his departure, the commander, Sixth Heavy Cruiser Division, [Rear] Admiral [Aritomo] Goto, called on us to say farewell. His is the last force that goes out, leaving here tomorrow.

I'm in high spirits. I stared at the weather chart, wondering how they are doing on that task force which is supposed to be heading east through northern seas. They will be experiencing many hardships and difficulties. May God grant them two days' fine weather for refueling!

[At this point Ugaki recorded the Hull note of 26 November in its entirety, adding that this would greatly disappoint Nomura and Kurusu. The United States had not "accepted a single demand of our empire. . . . How they insult us!" Ugaki saw no further room for reconsideration: "The only way for us is to make short work of the United States." No diplomat, however moderate, would "have the courage" to continue talks any longer.]

Sunday, 30 November 1941. Fine. We left Hashira Jima at 0400 and moved out off Bungo Channel through Iyo Sea rounding Nuwajima Channel. We engaged in ocean training, which I thought might be the last one. This exercise might be called a special training of the main force except for the air fleet. I initiated this exercise for practice and many defects were found.

We trained in many categories: range-finding at Iyo Channel, high-speed passing through mineswept channel, main guns shooting at imaginary targets, assault of a destroyer division, night firing of auxiliary guns, watch and searchlighting. What was most annoying during the exercise was trouble in the torpedo defense equipment, which will have to be repaired.

As it is just before the opening of war, we laid stress on the watch against submarines. At night information about the strictness of enemy activities was reported.

Monday, 1 December 1941. Fine. Stayed on the bridge to supervise the training last night, with only an hour's catnap. At 2000 we passed through Nuwajima Channel and entered the anchorage at 0100.

At length 0000 hour of the 1st passed. The time of decision has arrived. Is there still any room for us to reconsider?

The commander in chief, accompanied by the adjutant, left for Iwakuni, where he will entrain at 1600 to be received in audience by His Majesty and be granted His Imperial Rescript in the capacity of representative of the navy about to go into battle.

[Ugaki had drafted a reply for Yamamoto to make to the emperor upon receipt of the rescript and of any questions which might come from the throne. Ugaki had plenty to keep him busy in Yamamoto's absence.]

At night a confidential telegram, sent at 1700 1st, came from the vice chief of the Naval General Staff, indicating that the top secret message sent days ago should be opened. Thus I found officially that our empire had decided to open war against the United States, England, and Holland during the first ten days of December, as indicated by Imperial Japanese Naval Order No. 9. The order said that the Combined Fleet will start for _____ and _____ Area Fleet for _____, and their Naval Stations will be _____. [The blanks are Ugaki's.]

But the time and date when war will be opened, that is, when arms will be used, will be ordered later. At the same time, general principles for executing the operation will be issued by Imperial Japanese Naval Directive.

Thus everything has been decided. Although I had no specific authority to notify each fleet commander in chief, I sent confidential telegrams to them, pending issuance of the order about X-Day: "Decision made. Date and time will be ordered later."

The radio reported that an Imperial conference was held this morning at 0800, and ended in thirty minutes, explaining that Japan is even now contriving a policy of requesting the United States to reconsider this problem, despite this pressing situation, still hoping for a peaceful solution.

[*While the Hull-Nomura-Kurusu talks continued, the Imperial conference of 1 December 1941, did in fact determine upon war.*][26]

It was also reported that President Roosevelt, who had been at Warm

Springs for recreation, hurriedly came back to Washington. This, as I had foreseen, is proof of the extreme difficulty in opening war while appearing unconcerned. This is partly due to poor diplomacy, and partly to the inevitable movement of military forces.

The British occupation of Thailand might happen earlier than our X-Day, while it is reportedly said that the British fleet is approaching the Asiatic East. Of course it's natural that those events should happen, yet I hope things will work out as quietly as can be expected.

Tuesday, 2 December 1941. Cloudy. Our task force has entered western longitude. A high atmospheric pressure luckily happens to be just behind them, following them eastward; they'll be able to refuel, I'm sure. They're blessed with this favorable weather just at a critical junction when they'll have to decide whether all the forces could participate in the surprise attack, or to abandon those ships which could not be refueled. Providence has miraculously decided for us, so to speak.

[Here Ugaki expressed his view that this war was "sacred," and as long as all concerned were ready "to die as martyrs for our empire with single-minded loyalty to His Majesty," heaven would protect them. Meanwhile, he would do his part.]

We must have an address of instructions from the commander in chief just at the opening of war. Expecting this, I had ordered the staff to draft it, but no idea seems to come into their minds. I have been trying to draft it myself, and came up with this: "The fate of our empire depends upon this war. Let every man do his duty, exerting his utmost effort." I showed this to Staff Officer Watanabe, asking him to consult with the other staff officers. A little later he came to me and asked for some changes. I promised to take these into consideration.

[*Watanabe asked that only two words be changed, believing them somewhat archaic. Evidently he had in mind Admiral Horatio Nelson's famous signal at Trafalgar: "England expects every man to do his duty."*][27]

Think of the signal which Commander in Chief Admiral [Heihachiro] Togo sent [by Z flag at the battle of Tsushima]: The fate of our empire depends upon this fight. Every man is expected to act with his utmost efforts." My draft bears comparison with this. Under any circumstances, war decides the fate of a country. And, in my personal view, the present war stakes the rise and fall of our empire. This is the firm belief of all who are going to engage in this conflict. Though the natural tendency is for men to think that events connected with them seem more important than anything in the past, such as the Sino-Japanese War or the Russo-Japanese War, yet the war this time is truly a little different from those. Though posterity may regard it as nothing unusual, yet I look upon this as one in which Japan fights against all the nations of the world. This crossroads will determine whether or not Japan will be able to go it alone in the future.

At 1700 I received a telegram from the vice chief of the General Staff to open Imperial Naval Order No. 12. That order says we are authorized to use arms after 0000, 8 December. The Chinese Area Fleet and each naval station will activate their arms by the report of the first attack by the Combined Fleet. Thank goodness!

At 1730 I sent a wireless to the Combined Fleet: "Climb Mt. Niitaka 1208." This meant that "X-Day has been fixed at 0000 of 8 December." This will be communicated to all forces tonight. What will they feel who are doing their duty in the Combined Fleet? I hope everyone will do so at the risk of his life. I don't mean that only our subordinates should rush into the jaws of death, but that I myself will follow them all. Only one thing matters—everything is for the sake of His Majesty and our dear country.

[A liaison officer from the Naval General Staff brought Ugaki instructions about operations against commercial shipping, and Ugaki passed the word along to those concerned. Then he received a message from the army that seven ships of unknown nationality were heading north off Taiwan, but Ugaki did not know whether this was accurate.]

President Roosevelt came back to Washington and talked with Hull and Stark. It was also reported that Nomura and Kurusu had an interview with Undersecretary of State [Sumner] Welles for an hour. In diplomatic negotiations, the best policy is to drag on as if success were probable.

Japanese people in the United States will understand what I have been saying all these years.

In Singapore, Malaya, and the Philippines, tenseness has begun to prevail among the people. We must have patience until the 8th of this month.

The Second Fleet[28] has been a little panic-stricken of late: there is a hint of its proposing to the army that X-Day be moved up. Nervousness and too much fear of the enemy are two things to be aware of.

[Ugaki noted some minor cabinet changes. Yoshiaka Hatta became minister of railroads, while Minister of Agriculture Ino took on the additional duty as minister of colonization. This would free Foreign Minister Togo to handle diplomatic affairs only.]

Wednesday, 3 December 1941. Fine. The lowering sky has cleared up. It became so hot in the afternoon that we were forced to put the ventilator in operation.

In the morning Commander in Chief Yamamoto must have been received in audience and been given His Rescript. He is supposed to have an interview with princes Fushimi and Takamatsu.

[*Admiral Prince Hiroyasu Fushimi was chief of the Naval General Staff from 1932 to 10 April 1941. Commander Prince Takamatsu, a brother of the emperor, was a member of the Naval General Staff. Ugaki had operational matters to think about.*]

It is reported that a British battleship, *Prince of Wales,* arrived at Singapore on the 2nd, and four other battleships were reported lurking in the Indian Ocean.

[Staff Officer Miwa returned to *Nagato* from a field trip and reassured Ugaki that the rumor that "symptoms of disturbance" had appeared in the Second Fleet were only rumor. A letter from his son Hiromitsu also convinced Ugaki that matters at his home were proceeding smoothly. His thoughts turned to the Pearl Harbor expedition.]

The sea on which our task force is moving is covered with an atmospheric pressure; there will be no change on that sea for the time being. This condition coincides with the weather map of 13 November 1936. A moderate breeze will keep blowing over the sea surface for a few days. What a providential gift that is!

President Roosevelt and the secretaries of war and the navy put their heads together, along with the chief of staff and the chief of naval operations. And, in conference with Hull, Kurusu and Nomura on the 2nd, he asked our representatives for an explanation of the new situation and of our intentions hereafter. Don't you know that a big dagger will be thrust into your throat in four days? I pray to God nothing will happen until that last judgment! It all depends upon Providence.

A telephone message from Tokyo advised that the commander in chief of the Combined Fleet will arrive at Miyajima at 0600 tomorrow, instead of flying by plane, owing to unfavorable weather. That's all right.

Thursday, 4 December 1941. Partly cloudy. A great many changes and promotions occurred in the U.S. navy and telegrams are being dispatched very actively. On the other hand, application for fuel funds in November and in December in the (U.S.) Central Ammunition Bureau from the Hawaii Munitions Branch does not show any increase. This makes a good chance for us. It isn't unfair to assault one asleep. This ensures a victory over a most careless enemy. No other means of frustrating this numerous and big enemy can be found but to baffle them at the start.

Public opinion seems not to be stirring so actively. This will help us, together with slippery diplomatic negotiations. The Japanese have to exercise some tact in dealing with such cases. You have my praise!

Last night the Naval General Staff sent us a directive stating that the landing of the Dispatched Corps of Malaya should be done according to the A method. This accords with the opinion of the commander in chief of the Southern Expeditionary Fleet, who has expressed it before: I sent it by wireless.

[*The A method was a surprise landing operation on Malaya to be launched simultaneously with the Pearl Harbor attack.*][29]

The said force left Sana today heading south. The main forces of the southern force—First Division of the Fourth Heavy Cruiser Division, Second Division of the Third Battleship Division, plus two destroyers—left Bako (Formosa) today to cover the Malay Dispatch at the China Sea. The British Navy, it was reported, organized the Far Eastern Asiatic Fleet, with Commander in Chief [Vice] Admiral [Sir Tom] Phillips and flagship *Prince of Wales,* in parallel with the British Main Fleet and the British Mediterranean Fleet. This explains to me the reason for the hurried voyage of *Prince of Wales* via southern Africa. After we have dealt a decisive blow to her, our next game will be the King—*King George V or VI.*

Lieutenant Commander Suguru Suzuki gave us an address about his trip around Hawaii on board the *Taiyo Maru;* he was sent from navy headquarters for that purpose. It may serve as information for us, but it is a little too late for the forces who will attack there.

[*Ugaki wronged Suzuki, who had thoroughly briefed Nagumo and his staff at Hitokappu Bay on 22 November 1941.*][30]

They have no alternative but to head for that place on the supposition that there will be an enemy fleet there. If it can't be found at Lahaina, they'll be floating some place on the ocean. Then they can be located by subs which will catch them in a network.

[A report that the commandant of the Fourteenth Naval District at Honolulu had sent out a "concise and urgent message" disturbed Ugaki, for he feared this might indicate that the Americans had discovered the presence of Japanese submarines. Later, however, he was relieved to learn that the United States had made no changes in position. On the other hand, Japanese planes discovered six submarines near Palau, which Ugaki took to indicate that their opponents had begun to deploy.]

Friday, 5 December 1941. Fine. At 0830 the commander in chief returned to the ship. His Imperial audience, Imperial grant of his [Hirohito's] words and his [Yamamoto's] reply to it—all went without a hitch at Tokyo, he told me. And there was no inquiry from him [Hirohito].

[Yamamoto told Ugaki that Naval Headquarters seemed to have "no definite ideas"; the Combined Fleet would take the lead. In fact, Yamamoto told the chief of the Naval General Staff and the navy minister not to interfere too much "and thus set a bad precedent in the navy."

He added that the emperor recognized the inevitability of the war and "seemed very serenely bright." Less exalted matters took up Ugaki's attention.]

Commander [Shigeru] Fujii was appointed staff officer for military policy, and arrived here. His help will much encourage me, because he has six years' experience at the Bureau of Military Affairs, and has a talent for writing, too. It's very economical to have both brains and a fine pen in one man. This reminds me, with respect and affection, of [Vice Admiral Seneyuki] Akiyama.

[*A noted strategist, Akiyama served as senior staff officer of the Combined Fleet under Togo at the time of the Russo-Japanese War. He was extremely skilled in writing. Ugaki next recorded a worrisome incident.*]

It was reported that two submarines were discovered somewhere near Kondor Island.

The friendly plane which had started from Taihoku (Taiwan), carrying important army operational orders for Canton was reported missing, due to unfavorable weather. According to a telephone message from Tokyo, it was feared that the Chinese Army captured the crew, with important documents. These documents are sufficiently like the Imperial Japanese Naval Orders to indicate whole phases of the war, for they will disclose the decision to open war in the first ten days of December, and that operations thereafter would be in accord with the Imperial Japanese Military Order. This worries me a little. Meanwhile, there came a report saying that fighters in the Philippines were alerted for action at twenty-five minutes' notice. We must be very watchful while I interpret the true meaning of this. I sent a wireless: "Be watchful."

[That evening Ugaki composed one of his brief poems and wrote it on a number of postcards, to be posted to relatives and close friends at the outbreak of war.]

Saturday, 6 December 1941. Fine (X-2), [that is, two days to go before X-Day]. Wrote letter to Hiromitsu. In that letter I enclosed another envelope to be opened at my special communication which might reach him later on; the additional envelope contained a bit of my hair and nail-parings as a memento. Don't ask me where I took that hair from, for there is still plenty of hair on my head!

Once I hoisted my admiral's flag on board *Tone*. I sent this to Hiromitsu in that special envelope with one of my writings which bears the short poem given above, for there will appear no other occasion of hoisting that flag while I am a rear admiral.

In the afternoon an antitorpedo net was experimentally equipped on *Nagato's* starboard. At present, the operational situation is quite all right.

Hawaii is just like a rat in a trap. Enjoy your dream of peace just one more day!

It was reported that an attack order was issued to our force against a large type enemy plane (British) which kept contact with our convoys of the force dispatched to occupy southern Thailand at Siam Bay at a spot on the southern coast of French Indochina.

It was also reported that the Saigon Communications Unit sent out some urgent wireless. We could not receive that message, but I wonder if it was sent for the purpose of ordering an attack on that British plane.[31] Thus what is most worrisome is what may happen at Siam Bay tomorrow. If it should come to the worst, there will be some clash between the two parties. In such case, if the United States does not make a positive move, I think it might be best that the day [to open hostilities] remain decided as day after tomorrow, as planned.

One of my staff officers proposed a change. But, in my opinion, it will be a great disadvantage at this critical moment for us all to change the directions that have already been sent, for it will unsettle the officers and men, and since the principle has been to accept a risk whether we win the horse or lose the saddle. What I fear most is that our forces may lose sight of strict control. Tomorrow's possible trouble might be no more than a skirmish between planes of ours and the enemy's. We must not be so cautious as to cause uneasiness. Therefore I turned down his proposal. Well, how will it come out tomorrow?

Indeed, we await the day with our necks craned. Nothing in the whole world will be more eagerly awaited than this. What a big drama it is, risking the fate of a nation and so many lives!

Don't worry! Let things run their course. During that course, divine will will work out well. This belief is our greatest advantage.

Sunday, 7 December 1941. Fine. At 0000 hours we were honored with the Imperial Message to the Combined Fleet through the Tokyo Naval Communications Center. We immediately sent our answer by wireless. I let it be read to all our ranks and ratings.

Further, at 0600 I sent the commander in chief's message by wireless. The message was polished in style many times, so as to express strength in very concise phrases. I drafted it: "The fate of our empire depends upon this expedition. Each of you will do your duty, wearing yourselves to the bone." How this message will impress all the ranks and ratings on their ships already deployed on the Pacific!

[*In Romaji the message reads: "Kokoku no kohai kakarite kono seisen ni ari, Kunkotsu-saishin ono-ono sono nin o matto seyo." For all his pains, Ugaki had changed his first draft by a mere three words.*]

According to the sortie order, ships have been ready to make 14 knots in four hours since 0800. We finished taking on board about four hundred rounds of 40-cm new shells and cut any connection with land; everything was fully prepared.

At 0900, Vice Admiral Takasu, commander in chief of the First Fleet, and his chief of staff, [Rear Admiral Kenzo] Kobayashi, visited us. In the afternoon, [Rear Admiral Torao] Kuwabara, commander in chief of the Third Carrier Division, came. They all seemed merry and pleasant. As *bujin* or military men, they were only too glad to meet this opportunity.

No special telegram has reached here from the convoys dispatched toward Siam, contrary to my expectation of some trouble between the two parties, and I wonder if rain held them up. Nonetheless, my guess was right. What Staff Officer Miwa feared was nothing but an imaginary lion in the path. He said to me that I bested him this time. Naturally England will show Dutch courage, but it's sure that she won't willingly fight in the Far East. Seeing that a Japanese convoy was heading west, she might think that it was headed for Thailand, not for her own territory. She won't have the courage to open fire on us, so their surface ships won't come northward. As yet they have neither preparation nor resolution to do that.

I had insisted that our convoy would pass without any big hitch until evening. Just as I had predicted, the sun set with no incident. In that part of the world it will be night two hours from now. If our convoy is not sighted on its way to its landing spots after noon today, we may assume that its landing will be a success. However, I had a telegram message from the Naval General Staff stating that an army aircraft had shot down an enemy seaplane off Kamo Point around 0900. The downed plane seemed to be British, it added. Anyway, I've taken such happenings into consideration.

There has been no other important telegram or telephone call. By this silence I can sense that every force is moving on silently and stealthily. It's highly certain that our first attack will succeed.

Our program to be carried out tonight between our country and Thailand is as follows: First, passage of our Imperial troops through Thailand with use of port facilities; second, mutual defense, if circumstances permit. These have been progressing. It was all for the purpose of preparing a way for us to secure Thailand as a friendly state that our empire took the trouble of returning her lost territory by mediating the dispute between Thailand and French Indochina after our occupation of the latter. At this last moment, if we transact this matter with grim resolution, that country will have no alternative but to submit to us. The coming operations are supposed to take several countries as our opponents. Such arrangements and negotiations so that our military strength may be used against Thailand, which is so small and weak, will be the worst policy. We can pull our weight against such a small state successfully.

What has become of the negotiations between Japan and the United States? On the 5th a short interview was held, but, anyway, the United States will be notified at 0400 tomorrow (Central Standard Time) to the effect that our empire will take free actions and movements. That's all right. It was reported that at Manila yesterday an urgent call was issued to the people there to evacuate all personnel. Some commotion seems to be stirring. A report says that both England and America are generally observing the movements of Japan who, in their opinion, will act to gain his ends but will not yet fight for some time. That's enough, anyway. Don't you know that the whole world will be panic-stricken within several hours to see such a world-shaking scene enacted?

From my point of view, the process and steps that our empire has taken concerning this war will be worthy of full marks.

[Here Ugaki listed these steps, which may be summarized as follows:

1. War preparations were well advanced, although complete preparedness never could be attained.

2. The army, traditionally obsessed with Russia, had "awakened to the importance of the southern areas," if only temporarily.

3. The Tripartite Alliance and occupation of French Indochina had clearly established the United States and England as the enemies and if Japan were to fight them, they had "better start while the war situation in Europe is developing favorably to Germany and Italy."

4. Japan had come to realize that it could not establish the Greater East Asia Co-Prosperity Sphere without first destroying England and the United States. "And our nation is quite tired of the [China] Incident and they want something else at present."

5. The occupation of French Indochina had more of an effect on the United States and England than Japan had anticipated, resulting in the freezing of funds. Oil on hand was "far from enough to supply the home industries. And what oil is produced at home is nothing but a drop on a hot stone." This had convinced the Japanese that they had to fight to preserve their independence.

6. American war preparations were proceeding apace, so now was the time to strike. "If it is delayed two or three years, the material balance between Japan and the United States will become beyond comparison."

7. Although the Soviet Union was proving unexpectedly tenacious, the Japanese estimated "that Russia will not fall in with England and the United States this winter."

8. Strong elements in the navy had insisted that if the opening of war

was delayed beyond December, it should not be started at all for some time to come.

9. Research had tended to show that if Japan conquered the rich resource areas of southeast Asia and procured supplies from them, they could continue fighting as long as necessary. "Those in authority" had become convinced of the truth of this concept.

10. The United States had been "too stiff" diplomatically, which in Ugaki's opinion "was rather a break for us," as "not even dovelike persons" wanted to continue negotiations.

11. "The national policy was in accord with strategy, and the latter was stronger than the former."

12. This was the time and the opportunity, "and if this chance had been missed, it would have been difficult for us to stand up again."]

2
No Greater Victory
8 December 1941–28 February 1942

HERE BEGAN *days of glory for Japan's armed forces and days of frustration for the Allies. Pearl Harbor, Guam, Wake Island,* Prince of Wales *and* Repulse, *the Philippines, the Netherlands East Indies, Hong Kong, Singapore—names that rang with the music of victory in Japanese ears. Naturally, Ugaki reveled in this series of successes.*

Pearl Harbor caused him one disappointment—the task force's failure to follow its astounding success with a second major attack. Ugaki never really forgave Nagumo for his decision to retire, and his disdain for Nagumo surfaces several times over the succeeding months.

Causes for complaint, however, were few and far between during this period. The Japanese Army was victorious wherever it set foot, and Ugaki was sufficiently fair-minded to give it a word of praise. In fact, Japan's conquests were running ahead of schedule, and Ugaki pondered what should be the second phase.

After Pearl Harbor, the navy's successes in these months were relatively minor but came steadily. Yamamoto's men sank the old carrier Langley *and seriously damaged the* Saratoga—*not for the last time confusing her with the* Lexington. *The Nagumo Task Force shot up Darwin, Australia, and at Badung Strait other Japanese ships engaged in what Ugaki called "the first sea battle worthy of the name" since the war started. The Japanese sank one ship and damaged two others; they claimed to have sunk five and seriously damaged two more. This established a pattern of exaggeration prevalent throughout the diary. Ugaki was not being deliberately deceptive; he could only record what the battle reports told him. Therefore, all such reports—Allies' included—must be viewed with a skeptical eye. The truth had to await the end of the war and comparison of records.*

Events gave Ugaki a rather low opinion of the opposition. Ever the professional, however, he thought the Japanese could have done better, and did not hesitate to record with indignant disgust what he considered to be their mistakes. He could, also, spare an admiring word for the enemy when praise was due

42

for the Americans who raided the Marshalls or for the British defenders of Hong Kong.

Ugaki was too intelligent to take this burst of success for granted. He antici-pated that the war would last five to ten years, and worried that the Japanese people would not be ready for such a long ordeal. For the present, he was alert to the possibility of U.S. submarines, even in the Inland Sea, and fretted that at all costs Tokyo should be protected against air raids.

Inevitably, Ugaki reveals many aspects of his own personality. He was an enthusiastic huntsman, and whenever possible he went ashore to bag ducks and other game birds which he and his messmates enjoyed eating. He could be caustic in his criticism of an officer for what he considered stupidity or cowardice, but he could worry over the missing-in-action son of an old friend, and pray sincerely for the souls of the men lost in battle or in accidents. Ugaki had a spiritual side, and he believed firmly in the hereafter and in the intercession of his deceased wife, Tomoko, to whose memory he was devoted. His fascination with suicide is again evident in his concern for and lauding of the midget submariners at Pearl Harbor and his praise for an officer who went down with his ship although he could have saved himself easily.

This section ends on a high note for the Japanese—the beginning of the battle of Sunda Strait.

Monday, 8 December 1941. Fine, warm. X-day. The long-anticipated day has arrived at last. I awoke at 0300 on my own. After leaving bed, I was having a smoke when [Air] Staff Officer [Commander Akira] Sasaki hur-ried into my room and reported, "At 0319 wireless TO is being sent repeatedly." ["To" *is the first syllable of* Totsugeki (*charge*).] With this I knew that the attack order had been issued to the two hundred planes of our task force which had been approaching Hawaii, and the first attack on Pearl Harbor was under way.

Then I confined myself to the operations room and listened with atten-tion to every telegram: "I torpedoed enemy battleship with great war result," or "I bombed Hickam Airfield and got a great war result," which were wirelessed by our friendly planes, as well as enemy wireless messages which were most interesting. We can see the fighting situation so clearly. Enemy consternation is beyond description. It is their breakfast time at 0320 [Tokyo time]. While they were at their breakfast table, great masses of Japanese airplanes came like bolts from the blue; I can imagine their utter surprise. The following are some examples to show their uproar:

1. All ships sortie from Pearl Harbor.

2. An order to sweep magnetic and moored mines in the waters south of Ford Island.

3. An order at 0415—the commander in chief of the Asiatic Fleet will operate according to Operational Plan No. 4.

Other such orders were given in succession. Such information was sent as: enemy transports (nationality unknown) or six naval vessels were being sighted; a destroyer and six ships were approaching the shore on fire; and so forth, and it is estimated that they fought among themselves.

[*Ugaki gave a few other instances. Evidently the Japanese had picked up garbled bits of American messages. Certainly Ugaki exaggerated U.S. confusion very little.*][1]

We assume that the second air raid came an hour later than the first one, at which time the five midget submarines, after being released from their mother ships, were to have attacked enemy ships in harbor. I suppose the enemy mistook these for mines, which were ordered swept. I shall be very happy if these midget subs will return, but if they don't, who will make public their pains and merits? I regret their efforts can only be estimated by enemy situations at a later time.

[*One might gain the impression from Ugaki's diary that the only action of the second wave was the midget submariners, which were totally ineffective. He had no word for Nagumo's airmen, whose skill and bravery brought about results.*][2]

On the other hand, our units succeeded in landing at Bataan.

I received a wireless message that the Eleventh Air Fleet had decided to postpone its departure for the air raids until 0800 owing to dense fog in Formosa, but it seems that the attack was to be executed at 1330, judging from later messages.[3]

In the Malayan area, our forces reportedly succeeded in landing at 1330, but it's quite dubious whether the landing at Kota Bharu, which is more important, was a success or not. I understand that after the first landing the rest apparently withdrew. I am very worried about this issue.

At 1000 I called in the skippers and chiefs of staff of the ships and had our staff explain the war situation to them as far as possible. I also gave them instructions concerning the forthcoming operation the Main Body was going to take.

As the present war situation is generally progressing at a favorable pace, as I had presupposed, our Main Body left port as planned cutting off telephone contact with the Naval General Staff, coming through Bungo Channel (which was mineswept) at the speed of 14, 16, and 18 knots an hour around 0830, and sailed for the south under strict watch (in the direction of about 140°).

At 1045, a Privy Council was held and the Imperial Declaration of War against England and the United States issued. After this, His Majesty summoned the ministers of the army and navy, giving a special message to the fighting men; the two answered him for all those men.

[At the end of his entry for 8 December, Ugaki copied into his diary the text of the Imperial Rescript declaring war.

[Here he mentioned some miscellaneous action. Thailand had agreed to let Japanese troops pass; Germany and Italy would soon declare war against the United States; the China Area Fleet had commenced an assault upon Hong Kong. "On the Yangtze River an American ship [the river gunboat *Wake*] was captured." He summarized the war results as reported by the participants.]

Generally speaking, this is a great success—first come, first served.

Tonight the chief of the Naval General Staff sent us a congratulatory telegram upon our glorious victory. I put off our answer until we entered port, because we were in the midst of movement on the one hand, and on the other this result should be counted, in my opinion, as only a trivial one.

Tuesday, 9 December 1941. Partly cloudy. X + 1 day. Telegrams of congratulation on the war results came in from the navy minister and the chief of the Naval General Staff, the army minister and the commander in chief of the Southern Army, but, just like last time, I did not hasten to answer.

The United States and England declared war against Japan this morning.

A wireless interception told me that the U.S. secretary of the navy sent the following to all ships and chiefs of U.S. naval stations:

> The first treacherous attack of the enemy navy gave a tremendous shock to us who are in charge of war. Now no time is to be lost. Our nation wants as many ships, as many guns and personnel as can be obtained, the sooner the better. Not a second will be lost in hesitation. Navy, stand up! What I have said is the real road the navy should tread and what our people earnestly want. Frank Knox.

How crazy this is at the eleventh hour! This means an absolute "knockout."

My headache was the occupation of Kota Bharu. But, according to the Third Destroyer Squadron report, they are engaged in hard fighting, their landing craft having drifted away, but the Takumi Force has already occupied the enemy airfield, as was revealed later. I was much relieved at that.[4]

At the report from our sub *I-65* at 1513, that he sighted two enemy capital ships at _____ miles off _____ [Ugaki's blanks] of the Malay Peninsula, at the speed of 14 knots an hour, our operations room suddenly became excited and strained. All sorts of orders were issued at once: "Sub will keep contact with these enemy ships"; "The Southern Expeditionary Fleet will call up all its strength at once"; "The Second Fleet will make haste in turning southward." Can the planes fight? Is there time enough before nightfall? Will the sub be the sole figure on the scene? What interesting subjects these should be! After the report from the plane that had been keeping in touch with the ships was cut off, it was reported that another sub once and the Seventh Heavy Cruiser Division⁵ once sighted these enemy ships, but nothing happened except these reports. The opportunity was not ripe to attack them yet.

The process was as follows: At the first report that enemy ships were taking a course of 20°, our surface ships joined so as to meet them in due time. But soon after this, they turned and we missed a long-awaited opportunity. We missed a happy chance for an ideal night battle with the cooperation of plane, submarine, and surface ship. What a pity! What were we doing to lose such a chance!

What can be the purpose of the British fleet's northward voyage? Is it to interrupt our landing at Kota Bharu? Do they intend to find some nice game in attempting guerrilla warfare? Or are they going to adhere to their old principle of fighting the enemy wherever they sight him, and then display their valor after controlling the enemy? From our point of view, it is too headstrong, but their conduct of outrageous audacity is praiseworthy. I don't know if they know or not that subs, mines, several heavy cruisers, two high-speed battleships, and considerably predominant fighter planes are in the southern part of French Indochina. To think of such defense!

At first it was reported that the battleship was estimated as *Repulse* but later as the *King George* type. According to the reconnaissance report of the morning of the 8th over Singapore, the following were sighted there: *Prince of Wales* and another battleship, four cruisers, and several destroyers. Then are the ships that our sub sighted another outfit?

Be that as it may, it is a great regret that we could not send them to the bottom of the Pacific. I will put down roughly my intuitive estimate of the causes of our miss:

1. There was a two-hour gap between the time of discovery and the time of reporting it. This gap delayed everything that should have been done thereafter. But we must not overlook the merit of *I-65* who sighted them.

2. At that time, subs were deployed so that they were ordered to keep in touch with each other, but in vain. Was it partly because of their low speed (13 knots) and partly that the distance between subs was too big, or the location of the enemy ships was not exact enough, I wonder?

3. Was the weather not favorable to us or did a shower prevent sight?

4. Air contact could not be kept continuously. It seems that efforts on the part of the surface ships to keep contact weren't sufficient. By the way, one of the most important conditions is that the location of enemy ships should be made as clear as possible.

5. It was too late to have our attack planes at the battle scene, being already late at night, and the situation was such that to distinguish friends from enemy was difficult.

6. The first plan of the commander in chief of the Southern Expeditionary Force was good. But in his plan the commander in chief of the Second Fleet overestimated the distance. Though in effect the latter was senior to the former from the standpoint of control and command, yet I wonder if the latter rather overawed the former Southern Expeditionary Force. That is, the Southern Expeditionary Force should have made contact with the enemy; I cannot agree with the idea that the Southern Expeditionary Force and the Second Fleet should join in attacking the enemy by surface ships, turning the attack tonight over to the sub squadron and air forces. In a word, they tried to be too adroit and instead were outmaneuvered.

7. At the time of the enemy turn at 20°, our forces tried to concentrate all our forces at the enemy's head; this caused us to lose a chance of nabbing the enemy when he reversed his course. So much for the British ships, for we have tomorrow. Anyway, you will hear of it some time tomorrow. We can't remain without any retaliation after being made such fools of.

Last night there was a telegram that our task force will return through L point via first course with the report of the war result. This is open to criticism as sneak-thievery and contentment with a humble lot in life. Since our loss is not more than thirty planes, it is most important for us to expand our results.

[*Ugaki referred to Nagumo's decision to retire without launching another full-scale attack on Pearl Harbor. He continued in this vein.*]

At the news from the task force mentioned above, my staff officers proposed a new plan that our fleet also head for the same course. But I didn't agree with that. I ordered them to wait for today's war process, because I had my own idea. Although most of the enemy battleships were made unnavigable and many planes lost as a result of our attack, yet several cruisers and CVs are probably able to come out for battle. But they could hardly have enough courage to make a long chase because of supposedly insufficient battle preparations. Last night two destroyers assaulted Midway Island from the western part, but I wonder how much damage these two ships could give the enemy, even though the report says the attack did considerable damage to enemy installations.

Then I proposed that they make another attack on that island, and they agreed with my idea. And there was another who insisted on assaulting Hawaii again, which is fairly reasonable.

[*This probably was Kuroshima, who urged this at a staff meeting the next morning.*][6]

On this matter we discussed the following questions again:

1. In the second attack, we couldn't expect surprise. We could surely expect good results, yet our damage would not be small. There is some chance of enemy carrier planes attacking our flank. This could result in a heavy blow to us. And we don't know the extent of the damage to the enemy air forces.

2. Such a plan is not ready yet. To take it up again afresh is not an easy task. On the other hand, our force will have to send out wireless telegrams, to its disadvantage. Moreover, if they remain on the sea near there, the center of atmospheric pressure will begin to move, and refueling will become difficult.

3. How to keep up morale is most important. Who can say it is better to force this operation again among those who experienced the beginning and the end of the last operation? They gave it their utmost effort. It would only make them angry at the idea if we try to force this on them. We cannot force others too much.

If I were the commander in chief of the task force, I would be prepared to expand the war result to the extent of completely destroying Pearl Harbor, by encouraging my subordinates at this critical time. But I should not measure others by my standard; I should confine myself to myself. So, as I had proposed, the assault on Midway was decided upon; the following was wirelessed to the commander in chief of the First Air Fleet: "If the circumstances permit, the task force will attack Midway by aircraft on its way back. It will try to destroy the Midway base so that it cannot be used again as a base."

We are sailing at 140° as usual, but as nothing happened, speed has been lowered to 14 knots since evening.

Today small units made an air raid on the Philippines.

England and the United States must be in commotion now, but no other news but radio is available.

Wednesday, 10 December 1941. Rainy. X + 2 Day. At 0830, we turned to 90° in order to pass between Haha Jima and Iwo Jima. In accordance with the report from our plane advising that it had sighted a track of some fishing boat at fifty miles northwest of northern Iwo Jima, since 1130 we began to navigate in a zigzag course at 16 knots, heading a little northward. Rain began to fall since morning owing to low pressure.

The landings at Aparri and Vigan were made as scheduled. In the former, it was done without being discovered or encountering any resistance, but in the latter there was air resistance, and, as a result, the enemy's sweeping machine-gun fire exploded mines on the No. 10 minesweeper. Five officers and petty officers with seventy enlisted men were killed and twenty persons wounded. The minesweeper at last sank at 1130.

[*This was the occasion of the highly publicized supposed sinking of battleship* Haruna *by Captain Colin P. Kelly, Jr., USA, off Aparri. It later developed he had attacked heavy cruiser* Ashigara *but, as Ugaki indicated, the only loss to Japan was a minesweeper.*][7]

We sustained further minor damages. Landing at Guam was a success, and the island was occupied.

What has become of last night's prey? The enemy began to turn southward, our sub chased them and fired torpedoes, but in vain. Also, mines didn't touch them. The last resort was to use planes for an attack. The Second Fleet and the Southern Expeditionary Force have also given up pursuit and have begun to steer northward. A telegram was received saying that planes left for battle at 1100. Everyone was beaming with smiles at the report "Enemy sighted." Judging from a wireless sent between the planes that participated in the fight—"Where is the other battleship?"—I am sure one was sunk, but the details are unknown. Another bomber reported two hits on the target, which sank instantly, with a destroyer rescuing some of her crew.

According to later information, torpedo bombers (fifty-one planes) scored many hits on two ships. *Repulse* sank at 1420 and *King George* also sank at 1450 as she fled to the east with her body listing to port. Our damage: Three planes shot down, and a few planes were forced down in French Indochina owing to moderate damage. No greater victory than this will be won![8]

What name shall I give to this naval engagement? In this case again the credit has to be attributed to aircraft, so my idea—"Kamo Point Sea Battle"—will not be appropriate. Afterwards it was revealed that the ship we had estimated to be *King George* was *Prince of Wales*. The ship had been sent here in a hurry as flagship of the commander in chief of England's Far Eastern Asiatic Fleet. But her headlong movement caused a sad end, her dead carcass sinking deep in the ocean. (The part where the ship sank is not deeper than fifty meters; it won't be too difficult to refloat her. I think that in the near future the ships will join the Japanese nationality of ships. I hope they won't turn into seaweed too soon.) I cannot but recognize the remarkable power of airplanes, seeing the results since last night. These battleships that had participated in the sinking of *Bismarck* proved to be poorly equipped for a defensive battle, though they were the newest and most powerful ones. In the long run, this is a long-way-around method of taking revenge. [*In Romaji,* Edo no kataki o Nagasaki de utsu. *Tokyo (Edo) is a long way from Nagasaki, but vengeance may be exacted far from the scene of the original offense. Ugaki meant that* Bismarck *had been avenged a long distance from the scene of her destruction.*]

As a result of this action, the opinion that battleships are nothing and airplanes are everything will become active. The war results of these days, gained on both the eastern and western part of the Pacific, will be worthy of great praise. While I was engrossed in these war results, at 1600 another report was intercepted for our side from the planes around Chichijima: "Enemy main forces sighted at 40 miles south of Haha Jima, advancing in zigzag movement." What a thing! These are simply our main forces! Immediately a warning was wirelessed, and a first disposition was issued to prevent mistaken bombings. Afterwards the plane retracted her wireless.

At the same time, the commander of the Seventh Land Base asked me if any friendly subs were moving near there. I answered, "None." Then the next report said that an enemy sub was sighted at forty miles south of Haha Jima, and they attacked it. The location was just in front of our course. Later we changed course to the south and increased speed. In the meantime, it was revealed that the sub was four subs, judging by their wireless. At dusk we turned to 35° and increased speed up to 20 knots to deceive enemy subs. It is not certain whether they were following us or have discovered us. The sensitivity [radio audibility] is too high. Uneasiness pursues me. At 1910 our patrol boat discovered another sub at forty miles to the rear of us. How dangerous our invisible enemy is!

[*To the best of our knowledge, no U.S. submarines were in Japanese waters at this time.*][9]

Since launching patrol planes from the light carrier *Hosho* was delayed due to misjudgment, she had to recover them after dusk with lamps lighted on deck. How dangerous that is! Visibility is very low in the dark.

In fear of our position being found, an order was issued to maintain radio silence and even refrain from using flash signals as much as possible. Owing to these, *Hosho* and three destroyers were missing after they left the Main Body.

According to a telegram from the chief of the First Bureau of the Naval General Staff, another battleship was found sunk on the afternoon of the 9th.

As for the desperate efforts of those midget subs, two of them have succeeded, judging from their telegram "*Tora,*" meaning "I have succeeded in surprise attack." ["*Tora! Tora! Tora!*" (*"Tiger! Tiger! Tiger!"*) was the code signifying surprise had been achieved. Despite Ugaki's belief, no Japanese submarine did any damage at Pearl Harbor.] But even until now, they haven't been saved on board ship. My heart aches to think of that. I heartily regret that their immortal spirit will remain in the dark.

[Here Ugaki recalled the farewell party held at Kure on 17 November 1941, when the midget submariners had their pictures taken and wrote autographs with short mottoes. Ugaki listed these and expressed his wish to show the framed picture to the emperor some day.

[The Combined Fleet received an Imperial Rescript commending it for the results achieved, which "profoundly impressed" the recipients.]

The Southern Area Forces have occupied the Gilbert Islands and established bases.

The radio reports that the air defense commander of Hawaii; the commander in chief [*respectively, Major General Frederick L. Martin, commanding the Hawaiian Air Force and Lieutenant General Walter C. Short, in command of the Hawaiian Department*]; Admiral [Husband E.] Kimmel, commander in chief of the U.S. Fleet; Admiral Stark, chief of naval operations; or Secretary of the Navy Knox should be court-martialed. This tells us so much about the shock they received. It is a gross error for the authorities to want to punish their subordinates when some misfortune occurs, when a state wants to force its national policies, that state must be sufficiently prepared for war to carry them out. It is natural that he should be defeated when he is not fully prepared to back up his braggadocio, and responsibility always rests on the president. Shall we send our judge advocates there to defend those officers, saying that Japan should be accused instead, since it was Japan that attacked there? Ha! Ha!

Tonight we took a southwestern course at 18 knots, under strict watch.

[On Thursday, 11 December 1941, the "absurd affair" of the missing ships, CVL *Hosho* and three destroyers, was resolved when they were discovered some five hundred miles away on the eastern side of the Bonin Islands.]

The Main Body had sailed out to sea with the main purpose of receiving the returning task force, but it was decided that the Main Body's operation be suspended, first because no enemy threatening the task force has been observed, and, second, it has become necessary to send out a destroyer squadron to the returning task force to strengthen its anti-sub guard. We decided to turn west at 0600, and northwest at 0900, then headed for Bungo Channel. It rained all day today, heavily sometimes. At night, enemy wireless communication between the subs and Cavite is quite heavy. It is estimated that enemy subs are lurking on waters not so far from us. We must be very watchful, since a report came in from the Kure Naval Station saying that one of its training planes sighted something like an enemy sub on the northern point off Sata Point—in the Inland Sea.

This morning the Southern Ocean Force tried to occupy Wake Island, but it seems a considerably hard job. The commander in chief of the Fourth Fleet gave an order to withdraw all the force together, if circumstances required. Enemy strength on the island is estimated to be much more than prefigured, but not so many as to require withdrawal. Details of the operation's progress are not yet known. Our Philippine Air Force rendered a great service by attacking enemy planes and other equipment around Manila: Shot down and destroyed planes, 106. No more than fifty planes have been left for the enemy. What are the army planes doing? They should be rather pitied. In the announcement of war results, the army pretends to have participated in all battles and that all the aircraft shot down were due to the army air forces. But in war, real ability is everything. Such a trivial cheat will be disclosed to all the people within a short time.

[Ugaki took note of the declarations of war between Germany, Italy, and the United States, and reflected upon the situation.]

Now it has really turned out to be the Second World War. Everything connected with future operations and leadership of the new world order rests upon the shoulders of our empire. The whole world will revolve around our empire, which forms an axis. We must stress this idea.

[Ugaki mentioned that a treaty had been concluded with Thailand. He declared that Japan must consolidate her hold upon the southern region before the spring thaw, when the Soviet Union might join with the United States and England. He reminisced about the division of opinion as to the advisability and timing of the Pearl Harbor attack. "But now we have achieved the expected result by the daring attack to the east, a fact which deserves congratulations." He ended the day's entry by reproducing the new Tripartite Treaty concluded on 11 December between Japan, Germany, and Italy.]

Friday, 12 December 1941. Cloudy. X + 4 Day. At dawn this morning, landings at Legaspi on southern Luzon Island succeeded. The defense at that place was quite firmly prepared and the enemy reinforced, too, it was reported, but the landing was made quite easily. Fear is often greater than the danger.

Details of the occupation of Wake are not yet known, but the chief of staff of that fleet asked me for another carrier as a reinforcement. I fear the fleet will withdraw in the end with much damage. As there were too many obscure points in the telegram, I put off the decision for a little.

The watch against subs has been strict since the night before last. Beginning at 0800, speed was heightened to 18 knots, zigzagging. While I was bathing in the rest room, suddenly I heard "battle disposition!" Then I was informed of the approach of an enemy sub. I hurried up to the bridge. Our patrol plane dropped a bomb at 3.5 or 4 kilometers, starboard, in the direction of 340°. I ordered my ship to turn port at 90° with speed of 20 knots. Two destroyers were sent to make a depth charge attack. During our dodging movement we could intercept enemy wireless between subs:

A. How are you doing?
B. O.K.
C. Nice, nice.

If heard in peacetime, that might not sound like a hostile interception, because it was nothing but ordinary conversation, but at that time it was an ominous communication to us. We could ascertain by the sensitivity that at least two ships were around us as well as know the distance of these subs.[10] These communications will be useful for a war of nerves, but, upon reflection, such private communication between personnel in charge of wireless should be strictly prohibited. This is an example by which we can judge the American navy. It is very rare that U.S. subs move alone; they always operate with a companion. Is it for the sake of safety, or to dispel loneliness?

Visibility tonight is not good, if not poor. As darkness fell, we changed course to 0° heading north.

[Here Ugaki faithfully recorded another Imperial Rescript, congratulating the fleet's arm for sinking the British ships, and Yamamoto's reply.]

Saturday, 13 December 1941. Cloudy. X + 5 Day. After passing through Hayasui Channel, at 0230 our fleet headed eastward with antimine and torpedo equipment hauled up. On our way, we challenged three boats, which proved to be subchasers from the Kure Naval Station. These were sent against the enemy subs discovered a few days ago. After passing through Kudako Channel, we arrived at the buoy at 0630. I do not feel tired, though I have had little sleep. This is partly owing to the excitement caused by my feeling of responsibility and partly to that metabolin which [Kaoru] Miyake gave me. In action, physical power is everything.

During my little nap, the adjutant captain called me, saying there were guests. At 1030, the chief of the Education Bureau, [Rear Admiral Sakae] Tokunaga, Adjutant of the Naval General Staff [Capt. Zensuke] Kanome, representing the navy minister and the chief of the Naval General Staff respectively, with the chief of staff of the Kure Naval Station, [Rear Admiral Torahiko] Nakajima, to extend hearty congratulations. I said to myself, "Don't make a mountain of a molehill," but appreciated their words anyway. "At the very start everything went quite favorably for us. But it is just a prelude; the drama is not yet on. I'm not so satisfied with our initial results, but of course I'm not off my guard. I am going to do my bit all the more. When you see your chiefs after you return, tell them this, please." They all left at 1330.

The assault on Wake Island ended in failure, as I had feared, with two destroyers sunk (_____) [Ugaki's blank][11] and some killed or wounded. All the forces except those withdrew. Accordingly, a part of the ask force was ordered to help attack Wake at the request of the chief of staff, Fourth Fleet. No report of Midway air raids came. I much wonder if that is due to some new idea of attacking or to some difficulty in refueling. Sending our wireless telegrams is too dangerous.

In the evening a report came from destroyer *Sanae* of the Kure Naval Station that an enemy sub was sighted at three miles near the Okinoshima Lighthouse. Is it one of those that we met during our voyage, or another one? It is not certain. But it was at the time when *Hosho*, which had left the Main Body, should enter the harbor. I sent a destroyer division and some planes to watch and guard.

I read the newspapers since the 7th and got the impression that the people's mental attitude is rather satisfactory, but I fear their zeal will cool in the course of time. For the time being, they will not cool down, thanks to the splendid war results. But when the war becomes protracted, can our leaders and authorities lead our nation for as long as five or ten years, maintaining the people's morale and overcoming every difficulty?

Today our Philippine Air Force attacked the enemy and did considerable damage to them.

Sunday, 14 December 1941. Cloudy. X + 6 Day. The way to operations in the southern areas has been paved opportunely. In a military decision, it is everything to catch the rising tide.

[Another submarine scare that morning convinced Ugaki that "enemy subs have sneaked into the Inland Sea." Defenses of Bungo Channel had been strengthened but were still "makeshift"; if a U.S. submarine wanted to enter, it could do so quite easily.]

Monday, 15 December 1941. Cloudy. X + 7 Day. A report says that the attack against Midway Island was abandoned owing to bad weather, and the forces are on their way back via L Point. This disappoints me very much. The best strategy will be to strike Wake Island first, then Midway. Perhaps this game will be a winner.

[According to Ugaki, the war, Pearl Harbor, and sinking of the British ships had been given official names. For a variety of reasons, Japanese radio was "too noisy to hear." This worried Ugaki: "Unless some counter-measures are taken, this information facility will be useless." The Diet had been summoned for a two-day session, and Ugaki was "eager to hear what public opinions are reflected in it."]

Tuesday, 16 December 1941. Cloudy. X + 8 Day. Cloudy with rather strong wind. Winter has come.

Representatives of the First and Second Battleship Divisions and the Third CV Division held a research meeting on the subject or "our movements during this time."

Early this morning, a report of a successful landing at Mili reached us.[12]

According to new orders issued, the task force changed its course, and is expected to enter Truk Harbor on the 22nd. It is the most natural course for them. For the task force to cooperate with the Southern Ocean Forces and make a quick job of it is the best tactic at present. And, in my opinion, to strike Wake Island on their way to Truk will be the better policy; but I wonder how it will come out.

At about 0900, Captain Tomioka, chief of the First Section, Naval General Staff, came with [Cmdr. Shigeshi] Uchida [of its Operation Section] to discuss the estimated state of the war.

My ideas about this matter have already been handed to the senior staff officer in a paper; what the Naval General Staff thinks about it and what the Combined Fleet does are almost the same. But I was told that the army is looking for the chance to attack Russia after the successful end of the first-period operations; what a mean spirit it has!

Today again hunting enemy subs was carried out throughout the Inland Sea, using planes and boats; nothing particular happened. A large group of dolphins was reported seen at Iyo Bay; this might have caused some misjudgment. The Kure Defense Unit reported that two enemy subs were considered damaged; one at the time when unusual turbulence was observed in a minefield, and another at the time when destroyer *Sanae* attacked while CVL *Hosho* was entering port.

The opening ceremony of the extraordinary Diet session was held today. The premier gave a speech, then reported the war results. Admiral Shimada, the navy minister, was at his best. His report brought down the whole house. This is symbolic of the people's gratitude. We must do our best to justify the people's trust in us.

Once the task force wirelessed us they were headed for Truk, but later sent another message that they are coming back to Japan Proper due to refueling problems. This made everything so confused. Then I ordered them to strike Wake Island on the way home with a part of their force.

Today construction of *Yamato* was completed and she entered the Japanese Navy's Vessels List. *Yamato* was included in the First Battleship Division. A great addition of strength to us!

[On Wednesday, 17 December 1941, Nagumo's action report of the Pearl Harbor attack came in, and Ugaki recorded it verbatim. In brief, the task force claimed to have sunk four battleships, one cruiser, and an oil tanker; severely damaged two battleships, two cruisers, and two destroyers; and inflicted moderate damage upon two battleships and seven cruisers. In addition, they claimed to have shot down fourteen planes and destroyed 450 on the ground. All this at a cost of twenty-nine aircraft lost.

[Nagumo added, which must have pleased Ugaki, "In addition to the above-mentioned results, it is certain that extraordinary results were obtained by the most valiant attacks by the special attack units of the submarine force."

[*Under the circumstances, this report was not too far off the mark. No oil tanker was hit, and the Japanese overestimated the cruiser strikes; however, they failed to report other ship damage. The report badly overestimated damage to U.S. aircraft. And, as mentioned, the midget submarines did no damage. But Ugaki had plenty to be pleased about.*]

By the help of Providence, we have at last obtained such brilliant results! Nothing can be more praiseworthy. With the entry of that huge *Yamato*, the ratio of 5–5–3 [set at the Washington Naval Conference of 1921–22] turned out to be reversed. Instead of by treaty, we retaliated against the enemy with real power. This ought to teach them a lesson. Our twenty years of hard pains have now borne fruit. Here I express my hearty thanks to our great seniors who strove so hard.

But a blow to Hawaii must have stung them [the United States] to the quick. So we must bear in mind, on reflection, that they have an enormously predominant air strength—planes and carriers—and we cannot forecast what game they will play to revenge this mishap. Of this future threat we cannot be too careful.

It seems that the destroyer *Shinohome* sank, leaving a big fire and pillar of white smoke in the air, at fifteen kilometers north of Baram Lighthouse on northern Borneo. Sunken destroyers amount to three so far and two minesweepers. Damage to small vessels is comparatively not small. The cause of their sinkings is most likely due to explosion of their depth charges on board.

[The United States had announced the damage at Pearl Harbor, and Ugaki noted that in actual numbers of ships sunk there were points of resemblance between the two reports; however, there was "much difference" in the names of ships.]

According to the scout report of the plane dispatched from the sub, four battleships, one of which had a basket type mast, were found to be damaged in Pearl Harbor, but the degrees were not observable (or if any one was sunk or not), and a CV and several others were observed.

Thursday, 18 December 1941. Ideal weather. X + 10 Day. In the Seventy-eighth Extraordinary Session of the Diet, an extraordinary military expense of twenty-seven hundred million yen and other bills passed both houses, and the Lower House closed today. [Ugaki recorded a Diet resolution praising the Imperial Army and Navy for its "sweeping and successive victories" and added his opinion.] The words were well chosen and the expression is nicely high-sounding. What I want the nation to realize is that they have to bear ten more years' hardships and difficulties, and keep cool heads toward our present victories.

It was reported that two subs—*RO-66* and *RO-62*—collided with each other during their patrol near Wake Island last night, and sank in a moment. What an unhappy accident that is! That island is bewitched. I decided to send the Eighth Heavy Cruiser Division, Second CV Division, and two destroyers of the task force to the Fourth Fleet temporarily with a determined view to ending our assault this time.

It came to this: The task force would sail around the south of Iwo Jima to evade enemy submarines, and two destroyer divisions would be sent to guard the force.

Friday, 19 December 1941. Fine. X + 11 Day. At about 0700, our patrol plane sighted an enemy submarine near Kominazejima, so *Hatsuharu,* a destroyer, gave it a successful blow. Oil came out on the sea. And again, at about 1100, another was seen very near Yashima, and the destroyer *Sanae* reportedly attacked it with depth charges. The Kure Naval Station was so rash as to ask us how to deal with the sunken sub after her position was confirmed, but I am afraid that nothing will be found but an oil tube when the area is examined. At evening, the sub which had been attacked at Yashima Island was recognized to be running toward Hayasui Channel. This time did we again miss our game, I wonder? It was just on the other side of the island that the sub had been lurking. Beware the Ides of March!

On top of the Combined Fleet's report of the [war] results, Naval Headquarters released information about the activities of our midget submarines, which added luster to the war results in the newspapers. Since the Washington press reported that the United States caught some of them in and out of Pearl Harbor, Japan could not but announce it. In a sense, it is good that the merits of the brave men who dared the attack in the face of death have been made public. What I regret is that the United States will take defensive measures against the use of that sort of sub, which was under consideration for use on the western coast of the United States in the future.

[Ugaki closed the day with one of his brief poems in praise of the "shocking blows" the Japanese had given their enemies.]

Saturday, 20 December 1941. Cloudy. X + 12 Day. At 0400 the landing at Davao ended in success, under close cooperation of the army and navy. Imagine the joy of all the Japanese who had remained there until now! A few days later, our air force will move down there and will keep the enemy from entering the Sulu Sea area.

The spouting of oil from the enemy sub has not yet been definitely ascertained. In the afternoon, one of our planes of the Oita Air Corps sighted a track of oil flowing toward Moshima. A picket boat immediately bombed and attacked it. No enemy that has once entered the Inland Sea can be allowed to escape. An entrance will be repeated hereafter. What is important is to kill them before they form a habit.

[That afternoon Navy Minister Shimada came to Iwakuni Air Corps to congratulate the Combined Fleet. Yamamoto entertained him and Admiral Takasu of the First Fleet at a party. The occasion was spoiled for Ugaki by a toothache—"another battle in my mouth!" Yamamoto and Shimada were old friends, having been classmates at Eta Jima, and they had a long talk until it was time for Shimada to leave for *Mutsu* where he spent the night.

[Among Shimada's group was Captain Chikao Yamamoto, assigned to the First Section, General Affairs, Naval Air Administration Headquarters, who had once served under Ugaki at the Naval General Staff. "He talked freely about the future of Japan. I have come to love human companionship since I have been out of the world."]

Sunday, 21 December 1941. Rain. X + 13 Day. This morning the minister came to the ship to join our breakfast and left the ship after a picture was taken including us all. He was to fly to Tokyo, leaving Iwakuni. In appreciation of the many gifts that were brought from Tokyo, we gave beef in exchange. It seems that no cows are raised in Tokyo at present. A little past noon, *Yamato* entered the harbor and lay west of *Nagato*. It made us feel that much has been added to the power of the Combined Fleet. It has been reported that the "shakedown" shows the ship has enormous ability, but it will take a lot of time before the ship can be fully prepared to receive the whole headquarters of the Combined Fleet with complete assurance; training for that is not going to be easy. The captain of the ship and others have been working very hard.

[Ugaki noted that weather had been unfavorable in the southern area following a typhoon. He had heard nothing further from the Wake Island campaign. "Many letters have come to me from my relatives and intimate friends appreciating my efforts."]

Monday, 22 December 1941. Cloudy. X + 14 Day. At 0500, our Philippine Assault Forces entered Lingayen Bay and landed there safe and sound. It should be noted that they encountered no enemy resistance. I sense that the enemy has lost her fighting spirit. The newspaper says the United States will defend Singapore even after they abandon the Philippines. But can those who once have abandoned the Philippines keep Singapore? I very much doubt it. And Hong Kong has not many days left. I don't doubt that Singapore will fall sooner than we expect.

Two destroyers of the Seventh Destroyer Division that made night bombardments on Midway Island made port. I appreciated their service.

Tuesday, 23 December 1941. Fine. X + 15 Day. Left the ship at 0845 for *Yamato* and inspected it. It gave me the impression that it was built pretty well, but some points should be improved. These may be due to old ideas. Much research and investigation about these will be necessary.

When I came back to the ship a little after 1100, there was a report that a sub, which seemed to be an enemy, was sighted west of Tsurishima Channel, and our picket vessel attacked it immediately. But according to the later report from the destroyer sent there later, the plane mistook a whirlpool in Soto Channel for an enemy sub. Such incidents are sure to be repeated, especially in trivial matters. I fear that mistakes of that sort have been made many times. In my opinion, enemy subs have a very poor fighting spirit and their ability is very low; how can such subs enter Bungo Channel into the Inland Sea? But it's too early to be relieved about them, unless we obtain abundant and conclusive evidence that they have never entered the Inland Sea, and that all our experiences until now have been due to mere suspicions and misgivings. It is urgently necessary to gather together in one room all those who were concerned with the discovery of enemy subs and have them describe the circumstance of their experiences with the utmost frankness or to train them to grasp the real conditions of submerging subs, using our subs to demonstrate. I have many times given a suggestion to the staff about this, but they have not yet put it into practice, to my regret.

[At 1245 Ugaki left *Nagato* to inspect the supply ship *Irako*. He was quite satisfied, noting that storage for vegetables had been enlarged "and the cake equipment is excellent." Then he returned to business.]

Captain Minoru Togo, skipper of the supply tanker *Shiriya*, reported on his supply mission accompanying the task force and complained that his ship could hardly make more than 8 knots, even though he tried very hard, which proved to be very disadvantageous, especially so when enemy subs were often sensed moving around, or when he wanted to evade enemy subs which had been sighted previously. [*Captain Togo was the son of Japan's great sea hero, Admiral Heihachiro Togo. His tanker,* Shiriya, *was part of the Midway Neutralization Force.*] It's absolutely necessary for naval supply ships to have at least 20 knots in this future. This applies also to civilian ships in the service of the navy or army. First of all, more serious efforts should have been made in building more efficient, excellent ships in peacetime.

One of the hardest nuts to crack, the attack on Wake Island, might have been finished this morning, but, contrary to my expectation, no report has come out. Not only the senior staff officer but all of the staff were almost impatient. At last, at about 1100, a telegram message came that the attacks had been made. They approached the coast at 0035, began to land against furious enemy resistance, besides high seas; at about 1100 the occupation of both islands was finished. This is a great relief.

[Ugaki expressed his sympathy with the commander in chief, Fourth Fleet, for "the awkward position into which he was thrown" in this unexpectedly difficult campaign.

[Ugaki suffered a painful personal loss on this day when the aircraft piloted by First Lieutenant Teiji Nishimura exploded upon takeoff near Legaspi. He was the son of Admiral Nishimura, now in command of the Second Destroyer Squadron, a good friend of Ugaki's, and the young man had studied under Ugaki.]

At sunset some portion of the task force appeared, heading north at the eastern part of Kudako Channel, and anchored at 1830. Immediately I went to *Akagi*, the flagship, to welcome the victorious men and express our thanks to Commander in Chief Nagumo and Chief of Staff Kusaka.

1. In this successful operation, everything went on so smoothly in any urgent case that we cannot but believe that the gods have protected us all.

2. Under the condition of radio silence, the greatest effort had been made to keep all the ships of the fleet together.

3. All the personnel of the supply ships under their commander were most self-sacrificing, with skill worthy of high praise.

4. The chief of staff himself got a little angry at the order to attack Midway by air strength, although the order had a condition of "if possible."

These were some of their opinions. The extent of our loss is twenty-nine planes lost and fifty-five personnel killed. If carriers, say two, had been lost, all would not be in such spirits.

Wednesday, 24 December 1941. Fine. X + 16 Day. Landing at Lamon Bay [on the east coast of Luzon] was a success early this morning, with little resistance on a fine day.

The commander in chief of the First Air Fleet and others came to the ship at 1000. The chief of the Naval General Staff, Admiral Nagano, came to the ship at 0930, delayed by some train accident. Then everyone heard the battle report of Operation Hawaii, followed by a drinking party. A picture was taken.

After 1100 we left *Nagato* for *Akagi*, flagship of the task force, where Admiral Yamamoto gave an address to commanders and officers of the task force, followed by an address by Chief of the Naval General Staff Nagano. Pictures were taken and toasts followed. We came back to the flagship at 1240.

I accompanied Admiral Nagano and [Vice Admiral Eikichi] Katagiri, chief of the Air Administration Department, to *Yamato* for inspection. After that, the two left for Iwakuni at 1500.

I had a severe toothache, so lay down on my bed for an hour at sunset, but it didn't seem to help.

Thursday, 25 December 1941. Cloudy. Jolo [in the Philippines] was successfully occupied this morning.

In the invasion of Kuching [capital of Sarawak] enemy ships attacked one destroyer, *Sagiri,* besides four transports. Torpedoes struck the former, too, and she sank due to the explosion of explosives and the mine-storage. Half of the crew were saved.

Many destroyers and minesweepers have been sunk by the same cause. Immediate countermeasures should be taken. Depth charges should be protected by sandbags and powders should be those that will not explode from near explosions.

Soon after I got into bed, the report of the fall of Hong Kong came. It seemed that they had a hard fight with the English troops who defended well. Indeed the English troops should be praised.

[Ugaki began his entry for Friday, 26 December 1941, by recording the loss of a minesweeper and a transport in the Kuching Sea. The Southern Expeditionary Force had asked for carriers, but according to Ugaki, they had "no spare strength for the Fleet. . . . At noon military disposition was changed to Second of the First Operation."]

We have to investigate and study the organization, route, and time of U.S. task forces' assaults (including air raids), together with the means of destroying them all. It is most certain that, after their new organization of the forces, the United States will come against us for retaliation. If we could destroy them completely, for the time being they will be baffled in attempting anything. This must be done by all means.

Tokyo should be protected from air raids; this is the most important thing to be borne in mind.

[Ugaki noted that on the previous day he had received a letter from Captain Binpei Inoguchi, dean of the Naval Gunnery School, who was a bit disgruntled because he had hoped for great things from the "big guns in the Malay Sea Battle . . . but this time again the credit turned out to be attributed to the air forces." Ugaki thought his feelings quite natural; still, the "big guns will have their chance some day."

[Ugaki also remembered that Nagano had remarked, "The occupation of the southern part of French Indochina was very useful, wasn't it?" To this Ugaki replied, "It formed an immediate cause of the American-Japanese war, but was absolutely necessary to the operations following." As Nagano had not participated in planning for that occupation, Ugaki concluded that he was not boasting, but sincerely praising the navy. This pleased Ugaki.]

When results turn out well, we should be praised for our farsightedness, but if the opposite, we should be blamed for it. Such is the way of the world. In due time the Tripartite Alliance will display the merit I had expected.

What is most important is to lay stress on what is considered most important from the national point of view, and do it definitely. It will be too late if we wait for public criticism. This must be borne in mind strongly by those who want to do great deeds for the state.

Saturday, 27 December 1941. Partly cloudy. Today there was no big change in the war situation. But in Malaya, things are progressing favorably; the army is speeding down to the south through two passages, east and west; army planes have attacked Rangoon three times and have shot down many enemy planes.

The newspapers are full of the big news of the fall of Hong Kong.

A report said that the advancement of the Eleventh Air Fleet to the south is not very speedy, but after investigation I found its progress is as scheduled; however, the attack on Davao is a little slow compared with the program.

I requested the commander of our air force in Mili to keep watch over Kuching Bay because we sustained a loss there. He answered that it is almost impossible to do so because it is like trying to protect Kobe by using planes from Kasumigaura. I think it is quite natural and reasonable for him to say so. According to report, fighter planes have only fifteen minutes in the air unless they are equipped with disposable gas tanks. Let both sides have their say, but it is best that they meet each other half way and not discuss how to contrive the best means.

Enemy subs attacked and torpedoed a special ship, *Nojima,* which had been sent for the purpose of supplying coal at Camranh Bay [in Indochina] on the southern sea off Hong Kong. Being pierced through the second hold, with heavy leaking, she entered some port on the China Sea. The disposition is appropriate. It seems that the torpedo went through it instead of exploding. Some in the operations room said that the body of the ship was so rusted that the point of the torpedo did not have enough shock to explode when it hit! Everyone smiled at this. Anyway, they still have some composure.

Today and tomorrow I arranged to train the observers on the planes by showing what submerged subs look like, demonstrating with subs of the Submarine School. Is any difference perceived between a sub which is merely under water and one which has been attacked and sunk? I want to hear what the crew has to say about that.

Chief of the Second Section of the Naval General Staff [Captain Taro] Taguchi came to the ship with [Commander Reizo] Tamura, a member of the Communications Section.

[Ugaki dropped his narrative of events to muse briefly on the qualities of leadership and the need for knowledge of the enemy's movements so that the Combined Fleet might "take suitable countermeasures."]

Sunday, 28 December 1941. Cloudy and fine. Yesterday the commanding general of the China Dispatched Troops and the commander in chief of the China Area Fleet were given His Imperial Rescript in appreciation of their merits in occupying Hong Kong.

No great change in the war situation occurred today.

An antisubmarine net was fixed up today in the area where the fleet is at anchor; this will save half of the patrol ships that have been in position day and night.

Monday, 29 December 1941. Partly fine, wind getting stronger. At around 1330, the Eighth Heavy Cruiser Division was seen to the far east heading for Kure. Glad to see it again! It was the heavy cruiser division that I commanded most sincerely and pleasantly, though my tenure as its commanding officer was only slightly more than three months. I felt like a father who welcomes back his son after he has achieved a glorious victory.

Half an hour later, the Second CV Division was also seen heading north. I greatly appreciate the great efforts of Rear Admiral Tamon Yamaguchi, its commanding officer and a classmate of mine.

In the evening Staff Officer Miwa came back from Tokyo. He said that there was no big change in the central authority there, though a number of changes on minor matters. Anyway, there wouldn't be major changes on immediate problems.

[Ugaki worried somewhat about the fact that the government did not seem to him to have "a basic policy" on the problems of dealing with occupied areas. He was concerned because "the basic policy will have an important bearing on how to use the armed forces when those areas are occupied." He concluded that the empire lacked "talents in colonial ventures, though displaying merits in war."]

Tuesday, 30 December 1941. Fine. The land operation on Malaya is making rather rapid progress. In the Philippine theater, our Lamon Bay landing force is advancing from southeast of Manila and our Lingayen landing force from its north. Both forces have already advanced half of the whole way. Overseas cables repeatedly reported the crisis both theaters are facing.

Staff Officer Watanabe was sent today by plane via Tokyo to the Fourth and Sixth Fleets' headquarters for briefing.

[In pursuit of his worry about occupation policy, Ugaki decided to work up a draft of his thoughts and have Commander Fujii take it to Tokyo. He had some qualms: "In the China Incident, everybody tried to put his nose into it to spoil everything." Still, he thought that the "simple and frank view from a field officer" could be appropriate. He thought those "in charge of naval administration" sometimes came up with "poor designs." On the other hand, he had no doubts about the Dutch East Indies. "It is enough for us to inform Germany of our determination on what to do with it." In any case, it was now up to Japan "to play a leading role in establishing a new order in the world."]

Wednesday, 31 December 1941. Cloudy. Around 1130, Second Division Commander Yamaguchi came on board for briefing. It was a great pleasure to see him in very high spirits.

He expressed his view about the task force's return movement. Though it agrees with what I thought, it is considered better not to mention here.[13] I felt greatly encouraged to be shown aerial photos taken from his planes showing enemy warships evidently capsized in Pearl Harbor, as well as damages on Wake Island.

In the afternoon, I had a molar tooth in my left upper jaw pulled out; it had annoyed me greatly for the past two years.

At 2030 we all ate noodles for New Year's Eve in the cabin. Such customary decorations for the new year as rice cake, pine, bamboo, and Japanese apricot were well prepared there. I think it is too much to have such decorations when we are in a great war. I can't help having sympathy for those men in the battlefield who have no time to celebrate the joyful new year.

This year, the sixteenth year of the Showa era, which should be marked as an eventful year not only in Japanese history but also in world history, will end very soon. I am deeply engulfed in an overwhelming amount of emotion and thought.

Thursday, 1 January 1942. Fair. X + 24 Day. I greet the first new year of the Pacific war and the sixth since the China Incident started. I hope that we attain the object of the war speedily, as well as for the prosperity of the imperial family and an epochal expansion of the nation.

It has been only twenty-five days since the war started, yet operations have been progressing smoothly and we have enough reason to hope for completion of the first stage of the war before the end of March. Then what will come next?

Shall we be dragged into war with the Soviet Union, owing to a rash and thoughtless act of the army? Or will the United States and the United Kingdom recover their strength sufficiently to fight a great decisive battle in the Pacific? [*The concept of a great all-out battle in the western Pacific between the Japanese and American fleets was a staple of Japanese naval thinking. The Japanese planned to lure the U.S. fleet westward, whittling it down as it moved onward, so that by the time the Americans reached Japanese waters, the Combined Fleet would be able to destroy it. This was strictly a ship versus ship concept.*] Anyway, the future is filled with brightness. The course of events during this year will determine the fate of the war, so we must work hard, exerting every effort. The main thing is to win, and we surely will win.

The New Year's ceremony, salute to the emperor's portrait, drinking the toast, and picture-taking were carried out as usual.

The Wabimi detachment of the army, which had landed at Kota Bharu, continued its southward advance along the east coast of Malaya and captured the enemy air base at Kuantan yesterday morning. This project was not as simple as it looked, however. Originally it was planned to transport the troops by sea, but instead they succeeded in attaining the objective by marching overland. Their deed deserves commendation.

At 1630, the submarine *I-3* reported sighting an enemy carrier with two cruisers at a point one hundred miles bearing 230° of Oahu on course of 270°. [*Possibly* I-3 *had spotted* Enterprise, *which stood into Pearl Harbor on 31 December 1941 (1 January 1942 Japan time)*[14]. *Ugaki was quite unconcerned.*]

What do they intend? Is it merely a patrol in the near sea? Or will there be an air raid to avenge our raid on Midway? Anyway, there are not enough of them to make a hit-and-run attack on our homeland. It will be a nice game for us.

This enemy can be destroyed by placing in its path a submarine flotilla being readied in Kwajalein, and letting another sub flotilla, now on return voyage from the west coast of the United States, sweep from the rear, and advancing medium torpedo bombers and flying boats to Wake Island. It is only regrettable that we have no fighter planes at Wake. At the same time, the Task Force now making preparations at Kure should be readied for immediate action as a precaution.

Friday, 2 January 1942. Fair with strong winds, cold. The Sixth Fleet (submarine force) has given necessary orders and deployed its submarines against the enemy carrier and cruisers discovered near Hawaii yesterday. But we had no further report of sighting the enemy again, and we seem to have missed him due to our inferior speed.

The commander in chief said, "In the naval conference Japan opposed abolishing submarines on the grounds that they were defensive weapons and never offensive, and now they seem to have really become defensive. However, if they can sink a warship, their spirits will rise." It is too bad for the officers and men of the submarine service that they have not yet sunk any important man-of-war, only merchantmen. I fear this might lead to a premature conclusion.

The army continued its swift advance in the Philippines and reached thirty miles north of Manila at dawn this morning. The Forty-eighth Division has been ordered to enter the city. In the evening, the radio reported it was only five miles away. And it has become certain that entry will be made tomorrow.

Pictures of the battle of Hawaii were published prominently in the papers on New Year's Day and the people seemed to be delighted with them as the best of presents.

After completing its refitting, the Ninth Light Cruiser Division came into port and Rear Admiral Kishi, in command, came to visit us. He insisted on being sent to the Pacific promptly. Staying in the Inland Sea did not count as being in the war, he said. I don't know whether that's so or not, but training must come first in any case.

Saturday, 3 January 1942. Fair, the winds died down. A ceremony was held at the usual hour. The van of the Forty-eighth Division and a part of the Naval Communications Corps entered Manila yesterday evening, the main force at 1000 this morning. There was no resistance at all except the burning of oil tanks.

Where did the garrison force and its commanders flee? It is said they fled to Port Darwin in Australia or the fortress of Corregidor. Manila fell quickly enough; but Corregidor, at the entrance to the bay, is heavily fortified with many cannons, including 30-cm guns. Unless this is disposed of, it will be impossible for ships to enter the bay. To accomplish this without too much sacrifice, it will be best to attack it from the air with 800-kg bombs and finally make a forced landing from the bay. Anyway, its existence is troublesome.

[That evening the skipper of the submarine *I-16*, which had taken a midget sub to Pearl Harbor, returned to Japan and reported to Ugaki. With him was Sublieutenant Keiu Matsuo, a midget sub expert who had participated in a spy mission to Hawaii in October 1941.[15] As always, Ugaki was filled with sympathy for the minisub mission. He recognized that much remained to be done in perfecting this technique.

[Even as they talked, Ugaki was suffering from his long-standing problem, toothache, having had to postpone an extraction.]

Sunday, 4 January 1942. Fair. No further information has been received about the carrier and two cruisers found near Hawaii. We also especially ordered the radio traffic around the Fourth Fleet watched, but it did not appear to be taking any precautions.

Despite the damage received on Greenwich Island, an attack on Rabaul was ordered today. If the enemy takes any action, he may air raid Wake on or about the 6th. So we asked the chief of staff, Fourth Fleet, to send in his judgment of the situation. Effective yesterday, the Southern Expeditionary Fleet was renamed First Southern Expeditionary Fleet, and the Third Southern Expeditionary Fleet was newly established to take charge of the Philippines. Vice Admiral [Rokuzo] Sugiyama was appointed its commander in chief. These actions were taken on the occasion of the fall of Manila.

The Third Fleet is going to be dispatched south for operations in the Dutch East Indies. I consider these changes quite fitting for the occasion. Accordingly, we have made changes in the names of the Combined Fleet orders.

In the morning, eight enemy four-engined bombers raided Mararag anchorage near Davao from the northwest at an altitude of seven thousand meters. A 250-kg bomb hit *Myoko*, flagship of the Fifth Heavy Cruiser Division, at anchor there, damaging Nos. 1, 2, and 3 turrets and causing over sixty casualties. The flag was moved to *Nachi*, and it was decided to send *Myoko* to Takao.[16]

Besides two patrol planes which had been in the air, almost all the aircraft were launched. They fought hard, with antiaircraft gunfire, but the enemy escaped at high altitude.

It was not a good idea to concentrate many vessels there at this time, as the division commander's recommendation stated. Did they come from Ambon? We shall have to do something about that area promptly, too.

Staff Officer Sasaki returned this evening from a hurried trip to Takao to have a talk with the Eleventh Air Fleet. I was glad to hear that all the air fleets in the south were full of life, with operations moving along splendidly. Their morale was high, and they were saying that the enemy was weaker than the Chinese because their losses were unexpectedly light.

Monday, 5 January 1942. Fair, cold. The chief of staff, Fourth Fleet, sent in his judgment on the situation in response to our inquiry of yesterday. Also, a separate telegram came in from the commander in chief, Sixth Fleet. They were about the same as our views. As we can take considerable precautions against Wake and the Marshalls, no orders were issued to them especially.

The task force completed most of its preparations and left Kure today. It started to recover aircraft. It was decided to have the task force search the seas northeast of Marcus en route to operations in the Rabaul area as a precaution against an enemy surprise attack on the homeland.

We shall be able to finish first-stage operations by the middle of March, as far as the invasion operation is concerned. What are we going to do after that? Advance to Australia, to India, attack Hawaii, or destroy the Soviet Union at an opportune moment according to their actions?

In any case, we must establish our plans by the end of February. I have decided to have staff officers study it. The senior staff officer seems to make it a premise to keep the war in the south because he thinks, if left alone as it is, the army will bring about a break with the Soviet Union. However, this must be based on the attainment of the war objectives as its main issue.

Not only is the eventual recovery of the United States certain, but it is also clear that the British will increase their strength in the Far East. It is unthinkable that the Soviets of themselves would seek trouble with Japan for the present; but if they face downfall in Europe after the German spring offensive, the United States will insist on using Soviet territory. Thus, we shall be brought into war with her.

On the other hand, it may become necessary to share a victory when the Germans succeed. Should we extend the theater of war unnecessarily wide, we would lose flexibility in conducting operations. We should limit the operations within the scope of capturing and maintaining the resource areas necessary for the country's self-sufficiency.

It may well be all right to engage in operations that would induce disintegration of the British empire, if not much fighting strength is needed. But it is most essential to have fighting strength in reserve. The wisdom of invading Hawaii will be another issue, and it can be undertaken only after we have won a decisive sea battle.

I have also proposed to send submarines to the Panama Canal and the Bombay area in the Indian Ocean for raiding operations. There are lots of things to study. The Combined Fleet headquarters never sits idle. The execution of this great war is an unprecedented major responsibility bestowed upon us.

As it happens, because of the New Year banquet today, we had a sukiyaki dinner, but I could not enjoy it on account of my teeth. Their treatment in the mornings and evenings is quite troublesome, but still I go to the dentist, thinking I might be handicapped at important moments unless I have them fixed now.

Tuesday, 6 January 1942. Fair, warm. An American radio reported on the 4th (5th here) that a carrier and cruisers narrowly escaped a Japanese submarine attack at Lahaina North Channel, and planes were believed to have sunk the submarine. They must be those ships reported to have sortied from Pearl Harbor the other day, and we got the information we wanted through the enemy. Accordingly, we have decided to cancel the task force's search in the Marcus area.

If the enemy has brains, he may proceed stealthily toward us while making an announcement like this in plain language. We have made an enquiry to the Sixth Fleet about this. If the submarine does not answer, it must have been lost. If such an enemy has not been sighted, it must have been a misjudgment or a false report on the part of the enemy.

[That afternoon Yamamoto, Ugaki, and other officers inspected various shore positions. At Omishima, Ugaki noticed that few young men were working in the tangerine groves and paddy fields and wondered whether they had all gone to war or might be working abroad. At Nasake Jima, Ugaki fretted because the two batteries supposed to command the strategic east and west channels of Moroshima were actually small caliber, short-ranged guns "of ancient make." Although the scenery was beautiful, he definitely felt sorry for those posted in this location.]

We had an excellent afternoon's exercise, and I told those who did not go that, if they wanted to go ashore, they had better climb Omiyama.

Vice Admiral [Gunichi] Mikawa, commander, Third Battleship Division, came to confer today. His division is going to carry out all kinds of practice firing in Iyonada tomorrow and is scheduled to leave for the south as a part of the task force the day after tomorrow.

Wednesday, 7 January 1942. Rain, later cloudy. As no Sixth Fleet submarine happened to attack the carrier or cruisers lately in the Lahaina area, that fleet reported that the enemy must have announced the event on the 1st, purposely changing the date. That may be so, or it may have been an enemy mistake in identification.

Anyway, it can be determined that the enemy will not come to the Wake area in view of the fact that reconnaissance by a seaplane sent from a submarine in the evening of the 5th ascertained that enemy carriers were in port.

On our inquiry about its patrol disposition, the Fifth Fleet ordered the Twenty-second Division and *Kimikawa Maru* to advance swiftly. Such inquiry must be made with much caution, as it has a considerable effect over a wide area. Yet it is not good to be idle, taking no precautions. They should be especially alert, as the light cruiser *Kiso* and others are under repair at Yokosuka.

The principal officers of the First Air Fleet came to visit us and we had lunch together. They have finished preparations, received planes, etc., and are scheduled to leave for the south early tomorrow morning.

As for the Rabaul operation, it has been decided that the task force is to cooperate with the Southern Force chiefly in attacking enemy planes and vessels and, in case of attacks upon enemy ships, to command the ships of the Fourth Fleet in the vicinity, if necessary. Seniority in the chain of command is always a problem.

An agreement is being worked out among the concerned forces for an invasion of Java Island to be made on around 26 February. Isn't that early? At this rate, we shall be able to finish the first-stage operations by the middle of March, as expected.

It started to rain before dawn, but soon cleared up. Then northwest winds blew in with velocity reaching fifteen to twenty meters. The torpedo net sustained great damage. We must think of something else.

Thursday, 8 January 1942. Fair. One month has elapsed since the war started. The 8th of every month has been designated as a memorial day for the issuance of the Imperial Rescript instead of the day of service for the rise of Asia as heretofore maintained.

[This decision triggered some reflections on Ugaki's part as to the future of the nation. He wanted an aggressive policy instituted to win the war and greatly expand "the imperial fortunes." Such a program would require a high level of statesmenship, and he feared that Japan had no statesmen capable of envisioning and carrying out a broad national policy. Unless such came forward, all the achievements of the armed forces would have been in vain.]

The British Indian Army commander, [Field Marshal Sir A. P.] Wavell is to command the whole forces in the western Pacific theater, with the recently appointed Malayan commander [Lieutenant General Sir Henry] Pownall as his chief of staff. The commander in chief of the U.S. Asiatic Fleet, [Admiral Thomas C.] Hart is to command the fleets under Wavell. Furthermore, Chiang Kai-shek is said to have command of China, French Indochina, and Thailand. That makes me laugh.

We shall not be afraid of them even if they come with an array of all the clever, brave, and fierce generals and admirals in the Allied nations. Don't they know that they will soon be looking for places to hide, after exposing more than ever the weakness involved in the Allied forces? Wait two months more! I can ony advise them to enjoy the remnant of their lives in the meantime.

A report came in this evening that a submarine of the Fourth Submarine Division, on her way back from the west coast of America via the waters near Hawaii, sank an enemy carrier of the *Langley* type between Johnston and the Marshalls at 0700. The torpedo staff officer just missed a prize of a dozen beers, as it was not a *Lexington* type.

[*Converted from a collier into a carrier in 1922,* Langley *had long been a seaplane tender. Whatever the submarine sank or thought it sank, it was not* Langley, *which survived until 27 February 1942.*][17]

The Dutch East Indies Force with the Third Fleet as its main body sortied from Davao for the invasions of Tarakan and Menado to be made in the early morning of the 11th. The British, the United States, and the Dutch seem to have obtained information about this. I would like to urge them to put up a little fight instead of withdrawing to the Java Sea. However, a battle is an impetus and they may not be able to do anything about it.

The task force (minus Fifth Heavy Cruiser Division, Second Carrier Division, and *Kaga*) left this morning headed south for the second-stage operations.

Friday, 9 January 1942. Partly fair with strong winds. Enemy planes in Malaya are said to have been increased to 134 according to reconnaissance. Some reinforcements seem to have arrived. We shall only destroy them.

The preparations of the Fifth Fleet and Yokosuka Naval Station against an enemy air raid on the Tokyo area are insufficient. I feel it necessary to increase their strength in the near future and to revise the plan. We should never allow the enemy to raid Tokyo.

The Eighth Heavy Cruiser Division left Kure and dropped anchor in the anchorage for the night. Rear Admiral [Hiroshi] Abe, its commander, wanted to come on board but could not do so due to the rough sea, and sent in a signal. He is leaving for the Rabaul operations with *Kaga* early tomorrow morning. I wish him success in his further efforts.

[As a light touch in the midst of war preparations, Ugaki noted that at the previous night's dinner an amiable argument arose as to whether or not a seagull had webs. Ugaki and the fleet engineer voted for no webs, which mistake cost them a dozen beers.]

Saturday, 10 January 1942. Fair. Yesterday's gale died down at last and every ship had trouble repairing the torpedo nets. What a nuisance!

The advance along the west coast of Malaya is progressing most favorably. The enemy on Bataan Peninsula in the Philippines is resisting stubbornly, but is being driven back gradually by our fierce attack and seems to be running short of foodstuff. Starving the enemy has been a capital method of war for ages. They may have a fair amount of food at Corregidor, but how long will it last with the enemy who is used to a luxurious life?

Sunday, 11 January 1942. Cloudy. The Dutch East Indies Force, which had been quietly preparing, succeeded in landing its first wave at midnight last, and the second at 0400 at Tarakan.

Also, they successfully landed at Menado on the north tip of Celebes at 0600. They must have tried to capture Kakas Airfield with the 101st Unit Paratroops. We had worried a great deal about its delayed training and preparations, and I hope they have succeeded satisfactorily in their first use in actual combat.

They have reported that the weather was fine and most suitable for flying, and also that enemy planes attacked both places, but nothing else yet.

The Second Carrier Division left Kure and dropped anchor in the northern anchorage. Rear Admiral Yamaguchi and his staff came to visit us.

Navigation Staff Officer [Commander Shigeru] Nagata left at 1000 by plane to the Davao area for liaison and conference with the staffs of the Second and Third Fleets.

Kanko Maru of the First Gunboat Division, patroling off the south of Davao the day before yesterday, sighted an enemy periscope [of USS *Pickerel*] close ahead and three traces of torpedoes at the same time.[18] In spite of her efforts to evade them promptly, one of them hit her, flooding her Nos. 1 and 2 holds and disabling the main engine. While they were doing their best in damage control, the hull broke in two before the bridge and sank. Three were killed in action and others, including injured men, were all rescued.

[Ugaki noted with pride that her skipper, Lieutenant Commander Hoichi Noguchi, chose to go down with his ship, although it appeared he had had plenty of time to escape.]

Starting from today, I am going to draft the principle of directing operations according to the judgment of the situation.

Monday, 12 January 1942. Fair. The landing operation at Tarakan yesterday was a real success. But, as the local Dutch commander surrendered at 0800 this morning, the commander, Second Escort Force, sent in minesweepers first, intending to send the Fourth Destroyer Squadron in later, when the fort began firing on the minesweepers at noon, and gunfire and mines sank minesweepers Nos. 13 and 14. In his report, he expressed regret for his failure to complete the operation flawlessly. I felt sorry for him. However, when the enemy surrenders, we should wait until his order of general cease-fire has prevailed and let him indicate the minefield and other hazards.

On such occasions as this, there is always a competition to be first between the army and the navy. Though this spirit is not necessarily bad, sometimes it brings undue troubles. The basic reason is that there are some delicate differences between the army's and navy's standpoints which cannot be expressed in words. This is also the reason why a local agreement between the navy and army in Manila has not been concluded.

Everything is going well in the Menado area. The paratroops secured Kakas Airfield with a few casualties, including three officers. Two flying boats alighted on Lake Tondano with medical personnel. The naval landing party which landed at Kama seems to have joined the paratroops by advancing around Lake Tondano.

[Ugaki facetiously observed that this was "a very nice spot" and perhaps he should acquire a few acres to build himself a villa. A more realistic source of glee was the telegram which his torpedo staff officer, Commander Takayasu Arima, brought to him. It claimed that *I-8* had sighted *Lexington,* a heavy cruiser, and two destroyers. The submarine fired and claimed two certain torpedo hits. Sounds of explosions and lack of traces when they surfaced convinced the Japanese that *Lexington* had sunk.

[*Actually,* I-8 *struck* Saratoga, *not* Lexington. *Although damaged, she was able to reach Pearl Harbor and thence Bremerton for repairs.*[19] Ugaki had more to say about undersea warfare.]

Quite a few of our submarines are sweeping the area. So, even if the crippled carrier escaped sinking, other subs would easily catch her again and the heavy cruiser too, if lucky.

The officers and men of the submarine service have gone through endless hardships up to now. But, having sunk *Langley* the other day, and if they sent *Lexington* to the bottom now, their hardships have paid off. They also have proved that submarines are indispensable.

I shall be very happy because I have regretted the growing trend to underestimate their ability, dazzled by the brilliance of the air activity. The torpedo staff officer will get the five dozen beers which the commander in chief promised.

[That morning Ugaki inspected the light cruiser *Oi*, flagship of the Ninth Light Cruiser Division, which had been recently remodeled, greatly increasing her torpedo fire power. Not satisfied with his staff's plans on how to use her, Ugaki, with the concurrence of her skipper, Captain Nobue Morishita, wanted further study to take advantage of her torpedo power.]

Tuesday, 13 January 1942. I wonder if we really did sink *Lexington*. If we did, a fair amount of flotsam should have been left in the neighborhood, and at least destroyers should have remained to rescue survivors. But another submarine found only some oil slick at a point about one hundred miles southeast of this point.

Our submarines appear to be greatly menaced by bombing and depth charges, but I wonder if they cannot remain a bit cooler. This seems to be quite a difficult problem. The commander in chief Sixth Fleet recognized the sinking and ordered the Second Submarine Force to return to Kwajalein.

The combined air strengths of the army and navy, with fighters, carried out a large air raid on Singapore today, but I regret that the naval aircraft either turned back halfway due to bad weather, or bombed blindly and could not attain results like the army planes.

[Imperial Headquarters Naval Section ordered that the division be escorted from Moji to Takao in Formosa, and the fleet decided to assign this duty to the Ninth Light Cruiser Division, which was practicing torpedo firing.]

Wednesday, 14 January 1942. Partly fair. The Ninth Light Cruiser Division returned in the early morning and sailed for Kure after 0800. The division commander visited us in the meantime. He seemed braced up by receipt of the operational order, but I regret that he had to give up firing practice on account of bad weather.

An army plane reported a large type carrier in Singapore and the Southern Expeditionary Fleet ordered it attacked. While the army planes are continuing great activities, naval aircraft have lost a great deal of their offensive power due to bad weather.

A reconnaissance plane sighted thirty submerged enemy submarines heading north to the southwest of Celebes. This sighting was said to be certain, although the number was doubtful.

A submarine of the Sixth Submarine Division found USS *Houston* and two destroyers to the south of Timor. While she is chasing them, another submarine has been put on wait anticipating that they are bound for Port Darwin. The game is plentiful. The main thing is the actual result of attacks.

After four days' toil, I have finished the principle of directing the operations. The conclusion is to take Midway, Johnston, and Palmyra after June, send our air strength to those islands, and after these steps are almost completed, mobilize all available strength to invade Hawaii, while attempting to destroy the enemy fleet in a decisive battle.

I wonder how many will agree with this plan. My reasons for this conclusion are shown below:

1. What would hurt the United States most is the loss of the fleet and of Hawaii.

2. An attempted invasion of Hawaii and a decisive battle near there may seem a reckless plan, but its chance of success is not small.

3. As time passes, we would lose the benefit of the war results so far gained. Moreover, the enemy would increase his strength, while we would have to be just waiting for him to come.

4. Time is an important element in war. The period of war should be short. Though a prolonged war is taken for granted, nobody is so foolish as to wish for it himself.

5. After the German invasion of England, there is fear that our navy's operations will face increasingly heavy pressure.

6. The destruction of the U.S. fleet would also mean that of the British fleet. So we would be able to do anything we like. Thus, it will be the shortest way to conclude the war.

I have given this to the senior staff officer for further detailed study. The staff officers have not yet submitted any answers.

My toothache has gone at last.

Thursday, 15 January 1942. Fair. No news has been received yet regarding the enemy found yesterday.

The imperial headquarters announced last night that USS *Lexington* was considered sunk, with detailed descriptions of the situation under which submarine *I-8* sighted and torpedoed her the other day. This morning's papers took it up with banners. I hope this sunken ship never appears in the paper or on the sea in the future. The navy is not supposed to lie.

[*In fact,* Lexington *survived until the battle of the Coral Sea, 8 May 1942.*][20]

The Second Battleship Division returned from Kure. How about action reports of the amorous kind?

Friday, 16 January 1942. Partly fair. It has become certain that the USS *Houston* did not go to Port Darwin, but is in a spot southeast of Celebes. Our submarines have waited for her in vain. In addition, the cable they tried to cut off that port could not be caught; the grappling wire was cut instead. I sympathize with the regret that the Twenty-eighth Submarine Division must feel.

Based upon the report of thirty enemy submarines heading north, the Second Destroyer Squadron and others carried out a submarine hunt one night, but there seems to have been no result. Have they turned back to the south? If so, they must be said to have no fighting spirit. It may be necessary to teach them how to use submarines.

An enemy battleship was found in Singapore. Accordingly, bombers and fighters sortied early this morning, but we have received no good news yet.

Immediately after bombings were made on land, a reconnaissance plane found an enemy battleship speeding at 30 knots on course of 240° at a point twenty miles west off the southwest shore of Singapore. Just missed her! However, if she proceeds north through Malacca Strait, she will still be within our bombing range tomorrow morning despite her high speed. In addition, two submarines of the Submarine Division will reach the north end of Malacca Strait tonight and start a search on course of 140° from 0200. I hope they will achieve success tomorrow by keeping good cooperation between planes and submarines.

Anyway, it is amazing to see that this battleship dared to appear in Singapore. What was her mission? It must have been an attempt to transport reinforcements, taking advantage of the great capacity for loading and the superior speed of the *Renown* type battleship.

It is a great pity that our naval air force's advance and establishment of bases on the west coast of Malaya have been delayed.

Saturday, 17 January 1942. Fair. Cold winds were fairly strong. There has been no news about the British battleship which escaped from Singapore. Our planes only bombed targets ashore.

The USS *Houston* entered Darwin last night. Our submarine sighted her at ten thousand meters but could not attack her.

The chief of the Education Bureau, chief of the Third Section of the General Staff, and others came to see *Yamato*'s combat practice.

Staff Officer Watanabe, who had been sent to the Fourth and Sixth fleets since the end of last year came back this morning. He had a lot to tell about Guam and Wake. I was glad to hear that they were all of good cheer and morale was high.

The skipper of the submarine *I-68* came to report on the occasion of her coming back to Kure for repair. He told us of the fierceness of enemy depth-charge attacks off Hawaii.

I watched the film of the capture of Hong Kong for a little while tonight.

[Sunday, 18 January and Monday, 19 January were almost entirely occupied with routine firing practice at sea, Yamamoto temporarily moving his flag to *Yamato*. On Monday, *Yamato* almost collided with a sailboat; in trying to avoid her, the battleship's tremendous inertia nearly sent her aground on Nuwa Jima. In the afternoon they returned to Hashira Jima and moved the flag back to *Nagato*.

[Ugaki was much gratified to receive a friendly note from the secretary to His Imperial Highness Fleet Admiral Prince Fushimi.

[On Tuesday, 20 January, Yamamoto aboard *Nagato* went to Kure to visit the sick and wounded at the Naval Hospital, but Ugaki was too busy to go along. That evening, the two admirals and others had a party ashore, their first in a long time.

[On Wednesday, 21 January, Ugaki merely noted that the weather was fair, and on Thursday, the 22nd, that there was "no great change in the war situation."

[Ugaki's only war notation for Friday, 23 January, was that Japan's forces landed at Rabaul and Kavieng at 1400. Then he hosted a small dinner party.]

Saturday, 24 January 1942. Cloudy. Our forces successfully landed on Balikpappan and Kendari at 0200. Upon receipt of a false report that a cruiser was entering the port of Balikpappan, our Dutch East Indies Force started for the south.

[At 1000 *Nagato* left Kure for Hashira Jima. Later an order was issued to "change into the 3rd strength disposition of the 1st stage operatons."]

Sunday, 25 January 1942. In Balikpappan a special transport, a tanker, and a patrol boat were damaged. It must have been due to enemy submarines and planes which sneaked in there. [*Neither planes nor submarines caused the damage. Four U.S. destroyers penetrated the anchored Japanese convoy, sank four transports and a patrol craft, and damagd a few other ships.*][21] Besides, the light cruiser *Nagara* and destroyer *Hatsuharu* collided in a squall. Generally, damages sustained seem to be increasing. Though we should expect some as we advance further into enemy territory, we can't be too cautious.

At 1000, chief of the Naval Ship Administration Department, Seiichi Iwamura, the superintendent of Kure Naval Arsenal, and others came aboard. I explained and presented to them our current fleet requirements. It is difficult to obtain much result from negotiations with lower officials, but today it may be more effective.

From 1300, the staff officers explained the present situation of the operations and also those being planned. After that, Staff Officer Fujii gave a report on the situation in the Philippine area.

The central authorities are still indecisive about future general operational policy, while the General Army Command have many matters pending. On this occasion we must establish a definite policy promptly, but the staff officers keep on saying they are studying it, and it is getting nowhere.

According to the detailed telegram received yesterday concerning the attack on the USS *Lexington,* she seems to have been sunk for certain. Foreign news, except the American, disclosed this, but the American authorities don't deny it, and public opinion is said to be aroused.

The army force, having entered Burma over pathless mountain ranges, is ready to attack Rangoon in earnest. I am pleased.

[On Monday, 26 January, Ugaki's thoughts were mostly of the international scene. He thought Thailand wise to have declared war on the British at noon on the 25th. Her troops had joined in attacking Burma, and Ugaki suggested that Japan should reward her by giving her the land south of Moulmein.

[Japanese forces moving south in Malaya had reached within eighty kilometers of Singapore. Ugaki also congratulated army planes for their raid on Palembang, Sumatra, "said to be the farthest and longest attack by army aircraft on record."

[The report of the commission on the Pearl Harbor attack, headed by Associate Justice of the Supreme Court Owen J. Roberts, was published,[22] and Ugaki commented upon some of the American mistakes revealed therein.]

It condemned Commander in Chief U.S. Fleet Admiral Kimmel and Commander Air Force [sic] in Hawaii General Short, who failed to take necessary measures in spite of the warning given on 27 November by the army chief of staff and chief of naval operations. Further, they did not take any action even when a report was made to their chiefs of staff of a destroyer attacking a submarine which was found by a ship in the prohibited area near Pearl Harbor one hour before our attack on 7 December. Also, a radar operator reported approaching planes, but the officer in charge let it alone, judging it to be friendly planes scheduled to fly in at about the same time. Moreover, the fate at the harbor entrance remained open until after 0800, after letting in two minesweepers during the night.

Even if they issued the general warning before handing over the note to Japan, it was natural that they did not think we would come far away to Hawaii right away. This negligence seemed to result in their unpreparedness.

Before accusing others, did both army and navy chiefs, as well as Hull and Roosevelt, really think that Hawaii was in danger? Just a general warning should be considered a mere excuse for evading responsibility.

This afternoon the staff held a meeting to study operational plans, but denied me admittance because they would not be able to say what they liked if I was there. One day's delay now could result in a tremendous delay in the future.

Tuesday, 27 January 1942. Fair. Thanks to the faulty forecast of northwest winds freshening with extended high pressure, it was comparatively warm today, too.

The senior staff officer came to explain the operational policy of the future that the staff studied yesterday. They also studied a decisive battle between both fleets to be fought when we attempt to invade Hawaii. But they failed to discover any good plan for destroying the land-based airpower, and they concluded it better to operate toward the west at this stage of the war.

Despite some differences between their ideas and mine, I approved it, because it was what I originally thought of, and there was no need to carry it out forcefully at great sacrifice and with less chance of success. Their idea is the same as mine, only in reverse order.

However, the following points should be noted when it is shaped up into an actual plan:

1. The Soviet Union is not likely to go to war with us. But enough preparations should be made not to be surprise-attacked during our advance toward the west. Special care should be taken in making our army forces in Manchuria ready.

2. Measures must be taken against U.S. task force operations.

3. The operation should not be started before the regrouping of the forces after the first-stage operations are completed. If possible, it should be launched simultaneously with the German operations against the Near and Middle East. However, the land operation through Burma may be continued notwithstanding.

4. The objects of the operation should be made clear from the beginning:

    a. Destruction of the enemy fleets.
    b. Invasions of strategic points and destruction of enemy bases.
    c. Furtherance of the anti-British movement in India.
    d. Connection between the Axis powers in the east and west.

Wednesday, 28 January 1942. Fair. There has been some trouble regarding the sequence of the Dutch East Indies operation. The central authorities and the field commands exchanged some telegrams, but nothing serious happened.

Plans have been revised so as to advance overland to Banjermassin in view of the difficulties in making a sea-borne landing there as well as possible losses, and also to take Bali Island instead or sending fighters there before the Java operation. Is this really a good plan? I hope they will get on all right in capturing Bali, which is only a stone's throw from Surabaya.

[The previous night, the text of the military agreement between Japan, Germany, and Italy had been received. Ugaki was highly skeptical about it. "Its contents were entirely hackneyed" and he suspected that the Germans had little if any intention of carrying it out. In Ugaki's opinion, Japan should not stick too closely to this agreement in deciding upon operational policy.]

Thursday, 29 January 1942. Fair. In the evening, Staff Officer Fujii submitted to me the principle he drafted for directing the Great East Asia War. There is fear of causing a flare-up when we urge it upon the central authorities in Tokyo, so I decided to study it more thoroughly.

Staff Officer Miwa brought in a plan to send the task force off the south coast of Java, where a second Dunkirk is likely to take place at the time of the Java invasion. I pointed out some matters for his reconsideration.

The submarine *I-124* has not been heard from since the night of the 19th, when she was patroling off Port Darwin. Fearing she might be having trouble with her transmitter, another sub was sent to meet her on her return route, but she failed to come home. On the other hand, the British announced the sinking of a submarine in the Pacific, somewhat coinciding with this event. It must be surmised that her skipper and crews went down with the ship. It is regrettable.

The submarine *I-61* which sank by accident in Kyushu on 1 September last year was refloated, thanks to indomitable efforts of the salvaging party. Sixty bodies were recovered. This, too, deeply moved me.

Friday, 30 January 1942. Fair. I okayed the principle for directing the war, submitted last night, after carefully studying it and instructing that some points be corrected. With regard to sending the task force to the south of Java, I contacted the chief of staff, First Air Fleet, who happened to be in Tokyo. As he also wished this done, it was decided to send the force there, though some damage must be anticipated.

[Commander Yugi] Yamamoto, an officer of the Naval General Staff, came for a liaison mission, but did not bring anything important to talk about. On the other hand, I hammered home our ideas to him.

Saturday, 31 January 1942. Fair. Leaving the ship at 0810, I accompanied the commander in chief to *Chiyoda* to inspect the lowering of and attack training of midget submarines. Efforts of those concerned in a gale were great and the spirit of the young skippers was really high. It was quite reassuring.

Thus we can hope those midget submarines penetrate into enemy bases and sink major vessels. Hoping to promote their future use, I asked the commander in chief to inspect them today. After watching the practice attack, we left *Chiyoda* near Maejima and returned to the ship by the admiral's boat at 1130.

Submarine *I-60* in the south has not been heard from since 12 January and failed to return on the scheduled day. She may have been lost, too.

The U.S. radio is exaggerating our losses and trying to hide their own. It is quite laughable; they are usually megalomaniacs by more than ten-fold. The loss of their friendly forces, such as the British and the Dutch, are announced as they truly were to some extent. They seem to think that if they themselves are all right, they don't care for others, even friendly nations. Their meanness even exceeds that of the Chinese.

January has gone, and at 0230 of its last day a landing on Ambon succeeded. This is one of the few cases behind schedule. It was deemed necessary to cut off this line earlier, but the operation did not progress as desired.

Sunday, 1 February 1942. Rain, later cloudy. Before 0700 a report came in of an air raid on the Marshalls. They have come after all; they are some guys!

From about 0400 an enemy task force consisting of a carrier, three cruisers, and several destroyers air raided and bombarded Wotje, Eniwetok, Kwajalein, and Jaluit. At first, they reported it to be two battleships, and anyway they were not certain about the enemy strength. The Fourth Fleet thought there were other carriers. The position of the enemy was not accurate either, They made mistakes in coding. After experiencing defensive weakness ourselves, we cannot laugh at the enemy's confusion at the time of the surprise attack on Pearl Harbor.

[*These raids were conducted by two carrier groups, respectively, under Vice Admiral William F. Halsey, Jr., in* Enterprise *and Rear Admiral Frank Jack Fletcher in* Yorktown. *Results were disappointing from the American standpoint.*[23] Ugaki recorded Japanese actions taken in consequence.]

Medium torpedo bombers and other planes which had been in Truk for the Rabaul operation, as well as the Sixth Light Cruiser Division, were ordered to advance to the east swiftly, while several submarines of the Sixth Fleet sortied promptly to take up positions. The task force, which happened to be in Truk, sortied at 1100 and headed east. These steps were taken at the discretion of those commanders in chief concerned.

While we are being attacked in the south, it is also necessary to take precautions in the north, that is, for the east coast of the Japanese homeland. So we alerted the Fifth Fleet and after noon ordered the Third Station against the U.S. fleet with the organization as it is.

The enemy's attempt was most timely because our operations were focused in the southwest Pacific and the defensive strength in the Marshalls was thin. In addition to a fairly big result, they achieved their purpose of diverting our strength. Carriers closed in and heavy cruisers' bombardment was also most daring. It seems we have been somewhat fooled.

In exchange, we only hit a heavy cruiser with some bombs which caused a fire at midship and temporary loss of speed. (*This was* Chester, *assigned with two destroyers to bombard Maloelap Atoll.*][24] It's a pity to think that had those planes from Truk been earlier, we could have attacked them effectively, taking advantage of tonight's full moon.

There is little chance of the enemy coming up again tomorrow morning. Anyway, we have missed the game.

They will announce this as a great success on a grand scale and will repeat this kind of surprise attack. Pearl Harbor was a complete surprise, but we cannot say the same for this, which happened during the war. Our carelessness in being ignorant of the enemy approach until he was so close was extremely regrettable.

However, at about noon yesterday the Sixth Communications Corps issued a warning that the enemy was planning some offensive, but it arrived too late this morning. We must admit that this has given a most effective lesson to those who, intoxicated with the sinking of *Lexington* and the favorable turn of operations, thought the enemy incapable of carrying out air raids. I thought that the enemy was up to something, judging from the words of the heads of the American government at Congress lately, operations bureau intelligence based on reports of agents, or from the concentration of enemy submarines in the Marshall area. And it finally turned out to be true. That certainly provides food for thought.

There have already been several cases which eventually turned out adversely because of my indecision. In spite of my feeling some apprehension, or contrary judgments, I refrained from giving my decisions in order to save the face of the staff officers who drafted the idea or after being forced to give in to their strong one-sided arguments.

A battle contains many unknown factors. Intuition, instinct, or sixth sense, even when it is right, tends to be ignored when many people or insensitive people are consulted. I can see now why Hitler, having supreme power and being dictatorial in decision and execution, is so successful in doing unexpected things and is called an expert on the administration as well as the leadership of the armed forces. It is because he has this distinct, strong intuition and acts upon it decisively.

This intuition cannot be simply called instinct or presentiment. This, of course, owes much to talent, but its function will not be complete unless based on full knowledge of the enemy as well as ourselves—and everything in the universe.

Only after experiencing all kinds of hardships and difficulties will a gem increase its brilliance. Gems should be polished. I will try to put into practice all that I feel in the future. This does not mean that I would not listen to others' opinions, or that I would insist on my own.

Our losses were fairly big, including a few auxiliary ships, in spite of our shooting down six planes and inflicting some damage to a heavy cruiser.

[Ugaki ended this day's entry with a brief tribute to a former Naval Academy classmate, Rear Admiral Yukicki Yashiro, commander, Sixth Naval Base Force, killed in action in the Marshalls raid. He was the first Japanese admiral killed in the war.]

Monday, 2 February 1942. Cloudy, the winds died down and warm. The enemy who surprise-attacked the Marshalls yesterday seemed to consist of two task forces. Our shadowing float plane lost contact with them in the afternoon and even at night they maintained radio silence. It is likely they have withdrawn to the Palmyra area. The enemy radio is said to have announced this attack's achievements. They claimed nothing big was in the atoll, but that local enemy forces were destroyed with two ships sustaining some damage and eleven planes missing.

This incident was really "a reproach that went to the heart." It has been nearly two months since the war broke out, and there is no reason why he [the enemy] should be doing nothing. We must admit that this is the best way to make us look ridiculous. Adventure is one of their characteristics. They took advantage of the situation when we were busy fighting in the south and west, and attained their object of restraining our southward advance in addition to the actual damage.

They will adopt this kind of method in the future, for it is the easiest for them and the most effective. And the most probable move they would make would be an air raid on our capital. Not only have they already prepared ten converted carriers, but they will intensify this kind of attempt by utilizing superior merchant ships and by replenishing air personnel and material.

It was fortunate for us that the enemy only scratched us on this occasion and gave us a good lesson instead of directly attacking Tokyo. I have written down what I thought as information for the staff.

On 31 January our army force in Malaya reached Johore Bahru, the southernmost point of the Asian continent. Their advance and attacks are brave and swift, and really marvelous.

We sent Staff Officer Fujii to Tokyo, taking with him [our plan] for directing operations and the policy of administering the occupied territory, etc.

Tuesday, 3 February 1942. Cloudy. In view of their method of attack and radio intelligence, it was ascertained that the enemy which attacked the Marshalls consisted of two task forces, one coming from northeast of Wotje and another from southeast of Jaluit. They carried out level bombing, dive bombing, and torpedo attack in that order, at great intervals, but their skill in each was far inferior to ours. The local air force on the spot reported this.

Five enemy cruisers and a destroyer are at Bangka on the east coast of Sumatra. They are nice targets for the Twenty-second Air Flotilla. Furthermore, two battleships were said to have been discovered in the Surabaja area. We would like to get them all.

A detailed agreement on the invasion of Palembang has been concluded between the First Southern Expeditionary Fleet and the Thirty-eighth Division.

[Temporarily leaving the war, Ugaki related how that morning he had gone ashore to shoot. He made a good bag, and that evening had a sukiyaki dinner featuring his game.]

Wednesday, 4 February 1942. Fair. It was sunny and warm today, too. The weather officer jokingly said the atmospheric condition had also changed because of the war.

The report of the battle in the Marshalls of more than ten thousand words came in from the commander in chief, Fourth Fleet. It was the largest telegram since the war started and took quite a time to decode. The damage sustained at various places added up to more than initially reported. The Fourth Fleet has its own excuses, but I still can't help regretting that we were surprised.

The Eleventh Air Fleet's attack on Java achieved great success, destroying seventy enemy planes.

Considerable difficulty was experienced in the occupation of Ambon. Not only that, an enemy mine sank Minesweeper No. 9. Both Nos. 12 and 17 were damaged and disabled when they exploded enemy mines by sweeping cable. The method of sweeping mines in shallow waters must be restudied.

A lookout post reported at 0500 sighting an enemy submarine at the southern end of Nuwa Jima Channel. We will have troubles in guarding. The truth [of the report] should be ascertained more definitely.

[That afternoon Ugaki heard reports from two high-ranking submarine officers. One of them, Captain Sasaki, had commanded the First Submarine Division, which took the minisubs to Pearl Harbor.]

Thursday, 5 February 1942. Fair. Our plane sighted three Dutch cruisers (*Java, Sumatra*), U.S. cruiser *Marblehead,* and eight Dutch destroyers sailing southwest of Macassar yesterday afternoon. Medium torpedo bombers concentrated attacks upon them, sank one *Java* type and seriously damaged the *Sumatra* type which, however, did not sink. Fairly heavy damages were also inflicted upon the other two cruisers.

[*This force under Rear Admiral K.W.E.M. Doorman, RNN actually consisted of his flagship, light cruiser* De Ruyter, *heavy cruiser* Houston, *light cruisers* Marblehead *and* Tromp, *four Dutch and four U.S. destroyers. Although* Houston *and* Marblehead *were heavily damaged and* De Ruyter *less seriously, none sank.*][25]

Furthermore, planes of the Second Carrier Division destroyed and set on fire a transport of five thousand tons heading for Macassar under destroyer escort. They planned to continue the attack into the night. That would have been effective if they carried it out, but they could not. They resumed their attack this morning, but it ended without our receiving any good news.

The landing on the Bangka and Palembang area has been postponed for two days and has been set for the 12th. The army's advance in Burma is continually going forward. They crossed the Salween River after capturing Moulmein.

The high command in Tokyo is against an invasion of Port Darwin. In order to destroy it thoroughly we are to capture Dili as well as Koupan at the same time. An instruction will be given shortly with regard to the capture of the Andamans. The chief of the Operations Bureau of the General Staff informed us of the above yesterday.

What is the high command's reaction to the details of the westward operations? There is no sign of it yet.

It was pleasantly sunny and warm until about noon today, and it felt like spring on deck.

> What's the matter with you people? Fighting,
> Waging war, when flowers are blooming?

We are really trying hard, hoping to make a clean sweep of the enemy at least before the cherry blossoms bloom.

Friday, 6 February 1942. Cloudy. Leaving the ship at 1000, the commander in chief and eight staff officers went to inspect a special battery at Ohbatake-Seto.

[Apparently this inspection combined business with pleasure. The battery was located in the garden of a private residence. The owner served them "a sumptuous lunch." Ugaki tried his luck with his shotgun, but the ducks were too wary for him.]

The results of the air attack on the 4th in the Java Sea exceed the original estimates. At 1130 and 1330, under heavy enemy gunfire, seventeen land torpedo bombers of the Kanoya Air Group and twenty-four of the same from Takao and the First Air Group attacked the combined Dutch and American fleet sailing at 24 knots on a southeasterly course thirty miles south of Kamboan Island. The following damage was inflicted upon the enemy fleet.

The first ship, of the *De Ruyter* type, surely sank soon after being hit by two 250-kg bombs and four near misses of the same. The second ship, of the *Java* type, sank instantly from two 250-kg bombs. A 60-kg bomb and a near miss damaged the third ship. Hits from ten 60-kg bombs and near misses amidship from two 60-kg and two 250-kg bombs heavily damaged the U.S. heavy cruiser. Only the U.S. *Marblehead* seems to have escaped unscathed. I wonder how they are feeling.

As preparation of bases at Kuantan, Kuching, Iedo, etc., were delayed, the landing operation on Sumatra could not be made until about the 18th, the First Southern Expeditionary Force appealed [for reconsideration]. On the other hand, the Second Fleet pressed for an early execution regardless of losses in view of the overall situation. Thus they are pitted against each other. So, after consulting with Tokyo on the matter, a suggestion was sent to the Second Fleet's chief of staff not to hurry so much.

Staff Officer Fujii telephoned from Tokyo. He said that they had no concrete plan about the next operation, but he was trying to educate them, using our plan, and was making progress. We have also drafted the principle of directing the operations.

Saturday, 7 February 1942. Partly fair. Today's papers headlined reports on the battle of the Java Sea. Although I don't think much of it, I'm pleased that we have sent the main force of the Dutch East Indies to the bottom and also inflicted heavy damage to an American cruiser. (She is said to be a heavy cruiser.)

The policy which the Second Fleet adopted with the reinforcement of the task force is quite agreeable. It will be interesting to see if a second and third Dunkirk will take place in the south of Java, as the staff says, so that big British fishes may be bagged.

Each unit fought well at the time of the enemy raid on the Marshalls the other day. As it was deemed necessary to say something to them, although there were some points to which their attention should be invited, we sent a message to the commander in chief's Fourth and Sixth fleets, praising their deeds mildly while asking them to remain in a state of preparedness.

The supply ship *Irako* finished her maiden voyage supplying fresh food to the southern area and returned to the anchorage here. Of her load of five hundred tons of vegetables, she couldn't distribute more then two hundred tons. Shipping traffic should be arranged more effectively.

The ship brought back eighty tons of sugar from Saipan, which was quite an appropriate step. But I can't approve of the paymaster's plan to supply it to the navy. The navy is not so short of sugar; the civilians are suffering most. Our dear children should be considered first. Even in this time of shipping shortages, one should be more broad-minded and look at things from the national standpoint.

Sunday, 8 February 1942. Partly fair. It is said that the leading ship in the battle of the Java Sea was ascertained to be an American heavy cruiser, as a result of interpretation of an enlarged photo. The local air unit reported this.

According to a telegram from the chief of the Communications Department yesterday evening, telegrams from four to five ships were intercepted in the direction of about 50° of Owada, north of Tokyo. This makes us wonder if the enemy is attempting a surprise attack on the homeland. The areas concerned were accordingly alerted, while a special force was ordered formed with the Second Battleship Division, Ninth Light Cruiser Division, Third and Fifth carrier divisions, and two destroyers under the command of the commander in chief, First Fleet, in preparation for an emergency. An order for sortie was not issued as nothing definite was heard until midnight. The First Fleet command acted quite well in making preparations.

Monday, 9 February 1942. Partly fair with fair winds. A part of our invasion force landed near Macassar last night and the rest succeeded in landing at Macassar at 0400. An enemy submarine [*S-37*] torpedoed *Natsushio* of the Fourth Destroyer Division south of there [on 8 February.][26] She escaped sinking but was rendered unnavigable.

The First Southern Expeditionary Fleet set the date of landing on Banka and Palembang as the 15th. This landing date had been a matter of controversy for some time.

Tuesday, 10 February 1942. Partly fair. *Natsushio* finally sank after 0800 on the 9th.

Our army forces, which had been preparing an attack on Singapore since the 8th, after bombings and bombardments, crossed Johore Strait from the northwest at midnight of the 8th/9th. They must have gone through many hardships. This afternoon's radio further stated they captured Tengga airfield.

Leaving the ship at 0600, I went shooting from off Yuu to Takara Jima and returned to the ship at noon. I had bad luck today and only bagged two [birds].

Yamato finished her repairs and returned here from Kure.

[Wednesday, 11 February 1942 was the 2602nd anniversary of the accession of Japan's first emperor. Ceremonies were held in the ward room, and the event moved Ugaki to hope that, "with one hundred million hearts beating as one," the Japanese could overcome all hardships.]

Our Imperial Armed Forces which advanced into Singapore have captured Mantai Hill overlooking the town and the harbor.

The orderlies were busy preparing for the changing of flagships. As it was noisy, I went shooting from after 1400.

The army unit which advanced overland from Balikpapan have captured Danjermassin today.

[On Thursday, 12 February 1942, Yamamoto shifted his flag to his new flagship, *Yamato*.)

Friday, 13 February 1942. Fair. What has happened to our force which advanced to Singapore? Little seems to have developed there.

[That afternoon Rear Admiral Takeda, commanding the Twenty-fourth Division, and his senior staff officer, Captain Kiichi Shintani, came to the flagship to report on their activities. Ugaki was not impressed, observing acidly that however detailed their reports, all they had done was sink two American merchantmen. They should consider how better to use this division in the future.]

Saturday, 14 February 1942. Cloudy. I thought something must have been wrong about the delay in capturing Singapore, and sure enough there was a great deal. The big guns of the enemy fort which had been directed to the sea unexpectedly turned around and displayed their might on the back hill our force had occupied, and it has become necessary to devise some countermeasures. There seems nothing else to do but bomb them heavily and cover the flank gunfire while attempting to break into the fort in the meantime. I hope it will not be a repetition of Bataan Peninsula in Manila Bay.

On the other hand, Ubin Island was taken on the 8th, and a naval force dispatched on land previously is said to have captured the naval port of Seleter and hoisted the rising sun ensign atop the headquarters building.

Enormous numbers of transports have been sailing to the south from Singapore in the last few days, escorted by a fair number of cruisers and destroyers. The British have experienced evacuations at Norway, Dunkirk, or at Crete in Greece. Once decided, they make preparations early and embark ships at night to alleviate possible loss. In spite of our fairly big air strength, attacks against these vessels seen to be rather mild. So I have warned the concerned chiefs of staff against this point, as the Java operation will be coming up soon.

Army paratroops landed on Palembang airfield at 1130 and succeeded in capturing it. [The Dutch defenders soon killed them.][27] The army had wanted the announcement of the use of naval paratroops withheld until this attempt was completed. Now it can be released.

Along with our operations in Andaman and Burma, the British Fleet in that area is expected to make counter activities. Accordingly, we have decided to carry out an operation, dispatching the task force to the Indian Ocean east of Ceylon to launch a surprise attack on Ceylon at a favorable opportunity. Its time was set at about the end of March.

We have issued a plan to hold table maneuvers from the 20th of this month, mainly to study the second-stage operations. We are pressed for time as usual.

[Sunday, 15 February 1952, was Ugaki's fifty-second birthday, and his shipmates treated him to a special breakfast. He promised himself to remain in shape physically, the better to "fulfill the heaven-sent mission myself and comfort the souls of my deceased parents." Business soon caught up with him.]

Before lunch a staff officer brought in a telegram reporting that three enemy cruisers accompanied by six destroyers were headed north-northeast of Banka Island at 0900. The commander in chief, First Southern Expeditionary Fleet, issued an attack order at the proper time. But when a plane reported there were three battleships, three cruisers, and eight destroyers, he ordered heavy cruiser *Chokai,* Seventh Heavy Cruiser Division, light cruiser *Sendai,* light cruiser *Yura,* and destroyer divisions, which were only about one hundred miles from the enemy, to withdraw temporarily. His idea was to have a decisive battle with the enemy fleet after the air force had destroyed the battleships.

Though this seemed like a proper decision, reconnaissance later determined that there were only cruisers with no battleships. The planes of CVL *Ryujo* and others attacked, but seemingly with no success. It was regrettable that we missed such an easy target, but they will fall prey to our planes some day. My only regret was that we couldn't destroy them with gunfire as a test to prove its might.

[*Although Admiral Ozawa's aircraft inflicted little actual damage on Doorman's ships, Doorman had no fighter protection and decided to retire to the Java Sea.*[28]

[Ugaki had just retired to his cabin after dinner when a staff officer informed him the British at Singapore had decided to surrender. According to Ugaki's information, the Twenty-fifth Army commander met the Singapore commander, Lieutenant General Arthur E. Percival, and they agreed to unconditional surrender at 2200. This news sent Ugaki's spirits soaring. He sent for *Yamato*'s skipper and a few other officers, and they celebrated until around midnight. Almost as an afterthought, he noted the capture of Muntok on Banka Island at 0400.]

Monday, 16 February 1942. Fair. We were busy receiving congratulatory telegrams on the fall of Singapore and sending replies to them. The imperial aide-de-camp [Vice Admiral Tomoshige] Samejima arrived from Kure at 1045 and conveyed their majesties' messages.

[Like the loyal subject he was, Ugaki recorded both messages in full. The empress had added a special gift for Yamamoto, "an embroidery of a plane on the background of an ensign, which Her Majesty had hand-embroidered herself." Ugaki also recorded the Imperial Rescript which the emperor gave to the Southern Area Army commander and to Yamamoto.

[On Tuesday, 17 February 1942, Samejima left for the China Area Fleet. Premier Tojo had delivered a speech to the Diet, and Ugaki summed up its main points, which were concerned with how to control Greater East Asia in the future. These coincided with Ugaki's ideas, so he approved. He spared a thought for the Allies.]

On the 7th, Commander in Chief Hart ceded his position to the Dutch Vice Admiral [C.E.L.] Helfrich, owing to illness. A Surabaja-Shanghai dispatch reported yesterday that Hart went down with *Houston*. As I thought, this turned out to be a trick played by the Naval General Staff, and the staff officers who had drunk the beer given to the commander in chief had to disgorge it today. It was perfectly ridiculous.

[All the newspapers, wrote Ugaki, featured "Fall of Singapore" editions. The former British stronghold henceforth would be called Shonanto (Singapore).]

Vice Minister Michio Yuzawa was promoted to home minister today. This was a necessary step prior to the election in April and also relieved the prime minister of one of the three positions he held concurrently. It was necessary for the cabinet to consolidate its foundation now, as some people were criticizing it, though it seemed to be doing all right generally.

[Wednesday, 18 February 1942, was a day of victory celebrations. For the first time since 1938 the entire imperial family appeared "to receive public congratulations."]

Thursday, 19 February 1942. Fair. At 0600 the First Battleship Division went out to Iyo Nada in the rain for training. This was the first time after *Yamato, Mutsu,* and *Nagato* were made first, second, and third ships of the line today, and the exercises were mainly to compare their maneuverability.

The task force surprise-attacked Port Darwin on a large scale up to 0800 and sank three destroyers, one sub chaser, and eight merchant ships. All of twenty-eight planes were also destroyed and installations, too. I am sure all the Australians were shocked and scared stiff.

[*This was a combined attack by four carriers under Admiral Nagumo of Pearl Harbor fame, with two battleships and three heavy cruisers under Admiral Kondo. Allied losses included the U.S. destroyer* Peary *and army troopship* Meigs, *an Australian troopship and freighter, three merchantmen, two corvettes, and a Norwegian tanker. The U.S. aircraft tender* William B. Preston *was damaged, and a merchantman had to be beached. In addition, eighteen Allied aircraft were destroyed, and Port Darwin itself so badly shot up it had to be abandoned temporarily.*][29]

On the other hand, our navy's Dutch East Indies Force carried out a landing on Bali in cooperation with the army and captured the airfield, meeting no resistance.

Bombing from enemy planes damaged an army transport. The airfield is ready for fighters to use, which is most convenient. Planes should be advanced there right away.

While escorting and supporting the convoy, the Eighth Destroyer Division met one *Java* type, one *Locarno* type [probably *De Ruyter*], and three destroyers [probably *Piet Hein, Pope,* and *Ford*] during the night. As a result of the ensuing battle, the Dutch cruisers narrowly escaped in the direction of Surabaja, two of the remaining destroyers were sunk, and another seriously damaged. In this engagement *Michishio* was disabled.

[*In this engagement in the Badung Strait, the Japanese sank the Dutch Destroyer* Piet Hein *and severely damaged the U.S. destroyer* Stewart *and the Dutch light cruiser* Tromp. *The Japanese destroyer* Michishio *was disabled but survived.*][30]

Friday, 20 February 1942. Fair. Following a briefing from 0830, the first table maneuver was held. Its purpose was to study operations after the middle of May following completion of the first-stage operations—substantially the Indian Ocean operation.[31]

[A number of high-ranking officers, including Prince Takamatsu, visited *Yamato.* Ugaki learned for the first time that Vice Admiral Mitsumi Shimizu, commander in chief, Sixth Fleet, had been wounded and would be replaced by Vice Admiral Teruhisa Komatsu of the First China Fleet.]

Captain [Wataru] Nakase, chief of the First Section of the same bureau [Naval General Staff] also came and conferred with us on the questions of double promotion and also of education. The northwest winds were strong and it was cold today.

A search plane sighted a large enemy force on course of 315° at a point 450 miles 65° of Rabaul at 0900. The Fourth Fleet has issued an attack order.

The First Air Group, now in Ambon with nothing much to do, was ordered to advance swiftly to the Truk area to go under the command of the Fourth Fleet. Toward evening the enemy was reported to have altered course to 135° with the speed of 15 knots.

While we are eager to get him this time, the enemy apparently has withdrawn again, suspecting that his attempt has been disclosed. Though it was said to be a large force, a powerful force, or the main force, nothing has been said about its content. Without this information, the higher command cannot take proper measures. After all, it seemed to include one battleship, one carrier, three cruisers, and destroyers.

[*This was Vice Admiral Wilson Brown's* Lexington *group, consisting of the CV, four heavy cruisers, and ten destroyers.*][32]

Against this enemy seventeen medium torpedo bombers attacked from Rabaul, but only two returned. Accurate enemy long-range antiaircraft gunfire [actually, it was very poor] and interceptors destroyed the rest. Besides, they could do no more than disable a heavy cruiser or a destroyer. It was most regrettable.

The reported enemy course of 135° was a telegraphic error; its real course was 315°. His subsequently reported course at night made us think he might come in. Though I wish to get them this time if they should come, I cannot help regretting the huge loss of the bombers.

Our force landed on Koupan in Timor this morning. The landing force consisted of an army unit and a naval landing party. It took the airfield without any resistance.

On the other hand, the force which took Dili met strong resistance, but captured the airfield.

[Ugaki remarked that the government had taken great pains not to antagonize the Portuguese in connection with this landing, assuring the Portuguese minister that they would respect Portuguese sovereignty and eventually evacuate.]

Saturday, 21 February 1942. Fair. This was the second day of the table maneuvers, continued from yesterday.

We have not been able to find the enemy east-northeast of Rabaul at the estimated point in spite of searching since this morning. We have no idea whether they have turned back or not.

Further, flashing lights were sighted on the horizon southeast and south-southeast of Wake Island last night. Search was accordingly made in the area this morning but also with no result. While we are thus occupied in the south, couldn't the enemy come from the north? Alert should be maintained.

[That night Yamamoto hosted another sukiyaki party, with the commander in chief, First Fleet, and his chief of staff as guests of honor.]

Sunday, 22 February 1942. Cloudy, later rain. This was the third day of the table maneuver; we finished the actual performance this morning. The idea of the operation in the Indian Ocean was not good. Though we landed on Ceylon, we missed the main force of the enemy fleet and were hindered by the enemy local air strength. We need further study for its actual execution.

The fighting of the Eighth Destroyer Division at Badung Strait was splendid. They sank two Dutch cruisers, three American and Dutch destroyers, and seriously damaged two others. It should be announced to the world by the name battle of Badung Strait, as it was the first sea battle worthy of the name since the beginning of the war. It was really a fine night battle with a destroyer division. Its commander is said to be a younger brother of Rear Admiral Hiroshi Abe.

Nothing has been heard of the enemy northeast of Rabaul since then. According to an investigation of aerial photos of the Twenty-fourth Air Flotilla's attack, it is said to be certain that a carrier other than the *Saratoga* type was sunk. That may be true in view of the way the enemy withdrew. Such damage ought to have been inflicted, considering such a great loss.

Monday, 23 February 1942. Fair. In view of the fact that the enemy fleet and a fair number of planes still remained, the schedule for the landing on Java was put off by two days to the 28th.

[Another group of naval VIPs, including Prince Takamatsu and Major Prince Tsunenori Takeda, came to observe the table maneuvers. Ugaki learned that the Army General Staff anticipated "nothing serious" with the Soviet Union that year, and General Yoshijira Umezu, commanding the Kwantung Army, had the army under control. But the chief of the Operations Bureau, Naval General Staff, warned against relaxing precautions against the Russians.]

Tuesday, 24 February 1942. Rain, later cloudy. A patrol plane from Wake found two heavy cruisers, two light cruisers, one carrier, and four destroyers after 0500 as near as ten miles from the island. As usual, it was difficult to determine the truth as to ships, carriers, or destroyers.

The enemy attacked the island with seven carrier planes and fifty carrier bombers and also bombarded from cruisers. We shot down two enemy planes and our shore batteries started a fire on an enemy cruiser. The enemy retired at high speed in the direction of 40° to 60°.

A flying boat contacted the enemy force well, and over a dozen medium torpedo bombers from Luot attacked it, making a hit with a 250-kg bomb on the stern of a cruiser, which dropped out. I regret we did not get enough results.

[*Halsey's* Enterprise *group raided Wake on 24 February 1942. They sank only a small patrol craft and lost one of* Enterprise's *dive bombers and its crew.[33] Ugaki now waxed sarcastic about the United States.*]

For the Americans, today is called Washington's birthday, and President Roosevelt was going to make a fireside talk. They had to do something, or the existence of the U.S. Navy would have been doubted.

Though they have a certain flair for strategy—having a task force each in the north and south, maintaining cooperation between the two—there is nothing much to praise in their actual actions. Only their bold practice of bombarding directly at close range or launching planes should be called quite daring. Some day we shall teach them a lesson; we will have a good chance of destroying them.

Our forces which had minesWept the Singapore area succeeded in opening the channel yesterday. Part of the fleet accordingly entered Seleter Naval Port, replacing the Union Jack.

Our repeated air raids have wiped out the enemy's air power in eastern Java. Now only sixty or seventy planes remain in the west. The invasion of Java is now just a matter of time. The enemy must know well that Java is doomed by our capture of Bali, the paradise of the world, only twenty-two kilometers away. The Americans and the Dutch are complaining but they can't do anything about it. This is part of our strategy.

A low pressure suddenly approached since this morning and the rain started, making the use of a specially prepared fleet plane impracticable. The two princes returned to Tokyo by train.

Wednesday, 25 February 1942. Partly fair. No great change in the war situation.

Thursday, 26 February 1942. Light rain, later cloudy. It was calm before the invasion of Java and there was no big change. A carrier of the *Ranger* type accompanied by a submarine was sighted at a point 345 miles bearing 220° off Koupan on course of 330°. They were probably heading for Tjilatjap.

After dinner we saw a newsreel of the action of the naval paratroops in Menado and I was deeply moved by the first success of its kind in this country, splendidly accomplished.

Friday, 27 February 1942. Fair. The maneuver of the First Battleship Division was put off until tomorrow, owing to bad visibility. It was foggy with south winds and made me feel that spring was just around the corner. March will soon be here and the completion of the first stage operations is quite close, too.

The carrier we found yesterday might be *Langley*, which was supposed to have been sunk, according to the intercepted enemy message, "Sixteen enemy planes are attacking me."

[*This was indeed* Langley. *Planes from Japan's Eleventh Air Fleet damaged her so badly she had to be scutted by her two escort destroyers.*[34] Ugaki was dissatisfied with the attack reports.]

A submarine which attacks submerges after an attack and fails to confirm the sinking of the victim. Planes also count the same loss twice or three times, or report a sinking for certain without waiting to make sure of it. In this way, they are finally recorded as sunk. This is not intentional but is the natural course of events. Thus a great difference occurs between enemy announcements and ours, all the more so because the enemy makes the loss of ours double or several times more, and tries to obliterate his own, much worse than the Chinese did in the past.

A friendly fighter strafed the submarine *I-5* in the Java Sea and seriously wounded the skipper and others. It is needless to stress the importance of friendly identification.

Three cruisers and destroyers on an indefinite course have been reported at a point about thirty miles northwest of Batavia.

[*These were the cruisers USS* Houston, *HMS* Perth, *and* Exeter, *with the destroyers USS* Pope, *HMS* Encounter, *and HNMS* Evertsen. *A delay in starting kept the latter from catching up to the cruisers.*[35] More ships had been sighted, as Ugaki reported.] Besides, several cruisers and destroyers were sailing east-northwest of Surabaja. I hope for the safety of the Batavia invasion force, heading south to the west of Borneo for tonight's landing, and of the Surabaja invasion force sailing southeast of Borneo.

Two or three destroyers and forty merchant ships are in Tjilatjap, several cruisers and destroyers and forty merchantmen off Surabaja, also a fair number of ships in the Batavia area. We must take measures to capture these.

Many captured ships had been added to the list of Japanese warships and were paraded in the Triumphant Naval Review at the conclusion of the Russo-Japanese War. On this occasion, we must get hold of some fairly big British, American, and Dutch warships.

In addition, about one hundred enemy merchantmen represent at least three hundred thousand tons. Shortage of shipping is a loud cry prevalent now. This is the usual excuse of the central authorities for their hesitation in making operations to the west, to the south, and to the east. The most effective thing, from the national point of view, would be to gain the three hundred thousand tons now and shut up these excuses.

One way to prevent their escape would be by a diversionary movement by a powerful force, while making the enemy seek an early surrender by developing the air and land operations. Direct operational forces should themselves devise and execute plans. The show is at its climax now. We cannot expect such a big game as this even if we carry out large-scale operations in the future.

Though the invasion force was scheduled to enter the roads tonight, the commander, Fifth Destroyer Squadron Escort Force in the Batavia area, postponed it by one day on account of the enemy situation.

Saturday, 28 February 1942. Fair. The Surabaja Area Force, consisting of the Fifth Heavy Cruiser Division and others, sank three enemy cruisers, six destroyers, and damaged others in the battle off Surabaja fought at daylight and night, starting yesterday evening. The United States' heavy cruisers were not equipped with torpedoes, and a defect was now disclosed in the fact that they were easily destroyed in a gun-and-torpedo-fire battle.

[*This engagement continued into 1 March where Ugaki discussed it in more detail.*]

3
A Second Victory Celebration
March–May 1942

MARCH OPENED *on a high note for the Japanese, with the sinking of three Allied cruisers and three destroyers at minimum cost. Elsewhere the march of Japanese victories continued, interrupted only by such ineffectual American efforts as Halsey's raid on Marcus Island and the activities of American submarines. Rangoon, Batavia, and Surabaja all fell, and, with the surrender of the entire Netherlands East Indies, Japan held a victory celebration. This made Ugaki somewhat nervous. Suppose there was an air raid "over the heads of the rejoicing multitude?"*

In April Nagumo added further luster to his already shining record with his task force's attack on Ceylon. This resulted, among other things, in the sinking of major British vessels—CV Hermes *with her escort destroyer* Vampire *and the heavy cruisers* Dorsetshire *and* Cornwall.

History repeated itself when Yamamoto secured the Naval General Staff's approval of the Combined Fleet's Midway plan by strongly hinting that otherwise he might resign. Planning and practice for Operation MI occupied much of the Combined Fleet's attention during this period. One could wish that Ugaki had been more detailed in his reporting of these activities, but, no doubt for security reasons, he confined himself to generalities.

The famous Doolittle raid of 18 April 1942 on the Japanese homeland agitated Ugaki far beyond what the meager results would seem to call for. But, as we have seen, he had expected the Americans to try to attack the Japanese homeland and set a high priority on frustrating any such attempt. The Doolittle exploit destroyed his "firm determination never to let the enemy attack Tokyo or the mainland." He keenly felt his own and the navy's failure in this regard.

In May 1942 Yorktown *attacked Tulagi with relatively minor results. Corregidor surrendered, and Ugaki was relieved that at last the Japanese fleet could "move in and out of Manila freely." Early in May came the major naval battle of the Coral Sea. The Americans had the worst of it operationally, with* Lexington *sunk and* Yorktown *badly damaged. They also lost two valuable tankers,* Neosho *and* Sims, *which the Japanese mistook for a carrier and a cruiser, respectively. For their part, the Japanese lost the CVL* Shoho. Shokaku *was so*

98

badly damaged and Zuikaku *lost so many aircraft that neither of these big carriers could participate in Operation MI as planned. Furthermore, the Japanese objective—to capture Port Moresby—had to be postponed and was later abandoned. Strategically, Coral Sea was an American victory. As Ugaki wrote in a moment of unusual pessimism, "A dream of great success has been shattered."*

Between actual engagements during these months, Ugaki gives a broad picture of the day-by-day activities of a navy at war: training aboard ship, outfitting with and testing of armament and shells, plans and briefings, and the inevitable mistakes and accidents.

This period ends with the Combined Fleet on its way to Midway. Convinced of Japanese superiority and seriously underestimating the Americans, Ugaki and his colleagues confidently expected another rousing victory.

Sunday, 1 March 1942. Fair, later cloudy. We left Agenosho at 0700 and after practicing recovery of planes returned to Hashira Jima anchorage at 1215.

Before dawn this morning, we made successful landings both at Surabaja and Batavia. Enemy cruisers penetrated our landing scene and we sank two of them. We also suffered a little damage to a destroyer, while a transport was sunk and three were seriously damaged. The enemy is now fighting back desperately, as this is a showdown.

[*In the Sunda Strait action of 28 February–1 March 1942, the Japanese sank the cruisers* Perth, Houston, *and* Exeter *and the destroyers* Evertsen, Encounter, *and* Pope. *The Allies damaged the destroyer* Harukaze, *slightly damaged the cruiser* Mikuma, *sank one transport, and forced three others to beach themselves. The Fifth Air Force evacuated Java.*][1]

Rear Admiral Takijiro Onishi, chief of staff, Eleventh Air Fleet, was ordered back to the Naval Aeronautical Department to become chief of its General Affairs Bureau and came to report on his way to Tokyo from the front. While many of his views were justifiable, he claimed that the center of armament is now in air power, and the big-ship-and-gun policy has turned into just an armament for surprise attacks. His assertion was based only upon our past operations along the island chain from the Philippines to the Dutch East Indies.

I believe this matter needs further study. The use of land-based air power over a huge expanse of water is difficult. Are the carriers enough to advance air power?

Navy Minister Shimada also often expressed his opinion that the construction of [the superbattleship] *Musashi* should be held off, but was restrained by Fukudome, the chief of the Operations Bureau, who asked him to wait, Fukudome himself told me. All general opinion is like this. If we had a sure way to neutralize enemy battleships, there would be no need to spend billions in yen and materials to build our own.

Monday, 2 March 1942. Rain, later clears up. We had a light rain since before dawn, and it has already begun to feel like spring.

Rear Admiral Onishi left at 0800. He said he played chess with the commander in chief last night with a result of three wins and four losses. As he himself said, he may be one of those who spends the war on a chess board.

[*Yamamoto was an inveterate chess player. He not only enjoyed the game, he believed it kept his mind alert.*][2]

According to the statements of POWs, in the battle off Surabaja a Dutch vice admiral commanded the six cruisers, only one of which was sunk. Another dropped behind in the daylight battle, and one was seen dropping back in the night battle. This proves that there was a big difference between the actual loss and what they saw and reported.

As to the *Java* types, they were supposed to have been sunk at the battle of Bali.

The commander, Third CV Division, completed his mission of transporting planes for CVL *Zuiho,* and on his return came on board to report.

Tuesday, 3 March 1942. Fair. It was the festival of peach blossoms, but didn't feel like it to me.

A telegram came in to the effect that *Chiyoda's* midget sub No. 13 sank during training last night, and they were making every effort to locate her. *Nisshin* and destroyer *Yakaze* were dispatched for rescue and the torpedo staff officer went to the spot. Three crewmen were on board, and I hoped for their early rescue.

A meeting to study the first exercise of the First Battleship Division was held from 0830 in *Yamato's* ward room. Fair progress has been made in skill, but not enough. I fear the morale of the Main Body is stale after a long stay in home waters. I have encouraged them, but we must study methods of training afresh and at the same time engage in some operational action.

Before we fight a decisive battle with the American fleet, an engagement with the British is, of course, desirable, without the need of referring to the lesson obtained in the battle of the Yellow Sea on 10 August 1904 prior to the battle of Tsushima on 27 May 1905. Anyway, from the standpoint of the whole fleet's morale, it will be absolutely necessary to sortie for operations in the Indian Ocean in May.

As *Java* and *De Ruyter* type cruisers appeared in the battle off Surabaja, the war result of the Eighth Destroyer Division of the other day has been corrected.

Our landing forces in Surabaja, Batavia, and the central part of the island all seemed to be advancing rapidly.

The army offensive on Bataan Peninsula has stalemated, and they started mopping up the enemy on the other islands of Mindoro and Cebu in cooperation with the navy. This must be termed the poorest strategy—to surround the most important center from a distance and to touch elsewhere. In this way, the peninsula and Corregidor will remain until the last and it will only make [General Douglas] MacArthur a hero. It will badly affect the future course of the war and also the administration of the Philippines. The dismissal of [Major General Masami] Maeda, chief of staff, Twenty-fourth Army, was said to be on account of this.

Wednesday, 4 March 1942. Fair. Midget sub No. 13 was located by sweeping at 2300 last night. There was no answer to underwater signals from a submarine or knocking on the hull by divers.

[Ugaki flew to the scene of the accident to learn what had happened, then returned to report to Yamamoto. Later they discussed personnel matters with Captain Tsuneo Shiki of the Personnel Bureau and Commander Sadamu Sanagi of the General Staff.]

While we were having a sukiyaki dinner, a delayed telegram arrived stating that an enemy task force including carriers raided Marcus Island and demolished the radio station, burned drums of gasoline and caused some casualties. We talked about this for a while. They would scarcely come to Tokyo Bay on this trip.

[*Halsey*'s Enterprise *group raided Marcus Island on 5 March, losing one scout bomber.*][3]

We heard the report of Staff Officer Fujii's trip. While it contained interesting news, there were many points we should consider, together with the views of those having superior powers of observation.

Thursday, 5 March 1942. Rain. We sailed out at 0745 and experimented in the rain the effect of contact by floating mines on a battleship. Those that dropped below the bow wave at 12 knots were not activated, but the two coming right in front of the bow were found to have possibilities of exploding. We entered Kure port at 1100 and took a buoy off the port.

[Rear Admiral Shigeyoshi] Miwa, Third Submarine Squadron commander, and [Rear Admiral Chuichi] Hara, Fifth CV Division commander, came to visit, and Vice Admiral Jo Tayui, chief of staff, China Area Fleet, stopped by on his way to his new post.

While we were on our way to Kure, we received through the Naval

General Staff a report from a patrol boat of sighting thirteen unidentified planes heading west at a point 340 miles bearing 100° of Inubo Zaki. Accordingly, we ordered the Second Battleship Division, which we passed near Yakataishi in the opposite direction, and others to stand by for an attack, but had to cancel the order afterward on finding the report was an error in decoding. A small error can cause a lot of trouble.

Batavia was taken today and we celebrated.

[Ugaki spent most of 6 March 1942 shooting, and stayed ashore that night.]

Saturday, 7 March 1942. Fair. The army in Burma captured Pagu this afternoon. It was reported that the enemy proposed a cease-fire in the Bandung area.

Sunday, 8 March 1942. Fair. A naval funeral service was held at a temple at 1000 for Lieutenant [Akira] Kanda, Sublieutenant Mifu, and Warrant Officer Shiraishi (each promoted one rank) of the midget sub which sank on 3 March. I attended it together with the commander in chief. I was filled with sympathy.

The army unit which had captured Pegu made a swift further advance and took Rangoon this morning. Also we got splendid news of the capture of Surabaja. It has been just three months since the outbreak of the war, and it is about twenty days ahead of schedule.

Monday, 9 March 1942. Cloudy, later rain.

[Ugaki spent most of this day shooting, returning to the ship at 1515, when he picked up his narrative.]

While Bandeong has been proposing cease-fire, the commander, Dutch East Indies Army, surrendered unconditionally this afternoon. Everything had been quickly settled one after another while we were at Kure.

Tuesday, 10 March 1942. Partly fair, thick fog in the morning. *Yamato* left port alone at 1000 and moved out to Hashira Jima anchorage, while *Nagato* and *Mutsu* remained at Kure for more repair work.

Lae and Salamaua, which were captured on the 8th, were attacked from about 0730 for about two hours by approximately forty planes, including carrier torpedo-bombers, bombers, fighters, and land aircraft. They attacked mostly vessels. Light cruiser *Yubari* and some destroyers of the Sixth Destroyer Squadron were slightly damaged, and several transports received fairly big damage.

We found the retiring enemy task force, including *Saratoga,* two heavy cruisers, and five destroyers at 1400, but we missed them again, only shooting down four planes. It was most regrettable.

[*This was Vice Admiral Wilson Brown's task force centering around* Lexington *and* Yorktown. *They struck from the Gulf of Papua over the Owen Stanley range. They sank a minesweeper, a freighter, and a converted light cruiser, losing only one plane and pilot.*]+

Enemy submarines are becoming active, appearing off Shioya-Misaki and to the east of Shanghai.

The fleet strength disposition was changed to the Fourth Stations in the first stage operations.

Effective today, the Third Fleet was reorganized into the Second Southern Expeditionary Fleet.

[Ugaki ended the day's entry with the Imperial Rescript praising the action in the East Indies area.]

Wednesday, 11 March 1942. Cloudy. We have not yet received any information about the task force which raided yesterday.

In view of the fact that the Hawaii area was put on a strict alert around the 3rd, and the intensified activities of enemy subs in he seas near our country, it is judged that the enemy may be preparing for an air raid on Tokyo and the Bonin Islands, cooperating from the south and north. Accordingly, we issued orders calling for the guard force mentioned in "Tactical Method No. 3 against the U.S. Fleet" to sortie at an appropriate time and also for the Fifth CV Division, then on its way to the Southwest Area, to head for Chichi Jima.

It's annoying to be passive. Warfare is easier, with less trouble, indeed, when we hold the initiative.

Thursday, 12 March 1942. Cloudy. The Twenty-first Air Flotilla moved to Kisarazu, a southeast suburb of Tokyo, and carried out a search of the eastern sea today. At 1030 the code officer dashed in with a telegram from a plane reporting "the enemy sighted." But in it no position was mentioned and the enemy was only said to be 95 km bearing 30° from the friendly force and with no plane number. This may be the distance and bearing from a patrol ship of the Fifth Fleet. In any case, he said there was no doubt about the wave used in transmission.

So we got in touch with Tokyo and investigated Kisarazu. We had a reply in the afternoon saying that all search planes were keeping contact with the base, but no plane transmitted such a signal.

It turned out to be a practice communication of the Second Battleship Division's plane and happened to be picked up by multiplied frequencies of the wave. We should be careful, as there are many cases of fuss due to bad judgment or errors in communication. The Diet in recess opened its session, and a second victory celebration was held today all over the country, hailing the surrender of the entire Dutch East Indies and the fall of Rangoon.

If real enemy planes raided amidst the festivities, the mere thought of the result makes me shudder. A great air raid over the heads of the rejoicing multitude! I think it is better to stop such celebrations. We have no time for relaxation as we still have many more difficulties ahead of us. How can we decide it is a victory so early?

Friday, 13 March 1942. Partly fair. Today's search has not yet sighted the enemy. The Communications Corps still says the enemy is likely to come. He won't come when we're waiting and will come when we're not ready— this is what usually happens.

Our forces landed on points in North Sumatra on the 12th; the enemy seems to have no will to fight.

[That afternoon Ugaki was "just itching to go shooting," and did so.]

Saturday, 14 March 1942. Rain. Though it rained here, the sea east of Tokyo was mostly fair. We continued air patrol against the enemy, but nothing was sighted except friendly patrol vessels.

Staff Officer Fujii returned from Tokyo. The principle of directing the war passed the liaison conference, but they only wanted to enlarge the war results and didn't decide on any practical plan which meant a positive operation. The causes are:

1. The army took its usual attitude of refusing it once, as the opinion of the Combined Fleet was presented as that of the navy, when they had no opinion of their own.

2. There was no reserve army strength. It was difficult for them to extend the scope of the war more than the present scope because of considerations against the Soviet Union.

3. In preparation for the general election to be held in late April, they wanted to utilize the shipping bottoms to pacify the atmosphere of discontent, as the nation is experiencing a fair amount of shortages at present. (From the standpoint of the prime minister as well as the war minister.) [Tojo held both portfolios.]

This sounds reasonable to a certain degree and I have nothing against the purport. But I think they will follow us without fail if we keep on pressing persistently, taking into account that it will be delayed about six months from the time of our initial idea. In the meantime, we had better show them what the navy or the Combined Fleet can do.

Sunday, 15 March 1942. Cloudy. It has become clear that the brisk enemy radio activities and air patrols in the Hawaii and Midway areas were their precautions against surprise attack, occasioned by the night attack on Hawaii and reconnaissance of Midway by our flying boats. So we ordered the return of the guard force to its base and the Fifth CV Division to the task force.

[*On the night of 3–4 March, two Japanese flying boats had dropped four bombs on Oahu but did no damage. On 10 March an aircraft of the same type was shot down off Midway.*][5]

Monday, 16 March 1942. Our forces are extending the front line in North Sumatra.

I am suffering from the noise of hydraulic machinery for the turret in the morning, afternoon, and even after supper. After this ends, the diesel generator takes its place during the night. I have tried hard to get used to them but it has been all in vain. My contemplative faculty is gone now.

[On Tuesday, 17 March, Ugaki made no comment beyond the fact that there had been no change in the war situation, and he made no entries for Wednesday, 18 March, or Thursday, 19 March. His entry for Friday, 20 March, covered details of experimental firing at Kamegakubi experimental range where he conferred with Rear Admiral Choso Suzuki, chief of the Gunnery Experimental Department.]

Saturday, 21 March 1942. Fair. The ceremony on the occasion of the vernal equinox was held at 0915. I prayed for the souls of the imperial ancestors, my parents, and that of wife Tomoko.

When I went to the Admiral's cabin for lunch, the staff officers congratulated me for being decorated with the Third Order of the Golden Kite.

[This award was for his service in the China Incident, and for most of his entry Ugaki waxed reflective over that service, fondly recalling his devoted wife.]

Without her help I could not be as I am now, or I could not have been appointed to such a post of distinction as chief of the Operation Bureau right after my promotion to rear admiral, and complete that duty. On receiving this honor today, I could not help loving her anew and I want to dedicate the whole honor in her memory. Coincidentally, today is the Buddhist day of prayer.

The guard force returned after sunset and the chief of staff, First Fleet, came to report.

Sunday, 22 March 1942. Cloudy, later light rain. Leaving the ship at 0800, I went to Kamegakubi range again with the chief of staff, First Fleet, and the skippers.

[Here again Ugaki described some of the firing details, then continued.]

While we were watching from a hilltop, I heard a report from Commander [Kumataro] Nakao, who as a member of the Education Bureau had been to Sasebo to investigate the fighting of the Fifth Heavy Cruiser Division in the battle off Surabaja. It was said that for an hour the heavy cruisers continued gunfire action at 25,000 to 26,000 meters, a long distance for them, and expended almost all the main battery shells. Still they could not destroy the enemy cruisers. They also fired 121 torpedoes, only one of which hit a destroyer.

Though they said they adopted long-distance tactics for self-preservation against the superior enemy in the presence of a convoy of dozens of transports, they displayed lack of skill in their first battle.

After inspecting the condition of splinters by stationary bursting of 36 and 40 cm common projectiles at 1600, we left the range.

Monday, 23 March 1942. Foggy. At 0800 *Yamato* and *Fuso* changed anchorage to the east of Iseko Jima in the north. Owing to the spring fog, we couldn't carry out antiaircraft firing practice of the main batteries originally scheduled at 1000 until 1300.

Vice Admiral Teruhisa Komatsu, the new commander in chief, Sixth Fleet, arrived on board *Katori* and came to visit us at 1640.

A landing was made at Fort Blair in the Andaman Islands at 0630. There was no resistance, and the place was easily taken with the disarming of twenty-three principal British officers and three hundred Indian soldiers. The British soldiers, women, and children were said to have been evacuated about ten days before.

MacArthur, the U.S. commander and the hero of Bataan Peninsula, and his wife with other staff officers escaped to Australia on two planes. He has become the anti-Axis nations' idol and has been assigned as commander of Allied forces in Southwest Asia. He stressed the urgency of American support in fighting strength and materials for the defense of Australia. Is he a great general or a crazy one?

Tuesday, 24 March 1942. Rain, later fair. The chief of staff, Sixth Fleet, accompanied by the commander, Eighth Submarine Squadron and his senior staff officer, came to consult about the delay in their next departure because of the remodeling and training of the midget subs. Readiness being the prime requisite, we could not but agree with him.

Regarding the shipment of essential arms from Germany, the Germans want Japanese submarines to go over there, as it is impossible to load them on a German submarine. I wonder if it is possible to load them on a Japanese submarine, and if this can't be managed by going half-way. Anyway, as the question has been pending, we have made up our minds to dispatch them.

The communications and engineer staff officers, who had been dispatched to the southwest area, landed on Iwakuni via Shanghai and Kanoya and returned to the ship.

[Wednesday, 25 March, was devoted to reports from various staff officers and commanders.]

Thursday, 26 March 1942. Cloudy. [Rear Admiral Masakichi] Matsuki, chief of the First Bureau of the Naval Ship Administration Department, came from Kure in the afternoon. We conferred about the problem of damage control of capital ship turrets and the antiaircraft projectiles of the main battery. After we had dinner together, he stayed the night on board *Nagato*.

Friday, 27 March 1942. Fair and hazy. The First Battleship Division left Hashira Jima anchorage at 0700, carried out navigation practice in the fog and aircraft recovery practice in the morning and in the afternoon antiaircraft firing, spotting exercise, and air attack exercise. At night lookout and searchlight practice was conducted. Dropped anchor near the entrance in Tokuyama Bay at 2300.

Saturday, 28 March 1942. Cloudy. Today's exercises were postponed until tomorrow owing to bad visibility.

[Ugaki feared the decision came too late to catch *Fuso*, which was towing the target from Hashira Jima anchorage.]

Sunday, 29 March 1942. Rain. Late last night, as a result of studying enemy communications traffic, the chief code officer expressed his confident judgment that the enemy task force would air raid from east of the Marshalls this morning. So we relayed this judgment routinely to the chief of staff, Fourth Fleet.

This may have been a misjudgment, as nothing happened this morning. But the Fourth Fleet should have no bad feelings and appreciate our kindness.

Monday, 30 March 1942. Cloudy, later fair. Since last night, staff officers had been studying the contents of the second stage operations which they had drafted with painstaking effort. They scrutinized them again this morning.[6]

Though it was drizzling in the morning, we left the anchorage at 0900, thinking it could clear up later on. We started training after casting anchor simultaneously off Mitajiri. We weighed anchor soon afterward and from 1230 started an air attack exercise by planes of the Third CV Division, but we waited in vain as the attacking planes didn't come, due to a mistake in communications.

[For the rest of this day, the fleet conducted firing practice, returning to Hashira Jima at 2130.]

Tuesday, 31 March 1942. Fair. I presided at the conference studying yesterday's First Battleship Division practice, which was held in the ward room at 1400. In general they seemed capable of executing operations without much difficulty, but it was regrettable that we could not yet have confidence in the important gunfire. I hinted at the participation of the Main Force in the coming operation and urged that everyone do his best.

My recent awards of the Orders of the Golden Kite and the Rising Sun have been announced by radio and in the newspapers, so letters of congratulations are pouring in.

Wednesday, 1 April 1942. Cloudy. April has come and spring is here. But some are serving in the broiling sun of the south, while others are in the northern sea where the winds are still piercingly cold. The spring is greeted in different fashions.

Mopping-up operations in the western part of New Guinea have started. Our force landed without resistance and the enemy command surrendered. There won't be much serious activity in the future, either.

The landing on Christmas Island also succeeded, so it will be possible to obtain some phosphate. If this can help increase farm production it will be all the better.

Captain [Sutejiro] Onoda, a staff officer of the Naval General Staff, came on board for liaison.

[*Onoda was the liaison officer between the Naval General Staff, Navy Ministry, and Army General Staff.*]

Thursday, 2 April 1942. Fair. The sea was absolutely calm, without a ripple. The number of telegrams is a barometer of operations, and it's very low now.

At the time of capturing Christmas Island, light cruiser *Naka*, flagship of the Fourth Destroyer Squadron, was struck by a torpedo from an enemy submarine and sustained a fair amount of damage. It was decided that light cruiser *Nagara* tow her.

[*The U.S. submarine* Seawolf *put* Naka *out of action for a year.*][7]

Friday, 8 April 1942. Fair. The ceremony in honor of Emperor Jimmu was held at 0845 according to the summer routine.

[That afternoon Ugaki went shooting. He noted that the many people taking advantage of the low tide to gather shells seemed to be doing so almost as a duty instead of for pleasure.]

Saturday, 4 April 1942. Fair, later cloudy. We celebrated the birthday of the commander in chief with whole fish at breakfast.

Ceremonies of awarding the Second Order of the Golden Kite and the First Order of other decorations were held at the palace today. In the morning Ohno from the personnel bureau brought the decorations of the First Order of the Rising Sun and the Second Order of the Golden Kite [for service in the China Incident] and handed them to the commander in chief. The commander in chief was quoted as saying, "Is it all right for me to receive such things?" I congratulated him right away. He said, "Those who served in the Naval General Staff deserve to receive such honors, as they did something for the war. But I did nothing except when the U.S. gunboat was sunk near Nanking."

[*Yamamoto referred to the bombing of the U.S.S.* Panay *in December 1937. He was navy vice minister at the time and helped smooth out the delicate situation, publicly thanking Washington for accepting Japan's formal apology and promising that the navy would be more careful in the future.*[8]

[Ugaki continued his day's entry observing that Yamamoto looked "a bit bashful" at the sight of the gaudy decorations, protesting, "I can't wear things like these, I'm too self-conscious." That night the staff saw newsreels of action at various fronts.]

Sunday, 5 April 1942. Rain. The wind's velocity reached twenty-five meters per second mixed with rain. The cherry blossoms will be ruined.

Today was the scheduled date for the task force to attack Ceylon. The low pressure in the Bay of Bengal has passed to the north, and though there are showers the weather seems suitable for a surprise attack.

Due to the long distance, direct receipt of messages from the planes was impossible, but past noon we picked up an enemy signal of "1045 air raid alert in Colombo."

The enemy seems to have found one battleship and two cruisers. The situation is different from that at the time of Hawaii, as this time we are trying to attack Trincomalee and Colombo under strict surveillance. I hope there will be no damage to our force.

Staff Officer Watanabe has been in Tokyo to consult with the high command on the second stage operations plan. And he telephoned back that the Naval General Staff seemed to have reluctantly agreed to it.

[*This was the Midway plan. As in the case of Pearl Harbor, the Naval General Staff caved in when Yamamoto exercised a bit of genteel blackmail, hinting he might resign if he did not get his way.*][9]

Monday, 6 April 1942. Fair. In the air raid on Ceylon, the task force shot down sixty enemy planes, damaged more than a dozen merchant ships, and bombed installations in Colombo. Besides, two British heavy cruisers of the *Cumberland* type were sunk at a point about two hundred miles south-southwest of Colombo.

[*In the attack on Colombo, the Nagumo task force sank a destroyer and an armed merchant cruiser in the harbor, seriously damaged shore installations, and shot down twenty-four RAF aircraft. Later that same day, Nagumo's fliers sank the British heavy cruisers* Dorsetshire *and* Cornwall.][10]

The land-based air force of the First Southern Expeditionary Fleet sank one cruiser and one minelayer at Calcutta, while a task force of the same fleet succeeded in sinking thirteen merchantmen in the Bay of Bengal.

[For 7 through 9 April Ugaki recorded nothing of an operational nature. He spent some time ashore making purchases and strolling amid the "remnants of cherry blossoms."]

Friday, 10 April 1942. Rain, later cloudy. According to telegrams, the air raid of Trincomalee seems to have been a great success. The carrier *Hermes,* one light cruiser, and a destroyer were sunk. Fifty planes were shot down, while installations and merchant ships were greatly damaged.

[*In the attack on Trincomalee, the Nagumo task force sank a merchant ship, shot down fourteen RAF aircraft, and damaged shore installations. That afternoon at sea they sank the carrier* Hermes *and her escort destroyer* Vampire, *as well as a corvette, an auxiliary vessel, and a merchant ship. From 5 through 9 April 1942 Japanese forces (Nagumo's and those of Rear Admiral Takeo Kurita), the carrier* Ryujo, *and six heavy cruisers sank a total of twenty-three merchant ships.*][11]

[On the afternoon of 10 April, Ugaki accompanied Yamamoto on a visit with Prince Fushimi.]

Saturday, 11 April 1942. Fair. [This morning Prince Fushimi returned the call. After he departed, *Yamato* left port for training exercises. Ugaki had news from the Philippines to record.]

It has been eight days since the general attack was started on Bataan Peninsula. Though the enemy proposed to surrender, we did not accept as he did not include Corregidor in the surrender terms. So fighting continued.

[For 12–15 April, Ugaki recorded only routine activities, such as a lecture on damage control by Commander Yoshiyuke Takeshita and a presentation on the battle off Surabaja by Commander Nakazawa of the Fifth Heavy Cruiser Division.]

Thursday, 16 April 1942. Rain. Vice Admiral Yasuo Inouye, commander of the First Escort Force, came on board at 0900 to report. His force was newly organized on the 10th in view of the necessity of controlling the surface escort.

At 0915 Vice Admiral Komatsu, commander in chief of the Sixth Fleet with his staff; commander, Eighth Submarine Squadron with his staff; the skippers, seven officers, and petty officers of the midget subs, as well as the skippers of *Nisshin, Chiyoda,* and *Aikoku Maru* came on board. The commander in chief delivered an address to them. After that, we drank farewell cups as they were going to leave the homeland with important missions at the outset of the second stage operation.

I wanted to give them a hearty send-off and wish them a brilliant success and the best of luck. Especially to those young sublieutenants and ensigns of the midget sub crews, being confident of their skill and with firm determination to die for their country, which I could sense, must be called noble and exalted. With this spirit the foundation of the empire can be considered safe. Again I wish them the best of luck in the war.

They left the anchorage at 1100. The A Submarine Force headed for the south Indian Ocean via Penang, and the B Force for Port Moresby and the east coast of Australia via Truk. Spring rain was falling gently as if it was lamenting over their departure.

Friday, 17 April 1942. Cloudy. The Fifteenth Destroyer Division arrived from Kure and sortied right away to reinforce the Third Southern Expeditionary Fleet.

[The rest of Ugaki's day was uneventful.]

Saturday, 18 April 1942. Partly fair. An enemy task force attacked our homeland!

A telephone message from the Naval General Staff after breakfast (0730) stated that they received a report from No. 23 *Nitto Maru*, a patrol boat of the Fifth Fleet, of sighting three enemy carriers at a point 720 miles east of Tokyo at 0630. [*This was the famous raid by 16 B-25s under Lieutenant Colonel James H. Doolittle which took off from* Hornet.[12] *Task Force 16 under Halsey contained two, not three, CVs—*Enterprise *and* Hornet.]

The fleet staff plunged into activities at once. We issued an order to activate Tactical Method No. 3 Against the U.S. Fleet, then successively sent out the necessary orders.

Heavy cruiser *Atago,* flagship of the Second Fleet, returned to Yokosuka yesterday, and the commander in chief and his chief of staff and the senior staff officer were at the Naval General Staff. Thereupon we placed various kinds of vessels in the advance force temporarily, let the guard force support it and ordered the task force on the way home from west of Formosa to proceed to the east of the homeland.

No. 23 *Nitto Maru,* a fishing boat of ninety tons, has not been heard from since her first signal. *Awata Maru, Akagi Maru,* and other auxiliary cruisers of the Twenty-first Division were sent to the spot, but they were only attacked by enemy planes or sighted those planes and did not find the enemy itself. Though some patrol boats reported the enemy position in the afternoon, the Kisarazu Air Group of the Twenty-sixth Air Flotilla failed to make contact with the enemy. Many difficulties seem to have been encountered in searching. The discontinuous weather line passed the spot just a while before, so visibility was very poor.

At 1300 we received news of an enemy air raid on Tokyo from the Naval General Staff. Then much information came in reporting an enemy plane made a forced landing in the Chiba area, Yokohama, Kawasaki, and Yokosuka had been air raided and so on. [*None of Doolittle's planes was lost over Japan.*] But many reports were of a doubtful nature, and it was hard to guess the object of the enemy attempt. The Third Submarine Squadron, which had been about two hundred miles west of the enemy, issued an order to stand by for an attack.

There has been no certain report of the enemy position, and none of our forces made contact with the enemy. As locating the enemy is the first requisite of everything, we ordered pursuit to the east.

Sunset in that area was 1700 and I was getting impatient. Thirty-two medium torpedo bombers and twelve Zero fighters from Kisarazu sortied at 1300, but had to turn back after reaching seven hundred miles out.

Having been discovered by our patrol line, and anticipating our submarines ahead, as well as intercepting radio activities of our planes and ships, the enemy apparently launched several of his long-distance bombers (twin motor Martins or B-26s [actually B-25s], smaller than our medium bombers), thinking it impossible to attack the next morning. They bombed nine spots in Tokyo with incendiary and other bombs. Twelve were killed, over one hundred wounded, fifty houses burned, and fifty more completely or partly destroyed. Also bombed were Yokohama, Yokosuka, Nagoya, Wakayama, and Kobe. At Yokosuka some damage was caused to the bow of *Taigei* in dock. One of them was said to have raided Niitsu in Niigata Prefecture where the oil wells are situated.

These planes must have been few, and it isn't clear whether they returned to their mother carriers, went over to the Siberian coast or China, or the crews were rescued by a Soviet ship that had been in position about two hundred miles south of Ashizuri Zaki.

[*In fact, the Soviet Union did not assist in any way.*]

On the other hand, the enemy force seemingly withdrew to the east after launching the planes. We have missed him again and again. This is more than regrettable, because this shattered my firm determination never to let the enemy attack Tokyo or the mainland.

If the enemy carried out attacks from such a long distance, which is about the same as an expected one-way attack, we shall have to revise our countermeasures fundamentally, studying their type planes. In any case, this is one up to the enemy today.

As we have no information whether he'll attack again tomorrow, going north toward Hokkaido or south heading for Marcus and Wake, we shall have to let it up to him.

Sunday, 19 April 1942. Cloudy and rain at night. Yesterday's air raids were made on Tokyo, Kawasaki, Yokosuka, Nagoya, Yokkaichi, Kobe, and villages in Wakayama Prefecture. The enemy used over twenty 40- to 50-kg bombs and incendiary bombs. They also strafed at times.

They came in from the direction of Chiba, and after raiding places one after another from the east, two of them went south over Kitan Strait, five flew to the southwest from a point east of Toizaki. If another one attacking Niitsu in Niigata is counted, there were eight or nine planes. Total casualties were 363 and the loss of houses reached about 350. The reason for the comparatively large number of casualties versus the number of bombs might be splinters from our own antiaircraft firing.

One of them crash-landed on the water near Nanshang and its five crew members were captured by an army force last night. According to their words, they started from a Bayer Island (no such place on charts) west of Midway or took off from a light carrier *Victorious*. They also said they reached Balt Island in the Aleutians on the 14th from San Francisco and left there on the 18th. There was no airfield on the island with a garrison of 150. Also, they said planes of the same kind were still on the carrier.

They never told the truth. It couldn't be helped, as the interrogators must have been some army officers of lower rank with little knowledge of foreign languages and the sea. We must investigate further promptly so that we can take proper measures for the future. However, it is evident that there were thirteen North American B-25s with five crew members each, and they were directed to land at Hangchow.

On our side, No. 23 *Nitto Maru* and *Nagato Maru* have not been heard from and about three others were damaged in the eastern patrol line. A fair number of them sighted planes but only one saw the enemy ships.

After disturbing our picket line, didn't they turn back and retire in a northerly direction?

Search planes from Kisarazu did not find the enemy today and those who went out to the northeast turned back to a point about four hundred miles away due to rain. Four enemy planes were reportedly seen heading north by *Kurita Maru* from early morning until 0800, and two ships, seemingly enemy destroyers, were seen in the north, too. An enemy raid on the Hokkaido area tomorrow morning appears likely.

It was regrettable that the Second, Fifth, and Sixth fleets and Eleventh Air Fleet were rushing after the enemy but nothing was gained. A part of the forces was ordered to resume disposition for the first term operation, to be ready for the next operation.

What the enemy intended in this attack, I suppose, was to launch long-distance planes from converted carriers after closing in our homeland supported by carriers, heavy cruisers, and destroyers. After flying over our homeland, the bombers were to go to the mainland of China, where they would use bases for carrying out raids on our country.

In view of this recent success, undoubtedly the enemy will repeat this kind of operation while attempting raids from China. Therefore, we must take steps to watch far to the east and, at the same time, always keep a sharp lookout on the threat from the west. As I felt the necessity of drawing up a definite plan now, I expressed my views to the staff officers, hoping they would use them as their guide.

At lunchtime an alert was issued in the Osaka district as three mysterious planes were said to be heading north. We were alerted here, too, but they turned out to be [Japanese] twin-motored army planes.

Monday, 20 April 1942. Rain. An overnight spring rain continued until evening. It moved eastward and started to rain in the Yokosuka area since this evening.

The enemy did not come to Hokkaido. We had no information at all about the enemy, except some reports such as a patrol boat being bombed or receiving a few rounds of gunfire from a likely destroyer which could serve as some material for judgment. I guessed he must be somewhere about 350 miles southeast of Etorofu Island in the Kuriles, a position just outside the search range of our medium bombers from Kisarazu.

We ordered the air units to search this area, while at the same time ordering the commander, Advance Force, to unify the forces in the area.

By evening the report of enemy bombing turned out to be false, so we ordered Tactical Method No. 3 Against the U.S. Fleet suspended, and the first term station resumed. There was nothing else to do but let the Fifth

Fleet, Twenty-sixth Air Flotilla, and Third Submarine Squadron continue vigilance.

The enemy, already withdrawn far to the east, through radio must have observed our confusion with contempt. Thus, our homeland has been air raided and we missed the enemy without firing a shot at him. This is exceedingly regrettable.

Tuesday, 21 April 1942. Partly fair with strong winds. American war prisoners captured at Nanchang had been sent to Nanking, where they told the truth at last. Sixteen planes were loaded on board the carrier *Hornet,* which left the West Coast on 1 April with two cruisers, four destroyers, and a supply boat. They came direct, without touching a port on the way, until they sighted our submarine on the 18th. Thereupon they launched thirteen planes. These flew almost due west and reached the Boso Peninsula, where they carried out attacks. The flyers were all volunteers.

A Soviet ship supposed to have cooperated with the attack of these planes was sighted to the north of Kishu Peninsula. The First Fleet, which was heading east in the neighborhood, inspected her.

While a destroyer was escorting her with the aim of bringing her to the southern tip of Kishu Peninsula for further investigation, contact with her was lost as a position about fifty miles bearing 200° of Shiono Misaki yesterday afternoon. Since then she has not been found, in spite of aerial searches sent from Komatsu Jima and Kanoya.

An officer and ten petty officers were on board this ship. If she is lost in this way, it will be most disgraceful for the Imperial Navy. What a troublesome captive she turned out to be!

According to a report of sounds of a great formation in the Hangchow area, Chekiang Province, an alert was issued in Kyushu district. In the fleet, we only intensified the lookout.

False reports come in every day. By the time we ascertain their reliability, it will be too late to take measures about them. The main thing is to have more reliable sources. We should be more careful about this, as we had another case of the same kind in Kobe and the Osaka area the day before yesterday.

Wednesday, 22 April 1942. Fair. More truth has been added to the statements of the POWs captured at Nanchow. *Hornet* left the states with two cruisers and four destroyers and was joined on the way by another carrier, cruisers, and destroyers. At takeoff, the relative wind velocity was twenty meters per second. The length of her flight deck was seven hundred feet and takeoff run 550 feet.

How the sixteen planes were accommodated remained unsolved. Work harder to resolve the riddle!

The Seventh Heavy Cruiser Division returned with flying colors at 1330. Its commander, Kurita, his staff officers, and the shippers came to report. Marks of toil were deep in their faces. They left for Kure at 1400.

Ryujo of the Fourth Carrier Division arrived alone in the evening, and [Rear Admiral Kakuji] Kakuta, its commander, came on board at sunset to report.

Both commanders expressed their desire to let their officers and men have long-term leaves during their stay in port. Though I can appreciate their feelings, leaves can't be permitted beyond the standard already set, under the present circumstances in which anything might happen. The officers in command should understand this point well.

[During the evening firing practice was conducted as well as training in communications. Ugaki had a special word of praise for Staff Officer Captain Yasuji Watanabe.]

Thursday, 23 April 1942. Fair. Captain [Norio] Sugiura, chief of the Third Section of the Naval General Staff, came to consult us on the planning of armament, and Captain Kami, a staff officer of the Operations Bureau, brought their judgment on the war situation. At night we heard their views and also expressed ours as follows:

The construction of battleships should be withheld after the third ship and the power thus saved concentrated on the construction of carriers. That of the super-heavy cruisers should be withheld too, as they will be delayed in any case. The construction of submarines should be greatly speeded up.

What we regret most is the insufficient production capacity of aircraft. Now is the time to concentrate all the resources of the country on naval aviation, and yet all they do is compete with army aviation just the same as before the war. We request that the government reconsider from the overall viewpoint.

[At the end of his entry Ugaki expressed his pleasure in letters from his son Hiromitsu and from an old friend.]

Friday, 24 April 1942. Fair. In the afternoon Captain Minoru Ota, designated commander of the Midway Landing Force, Captain Kanae Monzen, its construction unit leader, and three landing party commanders came to consult with us at our request. All of them seemed optimistic and convinced of success. It was most reassuring and I wished them luck.

[On Saturday, 25 April, the First Battleship Division conducted firing practice, and Ugaki took respectful note of the rite held in Tokyo, enshrining at Yasukuni the souls of over ten thousand new war dead.]

Sunday, 26 April 1942. Fair. This was the second anniversary of the death of Tomoko. I got up early and prayed for her soul in heaven.

[Ugaki hoped that next year he would be in a position to "do something suitable" in Tokyo in his late wife's honor.]

Monday, 27 April 1942. Cloudy, later rain. A meeting was held from 1300 to study the recent first-degree exercises and other training.

After 1600, Commander in Chief Kondo of the Second Fleet with his Chief of Staff [Rear Admiral Kazutaka] Shiraishi and other staff officers came to visit us. We had dinner together.

I stopped smoking since yesterday. Besides my throat hurting a bit, I felt drowsy all day and in rather a languid condition. I may be suffering from nicotinism. But stopping smoking made me worse. To be moderate in everything is the best policy.

Tuesday, 28 April 1942. Cloudy, light rain. A conference was held from 0830 to study the first stage operations with all the commanders in chief, commanders, and their staffs now in home waters, and, as far as possible, even some staff officers of the fleets now actually engaging in operations. It was conducted under supervision. By the middle of the afternoon we had finished hearing reports outlining the action of each force as well as the war results achieved. Then war lessons, views, and opinions were discussed.

Thinking that the meeting did not seem to yield many results as it went on today, I tried to devise some means to improve it.

Wednesday, 29 April 1942. Fair. We met the emperor's birthday in the middle of war, and the ceremony was held at 0805, earlier than usual. We saluted the emperor's portrait afterward.

At 0830 Nagumo, commander in chief, First Air Fleet, and others of the task force came to report.

From 0915 we resumed the meeting begun yesterday, and I did fairly well in directing it. As a result, discussions were more actively exchanged, achieving good results. It became more significant with an address delivered by the commander in chief at its conclusion.

[*No doubt for security reasons, Ugaki was very reticent in his diary about the content and discussions of most of the meetings, briefings, and table maneuvers in which he participated. The late April discussions centered around the plan to capture Midway Island and destroy the U.S. Pacific Fleet. At this particular session, Yamamoto warned all concerned against self-satisfaction based upon their thus-far successful operations.*]¹³

We should make use of these war lessons, and, adding new ideas to them, must go ahead on the second stage operations.

Thursday, 30 April 1942. Fair. A ceremony for the regular festival of the Yasukuni Shrine was held at 0805. After that, the commander in chief, his staff, and other members of Combined Fleet Headquarters had a photo taken to be inserted in the memorial album of the war.

Sectional meetings of the first stage operations were held today and I instructed each staff officer to attend them. Aerial warfare and gunfire battle were studied aboard *Yamato*. Each made an effective study.

An enemy plane to the east of Rabaul reported in plain language the sighting of a big convoy escorted by two destroyers on the course 200° with the speed of 10 knots. This was one or a few days too early for this to be our invasion force for Tulagi or Port Moresby. In any case, we shall have to expect a concentrated enemy attack, and we should give sufficient consideration to this.

Today was an election day for the House of Representatives and the poll was held all over the country.

Friday, 1 May 1942. Fair. A table maneuver of the second stage operations was to be held on board *Yamato* from today for four days. I participated in it all day as its superintendent, chief judge, and commander in chief of the Blue Force in one.¹⁴

The weather was fine today and the temperature rose.

Saturday, 2 May 1942. Fair, later cloudy. At 2315 last night an enemy submarine [*Drum*] attacked the seaplane tender *Mizuho* on her way from Yokosuka to Hashira Jima anchorage after finishing her fitting, at a point forty miles bearing 220° of Omae Zaki. She listed by 23° and an induced fire broke out. Though she seemed to be holding out at around 0200, flooding and listing increased from about 0300. All hands abandoned ship; she went down at last at 0416.

Heavy cruisers *Maya* and *Takao*, cruising nearby to her rear, went to her rescue at once; her crew was taken aboard *Takao* while that ship depth-charged. Seven officers and ninety-four petty officers and men were missing, while seventeen were seriously wounded and fourteen slightly wounded.

The two ships turned back to Yokosuka and the wounded have been sent to hospital, the rest to Tateyama Air Base. This was the greatest loss so far, to my great regret. I am sorry that little can be done against an enemy surprise attack in full moonlight.

A warning against enemy submarines was issued in the name of the chief of staff.

The table maneuver was on its second day today.

[Ugaki had a letter from his son, sending some snapshots, and telling him how the anniversary of Tomoko's death had been remembered.]

Sunday, 3 May 1942. Rain. The table maneuver was held on the fore mess deck, and we made all speed to bring the scene up to an invasion of Hawaii. The methodology should be carefully planned, and it is most essential to conduct further training and planning before its execution.

According to radio intelligence, there were comings and goings of enemy task forces in Hawaii around the 25th and 27th. One of them seemed to have headed for the south.

[*The "comings" was Halsey's Task Force 16, back from the Doolittle raid. The "goings" was Task Force 17, centering around Rear Admiral Frank Jack Fletcher in* Yorktown *and Rear Admiral Aubrey W. Fitch in* Lexington, *already en route to the Coral Sea.*][15]

We succeeded in landing on Tulagi today, but we are in considerable doubt about the voyage and landing of the Port Moresby Invasion Force. A war of attrition of aircraft was repeated almost every day both at Rabaul and Lae, with losses accumulating. Half of the fighters we were unloading at the Kwajalein area were therefore rearranged to be sent to Rabaul on board *Kasuga Maru*.

[*On 4 May B-26s of the Fifth Air Force bombed Rabaul, while P-39s and B-17s struck at Lae.*][16]

Monday, 4 May 1942. Partly fair. In the forenoon on the fourth day of the table maneuvers, we studied its past development.

Soon after it started, a report came in from Tulagi, occupied only yesterday, that six bombers and five torpedo bombers came to attack until 0600, then fifty enemy planes. The Nineteenth Division, *Okinoshima*, destroyer *Mikazuki*, patrol boats, and transports were stationed there. The enemy continued his attack through the afternoon. It was evidently a raid by an enemy task force.

[*This first attack by twelve torpedo planes and twenty-eight dive bombers, a second raid an hour later by eleven torpedo planes and twenty-eight dive bombers, and a third attack by twenty-one dive bombers came from* Yorktown. *Results of all this air power were minimal—the destroyer beached, three small sweepers and four landing barges sunk, and minor damage to several other craft.*][17]

The Port Moresby Invasion Force and Task Force headed there, but the distance was so far there was hardly a chance of catching the enemy. The enemy seems to have attacked after detecting our situation fairly well.

We must anticipate further enemy attacks before the invasion of Port Moresby. I earnestly hope the South Sea Force will take proper action and fight hard.

A briefing on the second term operations was held from 1330, and I was glad to have generally coordinated the concept of each force.

Although some forces haven't enough time to make ready, we have decided to carry it out as originally planned, since a delay could be unfavorable in view of the moon's age, and also we fear that delay would only benefit the enemy. I hope every force will make every effort in preparation, in training, and in setting up its operational plan.

The northeastern part of the homeland was alerted as a patrol boat was said to have sighted an unidentified plane heading west at a point about 250 miles east of Yokosuka. Later, a patrol boat at a point about 650 miles bearing 83° of Tokyo Bay reported the sighting of two big and small vessels, apparently cruisers, although this was not clear due to the clouds.

By nightfall the area west of Osaka was also alerted, and the vessels in the anchorage assumed second stations. We cannot be too careful in such cases.

I could not help being a bit tired after a week of continuous conferences starting with the war lessons, table maneuvers, and briefings.

Tuesday, 5 May 1942. Fair. Today was Boy's Festival. The carp banners were not to be seen, but fresh green of the isles was at its height.

[*A part of this ancient festival is the flying of paper or cloth banners shaped like carp. Ugaki expressed himself further in poetry:*]

> All day long, verdant isles fresh to see,
> Around us, floating on the sea.

At 1600 the breech-block of the left gun of *Hyuga*'s turret No. 5 was blown off at the seventh salvo during firing battle practice in Iyo Nada. The blown-off canopy landed on the port side upper deck. Flames from the gun platform ignited normal charges for two rounds, further penetrated the shell magazine, and white smoke came out of a voice tube from the powder magazine.

Though flooding powder magazines of turrets Nos. 5 and 6 saved the ship, damage was quite serious. Except for the right gunner, who escaped by being blown out on the upper deck, all of those in the gun platform and half of those in the shell magazine were either killed or wounded. Altogether, fifty were killed and eleven seriously wounded, including re-corders from other ships.

The division stopped practice at once. *Hyuga* and *Fuso* entered Kure while *Ise* and *Yamashiro* returned to Hashira Jima anchorage at midnight.

It is regrettable that such an accident happened during wartime, thus losing many officers and men not in combat. What was the cause? We must investigate thoroughly whether it was due to bad handling or to defects in the breech mechanism.

While most of the enemy on Bataan Peninsula have surrendered, the Fort of Corregidor still continued resistance. Our force ventured at land-ing at last at 2300, taking advantage of the moon.

We received imperial orders for the invasions of Midway and the western part of the Aleutians.

Wednesday, 6 May 1942. Fair, later cloudy. At 0800, a flying boat sent out from Tulagi found the enemy task force which attacked Tulagi heading south at 20 knots at a point 450 miles south of the island. Though the Fifth Heavy Cruiser Division and the Fifth Carrier Division are chasing it from the east and the Moresby Invasion Force from the north, the chances of catching the enemy seem slim. Once again we will miss the enemy by a small margin.

On the other hand, *Awata Maru* sighted a formation of nine large planes flying northward at a point east of the homeland, and an air raid warning has been issued. They may raid the Tokyo area tonight.

The Fort of Corregidor hoisted a white flag at noon and surrendered. It has been regretted that it held out from the beginning until the last, but now the fleet can move in and out of Manila freely.

Thursday, 7 May 1942. Rain. Yesterday's enemy task force appeared to the south of Rossel Island, southeast of New Guinea. Reportedly it consisted of one battleship, one heavy cruiser, two light cruisers, and five destroyers with a carrier of the *Saratoga* type. Furthermore, one carrier, one cruiser, and three destroyers were said to be found in a position south of Tulagi. The latter, being 160 miles south of the Fifth Carrier Division, can be wiped out with one blow, while the former will be nice bait for the medium torpedo bombers from Lae and Salamaua.

While we were waiting for good news since early morning, a report came in that enemy planes attacked CVL *Shoho,* accompanying the Sixth Heavy Cruiser Division. Six bombs and three torpedoes struck her, and she sank in twenty minutes at 0830.

[*Planes from both* Lexington *and* Yorktown *participated in the attack on* Shoho.][18]

Further, it was found that the enemy to the east were tankers instead of carriers. Attacking them delayed the westward movement of the Fifth Carrier Division. At 1400 they launched torpedo bombers from a long distance, but almost all were annihilated in the ensuing serial combat.

[*These were the tankers* Neosho *and* Sims. *Believing them to be respectively a carrier and a cruiser, the Fifth CV Division attacked in force, sinking* Sims *and damaging* Neosho *so badly that she had to be scuttled four days later. Later, the Fifth CV Division sent out twenty-seven aircraft seeking the U.S. carriers. Of these, twenty-one were lost either in aerial combat or by crashing into the sea upon attempting recovery aboard* Shokaku *and* Zuikaku.][19]

On the other hand, the medium bombers were supposed to have sunk a battleship, but its type was not clear. Besides, they inflicted big damage on a heavy cruiser with two hits and a near miss. A flying boat contacted the enemy in the evening and three planes were said to have launched night torpedo attacks, but the result was doubtful.

[*Apparently Ugaki referred to the attack on the support group under Rear Admiral J. G. Grace, RN (cruisers* Australia, Chicago, Hobart) *with destroyer* Farragut. *The attackers claimed to have sunk a battleship (probably the cruiser* Australia), *damaged a cruiser, and also to have torpedoed a battleship of the* Warspite *class. Actually, Grace's group suffered no damage.*][20]

The commander in chief, Fourth Fleet, ordered the Sixth Heavy Cruiser Division and Sixth Destroyer Squadron to carry out an attack tonight. Not only is this a difficult task, but these forces' southward advance is slow. Converted from the naval transport *Tsurugizaki*, CVL *Shoho* was commissioned early this year and included in the Fourth Fleet. I am sorry for her short life. Part of her fighters were rescued, but I am worried about her torpedo bombers.

A dream of great success has been shattered. There is an opponent in a war, so one cannot progress just as one wishes. When we expect enemy raids, can't we employ the forces in a little more unified way? After all, not a little should be attributed to the insufficiency of air reconnaissance. We should keep this in mind.

Two enemy carriers still remain, while our torpedo bombers were annihilated. It will be risky to carry out an invasion attempt before destroying them. Moreover, to make contact with the enemy tonight seemed impossible. In view of these [considerations], we suggested to the chief of staff, Fourth Fleet, that they put off the invasion of Port Moresby as the local situation warranted.

A summary of the situation today is as follows:

At 0800 a plane from the Twenty-fifth Air Flotilla sighted two enemy battleships (USS *California* type and UK *Warspite* type), one Australian cruiser of the *Canberra* type and destroyers at a point 115 miles bearing 200°

off Deboyne Island. Most of the Twenty-fifth Air Flotilla's land-based torpedo bombers attacked them, sank a battleship with torpedoes, and seriously damaged another battleship and the heavy cruiser. The latter was considered sunk, too.

The weather in the north was fair, but it was cloudy with showers in the south, so they could not find the enemy carriers.

By 1635, a Yokohama Air Group flying boat sighted one carrier, one heavy cruiser, two light cruisers, and four destroyers at a point 170 miles bearing 241° of Rossel Island. This led us to think that there were two enemy groups, one centering around the battleships, another around carriers. Besides them, there were a tanker and three destroyers to the east.

[Ugaki closed this day's entry by noting that Corregidor had been captured completely by 0800, and that the British had landed on Diego Suarez. He reflected that the British and Americans had been putting more pressure on the French since Pierre Laval became head of the Vichy Government.

[He began the entry for Friday, 8 May 1942, by recording the emperor's congratulatory rescript to the commander in chief, Combined Fleet, and Southern Area Army commander, with Yamamoto's reply thereto.]

Early this morning, a Fifth Carrier Division plane found the enemy group of yesterday evening at a point thirty miles south-southeast of Rossel Island, sailing on course of 120° at 16 knots. Its position was two hundred miles from our task force.

All planes were launched by 0715 and attacked the enemy at 0940. Ten bombs and over eight torpedoes hit a carrier of the *Saratoga* type, and several bombs and three torpedoes struck another of the *Yorktown* type. Their sinking was not confirmed but is considered certain. Dozens of enemy bombers came north at 0740 and attacked our force three times from about 0840 to past 1000. Three bombs hit *Shokaku*, the second ship of the Fifth Carrier Division, causing a fire. Her planes had to be shifted to her sister ship *Zuikaku*.

[*This was the major action at the Coral Sea. The United States lost* Lexington, *and* Yorktown *was seriously damaged. Convinced that* Lexington *had already been sunk, the Japanese reported her as* Saratoga, *then under repair at Puget Sound.* Shokaku *was so badly damaged and* Zuikaku *lost so many planes that the Fifth CV Division had to be counted out of the Midway plans. Despite the United States' losses, Coral Sea was a strategic victory since it accomplished its purpose—denial of Port Moresby to the Japanese.*][21]

While we were expecting further attacks on enemy battleships and others in the afternoon, a report came in stating that they could carry out the afternoon attack. The commander in chief, Fourth Fleet, despite his praise for the morning's exploits, ordered the task force to stop the offensive and come up to the north. His object was not understandable, so we sent a message to his chief of staff, demanding to know the reason for issuing such an order when further advance and attack were needed.

Not only did they not reply to our inquiry, they postponed the invasion of Port Moresby indefinitely. They were going to carry out the occupation of Ocean and Nauru Islands as scheduled and put the forces in defensive positions.

Thereupon our staff officers became very angry and demanded that we send a strongly worded telegram to the chief of staff. They charged that the Fourth Fleet had fallen into defeatism after losing *Shoho*, so an order calling for exploitation of the battle achievement and destruction of the enemy remnant should be sent to them.

Not only was it too late to turn back, but wasn't it more advantageous to send them some good advice to support the Moresby invasion? The previous telegram brought home to them the need to advance. Thinking that a further request would only make them [the Fourth Fleet] more confused, I asked them to think it over. But its spirit should be respected, of course, so we finally issued an order in the name of the commander in chief to the commander in chiefs of the Fourth and Sixth fleets and Eleventh Air Fleet.

Cases in which pursuit is discouraged, overestimating one's own losses, thus failing to enlarge the gain in a battle, have often been observed in past war history, and this is another case. Even if a second attack today was impossible, flying boats from Tulagi or float planes of the Fifth Heavy Cruiser Division could shadow the enemy, as all the enemy carriers had been destroyed. In the meantime, our task force could approach the enemy, joining the Sixth Heavy Cruiser Division and Sixth Destroyer Squadron, and attack in cooperation with aircraft or at night. In this way, the enemy could have been destroyed. This precious lesson should be driven home.

This evening Imperial Headquarters made public the war result since yesterday and made it out to be the most significant gift to the nation on the occasion of the fifth memorial day of the issuance of the Imperial Rescript [upon the start of the war]. The people will be very pleased, but I could not help feeling somewhat dissatisfied.

Our army forces in Burma advanced through Lasio and Burmo, further crossed the frontier into Yunnan Province and took Yuanchan and Lungliang. Thus, the Burma Road is now completely in our hands. What is the Chungking government going to do?

Saturday, 9 May 1942. Fair. As a result of last night's urgent operational signal, the Fourth Fleet revised their order to a little more positive one, but the chance had already been lost. The Sixth Heavy Cruiser Division refueled at a point north of Tulagi today and reported ready for sortie by noon. Movements of the task force had been unknown.

Though flying boats, medium bombers, and float planes tried hard to find the enemy in the Coral Sea, none was sighted except an enemy float plane that a submarine spotted on its way south. It is quite natural for the enemy to run away with all speed. It was too bad that we did not even try to confirm the war result yesterday afternoon.

Today's papers all reported the result of this battle in large type.

Since last night I had given deep thought to the wisdom of resuming the invasion of Moresby. This morning I received a signal from the chief of staff, Fourth Fleet, inquiring about this issue.

Unless provided with powerful carrier air power and fast army transports, I think it might be postponed until July. Unfortunately, the telephone cable from the flagship was out of order, so we got in touch with Tokyo, using the telephone line of *Hyuga*'s buoy and also sending a staff officer to Kure.

As a result of telephone negotiations, it was learned that replenishment of the float planes, reinforcement of carriers except *Kaga*, and changing transports were all impossible at the present stage. Moreover, it is very difficult to transport army landing troops on cruisers and destroyers. The army had also been deeply concerned with the past weakness of the Southern Detachment, and decided to replace it with the Seventeenth Army.

Considering all these things, it was decided to resume the operation in July. We could carry it out now if we want, but it is no use as long as the command taking charge of the operation is not yet firmly determined. *Fuso* and *Ise* of the Second Battleship Division went to Kure.

Sunday, 10 May 1942. No information about the enemy was received except for a flying boat from Tulagi sighting an enemy flying boat. In spite of the papers highlighting the battle of the Coral Sea, I was sorry for not having enlarged its result. Besides the congratulating telegrams sent from various circles, the Germans and Italians were extremely delighted too.

Announcements made by the United Kingdom and the United States are still pretending to be strong. God only knows which is true! I regret that I don't know myself.

Monday, 11 May 1942. Partly fair, rain at night. Two torpedoes hit *Okinoshima*, flagship of Rear Admiral [Kiyohide] Shima, commander, Nineteenth Division, before dawn this morning, while she was engaged in sub hunting northeast of Rabaul. She was flooded and set on fire. We fear for her fate though many vessels have gone to her rescue.

[*The U.S. submarine* S-42 *sank* Okinoshima, *flagship of the invasion force headed for Ocean and Nauru Islands.*]22

The First Battleship Division left Hashira Jima anchorage at 0615 to go out to Iyo Nada. Assault practice by planes of the First Air Fleet, anti-aircraft firing, running engine practice, and emergency maneuvering were carried out. Starting at 1630, main battery firing, then secondary battery normal charge firing took place. We cast anchor at Agenosho after 2200.

Having acknowledged the return of the Fifth Carrier Division to the homeland, the Fourth Fleet activated the invasions of Nauru and Ocean Islands.

Tuesday, 12 1942. Rain. Leaving Agenosho at 0700, we carried out refueling practice in tow and spotting practice and returned to Hashira Jima at 1615 through extremely poor visibility.

Every effort had been made since yesterday to save *Okinoshima,* but she capsized and sank at 0640 while being towed at a point quite close to Buka. Moreover, a submarine [S-44] attacked the repair ship *Shoei Maru,* which had gone to her rescue. She sank at 1430 at a point nine miles bearing S44W from Cape St. George.

Besides, we paid in fairly big sacrifices of our own in this battle, including destroyer *Kikuzuki,* which went aground and sank, and *Tama Maru,* sunk by bombings.

Wednesday, 13 May 1942. Foggy, later clears up. We left at 0945 for Kure which we reached at 1230. The naval port of Kure is filled with vessels being fitted and readied.

[Here, as was Ugaki's patriotic custom, he recorded the Imperial Rescript from the emperor to commander in chief, Combined Fleet, on the battle of the Coral Sea. Yamamoto's reply was slightly ambiguous, and Ugaki hoped their forces would get the point.

[On Thursday, 14 May 1942, Ugaki attended the funeral of those killed in the accident to *Hyuga*'s turret.]

Friday, 15 May 1942. Fair. A flying boat from Tulagi sighted an enemy task force consisting of two carriers, four cruisers, and six destroyers at a point about 455 miles bearing 98° of Tulagi. They were heading west at 15 knots at first, then turned back and increased speed to 20 knots. Frequency of enemy plane flights in the Hawaii area increased on the 8th. Supposing that a task force left there then and sailed south at 14 knots, it would just reach this point. It must have come in a hurry to reinforce because of the last battle.

[*This was Halsey's Task Force 16, centering around* Enterprise *and* Hornet,

which headed south on the chance of reaching the area in time to participate in
the battle of the Coral Sea.][23]

But, seemingly upon receipt of reports of the enemy sub which sighted
and attacked our Nauru and Ocean invasion force and *Okinoshima* west of
Buka, this task force is considered to be operating to attack our force,
assuming that it would go around east of Solomons to the south. If this
enemy comes up north, our Nauru-Ocean invasion force will be put in
danger. We have to be prepared against this.

In the afternoon, the Fourth Fleet ordered the invasion attempt suspended, the invasion forces to be withdrawn to the direction of Truk.
This, too, had to be put off until July, and we notified its chief of staff
accordingly.

Saturday, 16 May 1942. Fair. No information was received on yesterday's
enemy task force after our shadowing flying boat withdrew in the afternoon. I wonder whether they have gone south or north.

Sunday, 17 May 1942. Light rain, later cloudy. Returned on board at 1000.
There was no change in the war situation.

Aircraft carrier *Shokaku,* which fought bravely in the battle of the Coral
Sea and was hit by three bombs, returned to port and cast her anchor in
the evening. She could not be moored because of damage. I inspected her,
accompanying the commander in chief, and thought she was very lucky to
have got off lightly with such damage. We paid our respects to the forty
killed on the planes and over sixty others who died on board and com-
forted the wounded, most of whom had burns. I felt very sorry for them.

[Captain Nakase of the Personnel Bureau came to fleet headquarters to
confer with Ugaki on a delicate problem. The midget submariners killed in
the Pearl Harbor attack had immediately been given double promotions,
an honor not accorded the airmen who died there. (This was a sore point
with the naval air arm.)[24] At this conference the decision was to consider
each case on its merits.]

Monday, 18 May 1942. Cloudy, later light rain. Colonel [Kiyonao]
Ichiki, the commander of an army force, accompanied by a staff officer and
another, came to pay respects after conferring with the Second Destroyer
Squadron on the joint Midway operation. After talking for a while on the
weather deck, they took their leave.

[That afternoon Ugaki bundled up his Order of the Golden Kite, his
diary, and his spare clothes, and entrusted them to the commandant of the
naval barracks.

[*Yamato* sailed at 1000 on Tuesday, 19 May 1942. Ugaki was quite upset with the skipper of the new carrier *Junyo,* which almost sideswiped the superbattleship.]

We received the calls of the commander in chief, First Fleet, and the commander in chief, First Air Fleet. The latter's chief of staff, Kusaka, again expressed his view on the double promotion issue, but it was settled so as to follow the policy already determined.

Commander Uchida, a staff officer of the Naval General Staff, brought with him Imperial Headquarters orders and directives for operations in New Caledonia, Fiji, Samoa, and Port Moresby.

[From Wednesday, 20 May, through Saturday, 23 May, *Yamato* participated in training for the second stage operations.

[On Sunday, 24 May, Captain Sakae Takata of the Military Affairs Bureau and Captain Yoshio Yamamoto, slated to become chief of that bureau's first section, came to consult with the fleet headquarters about switching commands between line and engineer officers. Ugaki had no objections, for "it would not affect operations much," but all concerned decided to consult the fleet before taking action.]

Rear Admiral Chuichi Hara, commander, Fifth Carrier Division, came in the afternoon and reported on the battle of the Coral Sea. What he said was true indeed. He said as follows: They were so unlucky on the 7th that he felt like quitting the navy. The next day, the 8th, they managed to inflict some damage upon the enemy, but they also were hurt. Under such circumstances, he could decide nothing by his own will. When ordered to go north, he was glad to do so, and attacked when so ordered. Though he had the enlargement of the war result in his mind, he had no confidence that he could do so.

Monday, 25 May 1942. Cloudy. A limited table maneuver of the Midway and Aleutian operations was held from 0830. A conference to study it was held in the afternoon and a briefing of the second stage operations from 1500. After that, Rear Admiral [Takeo] Takagi, commander, Fifth Heavy Cruiser Division, reported on the battle of the Coral Sea.

From 1815 we celebrated the commencement of the second term of the second stage operations with *sake,* a gift from the emperor, and a lunch basket on the upper deck.

[On Tuesday, 26 May, Ugaki and his colleagues studied past fleet exercises, which Ugaki believed "yielded many results." Then he had some bad news to record.]

At 2330 last night, an enemy submarine [*Salmon*] attacked the repair ship *Asahi* on her way home from Singapore at a point 120 miles south-south-east of Cam Ranh Bay. Two torpedoes hit her side and she sank an hour and a half later. Remembering her meritorious service since the Russo-

Japanese War, it was extremely regrettable that she sank to the bottom together with all the machinery.

Staff Officer Miwa was dispatched to Tokyo to meet the senior staff officer of the Fourth Fleet, who was coming up there regarding the resumption of the Moresby operation.

[A letter from the chief of the Personnel Bureau to Yamamoto arrived that morning, consulting him "about a reshuffle of flag officers." Ugaki lost no time in replying, adding "a request for proper settlement of the double promotion problem." He gave this reply to Miwa to take with him.

[Wednesday, 27 May, was Japan's Navy Day, celebrated on the anniversary of the battle of Tsushima. Ugaki pledged himself "to answer to the souls of our predecessors by attaining the objective of this war." He wrote a few personal letters and sent his housekeeper instructions to be followed in his absence.]

We heard the report of the torpedo staff officer from 0830. There are still some points I cannot understand about the Fourth Fleet's actions in the battle of the Coral Sea. Its relationship with the Eleventh Air Fleet did not seem to be very good, either. It may all boil down to the matter of personal relationships.

Installation of radar on *Ise* and *Hyuga* was completed at last, and Rear Admiral [Yukitake] Nikaido, Director of the Technical Research Institute, came to visit us. Will they (the radar mechanisms) really display their full value? I hope they won't prove useless after all this waiting.

The task force sortied at 0600. I wish them good fighting.

[*Ugaki referred to the sortie of the Nagumo carrier force*—Akagi, Kaga, Hiryu, Soryu, *with their support units—for the anticipated Midway engagement.*][25]

Thursday, 28 May 1942. Slightly cloudy. In the afternoon the commanders in chief of the First and Second fleets came on board to say farewell before sortie.

No special movements were seen on the battle front except for considerable air activities over the northern district of the Australian east coast. They are considered a sign of some action, but we can only stop them by launching a heavy blow upon Port Moresby.

[That evening *Hyuga* returned to the fleet, her accident damage repaired and her new radar working well. Ugaki noted that at least thirteen enemy submarines were supposed to be operating near Japan and the Marianas; therefore, "utmost care should be taken in tomorrow's sortie."]

After having my hair cut and teeth fixed, I put various things in order and felt calmness in my mind, having nothing to worry about, only to await tomorrow's sortie. This may be the calm before the storm. I firmly believe that God will bless the Combined Fleet. We will go on a major mission to the east in high spirits to inflict heavy damage upon the enemy.

Friday, 29 May 1942. Clear. At 0500, the Invasion Force, consisting of most of the Advance Force (Second Fleet), sortied from the bay.

At 0600, the Main Body left Hashira Jima anchorage. The Ninth Cruiser Division, First Battleship Division, Second Battleship Division, *Chiyoda,* and *Hosho,* in that order, steamed through Bungo Strait to the south after passing the Inland Sea. Speed was 16 knots. At 1500, the force arrived at the outer end of the east channel, where the Third Destroyer Squadron joined the force as a screen. The destroyer squadron had been in that area since the night before last to clear the area of enemy submarines. At 0230 an enemy sub was detected at a point bearing 220° forty miles from Okinoshima and again this afternoon detected another one in the same area. In both cases depth charges were dropped. Vessels from Kure Defense Squadron also made their utmost efforts in cooperating with us.

After passing the channel, speed was increased to 18 knots on course of 150° until evening in order to pass rapidly through a dangerous area. Fortunately, nothing happened. Then paravanes were lifted and the course set at 120°.

At night the light of the nearly full moon was so bright that I thought for a while that, were they Japanese subs, they could make effective attacks upon our force using night periscopes.

Yesterday afternoon enemy land-based planes came to attack Tulagi, and at night twelve carrier-borne planes came to attack there, taking advantage of the moonlight. Some fuel dumps were set on fire and others damaged. Enemy movements, which had been suspected for some time in the direction of northeast Australia, must have meant this. If the enemy has guts, he will come to capture either Tulagi or Rabaul.

Since necessary preparations were completed before the sortie, there has been no need to send radios since the force left the anchorage. Even exchange by telephone was suspended to maintain strict radio silence. Likewise with the preceding forces. Though we are keeping silent, we are sufficiently alert.

As we haven't had any fleet maneuvers lately, the movement of the destroyer squadron in the screen position is very unsatisfactory and constant vigilance has to be maintained. The movement shifting to a night fleet disposition was just like taking kids to their beds.

[On Saturday, 30 May, the Main Body of the Midway Invasion Force kept moving toward the objective, increasing speed and zigzagging. High winds and rough sea forced speed reduction and altered formation to a parallel column. Ugaki was still nervous about U.S. submarines.]

According to radio interception, an enemy sub supposed to be either ahead or in the vicinity of our Transport Force dispatched a long, urgent message to Midway. If the dispatched message was a report of discovering our force, it would surely serve to alert the enemy, thus contributing to making our game in battle heavier.

[Rains continued on Sunday, 31 May, and submarines were reported in the area through which the Main Body was passing, so "a considerable alert" was maintained; however, the weather prevented antisub scouting by aircraft from *Hosho* and Chichi Jima.

[That evening, two patients from destroyers were transferred to *Nagato* for surgery.]

A radio interception indicates that enemy planes and subs in the Aleutian Islands, Hawaiian Islands, and the mid-Pacific are engaged in brisk activities. Exchanges of urgent messages are at a very unusual rate. Certain indications make me suspect that they are taking countermeasures against our suspected movement rather than engaging in operations based on their own initiative.

A sonar device could have detected our sortie from Bungo Strait. May they not have suspected a movement of our northern force through radio intelligence or a report by a Russian vessel? The worst possibility is that they might discover our transport force leaving Saipan on the 28th. Judging from its course and strength, they could suspect that the force was heading toward the Midway district.

Since the said force is not provided with carrier-borne air cover, except for the Eleventh Seaplane Tender Division, it is not impossible that enemy subs may discover this force. Its premature discovery might lead to a showdown with the enemy force, which is rather welcome, but a concentration of enemy subs on the scene is not welcome at all. Be that as it may, for the time being there is no need to change our plan.

The east detachment of the Eighth Sub Squadron is scheduled to converge upon Sydney and attack *Warspite* and two heavy cruisers in that harbor with midget submarines, taking advantage of tonight's moonlight. Can they successfully knock out the remnant left from the Coral Sea battle? The west detachment of the same force is operating off the east coast of Africa.

No news has been heard from it yet, but it is most desirable that it launch a surprise attack upon a British fleet reportedly concentrating in the north of Madagascar and the east coast of South Africa. It is earnestly hoped that the detachment would not miss a big game after sticking too closely to the original refueling schedule or spending too much time in reconnoitering not-so-very-important points.

[*The planned attack on Madagascar consisted of five submarines under the command of Rear Admiral Noboru Ishizaki. I-16, I-18 and I-20 each carried a midget submarine aboard, while I-10 and I-30 each carried a seaplane. This force had been under way since 30 April.]*[26]

4
Don't Let Another
Day Like This Come
June–July 1942

THE FIRST *few days of this period
Ugaki kept busy with the difficulties involved in shepherding a huge fleet to its
destination—fog, stray ships, refueling—all while maintaining radio silence.
He also followed the exploits of his favorites, the midget submariners, at Sydney
and Madagascar.*

*Midway fell on Ugaki with the impact of an avalanche. The Japanese were
not totally unrealistic, and understood that their plan to seize American territory and lure out the U.S. Fleet posed certain dangers. They could have
accepted the loss of a ship or two, but to lose four carriers with all their aircraft
plus a heavy cruiser was almost beyond comprehension.*

*Along with the psychological shock of decisively losing a battle the Japanese
had fully expected to win, and the consequent loss of ships and lives, Ugaki
experienced deep personal sorrow when an academy classmate, one of his closest
friends and colleagues, Rear Admiral Tamon Yamaguchi, chose to go down
with his flagship, the CV Hiryu. Ugaki is torn between his grief at this loss
and his pride in Yamaguchi's nobility, as he saw it, in thus fulfilling his command responsibility.*

*For three days Ugaki had neither the time nor the inclination for his diary.
Then his professionalism asserted itself and he set out to relate the action as he
knew it, and the whys and hows of this most unexpected debacle. One of his duties
as chief of staff was to analyze fleet engagements so that Yamamoto and his staff
might profit by the experience. It is natural, then, that he put the cart of analysis
before the horse of action. To maintain the integrity of the diary, we have kept his
format; however, we suggest that the reader unfamiliar with the action at
Midway skip from the end of the 4 June entry on p. 138 to the spot on p. 148 where
Ugaki resumed his day-to-day narrative and continue through 9 June. Then the
reader can turn back to p.138 and read Ugaki's analysis with heightened understanding.*

*Ugaki's comments are intelligent and well considered. Some of his conclusions
are valid. Indeed, it is ironic that he should see many of Japan's mistakes so*

clearly after the fact when he had presided over several table maneuvers designed to catch just such inconsistencies. Some of his thoughts are not so clear-sighted, and they include no suggestion that the United States had broken the Japanese Navy's operational code, JN 25, in which the messages concerning the Midway operation were sent. Ugaki did not suspect such a thing until 30 July.

Yamamoto's Main Body was far to the rear of the advance forces, so Ugaki saw none of the action first hand. His account is based upon information fed to Yamato *from the units engaged. For this reason, Ugaki's remarks concerning the discussions aboard the flagship have more immediacy and are more informative than his attempts to second-guess Nagumo. Ugaki gives us a vivid picture of the suggestions put forth to salvage something from the wreckage and their abandonment one by one. Particularly touching is his account of the decision to scuttle* Akagi, *the noble flagship of the First Air Fleet. Yamamoto had once served aboard her, so the decision caused more than professional anguish.*

The rest of June and all of July are anticlimactic, as Combined Fleet Headquarters engaged in such matters as how to reschedule fleet operations and how to rebuild the naval air arm. In view of the scope and urgency of these tasks, one is surprised to find the entire entry for 1 July devoted to the old question of double promotions for those who died at Pearl Harbor. Planning went forward for a campaign in the Indian Ocean, with the ultimate invasion of India, but the latter concept had to be postponed. One has the impression of confusion, and that Midway had left the Combined Fleet without viable alternate plans. Ugaki fretted over the lack of new and original weaponry.

During this period one catches glimpses of Ugaki the man. It is somewhat astonishing to discover that Ugaki, so steeped in naval tradition, should not only have been permitting but encouraging Yamaguchi to go over Nagumo's head, and to carry tales on his superior. Perhaps Ugaki felt that the special bond between Eta Jima classmates excused this breach of naval protocol.

Ugaki appears in a more sympathetic light as he mourns the death of his pet dog. He had worn his hair long; now he cut it short to signify a new beginning after Midway, to express sorrow at the death of his dog, and in anticipation of hot weather. At a brief visit to his home he was cheered to find "a cute kitten." As always, he was sure that Tomoko's spirit watched over him and protected him.

[Monday, 1 June 1942, on which date the fleet should have changed into summer uniforms. But Ugaki considered the move premature and postponed it "until further notice."

[There was a submarine scare, and the Main Body took evasive action, but Ugaki questioned the report because a staff officer had seen whalespouts.

[That afternoon, a search plane failed to locate the tanker train. The

Ninth Cruiser Division and two destroyers were arranged to steam ahead to refuel at Point "H" early in the morning.]

A flying boat from Wake Island sighted an enemy sub each at points four hundred to five hundred miles north-by-northeast and northeast from the island. Moreover, another flying boat from Wotje Island sighted an enemy flying boat at a point five hundred miles north-by-northeast from the island and attacked it.

Out of over 180 radio exchanges observed in the Hawaii district, as many as seventy-two were tagged "urgent." We believe that the enemy are preparing to meet us, after having strongly suspected our movement. It has become especially almost certain that they have deployed subs in the vicinity of six hundred miles bearing southwest of Midway Island and have intensified their guard together with planes.

At night an urgent telegram came in from the chief, First Bureau of the Naval General Staff, which said that, according to broadcasts from Sydney and San Francisco, three Japanese midget subs attacked Sydney Harbor last Sunday. As they attacked, it is supposed that they must have inflicted considerable damage on the enemy. Pray to God for the safe recovery of their crews!

Tuesday, 2 June 1942. Rain. It is learned from an unidentified station in Australia that three Japanese midget subs attacked only harbor vessels and two of them were sunk by depth charges, the remaining one by bombardment.

[*The Japanese claimed the midgets sank the battleship* Warspite. *In fact, this operation succeeded only in damaging an old ferryboat in use as a barracks, killing several sailors. None of the minisubs or their crewmen survived.*[1]

[Ugaki was especially disappointed because, unlike the Hawaii operation, only well-trained crews participated in this attack.

[The bad weather that would plague the Main Body on its voyage to Midway worsened. *Toei Maru* and two other tankers were not sighted until 1130. "Refueling was then made to the hungry kids—the destroyers. They are really kids who need much care and attention." Because of the weather, further refueling was suspended for the day.]

Wednesday, 3 June 1942. Rain. Sunrise was 0315 according to the time we are using. Since we are still using Japanese standard time, the daily work cannot be done within the usual time concept.

After last midnight, a considerably thick fog shrouded the force from behind, so that the next ship from us was hardly visible. Searchlights were turned on and fog beacons towed. The thick fog cleared up before 0100. Fog during a wartime cruise is the most difficult navigational hazard to overcome, as we cannot use radio, and have to refrain from excessive use of sound signals and light signals out of [security] considerations.

[At dawn, three tankers—*Toa Maru, Toei Maru,* and *San Clemente Maru*—were available, and the remaining five destroyers refueled, assuming position after 0700.]

Sendai, flagship of the Third Destroyer Squadron, and one destroyer were missing from the force this morning, most likely due to yesterday's poor visibility or the Main Body's reduced speed. As they are assumed to have gone ahead of the force, it was decided to dispatch a *Hosho* plane to locate them.

None of the midget sub crews who made the surprise attack upon Sydney were recovered, and the mother sub suspended its search.

[As was his custom where midget submarines were concerned, Ugaki made a rather lengthy entry about both the Sydney and the Madagascar missions. He tried to console himself with the thought that, even if the Sydney attack failed, the Australians must have received a "tremendous" shock.]

[*Ugaki had little information about the Madagascar venture, which actually did not do too badly. Two of the midgets reached their target area. I-18's midget did not, as the mother sub encountered difficulties and arrived at the launching site too late. The minisubs torpedoed the 6,993-ton merchantman* British Royalty, *which sank, and the battleship* Ramillies *which, although heavily damaged, saved herself by jettisoning her fuel and ammunition. One midget sub escaped out of the harbor only to go aground. Several days later a British patrol encountered the two crewmen. They refused to surrender, and the British shot them dead. In 1972 the site of the incident was confirmed and in 1977 a monument was erected.*[2]

[That afternoon, 3 June, what they thought was a merchant ship was sighted far to the north, and the Main Body changed course to evade. It turned out to be the Japanese patrol ship No. 7, *Nankai Maru,* and Ugaki regretted that the Main Body did not approach her, so that the gallant little ship "might have been cheered by the sight of our Main Body majestically steaming east."]

At 1315 a search plane located *Sendai* and the destroyer *Isonami* forty-three miles ahead of the Main Body. Being informed of our position, they immediately reversed course and finally joined before 1600. This was a consequence of maintaining radio silence.

Thursday, 4 June 1942. Cloudy. No rain since last night, but the sky was entirely covered with thick clouds, as hitherto.

At 0500, at a point 35° north and 165° east, the guard force separated from us. Consisting of the Second Battleship Division, Ninth Cruiser Division, twelve destroyers, *Sacramento Maru,* and *Toei Maru,* the force is to proceed on course of 45° at nine knots while refueling on the way to act as a support for the Northern Force. [*Ugaki mistook the names of these two tankers. They were, respectively,* San Clemente Maru *and* Toa Maru.] The Main Force, comprising the First Destroyer Division, the Second Destroyer Squadron (eight destroyers), *Hosho* with one destroyer, and *Toei Maru* is to steam on course of 90° to act as support for the Southern Force.

The Aleutian operation commenced at 0100. The Second Task Force centering around the Fourth Carrier Division and the second section of the Fourth Cruiser Division launched attacks upon Dutch Harbor at 0107 after having closed in Unalaska Island since last night.

[*This attack upon the Aleutians was designed both as a diversionary tactic to distract U.S. attention from Midway, and to cut off what the Japanese thought to be a possible U.S. route to invade Japan.*][3]

Junyo's carrier-borne force turned back on the way due to foul weather, but *Ryujo*'s force succeeded in attacking the island. The enemy radio station on the island suspended transmission for a while but resumed after 1700. Enemy planes seem to have attacked the force when it was about to launch the second attack. Presumably the situation is not serious.

On the other hand, a report came in that an enemy plane sighted the invasion force accompanying twelve transports at a point six hundred miles from Midway at 0600, and the No. 16 Minesweeper Division was fighting. A premature exposure! If its early close-in is unavoidable out of consideration for its slow speed, our task force's first attack on Midway on N-2 day [two days before the projected Midway landing] should have been made one day earlier. This problem was brought up in a briefing conference before the sortie, but the date of an aerial attack was not advanced because of the task force's preparation time.

[*The sighting of the invasion force was made by Ensign Jack Reid's PBY 8Vss, that of the minesweeper division by Ensign Charles R. Eaton's PBY 6Vss. The Japanese expected, even hoped, that the invasion force would be sighted and thus deceive the United States into thinking it was the main attack force coming in from the south. But this was not supposed to happen until 6 June, N-1 Day.*[4] The sighting made Ugaki somewhat nervous.]

It is now apparent that this sighting led the enemy to suspect our intention. The enemy force in the Hawaii district will surely take measures to cope with this sighting. Care should be taken about this, I believe. In the afternoon a report came in from the commanding officer of the Second Destroyer Squadron that nine B-17s came to attack our invasion force but inflicted no damage. Now action is imminent.

[*This report was accurate. Nine B-17s under Lieutenant Colonel Walter C.*

Sweeney attacked the Tanaka force and claimed a number of hits; actually, neither side inflicted or suffered damage.[5]

[In the afternoon fog came in, so zigzagging was suspended, and the destroyer screen drawn in. While these measures were being taken, the fog thickened, and Ugaki found it a major problem.]

Since fog came in from ahead with an east wind of five meters, there was little prospect of ascertaining when it will clear up. Yesterday the task force broke radio silence to order its new course and speed by radio, and now it is considered that the task force probably met this same fog and had no choice under the circumstances but to carry out subsequent operations as scheduled.

I have the feeling that even the midst of the Pacific is small. All I hope now is that there will be no trouble in the task force's air attack upon Midway Island tomorrow.

[*At this point we suggest that the reader might move to p. 148 through 8 June, then return here to Ugaki's analysis.*]

Friday, 5 June 1942. Thick fog. Since operations on the 5th, 6th, and 7th were so urgent, I couldn't find time to put the daily account in this war diary. I feel like a week or ten days have elapsed since then. As I have some time today (8 June) to spare, I'm going to write down first the main problems in my head.

Main causes for the failure of this operation:

1. There are questions as to whether the enemy knew our plan, apart from its extent. These doubts are endorsed by the fact that the enemy defense in this district has been intensified of late, in addition to brisk submarine activities and their concentration of forces. Whether the enemy discovered our plan by their subs sighting our invasion force leaving Saipan on the 28th or the sortie of our Main Body and others from the Inland Sea, whether the enemy suspected a reinforcement movement of our northern force through information from Russian ships, or whether the enemy found out, either based upon security leakage from messages sent from our army forces in the homeland, or based upon judgment of general radio intelligence—all these can't be ascertained. But much suspicion about these questions is not lacking.

[*Actually, U.S. Combat Intelligence had broken the Japanese naval code JN 25, enabling the Americans to get a very good fix on Japan's Midway plan.*][6]

The enemy couldn't possibly have advanced its task force from Hawaii to the north of Midway Island by merely discovering our invasion force on the 4th. The possibility that the enemy's powerful task force left Hawaii on 30 May can be confirmed by increased flights of the many planes in that district since that day.

[*Task Force 16*—Enterprise, Hornet, *and their support ships—sortied from Pearl Harbor on 28 May, the same day—29 May Japan time—that Yamamoto's Main Body left Hashira Jima. Task Force 17*—Yorktown *and her escorts—left on 30 May.*]

It's impossible to judge that the enemy just happened to meet us on its way westward with an offensive intention (for instance, an air-raid on our capital). This can be reasoned by the fact that the enemy strength included not only all the remaining three carriers (*Yorktown, Enterprise,* and *Hornet*) but two converted carriers with several powerful cruisers and more than a dozen destroyers.

[*Actually, the United States had no converted carriers at Midway. Ugaki goes on, making a parenthetical statement.*]

(The Naval General Staff in Tokyo had sent in its judgment that the enemy had not yet suspected our intention, and I wrote in this diary my impression upon receipt of those messages as they came in.)

[In the margin of Ugaki's page the following was added, apparently later: "The U.S. Navy later announced that they had anticipated the Japanese attempt, adding that it was a Japanese characteristic to make another active action following the victory of the Coral Sea battle."]

2. Our reconnaissance of the enemy was insufficient. An advance attempt to reconnoiter the Hawaii district by Type Two flying boats couldn't be carried out, as two enemy vessels were in French Frigate Shoals. In addition, Wake Island couldn't afford enough sea area for them to take off. So our operation had to be made without any information on the enemy force and activities in Pearl Harbor. (Had we had a sufficient number of these flying boats, we could have remedied this defeat to some extent.)

[*The Type Two flying boat was then Japan's best long-distance reconnaissance aircraft, with a radius of two thousand miles, speed of 235 knots, and a payload of ten 250-kg. bombs.*][7]

Unlike the Pearl Harbor operation, in which the surprise element could be expected, the Midway operation lacked such an element. Nevertheless, we admittedly didn't sufficiently consider searching the sea area by submarines and other means. That is, only *I-168* was positioned around Midway and the other fifteen subs of the Third Submarine Squadron, the Fifth Submarine Squadron, and the Thirteenth Submarine Division were positioned on the north-south line six hundred miles west of Hawaii to meet an enemy force expected to come from Pearl Harbor as reinforcements.

[*In any case, the U.S. task forces had passed the Japanese reconnaissance line before the submarines were in position.*][8]

Even if we didn't consider the enemy had suspected our intention, at least we should have either positioned an element of our force at an expected enemy attack area to meet a powerful strike, or made a sweeping search from Midway toward Hawaii. Either one of these steps would have served, for one thing, as a means to obtain information about the enemy and at the same time a measure for protecting the flank of our task force. I seriously feel it to be a grave responsibility of our headquarters that we failed to take these steps.

[*Before Midway, Japanese strategists, devoted to the offensive, begrudged the aircraft and manpower for reconnaissance. Not only was the preliminary search plan for Midway inadequate, but air reconnaissance from the Nagumo task force itself was faulty.*][9]

3. An unexpectedly large enemy force attacked our task force at its most vulnerable moment.

The enemy had only two carriers in operational condition and contact with them had been entirely lost since they were seen east of Tulagi for a while on 15 May, after having come down from Hawaii for the Coral Sea battle. Although they were estimated to have returned to Hawaii, we never expected them, even including another one and two converted carriers, to ambush our force near Midway Island.

A carrier force has a vulnerable point when the enemy forestalls it, especially so when it's concentrating its attack upon another target, because it not only lacks a sufficient defensive force, namely interceptors, but it isn't in a position immediately to switch its attack upon the new enemy carrier. In all sea battles since the outbreak of the war—namely, the Pearl Harbor attack, the attack upon Port Darwin or the attack upon Ceylon—we achieved brilliant success under circumstances where no powerful enemy air force was in the operational area. It was just like striking a sitting enemy.

In the conference assessing the Combined Fleet's first stage operation held toward the end of last April, the First Air Fleet chief of staff, Kusaka, stressed, citing the sword theory, to the effect that a carrier-borne air attack should be launched with a concentrated single stroke after sufficient study and minute planning.

[*Kusaka based this theory upon* Kinshicho-Oken, *a form of swordplay where one works in close to the opponent, holds the sword over his head, strikes downward, then returns to the original position.*][10]

Upon hearing his remark, I felt considerable apprehension about it, because I thought, unlike land warfare, it is not easy to make sufficient studies beforehand or thoroughly to reconnoiter over a vast sea area, where forces can move anywhere. Measures to cope with any change of circumstances are important.

Second Carrier Division Commander Yamaguchi had always been actively with the task force, and had been so unsatisfied with the thinking of its headquarters that he went so far as to recommend his own views more than once during the past operation. He told me three times that the First Air Fleet headquarters had never taken steps to expand its achievement in battle, grasping an opportunity to do so, or to cope with a change of circumstances.

I think his remarks generally hit the point, and as I agreed with him, I told him that he should continue recommending his views as much as possible in the future, too. When asked who was leading the headquarters, he said, "The commander in chief doesn't say a word, and both the chief of staff and the senior staff officer lack boldness, although I don't know which one is more so."

Hearing this, at that time I worried deeply whether the First Air Fleet would be able to accomplish its mission in future sea operations in which every kind of change must be expected to happen.

When asked in the battle-lesson studying division what the First Air Fleet was going to do in case an enemy air attack forestalled it in an engagement, or flanked it while it was engaged in an air raid upon an enemy land, the First Air Fleet chief of staff simply said that the fleet would operate so as not to let such an event take place.

To a further question in this connection, [First Air Fleet Air] Staff Officer [Commander Minoru] Genda said that the fleet was going to have two or three bombers equipped with additional fuel tanks so that its radius of action could soon be extended to some 450 miles. When it got them, the fleet intended to employ them, together with the cruisers' seaplanes, in searching the fleet's flank. But at that time he admitted pessimistically there would be no alternative but to depend upon interceptors presently in the air for defense of the fleet if an enemy forestalled it.

I thought that this remark considerably roused their attention to this problem. In addition, I asked them to deepen their attention by citing similar cases occurring in a war game prepared for this Midway operation—once in a Midway invasion operation and twice in a Hawaiian invasion operation.

In the operational briefing before the commencement of this operation, the First Air Fleet headquarters took this problem more seriously and presented a plan for arranging its attack upon Midway in two stages, the second wave being kept in readiness to meet an enemy sea-air force. This relieved me a little bit.

Finally, in the studying conference of a war game covering the Midway-

Aleutian operation, the Combined Fleet's senior staff officer, Kuroshima, gave as his personal opinion that we must not depend upon the air force too much; the surface force must be prepared to sacrifice itself in its place when necessary. Therefore, at the end of the conference, I said that I shared his view, adding that a good use of the air arm was to seek victory by hitting the enemy's weak point, but there could also be cases in which this principle couldn't be applied. Also, I invited their attention to the vulnerability of the carrier, quoting the views of Fifth Carrier Division Commander Hara, who had come back to the homeland from the Coral Sea battle the other day.

As stated previously, we failed to make good use of submarines in reconnaissance and supported the flank of our force in spite of that apprehension. I must accept a grave responsibility for this flaw in our operational plan.

Considering this point, a battle lesson is derived that elements of the submarine force should be placed under the command of the task force commander, as in the case of the Pearl Harbor operation.

What I couldn't understand in this operation is what steps the task force took against the newly discovered enemy when it received reports from a *Tone* plane saying that "a large enemy force sighted to the east, near," and also "many enemy carrier-borne planes heading for the main force," after the first wave had been launched. This should be investigated later.

The task force could not launch its second-wave planes and depended for its defense solely upon escorting fighters presently in the air. This seemed to intensify our damage. Couldn't the conflagration have been prevented to some extent had those planes been launched before the enemy attack, thus minimizing the inflammable material on board ship?

[*Ugaki never erred on the side of charity in judging Nagumo. Actually, the task force's situation was much more complicated than Ugaki's diary indicates.*][11]

4. To the enemy's advantage, they attacked our force while our carriers were concentrated in one group, offering many eggs in one basket.

With the number of carriers in use gradually increasing, a view has been advocated that they could be better used from dispersed positions, whereby attacks could be launched from different directions or an attack range could be extended by using another carrier as a relay base for attack or return to the mother carrier. This view gained strength when I was teaching at the Naval War College and later proved effective when applied in a fleet maneuver while I was senior staff officer of the Combined Fleet.

Later, however, an air fleet was formed from the viewpoint of controlled use of carrier strength, placing emphasis on concentrated use of carrier-borne planes. From the outbreak of the war, this policy has been followed and proved successful. This concentrated use of carriers has advantages, making it possible to command them so that their movement can be concealed, combined defense against an enemy attack is facilitated, and a combined simultaneous attack can be launched.

In consequence, the First Air Fleet headquarters entertained the view that its strength could possibly be expanded to as many as about nine carriers, for it would be possible to command that number in the same area. Furthermore, in a war game held for the second-stage operation, the same headquarters arranged to use as many as twelve carriers, even including ones of inferior speed and quality, in one group for an attack upon Hawaii. In a conference to study the war games, I asked the same headquarters to study this problem further, pointing out that that concept was not considered adequate.

In the Coral Sea battle, *Shokaku* was damaged and *Zuikaku,* too, needed repairs. In addition, the Fourth Carrier Division was employed with the northern force. As a result, the only carriers available for the Midway operation were the four of the First and Second CV divisions. So it could not be called excessive concentration of carrier strength, as such strength naturally should be concentrated in one group.

As it turned out, however, according to reconnaissance reports, the enemy force was reported first as a large enemy group, then followed by five cruisers and several destroyers, what seemed to be carriers, then two cruisers and two carriers with cruisers and destroyers. These reports showed that the enemy force was divided into two or three groups over a vast area extending one hundred miles from north to south.

On the other hand, the enemy sighted our carrier force in one group and concentrated their attacks upon it. The first enemy attack set huge fires on *Akagi, Kaga,* and *Soryu. Hiryu* alone escaped that enemy attack and succeeded in scoring hits with five 250-kg. bombs upon a *Yorktown* type carrier and two torpedoes on another one of the same type with planes reserved for the second attack, in addition to fifty enemy planes shot down. But subsequent enemy attack rendered her unfit for engagement.

[*Contrary to Ugaki's entry, the first American strike did not hit the task force. They had been under unsuccessful attack by several groups of Midway-based and carrier-based aircraft before the successful dive bomber attack. Nor had the Japanese sunk two American carriers, although convinced that* Hiryu's *airmen had done so. Actually they hit* Yorktown *on both attacks.*][12]

This may lead to a view that, had our carrier force been more powerful, it would have been able to prevent the attack and also destroy the enemy.

At the same time, however, the battle could be said to have revealed disadvantages involved in having the carrier strength in one group. But Second CV Division Commander Yamaguchi was opposed to the idea of dispersing carrier strength when I talked with him previously.

After all, it seems, a conclusion is reached that more than two air fleets or task forces, each consisting of four to six carriers, should be employed in separate groups.

5. The front area of our invasion plan was expanded too widely. It was impossible to continue the operation under the circumstances when all the carrier strength available to us were *Hosho* with only six old type bombers (type 96 with unretractable landing gears and now out of production) and *Zuiho* with nine fighters and nine bombers, while the enemy still had one carrier and two converted carriers in perfect condition in the nearby sea under cover of the half-damaged air base, and furthermore they could expect a reinforcement of planes from Hawaii.

The Fourth Carrier Division of the northern force was ordered to move down south, but, contrary to our expectation, the force was still near Dutch Harbor under cover of foul weather. It could not come down to reinforce before the 9th.

On the other hand, the problem of how long the landing force could remain at sea had to be considered. The only means left for us to carry out an operation without previous planning would be to dash to the island with all forces combined into one group, but this attempt would only add to our sacrifices. Therefore, we had no alternative but to suspend the operation.

This plan was made before the Coral Sea battle. After we learned that the Fifth CV Division could not participate in this operation, the plan should have been revised so that one mission would be finished before dealing with another. I think we can't escape being blamed for negligence in not having taken the necessary steps in spite of such necessity. For that failure we have to take responsibility, too.

We should also have considered a plan to shorten the distance between each group with a determination to launch a forceful attack after the landing force was discovered on the 4th, or to order the second attack force south, calling off the northern operation for a while.

The reason why a night engagement was ordered that night and an account of why it was called off later:

As a result of the enemy attack, *Soryu* and *Kaga* went down first, while *Akagi* was disabled. Thereupon, Commander in Chief Nagumo transferred his flag to *Nagara* and continued fighting with *Hiryu* alone. But she was also disabled after attacking two enemy carriers. Under the circumstances it was impossible to continue the operation unless the enemy, especially his carriers, was destroyed.

Fortunately, the second half of the Third Battleship Division, Eighth Cruiser Division, and Tenth Destroyer Squadron were only one hundred miles west of the enemy force. In addition, the first half of the Fourth Cruiser Division, Fifth Cruiser Division, Second Destroyer Squadron, and Seventh Cruiser Division belonging to the invasion force (namely, the Main Force of the Second Fleet) were in a position to cooperate with the above force if the later took positive steps against the enemy after sunset. The Main Body was also in a position to support our night engagement force next morning, after steaming east.

No way was left to destroy this enemy except by a night engagement. The fate of this operation entirely depended upon the night engagement. Furthermore, as we thought it to have a great deal of possibility for success, with firm determination we issued a decision to catch up with the enemy for the kill (at 1615).

[In the margin of this entry, the following was added: "The last air reconnaissance report seemed to say that the enemy was heading west."]

Sunrise time: 0152; sunset time: 1543; and the moon age: 2.1 (two days, one hour.)

However, unexpected events took place one after another, making it impossible to materialize this plan.

After *Hiryu* was damaged, the movement of the task force became entirely passive. Not only did it fail to try to shadow the enemy force with seaplanes before darkness fell, but it didn't proceed toward the enemy; a report came in saying that *Nagara* was withdrawing to the northwest, escorting *Hiryu*. Whether the withdrawing force included all of the task force or not was unknown, though it was considered probably to include all of the force.

The Second Fleet commanding the night engagement force (excluding the Seventh Cruiser Division which became the base bombardment force) steamed eastward to commence a sweeping search toward the east after midnight.

Although several hours elapsed after sunset time, 1543 (standard time), no information on the enemy force was available. Only four hours were left before sunrise. At 2030 I concluded that there was little prospect of challenging the enemy with a night engagement before dawn, and warned the operations room through a voice tube not to let the night engagement force go too far, thus bringing the situation after dawn beyond control. At 2115 an order calling for joining the Main Force (after suspending the night attack) was issued.

When an operation turns out to be a failure and distress sets in, it's quite natural for a human being to be discouraged and apt to seek only passive actions, thus leading to losing an opportunity to strike back at the enemy. There is a great deal of difference, with regard to their attitudes toward the night engagement, between the task force, which saw a tragic scene in battle, and the invasion force which hasn't yet engaged in battle. Further investigation needs to be made of the circumstances which then prevailed, but it is my view that no other means than a strong lashing order by the supreme command could do anything to remedy the prevailing situation.

Furthermore, the night engagement plan, upon which the final outcome of this operation gravely depended, lost a chance of success and an order had to be issued to join the Main Force. (In an order issued by the commander in chief of the Second Fleet calling for a search, it was apparently observed that he had little hope of making it successfully.

[*It's highly unlikely that the projected night engagement could have succeeded. Rear Admiral Raymond A. Spruance, in command of Task Force 16, had no intention of risking his two remaining carriers by sailing within range of Japan's surface forces.*][13]

Account of issuing an order to attack Midway base:

Midway base was attacked by the first wave but no more. On the other hand, the enemy task force damaged our carriers one after another. Nonetheless, *Hiryu* was still operational, while the night engagement plan was under way. Whether this night engagement could succeed or not was considered to depend upon how much damage the first wave attack had inflicted upon the enemy base on the island. So an inquiry with regard to this point was sent in my name to the chief of staff, First Air Fleet, after its flag was transferred to *Nagara*, but no reply was available.

Judging that the base was not sufficiently destroyed in view of the prevailing circumstances, it was thought that unless it could be completely destroyed before dawn, enemy reinforcements would be sent to the island even tonight, not to speak of tomorrow, thus making our landing on the island more difficult. Therefore, an order to bombard the island was issued and the Second Fleet assigned the Seventh Cruiser Division for that mission.

Although I doubted the effectiveness of bombing an air base by 20-cm. shells, in addition to the risk of attacks by enemy subs, the staff officers strongly urged that it be done as no other way was left. So I approved. But, at that time, I had a plan in mind to force through this operation with all fleets continuing the eastward movement.

Since the Midway bombardment force was expected to close the island about midnight, namely one hour and a half before sunrise time, its withdrawal from the island was feared to involve extreme danger. As expected, the Second Fleet headquarters sent in a recommendation to the same effect, pointing out that the Seventh Cruiser Division would not be able to commence bombardment shortly before dawn.

Indeed, it would be a hopeless as well as a dangerous venture. Considering that the sooner it was suspended the better, an order to call it off was issued before the issuance of the order to give up the night attempt.

P.S. When we finally decided that to launch a night engagement was impossible, staff officers came up on the bridge with a plan to bombard the island with 40-cm and 36-cm shells of battleships after they bravely closed the island the following daytime. They ought to have known the absurdity of attacking a fortress with a fleet! Under the circumstances, where not only is the enemy air base operational with a considerable number of land-based planes available but enemy carriers are still sound, even powerful battleships would be defeated by enemy planes and subs before they could use their gun power.

If the landing force could be kept at sea for some time longer, it would have to wait for the coming of the second task force from the north. Even though we lost four powerful carriers, we still have eight carriers, including those scheduled to be completed before long, so that we need not be discouraged at all, as we can still hope to make good use of them in the future.

Pointing out that it is a plan of a fool without a brain to challenge a hopeless game of *go* again and again out of desperation, I earnestly persuaded them to reconsider the bombardment plan. Accordingly, those in the operations room restudied the plan and agreed to call off the plan after they regained calmness.

[*These schemes to attack Midway might have succeeded, for Ugaki greatly overestimated the U.S. strength remaining available on Midway.*][14]

Nothing is more regrettable than that a grave responsibility of deciding the fate of the empire in directing overall operations should be fulfilled under such circumstances as these.

Problem of disposal of *Akagi*:

After being attacked, *Soryu* went down at 1615 and *Kaga* at 1526. On the other hand, *Akagi* was set ablaze after enemy dive bombers dropped three 250-kg. bombs on her fore, midship, and astern. When the fire became uncontrollable, all her crew members abandoned ship at 1630, bringing pictures of the Imperial family with them. After they transferred to other ships, her skipper sent a cable to the commander in chief, First Air Fleet, asking his permission to sink the ship with torpedoes from a destroyer, as her sinking had not yet been confirmed.

Under the circumstances when, although the sun had set, we still intended to launch a night engagement and the whole fleet was expected to steam east, why was there a need to sink her prematurely? Accordingly, an order was issued to "immediately suspend disposal of her."

Then destroyers of the Fourth Destroyer Division and Seventeenth Destroyer Division remained standing by her. When we decided to call off the invasion plan because there was little prospect for the planned night engagement, however, we had to decide what to do with *Akagi*.

Since the commander in chief said, "Shall we dispose of her on my responsibility?" I agreed with him, though the senior staff officer opposed it. In the meantime, time had passed by while we sent off cables inquiring about her condition. Finally, there wasn't much time left before dawn, and at last we issued an order to dispose of her. This was at 2350.

The reasons for such a decision are as follows:

1. *Akagi*'s damage was serious. Under the circumstances in which her skipper, who had the ultimate responsibility, thought in his best judgment that the ship had to be abandoned and also sunk, it would be impossible to rescue her by towing. As the enemy still had powerful air strength, an approach to the scene could not be made without strong air support, which we lacked. No time should be wasted at a time when withdrawal of all forces had been decided, and disposal of her would be better made at night.

2. If and when the enemy captured her, it would not only be another disgrace but a serious disadvantage to us.

3. The situation when facing an enemy force is entirely different from that in peacetime. It is a matter of sentiment to think that it would be a graceful gesture to see *Akagi* once more, as the Main Body is expected to be considerably close to the scene tomorrow morning, or that she should not be sunk by our own weapons. It is indeed extremely unbearable, but we must not blunder from the overall standpoint for the sake of a sentimental feeling like this.

The commander in chief had once been skipper of *Akagi* and commanded the carrier division on board her. Now as a result of the unfavorable outcome of the operation, he, as commander in chief of the Combined Fleet, found himself obliged to issue an order to dispose of her. Guessing his feeling, I can't help shedding tears, but sentiment is sentiment and reason is reason, and I think he made the reasonable decision as commander in chief.

As the fog cleared up slightly after dawn with a prospect of visibility being improved soon, we let *Toei Maru* refuel *Nagato*.

[*Here Ugaki resumed his narrative of daily events.*] N-2 Day (5 June) was the first day to commence attacks upon Midway. At 2035 a *Tone* plane sent in the first report of "enemy planes in sight heading toward your force." At

0255 it sent in another report of "fifteen enemy flying boats heading toward your force."

At 1346 the *Hiryu* force ended its attack upon the island, reporting the need to launch a second attack.

[*Aircraft from all four carriers, not just* Hiryu, *participated in the attack upon Midway.*] While we supposed that our attacks must have inflicted considerable damage upon the island, a startling report came in from one of our search planes at 0440, saying, "What seem to be ten enemy ships in sight bearing 10° 240 miles from Midway, course 150° and speed 20 knots." Though the type of this enemy force was unknown, we immediately realized that the enemy force was there in readiness. So it was arranged to let *Toei Maru,* then refueling *Nagato,* simultaneously refuel two destroyers.

After 0500 another report came in stating that the enemy force consisted of five cruisers and five destroyers, accompanied by what seemed to be a carrier in its rear. At first we were in an optimistic mood, thinking that there was an enemy task force that we had been looking for, and how we should wipe out the remaining enemy force after our second wave, to be dispatched immediately, destroyed the enemy carrier.

[*It is difficult to believe that this happy-go-lucky attitude really prevailed upon* Yamato *at this moment. This was the first intimation they had received of any American force west of Midway, and it shot a major hole in their planning. The U.S. fleet was not supposed to emerge until the Japanese had taken Midway, according to the Japanese blueprint.*][15]

At 0547 a report came in that two more enemy cruisers were sighted at a point bearing 8°, 250 miles from Midway, but when a *Tone* plane said that it was going to return as its fuel was running short, the Eighth Heavy Cruiser Division commander said by return cable that it should continue shadowing the enemy force until about 0700, when a replacement plane was expected to arrive at the scene.

After the same plane reported "ten more enemy planes are heading toward our force at about 0600," not much change was observed until 0750, when a startling report came in from the Eighth Heavy Cruiser Division commander: "As a result of enemy carrier-borne bombers and land-based bombers attacks, *Kaga, Soryu,* and *Akagi* were set ablaze. *Hiryu* continued her attacks upon enemy carriers, while the task force is going to withdraw to the north for a while to regroup."

This sad report immediately changed the prevailing atmosphere in the operations room into one of deepest gloom, while steps were taken to proceed to the scene with increased speed to rescue the task force in distress.

Due to the prevailing fog, it took so much time for *Nagato* steaming in the rear of the formation to receive an order that impatience prevailed for more than one hour until she finally joined the Main Body. From about 1015 the force steamed ahead on course 120° at an increased speed of 20 knots. The prevailing fog was so thick that even the next ship couldn't be seen. Fog beacons couldn't be towed, only searchlights could be used as guide signals. Notwithstanding, the force managed to continue a high-speed run until the following morning.

The situation was far from what would be expected in peacetime. When the fog lifted to some extent, those destroyers which should have been on the starboard bow of the Main Body were often seen to the port bow near the Main Body.

Because of my warning, the relative position of the Main Body to the task force had been arranged to be shortened as much as possible—four hundred miles on N day and two hundred miles after N + 1 day. Contrary to plan, the entirely unexpected thus took place on N − 2 day. Fortunately, the Main Body had advanced by about one day farther than originally planned, mainly because it took less time to refuel than anticipated, and also that higher speed had been mostly used for fear that slower speed would be disadvantageous in submarine operations.

At 0920 we issued an order calling for withdrawal of the tanker train to the northwest, joining of the Second Task Force, and westward moving of the submarine patrol line. Following this, another order was issued calling for Attack Method C against the U.S. fleet, temporarily calling off the Midway and Aleutian landing operations and bombardment on Midway base with elements of the invasion force. All these steps were taken mainly with the aim of attacking the enemy force north of Midway. At that time, we still intended to resume a landing operation on Midway after attacking the enemy force. Accordingly, the landing force was instructed to be in the vicinity of 30° N, 174° E, so that it would not be too far away from the island.

In the meantime, the first report came in from the commander in chief, First Air Fleet, with his flag transferred from *Akagi* to *Nagara,* describing damage to his fleet as well as his intention of withdrawing to the north with all of his forces after attacking the enemy force, position . . . [Ugaki's omission] (received at 0920).

At 0930 a *Hiryu* plane sent in a report that a carrier was on fire, another one at 1136 saying that preparatory formation for charge had been taken, and another one at 1145 that torpedo attacks had been made on an enemy carrier with three direct hits confirmed.

Reports on the enemy situation varied, but it seemed that the enemy force consisted of three *Enterprise* type carriers, two or three converted carriers, five heavy cruisers, and fifteen destroyers, spreading over a large area extending over about one hundred miles from north to south.

[*This was a good estimate. The U.S. combat forces at Midway consisted of three carriers, eight cruisers, and fifteen destroyers. Obviously the Japanese mistook three of the cruisers for "converted carriers."*][16]

At 1500 a report came in saying, "*Hiryu* was hit by bombs and set ablaze. Time, 1430." The only remaining carrier, upon which we had pinned all our hopes, was finally damaged after inflicting damage upon two enemy carriers with single-handed good fighting. Alas!

At about 1536 a report came in from a *Chikuma* shadowing plane that the enemy force started to retire on course of 70° at 20 knots. Sunset time was 1532. The distance between the retiring enemy force and our fast-advancing invasion force was found to be one hundred miles.

Thereupon an order to pursue the enemy rapidly, intending a night engagement, was issued at 1615. Then reports came in one after another saying that *Kaga* sank only ten minutes after the end of *Soryu,* and then *Akagi* was abandoned, etc. We only hoped to pay off these bitter scores by means of the night engagement.

But the task force sent in a report (delivered at 1840 and decoded at 1920) saying: "Five enemy carriers, six cruisers and fifteen destroyers are steaming west at a point so-and-so at 1530. We are withdrawing to the northwest escorting *Hiryu,* speed 18 knots."

Since this action seemed to be passive, we issued an order calling for the commander of the invasion force to take command of the task force. Thereupon the said commander at 2040 ordered the task force to reverse its course immediately and participate in the night engagement which the invasion force would launch from the north.

Again another report came in (delivered at 1950 and decoded at 2210), saying: "The enemy still possesses four carriers (which may include converted ones), which are steaming west with six cruisers and fifteen destroyers. All of our carriers unable to continue fighting. We are going to catch the enemy force with seaplanes tomorrow morning."

Since no fighting spirit was observed in this report and also it was found that after all there was little prospect of materializing the planned night engagement, an order to "close in," giving the movement of the Main Body, was issued at 2115.

At the same time, resumption of the landing operation was finally given up and an order issued calling for designation of new refueling points, gathering the separated forces, and westward movement of the landing force.

Another misfortune fell upon us at night. The Seventh Cruiser Division, withdrawing to the northwest after the bombardment attempt on the island had been suspended, sent in a report which said: "At 2330 a surfaced enemy sub was sighted at 45° from the starboard bow, and while the division was making an emergency simultaneous turn to evade it, *Mogami*, the fourth ship in the column, hit *Mikuma*, the third ship, with her bow. Whether *Mogami* can make way was not yet ascertained, while *Mikuma* has little trouble in making her way. *Mogami* is under escort."

How distressing this is! Our earnest hope at present is to see the force withdraw safely. Then another report came in that *Mogami* was able to make a dead slow speed of 6 knots and was withdrawing due west under escort of *Mikuma* while the first half of the division is moving to join the Main Body. Joining the Main Body doesn't seem to make sense. What is most desired at this crucial moment is to provide escort to the crippled *Mogami* with all available forces.

Thus the distressing day of 5 June came to an end. Don't let another day like this come to us during the course of this war! Let this day be the only one of the greatest failure of my life!

Saturday, 6 June 1942. N − 1 day. Fair in the morning and cloudy in the afternoon. At midnight course was altered to 90°, maintaining a high speed of 20 knots. After dawn, visibility greatly improved, reaching fifty kilometers, with the finest day we have had since the sortie from the Inland Sea. Sunrise time was about 0140. Today was the very time that the First Battleship Division was going to enter enemy waters as the Main Body of our forces. Anticipating enemy air attacks, the strictest alert was maintained.

At midnight the invasion force was sighted to the southeast and course was set at 310° after it joined our force. According to schedule, the task force should have been in our vicinity. As it was not in sight, however, this course was chosen, believing that we had passed it. Later, the task force was found to be steaming forty miles northeast of our force, and course was changed to due north to close in that force before it came in sight and joined our force. It was regretted that a perfect meeting could not be made due to misunderstanding.

At report from the destroyer *Ukikaze*, dispatched at 2330 last night, was decoded at 0240, according to which we learned that *Hiryu* was being abandoned. Another report followed, saying that all the remaining crew of that ship were rescued except its commander and skipper who had remained on board the burning carrier, and she was finally hit by a torpedo under her bridge as the fire on board her showed no sign of abating. Rear Admiral Tamon Yamaguchi, a classmate of mine, and Captain Tomeo Kaku, an aviation expert, were thus lost. It is extremely regrettable.

[Here Ugaki briefly summarized Yamaguchi's career and their own association dating back to cadet days at Eta Jima.]

After *Soryu* went down, *Hiryu,* the only remaining carrier of the air fleet, continued bravely, fighting singlehandedly, and destroyed two enemy carriers, but she too finally went down, her strength exhausted. Sensing his grave responsibility as the commander, he went down with his ship composedly. Nothing could be compared with his supreme spirit, laying down his own life for his responsibility.

[Here, as "a memorial" to his friend, Ugaki recorded the messages Yamaguchi had dispatched during the battle. He also credited Yamaguchi with the Second CV Division's "brilliant achievements" from Pearl Harbor to Midway.

[He also recorded the description of *Hiryu*'s end, which Captain Toshio Abe, commander, Tenth Destroyer Division, had delivered to Watanabe aboard *Yamato*.]

Judging from his personality and character, it is considered certain that, after having seen that all the remaining crew boarded the rescuing destroyer, he composedly killed himself on the bridge amid upshooting flames and smoke.

In the morning a *Hosho* plane searching the rear of the force sighted *Hiryu* drifting, with several survivors on board, and fire still burning. Upon receipt of this report, *Nagara* was instructed to dispose of the ship for sure after rescuing the survivors, but attempts to that end were delayed until the afternoon when planes and the destroyer *Tanikaze* were dispatched to the scene. On her way there, *Tanikaze* was bombed twice and contact with her was lost for a while, causing some concern about her fate, but she managed to keep on course. She arrived at the scene in the evening to search the area, but found no trace of the distressed ship.

The task force, which failed to complete rendezvous from 0500 to 1400, was subjected to enemy air raids three times, with slight damage inflicted on the second half of the Third Battleship Division.

Though shadowing by enemy planes over our force was suspected from the sensitivity of enemy radio, squall-like low clouds set in toward evening, under which evasive action was taken and no actual attack was made upon our force. At 0400 the force reached a point 320 miles northwest of Midway, the closest distance to the island. The enemy attacked the task force, steaming in the near rear of the Main Body, but not the Main Body. Can it be that, after all, the enemy did not discover the Main Body and the invasion force?

Destroyers of the Tenth Destroyer Squadron, which had taken survivors of four carriers on board, came to join the force one after another in the afternoon. We intended to transfer them on board larger ships as soon as possible so that the wounded men might be given available treatment, but that was impossible in the face of the enemy. So an order was issued arranging their allocation to respective battleships and also their transfer at a refueling point tomorrow morning.

As there was still a great fear that the enemy might keep on coming upon us further, however, tomorrow morning's refueling point, set outside the six-hundred-mile circle from the island, had to be shifted to the west by one day's let. Accordingly, it was arranged to transfer the survivors temporarily to *Nagato* and *Mutsu*.

Mikuma and *Mogami,* heading west accompanied by two destroyers of the Eighth Destroyer Division, were attacked by eight B-17s at 0534 and *Mogami* further attacked, but fortunately sustained no damage. The skill of the enemy land-based air force was not at all high.

The Northern Operation Force sent in a cable asking that landing on the Aleutian Islands be carried out as originally planned against yesterday's order calling off the operation for a while. Accordingly, an instruction was issued leaving the execution of the landing operation to the discretion of the commander. Then we received his order to the Northern Operation Force calling for the landing, except for that of the Second Task Force, to be carried out as scheduled.

This morning, however, they changed their minds, for what reason we didn't know yet, and issued an order to suspend the landing operation for a while and reversing the course of all forces to the west. (This cable issued at 0315 was decoded at 0748.)

Without knowing that, we issued an order placing the Second Task Force back under the command of the northern force at 0700. [*The Japanese record of messages shows this dispatch sent at 0959 Japan time—1259 local.*][17] Seemingly encouraged by this move on our part, they decided soon after noon to launch a devil-may-care Aleutian Operation No. 5 Method on N + 1 day. Under what circumstances they reached this decision we can only guess, but an explanation should be made later on.

As the Midway operation was called off, the enemy is expected to strengthen efforts to defend and recapture those northern islands. In order to strengthen the northern force and, when an opportunity presents itself, pay off our scores at Midway, at 2020 we ordered the first half of the Third Battleship Division, Eighth Heavy Cruiser Division, one destroyer division of the Tenth Destroyer Squadron, *Kamikawa Maru, Zuiho,* Fourth Destroyer Division, Thirteenth Submarine Division, and Second Submarine Squadron dispatched to the north as reinforcements. But we arranged that the order should take effect after they had received the necessary refueling.

Sunday, 7 June 1942. Cloudy and foggy. N day, 7 June, finally came. During the two months of April and May, planning and preparations were made with great effort with this day as a goal. Before this target day came, however, the tables had turned entirely and we are now forced to do our utmost to cope with the worst case. This should be kept in mind as a lesson showing that war is not predictable.

When we were heading for tomorrow's refueling point of 33° N and 165° E after passing the original refueling point two miles from the enemy air base, at 1330 a report came in from *Mikuma*, saying, "two enemy carrier-borne planes in sight," and then another one saying, "attacked by six enemy bombers with one hit sustained." Enemy carriers seem to have pursued her. At 0645 she reported, "Attacked by a large number of enemy planes and one seaplane in sight." At 0745 another report came in saying that three seaplanes were shadowing her, which indicated that surface ships were in the nearby area. One bomb also hit *Mogami*, with slight damage sustained, and three enemy planes were shot down. Another report said that at 0800 enemy carriers and surface forces from the nearby area were pursuing them. They were heading for Wake Island, the present position being bearing 30°, 710 miles of Wake Island.

I had been worrying about their withdrawal and only early this morning suggested to staff officers that they had better head for Wake Island. No time must be lost now, so an order was issued to the invasion force plus the Eighth Heavy Cruiser Division to proceed and rescue them.

Leaving the first half of the Third Battleship Division behind, the commander in chief, Second Fleet, led the rest of the force and sped south at 20 knots. This was about 0930. At 1120 *Mogami* sent in a report in plain language saying that several dozen enemy planes had attacked her, with a result that she was hit by two bombs and set on fire, but was able to make way, while *Mikuma* was hit by five bombs and set on fire and stopped at sea. "At 1058 what seem to be enemy ships in sight, and a big explosion took place on *Mikuma* with little prospect of her being recovered." A destroyer division reported that it was rescuing eight survivors. At 1200 ten more planes came to attack them, and *Mikuma* was hit again with resulting big fire, while a bomb hit destroyer *Arashio* at her No. 3 turret, causing a fire. She was being steered by manual steering gears.

The enemy force seems to consist of one or two carriers as a nucleus, with accompanying cruisers. Admittedly, *Mikuma* was already doomed and, furthermore, other ships of the force might be wiped out. Not only that, in the worst case there would be no guarantee that the invasion force itself wouldn't be endangered.

Thereupon a decision was made that the Main Body proceed south with its full strength to prepare for the worst case and at the same time seek an opportunity to destroy the enemy force within air cover from Wake Island. An order to that end was issued accordingly. We realized that we had no alternative under the prevailing circumstances.

The enemy carriers concentrated in the Midway district are considered to be five or six, out of which only two have been destroyed so far. It is reasoned that the enemy still has three or four carriers, including converted ones on hand.

What is the strength of the enemy force coming after ours? It may be safe to assume that it consists of at least one regular carrier, two converted carriers, several destroyers, and cruisers. It is considered highly possible that this enemy force would tenaciously come after our invasion force tomorrow morning after it destroys the second half of the Seventh Heavy Cruiser Division and Eighth Destroyer Division and withdraw to the east for a while. Accordingly, it is considered best to force a close night engagement with the invasion force.

Otherwise, our force will have no choice but to charge into the enemy force with all our strength tomorrow morning, thus dispelling enemy planes each time they came over us and closing in the enemy force for the kill while attempting to destroy the decks of enemy carriers or their engines with all available planes mobilized.

Of course, if and when the enemy force happens to come within the attack range of our Wake Island air base, we would surely be able to see much chance for success, but it is highly doubtful whether it would come as close to the island as we hope.

[*In this Ugaki was correct. Spruance had resolved not to be lured within range of Wake's land-based air power.*][18]

And when we issued a Combined Fleet order, it was based upon a firm determination to take such a risk. An indescribable decision was needed, as we feared that the whole Combined Fleet would be damaged if the decision proved wrong.

At the same time, moving the tanker train south and a new refueling point were ordered because we feared that the invasion force, heading due south at 20 knots and having no seaplane search because of the prevailing fog, was not paying attention to anything other than rescuing the second half of the Seventh Heavy Cruiser Division.

As destroyers of the Third Destroyer Squadron and the Tenth Destroyer Squadron ran short of fuel—less than fifty percent of capacity—two hours before sunset time, it was decided to refuel from battleships as much as possible. Preparations were made accordingly, which took about one hour to complete. Then each column altered its course by 20° to starboard and each ship of the column made a simultaneous turn to starboard before refueling started at 12 knots. Viewed from *Yamato*'s No. 1 bridge, the sea didn't look rough, but actually it was pretty rough, causing considerable rolling and pitching when towing lines were passed to the refueling destroyers. The towing lines with each ship of the First Battleship Division were then broken, so speed was reduced to nine knots to continue refueling.

Darkness had already set in with poor visibility, and intercepted enemy radio activities indicated for certain that enemy subs were in the vicinity. But speed could not be increased and the course could not be altered. Furthermore, the force was disposed in echelon at 40°. It was difficult for the First and Third Battleship Divisions to refuel destroyers sailing alongside them under the circumstances. There was no choice but to refuel with resignation.

Battleships of the Third Battleship Division were still good at this kind of business, so good that they even refueled destroyers in the next turn under the dark of night. After refueling about 150 tons on the average to one destroyer, the refueling operation was suspended at 2030. At 2115 the formation was changed to normal and sped southward at 18 knots. It was a really rare test, indeed.

Since this morning the commander in chief suffered from a stomachache, which did not improve much in spite of treatment by a fleet doctor. This, too, is a source of concern in such a grave moment as this.

At 1225 *Mogami* reported that she was heading due west at 20 knots to lure the enemy toward our Main Force. That *Mogami* with her bow damaged managed to put up such a high speed, it is considered, is partly because her damage control has progressed and also partly because she made a desperate effort to get out of a trap. The commander in chief of the Second Fleet ordered her to change course to 300°.

Learning that an *Enterprise* type carrier [*Yorktown*] with three torpedo hits was adrift north of Midway Island, the *I-168* sub operating in that district was ordered early yesterday morning to sink her, and she sank the carrier at 1040 today.

At that time seven destroyers escorted the enemy carrier. As the said sub was subjected to their concentrated depth charges, she received considerable damage and was unable to submerge. After she retreated northward, she was going to return to the homeland.

Since the northern force issued an order to launch the Aleutian Islands operation on N + 1 day, the force has been advancing on the scene again and made a successful surprise landing on Kiska at 2220. Following that, a landing was successfully made on Attu Island, too. In either case, it seems that there was no enemy resistance.

Monday, 8 June 1942. From early morning, the invasion force made an air search to the southeast, but obtained no information about the enemy. The damaged *Mogami* and the Eighth Destroyer Division managed to join the rescuing force after they steamed west ahead of the invasion force. Despite their being considered doomed for a while, they managed to be saved with only the sacrifice of *Mikuma*.

Mogami had collided with *Mikuma* while evading an enemy sub, and was unable to move, but later managed to put up 20 knots after her damage had been repaired successfully. Though *Mikuma* was not damaged and was escorting the damaged *Mogami*, enemy attacks unfortunately sank her as a sacrifice for *Mogami*. The fate of both ships should be called a strange affinity, and also they displayed a beautiful relationship as comrade ships.

The enemy task force seems to have withdrawn from the scene since last evening, for search planes dispatched from Wake Island base obtained no information about the enemy. As we had no choice but to give up our intention of launching an all-out counterattack with the whole Combined Fleet, it was decided to secure the landing area with the northern force to be reinforced, thus trying to reduce enemy power at an opportune time, while the other forces would withdraw to the homeland hoping to make another try. Respective orders and instructions were issued accordingly (at after 2200).

At the same time we planned to form a diversion force with the first half of the Fifth Cruiser Division, one destroyer division, and one tanker, and have it dispatch false radio messages, using the same frequency as the task force and the Main Body, to the west, south, and east of Wake Island, with the hope of luring an enemy task force to the Midway district, while trying to attack it with our submarine and air force. Whether this attempt would work out is quite doubtful; however, we decided to try it as there was no other feasible way left for us at this moment.

Since Monday the Main Body headed southwest and gradually closed in on the designated refueling point. The invasion force followed suit from the rear. An occasional squall came in with visibility changing.

As *Yamato* and *Hiei* detected by sound-detecting devices to port what seemed to be an enemy sub after sunset, course was changed to evade it, and after dark course was changed again by 30° to port before returning to normal at midnight.

Tuesday, 9 June 1942. At midnight a 60° turn to starboard was made in two turns of 30° each. In the first turn, destroyer *Isonami* of the Third Destroyer Squadron, in the screen position for the First Battleship Division, collided with her starboard bow at the mid port of *Uranami*, also in the screen position. Though the incident took place a very short distance ahead of our force, nothing could be done about it.

Despite repeated warnings issued against turning movements of screen destroyers since the sortie, this deplorable incident took place. Caution should be taken against such incidents during an operation, as in this case and the case of *Mogami* and *Mikuma*.

The squadron flagship *Sendai* was left on the scene to take good care of them. Destroyer *Uranami* received damage to her funnel part, thus restricting the use of her boilers, but was able to make 24 knots. On the other hand, destroyer *Isonami*'s bow was chopped off by more than one meter, so that she could manage to make only 11 knots.

Instructions were issued concerning a movement of the diversion force and its operations policy. We fear that enemy subs may ambush us on our return voyage to the homeland, so we plan to restrict transmission of radio messages, but it seems unavoidable that, as the flagship of the Combined Fleet, we have left some smell on the way all the time.

Previously, it had been planned to have one of the screen destroyers transmit radio messages on our behalf from elsewhere after those messages were delivered to her, but so far there has been no chance of taking this step.

In the afternoon the invasion force joined us, but it consisted of only the first half of the Fourth Cruiser Division, the flagship of the Fourth Destroyer Squadron, and one destroyer division, the rest of the force being dispersed elsewhere.

We learned that the commander in chief's stomachache after all came from roundworms. His taking medicine against them got rid of the trouble, much to our joy.

Wednesday, 10 June 1942. Fine. Changed into summer uniform from today. Officers and men in summer shorts looked cool, but I still wear my winter uniform. Officers of captain and above seemingly hesitate to put on such summer uniforms.

The weather is fine today and the sea calm, making us feel very good. But this is not because of the weather and uniform; it is mainly because the battle situation has quieted. On the other hand, enemy activities in the northern district have gradually become brisk. How to secure that area is an immediate problem and also how to reduce the enemy strength there. I prayed for good fighting there in spite of the troublesome fog.

The most imperative problem at present is how to rehabilitate the hard-hit carrier-borne air force. Since we saw the need of meeting with the First Air Fleet's headquarters, we called *Nagara* in near *Yamato* and requested its staff to come on board the flagship. Those who came aboard after 0800 were Chief of Staff Kusaka, with minor wounds on his leg, Senior Staff Officer [Captain Tamotsu] Oishi, Air Staff Officer Genda, and the fleet secretary. They all had their winter uniforms on and seemed considerably exhausted.

Their first words uttered at the very moment we met: "I don't know what to say except to offer the utmost apologies." Naturally, they should do so.

After coming down to the chief's cabin, the chief of staff and senior staff officer reported. Kusaka said, "Admittedly, we are not in a position to come back alive shamelessly after having made such a blunder, but we have come back only to pay off the scores same day, so I beg you from the bottom of my heart to give us such a chance in the future."

To this, the commander in chief briefly but strongly said, "All right." (Their honest words, brief though they were, contained as much expression as a million words.)

Causes for the current failure, as summed up from Kusaka's reporting, are as follows. (Reference should be made to my observations described in the entry of the 5th.)

1. Rendezvous with refueling tankers could not be made smoothly. So, on the day preceding a high-speed run, a long-wave radio had to be transmitted because of the prevailing thick fog.

(Lesson: Radio transmission at a short distance from an enemy force is a most risky business. Even though its power is minimized so that it doesn't reach far, the said radio transmission was eventually intercepted by the Main Body.)

[*In fact, the United States did not intercept Nagumo's signal, so it played no part in the defeat. It is worth noting that at the Midway table-top maneuvers held on 24 May 1942, Ugaki had specifically authorized such messages when necessary to maintain "coordination among forces."*][19]

2. Searches on the flanks of our force were made with seaplanes of the Eighth Heavy Cruiser Division and bombers equipped with additional fuel tanks, but their departures were arranged to be almost simultaneous with that of the attack force so that they would not miss the area near the force because of the darkness before dawn. It was on its return leg that it discovered an enemy force, thus sighting the enemy task force belatedly.

(Lesson: As many search planes as possible should be dispatched as soon as possible. The area near our force should be covered with other planes after dawn.)

3. Each carrier prepared the first wave and the second wave—the first wave for attacks on the enemy base and the second for attacks on enemy vessels—so that all of them were at the same time put in confusion by

replacing fighters and recovering returning planes, and the enemy attacked before they could launch the second attack planes.

(Lesson: Four carriers should be divided into two groups, one prepared for the first wave attack with two carriers and another ready to launch its attack planes upon immediate notice with the other two carriers. It is advantageous to allocate another carrier exclusively for interceptors.)

Chief of Staff Kusaka remarked, "Since my appointment to the present post, training of the fleet has been based upon the principle that all strength be concentrated in one stroke after sufficient reconnaissance—and with success in all engagements. Therefore, I had no idea of changing this principle on the way."

4. After our attack planes took off, the carrier force was attacked by more than a dozen enemy land-based torpedo bombers, which were evaded and shot down, without our sustaining any damage, but it was dangerous. Then it was considered necessary to direct the second wave immediately to the enemy base. Torpedo bombers of the second wave were being reequipped into bombers when a report of sighting an enemy task force came in. Thus confusion and delay of actions ensued.

(Lesson: Searches to the flanks should be made as soon as possible, while reequipping of weapons should not be done prematurely until the nonexistence of an enemy force is confirmed. This defeat might be remedied to some extent by dividing carriers into mission groups.)

5. When a report of sighting an enemy task force came in, it was thought that our attack force without fighters would sustain heavy damage with little prospect of success, in view of the Coral Sea battle. Therefore, they planned to wait for the return of the first wave's fighters so that they might escort the second wave after refueling. Thus precious time was wasted.

(Lesson: An attack with escorting fighters is, of course, more desirable, but attack planes alone are able to inflict considerable damage upon an enemy. Especially, an enemy task force was sighted very close to our force. At a time when we will beat or be beaten, no time should be lost in indecision. Furthermore, a quick decision is all the more needed when there is danger that our damage would be doubled, having many planes ready for another attack prepared on a carrier.)

6. That we had disadvantage of too much concentration. (This is a view the commander in chief expressed on the 14th.) [*This parenthetical note, written in the margin, was evidently added at a later date.*]

All in all, we can't help concluding that the main cause for the defeat was that we had become conceited because of past success and lacked studies of the means and steps to be taken in case an enemy air force should appear on a flank while our force was launching an attack on one target—something which had worried me greatly and to which I invited their attention repeatedly—and, furthermore, failed to make a quick decision, still driven by a greedy motive of seeking ways and means even at the most crucial moment. (Reference should be made to the entry of the 5th.)

This is a matter for the utmost regret! Besides, this is not a natural calamity, but a result of human deeds. How can we do without caution and reflection? Grumbling is no use at all at this moment, however. I am writing this only hoping to make use of these bitter lessons in the future.

To Chief of Staff Kusaka I said, "As the Combined Fleet headquarters, we realize our own fault, for which we extend our regrets to the First Air Fleet. But this present setback has not made us at all pessimistic. We still intend to try the Midway operation again and also to carry out the southern operation. Our immediate problem is to supplement sufficient strength to the north to prepare for an expected enemy move there, thus seeking an opportunity to pay off our scores. Above all, how to rehabilitate the fleet air force is imperative at this moment, so we asked you to come aboard to talk over that matter with us." Then it was arranged to have separate talks on respective levels.

Kusaka said that when the First Air Fleet was about to transfer from the burning *Akagi* to *Nagara,* Commander in Chief Nagumo at first was unwilling, so Kusaka urged him, saying that he was responsible to fight to the end as long as his last man was still fighting, and he finally left the ship almost as if pulled by his men.

He also revealed his inner grief, saying that he was thinking various things, since all of the four carriers were lost with the division commander and all skippers except *Akagi*'s killed in action. So I tried hard to console him and explained to him practically how the defeat had not discouraged the Combined Fleet headquarters. After handing him consolation gifts and Y2,000, I let him and the others go back to *Nagara* in the afternoon.

When beaten by such a severe blow, everybody should feel deep grief. What to do with one's own life is naturally one's own concern, and especially so with those who have higher responsibilities. There is a great difference between those of a chief of staff and above and those of ordinary staff officers. I, as a man fighting at the battle front, have already made up my mind what to do in such a case. I can't help having sympathy for him, after thinking things over. One must not make a mistake in choosing between the overall philosophy versus the Bushido view.

After they transfered to *Nagara,* we let her, with two accompanying destroyers, go back to Kure ahead of the other forces.

Immediately after sunset, an escort plane dropped a bomb at a point bearing 30° and one hundred miles from Minami-Torishima, so we let two destroyers attack the suspected sub, while the fleet took an evasive movement to the north. When the fleet resumed normal course with a simultaneous 30° turn to port after running on the evasive course for a while, two torpedo tracks were sighted coming down from a point bearing 38° to port of and 2,800 meters from *Yamato*. The force immediately made an emergency turn to port so that they might pass by to port of the force. Though their tracks seemed to be rather feeble, nobody doubted them at that time. *Yamato* fired a total of six rounds of the secondary battery and the antiaircraft guns as a warning.

After darkness set in, course was changed to 300°, which was returned to normal 270° after midnight to head for the designated position for tomorrow morning.

[Thursday, 11 June through Saturday, 13 June, the Main Body continued toward the homeland uneventfully, except for the usual "fuss about enemy subs."

[On Sunday, 14 June, although hampered by rain and fog, the Main Body finally entered Hiroshima Bay and reached Hashira Jima anchorage at 1900.]

Wheat crops on the islands, which were turning yellow at the time of sortie, had been harvested, and farms on the islands were awaiting the planting of sweet potatoes. Only seventeen days have elapsed since the sortie, yet quite a change has taken place in the surroundings. It is somewhat dreary that the number of our ships seeing this changed scenery has been reduced.

Thinking back, this current move turned out to be a series of hardships. Five warships were lost and the Midway landing operation given up, while all the way, going and returning, we were troubled by bad weather!!!

What's the matter? Fog was the main enemy.
On both ways, go and return.

After 2000 Commander in Chief First Air Fleet Nagumo came on board to report. Though he was asked to come tomorrow, actually he came on board as the ship cast anchor. I think he was right to do so.

How comfortable it is to have pajamas on after having worn a uniform for a long time! In retrospect, I think I have endured hardships well and also have done what I should have done. These thoughts give me some consolation.

Monday, 15 June 1942. Fair. I used a pen for writing this diary while at sea, as it was inconvenient to use a writing brush and Chinese ink in a small room below the bridge. Now facing the desk in my own cabin, I deeply feel the pleasure of writing with a brush.

At 0900 we assembled the skippers of the First Battleship Division,

Chiyoda, and CVL *Hosho* to hear their reports of the operation. All of them had been unscathed through these movements and so were the hulls, armament, and engines. I appreciated the skippers' efforts to get through the fairly daring maneuvers. *Hosho* should be commended, too, for completing her duty with a small number of planes in the face of bad weather.

The commanders in chief of the Second Fleet and First Air Fleet, their chiefs of staff, and commanders of the Third, Fourth, and Tenth Destroyer Squadrons, and Eleventh Seaplane Tender Division assembled from 1330. We received the reports and also conferred with them on future policy.

Leaving the ship at 1630, I went to see the wounded of this operation on board the hospital ships *Mikawa Maru* and *Takasago Maru.* The former had 280 and the latter 338, and they were to leave here tomorrow morning for Kure and Sasebo to be hospitalized ashore. I was sorry for them and prayed for their quick recovery.

I had much mail after a long time. I was very sad to hear about the death of Ellie, my pet dog. She lost her appetite for a few days and died on the 2nd in spite of the care of a vet and shots by Hiromitsu. This happened while I was away at sea. She was buried beside her mother in the outer garden, the letter says. I remember she was eight years old. I wonder when I shall be able to visit her grave.

Tuesday, 16 June 1942. Fair. After hoisting the ensign, I called in a barber and had my hair cut very short, parting with the custom of longer hair since the fourth year of my lieutenancy. The commander in chief remarked at lunch, "I see a change in your hair, has it become too much of a bother?" I answered, "Well, it's because of the death of my dearest dog." "When? Not on the fifth?" he further asked. "A little before, on the second," I replied. Everybody looked at me. I did not feel myself changed, maybe because I could not see it.

Well, herewith I write down the real reason for my doing so. Originally I thought of having it cut on the occasion of the outbreak of the war last winter, but it seemed a bit premature. Thinking I should have to commit *hara kiri* or become a monk if defeated, I decided to wait.

Now this Midway operation turned out to be a failure, to my greatest regret, and I was firmly determined to start over again. I want to show this determination by my appearance, as well as expressing my sorrow for Ellie's death. Another reason is the expected heat inside the steel ship.

I wrapped the hair in a piece of paper, ostensibly to be dedicated to Ellie's soul, but it may be used as a memento of me when I die.

[That afternoon several naval VIPs from Tokyo visited *Yamato.* Vice

Admiral Ito, vice chief of the Naval General Staff, relayed a message from his chief that the emperor was not too concerned about the recent defeat; such things were to be expected in war. They were to keep up their morale and try again. Ugaki didn't know how true it was that the emperor was not too worried, but he was "overwhelmed with trepidation."

[On Wednesday, 17 June, Ugaki's classmate Rear Admiral Matsuyama, on his way to the South Seas, paid him a visit. Ugaki wished him "good fighting and luck." Ugaki had finished the tasks which had accumulated, and was "ready to rally again."

[On Thursday, 18 June, Ugaki was back at his desk, with over eighty personnel evaluation reports to prepare.

[Ugaki spent Friday, 19 June, doing nothing, although he had plenty to do. He "just spent the day."]

Saturday, 20 June 1942. Cloudy, light rain. Chief of the Second Bureau of the General Staff Rear Admiral [Yoshio] Suzuki, chief of the General Affairs Bureau of the Aeronautical Department Rear Admiral Onishi, Rear Admiral [Shipbuilding Iwakichi] Ezaki, and many others from the Naval General Staff, Ship Administration Department, and Aeronautical Department came on board at 1000. A conference was held on board *Yamato* from 1300 to study measures for improving carriers based upon the damages sustained in the last battle. Kusaka, chief of staff, First Air Fleet, presided. Detailed reports and lessons by survivors of *Akagi, Kaga, Hiryu,* and *Soryu* were so minute and enthusiastic that their statements alone did not finish before 2200.

Sunday, 21 June 1942. Cloudy. We resumed yesterday's conference from 0800 with limited attendance. Discussions mainly focused on the problem of carriers to be constructed in the future. Whether to be converted or newly built, there were no end of requests, and it seemed difficult to picture such a carrier however hard we tried.

Those four sunken ships were of almost the same construction and under the same conditions. They had to be abandoned, as fire spread out inside the ships, after being attacked with the most suitable weapons to bring about this condition. It is the first requisite to prevent such fires that even a match can easily cause. If this alone is done, fire will not result in dooming the ships. This point should be emphasized in refitting and new construction. All the statements of the lessons can be boiled down to this point.

But if the enemy employs the same torpedo attack tactics as we do, adopts large type antipersonnel bombs, or starts using rocket bombs as already used by the Germans and Italians, the situation will be entirely different. In such cases, a different view will be advocated. So the views expressed herein should not be considered as permanent ones.

Also, it is wrong to regard the carriers as useless unless they are re-modeled. The weak ships should be used as such, and we must be prepared to make sacrifices at certain times.

What we need at present is numbers, and no choice remains in this respect. The most essential thing at present is to prevent a fire caused by a single enemy shell or a bomb from induced ignition of our own bombs, torpedoes, or oil, which might doom the ship.

Our present shipbuilding program must proceed, adding necessary modifications to that end. We have no time to waste in discussions and conferences, even if they were not useless.

The commander in chief expressed these views when he addressed the conferees, but I further stressed it to important participants in the conference.

[After the conference, the engineer staff officer of the Second Carrier Division gave Ugaki an eyewitness account of the ceremony of leaving *Hiryu,* while Yamaguchi and the carrier's skipper, Captain Tomeo Kaku, remained behind. Ugaki also had a few kind words for the other two lost skippers, captains Jisaku Okada of *Kaga* and Ryusaku Yanagimoto of *Soryu.*

[On Monday, 22 June, a friend sent Ugaki eight shotguns with plenty of ammunition. The admiral was not sure of living until "the next shooting season." He was worried over Yamamoto, who "seemed to be brooding over something and losing spirit." But Ugaki did not feel close enough to the commander in chief to inquire as to the reason.

[Tuesday, 23 June, found Ugaki trying to catch up on his corres-pondence. That evening Rear Admiral Kurita, commander, Seventh Heavy Cruiser Division, came to the flagship and reported on the activities of his outfit in the Midway engagement.

[On Wednesday, 24 June, Ugaki tackled "the nuisance work of prepar-ing personnel evaluation papers" in a temperature barely under 90°. The successful test of a "recently perfected antiaircraft shell" cheered him up a bit.]

Thursday, 25 June, 1942. Rain. I was worried for a moment that a fleet plane might crash against a hill owing to the bad weather yesterday, but two staff officers, Miwa and Fujii, wisely took the train and came back this morning. We heard their report in the afternoon. We discovered that our views on future operations were not entirely in accord with those of the high command. We shall have to study them further. But an accord was generally reached on the reorganization issue.

In the European theater, Germany is involved in many weak points, but fortunately the situation is favorable at Kharkov, Sebastopol, and North Africa, which may cover these points. I anxiously hope so.

A rumor of Anglo-German peace talks is reportedly prevalent. I wonder if it is really true. Peace at this stage means a return of everything to prewar conditions. (They may give us oil in the Dutch East Indies.) Though this is not the time yet, we should pay attention to the fact that such a movement exists, while carrying out operations without giving it consideration.

[Ugaki had nothing to say about Friday, 26 June, other than noting that the weather was "partly fair."

[The navy minister, Admiral Shimada, visited *Yamato* on Saturday, 27 June. He came to discuss the navy's organization and "the reshuffle of flag officers." Yamamoto later passed on to Ugaki the meat of his conversation with Shimada. The latter had been received in audience when he reassured the emperor that the morale of the fleet had not been affected. The emperor said, "Tell the commander in chief to make further efforts." As usual, Ugaki was "deeply moved by His Majesty's consideration."

[Shimada left the next day, Sunday, 28 June, and touched Ugaki by inquiring about his family. This was typical of Shimada. As Ugaki noted, "His kindness as a superior touches the hearts of the men under him."]

Monday, 29 June 1942. Cloudy, later rain. A long-pending problem of additional payment for personnel serving in the fleet has been settled at last. Effective from 1 June, the new system gives more benefit to lower rank persons than to higher ranks. I shall be happy if this will make the life of petty officers and men easier.

Tuesday, 30 June 1942. Rain. Enemy activities were observed in the northeast coast of Australia or to the north. It is about time that the enemy starts taking advantage of his small success. I so warned the staff and, at the same time, ordered them to make a study of defense in general on this occasion.

At night a report came in that two hundred enemy troops with mortars attacked our garrison force at Saramaua from the north and the south at 0200. They were repulsed after two hours of hard fighting. Two float planes chased them after sunrise and inflicted fairly big damage on them.

More care should be taken to the north, south, and the center on this occasion. His independence day is the 4th of July.

Wednesday, 1 July 1942. Cloudy. Captain Nakase, chief of the First Section of the Personnel Bureau, came in the morning. He was ordered to come here in haste to hear the opinion of the commander in chief, Combined Fleet, prior to the final decision to be made by the navy minister on the pending problem of double promotions for those who died in the Pearl Harbor attack.

He outlined the proposal to us. The commander in chief had no objection to it, but he wanted me to ask the opinions of the staff. Accordingly, after discussions I stated the following as the opinion of the commander in chief:

We had done all we could and we thought the issue had been left to the discretion of the navy minister, who had the authority. But if we were further asked to express our views on the issue, ours were as follows: We consider the case of a covering fighter crashing into the ground while strafing as being hit. We could not believe it was due to the unskilled handling of the plane, as the pilot was an especially superior chief petty officer. Moreover, the daring spirit of not fearing to hit the ground was necessary in war. The double promotion should be given to him.

On the other hand, those who failed to return after all [*i.e., after the fighting was over*] deserved to be given the single promotion, as they must have lost their bearings. How to deal with the one killed on the plane after torpedoing and the two who became separated and missed making rendezvous after strafing, we left to the discretion of the navy minister. The latter two might be considered as possibly those who were later killed by American women with stones after landing on Niihau Island.

[*Only one Japanese landed on Niihau. After he had terrorized the unarmed islanders for about a week, he was killed by a native man. A resident Japanese who had joined the flier shot himself.*[20]

[Ugaki made no entry for Thursday, 2 July. The next day, Friday, 3 July 1942, the flagship participated in training in sound detection of torpedoes. "A nationwide warning was issued at 1900 as a precautionary measure."]

Saturday, 4 July 1942. Fair. At about 1000 a patrol boat sighted an enemylike carrier and two cruisers at a point three hundred miles bearing 200° of Jaluit on course 90° with speed 16 knots. Caution and attack were ordered the South Seas Force, Submarine Force, and the Land-based Air Force.

Staff Officer Miwa went up to Tokyo in the afternoon for consultation about the operation.

Sunday, 5 July 1942. Fair. Yesterday's enemy to the south of Jaluit turned out to be a false [report] after all, due to insufficient reconnaissance by the flying boat.

On the other hand, while *Chiyoda* was unloading at Kiska yesterday, an enemy submarine attacked the Eighteenth Destroyer Division in her escort outside the harbor at 0300. *Arare* was sunk and two others were damaged. It was extremely careless of them.

[The U.S. submarine *Growler* sank *Arare* and damaged *Kasumi* and *Shiranuhi.*][21]

Monday, 6 July 1942. Fair. I accompanied the commander in chief to the Navy Club at 0900 and heard the report of Rear Admiral Daigo, commander, Fifth Submarine Squadron. The squadron is going to be disbanded shortly and he will be assigned to the Naval General Staff.

Tuesday, 7 July 1942. Fair. This is the fifth anniversary of the outbreak of the China Incident. What a long time!

Yamato left Kure at 1300 and, carrying out antisub sound detection on the way, arrived at Hashira Jima anchorage at 1600.

The chief of staff, First Fleet, came to consult us on the movements of his fleet, as its Commander in Chief Takasu was going to be transfered to the Naval General Staff on the 14th.

Wednesday, 8 July 1942. Fair. As Vice Admiral Kurita was slated to be appointed commander, Third Battleship Division, he came to confer with us on turning over the command and other matters. Kusaka, chief of staff, First Air Fleet, came on board for briefing, as he is going up to Tokyo for consultation tomorrow.

It has already been seven months since the war started, and yet nothing new such as new weapons, etc., have been invented and furnished up to now. It's most distressing. Improvements and remodelings are all we're doing.

Since the outbreak of the European war, an organization has been set up to study war lessons. After this war started, many civilian technicians were included in the setup. But I can't help wondering what they're doing. Isn't there a need for us, who are actually using the weapons, to make requests to promote their studies?

The enemy of today is indeed aircraft. The effective range of an antiaircraft gun is less than eight thousand meters. If we could shoot down enemy planes before they reach their target by utilizing radar and using shrapnel shells with a faster firing rate, it would render the enemy harmless and prevent useless waste and loss. In such a case, couldn't the world situation be completely changed? Furthermore, if the complete detection of submarines is perfected, we would be invincible. Nothing is more urgently needed today than new ideas and devices. Something must be done by all means.

Thursday, 9 July 1942. Fair. The second section of the Third Battleship Division left for Kure and the first section of the First Battleship Division for firing practice.

I've finally finished writing the personal evaluation papers. That was some work!

Staff Officer Miwa returned from Tokyo in the evening with a new operational policy. The postponement of the New Caledonia, Fiji, and Samoa operations is agreeable, but the proposed positive operation in the western Indian Ocean is a matter of great importance. I can't approve it until I can be quite sure of its success after careful study.

[Ugaki made no entry for Friday, 10 July, beyond noting that the weather was "fair."]

Saturday, 11 July 1942. Fair. If this weather keeps on and winds do not blow, this year's rice crops will be really excellent. If the crop is increased by thirty percent, the people will be a little happier.

Vice Admiral [Naokuni] Nomura and Rear Admiral Abe sent in telegrams about the plans of Germany and Italy, respectively. Taking advantage of the favorable situation, they are going to attack Alexandria first simultaneously with an invasion of Malta.

Moreover, the shortage of fuel oil in Italy is a sad fact in time of war. They are said to be transporting 1,500 tons of oil by rail and refueling the warships, but only a part of them can move with it. We can't hope for the Italian navy's activities under such circumstances.

The Germans aren't advancing much farther north from Moscow. After breaking through its south, an element headed for the south of the Volga and another to the east. This is to cut off the Soviet industrial area from coal-, oil-, and foodstuff-producing countries. The food shortage in Germany is so acute now that they must make contact with the Far East to alleviate the situation. To that end they are reportedly aiming an eastward advance through Turkey with the final object of capturing the Caucasus.

If and when the situation in the Near and Middle East turns favorable, we shall have to advance westward in response, too. Attempts to reduce enemy strength and raid enemy sea traffic in the western Indian Ocean, which Italy craves, may be done by submarine, but it involves much risk to employ surface vessels in those attempts. I think we should capture Ceylon first, as ordinary tactics warrant.

This morning a telegram came in from the navy minister addressed to the commanders in chief of the Combined Fleet and China Area Fleet to send their chiefs of staff to the ministry by 1200 on the 17th. The main business is said to be concerned with the revision of the navy system. I must submit further requests on this occasion.

Sunday, 12 July 1942. Fair. Those reinforcements dispatched to the northern force started to come back one after another to Hashira Jima anchorage from this evening.

Monday, 13 July 1942. Fair. In the morning we heard the reports of Rear Admiral Takagi, commander, Fifth Heavy Cruiser Division, and Rear Admiral Kakuta, commander, Fourth Carrier Division. The result of their transmitting fake radios for diversion purposes was not effective.

Apart from June, the weather in the north sea was bad. It was foggy almost every day in July, unfit for any flight. No use employing a large force there!

[On Tuesday, 14 July 1942, Ugaki received a medal and citation awarding him "the Third Order of the Golden Kite and the Second Order of the Rising Sun with double rays," plus seven thousand yen, for his services in the China Incident. Ugaki was suitably grateful to the emperor, and expressed his intention of showing them to his wife's spirit when he reached home two days hence.]

Tomoko's spirit must be watching me all the time to share my joy with me. I can now show them to her before I wear them. Am I not fortunate?

The Third Fleet has been newly established, and Nagumo, commander in chief, First Air Fleet, has been appointed its commander in chief. He came on board to pay his respects, together with his new Chief of Staff Kusaka and other new staff officers.

Rear Admiral Hara, commander, Fifth CV Division, was appointed to command the Eighth Heavy Cruiser Division and came to report. We exchanged views frankly on the use of carriers. His views were mostly quite good, and what he said was generally in accord with mine. I encouraged him to express his views freely in the future in the fleet, taking the place of the late Rear Admiral Yamaguchi. He agreed heartily.

I heard the interim report on studies of the Indian Ocean operation at night, and I told the staff my intentions.

Wednesday, 15 July 1942. Fair. We conferred on operational policy this morning, continued from last night.

The policy against India which Staff Officer Fujii drafted upon my order was completed. After running through it, I ordered him to make copies of it.

[On Thursday, 16 July, Ugaki flew to Tokyo with the chiefs of staff of the Second and Third fleets. Bad weather forced a landing at Oi airfield, so they had to take a train for Yokohama. There Ugaki's son met him and took him home. "I missed Ellie's welcome, but I found a cute kitten instead."]

Friday, 17 July 1942. Fair and cloudy. Leaving home at 0930 by a car sent by the navy ministry, I went to the ministry and saw the minister, chief, and vice chief of the Naval General Staff. I told them our views first.

The commanders in chief of the naval stations and bases, the chief of staff, China Area Fleet, and we, the four chiefs of staff from the Combined Fleet, were invited to lunch by the minister at his official residence at 1230. From 1330, following an address by the minister, Captain Takata outlined the revision of the navy's system. After that, Captain [Kanei] Chudo, a section chief [intelligence] of the Naval General Staff, briefed us on the world situation in general. We left there after a little conversation.

Saturday, 18 July 1942. Fair. I saw Rear Admiral Onishi, chief of the General Affairs Bureau, and Vice Admiral Katagiri, chief of the Aeronautical Department. After hearing the condition of aircraft production, I expressed our wish to encourage them. Our main requirements were:

1. Increased supply of aircraft
2. New inventions and supply of weapons
3. Future policy of directing the war (execution of operations against India)

I believe I have impressed them a good deal.

[On Sunday, 19 July, Ugaki flew back to the flagship. There he heard a report from Captain Kaku Harada, skipper of *Chiyoda*, who had returned from Kiska. On the night of Monday, 20 July, submarines practiced attacking the anchorage. Ugaki made no entry for Tuesday, 21 July, beyond the notation "fair."]

Wednesday, 22 July 1942. Fair. An operational force of the Seventeenth Army seemed to have landed on Gona under the protection of the Eighteenth Division. [*On 21 July 1942, the Japanese landed troops at Gona and Buna on Papua and commenced to march over the Owen Stanley Range with the object of capturing Port Moresby.*][22] An enemy plane found our convoy and reported in plain language. Several planes came to attack the convoy.

Radio intelligence indicated the presence at Moresby of five squadrons of large type planes and seven of medium type. Though there was need to forestall them, so far no attack report came in. Was it because of the foul weather? Or didn't the enemy actually come to attack?

We thought up the plan for directing future operations. But the staff officers seemingly failed to produce any good ideas, probably due to the heat.

The Russo-German war developed in the latter's favor and Rostov is in danger, too. They are marching toward Stalingrad as scheduled. But an invasion of Malta is not getting on as Italy says. In the Alexandria district, too, not much progress has been made, perhaps owing to poor communications in the rear. This may be a war where everything doesn't turn out as expected.

[Thursday, 23 July, was so hot that Ugaki did nothing more warlike than copy "fine passages from a famous old tome." He continued his efforts on Friday, 24 July, broken only by a visit from Vice Admiral Shimizu, newly appointed commander in chief, First Fleet.]

Saturday, 25 July 1942. Fair. Vice Admiral Shimizu, commander in chief, First Fleet, and Vice Admiral Kondo, commander in chief, Second Fleet, were guests of honor at dinner.

According to the judgment of Osaka Naval Base, an enemy submarine in the south of Kitan Strait was supposed to be cooperating with the enemy task force, reporting our movements and weather conditions. But there has been no information yet about the east.

The Germans have entered Rostov, and are now near Stalingrad. I'm very pleased. The activities of these friendly nations are more welcome than ever before.

[Ugaki made no entry for Sunday, 26 July, or Monday, 27 July, beyond noting that the weather was "fair."]

Tuesday, 28 July 1942. Fair. As a staff officer concerned was asked to come to Tokyo on the occasion of concluding the central army and navy agreement on the Moresby operation, we dispatched Staff Officer Watanabe to Yokosuka by a float plane in the afternoon.

Earlier, we had proposed an operation aiming at reducing the enemy strength simultaneously with that operation, but it was rejected due to their placing more importance on the Indian Ocean operation.

I admit the necessity of listening to what the younger people say, but I can't help feeling that they are considering the war too rigidly. They don't seem to know that it depends largely upon momentum and chance.

And then, what are they planning to do in the Indian Ocean? We cannot agree with it readily. Unless we decide the sequence of the India invasion operation right now, we might miss the chance. It worries me to think that the basic principle of directing the war in accordance with new developments has not yet been fixed.

Wednesday, 29 July 1942. Fair. Destroyer *Ikazuchi,* towing destroyer *Arare,* which had been crippled at Kiska, left there for Maizuru. It is rather a difficult attempt.

Thursday, 30 July 1942. Fair. Watanabe returned from Tokyo by plane.

The navy proposed withholding the Chungking operation. The army is said to be in accord with the India operation in principle, but they are saying its time will be next year. And they request a traffic-raiding operation west of Australia. Shame on them! We can't do anything for the time being but take a nap. The United States is said to have known all about our strength disposition in the middle of April. They must have succeeded in decoding, which was the cause of our defeat at Midway.

[*Probably as a result of this conclusion, the Japanese made a major change in their JN 25 code on 1 August 1942.*[23]

[On Friday, 31 July, *Yamato* carried out firing practice, anchoring in Agenosho "after 2100."]

5
The Scene of a Fierce Battle
August–September 1942

WITH AUGUST *the tempo picked up considerably. The long, fierce struggle for Guadalcanal began, necessitating shelving the Indian Ocean project. To be near the scene of action, Yamamoto moved* Yamato *and much of the Main Body to the anchorage at Truk.*

That there was plenty of life left in the Japanese Navy was proved at the battle of Savo Island, one of the worst naval defeats in American history. Later, the carriers Enterprise *and* Saratoga *were badly damaged, and* Wasp *was sunk.*

On the other side, Japan lost the CVL Ryujo *and a number of other warships.* Yamato *herself had a narrow escape from a U.S. submarine, and Ugaki had praise for the Americans who had ventured this action at the very entrance to the anchorage at Truk. He wished Japan's submariners would be equally daring and attack U.S. warships, but oddly enough did not mention the feat of I-15 in torpedoing the battleship* North Carolina, *which had to return to Pearl Harbor for repairs.*

Ugaki was still nervous about the possibility of U.S. raids on the Japanese homeland. Another and more immediate worry was the scarcity of fuel, one of Japan's rationales for starting the war, and destined to be an ever-increasing problem. In some respects Ugaki was pessimistic during this period. He insisted that Guadalcanal would have to be secured by land warfare. On the other hand, he doubted that Moresby could be taken by land. He hoped for an invasion by sea. To his disgust, attempts to take the Milne Bay area on New Guinea failed. Never too enamored of the Japanese Army, Ugaki had his troubles with its representatives in the area, especially the army's habit of changing the date of scheduled operations. And of course there were the usual half-humorous snafus which are such a nuisance at the time and make good stories for the survivors.

Although perhaps other items came to his attention, during August and September Guadalcanal filled Ugaki's thoughts, so much so that he took a field trip to Rabaul to confer with the army officials engaged in this campaign.

September saw the savage battle of the Bloody Ridge on Guadalcanal. As usual when Japan suffered a major setback, Ugaki put down a thoughtful list of what, in his opinion, were its causes.

175

The naval situation at Guadalcanal was rather strange at this time. The Americans controlled the nearby waters by day; the nights belonged to the "Tokyo Express."

[For Saturday, 1 August, and Sunday, 2 August, the hot, fair weather continued. Again *Yamato* sailed out for training and returned to Hashira Jima anchorage at 1500 on Saturday. Throughout this exercise Ugaki "felt tired. . . . Maybe because of the heat."]

Monday, 3 August 1942. Fair. Captain [Kaoru] Arima, skipper of *Musashi,* came in the morning. Her official trials have been completed with results slightly better then those of *Yamato*. Commissioned on the 5th, she will come to Hashira Jima on the 10th.

Tuesday, 4 August 1942. Fair. Low pressure has not developed in the Yangtze Valley due to high pressure covering the south of the Japanese homeland, and the scorching weather has lasted for thirty-two days. It is record-breaking.

Staff Officer [Commander Masahiko] Asada of the Eleventh Air Fleet has been on board since yesterday for briefings. This morning he explained the situation of the Moresby operation as well as the strength disposition.

Our force has already advanced as far as Kokoda, and an amphibious unit is seeking to advance by sea in concert with the advance on land. They may encounter the enemy, but we can see the prospect of an invasion of Moresby. As the land-based air force in the area has been reinforced, I think a small loss will not discourage them.

Nobody has supplied a good plan for the next-stage operation for a long time, but the general trend has become more aware of the importance of destroying British sea power instead of emphasizing the traffic-raiding operation. I am quite agreeable to this trend, but the plan is still incomplete. It is desired that all the staff officers, including the senior staff officer, study it further.

As we have something to discuss with the Naval General Staff too, we decided to send staff officers Arima and Sasaki to Tokyo by plane early tomorrow morning, after briefing them on our outline policy.

[Wednesday, 5 August, passed with no comment from Ugaki beyond "partly fair." Thursday, 6 August, was cloudy. That afternoon Captain Takata of the navy ministry explained certain changes in the navy's officer system to take effect 1 November. "With this, the abolition of the engineer officer system and the pending problem of officers promoted from the ranks will be settled." The change would come about gradually. Ugaki noted that this was the first anniversary of his assignment to *Nagato*.]

Friday, 7 August 1942. Light rain, later fair. At 0520 the staff duty officer brought a report of the enemy attacking Tulagi on a large scale. We called [for] *Yamato's* leaving for Kure early this morning and racked our brains to contemplate countermeasures.

The enemy commenced its air raid and bombardment by battleships and cruisers from 0400, sunrise time there. It commenced landing. It took a considerable time before the enemy strength was made clear. There were one carrier, one battleship, three cruisers, fifteen destroyers, and forty transports. They seem to have made simultaneous landings on Tulagi and Guadalcanal.

At Tulagi all of seven flying boats were bombed and set on fire, while the garrison of seven hundred men fought back well. The last [radio] wave its communication corps transmitted was really tragic. At Guadalcanal the air strip was completed only about yesterday. The garrison there consisted of some twelve hundred, and in addition there are about two thousand laborers. They will not be captured easily, but the situation was unknown as no [radio] wave from that area could be heard.

[*Thus began the long Guadalcanal campaign. Ugaki seriously overestimated the number of transports involved—there were twenty-three, including four AKDs (converted destroyer transports) in the combined Guadalcanal and Tulagi landings. But he underestimated the support ships, which included the carriers* Saratoga, Enterprise, *and* Wasp.][1]

Twenty-seven medium torpedo bombers, eighteen fighters, and nine dive bombers of the Twenty-fifth Air Flotilla sortied at 0755. On the other hand, the Sixth Heavy Cruiser Division sortied at once, while the commander in chief, Eighth Fleet, boarded heavy cruiser *Chokai* in the afternoon and, along with the Eighteenth Light Cruiser Division under his command, headed for the battle area.

[*In the ensuing air engagement, the United States lost eleven F4Fs and one SBD, but saved the transports. The Japanese lost fourteen bombers and two Zeros.*][2]

This enemy employed a huge force, intending to capture that area once and for all. That we failed to discover it until attacked deserves censure as extremely careless. A warning had been issued two days before. Anyway, we were attacked unprepared. Unless we destroy them promptly, they will attempt to recapture Rabaul, not to speak of frustrating our Moresby operation. Our operations in that area will become extremely unfavorable. We should, therefore, make every effort to drive the enemy down first, even by putting off the Indian Ocean operation. We have made necessary arrangements accordingly.

Captain [Itsu] Ishiwara, senior staff officer of the Southwest Area Fleet, came all the way for consultation. The Second Fleet returned from Kure and the Eighth Heavy Cruiser Division from Maizuru.

Saturday, 8 August 1942. Partly fair. Yesterday's air attack on two enemy heavy cruisers was not so effective. We decided on a Combined Fleet operational order and issued it at 0100. It was decided that most of the Second and Third fleets and *Yamato* should sortie. Captain [Toshitane] Takada, senior staff officer of the Third Fleet, arrived last night on board a destroyer for briefing with us.

The Eighth Fleet searched toward Guadalcanal with float planes. They reported two destroyers and two transports outside of Tulagi port and seventeen transports inside. Further, one battleship, four cruisers, seven destroyers and transports were reported to be off the airfield at Guadalcanal.

The garrison on Guadalcanal is still fighting and those on Tulagi are also said to be resisting in trenches. They are enduring splendidly as only our forces can. Hold on as long as even one is alive! Thus they will be able to prevent the enemy from landing and using the airfield, pin down the enemy ships, and make our attack easier. We shall be able to send reinforcements shortly, and these brave men will be able to witness with their own eyes friendly forces destroying the enemy. Anyway, I am very glad to learn that those believed to have already been annihilated were still putting up a fight.

Even if we wished to send some encouraging message to them, there is no way to communicate except by dropping a message tube from a plane. It is regrettable indeed. The Eighth Fleet is going to surprise the enemy in Guadalcanal tonight. Come on, boys! Do your stuff!

Today's torpedo bombers are supposed to employ mostly torpedoes, as we suggested. Due to bad air conditions, we could not directly receive the result of the attack by the Twenty-fifth Air Flotilla, so we ordered retransmission. I believe they must have inflicted a fair damage in the roads.

As enemy activities by a fairly big force were suspected in the north in light of enemy communications yesterday, I warned the chief of staff, Fifth Fleet, to take strict precautions against possible enemy attempts following their attacks on Tulagi. And sure enough, five enemy cruisers and three destroyers attacked Kiska at 1500, bombarded the neighborhood of the base, and withdrew to the south. One of their spotting planes was shot down. Our loss was slight.

Our ordinary and midget submarines were deployed in that area, but the enemy was lucky enough not to be caught by them. We are confident of holding this area unless enemy attacks are made using carriers on a large scale.

The commander in chief, Third Fleet, and his chief of staff came on board after 1400. They were followed by the Eleventh Battleship Division commander, [Vice Admiral] Abe, and the Eighth Heavy Cruiser Division commander, Hara.

Intending to have a briefing of the Combined Fleet, Second and Third fleets on the 10th, I ordered the staff to speed up drafting the principle of directing the operations by that time.

[Sasaki and Arima returned from Tokyo, reporting that most of the fleet's requests in relation to the Indian Ocean and others had been accepted. Ugaki had to tell them that "the Indian Ocean operation was to be shelved for the time being." The Naval General Staff, he learned, "is only concerned with shipping as before."]

Sunday, 9 August 1942. Fair. Yesterday's search sighted no carrier. All the attacks seem concentrated in the Guadalcanal area, with attack results summed up by the reports as follows: two light cruisers and ten transports sunk, one large cruiser set on fire, one medium cruiser seriously damaged and listing heavily, two destroyers and one transport set on fire, and four planes shot down. This should be called a great result.

[*These results, reported by the commander of the Twenty-fifth Air Flotilla, were wildly off. The Japanese aerial counterattack of 8 August scored a hit on destroyer* Jarvis, *and a dive bomber, set afire, deliberately crashed on the transport* George F. Elliot, *leaving her a total loss. The Japanese lost seventeen torpedo bombers, at least two dive bombers, and two Zeros.*][3]

A report from the Eighth Fleet early this morning said that five enemy heavy cruisers were sunk by a sudden night assault. They might have seemed big ones in the darkness of night, but, even so, they were a fair result. Putting them together, we believed that all the warships and half of the transports have been sunk, and the fate of the battle has now been settled. However, according to a search this morning, the following ships were sighted at the Tulagi area in spite of the fog, and there was no sign of their leaving:

Sector C: one large cruiser, three destroyers, and three transports.

Sector D: one light cruiser, four destroyers, and fifteen transports.

Furthermore, a battleship was sighted trailing oil at a point ninety miles southwest of Guadalcanal.

Unless we launch all-out attacks after today, we have to realize that the enemy attempt cannot be frustrated. Besides, we should be aware of the fact that there exists a considerable difference between the recognized result of an attack and the actual one. So I ordered the staff to adjust their judgment on the situation every day in light of the enemy situation and our attack result so as to be ready for any change of plans.

The enemy, which appeared in the Kiska area yesterday, is said to have consisted of two large ships (likely a battleship and a carrier), four heavy cruisers, and ten destroyers.

The enemy force which left Hawaii on the 2nd of this month has been missing ever since. There is a possibility of its attacking the Tokyo Bay area around the 12th.

Furthermore, one or two battleships, two carriers, several cruisers, and over a dozen destroyers are in the Ceylon district. They might launch a surprise attack on the Andaman area. Now that they are active in all directions—from the north, south, east, and west—it is extremely important to counterattack them strongly.

At 1130 the chief code officer brought in a signal from a plane saying, "Enemy battleship is sinking." Later it was discovered that it was not a battleship but an *Achilles* type cruiser of 7,500 tons.

A summary report of the result of the Eighth Fleet's attack last night came in. It said:

> Two heavy cruisers of the *Kent-* or *Australia-* type sunk, two heavy cruisers of the *San Francisco* type sunk, and three of the same type set on fire and supposed to be sinking, as well as four destroyers sunk.
>
> Turret No. 1 of *Chokai* was disabled and the operations room destroyed with thirty-four dead. No. 12 torpedo tube of *Aoba* was disabled.

Other losses were slight.

[*This was the battle of Savo Island—one of the worst defeats in U.S. naval history. Four heavy cruisers and one destroyer were lost, 1270 officers and men killed, with 709 wounded. American losses might have been even worse if Mikawa had followed up his victory and struck troop transports. The Japanese suffered only damage to* Chokai *and* Aoba; *thirty-five were killed, fifty-seven wounded.*]+

As the movements of the Third and Seventh Submarine Squadrons had been slack and slow, we ordered them to annihilate the remnant of the enemy.

We also sent a telegram of encouragement to the commanders in chief, Eleventh Air Fleet and Eighth Fleet, appreciating their hard fighting and asking their further efforts to enlarge their achievements and to swiftly save the garrison now fighting hard all alone.

The Imperial General Headquarters announced at 1530 today the war results since the 7th, and also designated this battle as the battle of the Solomons. Those conceited British and Americans who regard the battles of the Coral Sea and Midway as supreme victories cannot say anything now.

Yesterday, the 8th, was the beginning of autumn in the calendar. The enemy must be feeling the autumn in the fortunes of war. The heat has been reduced with the rain of the other day. I feel much better now.

[Ugaki reported delightedly that, after a "heated speech" by Mohandas K. Gandhi, the National Congress Party of India passed a resolution calling for British forces to evacuate India. Since the British could not comply, "passive resistance" would arise all over India, "and in consequence India will fall into confusion." As the professed leader of East Asia, was Japan ready and able to help the Indians gain independence? If not, wrote Ugaki indignantly, "We are not worthy even as a neighbor, not to speak of as a leader." He hoped and expected that eventually the Indians would turn to Japan.]

Monday, 10 August 1942. Fair. All of the Twenty-fifth Air Flotilla's planes attacked the *Achilles* type cruiser yesterday and did not carry out reconnaissance of the Tulagi and Guadalcanal areas. This is regrettable. Two submarines penetrated the roads last night and saw no ships there. Air reconnaissance confirmed this this morning.

Apparently the enemy, which was severely attacked last night, withdrew by this morning. We have finished off most of the enemy surface ships, especially cruisers, but I regret we missed half of the destroyers and two-thirds of the transports.

Neither submarines nor planes ever reported the situation on land, not seeing that this would be important material in planning our operation. So we ordered them to investigate and report the situation promptly.

An enemy submarine attacked the Sixth Heavy Cruiser Division to the east of Kavieng, New Ireland, this morning, and heavy cruiser *Kako* was lost. [The U.S. submarine *S-44* sank *Kako*.][5] I can't see why *Chokai* and the Sixth Heavy Cruiser Division had to withdraw so far after an attack with slight damage. Maybe there was need to refuel, but I did not think it was so urgent.

They should have expected sub attacks, as the sea around Rabaul and Kavieng was infested with enemy submarines. Fortunately, three hundred survived, including the skipper and executive officer, and were all put ashore on the island.

An operations briefing among the commands of the Second and Third fleets was held from 1400 in the admiral's cabin. The discussion was based on the outline policy drafted by our staff. It ended at 1700.

Tuesday, 11 August 1942. Fair. According to reconnaissance by a fighter, it was attacked with machine-gun fire at Guadalcanal, but our force seemed to be continuing resistance. Many small craft here on the beach, and some of them were moving. The enemy was trying to use our dummy airfield while the real one, located about ten kilometers away, seemed to be quiet.

Several enemy ships were at Tulagi and a fighter was fired on by three antiaircraft guns. That plane must have had its hands full.

As it is essential to get in touch with our garrison force on the island and reinforce it in order to deny the enemy use of the airfield, we so suggested to the chief of staff concerned. It is annoying that communications are being delayed, due to congestion of telegrams at Truk, in addition to bad air conditions in the daytime.

The advance force sorties from Hashira Jima at 1700. *Yamato* left for Kure at 1300. On the way, a signal came in from the garrison in Ambon reporting that one cruiser, several destroyers, four submarines, and two transports were sighted heading west at a point five miles east of Ambon, and planes were ordered to attack. Accordingly, the Seventh Heavy Cruiser Division, Third Destroyer Squadron, and two destroyer divisions on their way from Melgi to Davao were ordered placed temporarily under command of the Southwest Area Fleet, But subsequent reconnaissance did not find the reported enemy.

Wednesday, 12 August 1942. Fair. Leaving the jetty at 0900, I returned on board. Our stay here this time happened to be at an important moment for directing operations. So I had warned the staff not to stay ashore for consecutive days. A fair number of them returned on board.

At about 1430, a report came in that a search plane from the Genzan Air Group that sortied from Misawa base after 1100 sighted an enemy float plane with U.S. markings which had made a forced landing on the sea at a point 490 miles bearing 112° of Cape Shiriya and strafed it. So the Ominato, Tokyo, and Kure areas were alerted.

Supposing the enemy task force was within a three-hundred-mile radius from this point, its position would be 720 miles from Inubosaki at the farthest. If the enemy attempts an attack after dusk, he will probably come tonight. So we requested the Third Fleet to move the fighters of the Second CV Division to the east. Besides the above-mentioned float plane, another one was seen flying in the same area at 1215 with slight differences in distance and bearing. As the existence of an enemy was thus confirmed, we issued an operational order to be on the alert. Furthermore, we also ordered a rapid transfer of the Second CVL Division's planes to the east, a sortie of the available submarines of the First Submarine Squadron, and also dispatched the Second Fleet, sailing off Shikoku this morning, to the east of Chichi Jima.

Thursday, 13 August 1942. Fair. We have been alerted on the second station since one hour before sunrise. On the other hand, we searched hard for the enemy, but found nothing. Shore liberty was permitted in the afternoon, but the alert was not eased.

Some enemies still remained in the Tulagi and Guadalcanal area, but now they are supposed to have been left behind with small craft when the enemy withdrew. Both the Eighth Fleet and Eleventh Air Fleet, therefore, turned out to be bullish.

The most urgent thing at present is to send a troop there to mop up the enemy remnant, rescue the garrison, and repair the airfield. The support force should simultaneously carry out operations as scheduled while invasions of Moresby, Ocean, and Nauru islands should be completed as well as attempting to reduce the enemy strength. I instructed the staff along this line.

Friday, 14 August 1942. Fair. Staff officers Miwa and Watanabe returned from Tokyo last night. They reported there will be a shortage of fuel in November of this year. I hope the Munitions Bureau will prepare so that operations might not be affected by it.

Fukudome, chief of the Operations Bureau, also revealed in a letter his fear of the scarcity of fuel, and wished to see to it that the Indian Ocean operation be made with only fleet tankers. He further hoped that the opinion of deeming the capital ship useless should not be advocated too soon, when nobody knew what would happen in the future, and as it also would affect morale. Finally, he stated that submarines used for the first time in actual war had proved not as successful as in fleet maneuvers, but after all they should be used principally in traffic-raiding operations, as in Germany.

[On Saturday, 15 August, *Yamato* returned to Hashira Jima. Sunday, the 16th, was busy if mostly routine. Ugaki and others inspected *Musashi* and expressed the hope that her crew would train vigorously so that she could be made flagship.

[That afternoon the commander in chief, Third Fleet, and his staff paid a farewell visit. "They sortied at 1800 in the order of Eighth Heavy Cruiser Division, Eleventh Battleship Division, and First CV Division to avenge Midway." Then Rear Admiral Ishizaki, in command of the Eighth Submarine Squadron, reported on the undersea operations in the Indian Ocean and off Africa.

[Ugaki expressed worry about "self-explosion of torpedoes" and hoped that after investigation this could be corrected. Obviously they had "learned something. . . . The result obtained by four submarines and two auxiliary cruisers in this operation was twenty-five ships, of which twenty-three were sunk and two captured."]

Information came from the chief of the Operations Bureau to the effect that the enemy in the Solomons had decided to withdraw. Maybe on account of this our lookout submarines sighted four enemy minesweepers coming to Guadalcanal from the east and also detected an enemy movement near Banicro Island of the Santa Cruz Islands.

It is necessary to prevent this enemy project and destroy others by taking advantage of this opportunity. But the Sixth Heavy Cruiser Division is still some distance away, and I regret that we shall not be able to drive them away tonight.

Monday, 17 August 1942. Light rain. Sortie from Hashira Jima. About two hundred enemy marines landed on Makin in the Gilberts from two submarines after 0300, and our garrison is fighting hard. The commander, Sixth Naval Base Force, ordered a rescue attack, but it is doubtful whether they can hold out.

[*Ugaki's figures were accurate. Two U.S. submarines*—Nautilus *and* Argonaut—*landed 222 marines on Makin, including the famous Second Raiders Battalion under Lieutenant Colonel Evans F. Carlson.*][6]

[Ugaki wondered what the reason was for this move, but, he boasted, "Anyway, such an enemy trick will be nothing to us."

[The main body of the Combined Fleet sortied at 1230 for the Truk area. Before they left port, Ugaki had a letter from Admiral Ito, vice chief of the Naval General Staff, conveying a message from the emperor. His Majesty had said to him, "I hear the major force of the Combined Fleet is going out to the Truk area, where enemy submarines are operating, as seen in the case of the heavy cruiser *Kako*. Of course, there is no need to worry, as competent Yamamoto is commanding."]

As to whence the enemy landed on Makin, some said from a destroyer, while others from submarines. But finally it was found that two hundred marines landed from two submarines. The garrison lost its contact after sending its last telegram, "We shall all die calmly," after 0900. But, according to aircraft reconnaissance, they were reported still fighting hard on the south beach at 1100.

Tuesday, 18 August 1942. Light rain, later fair. At about 1030, the sound of a submarine was reported detected to starboard, and then a torpedo. The fleet was like being handled by a leading seaman on the lookout. We took an urgent evasive movement, but nothing happened.

According to reconnaissance of Makin, the enemy has withdrawn and eleven of the seventy-man garrison remained. The enemy tried to destroy the island, preceding us in attempting a submarine-borne landing. We are already making preparations for that end, too, but I regret they preceded us.

The aim of this operation seemed to be to destroy our eyes at Makin, to defend Ocean and Nauru islands, and regain freedom of movement from that area while at the same time attempting to divert our efforts from the Solomon area. They will make surprise attacks on other islands in this way, and we must never relax.

[*The small Japanese garrison on Makin fought bravely, and nearly all died. This operation was a raid only, with no attempt at occupation.*][7]

A reinforcement of two hundred men was landed on Guadalcanal last night. The enemy attacked a certain lookout post on Tulagi today, and there was also a doubt about the enemy landing a reinforcement from four destroyers the night before last.

[*On 15 August 1942, four U.S. destroyer transports landed two officers and 120 men on Guadalcanal, as well as aviation gas and ammunition.*][8]

The information of the enemy's withdrawal sent from the chief of the Operations Bureau might be an enemy counterstratagem. The enemy does not seem to give up the place easily. And things appear to be getting brisk in that area.

A specially organized unit with six destroyers successfully landed a part of the Ichiki detachment to the east of our position at 0900 without opposition.

[*This was a detachment of 916 men under Colonel Kiyonao Ichiki, the same officer who had been scheduled to command the Midway landing force.*][9]

Wednesday, 19 August 1942. Fair. Enemy radio communications in plain language were frequent as enemy planes detected the movement of our reinforcements to Guadalcanal. The destroyer *Hagikaze* was bombed at Guadalcanal. The stern after turret No. 3 was set on fire and steering rendered impossible. She could still make 6 knots, however, and was to be sent to Truk under protection of a fellow destroyer. [A B-17 from *Espiritu Santo* scored this hit.][10]

With reinforcements on both sides pouring into this area, the fighting there is going to be intensified, as I expected.

Thursday, 20 April 1942. Fair. The sea was absolutely calm, like a pond. *Kasuga Maru*, originally with an inferior speed of 21 knots, could not make more than 20 knots due to a broken spindle of the engine fan. So two fighters were damaged when landing on her because of her insufficient speed. She is managing to fulfill her duty as a carrier.

At 0900 a search plane found one carrier, two or four cruisers, and nine destroyers at a point about 240 miles bearing 130° of Tulagi. It seemed to be heading north with the aim of either supporting Guadalcanal or attacking our reinforcements. In view of this new development, the situation had to be restudied.

[*This sighting was probably Task Force 18 under Rear Admiral Leigh Noyes, consisting of the carrier* Wasp, *three cruisers, and seven destroyers.*][11]

The Eleventh Air Fleet and Eighth Fleet ordered the Sixth Heavy Cruiser Division and the escort force of the Ichiki detachment to retire. This step was appropriate. We ordered the support force to sortie from Truk after finishing refueling and advance to the north of Tulagi.

A report from Guadalcanal after 1400 indicated a probable landing on the air strip by twenty enemy land planes including five fighters. [*On 20 August 1942, the CVE* Long Island *landed nineteen F4F Wildcat fighters and twelve Dauntless dive bombers with their crews at the former Japanese airstrip, newly renamed Henderson Field.*][12] Was the object of the enemy an attempt to transport planes? But we cannot consider that these were all the planes. Other light carriers may engage in the same mission, too. The most urgent thing for us is to destroy these aircraft immediately and render the airstrip unavailable by launching air raids and night bombardments upon it. Thinking we should not let the enemy consolidate its position, I got impatient, but our forces on the spot didn't move as we wished.

Deciding that the main force should also advance to the scene without touching at Truk in view of the support force's advance, I ordered the staff to draft the plan.

On the other hand, we ordered the Fourth Fleet and Eleventh Air Fleet to destroy radio stations and other military installations on Nauru and Ocean islands, and to keep watch upon them to prevent enemy flying boats from using them. The staffs were apt to be slow in dealing with these matters necessary for flank support.

From 0830 *Yamato* refueled destroyers and finished by 1700. The moon was on her seventh night, and we kept on 18 knots.

A landing party landed on Makin at 0900 today. Details were unknown and we were not certain whether the enemy was there or not.

[*This was probably the occasion when the Japanese captured nine marines inadvertently left behind when the U.S. raiders pulled out. At first well treated, the marines were later executed.*][13]

Friday, 21 August 1942. Cloudy with occasional showers. At 0830 a search plane found yesterday's enemy task force at a point about 250 miles southeast of Tulagi sailing on 230°. Furthermore, one cruiser and one destroyer heading west were sighted at a point some 150 miles east of Tulagi in the afternoon, but the cruiser was later found to be a transport.

On the other hand, enemy fighters on Guadalcanal took off at about 0400 and landed at 0530. They took off again, and the sound of small arms fire, heard in the airstrip area from 0200, couldn't be heard after 1000.

Some of the staff were of the opinion that the enemy must have surrendered because of the prompt attack by the Ichiki detachment last night. According to a report from the east lookout by nightfall, however, the detachment was annihilated before dawn this morning before they reached the airstrip. These were eight hundred picked soldiers who had successfully landed to the east of the enemy, and I'm afraid they didn't advance recklessly, underestimating the enemy.

[*Ugaki did Ichiki's men less than justice, for they fought bravely at the battle of the Tenaru River. Ichiki himself committed suicide.*][14]

An enemy destroyer entered Guadalcanal from the east in the afternoon, and three or four minesweepers seemed to follow her. Thus, the enemy foothold is becoming more consolidated than ours. We can't make light of them.

Meanwhile, enemy radio communications in Hawaii and the south were getting very busy with frequent urgent telegrams, which seemed to indicate the intensification of activities in the theater.

[*Coast watchers and U.S. reconnaissance aircraft had alerted the Americans to impending major Japanese action, which developed into the battle of the Eastern Solomons.*][15]

In spite of our warning, the Twenty-sixth Air Flotilla appeared to have sent out its torpedo bombers carrying torpedoes, vainly aiming at enemy carriers out of range. We haven't yet received a report covering the aerial combat over Guadalcanal. As I warned yesterday, it's a prerequisite to destroy the enemy planes and materials that have been unloaded there.

We altered the fleet course to 140° and continued our southward advance. Visibility was excellent in the moonlight and we sighted Grimeth Island about twenty miles to the port bow at 2310.

Saturday, 22 August 1942. Fair with occasional rain. We passed between Sasaon and Namocheck islands in the early morning. We reduced speed to 14 knots from the time the moon went down last night and proceeded south while sounding. Though many ships passed this route since the outbreak of the war, it was the first time for a giant ship like *Yamato* to pass. We certainly wouldn't like a *Yamato* shoal or something added to the chart! Caution should be taken against both submarines and shoals.

The destroyer *Kawakaze,* which penetrated into Guadalcanal last night, met two enemy destroyers instead of transports and sank one of them with six torpedoes and bombardment. [*The two U.S. destroyers were* Blue *and* Henley. Henley *towed the stricken* Blue *to Tulagi, where she had to be scuttled.*][16] While returning, she was strafed by enemy planes this morning and one man was seriously wounded. The skipper asked for instructions as to her movement because hospitalization was necessary for him as well as for another ordinary patient. Shame on that damn skipper with the rank of commander!

We saw no enemy except for several cruisers and destroyers at a point 250 miles southeast of Tulagi at about 0900. However, the enemy still kept four to six planes on guard over Guadalcanal on two-hour shifts, and yesterday's reconnaissance spotted over twenty planes on the ground.

We expected the Twenty-sixth Air Flotilla to attack today, but due to the bad weather they could not approach the island from the south. We have received no news about the fate of the Ichiki detachment. Though some doubts remain, the previous telegram telling of its doom seems to be true. Except for a doubtful report of over eighty casualties being sustained among our garrison force, today passed without incident.

The second echelon of the Ichiki detachment was moving slowly south at 8.5 knots. The Second Destroyer Squadron commander asked for direct fighter cover over the convoy, to which rest the Eleventh Air Fleet asked the support force centering around the Second Fleet to air raid Guadalcanal.

Unless something was done, there would be another disaster. Accordingly, we gave the following instruction in my name:

In addition to the enemy task force's position being unknown, our position should be kept concealed as much as possible. Guadalcanal should be attacked by the land-based air force on the 23rd. If this attack proves ineffective, the task force will attack on the 24th. In this case, if necessary, the convoy will postpone its arrival to the landing spot scheduled on the 24th.

In drawing up this directive, I had many things to suggest or request. It is regrettable that the staff is apt to stick to one matter, thus overlooking the overall picture.

The support force is maintaining strict radio silence, and so should our Main Body, but we couldn't help breaking it a few times every day. We communicated with Chichi Jima and Saipan and then with Truk by longwave. The reaching distance of long-wave was certainly short, but enemy submarines in the neighborhood would be able to detect our position correctly. This is another hardship to be endured.

We increased speed to 20 knots after *Kasuga Maru* joined at 1830 and proceeded toward tomorrow morning's refueling point, setting course for 100° from 1945.

[On Sunday, 23 August, *Yamato* refueled, while maintaining speed of 12 knots. After refueling, speed was increase to 18 knots, and the flagship continued toward the next rendezvous point.]

Except for a transport and three destroyers seen at Tulagi, no enemy was sighted today. And those ships also left port in a hurry, maybe on account of finding our submarine.

By 1600 the support and task forces respectively reached the designated points of two hundred and four hundred miles north of the Solomons, respectively. Search planes of the support force and a submarine coming south sighted Consolidated flying boats and carrier planes several times, but the enemy does not seem to have sighted our task force.

On the other hand, enemy planes shadowed the convoy escorted by the Second Destroyer Squadron, and it had to turn back.

In spite of our expectation, the attack force, consisting of medium torpedo bombers and fighters of the Twenty-sixth Air Flotilla, turned back, as they could not penetrate Guadalcanal roads due to low-lying clouds.

Somehow we must think of a better method of carrying out attacks. I feel the present methods are too naive and without aggressiveness. Both today and yesterday twenty-two enemy planes (all fighters) made a flight of about one hour and a half to the north and landed in the afternoon. What were they up to?

[*They were trying to find the Japanese transports that Rear Admiral Raizo Tanaka, in command of Desron 2, had moved out of range, as Ugaki indicated.*][17]

The Eleventh Air Fleet wanted the task force's attack on Guadalcanal executed immediately, while the latter wished to advance southward according to the enemy situation and attack early tomorrow morning. But in view of the probable existence of the enemy task force southeast of the Solomons, according to radio intelligence, and sighting carrier planes east of the Solomons this morning, we ordered tomorrow's operation as follows:

1. Land-based air force will carry out attacks as much as possible.

2. In case of not finding the enemy task force, our task force will attack Guadalcanal with adequate strength in the afternoon.

3. The submarine force will make a southward advance for one hundred miles.

4. The Kawaguchi detachment will sail out from Truk. How will the situation develop tomorrow?

Monday, 24 August 1942. Fair. The support force, consisting of the advance force, vanguard of the task force, and the task force itself withdrew northward last night. From 0200 this morning heavy cruiser *Tone,* CVL *Ryujo,* and three destroyers were dispatched south as a detachment at 20 knots.

Upon receipt of a report that over twenty enemy fighters left Guadalcanal base to the north at about 0900, we were worried about *Ryujo,* but nothing happened.

Since enemy planes still shadowed the second echelon of the Ichiki detachment, it couldn't advance southward and had to withdraw to the north. Meanwhile, at about 1300 a support force float plane reported sighting a large enemy force, but its strength and location weren't clear. Besides, contradictory reports came in, and we wasted time in confusion.

The Third Fleet launched its first and second air attacks, but the Combined Fleet and Second Fleet weren't informed of the enemy situation. It further ordered the Third and its vanguard force to attack at night. The Second Fleet finally ordered a night attack too, but receipt of that telegram was delayed.

Shokaku's first-wave planes seemed to have difficulty in finding the enemy due to an error of fifty to sixty miles in the reported enemy position. But they finally succeeded in attacking by 1600 and registered six hits of 250-kg bombs on a carrier of the *Essex* type, causing conflagration, while *Zuikaku*'s planes in the same wave set fires on another carrier and a battleship.

[*The "Essex type" carrier was* Enterprise, *badly damaged but saved by the excellent work of all hands. No other carrier was hit, nor was* North Carolina, *the only battleship with the American force, although several bombs fell near her.*][18]

Reports of these results reached us quite late after our enquiry about them. So we had trouble in considering the prospect of the night attack.

The second-wave planes failed to find the enemy. Night fell before the planes of these two waves were recovered with much difficulty, using searchlights in spite of the moonlight.

We lost contact with the enemy since before sunset. Though a float plane from light cruiser *Nagara* sighted an enemy cruiser, it failed to find the Main Force. Even the severely damaged carrier couldn't be found, so the commander of the night attack force gave up the attack and ordered withdrawal at 2200.

[*The "enemy cruiser" was the destroyer* Grayson, *which Fletcher had detached to rescue plane crews who might have had to ditch.*][19]

The time of its giving up was about the same as we thought it should be, and it seemed appropriate under the circumstances. Then we ordered them to withdraw but to be ready to attack the damaged ships after searching the area tomorrow morning.

In the meantime, the detachment, consisting of CVL *Ryujo,* heavy cruiser *Tone,* and three destroyers closed to two hundred miles north of Guadalcanal and at 1130 launched an attack force consisting mostly of fighters. They attacked the airfield in the afternoon and shot down fifteen enemy fighters.

On the other hand, over twenty enemy carrier bombers and torpedo bombers attacked *Ryujo,* and, in spite of her gallant fight, she was hit by a torpedo at her starboard engine room, disabled and listing 20°. After a while, the big fire was brought under control, but the list gradually increased. As there seemed no hope of rescue, "all hands abandon ship" was ordered. With the approval of Rear Admiral Hara, commander, Eighth Heavy Cruiser Division, on board *Tone,* she was disposed of. It was most deplorable. Again we lost a valuable carrier. [*Ryujo* fell to planes from *Saratoga.*][20]

On looking back over today's battle, we can see that the movement of our escort force with convoy of two transports and Eighth Fleet had been known to the enemy since the day before yesterday. Aiming to destroy them, the enemy task force advanced to the sea near Stewart Island, 150 miles east of Malaita Island, after going round to the northeast from south of the Solomons. After discovering our advance force and the *Ryujo* detachment, they directed their attacks mostly to the detachment and partly to our support force. But they didn't seem to expect to see our task force's CVs *Shokaku* and *Zuikaku.*

The appearance of the enemy in this area confirmed our judgment of the enemy situation and gave us the most favorable chance to test my cherished tactics of luring the enemy to come out so that we could destroy its big ones. So we should have bagged big game. On the contrary, we lost *Ryujo* while inflicting small damage to the enemy. The reasons for the failure are considered to be:

1. We depended too much on the search by flying boats. Though we ordered the Eleventh Air Fleet to search yesterday, by this morning the enemy hadn't been found.

2. A task force float plane found the enemy about two hundred miles to its south, but its report failed to arrive timely due to either too many errors or bad air conditions. Third Fleet headquarters did not communicate this to all fleets. Furthermore, as a revision had been made in code books, much delay occurred in communications.

3. The departure of the first-and second-wave planes was swift, but only the first wave could reach the target, as there was much error in reporting

the enemy position. Besides, sufficient consideration wasn't given to maintaining searches and also to a concept of search and attack.

According to the summary action report, the enemy was sighted at 1205, first wave took off at 1300, and carried out attacks at 1448. Second wave sighted no enemy. Planes recovered at 1700 to 1900. Sunset at 1615.

4. Contact with the enemy wasn't maintained, so that a night battle was made difficult.

5. Enemy attacks were concentrated on *Ryujo,* while most of our fighters were being used for the attack on the enemy base, so those available for the defense were few. This couldn't be helped, and she served as a decoy.

The enemy passed the line of our submarines for 2230 to 2240 and went south at 20 knots. Spot No. 15 sighted one carrier and several cruisers and destroyers, in addition to hearing sounds of a big group's passing. Spot No. 19 sighted one battleship, one carrier, and cruisers and destroyers. According to these, two carriers still remain intact. It was most regrettable that they couldn't carry out any attack though they saw a huge force passing in the moonlight.

Upon receipt of the report "enemy sighted," the Main Body was readied for 20 knots with an immediate notice. When it became certain, speed was increased to 20 knots and course set on 150°. But when the night attack force withdrew, we dropped speed to 16 knots at 2300. We crossed the equator at 1900.

Tuesday, 25 August 1942. Fair. The early morning search found our task force heading north at a point one hundred miles bearing 135° from us, and we joined it after 0900.

The second echelon of the Ichiki detachment was attacked since this morning. A fire broke out on light cruiser *Jintsu,* and *Kinryo Maru,* with the landing party on board, was also damaged. By visual signal we ordered the task force to dispatch a fighter cover to them immediately. In spite of CV *Zuikaku* being supposed to support them, *Kinryo Maru* exploded and had to be sunk by destroyer *Mutsuki.* And, later, an enemy plane attacked *Mutsuki* and sank her.

[*An SBD from Henderson Field struck Tanaka's flagship,* Jintsu, *and damaged her so severely that he shifted his flag to destroyer* Kagero. *The same Henderson group struck* Kinryo Maru. *A hit from a B-17 from* Espiritu Santo *sank destroyer* Mutsuki.]²¹

Last night we ordered that the second echelon's landing be made on the 25th and received a telegram from the Eighth Fleet so ordering. In view of the fact that light cruiser *Jintsu* was attacked this morning, however, we decided to call off that order.

[Deciding that "an excessive southward advance would be risky," the

Main Body withdrew northward to join the task force, zigzagging at 16 knots in brilliant moonlight.]

The First Submarine Squadron sub which sighted the enemy task force late last night tried hard to chase it and three times today found an enemy group consisting of one carrier, one battleship, and several cruisers, destroyers, and supply ships. Judging from its irregular movements, the enemy apparently was watching to the north. It seemed to be engaging in refueling and sending out search planes, some of which our search planes met. Moreover, there are reasons to believe he still has two carriers intact. We must be on the alert.

It is apparent that landing on Guadalcanal by transports is hopeless unless the enemy planes are wiped out. So the plan was revised to transport reinforcements by minesweepers and destroyers, which would shuttle from our place to that island at high speed every day. [*The Japanese destroyer shuttle became famous as the "Tokyo Express."*][22] Accordingly, we instructed the Eleventh Air Fleet and Eighth Fleet to consult the army in preparing for it. It appears that the Eighth Fleet shared this view.

As urgent and prerequisite as the transportation of reinforcements was to destroy the enemy air arm on the island as soon as possible. The island is so far away from our base at Rabaul that our attack forces often failed to reach there due to foul weather. The Eleventh Air Fleet earnestly requests carrier attacks on the island, but they couldn't be made without serious consideration.

It seems that the only way is to send some ground crew to Buka base, where *Ryujo*'s remaining planes, together with part of the task force's fighters, were transferred, and attempt to destroy enemy aircraft in cooperation with other air arms from Rabaul. So a suggestion was given to hurry up readying the Buka base.

Though we didn't receive it directly, it was learned by the Eleventh Air Fleet's summary report sent at about 2250 that a flying boat found one enemy carrier and several cruisers and destroyers to the south of yesterday's battleground at 1135 this morning. This must be yesterday's damaged carrier, with which I was much concerned. She seemed to be slowly retreating south at about 5 knots.

As we have adopted the new method of sending reinforcement by high-speed small vessels, the battle is expected to become a prolonged one, and the staff has drawn up a plan for the Main Force, advance force, and the task force to withdraw to Truk for briefings and unloading of unnecessary articles, aiming to sail south on the 1st of next month. But refueling can be done at sea, and no discrepancies were observed among the fleets during yesterday's operation. And the reason for our failure to achieve substantial gains in the battle must be attributed to lack of training. So I see no need to hold briefings. When in danger, unnecessary articles could be thrown into the sea.

In the meantime, the situation isn't developing to our advantage. Sinking our CVL *Ryujo* and damaging light cruiser *Jintsu* and others has raised the enemy's morale. No little possibility exists that the enemy will reinforce Guadalcanal and further launch positive actions. A withdrawal of most of the forces from the battle zone at this moment, leaving the Eleventh Air Fleet and Eighth Fleet behind, would discourage morale and would make it hard to meet the new enemy attempt. With the above reasoning, I rejected the staff's suggestion and decided to remain in the battle zone.

Moreover, by means of radio intelligence and submarines, the enemy would suspect the withdrawal of a major force. Going in and coming out of Truk would give enemy submarines an increased chance to attack, and it would not save fuel, either.

Wednesday, 26 August 1942. Fair. At 0500 we set our course to 270° and refueled three destroyers from 0800. The babies who get hungry every four days are quite a nuisance. We altered course to facing the wind from 1500, and got rid of the heat from the scorching sun, having a breath of air.

Our force succeeded in landing on Salamaua in eastern New Guinea before dawn this morning, but couldn't capture Rabi airstrip. Though this area tends to escape our attention, the capture of this airstrip would benefit not only the Moresby operation but also our operations in the Solomons.

[Ugaki recorded that the previous night one destroyer captured Nauru Island and another Ocean Island with no opposition. Ugaki was well pleased with this action; however, he added, "it is essential to send garrisons there promptly. We should never let Makin's case be repeated."]

[*The destroyers were* Ariake—*Nauru*—*and* Yugure—*Ocean.*]²³

Our air attack force from Rabaul raided the airstrip on Guadalcanal today and three medium torpedo bombers were shot down. Enemy fighters seemed to have been reinforced, and this area has become the scene of a fierce battle and of attrition. At last the staff has become aware of the gravity of the situation and began requesting concentration of strength and materials. I have been warning them that the fighting in that area would be intensified, but they didn't realize it until they faced the bitter reality. Under the present circumstances, it's of the first priority to secure Guadalcanal, and the destruction of the enemy fleet must be made the secondary one. We issued an operational telegram to this effect.

Thursday, 27 August 1942. Partly fair. At 0200, before I got fully asleep, a staff officer awakened me. The plight of our air power in the Solomons needed prompt attention. It became necessary to send the converted carrier *Kasuga Maru* to the Marshalls to ferry fighters of the Twenty-fourth Air Flotilla stationed there.

Accordingly, it was decided that the rest of the Main Body would go to Truk accompanied by two destroyers. Our course was then set to 300° with 20 knots at 0315.

[On this leg of their journey, Ugaki recorded that there was "not much change in the war situation," although there was "a strong possibility" of a U.S. task force southeast of the Solomons.]

One of our submarines, which had been chasing the previously damaged carrier, was attacked by an enemy flying boat. It was reported to have alighted on the sea and continued watching the submarine for nine hours.

[*Two Japanese submarines,* I-9 *and* I-17, *were attacked about this time, one by destroyers* Grayson, Paterson, *and* Monssen, *the other by an aircraft.*][24]

The advance force headed to the southeast after refueling yesterday and was shadowed by two flying boats today.

The capture of Rabi airstrip in the eastern end of New Guinea turned out unsuccessfully due to strong resistance. It was decided to send more landing party.

It isn't hard to imagine the hardship of the Eleventh Air Fleet fighting both in the east and west. They urgently ask for the task force's cooperation, but serious consideration should be given to its employment. Instead, we ordered the task force to send about thirty fighters to Buka, with the aim of having them attack Guadalcanal for about two days from there. In the meantime, the task force was to maneuver in the sea northeast of the island.

The Eighth Fleet ordered the start of the landing operation by small craft from today but later postponed it for another day because they thought thirty enemy planes remained. But their existence was deemed doubtful, as eight planes were caught in the bomb spread of yesterday's attack and nine were shot down in the air.

[Ugaki hoped that a typhoon headed for Kyushu and western Honshu would not damage the rice crop or the Second CV Division and the Main Body in hone waters.]

Including reports by *Zuikaku*'s fliers picked up by heavy cruiser *Chikuma*, it was ascertained that six bombs hit on what seemed to be a *Saratoga* type carrier emerging from an explosion reaching two hundred meters high. This was believed surely sunk. Besides, two 250-kg bombs hit the middle of another carrier, inducing explosion. The latter seemed to be the same one that a flying boat spotted to the south of the battleground the next day.

If two carriers passed our submarine line, there appear to be two carriers still intact, after fresh reinforcements joined.

The enemy radio announced today that two Japanese carriers, one battleship, one cruiser, and one transport were damaged and the battle was still going on. They did not seem to know about the sinking of our *Ryujo*, and did not mention anything about their own loss.

Our Imperial Headquarters announced one enemy carrier was seriously damaged and another damaged, while our small carrier was seriously damaged.

Friday, 28 August 1942. Cloudy. We took strict precautions, assuming second stations from one hour before sunrise. *Chitose*, damaged by a near miss, changed her schedule of passing the south channel, and cooperated with us in antisubmarine alert by joining us from the port side at dawn.

At 0600 we sighted the Truk Islands from a distance of fifty miles and headed for the north channel with two destroyers of the direct screen throwing depth charges at five-minute intervals to frighten potential enemy submarines. Soon after we changed course to 230° at 1331, we found bubbles of a torpedo firing at 3,500 meters bearing 140° to starboard. Three traces of torpedoes were then heading toward us.

We urgently steered to port for 30° to bear the traces to our stern. Two of them exploded on their way, while the remaining one came after us. It seemed about to hit us, but we just managed to dodge it to the stern. It was really with God's help. If we had not changed course after discovering the bubbles, we would have been fired at from close range. The self-exploding of the two torpedoes made our evasive movement easier. *Yamato*'s plane was just on the spot and could bomb the sub right away. The position of the enemy submarine was fifteen miles bearing 330° of Kita Island, and two destroyers and all the planes in the air concentrated their attacks on it. At the same time, the necessary warning was issued.

[*This may well have been the U.S. submarine* Flying Fish, *which caught a battleship in her sights but failed to score a hit. The sub was slightly damaged in the ensuing depth charge attack.*][25]

Two fleet tankers, *Shinyo Maru* and *Nichiei Maru*, which had been torpedoed and damaged outside the channel when entering the atoll the other day, had completed their repairs and were just coming up the channel to the north when they sighted a periscope at the same spot. At about the same time, a *Yamato* plane also sighted bubbles of firing and two traces of torpedoes about one kilometer further in front of the above position. So there must have been two enemy submarines and they seemed to have fired five torpedoes altogether against *Yamato*.

Seeing the insufficient strength of our antisubmarine operation, and also in view of the increased number of our ships going in and out of Truk recently, enemy subs apparently have risked themselves ambushing us at the very entrance of the atoll. Defying our threatening depth charge attacks, they dared to attack *Yamato* with a near miss. Their action deserves praise. I wish our submarines had the same courage and more determination to destroy the enemy, even at the sacrifice of themselves. Our submarines, which in these days could hardly make attacks upon the enemy in the Solomons area, in spite of sighting it at a close distance, should re-examine themselves.

The advance force of the Ichiki detachment succeeded in landing on Guadalcanal the night of the 18th at a point east of the airstrip. Then they advanced toward it and launched a night attack, but they met a strong defense of double barbed-wire entanglement along the east river. After dawn they were subjected to attacks by rapid-fire guns and planes. The casualties increased; they finally burned the regimental color and the commander killed himself. A lieutenant led the remnant of 128 [*this figure is not clear in the diary*] men and withdrew to the east. Seeking a position on the beach west of Cape Lunga, they were still opposing the enemy.

On the other hand, the construction detachment and garrison force under navy Captain Monzen, located on the west side of the river to the west of the airstrip, urgently needed help. However, the land-based air force's attack of last night, upon which we placed such hope, failed as they had to put about from the way due to bad weather. So did a daylight strike of today.

This morning thirty fighters were transferred from the task force to Buka airfield in accordance with last night's operational telegram order. We are placing much hope upon their activities after tomorrow. Furthermore, we plan to concentrate fighters and bombers in this region from various areas.

As the first attempt of the new method of landing from destroyers, the Eighth Fleet ordered landing of the Ichiki detachment and a naval landing party. But, perhaps because it got into the aerial attack range from Guadalcanal too soon and proceeded at slow speed, the Twentieth Destroyer Division was attacked persistently by twenty enemy planes. Destroyer *Asagiri* was sunk, destroyer *Shiratsuyu* rendered unnavigable, and destroyer *Yugiri* damaged. Its commanding officer was seriously wounded and died later. [*These attacks came from marine dive bombers at Guadalcanal.*][26]

The enemy did not find the Twenty-fourth Destroyer Division operating separately, but it turned back on receiving the above news. Then the Eighth Fleet ordered it to enforce at once but rescinded the order afterwards. Thus the first day of this landing method met with perfect failure.

Unless enemy planes are not destroyed by any means, it will be difficult to attain the aim.

One of our submarines found an enemy task force consisting of one carrier and many cruisers and destroyers southeast of the Solomons tonight, but couldn't attack it.

Yamato cast anchor in the second anchorage northwest of Harushima at 1530. Inouye and Komatsu, commanders in chief of the Fourth and Sixth fleets, respectively, came on board to visit us with their staffs.

Admiral Abe, in command of the Eleventh Battleship Division, and *Jintsu*'s skipper reported their actions in the battle. The former is waiting for the arrival of tankers and the latter is undergoing temporary repairs lying alongside the repair ship *Akashi*. Besides, there was destroyer *Hagikaze,* which was also damaged. How busy the business of war is!

[On Saturday, 29 August, *Yamato* sent staff officers Miwa, Sasaki, and Watanabe to Rabaul to confer at headquarters of the Eleventh Air Fleet, Eighth Fleet, and Seventeenth Army. Ugaki felt he should have gone also, but the rapidly developing war situation made this inconvenient at the moment.]

A destroyer found an enemy submarine at the north channel when she surfaced at about 2100 last night. But she submerged again before the destroyer reached within a thousand meters of her. Then the destroyer attacked her with depth charges by sound detection at 2200, and nothing has been heard of her since. Some oil patches were seen this morning, so some damage may have been inflicted upon the enemy sub. It is necessary to keep watch and persistently attack it in cooperation with the Fourth Naval Base Force.

Destroyer *Shiratsuyu* of the Twentieth Destroyer Division, damaged seventy miles north of Tulagi yesterday, was towed by destroyer *Yugiri* and withdrew under escort of destroyer *Amagiri*. Despite being shadowed by the enemy this morning, they got out of the danger zone 150 miles from the island in the afternoon. The enemy did not attack them, maybe on account of the fighter screen provided.

The Twenty-fourth and Eleventh Destroyer Divisions are slated to dash into the roads at Guadalcanal at full speed after sunset tonight. The commanding officer of the Twenty-fourth Destroyer Division said it was impossible to go into the roads unless the enemy planes were destroyed. And the Eighth Fleet command encouraged him by wiring that today's air attack seemed to have given the enemy fairly big damage. But actually the result was not satisfactory. Twenty-two fighters of the Third Fleet, which landed at Buka yesterday, sortied from there and only shot down four enemy planes, of which two were uncertain.

On the other hand, two transports, one cruiser, and two destroyers were reported to be at anchor off the east strip on Guadalcanal at 1200 today. The enemy also is trying hard to send in reinforcements. There is a chance of a night battle taking place tonight, and I hope it will happen after the landing is completed.

Our submarines found one enemy task force each east and southeast of San Cristobal Island. This led us to believe the enemy still has two carriers intact.

The Naval General Staff is worried about the situation in this area and plans to transfer the Twenty-first Air Flotilla to the Malaya and Sumatra areas, leaving the air operation in that region to the army. It also revised the agreement with the army so as to withhold the Moresby operation and settle the Guadalcanal operation first. Both measures are quite proper.

Sunday, 30 August 1942. Cloudy with light rain in the morning. The Twenty-fourth and Eleventh Destroyer Divisions succeeded in landing at about midnight last night without being attacked by enemy planes. A few planes were flying over the airstrip. They gave up an attack against the doubtful enemy ships at anchor and put about. This landing deserves congratulations.

Major General [Kiyotake] Kawaguchi, the detachment commander, now at Shortland, suggested the sea transportation of his troops be made by landing craft and refused to get on board destroyers *Amagiri* and *Kagero* to go to Guadalcanal. He said he did not receive such orders from the army command. The loss of the Twentieth Destroyer Division the other day appeared to discourage him, and there seemed to be some troubles between him and the Second Destroyer Squadron.

As eleven enemy planes were shot down today, it was considered better to take advantage of this by carrying out another destroyer-to-shore landing. So we wired the Eighth Fleet and Eleventh Air Fleet to this effect.

In spite of our submarine's report of seeing no enemy in the roads, this morning attack planes found a transport of three thousand tons and three destroyers or cruisers, and sank a cruiser or destroyer. [*This was* Colhoun, *a destroyer converted to a transport.*][27] Though the enemy is attempting reinforcements, the situation is turning in our favor by yesterday's air combat and last night's landing. What is needed now is one more push.

A submarine in the south sighted an enemy task force of one carrier, two cruisers, and several destroyers on patrol to the southeast of San Cristobal. This is the tenth time that they sighted enemies and always failed to attack. It is most regrettable. I am beginning to feel that the words of those who say the submarine is only good for raiding operations and scouting are almost admissible. I wish they would strike enemy warships even once just to disprove them.

A submarine which made an air reconnaissance of the Santa Cruz Islands found no military installations on Banicro Island, contrary to our suspicion, and instead one destroyer and six flying boats in a bay on the north side of Deni Island. Accordingly, the Sixth Fleet was ordered to attack them.

The tanker *Tatekawa Maru* arrived, so the Eleventh Division started its belated refueling. Another Third Fleet tanker also arrived from home waters. As fleet activities in this area increased, fuel consumption reached a huge amount, so the arrangement of fleet tankers reinforced by those belonging to the navy minister was strained to the utmost. This place is supposed to be an advanced naval base for this area, yet installations were exceedingly poor. Not even a fuel tank has been completed ashore.

Monday, 31 August 1942. Fair. Fine weather after the rain and the heat was fierce, but still it could not beat that at Hashira Jima.

The three staff officers dispatched to Rabaul returned on a flying boat and we heard their reports. I was glad to learn that those men at the front were not getting impatient as I had feared and morale was high, realizing the importance of the Solomons operation. But from another angle this could be interpreted as their lack of enthusiasm.

Though plane consumption was great, they said they could continue the current operation without any hitch as long as the replenishment of aircraft was maintained. The Eighth Fleet carried out the invasion of Rabi too soon as a preliminary to the Moresby operation. Its commander was Rear Admiral Matsuyama, commander, Eighteenth Division. Unless done with thorough planning and overwhelming strength, it usually ends up in difficulty, as in this case.

The Seventeenth Army's unit, which had advanced to Kokoda, found its rear communication exceedingly difficult. Its further advance is deemed doubtful. After all, it all comes down to how to secure sea transportation, and this means a further load on the navy. Unless Guadalcanal is settled, we cannot hope for any further development in this area. On the other hand, Rabi cannot be left as it is, even if we have to send an army force there.

The following message was brought to me from Mikawa, commander in chief, Eighth Fleet, and not a few points are justifiable, coming from a responsible commander in chief:

The staff of the Eleventh Air Fleet command, which is responsible for directing operations in the southeast area, consists of air officers, so they are not thoroughly competent to direct operations of the surface forces. The outcome is only natural. In other words, the commanders in chief of the Fourth and Eighth fleets ought to be senior to the commander in chief, Eleventh Air Fleet.

Today's daylight attack planes turned back due to bad weather.

The landing from destroyers succeeded last night. According to destroyer *Yudachi*'s report, enemy planes attacked them in the roads, but inflicted no damage. That was lucky.

The Kawaguchi detachment commander, who had been making trouble, finally embarked on board *Umikaze* with his troops at Shortland. Rear Admiral Raizo Tanaka, commanding the Second Destroyer Squadron, became overcautious in this landing after his flagship was damaged. He seems to have been much criticized. Consequently, the Eighth Fleet ordered Rear Admiral [Shintaro] Hashimoto, commander, Third Destroyer Squadron, to command the escort and transport duties right after his arrival.

I wrote the outline of the fleet's overall operations and gave it to the staff.

We ordered the advance and task forces to return to Truk after recovering the fighters sent to Buka on the 2nd.

One transport and one destroyer entered Guadalcanal from the east today, and those there since yesterday were moving between Tulagi and Guadalcanal.

So far our submarines have done nothing to enemy reinforcements. But a startling report came in from the submarine *I-26:* At 0446 this morning she fired six torpedoes with the bearing angle of 120° at a range of 3,500 meters against a carrier of the *Saratoga* type. Two minutes and forty seconds after the firing, the explosion of a hit was heard. She failed to confirm the result as destroyers attacked her for four hours after the firing. As the time of the run was too short, I wondered if the torpedo had self-exploded short of the target. But the fact that she attacked is to be commended.

[I-26 *had indeed struck* Saratoga. *She did not sink, but necessary repairs kept her out of the war for three months.*][28]

[Ugaki received word that a delegation of top brass from Tokyo could visit the fleet shortly, which convinced him that the high command was "gravely concerned" with his area.]

Tuesday, 1 September 1942. Fair. Yamazaki, commander, First Submarine Squadron, together with Mito, chief of staff, Sixth Fleet, came on board at 1400. He told us about the other day's battle southeast of the Solomons. He said from his bitter experiences that the enemy's antisubmarine precautions were very strict and sound detection swift, so that our attack movements will be rendered extremely difficult. The *I-15*, his flagship, was damaged and returned here the day before yesterday.

If a chase is difficult and an underwater movement dangerous, the only thing we can do is to lie in wait with many submarines and attack the enemy at opportune moments.

The Guadalcanal garrison reported the landing of forty enemy planes this morning. As a result of our recent attacks, about ten of them were believed to be still there, but now there were quite a lot of them again this morning. The enemy seemed to be trying to reinforce either from carriers or directly from Efate Island.

Furthermore, at 1100 one large transport and two destroyers arrived from the east at Lunga Roads. They are transporting personnel and material in increasing numbers every day. Our sneak landing succeeded yesterday, but it was small compared with the enemy transportation capacity. Moreover, an increase of enemy planes is a headache for us. When our troop strength on the island is reinforced enough to fight, we must try to recapture the airstrip at all costs, even staking its annihilation. Otherwise the situation will grow worse than ever.

We are in a plight in the Rabi area, too. Our naval landing party is facing its doom. We should devise means to evacuate them at once and try to revive the operation with the army force.

An enemy submarine attacked the tanker *Kyokuto Maru* outside the south channel. They may have been scared off the north and moved to the south.

Our planes turned back due to bad weather again today, so we could not attack Guadalcanal. As we thought it necessary for fighters of the Third Fleet to cooperate in tomorrow's attack, the return of fighter squadrons to the Third Fleet was changed to the 3rd.

[On Wednesday, 2 September 1942, Rear Admiral Tanaka, commander, Second Destroyer Squadron, visited *Yamato* to apologize for his failures of 29 and 30 August. Ugaki could understand his "mental suffering," so he "soothed him and gave him some comfort articles to cheer him up." Ugaki noted that the staff officers, with no command experience, tended "to be irresponsible and take extreme measures" in such cases.]

Battleship *Mutsu*, attached to the advance force, arrived here accompanied by destroyers in the morning. The Second Fleet wanted her to accompany them instead of the Third Battleship Division. But I wonder how effective she could be.

Staff officers Watanabe and [Lieutenant Commander Tatano] Aoki (logistics) were dispatched on a flying boat to Rabaul for briefings early this morning. I told them my views on the following three points last night:

1. In the end, Guadalcanal must be secured by land warfare, even with

sacrifices. There is no other way. Cooperation between planes and vessels, and how to deal with enemy counterattacks by our invasion and task forces immediately after the recapture, should be studied on this occasion.

2. Rabi is hopeless. Recover the survivors, and an attempt to recapture should be made with army troops.

3. An overland advance of the main force of the Moresby invasion is very difficult. Even if it could be done, it could not do anything more than make it. An invasion from the sea is considered to be the main course. Planning for this is necessary.

Two transports and three destroyers are still operating in Guadalcanal; our submarines there are only good for reconnaissance and never attack the enemy.

The enemy discovered last night's sneak landing at its halfway point. They had to suspend it and withdraw with a part of the landing force still on board. Altogether, five hundred of the Kawaguchi and Ichiki detachments remained at Shortland. The rest will be finished mostly with tonight's landing. *Tsugaru* is going there tonight with field guns aboard. I wish her success.

The Eighth Fleet announced that the result of this morning's attack was great, but it only destroyed a few planes on the ground and shot down two Grummans.

Meanwhile, our reinforcements seem to have landed in the Rabi area, but our force that had previously landed met enemy counterattacks and its contact was lost. Furthermore, an enemy cruiser accompanying a transport entered Milne Bay.

[*Ugaki referred to the relief force of 775 men under navy Captain Minoru Yano, which attempted to relieve the Japanese troops at Milne Bay, New Guinea.*][29]

Orders to attack enemy warships and planes have been issued one after another, but little result could be attained due to bad weather on the way.

[On Thursday, 3 September, a Japan Airlines flying boat brought a delegation of top army and navy brass from Saipan "for inspection and liaison" Combined Fleet staff officers briefed them "on developments since 7 August," explained future policy and their wants from the high command. Commanders in chief Komatsu and Inouye of the Sixth and Fourth fleets also attended.

Today's air raid on Guadalcanal could not materialize due to bad weather, and we had to put off the recovery of the Third Fleet's fighters until tomorrow.

The situation at Rabi was critical. The commanding officers of both naval landing parties were killed. One-third of the officers and about 560 men remained, but only two hundred of them were capable of fighting.

Though they dispatched their last sad telegram, some of them seemed to be still alive.

[Yano had cabled Rabaul on 2 September, "Situation most desperate. Every-one resolved to fight bravely to the last."][30]

Staff Officer Watanabe returned from Rabaul in the evening and reported that the army, Eighth Fleet, and Eleventh Air Fleet all wanted the general attack started around the 8th. As it was not just a local operation, however, but concerned the whole fleet, this command wished to start it around the 11th, when the fleet would be ready. The vice chief of the Naval General Staff was going to Rabaul tomorrow, so I asked him to keep this in mind.

Friday, 4 September 1942. Fair. *Yamato* moved to the first anchorage after weighing anchor at 0730, in order to await the arrival of the advance force and the task force.

Kasuga Maru, newly commissioned after changing her name to *Taiyo,* arrived accompanied by destroyer *Akebono* after completing her duty of transporting planes from Tarawa to Rabaul. She left again for Palau to resume the same kind of assignment.

After recovering its fighters at 1040 this morning, the Third Fleet was to come here. It is expected to arrive in the south channel at 1200 tomorrow, a little ahead of schedule.

Due to bad weather, our attack planes scheduled to go to the Solomons turned back again today.

This morning twelve enemy planes attacked forty landing craft engaging in sneak transportation since the 1st of this month. They are scheduled to land troops on the northwest tip of Guadalcanal at 0300 tomorrow.

Our troops at Rabi are still holding out and waiting for reinforcements.

A telegram came from the chief of staff, Eighth Fleet, advising that the Kawaguchi detachment would commence attacks about the 11th. Staff Officer Watanabe had flown to Rabaul to that end, but it was most fortunate that they so decided without awaiting his arrival.

Saturday, 5 September 1942. Fair. The Second Fleet arrived at 0930 and the Third Fleet at 1330. It was fortunate that they did not meet enemy submarines on their way. The anchorage has become quite lively. The commanders in chief of both fleets came in the afternoon and reported on the war situation.

After successfully landing troops, destroyer *Yudachi* and two other destroyers bombarded the airstrip, which was set on fire for some time, when they met two enemy ships. After about a forty-minute gun battle, the enemy returned lessening fire and seemed to be sunk. One of them, of the

British minelayer *Adventure* type, had a big induced explosion on her quarterdeck.

Yudachi's skipper is a commander who distinguished himself as skipper of destroyer *Oshio* of the Eighth Destroyer Division in the Dutch East Indies operation. He achieved a splendid deed again this time. There is a whale of a difference between him and the Twenty-fourth Destroyer Division commander of the other day. One full of fighting spirit is always rewarded with a victory. [*The sunken ships were the U.S. destroyer transports* Little *and* Gregory.]³¹

Among those landing craft proceeding to Guadalcanal, three were sunk by yesterday's enemy attack and two disabled, but the rest were heading for the landing point at 5 knots in the face of considerably rough seas. They seemed to have succeeded in landing at the scheduled time of 0300. (Actually, they succeeded in landing at 0530.) [*This parenthetical sentence was obviously added later.*]

Many casualties were sustained in the Rabi area and a wholesale evacuation was requested. It is to be carried out tonight. It was unfortunate indeed. [*This evacuation ended Japanese attempts to take over the Milne Bay area.*]³²

We telegraphed our future operational policy, which was the result of much study, to our command.

Sunday, 6 September 1942. Fair, shower in the morning. A flying boat with Prince Takeda, vice chief of the Army and Navy General Staffs, and others on board returned to Truk at 1430. A dinner was held with the commanders in chief of the Second, Third, Fourth, and Sixth fleets and vice chiefs of the Army and Navy General Staffs.

An enemy submarine attacked the chartered ship *Koryo Maru* with four torpedoes at the north entrance, but one passed in front and three passed under the bottom. An enemy transport with two destroyers were sighted heading north to south-southeast of Guadalcanal. I hope to destroy them tonight or tomorrow.

Staff Officer Watanabe returned after concluding an agreement between the commander in chief, Combined Fleet, and the commander, Seventeenth Army, regarding the coming Guadalcanal operations.

The naval landing parties in the Rabi area are really devoid of spirit. Last night's evacuees reached over 1,100. Considering the number at the time of landing being 1,800, and also the Sasebo No. 5 landing party being out of communications, the casualties were not heavy. The Kure No. 3 landing party commander was sent back because of a bullet wound in his lower thigh, and the healthy battalion adjutant accompanied him. What was the matter with them thus to desert their men?

The causes of this failure are considered to be as follows:

1. It was erroneously considered possible to take a defended airfield with naval landing parties alone.

2. In addition to our being too much burdened by the Guadalcanal issue, this landing operation was started thoughtlessly. Our forces accordingly were dispersed in three areas, including the one for Moresby.

3. The quality of the landing party was not good. Most of them were draftees of thirty to thirty-five years, lacking in perseverance and fighting spirit. Their actions in fighting were not proper. Their cooperative action from the north and south did not work out.

4. They were troubled with rain and athlete's foot. Moreover, bad weather hampered our planes' activities.

The Eighth Fleet should have been more thoughtful.

Mail arrived from the homeland today after a long time.

[On Monday, 7 September, top brass of the Second, Third, Fourth, and Sixth fleets and the Eleventh Air Fleet, among others, assembled at *Yamato* to discuss battle lessons, matters to be improved, and future operations.]

While we were eating lunch, the following signal came in and we all cheered:

Submarine *I-11* sighted an enemy task force at a point 270 miles bearing 145° of Guadalcanal at about 1000 yesterday, and a carrier of the *Yorktown* type was hit with two torpedoes and an explosion was heard.

After that, the submarine was attacked fiercely with depth charges and was unable to submerge on account of her damaged storage batteries. But she still withdrew. Anyhow, it was certain they got something this time. And that deserves congratulations.

[*The Japanese were unable to confirm the torpedoing of a U.S. carrier at this time, and U.S. records do not reflect this action.*][33]

Tuesday, 8 September 1942. Cloudy. In the morning, I thought of the need to change the current operational plans and its measures. At lunch time I said that we should hurry up refueling and place the readied fleet on short notice so as to meet an enemy attack from Guadalcanal and also an enemy reinforcement on a large scale.

One hour after lunch a report that the enemy was landing at Taivu Point with one cruiser, six destroyers, and six transports. Another telegram from the local army stated the army was trying to prevent the above landing with a part of the Kawaguchi detachment, and the detachment was also going to attack the airstrip on about the 11th.

[*This party consisted of the destroyer transports* McKean *and* Manley *and the patrol vessels* YP-346 *and* YP-289, *carrying marine raiders from Tulagi. Two other transports,* Fuller *and* Bellatrix, *were in the area but not a part of this particular operation. The Japanese apparently included them in the count of six transports. Kawaguchi retreated inland, making a stand at a major supply depot at Tasimboko, which the marines destroyed.*][34]

Moreover, the commander, Seventeenth Army, sent in a telegram stating that "as a powerful enemy invasion force has arrived at the Fiji area, I have requested the Kawaguchi detachment to hasten the commencement of its attack. We request that the Combined Fleet take up positions to meet the enemy promptly and make every effort to prevent enemy reinforcements. Awaiting your reply." My prediction of one hour before really came true. So we issued an order again changing the date of the general attack to the 11th. The date of two related operations, i.e., an attack on Nudeni Island and an advance of the float plane base, was advanced accordingly.

Though the Seventeenth Army had not yet consulted us on changing X-Day from the 13th to the 11th, we informed them that "the Combined Fleet has revised X-Day to be the 11th and started operational movements." It seems to me that even the Seventeenth Army turned out to be pessimistic upon seeing a powerful enemy reinforcement.

The enemy began landing to the east of our force today. It will be all right if the enemy is prevented completely, but otherwise most of the Kawaguchi detachment will be attacked both from the east and west, resulting in a serious situation.

Our force, which landed on the northwest tip of Guadalcanal from landing craft the day before yesterday, was found to be one-third of the original strength. This morning, the naval force commander on the island reported that it landed on the island safely and they were in high morale. But in the evening its regimental commander, Colonel Oka, sent in a telegram that only one-third of his force succeeded in landing, though the commander and the colors were all right, so searches were requested for the rest of his force.

Those who failed to reach the destination were in craft damaged by enemy attacks on the way and 350 men who were guided by a sub-lieutenant. Originally I thought the casualties would be one-third and the rest would reach the destination, but its proportion was completely reversed.

What would Major General Kawaguchi say after always insisting on a landing by landing craft? It ended up like this after days of hardship. It is most regrettable and, at the same time, we acutely feel the shortage in general fighting strength. Fortunately, the Aoba detachment [commanded by Major General Yumio Nasu], originally slated to be sent to Rabi, was on the way to Shortland after the original plan was changed. Then it was decided to send it to Guadalcanal.

Upon receipt of a report of sighting a large enemy force, the Eighth

Fleet decided to destroy it tonight with its own forces. Float planes of the Eleventh Seaplane Tender Division bombed ten enemy cruisers, destroyers, and transports in Tulagi at 1715. [*According to U.S. records, the only result of this air raid was the beaching of* YP-346, *with three of her crew dead.*][35]

The commander, Third Destroyer Squadron, was going to assault the enemy at Guadalcanal from Shortland, leading his flagship and destroyers—the Tokyo Express. I wish him success.

The enemy's favorite method has been to withdraw to Tulagi at night. As the order did not include this in its planning, a warning was sent to the Eighth Fleet.

[Wednesday, 9 September 1942, saw a comedy of errors. Destroyer *Akikaze* reported sighting "something like a periscope." The fleet immediately went to first station, all ships except the advance force changed anchorage, planes dove for the supposed sight, and a destroyer dropped depth charges. In the midst of what Ugaki called "the submarine fuss," the converted carrier *Unyo* entered the north channel. Half amused, half irritated, Ugaki wrote, "It was almost certain that the supposed periscope was her masthead. It must have been a case of one dog setting the whole town a-barking. It may be called an episode of war, but for those with responsibility it was a source of much trouble."]

Float planes bombed the enemy hiding in Tulagi last night after sunset, but the result was unknown. The Third Destroyer Squadron sank an enemy destroyer outside Tulagi and set fire to another one, which escaped into port. Why can't our forces get into port while the enemy can go in? Planes of the Eleventh Air Fleet could not get ready yesterday and neither did they succeed today.

Furthermore, another transport was sighted approaching Guadalcanal escorted by two destroyers. The enemy also seems desperate in attempting reinforcement. A big fire was reportedly observed at the airfield on the island last night. Anyway, it was a favorable incident for us.

Last night we received a telegram that ten enemy fighters attacked landing craft with the Sasebo No. 5 special landing party aboard at an island a few dozen miles north of Rabi. [The fighters were P-40s of the Fifth Air Force.][36] They were forced to discontinue further movement after being stranded there. They had intended to land north of Rabi. This was an unexpected mishap. We are going to get in touch with them by plane today and rescue them tomorrow night.

On the other hand, it was found that on Savo Island were another three hundred stranded forces that had intended to land on Guadalcanal by small landing craft. Getting stranded seems to be in fashion these days.

[On Thursday, 10 September, Ugaki want to Rabaul for liaison with the army, accompanied by staff officers Miwa, Watanabe, and Lieutenant

Commander Suteji Muroi, along with "a paymaster handling secretarial tasks."]

At about 0900 we saw the task force that sortied from Truk early this morning sailing southward to take up positions. We arrived at Rabaul at 1400 after circling the volcano at the mouth of the bay. At the headquarters I met the commander in chief, his chief of staff, [Rear Admiral Mumetaka] Sakamaki, and other staff officers. Later I visited Mikawa, commander in chief, Eighth Fleet, and his chief of staff, [Rear Admiral Shinzo] Onishi. Intending to sortie tonight, they went on board heavy cruiser *Chokai* at 1600.

Then I visited Seventeenth Army headquarters and met Lieutenant General [Harukichi] Hyakutake, its commander, and his chief of staff, Major General [Akisaburo] Futami, and was briefed on the outline operational plan by his staff officer, [Maj. Tadahiko] Hayashi.

Its plan solely depended upon a night assault, taking advantage of the jungle, and paid little attention to how to employ field guns brought on the island only with great difficulty. After asking some questions, I told the army commander that in view of the importance of this operation and the enemy's attitude, we should never be optimistic about the coming operation. Furthermore, I invited his attention to the increased importance of maintaining a close liaison between the army and navy, as it was a major operation covering several hundred miles with land warfare on Guadalcanal as its center.

[That evening, Ugaki shared the Eleventh Air Fleet's rather frugal dinner, then was quartered in the accommodation of the Eighth Fleet's senior staff officer. He learned that the army had postponed its general attack to the 12th.

[On Friday, 11 September, Ugaki met with senior officers of the Eighth Naval Base, Twenty-fifth Air Flotilla, and Twenty-sixth Air Flotilla, as well as the commander, Seventh Naval Base Force. That afternoon he visited a hospital atop a hill. At the moment, only 160 patients remained and additional wards were being constructed.]

After coming down the hill and a forty-minute drive, I reached Bunakanau, the western airfield on a hilltop. Just then that day's attack planes were returning from Guadalcanal. Together with [Rear Admiral Masanori] Yamagata, the commander, Twenty-sixth Air Flotilla, I listened to the combat reports. They shot down three or four enemy planes and one of ours was lost.

A B-17 made a rare visit in the morning and carried out reconnaissance. An alert was sounded.

Saturday 12 September 1942. Fair. X-Day. Leaving the quarters at 0515, I went to the east airfield and met the commanding officers of the Second,

Sixth, and Tainan air groups. The flotilla commander also came and we saw off fifteen fighters heading for Guadalcanal.

As the day before yesterday, our naval air forces attacked the enemy positions today and shot down thirteen enemy planes and lost three planes of our own. But the enemy reinforced twenty Grumman fighters there, and furthermore it was said that there were signs of their using B-17s there some time ago. They bring up planes as fast as we shoot them down. It is a problem.

Our army forces on Guadalcanal proceeded through the jungle without being sighted by the enemy yesterday and were going to begin attacks at 1600 today. Army headquarters were said to have celebrated a success in advance last night upon receipt of the above news. But I can't help entertaining much doubt about the success of the night assault with lightly equipped soldiers. They should be wary of their own conceit.

The Eighth Communications Corps reported that over a dozen enemy planes took off in the air after 1800, two of which asked for its radio direction to be found at about 2200 and also dispatched an SOS signal. This made us think that our army forces succeeded in the charge as scheduled. I went to bed hoping for their big success.

[*Thus began the two-day battle of the Bloody Ridge. The air attack from Rabaul cost the Japanese four fighters and ten bombers on 12 September 1942.*][37]

Sunday, 13 September 1942. Fair. I got up early and after breakfast closeted myself in the headquarters of the Eleventh Air Fleet to listen to incoming information. There has been no report from the Eighth Fleet's float planes, which were supposed to reconnoiter the spot last night.

On the other hand, the Third Destroyer Squadron ordered its destroyer divisions to charge, while a plane of the Eleventh Seaplane Tender Division sighted two bonfires with an interval of fifty meters, which looked like a signal for the capture of the airfield.

Two army reconnaissance planes left the base at 0430 and flew to Guadalcanal escorted by nine fighters. But the two became separated and their reports were contradictory. Aiming to land at the airfield if possible, Major [Koji] Tanaka came down to four hundred meters over the field only to find forty enemy planes still parked there. He immediately withdrew after making a proper observation.

Though these reports were vague, by putting them together we judged that almost surely the airfield had been taken. And this was sent out to those concerned from the Eleventh Air Fleet. Of course, we had some doubts about it, but we did so because we saw the need of promptly regulating the movements of the operational forces since I saw them conflicting. Also attributable was a human weakness brought about by wishful thinking since last night.

When the reconnaissance planes returned at 1400, however, we received their reports that they had fought enemy fighters. As there was no doubt about the existence of enemy fighters over there, we immediately sent out a telegram which said that the airfield had not yet been taken and canceled the previous one. The Eighth Air Fleet also dispatched a telegram about taking the field at 1030. Together with ours, it probably confused the movements of our operational forces for some time.

Nothing has been heard from the Kawaguchi detachment since the last telegram of the 11th. Both the army and navy concluded that the detachment must have confronted many difficulties in advancing through the jungle and postponed the commencement of its attack. It was accordingly decided to repeat the same operation tomorrow. My fears, which had been entertained for some time before, suddenly doubled, but not the others. [*There was little action at Bloody Ridge on 13 September beyond minor raids.*][38]

A search flying boat found an enemy task force of one carrier, two battleships, and three destroyers to the south of Santa Cruz. Our task force was sailing south to the northeast of Guadalcanal in concert with last night's scheduled army attack, and was six hundred miles away from the said enemy. As it sent in its intention of attacking the enemy tomorrow morning, I directed the staff to draw up our search tomorrow so as to cooperate with it.

As it was impossible to destroy an enemy air base on Nudeni Island with submarines, two destroyers of the Twenty-seventh Destroyer Division were dispatched. But enemy planes found them before they reached the destination and the enemy ran away.

[On Monday, 14 September, Ugaki attended a conference of the Eleventh Air Fleet. The commander in chief thought that the Kawaguchi detachment must have postponed its attack, hoping to join that night with the Aoba detachment, which had already joined the Oka detachment.

[Ugaki flatly stated this was "wishful thinking." The attack was already two days behind schedule, and he did not believe the two detachments could have made liaison. "Accordingly, my judgment was that the attempt must have ended in failure by meeting either an unexpected disaster in the jungle or a strong defense put up by the enemy in his rear. We should stop the optimistic thinking and think of countermeasures to meet a case of failure." Ugaki communicated this opinion to the army, but both commands "were dazzled by hope" and paid little attention.]

[*Ugaki's pessimism was justified. Kawaguchi lost almost half of his forces. At a cost of forty dead and 103 wounded, the marines held the ridge, thus keeping the vital Henderson Field in American hands.*][39]

[Ugaki had further cause for exasperation that day. He heard noises like machine-gun fire, and learned that an ammunition magazine had exploded. The explosions grew ever "bigger and more dangerous," and Ugaki, along with the commander in chief, Eleventh Air Fleet and his staff had to take refuge in a shelter in the garden. There they stayed for two hours, pinned down by their own ammunition. As Ugaki noted, "What an absurd accident!" If only they could have dropped all that firepower on the enemy! Meanwhile, the Communications Corps also had to take refuge. "Thus all the establishments within the danger zone stopped functioning at this important time of changing operations." The situation finally simmered down by 1600 and all concerned got back to work.]

Then the discussion returned to the outcome of the operation again, and I still said it was hopeless while Chief of Staff Sakamaki was as optimistic as before.

When we finished dinner, an urgent signal arrived from the Eighth Fleet. It said: "From Staff Officer Matsumoto dispatched from the Seventeenth Army to the front. Kawaguchi detachment seems to have changed its schedule to commence attacks at 2000 tonight."

Everybody cheered and the commander in chief looked as if to say, "There you are; my prediction was right." But I thought that "seems to" meant his [Matsumoto's] imagination and he was not saying it after any actual communication with the detachment. I couldn't help being skeptical about it. Saying, "If it is really like that, all the better," I left the room. And I was not happy either!

The following telegram came in from the naval radio station at Guadalcanal, which had remained completely silent since the day before yesterday: "Aoba detachment joined Oka unit yesterday and started the offensive from the west this morning. But it could not make any advance owing to enemy resistance, especially trench mortars, and withdrew to the south of the airfield by order of the Oka detachment commander."

It was most untimely that the naval unit had attempted to advance its communications equipment after the forward advance commenced on the 12th. Also, it was a fault on the part of the fleet not to have sent a naval liaison officer to the front.

The office house of the Eighth Fleet command sustained fairly heavy damage in today's explosion. A splinter struck right beside an armchair I used in the commander in chief's room, coming through the ceiling. I was lucky not to be there. Explosions continued spasmodically even after nightfall, and I had to move up to the commander in chief's quarters on a hilltop. I went to sleep with slim hope while explosions still continued.

[Bombs continued to explode until 0100 of Tuesday, 15 September. After admiring the "beautiful view of Rabaul Bay," Ugaki came down the hill at 0600 and inspected the damage. He reflected that, whether the explosion was due to sabotage or accident, "those who piled them up without any order and failed to take necessary steps to safeguard them could not escape their responsibility. Realizing that an enemy bomb could have caused all this, let this be a lesson for the future."]

No change was noticed except for a float reconnaissance plane observing field guns being fired five hundred meters north of the northern end of the Guadalcanal airfield from about 0230 to 0300 this morning. I told the staffs to completely renew their observations on the situation. At last they gave in.

Staff Officer Watanabe brought from the army command the first telegram sent from the Kawaguchi detachment commander yesterday. It read:

> The batteries of the eastern position commenced firing during the evening of the 12th as scheduled, but the main force was delayed by the difficult march in the jungle and was only able to carry out attacks at 2200 on the 13th. But enemy resistance was unexpectedly strong, so we suffered a great loss, including battalion commanders. We were forced to withdraw. After regrouping the remaining force on the west side of the west river, we are going to plan our move.

I can only say that this was what I expected.

I went to the Eleventh Air Fleet command and had the staffs draft a new plan right away. I also ordered them to revise the army and navy central agreement, draft a new local agreement, and commence negotiations with the army.

[Realizing that the army command had sustained a tremendous shock and seemed "at a loss about what to do," he moved to bolster their morale and help them "plan a comeback." Visiting Chief of Staff Futami, Ugaki encouraged him, urged that they try this operation again, and said that the navy would cooperate fully in transporting troops. Finally Futami "recovered his spirits" and was ready to try again. However, Ugaki feared that, in "character and capacity," he was not up to his job and might have to be replaced. As usual in the case of a major setback, Ugaki recorded his opinions as to its causes, which are thought-provoking and valuable.]

1. We underestimated the enemy determination to launch their first offensive, staking the president's honor for the intermediate fall election campaign and pouring in fighting strength despite repeated losses, as well as their thorough preparedness in defense and countermeasures.

On the other hand, we overestimated our strength displayed in the first stage operations and sought success in a surprise attack at one stroke with lightly equipped troops of the same (or less) strength as the enemy. (The Army General Staff, Seventeenth Army, and Kawaguchi detachment were all quite optimistic.)

2. While we were confronted with difficulties in air operations and transportation missions because of enemy air supremacy and bad weather, the enemy succeeded in sending in reinforcements, disregarding their losses, and consolidating their defense.

3. Little attention was paid to the utilization of field guns, except for the purpose of surprise attack. One of the 12-cm antiaircraft guns, transported to the island by *Tsugaru* with difficulty, was damaged in its sight when unloaded and was brought back, while another was landed near Taivu Point, hidden in the woods, and seems never to have been used.

The command system and coordination of the army were not perfect. Of those led by detachment commander Kawaguchi, those originally under his command were only two battalions, while another battalion and the remnant of the Ichiki detachment belonged to other units. Furthermore, regimental commander Oka was situated to the west, and there seemed to be no liaison between them. So they carried out attacks separately. They even failed to relate the postponement of the attack, so a part of them commenced its attack on the 12th.

4. The position where the main force of the detachment advanced was not proper. Not only confronted with many difficulties in advancing through the thick jungle, every battalion lacked liaison with each other, so that a coordinated attack became impossible.

5. A surprise attack can only be successful when it is carried out against an unprepared enemy. Actually, however, they were discovered earlier by sound detectors and other means. When they were unexpectedly subjected to concentrated fire, they were spiritually frustrated. Including over two hundred killed, the casualties suffered were 654, representing only ten percent of the original strength.

["In short," concluded Ugaki, "they made light of the enemy too much. Their operational plans should be more flexible." He sent his opinions to Yamamoto and "requested the necessary preparation as a whole to the High Command in Tokyo."]

A search plane sighted one carrier, one seaplane tender, and some destroyers heading south on course of 150° to the south-southeast of Guadalcanal. Probably they were on their way back after [delivering] reinforcement aircraft to Guadalcanal yesterday. The same plane further found nine transports heading north escorted by six destroyers to its southeast. This discovery eventually threatened the already hopeless army a great deal.

In the meantime, a float plane found an enemy task force of two carriers, two battleships, and seven destroyers further to the east. The time was 0830. B-17s were already operating from Guadalcanal, so our task force will not be able to move at will.

[*The two U.S. carriers,* Wasp *and* Hornet, *with their escort vessels, were covering a six-transport convoy bringing the Seventh Marine Regiment from Espiritu Santo to Guadalcanal.* Wasp *was escorted by four cruisers and six destroyers,* Hornet *by the battleship* North Carolina, *three cruisers, and seven destroyers.*]⁴⁰

Rear Admiral [Shigeharu] Kaneko, chief of the Communications Bureau of the Naval General Staff, together with his staff officer, Tamura, arrived here to investigate the communications conditions in view of their inefficiency.

At 1050 this morning the submarine *I-19* discovered an enemy group of one carrier, one cruiser, and three destroyers in her sector. Taking advantage of their turning around, she succeeded in hitting with four torpedoes. Later, *I-15* found this group and confirmed that the carrier of the *Yorktown* type sank at 1800. This is a success deserving congratulations.

[*Three of* I-19's *torpedoes hit* Wasp *and damaged her so severely that she had to be abandoned at around 1600 and was scuttled by destroyer* Lansdowne. *It is strange that Ugaki did not mention the exploits of* I-15, *which torpedoed* North Carolina *and destroyer* O'Brien. *Both were saved, but the battleship had to return to Pearl Harbor for repairs, and on 19 October* O'Brien *sank en route to the West Coast.*]⁴¹

[Apparently these successes did not reconcile Ugaki to the defeat on Guadalcanal, for he ended the day's entry, "It is not today that I realized our defeat; actually, I have known since the 13th. At 1800, I retired to the hilltop lodge. But, being unaware of our defeat, the hill welcomed me as before."]

Wednesday, 16 September 1942. Shower. Most of our medium torpedo bombers and fighters were sent out to attack the enemy convoy found yesterday, but they turned back on account of foul weather. According to a reconnaissance float plane's report, two transports entered and were unloading at Lunga Roads, while all the rest withdrew to the south for the time being.

[Much of the day Ugaki spent in conversation with various army and navy officers. He believed there had not been enough visiting between the Eleventh and Eighth fleets and the army. "They should drop in at each other's from time to time and talk."]

The Eighth Fleet command returned to its original quarters, so my quarters were moved to the room of the commander of the garrison force. It was near the entrance and the guards' telephones kept me awake. A few moments after I fell asleep, we had air raids twice. The noise of gunfire and small arms was terrible. Anyway, it was a night of little sleep. Now I can see the effectiveness of night raids.

[On Thursday, 17 September, Ugaki finished his mission "by concluding an agreement between the Combined Fleet and the Seventeenth Army in the morning." In the afternoon he drove around the island with Vice Admiral Masao Kanazawa, commander, Eighth Naval Base Force, inspecting various installations. The two admirals had "a pleasant talk and imbibed a fair amount of sake too." Ugaki accepted his hospitality on this, the last day of his stay in Rabaul.

[On Friday, 18 September, Ugaki noted that while the operation had failed, he had accomplished his mission. As the senior staff officer and communications staff officer of the Twenty-sixth Air Flotilla had come down with malaria, he left Muroi behind to help out.]

At 0530 I visited Vice Admiral Mikawa on the hilltop by car and bade good-bye after talking thirty minutes. I then visited Eighth Fleet headquarters and got back to my quarters for breakfast. I went to Eleventh Air Fleet headquarters at 0700 and then to Seventeenth Army headquarters, where nobody above the staff was present yet. It was just like the army as usual.

I got on a medium bomber and took off at 0835 and arrived safely at Truk airfield at 1445. Then I returned on board and reported to the commander in chief. After all, it was my domicile and I felt at home.

Early this morning a telegram arrived from Guadalcanal reporting that six transports, one heavy cruiser, two light cruisers, and twelve destroyers were in Lunga Roads and engaged in unloading. A large-scale attack with torpedo planes was planned, but it was decided to cancel it due to bad weather on the way. I learned this to my great regret only before my plane took off. The Third Destroyer Squadron dashed into the roads, only to find that the enemy had withdrawn three hours before.

[*Rear Admiral Richmond Kelly Turner, commander, Amphibious Force, South Pacific, decided to risk landing the marines at Lunga, and some four thousand landed safely with all stores.*][42]

Saturday, 19 September 1942. Fair. In the morning I took care of those items of business that had accumulated while I was away.

Rear Admiral [Gonichiro] Kakimoto, the Combined Communications Corps commander, arrived here with his subordinates. He was assigned to control fleet communications in the operational front. This order should have been issued a little sooner.

It was decided to reinforce the Seventeenth Army command by increasing its staff to eleven persons, and Colonel [Haruo] Konuma, its new senior staff officer, arrived here by plane. I hope with this measure the Seventeenth Army will become more trustworthy.

Sunday, 20 September 1942. Partly fair. The weather was bad again in the Solomons area and air attacks were impossible; therefore, our plan of having our support force go down south to strike the enemy and vessels at Guadalcanal after reducing the enemy air power by air attacks yesterday and today had to be rescinded. The necessary orders were issued for the support force to come to Truk to await orders.

The fleet's daily fuel consumption amounts to ten thousand tons lately, and the shortage of tankers was acute in the Rabaul area, as before. The fuel stock at Kure is said to have decreased to 650,000 tons, which is extremely discouraging. I hope it won't hamper the fleet's operational movements. It's also essential for the fleet to economize on fuel by refraining from unnecessary movements.

As antiaircraft firing in the Rabaul area was outrageously uncontrolled and unskilled, we decided to send competent officers and men from *Yamato* and *Mutsu* to teach them. They left here this morning.

Monday, 21 September 1942. Rain. The weather was bad as usual in the Solomons area. A competent air force attacked Port Moresby but the result was not known.

For some time, destroyers had provided transportation to Caminbo, the western tip of Guadalcanal. Tonight, however, enemy planes attacked them while they were unloading. This method is also dangerous on a moonlit night. Sneaking in by small landing craft should be carried out promptly.

Tuesday, 22 September 1942. Rain. No special change observed in the war situation. The commander, Third Destroyer Squadron, temporarily suspended transportation on moonlit nights.

The escort planning for the transportation of army reinforcements, which come from all places—the homeland, Korea, Hong Kong, the Philippines, Java, Sumatra—is very complicated. They appear to collect them, anything from anywhere, without any thought as to the bottleneck, the escorts.

[On Wednesday, 23 September, the advance force and the task force arrived back and their commanders in chief reported. Of the task force, Ugaki noted, "They just spent oil for nothing this time, but we should appreciate their hardships."]

Thursday, 24 September 1942. Fair. At 0705 a ceremony was held facing north on the occasion of the autumnal equinox. I closed my eyes and prayed for the souls of my ancestors and of Tomoko. We had appropriate dishes for the occasion, but I could not feel like autumn in this heat.

A new staff officer of the Seventeenth Army came on his way to his new assignment in the afternoon, together with two staff officers of the Army General Staff. Had they exerted more effort like this a little earlier, there would never have been a failure like that.

Friday, 25 September 1942. Rain. Weather was still bad and it was impossible to attack Guadalcanal. A trial landing was to take place today at the newly built airfield at Buin today, but it was not ready due to the rain the night before last. So fighters could not advance there.

In the meantime, transportation on moonlit nights is risky. We must do something, otherwise transportation will be much delayed, so that commencement of the offensive will have to be postponed. A serious study should be made to find a way to attack through foul weather.

Since this morning I have felt pain in my waist and slightly feverish. I hope I did not catch dengue fever or malaria while I stayed in Rabaul.

Saturday, 26 September 1942. Light rain, later cloudy. Contrary to the fact that for some time we had been unable to attack the enemy on Guadalcanal, the enemy has been constantly active. Seven B-17s raided Shortland at about 0900 this morning. Though the damage was slight, the situation demanded urgent attention, together with the damage sustained by light cruiser *Yura* the day before yesterday.

[*On 25 September a B-17 hit one of the after turrets on light cruiser* Yura.]+3

Meanwhile, the chief of staff, Southeast Area Fleet, requested a sortie of the support force because the enemy would probably raid the Shortland area. The radio intelligence section suggested that enemy radio activity similar to those noted prior to 7 August and before the battle of the Solomons was observed. Something may happen. Setting aside refueling of the capital ships, CV *Zuikaku* is not ready, though she will be ready tomorrow. It is admittedly one of the usual bad habits of this command that everything is planned on its own accord and is never prepared for an immediate sortie to meet the enemy. I warned the staff accordingly.

Of course training is important. But nothing could be more regrettable than if we should not be ready for an important matter bearing a great influence on the Guadalcanal operations after having advanced to this place.

I-33, under repair alongside the repair ship *Urakami Maru*, sank at 0923 due to an error of her key officers. What an incident!

[An accident to a submarine always discomfited Ugaki. In this case, to raise the bow, two of *I-33*'s officers gave permission to open the cock of the after main tank, with the result that she sank from the stern in two minutes, taking with her seven officers and thirty-seven petty officers and men. Ugaki thought there might be a hope, albeit slim, to rescue some of the trapped sailors. "It is significant," he noted, "that this incident was in no way due to a construction fault of the sub, but entirely to a blunder committed by her officers."

[The next morning, Sunday, 27 September, the senior staff officer of the Sixth Fleet, Commander Medori Matsumura, reported that this hope must be abandoned. All they could do was try to salvage the sub. Ugaki appointed Rear Admiral Takayanagi, skipper of *Yamato,* and two staff officers as an investigating committee.]

The commander in chief was scheduled to see a native dance after an inspection ashore, but it was postponed on account of the accident.

An air raid on Guadalcanal finally succeeded after a long time. I wonder how much damage they could inflict upon the enemy. Transportation to the island by means of destroyers and landing craft is going to be resumed from tonight. Moonlight still lasts, and I hope for success. (In today's attack they shot down several planes and bombed the airfield.)

[*Whoever reported these results to Ugaki was mistaken. The Japanese did not shoot down any U.S. planes at Guadalcanal on 27 September and, in fact, lost nine of their own fifty-three.*]++

Monday, 28 September 1942. Partly fair with squall. Staff Officer Watanabe, [Commander Toshikazu] Ohmae, Eleventh Air Fleet staff, Colonel [Masanobu] Tsuji, chief of the Operations Section, Army General Staff, and Hayashi of the Seventeenth Army arrived from Rabaul on a flying boat at about 1530. They are having a conference on operations.

The army asserted that, in view of the failure of the Ichiki and Kawaguchi detachments' attempts, further reinforcements were necessary, and they could not be made unless five more high-speed transports were added. Whether these transports could reach their target would affect our aerial operations, movements of the support force, and a bombardment attempt by our *Kirishima*-class battleships. On the other hand, a delay in this transportation attempt would detain the start of our next offensive, as the attempt would have to be postponed for another month because of the lunar age. I think a daring attempt must be made even if some loss has to be anticipated on transports.

Our attack planes engaged thirty-six enemy fighters over Guadalcanal today and seemed to have shot down about ten of them. However, a report from the garrison force on the island stated that thirty-six enemy aircraft took off thirty minutes before our attack, and the same number landed twenty-five minutes after the raid ended, and furthermore, eighteen planes, of which three were B-17s, landed later. Regrettably, the report included our loss of nine aircraft.

[*The Japanese sent sixty-two planes over Guadalcanal on 28 September. The Americans shot down one fighter and twenty-three bombers. The marines suffered no losses.*]⁴⁵

Why is it that results reported by our attack force and the reported number of planes taking off and landing on the island did not coincide, and only our loss was great?

An enemy submarine attacked the converted carrier *Taiyo* at a point about forty miles south of the south channel, and a torpedo hit her stern. She had been engaged in ferrying planes. She made 16 knots under her own power and entered port. Thirteen were killed or injured.

This happened right after I was saying to Captain Seiho Arima of the Second Escort Force that we were glad to see that our loss due to submarine attacks had decreased lately. Her damage could be repaired at the Fourth Repair Depot at Truk.

[Vice Admiral Nishizo Tsukahara, commander in chief, Eleventh Air Fleet, had been ill with dengue fever, malaria, and "a stomach and intestinal ailment." The Navy Ministry suggested that he be relieved for recuperation, "as operations in this area would be more intensified and it would take some time before they were settled."]

Tuesday, 29 September 1942. Fair with squall. An air raid was carried out on Guadalcanal today. The enemy aircraft used to take off about thirty minutes before the raid and land soon after it was finished. They were in great numbers, too. In view of this, we had to entertain some doubt about our fliers' claim of shooting down so many enemy planes. The daylight attack on that airfield now seems to be almost of no value.

Twelve B-17s attacked destroyer *Akitsuki* near Buka Island while on her way down to the south to intensify antiaircraft defense. But she displayed her value as an antiaircraft-purpose destroyer for the first time by shooting down one of them with no loss to herself.

Wednesday, 30 September 1942. Fair. *Chiyoda* arrived from Kure at 0900 with eleven midget subs on board. According to the skipper who came to report, training and readiness of the craft were still insufficient. I can't help feeling that we called them down too soon, disregarding these points. We shouldn't use them unless success is believed certain. Otherwise, judging from past experience, sacrifices would only be increased for nothing. I warned the staff accordingly and told them to let them keep on with their training for the time being.

We did not carry out an attack on Guadalcanal today and spent the day in readying planes. Transportation by destroyers will be carried out from tomorrow, avoiding moonlit nights.

Last night a submarine on the patrol line sank an enemy transport of seven thousand tons, accompanied by a destroyer, sailing on course of 190°. But she must have been on her way back after unloading, much to our regret.

Two planes, probably enemy, were sighted at a point 510 miles east of Tokyo on the patrol line last night. The Fifth Fleet issued a warning signal, and the Twenty-first Light Cruiser Division and First Destroyer Squadron sortied from Aomori Bay. Also, more than ten enemy planes raided Kiska yesterday and inflicted damage upon a submarine and others.

What's the enemy up to? I say, "Come on, we'll show you!" But I certainly would not like a surprise attack on the homeland at this juncture. In spite of a warning given by radio intelligence that something was going to happen in the southeast Pacific in these few days, nothing special has taken place so far. That was also all the better.

We received an advance notice from the chief of the Personnel Bureau to the effect that, effective 1 November, Vice Admiral Tsukahara would be appointed to the Naval General Staff and replaced by Vice Admiral [Jinichi] Kusaka.

[The Navy Ministry ordered the salvage of *I-33*, but Ugaki feared this would take quite some time, as only "poor equipment for that purpose" was in position.

[Ugaki also noted that the battle for Stalingrad, "expected to fall by early midsummer," was not progressing well. "Unless this city falls, the German operation will be upset. It is most essential for the axis powers to capture it at any cost."]

[Nor were things going well in North Africa, and the Allies had regained air and sea supremacy in the Mediterranean. "It is now time for the Axis powers to get through this hard time, making the utmost efforts."]

Today September is going to pass. Looking back, I find nothing has been accomplished this month.

6

The Chief of Staff Must Never Relax

October 1942–April 1943

Guadalcanal *continued to be the main Japanese preoccupation, so much so that their operational plans did not mention possible failure, because the campaign "can't be unsuccessful." But it could be, and was. By mid-December the Japanese knew they would have to abandon Guadalcanal. Meanwhile, however, three more months of warfare, stubbornly and bravely waged on both sides, had to be fought. In related naval actions, Ugaki's area of primary interest, both lost heavily, but the Americans were able to land reinforcements regularly, while the Japanese experienced ever-increasing difficulty in reinforcing their troops on the island. Ugaki recorded historically valuable reports of many of these engagements. Relying as he supposedly did upon reports of participants, especially naval aviators, these summations are highly optimistic from the Japanese point of view.*

Nevertheless, Ugaki was sufficiently realistic to record a worry over Japan's logistical situation. The fuel oil problem, always troublesome, was becoming acute. A shortage of shipping was reducing production of steel and aluminum. A large submarine returning from Europe with a cargo of new guns and spare parts struck a mine and sank. Then, too, the Japanese more and more would face the United States's "overwhelming air power." Thus Ugaki had to end his entries for 1942 on a pessimistic note, lamenting that Japan's plane for invasions on several fronts had been "scattered like dreams."

Chronic toothache, no respecter of rank, continued to give Ugaki pain and no doubt contributed to his somewhat sour outlook during this period. Although Yamamoto authorized a sharp memorandum stressing the folly of encouraging skippers to go down with their ships, Ugaki still harked back with admiration to Yamaguchi's death, and expressed his desire for eventually an "appropriate" place to die. He was sedately pleased to be promoted to Vice Admiral as of 1 November—evidently he had been of some use to his country.

Unfortunately, the diary for the first three months of 1943 is missing. Ugaki kept it for this period and it remained intact until after the war. According to Rear

Admiral Kameto Kuroshima, who was Yamamoto's and Ugaki's senior staff officer, he borrowed Ugaki's diary from one of the admiral's relatives when summoned as a witness to the military tribunal in Tokyo and brought the portion in question with him. He claimed that on the way there, he lost it on the train.

This is all the more regrettable as it would be of interest to have Ugaki's comments on the evacuation of Guadalcanal, when the Japanese took off some eleven thousand men almost under the noses of the Americans—a feat as remarkable in its way as Dunkirk. Also, one would very much like to have one of his detailed reports on the battle of the Bismarck Sea where U.S. aircraft inflicted considerable damage on Japanese transports and destroyers.

April 1943 was a busy and ultimately tragic month for Ugaki. The Combined Fleet flag had moved from Truk to Rabaul, arriving on 2 April. The move was to enable Yamamoto to take personal charge of I-Go, Japan's sweeping plan for operations against the Allies. In midmonth Ugaki came down with dengue fever; unluckily for him it abated in time for him to fly with Yamamoto on an inspection trip. On 18 April, U.S. fliers ambushed both planes. Yamamoto and those with him were killed; Ugaki's plane crashed offshore and he survived, although wounded. Not until a year later, on 18 April 1944, did he record a detailed account of these happenings.

Ugaki was transferred to the homeland for hospitalization and recuperation. He kept up his diary, but his son Hiromitsu refused permission to use the entries for this period when the diary was published in Japanese, claiming that they were purely personal and of no historical interest. Chihaya attempted to persuade Hiromitsu Ugaki's widow to allow us permission to publish these entries; however, she refused to go against her husband's wishes. Hence there is another, much longer, break in the diary until 22 February 1944, when once more Ugaki had an active role to play.

Something of a lull in the Pacific war occurred until mid-June 1943, with both sides making plans and building up. The next step for the United States was New Georgia with its strong air base at Munda. In related naval actions all concerned lost valuable ships and men in battles featuring miserable American torpedoes and effective Japanese ones. Munda fell on 6 August, and shortly thereafter the Americans abandoned the "island hopping" policy in favor of "leapfrogging," that is bypassing certain Japanese positions and leaving them to die on the vine. In November Admiral Koga, Yamamoto's successor, moved the fleet back from Rabaul to Truk.

[October opened with Ugaki fretting over the salvage of I-33, not helped by controversy between the chief fleet engineer and Captain (shipbuilding) Naosaburo Masukata, attached to the Combined Fleet. "It's outrageous that we can't do anything about it after sinking a ship in our own base," Ugaki exploded. He resolved "to salvage her with all the resources of the Fleet" and also to ask assistance from the homeland. "Otherwise, we'll have no excuse to offer the emperor and the victims."]

Friday, 2 October 1942. Fair with squall. It's gratifying that our aerial attacks have been successfully launched lately. In each sortie our fighters are shooting down almost more than ten enemy planes in dogfights.

An enemy submarine [U.S.S. *Sturgeon*] sank *Katsuragi Maru* at a point southeast of Rabaul yesterday, and most of the crew including the skipper were saved.[1] Three enemy planes raided Rabaul before dawn this morning and a bomb hit the stern of light cruiser *Tenryu*.

Three of the four destroyers engaged in last night's transportation attempt succeeded, while the remaining one had to turn back with rudder trouble which developed while evading enemy planes. Transportation by small craft seems to be quite a difficult proposition.

Kashima arrived in the fleet anchorage to participate in antiaircraft training.

I called in the chief of staff, Fourth Fleet, and told him that the commander in chief, Fourth Fleet, was assigned to salvage *I-33*. I also sent a request for some personnel to the high command for that undertaking.

Saturday, 3 October 1942. Fair with squall. The fighter attack on Guadalcanal succeeded again today.

At 1540, twenty enemy single-engined planes attacked *Nisshin*, which left Shortland at 0630 to transport army heavy armament to Guadalcanal. But she proceeded without damage. I hope she'll succeed in unloading at the scheduled time of from 2130 to 2330, because this outcome would greatly affect our future plan of bombarding the airfields and other locations.

[One of three torpedo planes raiding Shortland early that morning was shot down, and the Japanese captured a code book and some maps. Ugaki reflected that while "their skill in torpedoing was not so good," their flying technique was better, for they had flown from Australia "at night under a half moon." He added, "They must be satisfied, as for them it is quite honorable to be POWs."]

Refueling each ship of the main and support forces has been completed. Refueling is a prerequisite to an operation and yet, regrettably, it always tends to be delayed.

The communications staff officer brought a draft plan for recapturing Guadalcanal. I ordered him to restudy it, as some points were still insufficient. This plan, too, depended largely on how to maintain refueling.

The Eighth Fleet sent in the detailed schedule of the coming operations, made after consultation with the army. This sort of thing should be decided first, as it's essential to decide the movement of our fleet by estimating the enemy movements.

Staff Officer Muroi turned up today, as his dengue fever wasn't serious. Staff Officer Fuji got laid up with a cold, and hasn't yet appeared at the table for four or five days. The staff seems to be a bit tired. I would like to give them some rest, but can't do anything here. Wait about two months more!

Sunday, 4 October 1942. Cloudy with occasional squalls. Twenty-seven fighters attacked Guadalcanal yesterday. Finding no enemy, one group of them started strafing when all of a sudden enemy Grummans swooped to attack them. Though several of them were shot down, our loss amounted to nine, including those missing.

Last night enemy planes attacked *Nisshin* at the landing point. In spite of her damage by a near miss, the Second Division Command disembarked and unloaded 15-cm howitzers. She withdrew with a part of her load still on board. Ten enemy planes attacked her early this morning, but she arrived at Shortland safely without damage this time.

The Second CV Division left the Inland Sea for Truk. It's expected to arrive here on the 9th. Light cruiser *Kitakami* of the Ninth Light Cruiser Division left for Shortland with Maizuru No. 4 special landing party and others on board.

I approved an operational order after some correction. There has been a slight trend toward a lack of carefulness and minuteness in planning of late. I cautioned myself that the chief of staff must never relax.

Monday, 5 October 1942. Same kind of weather as yesterday. Two search planes lost contact in the southeast of the Solomons, one on its outgoing trip and another on its return way. Judging that they must have been downed by enemy fighters and also that there was much possibility of an enemy task force operating in that area, the Southeast Area Fleet issued an order exclusively preparing for this enemy tomorrow. This command also ordered the Sixth Fleet to carry out a search by submarines. What will be discovered?

[The fleet conducted training in spotting and identifying submerged submarines, with all the aircraft on the islands participating. "Henceforth," wrote Ugaki hopefully, "they can't mistake whales and porpoises for submarines."

[That afternoon the new chief of staff, Seventeenth Army, Major General Shuichi Miyazaki, with Captain Nakase of the Navy Ministry came to *Yamato* for briefing. Ugaki was favorably impressed. "I only hope he'll be all right in practice, too."

[In the afternoon of Tuesday, 6 October, experimental firing of projectiles to be used "in the coming operation" was conducted.]

Wednesday, 7 October 1942. Fair. Attacks by enemy planes and bombardments against our forces on Guadalcanal increased. Screening planes couldn't be sent today, so *Nisshin* turned back from her halfway point.

The airfield at Buin has been completed, but the forwarding of fighters there seems to have been delayed again. Everything tends to be delayed. It has become necessary to postpone X-Day to the 15th for landing and unloading the high-speed convoy.

An enemy submarine torpedoed and sank *Naminoue Maru* of an army convoy sailing from the Hiroshima area northwest of Rabaul. [*Naminoue Maru probably fell victim to U.S.S. Sculpin, which torpedoed and sank a transport in that area on 7 October 1942.*][2]

Vice Admiral Kusaka, newly appointed commander in chief, Eleventh Air Fleet, arrived here at 1330 from Saipan by flying boat. An operations briefing was held from 1400, gathering the important staff officers of the fleets. We then had dinner with each commander in chief. The briefing was over by 1630.

Chief of the Defense Construction Department of the army and party arrived here without notice. We decided to confer with him tomorrow.

The high command in Tokyo seems to be rather too sensitive in punishing commanders for their incapability in carrying out operations. After asking Commander in Chief Yamamoto's view on it, I wrote a letter to the chief of the Personnel Bureau. The commander in chief's view is as follows:

> Whatever they did under my command is my responsibility as commander in chief. If they fail once, use them again and they will surely succeed the next time.
>
> If we do not approve of the skipper surviving when his ship goes down after hard fighting, we shall not be able to carry through this war, which cannot be settled soon. There is no reason why we should discourage their survival, while we are encouraging the fliers to survive by means of parachute.
>
> In a war which must be carried out against tremendous odds, I, as commander in chief, could not help feeling reluctant in issuing orders if I had to ask our skippers not to return alive when their ships sink. Thinking of the resolution of Navy Minister Admiral [Gonbei] Yamamoto and the hardship endured by Admiral Togo at the time of the Russo-Japanese War, I am only trying not to be inferior to them.

The navy minister has authority to decide personal affairs while the commander in chief has the great responsibility of attaining the war aim and commanding the personnel thus appointed. Should there be any difference between the concepts of these two, in the end it would interfere with the commander in chief's leadership. The high command should be cautious about their words and deeds.

[On Thursday, 8 October, Ugaki participated in a conference aboard *Kashima* with members of the army and navy defense inspection team. "The army side fully understood the situation," wrote Ugaki, "and it decided to send five or six divisions in addition to twenty-five battalions of engineers and others to the Pacific area." They all dined together, the team being due to fly to Kwajalein early the next morning.]

While sailing toward Guadalcanal, *Nisshin* was attacked by more than a dozen enemy aircraft, including torpedo planes, but escaped from them owing to the good fighting of float plane fighters. Two of them made forced landings at sea, but their crews were rescued.

Transportation difficulties have reached their peak. In addition, the enemy started using the 150-cm searchlight set up at Cape Lunga since the 7th.

A ground service unit, which advanced to the newly built airfield at Buin, reported that it was unfit for operations at this time, as half of the planes would be overturned due to the strip's soft surface. How weak-minded they are! This is the time when every difficulty should be overcome. Don't grumble, but try to use it by all means!

[*The Buin base was completed "roughly" on 25 October, when some forty fighter aircraft arrived. But the conditions of which Ugaki complained still prevailed. After every squall about ten planes daily would suffer damage due to skidding.*][3]

The commander, First Submarine Squadron, Rear Admiral [Shigeaki] Yamazaki, isn't in good health. The commander, Third Battleship Division, Kurita, still has a slight fever. I hope they'll take care of themselves and recover soon.

[On Friday, 9 October, Tsukahara, slightly in better health, met Yamamoto ashore and inspected the salvage work on *I-33.*

[Kishi, commanding the Ninth Light Cruiser Division, reported in person, and Eighth Heavy Cruiser Division commander Hara forwarded his views on the operational plan.]

The commander in chief has become slightly sensitive lately, asking about minor matters and also mentioning them carelessly. So I cautioned the staff not to worry him too much.

The next operation is to be carried out with most of the Combined Fleet, and the army is now seriously undertaking it. It cannot be unsuccessful, though there may be ups and downs. That was why we didn't mention a case of failure in our operational plan. However, in order to ensure its absolute success, we still have some matters needing further study, so I ordered the staff to study them.

Whatever happens, we must succeed in the coming operation of recapturing Guadalcanal at any cost. In fact, we're now pursuing the second plan to meet the worst situation envisaged in the operational plan, drawn up immediately after the enemy surprise attack on 7 August. If even this fails, what other plans can we make? It would mean the Combined Fleet would become incapable of doing anything. If so, the commander in chief's stand and my responsibility would face many difficulties. I am trying to be well prepared for that from now on.

Saturday, 10 October 1942. Fair. Yesterday's large-scale fighter attack on Guadalcanal had to return without seeing the enemy. They gave us the complete slip. It was quite natural for them. We should use a trick, a new tactic.

Light cruiser *Tatsuta* and destroyers were attacked fiercely on their way back from the transportation mission this morning and sustained some damage.

The Seventeenth Army's battle command post, which landed on Guadalcanal last night, ordered Shortland to hurriedly send only victuals and ammunition instead of troops, as the Kawaguchi detachment was starving. Such might be the situation.

[*October 7th, 8th, and 9th saw considerable fighting between U.S. Marines and Japanese on Guadalcanal. General Hyakutake, in command of the Seventeenth Army, landed on the 9th to direct the campaign in person.*+

[Ugaki remarked that, before he left Rabaul, he had drawn attention to the need for supplies. "As transportation of personnel is much easier than that of equipment of material, those who participate in transportation are apt to transport troops only, neglecting the materials, ammunition, and foodstuff actually needed at the front."

[Ugaki's teeth had been bothering him, and one had to be pulled that day. He asked for it, "intending to leave it behind in case of my death."]

Sunday, 11 October 1942. Fair. The Second Fleet plus the Second CV Division left port at 1330. The Third Fleet also sortied from the north channel at 1000. They were going to take positions for the next operation. I saw them off standing on the weather deck with the commander in chief. I pray for their sure success.

We sent a telegram to the chief of staff, Seventeenth Army, to the effect that "the Combined Fleet set X-Day, the day after the convoy's arrival at the target, as the 15th and the advance task forces sortied from Truk this morning." While we thus let them know our movements, at the same time we intended by it to prevent them from further delaying the land warfare.

While refueling a ship alongside her at Kavieng, tanker No. 2, *Tonan Maru,* was attacked by an enemy submarine and took a torpedo hit. Both she and the ship under refueling managed to escape being sunk.

We used two-wave tactics for the air raid on Guadalcanal today. At about 1030, eighteen fighters dashed in over there, but they failed to engage in air combat. It seemed to be the best chance, as a rain squall happened to come from the northeast so that the enemy patrol planes would not be in the air. But seemingly they took off before our planes got there.

The second wave, consisting of medium torpedo bombers and fighters, intended to launch an attack one hour after the first wave but apparently failed to get there due to bad weather. It was most regrettable.

On the other hand, about ten enemy planes from Port Moresby braved the moonless night and raided our residential quarters with seventy bombs for the first time. One hundred and ten were killed or injured. The Eleventh Air Fleet asked for a reinforcement of fighters from the Third Fleet. We could not accept such a request to dispatch fighters from the very carriers which gallantly sortied only this morning. So we replied saying only, "Retaliate against the enemy by night attack."

As the loss of float planes of the Eleventh Seaplane Tender Division added up and one of its tenders, *Kunikawa Maru,* also developed engine trouble, we issued an order releasing her from the task force's command last night. The search in the eastern area hitherto assigned to her was then reassigned to the task force's own search.

The Sixth Heavy Cruiser Division is going to break through to Cape Lunga to bombard the airfield tonight. I place expectations on its attempt.

With the fleet anchorage almost empty, offering disadvantages for self-defense, *Yamato, Mutsu,* the Ninth Light Cruiser Division, the repair ship *Akashi,* and others moved to the south of Narushima after 1200. Anglers were very pleased and they lost no time in catching some fairly big ones. I wrote some letters after a long while.

Monday, 12 October 1942. Fair. Leaving here yesterday on their way to bombard the airfield on Guadalcanal, the Sixth Heavy Cruiser Division and destroyers *Fubuki* and *Shirayuki* encountered more than three enemy cruisers and several destroyers at 2130 at a point about eighteen miles west of Savo Island. In the ensuing night battle, they sank one heavy cruiser, seriously damaged an unidentified cruiser, and sank one light cruiser and a destroyer.

On our side, heavy cruiser *Furutaka* was rendered unnavigable and finally sank at 2330. A destroyer rescued four hundred of her crew, while destroyer *Fubuki* was also sunk. Heavy cruiser *Aoba* lost contact for a while, causing us worry, but it was soon found that she could still make high speed, although damage sustained above her deck was fairly great.

Its division commander, Rear Admiral Goto, was seriously wounded, so *Aoba*'s skipper succeeded to the command this morning. *Kinugasa*, the third ship of the line, appears to have fought valiantly. [*Actually, it was Captain Kikunori Kijima, Goto's senior staff officer, who took over command.*][5]

It seems to me that the enemy attempted a night assault with these surface craft upon our transportation attempts, considering their aerial attacks unable to prevent us.

Nisshin and *Chitose* succeeded in unloading at Guadalcanal and were returning safely via the southern course. But this morning, when they were still withdrawing, they were subjected to fierce enemy carrier plane attacks, with the result that destroyer *Murakumo* was disabled and destroyer *Natsugumo* sunk.

[*This was the battle of Cape Esperance. U.S. Task Force 64 under Rear Admiral Norman Scott, protecting a landing force under Turner, consisted of heavy cruisers* San Francisco *and* Salt Lake City, *light cruisers* Boise *and* Helena, *and five destroyers. It encountered Goto's Sixth Cruiser Division, consisting of heavy cruisers* Aoba, Kinugasa, *and* Furutaka *with destroyers* Hatsuyuki *and* Fubuki. *The Japanese lost* Furutaka *and* Fubuki, *while* Aoba *was damaged. Japan also lost Goto, who was mortally wounded. The United States lost only destroyer* Duncan, *with* Farenholt *and* Boise *seriously damaged.*

[*While this sea fight was going on, both sides accomplished their purpose. Japan's reinforcement group under Rear Admiral Takaji Joshima, in command of the Eleventh Carrier Division, landed 728 army personnel, with a large stock of material, at Tassafaronga. Turner's two large transports and eight destroyers managed to disembark the 164th Infantry Regiment of the American division. Destroyers* Shirayuki *and* Murakumo *of Joshima's command, having returned to the scene to rescue survivors, fell to Henderson Field's fliers.*][6]

On receipt of the first report of sighting the enemy last night, we ordered an early morning search by the land-based air force, while ordering the support force to proceed speedily to the south. The sudden encounter with the enemy gave me a shock, but I managed to get to bed finally at 0230.

A poor search should be blamed. Thus our great expectation placed on a bombardment by the Sixth Heavy Cruiser Division has come to naught.

Our planes sortied early this morning to search for and attack the enemy task force, but they only found two cruisers, one of which was leaking oil and dead at sea. Though we ordered them attacked, our planes missed them due to poor weather. Only a part of them bombed the airfield on

Guadalcanal. Meanwhile, one of our subs sighted one cruiser, two destroyers, and one transport heading north to southeast of that island.

Though our neutralizing aerial attacks hadn't yet achieved much and the requested bombardment by army guns had not yet been carried out, four transports were slated to leave Rabaul and two from Shortland tonight. We settled the landing date as the 15th. An all-out air attack was accordingly ordered for the 13th and a night bombardment by the Third Battleship Division on the following night, thus making our definite resolution clear.

[That afternoon Major General Miyazaki, chief of staff, Seventeenth Army, with the Eleventh Air Fleet's Captain Ohmae and Commander Genda—the latter the tactical genius of the Pearl Harbor plan—reached Truk from Rabaul. They wanted a reinforcement convoy and a Third Battleship Division bombardment, and "seemed quite relieved to hear that both had already been ordered." So they discussed future operations. Miyazaki would not go to the Seventeenth Army command post, remaining instead at Rabaul for liaison. After the talks, he and Ugaki "celebrated . . . in advance of a success."]

Tuesday, 13 October 1942. Partly fair with fair winds. At 0830 a search plane sighted one carrier, two cruisers, and two destroyers heading southeast at a point seventy miles southeast of Rennell Island. After 1200, one battleship, one cruiser, and two destroyers were found at a point eighty miles south of Stewart Island on course of 280° at 16 knots. Carriers were feared to be accompanying them, but they weren't sighted after all. [*These were probably the groups centering around* Hornet *and* Washington, *respectively, stationed for distant support of the Turner landing forces.*][7]

Had they been somewhere nearby, the Third Battleship Division under way south would have been within effective range of an air raid until evening. But fortunately nothing happened.

Besides these two large groups, two merchantmen, one destroyer, and several patrol boats were at Lunga Roads, while a light cruiser was reported cruising west of Savo Island.

We urged the absolute necessity of carrying through tonight's Third Battleship Division's bombardment by all means. In order to be prepared for a sudden meeting with an enemy, we also suggested dispatch of an element ahead of the force if necessary. These instructions were sent out because we hoped they wouldn't miss the main objective by sticking to small issues too much.

The land-based air force attacked Guadalcanal on a large scale today. Most of the enemy planes were caught on the ground at the time of both the first and second wave attacks. They reported that attacks were effective since about four places were set on fire. After sunset today, the army's 15-cm howitzers started bombardments with two guns for the first time, and one point was seen set afire. I think a chance of turning the tables has been grasped at last. It has been a long struggle and effort, indeed.

[*Two waves of Japanese planes bombed Henderson Field, followed by the newly landed heavy field artillery that the marines nicknamed "Pistol Pete."*][8]

The dauntless attack force, consisting of the Third Battleship Division and Second Destroyer Squadron, succeeded in breaking through off Cape Lunga from the west of Savo Island after 2100 without being found by enemy flying boats on their way. From 2330 they carried out indirect firing of the main batteries with three lights lit ashore as the leading target. Both float planes and the observation post set on the island were used for spotting. Altogether, 920 projectiles were expended. During the firing they maintained 19 knots. After completing the firing at 0100, they withdrew at 28 knots via the north of Savo Island.

Wednesday, 14 October 1942. Cloudy, cool. An unprecedented attempt to bombard an airfield at night with fourteen-inch guns attained a splendid result. The whole area of the airfield was turned into a mass conflagration of gigantic size with numerous flames shooting up. Induced explosions continued until dawn. And all this was done with no loss of our own. This proved that "if one dares to do a thing resolutely one will succeed."

[*Kurita's attack on Henderson was devastating. Of the ninety U.S. aircraft, only thirty-five fighters and seven dive bombers were operational, and most of the aviation gas supply went up in flames. Forty-one men were killed.*][9]

A night bombing on Guadalcanal was also carried out with three Type 96 medium torpedo bombers last night, one each in a run. We had long urged its need, but so far only in vain. Once inertia is overcome, a difficulty no longer proves insurmountable. A psychological reaction is really delicate.

Early this morning one fighter and several carrier bombers took off and landed again. Later, twenty carrier bombers arrived from the northeast, and their activities gradually became brisk.

Last night's attack supposedly gave a serious blow to the enemy. Two-thirds of more than eighty enemy planes originally observed at the field were believed destroyed, and the enemy seemed to be regrouping the remaining planes to meet us. Anyway, hoping to put the airfield out of use is a hope against hope. We should not be optimistic.

As at 0300 we thought the bombardment a success, we ordered the support force to advance southward and attack the enemy fleet. Ordering its supply force to hurry down south, it [the support force] seemed to be approaching Guadalcanal. Thereupon we warned it not to come within two hundred miles of it [the island] until the enemy task force was found, in view of Guadalcanal airfield still being used. This is an important point in using the bridle.

While the task force was advancing southward, an enemy flying boat shadowed it, so it took evasive action to the northwest for a while. Then this evening the task force moved toward tomorrow morning's rendezvous point.

Enemy planes discovered our Second and Third fleets today, but it was doubtful whether they also found the Second CV Division. The enemy might have been surprised at sighting our large forces. They are not in the area within easy reach of our search planes.

The enemy carrier groups were not seen anywhere today. The enemy sighted west of Rennell Island yesterday seemed to consist of two groups of almost the same strength. A *Chitose* float plane, operating from Indispensable Shoal as its stepping base, sighted what looked like a carrier through a break in the clouds. A group including yesterday's battleship was only sighted at about 1100 today at a point seventy miles southeast of San Cristobal Island. Accordingly, an attack with the support force was impossible.

The high-speed convoy consisting of four army and two navy transports concentrated at a point north of Isabel Island early this morning and proceeded south under the escort of the Fourth Destroyer Squadron with destroyer *Akitsuki* as its flagship. Though we had been pleased that the enemy did not discover it, about twenty enemy planes attacked it at 1400. Fortunately, however, they escaped from them. I thought there would be another raid. Sure enough, the same number of planes attacked it before dusk, and this time they [the convoy] got through the raid with slight damage. It reported back they would reach west of Savo Island at 2000. Sunset was never awaited more anxiously.

The weather in this area has been good these days, and today's air raid on Guadalcanal was also possible. Another attributable factor in protecting the convoy from enemy attacks was that all fighters from Buin and Buka bases as well as float planes from Shortland and Rekata could give air cover to the convoy. Heaven sides with us!

In the evening we issued an order calling for the advance force to attack an enemy to the south of the Solomons and the task force from the east to the southeast of the Solomons. However, each force had already issued its respective order to its command. So ours seemed to be a little late.

[Amid all this action, Ugaki worried about how to use *Chiyoda*'s six midget submarines and asked his staff to study the problem. Meanwhile the commander, Third Destroyer Squadron, intended to use them "at

Lunga or Tulagi after unloading them near Savo Island." The Combined Fleet staff suggested spotting them between Guadalcanal and Russell Island to support unloading the convoy. Ugaki was dead set against either plan, and the fleet finally ordered them unloaded at Caminbo base for use "only when especially needed according to the enemy situation." There had been remarkably little preparation before bringing them to the combat area, and it is no wonder that Ugaki was exasperated. "Though consideration to giving them a chance to participate in a battle since they were brought down here can be appreciated, what I am afraid of most is that it will only result in belittling human lives and arms, and sending them to certain death, yet bringing no contribution to the outcome of the operation."

[Ugaki also objected to the idea of a special landing from a submarine on Espiritu Santo. "The idea was not bad, but a reckless attempt without preparation and enough thought of success would not be encouraged by the commander in chief either."]

The most regrettable incident was the sinking of the submarine *I-30*. After the Indian Ocean operation she was sent to Europe and, after sailing around South Africa, arrived safely at a German submarine base in France where she delivered the documents and things entrusted to her. A big welcome given to her was made public in radio photos and announcements by Imperial headquarters. On her way back, she reached Singapore at 0930 yesterday, the 13th. After finishing business she left there for Yokosuka at 1600. But she struck a mine at the end of the swept channel south of the commercial port and sank.

All those aboard were rescued except about a dozen petty officers and men, but the new arms and parts which our navy needed most were lost. Their transportation to our homeland was the main object of her being sent to Europe. After covering more than eighty percent of the whole trip, she met this disaster in our occupied port. Nothing could be more regrettable. I also felt my responsibility to the high command and especially to the German authorities for the loss. At least the arms on board her should be salvaged by all means.

Seeing the great success of bombardment by the Third Battleship Division, the commencement of army artillery, and the air raid, I thought that yesterday was an extraordinarily lucky day, but after all it was just a moderately lucky one.

Captain [Saiji] Norimitsu, commanding the newly organized Sixty-first Destroyer Division, consisting of antiaircraft destroyers, arrived here on board destroyer *Terutsuki* and soon left for the south. Judging from the fighting of destroyer *Akitsuki*, I think these types are a success.

Six enemy torpedo boats from the direction of Tulagi attacked the Third Battleship Division during its bombardment last night. One of them fired a torpedo, but they were repulsed. On receipt of this report, we warned *Chokai*, flagship of Commander in Chief Eighth Fleet Kinugasa, and others scheduled to bombard the airfield tonight. [*Four, not six, PT boats were involved. They scored no hits, but bothered Kurita sufficiently enough that he withdrew. In any case, his ammunition was almost gone.*][10]

It was gratifying that the convoy succeeded in sneaking safely into the anchorage at 2200. *Chokai*'s plane found an enemy cruiser at a point five miles bearing 310° from Guadalcanal Island at 2130. I wonder if tonight's bombardment will be possible.

Chokai and Kinugasa fortunately succeeded in penetrating without meeting the enemy. They commenced firing at 2340 and each expended about four hundred rounds. One or two fires were observed but the effect was not so great as the night before. This was only natural.

[*According to U.S. records, 752 eight-inch shells hit Henderson in this bombardment. Mikawa was present aboard* Chokai.*]*[11]

Thursday, 15 October 1942. Cloudy. Since the convoy was undertaking unloading, at dawn we sent air cover over them with float planes, half of the fighters of the Second CV Division, and then land-based fighters. However, about twenty enemy aircraft each came to attack them three times—at 0100, 0930, and at 1100. *Sasako Maru, Azumasan Maru,* and *Kyushu Maru,* one at each time, were hit, set afire, and went aground.

Nankai Maru finished unloading in the forenoon and left the debarkation point accompanied by a destroyer. By 1000 about eighty percent of the unloading was over. Thinking it would be risky to continue unloading after that, the Fourth Destroyer Squadron commander ordered the convoy to retire and resume the work at 1700 after sunset.

[*Despite the damage to the fuel supply at Henderson, enough had been stored in outlying locations to enable army, navy, and marine planes to attack, grounding the three* Marus, *as Ugaki noted. In addition, Japan lost twelve bombers and five fighters. The U.S. lost three dive bombers and four fighters.*][12]

In the meantime, the task force sailed south as far as east of Stewart Island and found a light cruiser and a three-hundred-ton tugboat, towing what looked like a floating dock, and two transports further south of them. A *Chitose* float plane later reported finding the same enemy. We ordered the task force to attack, but their attack planes had already left to do so.

The distance between this enemy and the van force of the task force lessened in the afternoon, so we ordered him destroyed with suitable strength.

The advance force also reached a point about 180 miles north-northeast of Guadalcanal and undertook direct screening of the convoy with fighters. It also searched for the enemy in the area south of the Solomons, but they did not find anything big, the same as the land-based air force.

The enemy fleet seems to have withdrawn to the south. Since last night the communications traffic between their units has been brisk.

Our order to bombard the airfield tonight with suitable advance force strength was assigned to the Fifth Heavy Cruiser Division, heavy cruiser *Maya,* and the Second Destroyer Squadron. They were going down south with commence firing scheduled at 2200. At 1630 we ordered the support force to come up north after these two groups finish their mission, because they needed refueling.

At about 1200 an urgent report came in of enemy ships bombarding at Tarawa and Gilbert Island. At first they reported the enemy to be a battleship or three cruisers, but it finally turned out to be a cruiser of the *Augusta* type, which came up from the south. After the bombardment, she recovered her plane and withdrew south again. Was it simply a diversion? It was not smart of him. There was no damage and the Twenty-fourth Air Flotilla had completed its preparations to attack.

Heavy cruiser *Aoba,* damaged in the night battle of the 11th, entered port in the afternoon. The commander in chief left the ship at 1435 and went on board *Aoba* to pay homage to the souls of Division Commander Rear Admiral Goto and others killed in action. After inspecting the damage, he returned aboard at 1700.

Judging from what I heard about the battle, they must have been extremely careless and unprepared. They never realized the enemy's existence until the first and second ships received concentrated fire. Heavy cruiser *Kinugasa* fought almost alone. The commander in chief remarked, "I am confident of never losing this battle." His reasoning was that there were so many duds among the enemy shells. This is quite important and needs thorough study. At the same time, it is necessary to let the enemy know the reverse of the truth.

At 1842 the submarine *I-3* sighted an enemy task force heading north at 20 knots at a point 165 miles bearing 135° of the Guadalcanal airfield at the eastern end of the deployed line. Though its strength was not known, it seemed to be fairly strong. Its distance from our van force of the Seventh and Eighth heavy cruiser divisions, the flagship of the Tenth Destroyer Squadron, and four destroyers was only eighty miles, so they should, of course, attempt a night assault upon this enemy. Otherwise, in case the enemy has carriers, our van force could not escape aerial attack tomorrow morning.

On the other hand, should the enemy come up north in an aggressive action, it will offer the best chance for us to attack them. Accordingly, at 2145 we ordered the task force and the advance force to search and attack the enemy in the area east of Stewart Island and from the northeast of Ontong Java Shoal, respectively. However, it was a nuisance that an enemy flying boat had been shadowing our task force since about 1800. If they can evade it after the moon rises at 2115, fortune will be with us. But we should be prepared anyway for an enemy preemptive air attack early tomorrow morning.

It was later found by a report from a submarine that the above enemy consisted of several cruisers but no carriers. The van force of the task force could not launch search planes, maybe due to the rain. Apparently it gave up at 1900 and withdrew to the north.

The remaining two transports of the convoy were slated to resume unloading after sunset, but they turned and headed back to Shortland by order of the first convoy commander. Contrary to this, the Seventeenth Army desired to send in a convoy of four inferior-speed ships of 13 knots on the 18th. But we turned it down, as escorting is not easy and also because of the schedule of fleet refueling.

Friday, 16 October 1942. Cloudy. Four battleships, two cruisers, and several destroyers on course of 310° were sighted between Indispensable Shoal and Espiritu Santo Island at 1810. But we could do nothing about them.

On the other hand, at 0900 another enemy of one carrier, three cruisers, and five destroyers was sighted proceeding on course of 300° at a point sixty miles south of the eastern tip of Guadalcanal. After 1200, nine carrier bombers of the land-based air force sortied from Buin escorted by fighters. Furthermore, nine medium torpedo bombers started from Rabaul. But both of them failed to find this enemy, seemingly due to poor visibility. They only set an enemy tanker on fire on their way back. Thus they missed this good chance of destroying the enemy. The reason the support force failed to attack both of those enemies is partly due to a difference of phase in which it and the enemy were acting. Another reason might be that he operated after suspecting our movements by thorough searches. However, when an opportunity arises, a fight will be touched off. It is essential to create such an opportunity.

At 0840 Captain Yonajiro Hisamune and Captain Tamotsu Araki, skippers of heavy cruiser *Aoba* and heavy cruiser *Furutaka*, respectively, came and I heard their reports alone. They gave me an account of the other day, saying that they were revenged for the battle off Tulagi.

Though admittedly there was a need to complete preparations for bombarding the airfield, the search conducted in advance was insufficient. When they saw several ships to the west of Savo Island coming out of a rain squall, they thought them to be our *Nisshin* and *Chitose* on transport duty and approached them. Forming a perfect letter T deployment to them, the enemy opened fire with several parachute flares. They concentrated their fires on *Aoba,* which steered to her starboard, sending repeated signals of "I am *Aoba.*"

Her fire-directing tower, turrets, and bridge were disabled in a few minutes, and after firing only seven rounds of the main battery, not to speak of torpedo firing, she turned back and withdrew, extending her smoke screen. The division commander, his two staff officers, and the executive officer of the ship were killed by the same dud which fell through the front.

Furutaka was following *Aoba* at 1500 meters. Astonished by parachute flares suddenly dropped overhead, she steered to port for a while, then to starboard. An enemy shell hit a torpedo tube causing a big flame. Then the enemy rained their fire on her with this flame as a target. No. 3 turret and other torpedo tubes were disabled and a shell penetrated into the engine room. Though one of the four engines was available, the water feeding pipes of the boiler were damaged, making steam-raising impossible, and the engines finally came to a stop.

Then she listed gradually so that the ensign was pulled down and all hands ordered to abandon ship after three cheers for the emperor. The emperor's portrait was lost, as the bearer was killed. The skipper tried to commit suicide in his cabin on the bridge, but both a revolver and sword had been taken away from him. Then he went up to the bridge to tie himself to the compass, but nothing was available there. The executive officer looked after the skipper. While the skipper was ordering the executive officer to leave him, the bridge sank into the water. When he floated again, he said he was somewhere near the bow. She must have sunk from the stern.

Destroyer *Shirayuki* tried to rescue survivors by only starlight, but it did not get on well with a destroyer's small boats. Moreover, the survivors were scattered over a fairly big area of the dark sea. Fearing an attack by enemy planes the next morning, the skipper of the destroyer called off the rescue and withdrew. I felt most regret on this point.

Furutaka fired only thirty rounds and did not fire any torpedoes. However, after the second salvo, major damage was said to have been inflicted on the third ship of the enemy line.

The casualties sustained were as follows:

Aoba. Killed: 79 (8 officers included).

Furutaka. Killed: 33 (2 officers); Missing: 225 (16 officers included); Rescued: 518 (34 officers included).

[The surviving staff officers were aboard *Chokai* and Tokyo announced that a new division commander would not be appointed "for the time being." This "caused a peculiar situation," as Ugaki expressed it. He understood Captain Araki's feelings, and "soothed him, saying that the conclusion of this war was far off and difficult to achieve, so he should further his efforts in the future to serve the fatherland."]

There seem to be one or two more carriers and several destroyers besides the battleship and the carrier groups found today. And they can be considered the sum of the enemy fleet operating in this area. Unless this enemy is destroyed, the object of this operation will not be obtained.

But the enemy was maneuvering all the time, keeping some distance from our force. This was because the enemy was making reasonable movements after adequate searches discovered our movements. We cannot, therefore, get him with conventional methods. It is most essential to outwit the enemy so as to join battle. Moreover, this must be done within ten days. To that end, efforts should be made to create a chance of attack and take advantage of it. So I ordered the staff to study this.

[At 0705 those aboard *Yamato* held a ceremony, this being the "second day of the extraordinary festival of Yasukuni Shrine." Ugaki reflected that the number of souls enshrined there would be "sharply increased by the sacrifices of this war."

[He also noted that this was the anniversary of the beginning of this diary. He expressed the opinion that his entries would be "valuable materials in the future."]

Saturday, 17 October 1942. Cloudy with squall. A ceremony was held at 0705 on the occasion of the Harvest Festival. This year's rice harvest is expected to be sixty-seven million *koku* and very good, with a twenty-two percent increase over last year's. However, we won't be able to give enough domestic-produced rice to everybody who wants it, and we'll still have to rely on imported rice for not a small amount.

Except for one cruiser and two destroyers off Lunga, today's search did not locate any enemy. These destroyers bombarded our landing point at Tassafaronga under aircraft spotting. As a result, ammunition transported there only after great hardship was set on fire. Induced explosions continued until noon. The loss was not slight. More caution should be taken. [*This was probably the bombardment by the destroyers* Aaron Ward *and* Lardner *which ignited Japanese ammunition dumps.*][13]

The strength disposition for the general offensive was relayed from the chief of staff, Seventeenth Army. Judging from the fact that the army command post advanced from the beach, they seem to have recovered the left bank of the Matanicau river and made a further advance. Through the naval garrison force at Guadalcanal, they also requested a naval bombardment at about 1300 on the day of the general offensive. The Eighth Fleet also sent in a request to bombard with the Eleventh Battleship Division's large caliber guns just as the Third Battleship Division was employed the other day.

Maybe because this operation started from the navy's fault on the defense, the army seems to depend on the navy all the time and lacks the spirit of attaining the operational aim by themselves. Most of the requested personnel and material will have been transported by today's last attempt by naval vessels. They should not want too much, but try to attain the objective even at a sacrifice for the sake of saving their faces.

Though the Second CV Division's bombers failed to hit enemy destroyers off Lunga, the land-based air force's bomber attack sank one of them.

The landing of today's transportation by naval vessels was completed through the northern route without being attacked by enemy planes.

Sunday, 18 October 1942. Cloudy with rain squall. It was fortunate that the weather in the Solomons district continued good for more than a week, benefiting the progress of the operation. Bombing was possible both today and yesterday.

We have been racking our brains these days to think of some plan to destroy the enemy fleet. The staff say they have no first-rate idea.

While I was writing this, the torpedo staff officer brought in a report from our submarine, the second from the west in the deployment line. It said that at 1620 she sighted an enemy group of one battleship, two cruisers, and three destroyers just passing our deployment line on course of 60° at 12 knots. The position was about one hundred miles south of the eastern end of San Cristobal Island. The moon was on her eighth night and visibility was fairly good. Thinking that they were ambushing the enemy, I waited for good news.

Whenever there was an enemy battleship group, there was always a carrier group operating nearby. So we may see an enemy carrier group tomorrow morning, but both advance and task forces will be unable to make it, as it will be pretty far up in the north then. They cannot maneuver at will now, through fear of running short of fuel. Despite my request to the staff, we shall miss the enemy again this time. But it can't be helped.

The tanker *Kenyo Maru,* attached to the advance force, arrived with an empty stomach. As she had no time to go back to the homeland to fill up with fuel, she took forty-five hundred tons each from *Yamato* and *Mutsu* and some from *Nissho Maru.* She will leave here tomorrow morning, heading for the rendezvous point with the advance force.

In the afternoon two more ships came alongside *Yamato.* Battleships turned into floating tanks! The oil consumption was so much that even the full operation of tankers was not enough. The fuel storage at the homeland is also running short, and a strict order to produce fuel oil has been issued to the oil-producing area in the south. The fact that we now possess those resource-rich districts is our strong point anyway. And because of this we will not be beaten down.

Monday, 19 October 1942. Fair. In spite of the efforts of submarines, they could not get a chance to attack yesterday's enemy. On the other hand, attack planes turned back from the halfway point due to bad weather today. No other information was obtained on the enemy. Only two or three destroyers were operating in the Tulagi area.

The Nineteenth Destroyer Division headed for Guadalcanal to carry the chief of staff, Seventeenth Army, to that island and also bombard it afterward. Enemy planes attacked it on the way, and one destroyer turned back on account of a fuel leak.

The army's force, taking a roundabout route through the jungle, made better progress than expected and reached within one kilometer of the airfield on the 18th. At first it was reported able to commence the general attack on the 20th, but later it appeared to be changed to the 22nd. Well understanding the navy's standpoint, the chief of staff, Seventeenth Army, requested a definite answer about it, but so far no answer came in. So we decided on the 22nd as the date of the general attack and issued orders to the forces concerned.

An advance notice of the new assignments, dated 1 November, has been sent in, piecemeal. I'm to be promoted to vice admiral, too. Though without much ambition, I'm now going to be promoted to the rank of vice admiral on my own merits. I should be pleased with this as a proof of my worth to our country, shouldn't I?

Tuesday, 20 October 1942. Fair. During the night of the 18th, the army's Second Division command, both regimental commanders, and others completed their concentration at a valley on the upper reaches of the Lunga River. The army commander accordingly sent the following message to the commanders in chief of all the fleets and the chief of the Army General Staff: "The time is now ripe for us to engage the enemy once for all, and this morning the army ordered a general offensive commenced on the 22nd. We will fight gallantly and expect to respond to His Majesty's wishes by annihilating the enemy with one stroke."

It was full of spirit. So we instructed all the operational forces that a night assault against the airfield was to be carried out on the 22nd.

The Nineteenth Destroyer Division could not reach the landing point last night due to persistent enemy attacks and turned back. I wonder what happened to the army chief of staff.

Today's search found enemy destroyers, then three battleships and one heavy cruiser and others at a point 255 miles bearing 145° of Guadalcanal. A submarine also reported sighting a part of them.

At about 1840 *I-176* sighted two battleships, two cruisers, and several destroyers on course of 170° at 20 knots at a point 120 miles southeast of the eastern tip of San Cristobal Island. At 1915 she sent two torpedoes into a battleship of the *Texas* type. After two minutes, two loud sounds of induced explosions were heard. But she could not confirm the result due to a fierce attack by enemy destroyers. When she surfaced at 0030, the enemy had disappeared, so she gave up further chase. The enemy may have escaped with heavy damage. [I-176 *hit the heavy cruiser* Chester, *not a battleship.* Chester *made it back to Norfolk for repairs.*]14

Wednesday, 21 October 1942. Fair. This morning's reconnaissance spotted a group of two battleships, two cruisers, and several destroyers heading west at about sixty miles southwest of the position of last night's submarine attack and another one of one battleship, one cruiser, and two destroyers on course of 120° at 14 knots at a point thirty miles further east. It wasn't clear whether the latter was the one the submarine attacked last night.

Why does the enemy make such a movement with battleships? I suspect some political motive involved in it. Anyway, it will be made clear in a few days.

A cruiser was seen operating in the Tulagi area. Enemy carriers did not make their appearance, maybe because they could not refuel and replenish planes in time.

[Ugaki was disenchanted with the army, which advised that it had postponed the general attack to the 23rd "due to the topography in front of the enemy position." The navy agreed, having no alternative, but Ugaki was disgusted. "How unreliable they are!" The navy had repeatedly explained that "one or two days' delay would not mean much in land warfare, but it has a great effect on naval operational forces coordinating over vast areas." But the army could not seem to understand this. Determinedly fairminded, Ugaki ended the day's entry, "It might be our fault that we did not dispatch a naval liaison officer of senior rank on the spot."]

Thursday, 22 October 1942. Fair. A bomb hit was made on the stern of an enemy cruiser at Guadalcanal. The enemy battleship groups moved the same as yesterday, but we could do nothing about them.

Some time ago, enemy ships attacked patrol boats in the south of the Gilberts. The gunboat *Hachikai Maru* lost contact since this morning, when a cruiser and a destroyer attacked her. A flying boat sortied from Makin and bombed a destroyer.

Losses due to enemy submarines have increased recently. At a point west of Cape St. George, the supply ship *Onoe Maru* was hit by two torpedoes, one of which didn't explode. She was making 6 knots under her own power.

The army bombarded the airfield sporadically. The activity of the enemy planes decreased. According to an enemy flier who made a forced landing, they had about forty planes at present with another crippled.

The army undertook offensive action in the areas north of Mt. Austin and the left bank of Matanicau River and captured these areas. Tomorrow they are going to attack its right bank area from both sides. Taking a detour, the main force finished its deployment.

Yesterday's postponement of the general attack was due to the delay in advance through difficult terrain in front of the enemy position. Though enemy planes flew over our main force several times, apparently the enemy has not detected our plan. So far so good!

As the positions each force was to take on the next day of the general attack were not coordinated, we gave the standard to be followed by the advance force, task force, and main force of the Eighth Fleet.

On the 17th, a fire broke out in the generator room of CV *Hiyo*, flagship of the Second CV Division, and she could make no more than 16 knots owing to the damage. The commander, advance force, advised that after transferring a part of her planes to her sister ship *Junyo* and the rest to land bases, she would be sent back to Truk for repairs. It's too bad on this occasion, with a rare opportunity at hand.

Friday, 23 October 1942. Partly fair with rain squall. At 0800 two enemy battleships, one cruiser, and several destroyers were sighted at a point about ten miles further south from the usual point to the southeast of the Solomons. Later they split into two groups. They should be attacked tomorrow. Their daily movements, however, are considered to be supporting operations, seemingly with a great deal of political motive. But the whereabouts of the enemy carriers have been unknown for a few days. The enemy seems to intend to attack our task force's flank from the direction of Santa Cruz Islands after concentrating their remaining carriers, while luring our attention to the battleship groups. So we sent a warning to all forces.

The army diversionary force, supposed to carry out a night assault against the flank of the enemy position on the right bank of Matanicau River last night, could not undertake the scheduled action due to the thick jungle. It managed to start an attack at 1300. I was afraid that a delayed diversionary attack would not do much good. As it was sunset already, I expected them to start the scheduled general offensive when I was astounded by an urgent telegram sent from the Seventeenth Army commander immediately after sunset. It said that again they had postponed the date of the general offensive, to the 24th.

[Again Ugaki exploded in anger and frustration. He could understand delays due to "strong enemy resistance," but delays due to the terrain smacked of "insufficient preparation." He wondered if, in the future, naval plans in connection with land warfare should not be more flexible timewise, in anticipation of such unexpected changes. And only two days ago he had warned the chief of staff, Seventeenth Army, "that any more delay would not be permissible in light of fleet operations. But it turned out just like hammering on a cork. I lost face, too." The main point, however, was that the Japanese could not afford a failure. "We must succeed in recovering the island by hook or crook this time."]

In the previous entry I wrote that Sasebo No. 5 special landing party, originally slated to land on the north side of the peninsula for the Rabi operation, was attacked by enemy planes on the way and took refuge at Goodenough Island, where they were stranded on the beach. Since then, efforts to rescue them by destroyer have failed, and only a part of them was withdrawn with a submarine using a motor launch carried aboard her. However, even this had to be suspended, as enemy planes discovered this attempt. In the meantime, food was provided to them to await later rescue attempts. But today the enemy, about one hundred strong with machine guns and trench mortars, attacked them from behind. The enemy could be repulsed with a fair amount of loss, but our force also suffered some casualties. Its commanding officer sent back his grim decision that they need no more rescue. His tragic resolution must be appreciated. Isn't there any way to rescue them? Keep it up for a little more! We cannot stand still and see them left alone.

Saturday, 24 October 1942. Partly fair with squall. Last night's assault against the enemy position on the right bank of Matanicau River from the north side of Mt. Austin ended in failure. The Oka regiment doubled its disgrace. However, it may have served as a diversion.

[*This was a tank and infantry attack launched shortly before midnight by Major General Tadashi Simiyoshi, in command of the Seventeenth Army's artillery. Marine howitzer fire destroyed twelve tanks, and the Japanese suffered several hundred casualties.*][15]

The main force in the east seemed to have reached the scheduled line by 1200, so tonight's general attack had become certain. Evidently the enemy has not yet suspected our project. The enemy is said to be playing tennis on the south end of the airfield. We should charge into the enemy with a sudden, fierce attack regardless of sacrifices. They have to do it! Everyone is awaiting tonight's success with bated breath.

The commander in chief said to me on the upper deck, "The one who is waiting for its success most will be the chief of the Army General Staff." This is because he gave his word to the emperor that the army would succeed with the previous strength.

Having apprehensions in view of the progress of the land warfare and yesterday's shadowing by enemy flying boats, at 1850 the task force sent in its changed schedule for taking position tomorrow up north and moving southward only the day after tomorrow. The message originally transmitted before noon reached us so late as it was relayed by another ship. It's most deplorable. This wasn't done without some fear. Also it might be a case of the day after tomorrow being more advantageous, as the task force judged. On the other hand, it was feared that the task force's movement would jeopardize the general coordination and put the advance force in danger.

In case an attempt to regain the airfield fails, there are some other ways to meet the new development. So we sent an urgent order asking it to proceed as far southward as possible in accordance with the previous operational telegram order. Their attempt must be called an outrageous, arbitrary one. This command has the whole responsibility. Do not hesitate or waver!

At about 1900 we received a report of Guadalcanal in torrential rain at 1700. How will the army regard this? They were said to be quite confident of success, after reaching a point two kilometers from the airfield by 1200 and approaching the enemy through jungles without being spotted. This rain must have been a heaven-sent phenomenon. I pray for their success in a surprise attack, well inspired by the ancient battle of Okehazama, in which a Japanese hero achieved a brilliant victory taking advantage of pouring rain.

While the task force was located too far north, a fact which might be called disobedience to orders, our strength taking position in the southeast was insufficient. The advance force also lacked CV *Hiyo* for its originally scheduled movement. So I wondered how not to cause any discrepancy in the strategical position.

As I thought I could expect good news in the course of time, I went up to the weather deck and gazed at the brilliant moon of the fourteenth night. At 2335 we received an army telegram, "2100 Banzai," which meant the capture of the airfield. This settled everything. March, all forces, to enlarge the result gained! Hesitation or indecision at this moment would leave a regret forever.

[Henderson Field had not been captured, but the Japanese under Major General Yumio Nasu poured over the marine lines and fierce fighting continued all night between Nasu's men, the marines, and the soldiers of the 164th Infantry.][16]

Sunday, 25 October 1942. Cloudy. Seeing that each force was carrying out its mission, in gratitude upon receipt of the good news of capturing the airfield, at 0200 I went to bed quite relieved. However, a staff officer reported to me at 0450 a signal that "at 0230, the airfield has not been captured." What's the matter? Last night's telegram reported that "Kawaguchi detachment captured the airfield and the western force is fighting to the west of the field." No information has been received since then and an Eleventh Air Fleet reconnaissance plane reported that "fighting was going on at the airfield."

Anyway, the army's plan of capturing the field at one stroke has failed. Together with the use of reserve strength there still may be some hope for tonight's assault, but I can't help judging that the land warfare would be set back. Then I wrote down ideas of countermeasures for this contingency and handed them to the staff.

Soon after lunch we got the following telegram:

Control of the units was difficult due to the complicated terrain. Only an enemy position protruding from the south end of the airfield was taken, but the airfield has not been penetrated. Under regrouping since this morning. The force on the right bank of Lunga River pressed the enemy and reached to a point five kilometers southsouthwest of Cape Lunga. Four enemy planes took off and two of them landed soon afterward.

This was transmitted at about 0830. Then another signal said that the army would resume the attack tonight and was scheduled to charge in at 1900. If so, it will be all right. Now our last hope is that they will succeed tonight.

In accordance with last night's order, the task force advanced south with high speed and generally took strategical positions together with the advance force. But their search planes could not find the enemy.

An enemy B-17 then found the advance force which started to go up north. Thereupon we ordered as heavy an attack as possible on enemy positions and vessels at Guadalcanal by planes of the Second CV Division.

At 1116, however, a patrol plane sighted two battleships, four heavy cruisers, one light cruiser, and twelve destroyers on an irregular course at 14 knots at a point thirty miles east of Rennell Island. But it was so late that a support force attack was impossible, and the land-based planes could not reach them either. This failure was due to the fact that all the reconnaissance float aircraft of the Eleventh Seaplane Tender Division turned back due to bad weather in that area, so they could not carry out searches with Indispensable Shoal as a relaying base.

There was another report that two destroyers sortied from the direction of Tulagi and a light cruiser was also operating. Three destroyers of the Sixth Destroyer Division penetrated into the road with the aim of destroying them and also cooperating with the land warfare, but the enemy destroyers fled when some hits were inflicted upon them. Three transports were sunk. We suffered some damage from attacks by enemy planes.

[*These were the destroyer-minelayers* Trevor *and* Zane, *which brought much-needed ammunition and fuel to Guadalcanal. The three Japanese destroyers were* Akitsuki, Ikazuchi *and* Shiratsuyu. *After scoring a hit on* Zane, *the Japanese changed course under attack by U.S. bombers. Following this, the Japanese sank the tug* Seminole *and the patrol vessel* YP-284.][17]

The second attack force, consisting of destroyer *Akitsuki* and light cruiser *Yura*, under command of commander, Fourth Destroyer Squadron, also closed in from the north. *Yura's* fire-directing equipment was damaged and *Akitsuki* took a near miss at her stern. They were retiring to the north at reduced speeds, the former at 12 knots, the latter 23 knots. [*As Ugaki noted, both light cruiser* Yura *and destroyer* Akitsuki *were hit,* Yura *so badly the Japanese had to torpedo her.*][18]

We issued an order to attack the enemy fleet to the southeast of the Solomons tomorrow. Today's order was late in being sent out, too, due to long staff discussions. And as usual there was nothing new in the draft thus prepared.

Besides, they seem to have done nothing about a plan to direct future operations on Guadalcanal that I had ordered them to prepare. Unless they use their brains with a little more foresight, they can hardly direct the operations of the whole fleet.

The autumn full moon was not brilliant and no poem came to my mind. I went to bed early, placing a slight hope on tonight's army assault.

Monday, 26 October 1942. Fair. At about 0340 we received a report from our liaison staff on Guadalcanal stating that the army commenced the attack at 2200 last night but could not break through into the airfield by 0200. It was just as I thought.

[*The action on Guadalcanal cost Japan thousands of ground troops. The Americans also suffered heavy casualties—the Seventh Marine Regiment: 182 killed; the 164th Infantry Regiment: 166 killed and 182 wounded. But Henderson Field was still in U.S. hands, and Japanese plans thrown off schedule.*][19]

[Ugaki wondered how the Seventeenth Army could face the navy. He had asked if they had an alternative attack plan; now discovered that they had none, depending "only on night attacks which they thought was our favorite tactic and the enemy's weak point." In his opinion, "They should have prepared for both regular and surprise attacks and displayed the skill to use them properly." Ugaki pointed out in his diary that this failure had been repeated three times. "It was not a failure of the army alone and I was extremely sorry."]

At 1530 yesterday eight enemy planes attacked Hong Kong, and again at 0130 today it was air raided. Though the damage was slight, it must have been the action of American planes. We should never relax anywhere. It is getting busy both in the east and west.

[*This raid was by twelve B-25s and seven P-40s of the China Air Task Force (CATF). The Japanese interceptors shot down one each B-25 and P-40, but suffered heavy losses. During the night of the 25th through 26th, nine B-25s continued to pound the Hong Kong area.*][20]

After reading these reports, I went to bed early and thought about the future. At 0500 the first report of sighting the enemy came in. At 0115 a B-17 attacked the task force then under way to the south, which put about to the north at 24 knots. This move was proper. At 0450 its search plane found a large enemy group of one CV and fifteen others at a point 140 miles bearing 15° of Nudeni Island. [*This was Task Force 17, under Rear Admiral George D. Murray, consisting of CV* Hornet, *four cruisers, and six destroyers.*][21]

Now what we warned about the day before yesterday came true. As the whereabouts of the enemy carriers had been unknown for a few days, we had warned that it was necessary to take strict precautions to the east, considering the movement of the battleship group east of the Solomons to be for decoy purposes. A great sea and air battle is thus to be unfolded in the area east of the Solomons and north of the Santa Cruz Islands.

Except for the battle scene being within six hundred miles from enemy bases at Espiritu Santo, everything was favorable to us. In addition, the battle starting from early morning was estimated to last all day long today, so a night battle could achieve a successful result. Maybe we can make up for the failure of Guadalcanal off Santa Cruz.

At about the same time, a search plane also found three battleships, one cruiser, and ten destroyers (or one battleship, three cruisers, and eleven destroyers) on course of 150° at a point thirty miles west of Rennell Island. They were the same group found east of the said island yesterday. They must have closed in Guadalcanal last night to meet our challenge and proceeded southward since this morning. They were left to land-based air force attacks. [*This was Task Force 64 under Rear Admiral Willis A. Lee, consisting of battleship* Washington, *three cruisers, and six destroyers. This group was operating independently and did not participate in the upcoming battle of Santa Cruz.*][22]

Our task force swiftly sent out the first-wave planes at 0510, the second ones at 0600, and the third ones equipped with torpedoes at 0700. On their way they met the oncoming enemy planes.

At 0500 the advance force was located 120 miles west-northwest of the main force of the task force, and attempted to approach the latter on course of 70°. *Junyo* of the advance force reported she alone was going to dispatch ten fighters and nineteen carrier bombers, intending to attack the enemy at 0830.

Later, this commander, advance force, proceeded toward the enemy, leading the advance force while leaving *Junyo* with two destroyers behind under the commander of the task force.

At 0656 the first wave attacked an enemy carrier of the *Saratoga* type and set a huge fire on her. By this time, the entire enemy strength became quite clear. They were divided into two groups of one CV, one cruiser, and six destroyers each, with CVs as their centers. Each group was twenty miles apart. Another carrier was also sighted forty miles further northeast, so the enemy carriers turned out to be three altogether. Following the drifting of the *Saratoga* type carrier, another one of the *Yorktown* type was also left dead in the water. They also reported two battleships sunk.

[*Only two U.S. CVs,* Hornet *and the newly repaired* Enterprise, *were present at Santa Cruz.* Enterprise, *with battleship* South Dakota, *two cruisers, and eight destroyers made up Task Force 61 under Rear Admiral Thomas C. Kinkaid. The United States's losses were* Hornet *and destroyer* Porter *sunk,* Enterprise, South Dakota, *the antiaircraft cruiser* San Juan, *and destroyer* Smith *damaged, with about seventy-four planes lost from all causes, including accidents.*][23]

On our side, CV *Shokaku* was damaged and lost communication ability, while CVL *Zuiho* was set afire. Both retired to the northwest after becoming unable to operate planes. Heavy cruiser *Chikuma* of the advance force was also attacked by thirty carrier bombers and nine carrier torpedo bombers and was hit by bombs, sustaining fair damage. She was sent to Truk escorted by two destroyers. She still could make 23 knots.

[*No Japanese ships were sunk, but heavy cruiser* Chikuma, *CVL* Zuiho, *and* Shokaku *were damaged, the latter so badly she was out of combat for nine months. Air losses were at least one hundred planes and many of Japan's best fliers, including a legend in his own time, the ace Commander Shigeharu Murata, who had led the aerial torpedo attack at Pearl Harbor.*][24]

We still had two sound carriers, while the enemy had only one remaining. Dazed by small damage, the main body of the task force and the

Second CV Division were withdrawing to the northwest. If left under way as they were, they would be more than three hundred miles away from the enemy and eventually miss him. So we sent them a strictly worded attack order. A staff officer remarked that such movement would be advantageous for outranging the enemy. I wanted to shout at him, "Damn fool!" With this spirit, it would be impossible to hope for certain destruction of the enemy. We should keep this in mind.

We ordered an attack on the enemy north of Santa Cruz with most of our submarines and another one southwest of Rennell Island with a part of them.

The Second CV Division's summary action report made clear that the enemy was accompanied by two battleships. The attack planes of the Second Division hit a carrier amidship with more than three bombs. The *Saratoga* type one listed heavily to starboard. Besides them, another one was being towed by a cruiser and under escort of a cruiser and a destroyer. It was doubtful whether this one was still operating, but her speed was said to be 16 knots.

Added attack results of the Second CV Division included one bomb hit on a battleship, two bomb hits on a heavy cruiser, and six planes shot down. Four of our fighter and eleven torpedo bombers failed to return. The sinking of two battleships claimed by carrier torpedo bombers of the First CV Division was thus justified.

Damaged *Shokaku* and *Zuiho* got out of the seven-hundred-mile radius from San Cristobal Island, and three hundred miles from Guadalcanal by 1230. CV *Zuikaku* was placed under the temporary command of the commander, Second CV Division, and was speeding on course of 140° at 30 knots. It was a proper step, but regrettably it was late. The commander in chief, Third Fleet, transferred his flag to destroyer *Terutsuki* and was going to shift his flag to *Zuikaku* during a lull in the air battle.

Shokaku and *Zuiho* were sent back to Truk under escort of four destroyers. This was a proper step.

A *Zuiho* plane's report issued at 1420: "The enemy strength: one carrier, one battleship, two cruisers, and four destroyers. The carrier was drifting without fighter screen overhead. No damage on our side."

Summary action report of *Zuikaku*'s skipper at 1315: "Summing up the reports of the returned attack planes up to First CV Division's second wave, two carriers heavily damaged and an unidentified vessel exploded, the remnant of which is still seen."

Putting together these reports, it might be surmised that the enemy carriers were four altogether. Adding the following report, it was clear that we either sank or damaged all the enemy carriers. So it was now possible to annihilate the remnant.

Report from the commander, Second CV Division, at 1445: "At 1315 we torpedoed an enemy carrier of the *Yorktown* type, hitting with three torpedoes. Its sinking almost certain. One torpedo hit a cruiser, setting a big fire. They were among the group consisting of two battleships, three cruisers, and five destroyers."

A *Nagara* plane reported at 1610 that the northern group of three cruisers and six destroyers, which had been encircling an CV of the *Saratoga* type, abandoned the CV and commenced retiring due east at high speed. They seemed to have suspected the approach of our night assault force from the west. Thereupon the staff demanded that we capture the carrier and tow her in if the situation permitted. That is all right, if possible. Though it involved some risk, we sent a telegram to that effect in my name.

Two enemy forces were found to the west of Rennell Island this morning, but they probably were the same one.

In spite of last night's Combined Fleet order, the land-based air force lacked preparations for an attack on enemy ships and missed the enemy, although it was 650 miles away from our base, within our attack range. Our delay in issuing the order contributed to it.

Our shadowing plane observed some gunfire near the drifting enemy CV. It evidently came from enemy destroyers attempting to sink the crippled CV before their withdrawal. When our night assault force reached her, she listed 45° amid induced explosions. As she seemed hopeless, she was sunk. [*After* Hornet *was abandoned, U.S. destroyers tried unsuccessfully to sink her. Eventually Japanese destroyers finished her off.*][25]

The planes dispatched from *Nagara, Maya,* and *Isuzu* searched thoroughly, but could not find any major enemy except two or four destroyers fleeing at high speed to the southeastern or eastern directions. This appeared to be the end of today's battle.

A night battle against an enemy force retiring at high speed has little chance of success, as shown in peacetime training, unless complete contact is maintained before sunset and the distance between the two forces is short. The distance between the two forces at sunset today was about sixty miles.

The situation in the Guadalcanal area never left my mind, even while the others were absorbed in today's battle. And I gave a few cautions to the staff.

[A telegram came in from the chief of staff, Seventeenth Army, expressing regret that, despite "the wholehearted cooperation" of the navy, they had been unable to capture the airfield on Guadalcanal and hoped "for further assistance." Fleet headquarters sent a courteous reply; the navy appreciated their "continuous hardships," would cooperate in the future, and hoped the army would continue to attack the airfield.]

At 2230 we issued Combined Fleet Summary Action Report No. 1. It said:

> The Combined Fleet, operating in the seas near the Solomons, engaged the enemy fleet, which consisted of more than twenty ships, including four carriers, four battleships, and cruisers and destroyers in the sea north of Santa Cruz in the early morning of the 26th. All of the enemy carriers were destroyed by 2000, driving the enemy into confusion. We are now chasing the remnant with the whole strength of our night assault force.
>
> Summary of the battle result up to 2000 is:
>
> 1. Sunk: one *Saratoga* type carrier, one *Yorktown* type carrier, two new type carriers, one battleship, and one type unidentified.
>
> 2. Damaged: one battleship, three cruisers, and one destroyer.
>
> 3. Our losses: *Shokaku* and *Zuiho* incapable of continuing carrier operations, though both are able to make full power running. *Chikuma* hit with bombs and sailing at 23 knots. Telegram follows for our damage to planes.

CV *Hiyo* arrived in the morning and Captain Akitomo Beppu, her skipper, came to report. He expressed his deep regret at not participating in today's important battle, as his ship had been sent back here to repair the condenser and the damage caused by the other day's fire.

[That night, Ugaki retired to the weather deck where, inspired by the bright moonlight and the cool breeze, he composed two of his short poems. One was in honor of so-called *Saratoga's* sinking. It was not exultant but the respect of a good sailor for a fine ship.

[The next morning, 27 October, he recorded that the night assault force was able to accomplish nothing "except finishing off the crippled carrier." Nor did the morning's searches find anything but "enemy flying boats at Banicro Island." So the fleet ordered the support force to return to Truk, and issued a warning in Ugaki's name "to all operational forces not to spoil the hard-earned victory by relaxing security and precautions."]

The advance force rescued on the sea a sub-lieutenant of *Hornet* and a petty officer of *Enterprise*.

The fighting strength present which they knew for certain were CV *Enterprise*, CV *Hornet*, battleship *South Dakota*, one each of *Pensacola*, *Portland*, and *Indianapolis* type cruisers, and twelve destroyers. They left Hawaii on 16 October. The carriers have serial numbers in the following order: *Langley, Lexington, Saratoga, Ranger, Yorktown, Enterprise, Wasp, Hornet, Essex, Bonhomme Richard*.

[*The diary indicates this as a quotation; no doubt it is an extract from the advance force report concerning the two POWs.*]

(The one we disposed of last night had the number 8.)

The enemy builds and christens second and third generations of carriers, as many as we destroy. No wonder they do not need to change the names and numbers, but at present most of them are considered to be the missing numbers.

According to a later report from the task force, more than forty were shot down over the enemy and twenty-five over the task force, though the investigation was not yet completed. The remnant of the enemy that fled was estimated to be one battleship, five cruisers, and nine destroyers, including the damaged ones.

Submarine Group B searched, advancing southward, and at night it found the enemy battleship group coming southward from near Rennell Island. Two of the submarines attacked it, but they failed to score a hit, for the enemy made a great evasive movement. A sound like a hit was heard against a *Colorado* type. They were on course of 160° at 16 knots and supposed to be heading for Noumea.

At last the staff finished discussions about the future policy to be adopted for the Guadalcanal operation, and brought me their draft.

Just for a change I saw a newsreel. There were many in the audience. Had the army attained its aim at Guadalcanal, we would have had nothing to worry about.

[The next morning, 28 October, brought a telegram from the Naval General Staff expressing the emperor's satisfaction with the results, although he regretted the loss of "many capable fliers." The Tokyo radio also broadcast results from 25 August to 25 October, which Ugaki was sure must please the public.]

Though radio jamming was prevalent today, American Navy Day, they must have caught our announcement. I was confident that it served as the best present for Roosevelt.

The crippled carriers *Shokaku* and *Zuiho* came into port through the north channel at 1500. The two skippers, Captain Masafumi Arima and Captain Sueo Obayashi, came on board to report after sunset. *Shokaku* was hit by four bombs, *Zuikaku* [*Zuiho*] with one. But it was fortunate that both were hit after the planes had taken off. While they were waiting in my room prior to making their reports, I told them, "It was very good that with such damages you have managed to come back safely." On hearing this, they looked at each other and asked, "Is it all right as long as the ship doesn't sink?" So I replied firmly, "That's right, because we cannot alone remain unscathed while the enemy is destroyed." They seemed to be quite relieved.

It is only natural for a commander who had his ship damaged and who lost his officers and men in battle to have a deep concern about what his superior was thinking of him, while full of self-reproach. No one can understand this unless he has experienced it as a commander.

[Ugaki mused that in such cases a word from the commander in chief or the chief of staff meant a good deal to him. To receive the commander "with broadmindedness" and not speak of his errors was, in his opinion, a mark of leadership. "I have always treated commanders after their trying experiences between life and death with this in mind."

[Ugaki also recorded congratulatory telegrams from the navy minister, the chief of the Naval General Staff, and from General Hisaichi Terauchi, commander of the Southern Army. To these messages the fleet returned courteous thanks.]

Thursday, 29 October 1942. Frequent rain squalls. Leaving the ship at 0745, I went on board CV *Shokaku* to pay my respects to the loyal souls, visit the wounded, and inspect the damage. The damage done by four bombs after the bridge was quite severe. I marveled at the good luck that the damage did not reach any further below.

Then I went to CVL *Zuiho* and found that the one bomb hit at her stern had disabled her completely.

Vice Admiral Shigeyoshi Inouye was transferred from commander in chief, Fourth Fleet, to commandant, Naval Academy, and is due to leave here tomorrow. I expressed my deep appreciation for his arduous service for over a year in this southern district.

Captain [Keizo] Komura, in command of heavy cruiser *Chikuma*, came to report at 1330. He was wounded slightly and wore bandages on his head and face. The crippled *Chikuma* came into port at about 0930. She was attacked by forty-three enemy planes. Two bombs hit on the bridge and one on the torpedo tube compartment. A near miss inflicted a big hole at her side. She really owes her survival to well-executed damage control.

Staff Officers Sasaki and Watanabe returned from Rabaul and reported. The details of land warfare developments were not quite clear, but the main force's night assault ended in failure, as in past cases. The causes for the failure were almost the same as before, and there is nothing left to say about it.

Colonel [Takushiro] Hattori, chief of the Second Section of the Army General Staff, came from Tokyo by plane. I made him well acquainted with our opinions. He said the army intended to establish an area army by assigning seven divisions to this area including Port Moresby. Welcome, but it was also necessary not to be one step too late all the time. Furthermore, he told me that, in spite of the instruction given to the army's new chief of staff, the army repeated the same mistake as at Bataan Peninsula. Seeing that his idea was almost the same as mine, I felt a little bit reassured for directing future operations.

[The Fleet received an Imperial Rescript commending their efforts in the South Pacific. Late that night, the chief of the Naval General Staff sent another telegram, this time with an account of the emperor's words when presenting the rescript. Referring to Guadalcanal as "the place of bitter struggles," he expressed his wish that it be recaptured swiftly.

[Ugaki felt keenly "about His Majesty's anxiety over the failure at Guadalcanal." The fleet forwarded the emperor's words to the commander in chief of the Guadalcanal operational forces.]

Friday, 30 October 1942. Fair. The commander in chief left the ship at 0745 and paid tribute to the war dead on board *Shokaku, Zuiho,* and *Chikuma,* and inspected the damage. He returned at 1030.

The Third Fleet entered port through the north channel in the morning and the Second Fleet at 1500. Thus the whole fleet assembled at Truk, offering a grand spectacle. I was glad that no ship was missing this time.

Soon after sunset, the commander in chief, Second Fleet, and a little later the commander in chief, Third Fleet, came to report. They said that *Saratoga* was not there and the ships sunk were three carriers. There were not four, and the battleship seemed to be only one, also. The Third Fleet seemed to be proud of themselves for their success and blamed the Combined Fleet command for the failure of the land warfare on Guadalcanal. Of course, their regret and resentment can be appreciated, but isn't it true nobility not to blame others in the midst of one's success? We have also done our duty. I just treated them lightly.

A congratulatory telegram was received from the commander, Seventeenth Army, for the battle off Santa Cruz Island. I wanted to say something to him, but just replied simply.

Saturday, 31 October 1942. Fair with squall. We received a telegram of congratulations from Prime Minister Tojo and we thanked him.

There was no change in the enemy situation, but not a few enemy planes raided the Rabaul area at night.

Having lost many officers and men in the latest battle, the Third Fleet held a memorial service for them at 1200. The commander in chief attended it.

At 1530 Vice Admiral Baron Tomoshige Samejima, the newly appointed commander in chief, Fourth Fleet, paid his official visit. Outgoing Vice Admiral Inouye gave me a big macaw as a present. Under the circumstance that the next general offensive on Guadalcanal was not going to be made before the end of this year, I may perforce have time to play with the bird.

Captain [Kazuki] Niimi, the liaison officer on board the tanker *Toho Maru* came to visit me. He was a classmate of mine. He said the number of ships she had refueled since the Hawaiian operation last year reached over four hundred and the amount of fuel more than 110,000 tons. The recent refueling of the task force lasted for eight consecutive days, he added.

[Ugaki opened his entry for 1 November by recording the announcement of his promotion to vice admiral and celebrated by composing three two-line poems on the subject.

[Many officers of all types assembled at 0930 to hear Yamamoto address them about the battle of Santa Cruz. "After the address we gave three cheers for the emperor and drank the health of officers and men with sake, a gift from the emperor." Higher brass were invited to lunch. Ugaki thought this get-together was good for morale and "also for facilitating future operations by creating a harmonious atmosphere amid strained feelings." Later that day some officers arrived from Tokyo, "to make plans for replenishing the reduced air strength."]

Monday, 2 November 1942. Fair, later cloudy. Five enemy destroyers with two transports appeared between Lunga and Cape Taibo early this morning. After disembarkation, the destroyers bombarded our position and withdrew.

[*Two U.S. destroyers,* Shaw *and* Conyngham, *bombarded Japanese shore positions on the morning of 2 November.*][26]

A float plane reported that in its night attack it found an enemy airfield at a point 5.5 kilometers southeast of Cape Taibo. This was quite important. If it was difficult for the enemy to use the present airfield due to our bombardments, naturally they would construct second and third airstrips. If things were left unchecked, a second and third Guadalcanal would meanwhile be created in the eastern half of the Solomons. Constant reconnaissance is all the more essential and, at the same time, we must capture Guadalcanal as quickly as possible.

[The rest of the day was busy if routine. *Shokaku, Zuiho,* and *Chikuma,* with other damaged ships, left for home waters under destroyer escort. The Second and Third fleets held meetings to study the battle of Santa Cruz. The new chief of staff, Fourth Fleet, Rear Admiral Shunsaku Nabeshima, boarded *Yamato* "to pay his respects." That night Ugaki talked with Commander Tatsukichi Miyo, a member of the Operations Section, First Bureau, Naval General Staff, "and received information about various matters."

[Tuesday, 3 November, opened with a ceremony in honor of memorial day for the Emperor Meiji. Then various air officers met to study "operations since the 10th of last month." At noon the Seventh Heavy Cruiser Division, consisting of heavy cruiser *Suzuya* (flagship), heavy cruiser *Maya,* and the Second Destroyer Squadron left to reinforce the Eighth Fleet at Shortland.]

Wednesday, 4 November 1942. Fair. At 0630 CV *Zuikaku,* flagship Third Fleet, and heavy cruiser *Myoko,* flagship Fifth Heavy Cruiser Division, accompanied by two destroyers, left for home waters. *Zuikaku* had no damage herself, but she was sent back to reestablish the air arm of the First CV Division and for its training.

Three enemy cruisers. several destroyers, and two transports appeared off Cape Lunga and unloaded. After bombarding our positions, they withdrew in the evening. Our torpedo planes were sent out, but they failed again due to foul weather. This was really maddening.

[*Oddly enough, Ugaki did not mention that on the night of 2 November the Japanese succeeded in landing fifteen hundred troops with artillery near Koli Point. Here he probably referred to the bombardment of these new positions by cruisers* San Francisco *and* Helena *and the destroyer* Sterett.[27]

[On Thursday, 5 November, Colonel Suguru Arisue, slated to be senior staff officer in charge of operations when the area army was established in Rabaul, visited Ugaki with "an officer of the Army General Staff." Ugaki knew Arisue well and expressed his views to him "quite frankly."]

A transportation attempt employing sixteen destroyers is going to be carried out tonight via the northern route. I hope they'll be successful.

The submarine *Ro-65* sank in water thirty meters deep at Kiska early yesterday morning because of an accident. Seventeen lives were sacrificed. Who should be blamed for this?

Friday, 6 November 1942. Cloudy with squalls. Last night's sneak landing with sixteen destroyers apparently succeeded without hitch.

Enemy destroyers appeared again today from the direction of Tulagi.

We had selected Regata as an advance air base, but little progress so far has been made as the soil there is unfit for construction. So the Eighth Fleet issued an order to construct a new airstrip on Balale Island twenty miles east of Shortland. Any more delay cannot be permissible now. So we urged on them the need for selecting a suitable spot.

The sinking of submarines by accidents, not by hostile actions, has amounted to five since the outbreak of the war. Since it's most regrettable that this rate was so great compared with the combat loss of ten subs, the commander in chief issued a warning.

Saturday, 7 November 1942. Partly fair. Though the situation on Guadalcanal and the army's future intentions were unknown, we saw the need of sending a convoy shortly and issued an advance notice to make the necessary preparations, tentatively setting the 13th as the day of landing.

The navy was rather skeptical about the future after seeing three failures by the army. And its morale in general was low in spite of the success of the battle off Santa Cruz Island. We need a great deal of effort and preparations to lift it up and to make each force unite in a more enthusiastic spirit.

Chiyoda returned from Shortland yesterday.

The submarine *I-20* launched a midget sub carried on board her at a point five miles bearing 330° of Cape Esperance at 0222. This must have proved to be quite a threat, as the Honolulu station broadcasted "enemy submarine sighted off Lunga at 0759" to all vessels. I hope for success in its first attempt.

Sunday, 8 November 1942. Cloudy with squall. Staff Officer Watanabe accompanying Staff Officer Ohmae of the Eleventh Air Fleet returned at 1400 and made his report on the situation from 1500. The causes of the army's failure in the last general offensive, as well as the general situation, was made clear:

1. Difficult topography; much difficulty was encountered in moving troops and materials after landing and in advance movement in the jungle.

2. Personnel and material were sufficient. Eighty percent of the personnel and material transported were landed. In spite of the losses due to enemy plane and destroyer attacks, little shortage was felt in troop strength.

3. Poor command and leadership.

    a. The army's chief of staff was not on the spot. So control of the staffs was poor.

    b. Although the army placed the whole operational forces under the commander, Second Division, it later interfered too much.

    c. Officers of the Army General Staff and the division staffs were divided and interfered separately, without unity.

    d. The Second Division commander had chronic neuralgia, and division staff officers were incompetent.

    e. Insufficient reconnaissance. Incorrect judgment of the situation.

    f. The Kawaguchi detachment commander gave up his command. On the ground that the allotted front was unreasonable, he protested, and eventually was relieved of his command. The regimental commander was ordered to command the detachment.

g. The Oka force failed to follow orders. Disregarding the order to advance along the west coast, he advanced at his own discretion. When ordered to withdraw from the north side of Mt. Austen, he retired from the south of the mountain on his own judgment.

4. Insufficient fighting strength.

a. Excessive fear of enemy planes.

b. Disorderly manner of the Sixteenth Regiment's advance.

c. The Second Division had little hard combat experience, as it had engaged only in the easy Java campaign. Though high-spirited, they were not expert fighters. The Nasu unit, especially its left wing, knew nothing but bayonet charges.

d. Fatigue of the troops was great prior to the commencement of the offensive.

e. About one-third of the officers became sick.

f. Foodstuff and medicine grew less as it neared the front. Pilfering was prevalent.

As to the army's future operational policy, they reported as follows:

1. The Second Division will withdraw to the west, but the four mountain guns will be left to the south of the airfield and ammunition will be supplied to them.

2. The force which has advanced to the south of Koli—two battalions, one hundred remnants of the Ichiki detachment, and four hundred newly transported—will carry out guerrilla warfare in that area as long as the foodstuff lasts.

3. The area on the left bank of Matanicau River will be recaptured to retain the attacking front for the future.

4. Convoy transportation will be made as soon as possible to send personnel, ammunition of the Thirty-eighth Division, and store up provision for sixty thousand men for twenty days. The Fifty-first Division and a mixed brigade will be transported next month.

5. Offensive will be made after late December with the arrival of the above strength and the recovery of the Second Division's fighting strength.

Some opined that this plan would be good, but I wondered. I think it is necessary to prepare more ample plans after further reinforcements are made. The Thirty-eighth Division commander at Rabaul claimed that he could make it with his division and a mixed brigade. But we can't believe or trust what the army says. We must study it thoroughly and, if necessary, recommendation must be sent to the Naval General Staff.

We issued a detailed order for the current convoy transportation, based upon the policy of carrying it out at one time with as many ships as possible.

I ordered arrangements made to get in touch with Colonel Hattori, chief of the Operations Section of the Army General Staff, and ask him to drop in at this command on his way back to Tokyo. I believe it important at this moment to convey our views to the Army General Staff.

Monday, 9 November 1942. Fair, later cloudy with squall. Rice and wheat were supplied to the forces going out from *Yamato* and *Mutsu*. The job of keeping a battleship here is not limited to refueling alone.

In accordance with the Combined Fleet's order, CV *Junyo* and the advance force sortied at 1100 and 1545, respectively. The latter consisted of three cruisers and seven destroyers and seemed too small a strength as compared with four battleships of the Eleventh and Third battleship divisions. Only after being joined by the Fourth Destroyer Squadron on the way will their strength be enough for the job.

The main object of this operation is to support the convoy transportation slated for the 13th. But, since an enemy convoy was heading west from Hawaii and another one had left Aukland, they may have a chance to meet them.

Rear Admiral Hashimoto, in command of the Third Destroyer Squadron, visited us after entering port in the morning. They made extraordinary efforts in sneak landings from Shortland almost every day and just came in for servicing. Nevertheless, we had to order them to sortie again after barely finishing refueling to cooperate with the advance force. But the commander understood the situation and said the morale of the men under him was high. I was glad to hear it. Men with no complaints and without discontent are to be respected.

Colonel Hattori, chief of the Operations Section of the Army General Staff, arrived at 1400 on his way back from Rabaul. According to him, the situation on the front was much worse than was thought. The fighting strength was down from one-third to one-fourth. Nothing can be done unless enemy air strength is destroyed. An urgent problem is how to advance air bases. The commencement of the offensive is said to be on or about 20 January. How slow that is!

I expressed to him our views on the method of attack, strength, and the time of attack. As a result of talks with the staff, the target date was changed to the end of the year. Considering it necessary to relate our views to the high command at this stage, I decided to send a staff officer to Tokyo shortly and ordered preparations made.

The Allied forces of the British and Americans entered French Algeria and Morocco. The French are still resisting but the outcome is quite clear. The French also severed diplomatic relations with the United States.

Tuesday, 10 November 1942. Fair. One heavy cruiser, several destroyers, and three transports on course of northwest were sighted at a point about 150 miles southeast of Guadalcanal. I hope they will become prey to our attack tomorrow. There seem to be some enemy activities in the area southeast of the Solomons.

[*These ships were Admiral Scott's group of* Atlanta, *four destroyers, and three AKAs (attack cargo ships), transporting the First Marine Aviation Engineer Battalion, other marine personnel, and material.*][28]

The army force which evacuated Kokoda was being pressed further. Australian radio broadcasted brisk enemy air force activities in the Buna area. Utmost care should be taken not to make our force rats in a trap.

[On Wednesday, 11 November, the chief fleet surgeon, Surgeon Rear Admiral Ibuo Imada, left the fleet, scheduled to be superintendent of Kaijinkai Hospital at Kure.]

A short while after 0900 a search flying boat and a plane from Chitose Air Group found three battleships of the *Washington* type, two heavy cruisers of the *Chicago* type, six destroyers, and three transports cruising at 16 knots on course of 280° at a point about 190 miles bearing 129° of Guadalcanal. They must have been the source of enemy activities detected there before. Were there not *Saratoga* type carriers operating besides them? How shall we destroy this enemy?

[*The Japanese had spotted Task Force 67 under Admiral Turner, consisting of four transports, supported by two cruisers and three destroyers from Rear Admiral Daniel J. Callahan's TG 67.4. Ugaki's question about CVs was logical. Vice Admiral William F. Halsey, commanding the South Pacific force since mid-October, sent Task Force 16 under Admiral Kinkaid to the scene, but* Enterprise, *which had been under repair at Noumea, was still being repaired and far from being one hundred percent operational. She and her escorts did not arrive until 14 November.*][29]

Rear Admiral Yoshitomi, in command of the Seventh Sub Squadron, arrived from Rabaul on board the tender *Jingei*. He said Rabaul was air raided as usual, so the ships had to change anchorage every day. The submarines could not rest there.

We sank one enemy transport and a destroyer by today's air attack.

[*Aircraft from CV* Hiyo *attacked but sank no ships in this engagement and lost heavily in planes shot down. But near-misses badly damaged the U.S. transport* Zeilin.][30]

Thursday, 12 November 1942. Fair, squall. The enemy group we found yesterday daringly entered Lunga Roads beginning at 0300. These were three antiaircraft cruisers, probably those reported to be battleships yesterday, two cruisers, eleven destroyers, and six transports. The transports started unloading with destroyers guarding the outer circle and the cruisers in the inner circle.

Two squadrons of torpedo planes and twenty-nine bombers and fighters of our land-based air force sortied to attack them, but the enemy took refuge off shore. The torpedo attack was carried out at 1230. According to observations from shore, no hits were scored. It was also reported that a fair number of our planes were shot down because of brave charges amidst the enemy's defense gunfire. After the attack, the enemy soon came back to Lunga and resumed unloading. Their number was said to be the same as before. Then the situation became unknown as it got dark after 1700. On the other hand, the air force reported one heavy cruiser sunk and four ships set on fire. Was there another completely different group? The situation was hard to clarify.

[*This U.S. group consisted of Turner's four transports, with cruisers* San Francisco, Portland, *and* Helena *giving close support, and* Atlanta, Juneau, *eleven destroyers, and two minesweepers three miles out. Superb maneuvering saved the transports while fighters from Henderson and antiaircraft batteries riddled the Japanese aircraft. One of these deliberately crashed into* San Francisco, *damaging her and killing about fifty men. Destroyer* Buchanan *was also damaged, ironically by U.S. antiaircraft fire.*][31]

At breakfast time this morning, when I first received the report of the enemy group entering Lunga, I declared today's enemy would be persistent and made the following judgments:

1. The enemy's aims are to escort their convoy, bombard our positions, and prevent our reinforcement. The concentration of our convoy at Shortland is already known to the enemy. A shadowing B-17 detected the eastward sailing of a part of the Fourth Destroyer Squadron and its major part joining the Eleventh Battleship Division near Ontong, Java. In view of the above, I thought the enemy would be tenacious tonight.

2. Measures for us to adopt:

   a. Air attacks should be intensified.

   b. Enemy information should be obtained continuously.

   c. Eighth Fleet (heavy cruiser *Chokai*, Seventh Heavy Cruiser Division (*Suzuya*), and heavy cruiser *Maya* should make a prompt sortie.

   d. One destroyer division of the Fourth Destroyer Squadron, now on patrol duty between Guadalcanal and Russell, should join the former, and both be assigned to attack enemy fleets.

   e. In order to make its shore bombardment more effective, the Eleventh Battleship Division was going to use weak propellent charges in its main battery firing. This naturally involved a disadvantage in firing against enemy vessels. Its time of attack would be decided by the enemy situation.

f. The advance force should approach Guadalcanal tomorrow morning to recover our attack force, and also to be ready to meet the enemy fleet if necessary.

All the plans had been drawn up on the assumption that there might be an enemy in the road and also that the enemy might come to attack after the arrival of our convoy. Now that the existence of an enemy fleet is verified, they should be restudied thoroughly. Seeing the need to revise the plan, I wrote down the above-mentioned judgment and handed it to the staff. They appeared to discuss it well. But it didn't materialize, maybe because the senior staff officer refused to accept it, saying as before that a destroyer squadron as the van would be enough because the enemy would withdraw by nightfall.

Thinking that it would be too late anyway by the time I got their reply and also that the Eighth Fleet, the actual force concerned, would have already sortied and taken proper action, I passed it off without insisting on it. This resulted in a serious consequence a dozen hours later.

The lessons we learned:

1. When there is a difference between the basis of a plan and the present situation, and the enemy situation, it is essential to promptly devise a completely new measure afresh.

2. In case an enemy exists, the first requisite is to prepare against it. Unless tonight's bombardment by the Eleventh Battleship Division is successfully carried out, it will be impossible for the convoy to enter the road. We should get hold of the essential point and make it succeed. In the morning, an Eleventh Seaplane Tender Division aircraft sighted what appeared to be a carrier as well as fifteen small planes and one large one at a point 180 miles southeast of San Cristobal Island. But apparently it was shot down while still transmitting its report. We ordered a special search west of Santa Cruz Island tomorrow morning in anticipation of the enemy's coming up north.

Yesterday, *Hokoku Maru*, which had just gone out to the southern part of the Indian Ocean for a raiding operation, was hit by a bomb on her stern by an enemy patrol boat. Following explosions, she sank at a point three hundred miles southwest of Cocos Island. Her sister ship, *Aikoku Maru*, rescued more than 280 survivors. They seemed to have underestimated the enemy a bit.

[Ugaki noted two major changes in command. Nagumo was appointed commander in chief, Sasebo Naval Station, and Ozawa replaced him as commander in chief, Third Fleet.

[The fleet asked the high command to send construction corps and antiaircraft batteries to the Solomons area and sent two staff officers to Tokyo "to elaborate on it."]

According to the Eleventh Air Fleet's summary action report, its fighter squadrons saw the following battle results: one transport sunk; one heavy cruiser, one unidentified, and one transport set on fire; one heavy cruiser emitting black smoke; two destroyers emitting white smoke, and nineteen Grumman fighters shot down.

Had they really suffered such losses, they couldn't have come back again off Lunga.

The Eighth Area Army was newly established for the southeast area, adding the Eighteenth Army to the hitherto Seventeenth Army.

Area Army Commander	Lieutenant General Hitoshi Imamura
Chief of Staff, Area Army	Lieutenant General Rimpei Kato
18th Army Commander	Lieutenant General [Hatazo] Adachi
Chief of Staff, Eighteenth Army	Major General [Kane] Yoshihara

[This posed certain organizational problems for the Combined Fleet. "In conclusion, it boils down to strengthening the capacity of the Eleventh Air Fleet," Ugaki decided. "Its chief of staff and staff officers should be capable of directing not only aerial operations but also surface force operations, and of negotiating with the area army."]

The engineer staff officer, now in Tokyo, reported the situation as follows:

> The ships now being repaired at home will be generally completed as scheduled. *Shokaku* will be completed by March next year and *Zuikaku* by January, but *Chikuma* has not been decided yet.
>
> The stock of fuel oil at home is only one million tons. In the future the fleet must get fuel directly from the producing area as much as possible.
>
> The production of steel and aluminum have decreased, causing a great problem for the future. All these are due to the shortage of shipping bottoms.

[To this report Ugaki added, "The fleet should be greatly mindful of these points."]

Friday, 13 November 1942. Cloudy with squall. After sending its scheduled time of commencing bombardment on the enemy airfield as 2345, the dauntless attack force encountered several enemy cruisers and ten destroyers at 2350. Through poor visibility, our destroyers fought with torpedo and gun fire at the range of fifteen hundred to eight hundred meters. They seemed to have sunk three cruisers and two destroyers and damaged three destroyers.

[*The "dauntless attack force" was the raiding group under Vice Admiral Hiroshi Abe, Combat Division 11, with his battleships* Hiei *and* Kirishima, *light cruiser* Nagara, *flagship of the Tenth Destroyer Squadron, and a total of fourteen destroyers. Abe did not anticipate a sea battle; his mission was to knock out Henderson Field and kill as many marines as possible. On this truly unlucky Friday the 13th, both sides made costly mistakes. The United States lost heavy cruiser* Atlanta, *light cruiser* Juneau, *and five destroyers.* San Francisco *was seriously damaged. Admirals Scott and Callahan were killed, as was San Francisco's skipper, Captain Cassin Young, who had been awarded the Medal of Honor for heroism at Pearl Harbor. Five brothers, the famous Sullivans, were among those who went down with* Juneau, *which fell to the submarine* I-26.][32]

Fire broke out near battleship *Hiei*'s bridge and her communication was interrupted. Under these circumstances, it was considered unfavorable to carry out today's convoy transportation, so an order was issued to postpone its date to the 14th. Then submarines were ordered to take positions compactly east to west of Guadalcanal, while fighters were ordered to be ready for enemy planes.

Destroyer *Yudachi* of the Second Destroyer Division, which fought well, was hit in the engine room and fire broke out in the bow. She became unnavigable and all hands were ordered to abandon ship south of Savo. Destroyer *Mikazuki* rescued the crew and tried to sink her with a torpedo and gunfire, but her finish could not be confirmed on account of interference by an enemy heavy cruiser and planes at 0300.

A shell also hit destroyer *Murasame* in the No. 1 boiler room, and the No. 2 gun and a searchlight were damaged. She withdrew temporarily for repairs, then retired to the north at 27 knots. In addition, a destroyer seemed to be missing. (Eventually *Akitsuki* was sunk.)

As her steering gear room was flooded, battleship *Hiei* became unnavigable. The Eleventh Division commander ordered the rest of the attack force to retire and at 0600 moved on board destroyer *Yukikaze*.

Hiei's position was reported erroneously. Though five destroyers escorted her, six fighters for direct screen arrived on the spot only at 1135. In the meantime, an attack by about twenty carrier bombers rendered three of her boilers unusable in addition to serious damage inflicted on her above the upper deck. As the prospect of emergency steering was slim, the division commander ordered battleship *Kirishima* to hurry south to her rescue, intending to have her tow *Hiei* to Shortland. But seeing that it would be difficult under continuous air raids at daytime, he decided to run her aground at Camimbo.

Thereupon we sent a telegram asking for their attention that, in case of a steering gear being damaged, they should use a destroyer as a rudder by towing her astern at the side [of *Hiei*]. Later, enemy planes hit her with two torpedoes and she listed. As nothing could be done about her, the division commander sent in his intention of disposing of her. We replied by ordering him "not to do so" because it was necessary to make every effort to rescue her after nightfall. However, this order took a fairly long time to reach them, and they seemed to have sunk her. It was greatly regrettable.

[*Hiei was subjected to three bombing attacks on 13 November. The first was by nine bombers and six fighters from* Enterprise, *en route to the scene while still under repair. These flew on to Henderson Field and, after reservicing, went back after* Hiei *with eight SBDs and two more fighters. Two torpedoes struck the battleship, leaving her dead in the water. The third attack came from fourteen B17s from Espiritu Santo, which scored only one "possible" out of fifty-six tries.*][33]

In the afternoon a lead plane of the land-based air force found one battleship aground and listing, a small fire on a cruiser, two destroyers burning fiercely, and another destroyer on fire in a bay at the northern tip of Malaita Island. Later, another plane sighted two battleships or cruisers and a destroyer lying dead to the east of the bay. After ascertaining there was no mistake, we ordered the advance force to attack this enemy.

The existence of such an enemy group was rather strange, since Staff Officer [Lieutenant Commander Kusao] Emura reported the situation from Guadalcanal up to 1100 as follows:

> Twenty carrier planes and ten fighters flew west, while six fighters were in the air as cover. One heavy cruiser under escort of a *Portland* type cruiser was being towed, heading east at 2 knots. Another *Portland* type was damaged in the stern and was sinking. Two destroyers were on fire. Except for another destroyer, which escaped into Tulagi, no other enemy was sighted.

Judging from the result of yesterday's torpedo plane attack and the situation of last night's attack, there seemed to be a completely different group.

While *Kirishima* was on her way south to rescue *Hiei,* an enemy submarine attacked her with three torpedoes at a point north of Indispensable Strait. Though one of them hit her, it did not explode. Then she gave up the rescue and turned back north on orders of the advance force.

Meanwhile, the advance force postponed to tomorrow morning the requested reconnaissance to the north of Malaita, and ordered destroyers *Yukikaze* and others of the Twenty-seventh Destroyer Division, which were standing by *Hiei*, to attack the enemy in that area. This force, however, was considered insufficient, as they had many survivors on board. The advance force was supposed to be making haste in refueling, preparing for action after tomorrow.

One of our submarines converging to the east of Guadalcanal sighted two cruisers and destroyers heading south and fired at a *Chicago* type at a range of 2,500 meters. The sound of two explosions was heard, but she could not confirm the result due to a two-and-a-half-hour enemy attack.

The search to the south discovered a convoy of six transports with five destroyers heading east to southeast at 16 knots at a point sixty miles south of the eastern end of San Cristobal at 0915 and another group of one CV, two battleships, a cruiser, and four destroyers at a point two hundred miles south of the same island at 0800. The former was on its way back after finishing transportation, while the latter was believed to be starting its activities.

[*The first of these groups was Turner's, consisting of four transports, two cargo ships, three destroyers, and two minesweepers; they headed back to Espiritu Santo after unloading at Guadalcanal. The second was Kinkaid's Task Force 16, consisting of CV* Enterprise, *two cruisers, and six destroyers.*][34]

[The report of a U.S. force on Malaita proved to be in error; it was at Lunga Roads. So the fleet called off its search and attack order. "What a lot of trouble we have taken for nothing!"

[The rest of the day was spent in long, involved discussions on how to deal with *Hiei*. Although the division commander concerned twice appealed against the fleet's order not to sink her, the Combined Fleet headquarters was most reluctant to do so. As Ugaki noted, the situation was different from that of *Akagi* at Midway; Japanese ships were standing by her and she was within reach of land-based planes. First, it was decided to leave her in position with a submarine on watch. Yamamoto, however, feared that the United States might use pictures of her for propaganda. To this Kuroshima countered that no doubt they had already taken photos of her. She might be of use in absorbing enemy attacks away from the convoy. The day ended with *Hiei* still in position.]

Saturday, 14 November 1942. Rain. It was the worst weather we have had since we came down to this area, as a low pressure was staying nearby. It rained all day with winds reaching more than ten meters per second.

The war situation was quite complicated, too.

Both the morning search by planes and daylight search by the submerged *I-16* failed to locate *Hiei*. With the chrysanthemum crest on her bow, the ship seemed reluctant to expose her remains in front of the enemy. Or it may have been the will of God. It was in accord with what I wished, and I felt rather relieved.

Heavy cruisers *Suzuya* and *Maya*, joined by light cruiser *Tenryu* and a destroyer, under the commander, Seventh Heavy Cruiser Division, proceeded off Lunga at 2300 and shelled the Guadalcanal airfield and its vicinity with nearly five hundred rounds each ship. In spite of incomplete communication between ships, land, and planes, the shots fell between the new and old airfields. A fair result seemed to have been attained, with some places burnt up. They withdrew without any loss, taking the northern route. But neither did they sweep the enemy remnant off Lunga.

[*The attack by Rear Admiral Shoji Nishimura's bombardment unit left Henderson still operational, although it wrecked one dive bomber and seventeen fighters and damaged an additional thirty-two fighters.*][35]

Chokai, Kinugasa, and *Isuzu,* directly under the commander in chief, Eighth Fleet, supported the above-mentioned attack force partially on its way and met a terrible disaster on their way back. Enemy carrier bombers attacked them from the sea south of New Georgia Island to its northwest. *Kinugasa* was hit first, then *Isuzu* and *Chokai* were hit by near misses.

Kinugasa's steering gear was put out of order. She steamed at a slow speed under escort of destroyers *Makigumo* and *Kazagumo*. The torpedo officer took command of the ship as the skipper and executive officers were killed in action. With a good deal of flooding, she finally listed to port, capsized, and sank at 0920.

A fire broke out in *Chokai's* Nos. 4 and 6 boiler rooms. It was brought under control and she was capable of making 29 knots. *Isuzu's* Nos. 2 and 3 boiler rooms were flooded by a near miss so that she had to be steered directly at the stern. Both of them headed for Shortland, escorted by destroyer *Asashio*.

Chokai and the Tenth Destroyer Division left Shortland again in the evening after refueling there. These enemy planes were considered most probably to be coming from carriers. The Eighth Fleet requested the Eleventh Air Fleet to make a search to the south of the Solomons.

[*The attacking aircraft—six torpedo bombers, seven dive bombers, and seven fighters—came from Henderson, but some were in fact carrier planes, having flown off* Enterprise *to assist the marines. None of these aircraft were lost in this engagement.*][36]

A plane of the Eleventh Air Fleet's 707th Air Group sighted five large enemy planes and twenty to thirty small planes heading north at a spot 120 miles south of the western tip of Guadalcanal. After reporting the sighting of an enemy at a point three hundred miles southwest of Guadalcanal later, it has never been heard from.

[*United States records indicated that* Enterprise *was sighted around noon on 14 November, and her air patrol shot down the Japanese scout.*][37]

From early morning, an enemy B-17 shadowed the convoy escorted by the Second Destroyer Squadron, which entered Shortland yesterday afternoon and left there soon afterward at 1530. The plane reported in plain language that two carriers were among twenty-five vessels. Later it [the convoy] was subjected to enemy attack several times until the evening.

Nagara Maru and *Canberra Maru* were sunk. Two destroyers picked up their survivors and headed for Shortland. *Sado Maru, Brisbane Maru,* and *Nako Maru* were successively damaged. At 1420 the commander, Second Destroyer Squadron, started to withdraw to the northwest for the time being. Though his decision might be justified, this attempt must be carried out tonight by any means. At 1540, an order to turn back and resume the attempt was issued in the commander in chief's name.

[*The Japanese lost seven transports with their supplies and many men. Tanaka was able to transfer some one thousand men from each of the lost transports to his eleven destroyers and proceeded toward his objective with these destroyers and his four remaining transports. The United States lost five aircraft in this action.*][38]

At 1300 a search plane found four heavy cruisers and two destroyers heading north at a point eighty miles south of Guadalcanal and another group of one CV, two battleships, three cruisers, and several destroyers to its northwest. Another reconnaissance seaplane discovered two battleships further east. We wanted to attack them right away, but the land-based air force was not available. Its planes had gone out on a search and attack mission.

Accordingly, a warning was issued that these enemies might attempt to attack our convoy tonight, while a telegram in my name suggested that the convoy proceed along near Isabel Island, with the Second Destroyer Squadron concentrating its strength. The Eighth Fleet also requested the advance force to attack this enemy.

The convoy then consisted of only four ships and five destroyers of the Second Destroyer Squadron. [*Ugaki's figure of five destroyers is interesting, for U.S. records indicate Tanaka had his full contingent of eleven destroyers.*][39] They were to reach their destination at 2300, and in view of the delay and the enemy situation, they intended to go aground immediately. Approving their decision, we didn't give any special instructions. However, considering that running aground would reduce the efficiency of unloading, the Eighth Fleet instructed them to approach the shore with or without anchoring tonight and to run aground tomorrow morning if the enemy situation so warranted. The Eleventh Air Fleet shared this view, too. The experience was important.

The advance force [under Vice Admiral Nobutake Kondo], consisting of the flagship *Atago, Takao* with three destroyers, and battleship *Kirishima* with one cruiser and three destroyers, preceded by one cruiser and three destroyers, proceeded southward. They entered the Roads at 2130 from the west side of Savo Island and were to bombard the airfield while preparing for the enemy's counterattack on our convoy.

A report of sighting two cruisers and four destroyers heading north at a point twenty miles west of Savo Island came in from a plane. Then we picked up an enemy telegram of "I am in action" at 2030. Thus a night battle has started as expected. How will it come out?

[*Possibly this intercept came from the submarine* Trout, *which unsuccessfully attacked Kondo's group.* Trout *reported the encounter in plain language.*[40]

[Combined Fleet headquarters ordered a search for the next morning, and a "search-attack by the land-based air force." This tactic had not been too successful in the past, but, as Ugaki wrote, "We ordered it because it is sometimes necessary to try even when it is expected to be in vain."]

At 2215, we received a report of four destroyers and two heavy cruisers or battleships on course of 70° at a point fifteen miles west of Savo Island. [*This was Rear Admiral Willis A. "Ching" Lee's Task Force 64.*][41] The enemy apparently sent battleships, too, after learning the southward movement of our attack force. A night engagement between battleships will be fought for the first time tonight.

The losses sustained by the force directly under the command of the Eighth Fleet and the convoy during daytime today were due to the fact that the enemy task force closed in from the south. Judging from the enemy's movements yesterday, we anticipated it and considered it wise to postpone the attack another day for the sake of rearranging the battlefield and also in view of the approach of enemy vessels. But we had to be dissuaded, as any delay could not be permitted due to the difficulties of maintaining our air strength.

Nevertheless, the fact that the Eighth Fleet's withdrawal route and the convoy's course eventually were selected comparatively close to the enemy task force couldn't escape from blame as bringing about a disadvantage. In view of the convoy's inferior speed, it couldn't be helped. And yet, flexibility and the margin to meet a change in the enemy situation is necessary at any time.

According to a report front Staff Officer Emura at Guadalcanal, the enemy air strength as of about 1100 seemed to have increased to forty bombers, forty fighters, and three large planes. A cruiser off

Lunga appeared to have sunk at 0230, while an unnavigable *Portland* type seems to have been towed to Tulagi. No other ships were seen, he reported.

In view of the damage our convoys sustained, we twice requested the chief of staff, Seventeenth Army, to bombard the airfield by any means, as the outcome of the transportation attempt depended on neutralizing the enemy air strength. The army replied that they were planning to shell from 1600 today, morning and evening tomorrow, and early morning the day after tomorrow in view of the shortage of ammunition. They also said enemy planes attacking our convoy came from other bases, only using them as a stepping stone. But apparently they have ordered bombardment commenced at 1400.

At 2247 we received the following urgent telegram from the commander, advance force: "Guadalcanal attack force and the reinforcements are engaging with two new type enemy battleships and several cruisers and destroyers off Lunga at 2218. Tonight's shore bombardment called off."

Then the commander, advance force, ordered the convoy to go aground and *Kirishima* to withdraw to the north. The situation didn't seem favorable. Later, the following telegrams were received in succession: "At 2304 we are going to withdraw to the north after rearranging the battlefield." "Those who are pursuing the enemy should carry out attacks and withdraw to the north." "Report the condition of *Kirishima*."

Sunday, 15 November 1942. Battleship *Kirishima* fought two enemy battleships, one of which was a *North Carolina* type, and was seriously damaged. A torpedo hit on her stern made her steering impossible, and she was flooded. She tried once to reach Camimbo at her slowest speed, but there seemed to be no prospect of using the engine as ninety percent of the engine room crew were killed. All hands were then transferred to destroyers. We thereupon sent a telegram leaving her disposal to the discretion of the commander, advance force. At 0135 she capsized and sank at a point 8.5 miles bearing 285° of the summit of Savo Island.

[*Kirishima* fell victim to shells from battleship Washington. *In the engagements of 14 and 15 November, the United States lost three of Lee's destroyers, and* South Dakota *was badly damaged. The Japanese also lost the destroyer* Ayanami.][42]

We lost the two ships of the Eleventh Battleship Division, one each last night and the night before last. It couldn't be helped, as both sinkings took place after hard fighting. Destroyers rescued survivors of *Kirishima*, 1,128 in all, including her skipper.

Summary Action Report No. 1 from commander, Eleventh Battleship Division, issued at 2230 on the 13th:

1. While proceeding on the scheduled course after parting from the Main Force, from 0837 a B-17 shadowed us for about ten minutes. Fighters of the direct screen repulsed it.

At 1950 we encountered a heavy squall and entered Indispensable Strait through extremely poor visibility. Savo Island could not be seen. Considering the bombardment impossible, we turned back.

But soon afterward visibility improved a little and the observation post ashore also reported the weather to be fair, so we put about once again to resume movement for the bombardment.

2. Results: As reported by each force. After dawn, *Hiei* saw an enemy large cruiser [*Honolulu* type) sink after a big explosion.

3. Loss: As reported by each force.

At 2345, when we are about to open fire on the airfield, we sighted enemy vessels off Lunga, and I ordered them attacked. Then, from 2348 to 0100, we fought four enemy cruisers and ten destroyers at close ranges of six kilometers to two kilometers, and I believe we sank or seriously damaged all of them.

Summary Action Report No. 2 from the same commander issued at 1200 on the 14th:

1. Immediately after the commencement of fighting, enemy gunfire was concentrated on *Hiei*. More than fifty shells, as well as numerous machine-gun bullets, hit the foremast, antiaircraft guns, machine guns, searchlight, and other superstructures.

Gun firing became impossible for the time being, as the electric circuit of the main battery system and the control tower of the secondary battery were damaged. Fires broke out at several spots near the foremast.

Then the steering gear room was hit and flooded, rendering steering impossible. She then was navigated with the use of engines and reached a point west of Savo Island by 0400. But, as the rudder then stuck to one side, she eventually lost steering ability, so she circled in almost the same spot.

Destroyer *Yukikaze*, destroyer *Terutsuki*, and the Twenty-seventh Destroyer Division arrived on the scene one after another and engaged in rescuing and escorting her. As her communication facility was destroyed except the hand semaphore, I went on board destroyer *Yukikaze* temporarily to continue command of the whole force.

Under attacks of more than sixty torpedo planes and bombers coming from 0530 to 1030—three hits and numerous near misses—strenuous efforts were made to fight fire and flood. At 1230, when manual steering was made possible, after placing the fire at the fore-mast under control and the pumping of the flooded steering room proved effective, about twelve carrier torpedo planes came to attack her. Torpedoes hit the midship and stern on her starboard and the starboard engine room was flooded.

Then water gradually poured in from holes made in her side, and the listing increased. Pumping of the steering gear room became impossible, and all engines could not be used because of flooding.

Thereupon I ordered all hands to abandon ship and decided to sink her by our own hand. The transfer of her crew was completed by 1600.

When we were about to torpedo her with the Twenty-seventh Destroyer Division (minus *Ariake*), we received your order not to sink her. We immediately suspended the torpedoing and the de-stroyer division kept watch over her.

From 1700 we maneuvered to the west out of her sight for a while in order to avoid confusion with the Eighth Fleet. When we closed in again, we could not find her, though we searched for her for half an hour from 2300. Giving up the search at 2330, we proceeded so as to join the advance force.

2. Those killed in action aboard *Hiei* were about two hundred, including the senior staff officer, Eleventh Battleship Division, while many were wounded. Among them are the division commander, her skipper and executive officers, but the former two are fit for duty.

3. I am extremely sorry to lose many loyal, courageous officers and men and the valuable ship, in spite of everyone's good fighting.

4. Correction: "Four enemy cruisers" which appeared in my Sum-mary Report No. 1 should read as five cruisers (two new-type heavy cruisers, one heavy cruiser, and two light cruisers).

I believe the above reports are very well written. Dispatch Action Re-port from the commander, Advance Force No. 2, sent at 0951 on the 15th:

1. On receiving a report of an enemy heading north off Camimbo at 1645, we approached the enemy to destroy it first. At 2030 the van force, consisting of light cruiser *Sendai* and the Nineteenth Destroyer Division sighted the enemy and engaged it to the east of Savo Island from 2115. Then the direct screen force of light cruiser *Nagara,* the Eleventh Destroyer Division, destroyer *Samidare,* and destroyer *Ikazuchi* joined in the battle.

2. The Main Force en route to Lunga met more than two battle-ships heading west and engaged them in a fierce fight.

3. The destroyer squadron then pursued the enemy main force withdrawing to the southwest, and the direct screen force discharged their attacks upon this enemy northwest of Camimbo at about 2340.

4. Results achieved:

    a. Two heavy cruisers and two destroyers sunk.

    b. One heavy cruiser and one destroyer seriously damaged.

    c. One battleship (*North Carolina* type) hit by two torpedoes. In addition, three explosions of torpedo hits were heard at the time of the direct screen force's attack.

    d. One battleship (*Idaho* type) was hit by three torpedoes.

    e. Besides the above, one torpedo fired by destroyer *Oyashio* hit a battleship.

5. Our losses:

    a. *Kirishima* and *Ayanami* sank.

    b. Other losses are considered slight.

Thus the advance force withdrew to the north. In the meantime, the Third Battleship Division, Second CV Division, and others proceeded to the south for a while, but they turned back to the north.

The Second Destroyer Squadron had four transports go aground at Tassafaronga at 0200 and withdrew with ten destroyers at 0230 by our order. They are expected to arrive at Shortland tonight, taking the northern course.

According to the report from Staff Officer Emura, two of the transports started burning at 0640 by bombardments from the battery on Mt. Tai and strafing and bombing by the enemy planes. Further, at 0815 all four seemed to be set afire by gunfire from three enemy destroyers. However, they must have finished a fair amount of unloading by that time since 0300. Nothing more was seen in the area, except a destroyer that sortied from Tulagi and those three destroyers which bombarded Tassafaronga.

[*Bombers from* Enterprise *as well as marine bombers and army fighters participated in this action. The destroyer* Meade *would have been flattered to be recorded as "three enemy destroyers." She is credited with disposing of three Japanese transports, and later performed valuable service in rescuing survivors in this, her maiden action.*]⁴³

A search plane sighted two battleships at a point 160 miles bearing 154° of Tulagi at 0900, while a submarine found two battleships (one each of *Washington* and *Idaho* types) on course of 90° at 16 knots sixty miles northwest of the above point. These battleships seem to be the same and the very ones which appeared off Lunga last night. No information so far obtained on the enemy CVs. They seemed to have gone south, after parting from others yesterday afternoon.

Judging from the circumstances under which the enemy was sighted last night, yesterday's enemy was considered to be two battleships, two heavy cruisers, and eight destroyers. Even putting together the reported attack results, we seem to have missed two battleships, though damage was inflicted on two or three destroyers, which evacuated into Tulagi.

This is far from my aim of destroying the enemy with our loss representing one-third of it. We lost battleship *Kirishima*, heavy cruiser *Kinugasa*, and destroyer *Ayanami*. It is especially so when the loss of the transports is added. Out of the eleven transports, seven were damaged—six destroyers rescued 13,250 men on board. *Sado Maru*, one of those damaged, could be brought back to Shortland today, but it is still necessary to take steps about the six remaining ships. Concerns about these ships seemed rather slight as they were not naval vessels. We requested the Eighth Fleet to do all they could about towing, beaching them, or recovering their shiploads.

We also related the battle situation to the chief of staff, Seventeenth Army, and expressed our regret for failing to accomplish the convoy mission despite all our efforts, together with our future plans.

[*Both sides claimed the naval battle of Guadalcanal as a victory. But if victory means the accomplishment of one's mission—in this case reinforcement of Guadalcanal—it was obviously an American one. Turner landed all the troops and most of the material. Despite his rescue of 13,250 men (Ugaki's figure) aboard destroyers and his gallant efforts, Tanaka landed only some two thousand men and a small amount of ammunition and rice.*]++

Later, the advance force was ordered to go to Truk.

After 1400 a search plane found two cruisers midway between San Cristobal and Rennell Islands. One of them appeared to be towing another, for their speed was only 6 knots. The submarine force commander ordered a submarine, then engaged in the supply mission to Indispensable Shoal, to attack them.

Monday, 16 November 1942. Brief Action Report of battleship *Kirishima* came in:

> Following the Fourth Heavy Cruiser Division, we commenced firing upon an enemy battleship at the range of about ten thousand meters immediately after heavy cruiser *Atago* started her searchlight illuminations. Enemy gunfire also concentrated on us and inflicted more than six hits.
>
> Fire started at various sections, while the fore radio room was destroyed, hydrometers of Nos. 3 and 4 turrets stopped, and the rudder developed trouble.
>
> On the other hand, our first salvos of the main and second batteries

made hits upon two enemy battleships: Two of the main battery's first salvo made hits and especially one of them blew off the enemy bridge. At least ten hits were made upon them, but the enemy could not be finished off. At 2249 the distance between us and them was increased.

By this time most of the fires were brought under control, and all engines were still operable with their full power, but the steering gear room was completely flooded, so we couldn't make way at all. In the meantime, the engine rooms became intolerable because of the increased heat, and most of the engineers were killed though they had been ordered to evacuate. Only the central engine could make the slowest speed.

Then fires once brought under control gained strength again, so that the fore and aft magazines became endangered. Orders to flood them were then issued.

As light cruiser *Nagara* happened to close in, we asked her to tow our ship, but a negative answer was given. An attempt to prevent the flooding of the steering gear room also failing, the ship became hopeless.

Then we gave up the ship and asked destroyer *Asagumo* and destroyer *Terutsuki* to come alongside to transfer the crew to them. After we lowered the ensign and shouted three cheers of *Banzai*, Their Majesties' portraits were first transferred to destroyer *Asagumo*, which came alongside. When most of the crew had been transferred to *Asagumo*, the ship listed greatly so that we could hardly stand on her deck without help.

The ship finally went down at 0125 at a point eleven miles bearing 265° of Savo Island. Sixty-nine officers and 1,031 men were transferred on board destroyers.

My men fought well and displayed the noble spirit of service men. My only regret is that we could not sink the enemy in exchange for our ship because of the rudder trouble.

According to a report by the Second Destroyer Squadron commander who escorted the convoy, a total of 106 enemy planes attacked them from 0555 to 1520. The enemy planes were mostly divided into two groups and were considered to be coming from carriers. One transport was rendered unable to operate, four were set on fire, and another one listed. But four other transports could reach Tassafaronga, and two thousand men, 360 cases of ammunition for field guns, and fifteen hundred bales of rice were successfully unloaded. This amount of the staple foodstuff could not support our forces there more than several days. Even if the five thousand sick out of thirty thousand men now fighting there could be evacuated, a total of twenty-seven thousand men, including the current reinforcements, had to be supported.

As we are going to have an unfavorable moonlit night for the transportation attempt, it is never an easy task to envisage a plan to meet the requirement. Incidentally, we thought of a plan to half fill gasoline drums with rice, which could be jettisoned at sea at the destination for the receiver to pick up. *Yamato* made this experiment.

Our submarines looked for two enemy cruisers sighted yesterday, but so far in vain.

While the enemy's next move had been anticipated at the Buna district in view of enemy broadcasts, etc., an enemy force about one thousand strong landed on the left bank of the Zamboga River, seven miles south of it, this morning. At 1300 thirty fighters and bombers sortied and at 1700 sank three transports and set two others on fire, leaving only one undamaged.

Half of two army battalions originally slated to leave Rabaul tomorrow morning were changed to be transported by destroyers, expected to arrive there tomorrow morning. An army reconnaissance plane discovered a pretty big enemy airstrip about twenty-five miles southeast of Buna for the first time today. How careless they were! If and when Buna and Salamaua fall into enemy hands, the South Sea detachment now operating in that district would be cut off and our foundation for the Moresby invasion lost forever.

Some of the Seventeenth Army were reported to have advocated the wisdom of giving up Buna. That would be outrageous! In such a case, air raids upon Rabaul would be intensified, ultimately making it impossible for us to hold there. As Buna is located nearer to Rabaul than the Solomons, the threat from there would turn out to be a great problem for our national defense. The bud must be nipped to eliminate the enemy's chance of counteroffensives.

[*The landing Ugaki mentioned was by some of MacArthur's troops in fishing boats handled by natives. The Americans promptly began work on an airstrip.*][45]

Henceforth, battle developments will be centered in that district for a while. What a lot to cope with! Troubles usually come one after another like this.

Tuesday, 17 November 1942. Fair. It was said that the enemy force landed south of Buna were about one thousand strong, and it had not yet crossed the river. They seemed to have lost fighting spirit due to our attacks yesterday on the convoy.

This morning's search found only one landing craft in that district.

Fifteen hundred army strength embarked on eight destroyers, of which five would leave Rabaul at 0800 and the remaining three tonight to disembark them at Buna.

Just three months have elapsed since our departure from Hashira Jima anchorage. It is regrettable to see that our aim of that time has scarcely been attained. But it can't be helped.

Crippled destroyers entered port early this morning and the advance force also returned through the north entrance at 0830. It was lonely indeed that we couldn't see *Hiei* and *Kirishima* among them. Morale was lifted as it became almost certain, as a result of an investigation conducted by the advance force, that two or three enemy battleships had been sunk.

Vice Admiral Abe, commander, Eleventh Battleship Division, came on board at 0800. He looked sad with a bandage on his lower jaw. With a sorrowful face he reported losing two ships under his command. The feelings of those who come back after losing their ship in battle are always the same. He seemed to suffer especially for his sunken *Hiei*. He even confided that he thought he would have been better to have gone down with *Hiei*. I can well appreciate how he felt.

The reinforcement carried out by five destroyers to the Buna area safely reached the destination at 2340 and unloading was completed by 0230. Though enemy planes attacked on the way back, there seemed to be no loss. The other three ships scheduled to arrive there the same night were supposed to be safe, too. [*Probably Ugaki is referring to the two units of the special naval landing force under Captain Yoshitatsu Yasuda.*]⁴⁶

According to an air search conducted later, an airstrip under construction was found seven miles south-southeast of Buna, two runways at right angles five miles to its north, the very one found the day before yesterday, with three large planes and another single strip forty miles further away. Alert should be maintained at all times.

Yesterday many submarines were found dispersed more than one hundred miles of the Marshall and Gilbert area. In addition, there were signs of an enemy force secretly operating from the Hawaiian area, so Wake and the Marshall Islands were warned. At the same time, medium torpedo bombers were moved to Wake and the 701st Air Group from Tinian to Luot in the Marshall Islands. But nothing happened today.

Thursday, 19 November 1942. Fair. Three destroyers of the Eighth Destroyer Division entered Buna at 1700 yesterday and started disembarking soldiers. Enemy air attacks upon them were intensified and the unloading finally had to be suspended because of B-17 attacks. At 2030 a near miss damaged destroyer *Kawakaze* and a fire broke out in the fore. Being flooded, she withdrew ahead of the others at the reduced speed of 18 knots.

Destroyer *Umikaze* became unnavigable, her boiler and engine rooms flooded. Destroyer *Asagumo* was towing her at 9 knots from 2330 and withdrawing toward Salamaua.

On the other hand, about seven hundred enemy have come to attack Buna since early this morning. Although repulsed once, they returned to the attack after 0900. Their strength was unexpectedly great, and the airfield and village of Buna were said to have been encircled.

Dangerous! Should this point be captured, the South Seas detachment would be completely surrounded and become crippled. How can we break through this danger? We could hardly hold the Rabaul area should the enemy converge upon it fully utilizing all the airfields in eastern New Guinea. Now is the time when we must make every effort to rescue and secure the place. So I ordered that some good plan be thought out.

Friday, 20 November 1942. Partly fair. We received a report that our army force at Buna was engaged in bitter fighting on its coast area.

According to enemy communications traffic, an enemy force, most likely a reinforcement convoy, seemed to be approaching to the southeast of the Solomons. It was extremely regrettable that we could not do anything about it.

[Much of the day was taken up with reports. Captain Mikio Hayakawa, skipper of *Chokai,* told of her action on the 14th, meeting with Ugaki's approval. "The skillful way he evaded the attack was worthy of commendation." Then Captain Masao Nishida, skipper of *Hiei,* "made his tearful report." Ugaki was intensely sorry for him and tried "to cheer him up."

[Several officers arrived to supervise fitting torpedo nets around the ships, but Ugaki feared that if extended along *Yamato* and *Mutsu,* "they would hamper destroyers and tankers coming alongside them."

[Kuroshima and the junior air staff officer returned from Rabaul, reporting that "morale in general seemed to be low." Ugaki acknowledged that it might well be.

[The Buna situation continued to be a major worry. The main body of the South Sea detachment had not been heard from since November 9. "The first requisite" was destruction of the nearby enemy airfields. Perhaps the Twenty-first Mixed Brigade, scheduled to reach Rabaul on the 22nd, might carry out a landing operation near Buna airfield "and capture it at a stroke."

[A note concerning the battle of Midway, written by Commander Seiroku Ito, who had been Yamaguchi's senior staff officer, refreshed Ugaki's memories of his classmate's death. As late as November 1942 Ugaki was still under the impression that two U.S. carriers had been sunk in that engagement. "It was not without reason that he [Yamaguchi] could revenge the whole fleet by sinking two enemy carriers with only a few planes and CV *Hiryu* alone." Yamaguchi, recorded Ugaki, had combined "the cleverness of a skilled commander" with a fighting spirit. According to Ito's note, "He said he rejoiced in his good fortune of being able to die on the right spot at the right time." This was very much to Ugaki's taste.]

Those who can die at the right time and leave their spirit forever are fortunate. While having heavy responsibility of deciding the fate of the country, I can hardly fulfill my duty by only losing ships and sacrificing many men. It's doubtful whether I can have the most appropriate place to die, like Yamaguchi. The saying goes, to die is easy but to live is hard.

Saturday, 21 November 1942. Fair. Five destroyers, or two cruisers and three destroyers, and two transports entered off Lunga this morning and started unloading. But we can do nothing about them.

In the Buna area our forces were pressed from every direction and the situation appears critical. The Tenth Destroyer Division with eight hundred soldiers rushed there from Rabaul from early this morning. A B-17 shadowed it on the way. How will tonight's landing come out?

In view of the critical situation in the Buna area, we called in Colonel Tsuji, a staff officer of the Army General Staff and concurrently of the Seventeenth Army, too, for a conference. After agreements were reached on major points, we told him of our requests to the Army General Staff and the Seventeenth Army.

At 1430 Lieutenant General Imamura, the new Eighth Area Army commander, accompanied by his chief of staff, Lieutenant General Kato, and ten others came to visit us. Colonel Tsuji briefed them on the land warfare situation and our Senior Staff Officer Kuroshima on naval operations and our requirements.

Colonel Tsuji said he was going to telegraph the Army General Staff to send the Twenty-first Mixed Brigade to Buna at the end of this month, and try to capture the new airfield to its south if possible, with a regiment to be rushed from the Philippines.

Area Army Commander Imamura's general idea seemed to be that both army and navy would find it difficult to fight on the two fronts of Guadalcanal and Buna, and the rescue of Buna would be difficult also, as there was no means of pouring in a large force at one time. He seemed to be in favor of defending against the enemy offensive by securing the Lae and Salamaua line.

On the other hand, the commander in chief said it would be all right as long as there was a hope of attaining the objectives. He also wanted a sufficient study made, so that unnecessary sacrifices and troubles not be repeated one after another.

The Buna area has been entirely encircled. About fifty enemy planes attacked there today, and the situation worsened. It would not be good policy to press the reluctant area army and bring severe losses on ourselves. Therefore we reached a conclusion that our policy to be followed for the time being should be to wait and watch over the situation while securing strategic points on the one hand. This means we will have to give up Buna, to our great regret. [*Buna did not fall until 2 January 1943.*][47]

By the way, the activation of the command of the Eighth Area Army was set from the 26th of this month. No wonder he was not so enthusiastic!

It was decided to build a new airstrip at Cape Munda, and personnel and material were sent there last night and tonight. The enemy had already suspected the attempt. The fact that landing had to be made by small landing craft from outside the coral reef, seven miles away from the beach, was rather inconvenient.

It was decided to transport army troops from Manila by the Ninth and Sixteenth Light Cruiser Divisions. The Ninth Division commander, Kishi, came to visit in the morning, and they left here in the afternoon.

Sunday, 22 November 1942. Fair. A conference to study the sea battle fought on the 13th off Lunga was held on board *Yamato* from 0730. Fairly many attended. The views expressed were mostly based on fresh experiences of the actual battle and were very useful. As a result of the study, the following damage was believed to have been inflicted upon the enemy:

Night of the 12th: five heavy cruisers, two antiaircraft-purpose cruisers, and three destroyers were sunk. Two heavy cruisers, three destroyers, and one transport were seriously damaged. Three destroyers were damaged, of which two sank later.

Night of the 14th: two battleships, two cruisers, and four destroyers were sunk. One battleship was damaged.

[Ugaki ended the conference with an address. He pointed out that on both days the situation had been unfavorable. "Nevertheless, every force and ship fought hard, meeting the situation well, and attained a commendable result." However, "only four of the eleven ships of the convoy succeeded in reaching the landing point at Guadalcanal. Even they soon started burning on account of enemy air attacks and bombardment from land and sea, so men and material could not be unloaded sufficiently." As a result, the forces on Guadalcanal faced "an acute shortage of foodstuff and ammunition." For the future, "a steady supply" was planned, and the navy would establish forward air bases "and neutralize the enemy air strength when the bases are readied." He warned his audience that the enemy's "fighting spirit is high, too. . . . And there is no room for doubt that the area will become a decisive battlefield for both army and navy in the future. . . . Though we cannot train in the open sea, I hope you will devise every means to get ready for future battles."]

Commander [Advance Force] Kondo remarked that "in the battlefield no one can act beyond his subconsciousness, so it is essential to have enough training so that to act properly will come naturally." The commander in chief expressed his gratitude and respect for attaining the good result, overcoming many difficulties. The conference closed at 1130.

The Tenth Destroyer Division succeeded in landing eight hundred reinforcements at Buna last night, though a B-17 shadowed it on the way. Fifty planes attacked Buna yesterday, but the enemy bombardment was weakened and a lull seemed to prevail.

On the other hand, the South Sea detachment commander headed for the mouth of River Kubure with two battalions under his command. Other information said there was a plan to send them boats for crossing the river. They appear to be retiring on the left bank, after the enemy cut off their escape route. How about their fighting strength?

Monday, 23 November 1942. Fair. No special change was seen in the Buna area, but many planes were circling to its southeast direction. They seemed to be engaged in dropping supplies or in some new enterprise.

The chief of staff, Seventeenth Army, sent in that enemy aircraft attacks on our positions were intensified and the enemy seemed to be undertaking a positive offensive after discovering our fighting strength. We can do nothing about that, either.

On finding an unidentified plane at a point six hundred miles east of Tokyo at 1630 yesterday, Yokosuka Naval Station issued an air raid warning last night. Then medium bombers stationed near Tokyo Bay made a long-distance search, but found nothing.

A ceremony on the occasion of the Harvest Festival was held at 0705. This year's good crop is considered to have pleased the emperor, too.

I read through the high command's instructions based on the Central Operation Agreement between the army and navy, decided on the 18th of this month. This agreement doesn't include sufficient consideration of the situation in the Buna area, but it isn't necessarily unfit for the present battle situation in this area.

As a result of the staff study, we decided on a general policy of operations in this area. And it was in accord with what I first thought. We made up our minds to get on with it although we didn't know whether the army would agree with it. Its aim was to take the enemy airfield to the south while holding Buna.

Thirteen enemy naval vessels and transports and twenty planes are concentrated at Port Darwin. Judging that the enemy was up to some positive attempt, the Second Southern Expeditionary Fleet requested that one or two ships of the Sixteenth Light Cruiser Division be returned to the original outfit. The division was originally slated to transport army troops from the Philippines. So we ordered one ship returned to the division while ordering heavy cruiser *Kumano* and two destroyers on their way from Kure to take their place.

Tuesday, 24 November 1942. Fair. A patrol boat of the Fifth Fleet caused another fuss, since she issued a warning signal of a seeming enemy plane heading southeast at a point 530 miles east of Tokyo at about 0930. To what extent was [the report] reliable? Couldn't patrol planes find out? The situation must be clarified. Whatever happens, unless it's settled locally we can do nothing about it.

Staff Officers Miwa and Watanabe, who had been in Tokyo for liaison, returned at 1400. They caught cold from the cold weather at home and high altitude on the way back and made their reports while attending to their running noses.

They apparently achieved some success in making the high command realize the need of dispatching airfield construction equipment and anti-aircraft positions to the front. They also reported that the shortage of shipping bottoms was causing a drain of domestic fuel oil and a sharp drop in steel production. Moreover, the situation of the Axis powers was critical, too. There was nothing cheerful. I think we must encourage them, after winning a battle in this theater.

Lieutenant General Adachi, in command of the Eighteenth Army, his chief of staff, Major General Yoshihara, and others came on board at 1530. Our senior staff officer briefed them on current naval operations and our future policy. After that we had dinner together.

As rumored, they seemed to be more dependable than the Seventeenth Army. But most of them came from North China, so they didn't well understand the features of the southern district. Also, they didn't seem to have enough knowledge of the fervent fighting spirit of the American forces. Neither did they show much interest in comparative strength, theirs and ours.

The army commander said, "I was informed in Tokyo to take charge of eastern New Guinea, but I think this will be made definite after I receive orders from the area army upon my arrival at Rabaul. As to strength," he continued, "I have no original composite strength under my command,

and I am going to decide my policy after getting hold of my forces. I want to ask your navy's cooperation in transporting my forces to the front." He added that he was told in Tokyo to put up with smaller forces, as the capture of Guadalcanal was the first requirement.

So we lectured him on the necessity of studying the present situation well; of recapturing the enemy airfield in order to keep Buna; that a delay would help the enemy send in more reinforcements, making it impossible for us to continue operations, and of the need to prepare sufficient forces. We also invited his attention to the fact that defense positions to stop the enemy onslaught should be established and also that an advance to the front should be carried out after everything was made ready. Will they be able to accomplish their mission? I sincerely hope they will make a triumphant return, with the same high spirit they have now.

[At the dinner table, "the poor conduct" of the Sixteenth Regiment, composed of recruits from Yamamoto's home town, Nagaoka, came up. He had heard from men from Nagaoka who were to replace the Sixteenth regimental and battalion commanders, and he answered "encouraging them to clear the past dishonor. But most probably," he continued, "they will never come back alive." He added with a smile, "I, too, will not be able to go back home unless Guadalcanal is recaptured, so I am depending on your army." Despite Yamamoto's light touch, "really it was no laughing matter," as Ugaki noted.]

Wednesday, 25 November 1942. Partly fair with rain squall. The airfield at Buna is still being held. However, the enemy attacks by mortars and cannon were intensified under cooperation of air attacks, and our firearms are gradually being reduced. The garrison force requested an urgent reinforcement of army troops.

Two torpedo boats sortied for Salamaua the day before yesterday to transport base materials, etc., but had to turn back due to enemy air attacks. The attempt was resumed with the Second Destroyer Division yesterday, but this time, too, enemy planes attacked them twice at night. Destroyer *Hayashimo* was hit and fires broke out all over the ship. At 2330 she finally sank with induced explosion of torpedoes at a point thirty miles bearing 76° of Salamaua. The skipper and many of the crew were rescued.

The idea that destroyers, having a little superior speed and gunfire, could make it, whereas torpedo boats couldn't, was erroneous. We instructed them to carry it out by small landing craft.

Little chance was seen of encountering an enemy fleet or powerful surface forces in that area at present. So it should be censured as thoughtless to have carried torpedoes aboard. Anyway, the fact is that transportation attempts even to Lae and Salamaua faced such difficulties, not to speak of that to Buna.

The first attempt to transport foodstuff, etc., to Guadalcanal by submarines was carried out last night. But *I-19* gave up the attempt in view of the energy defense in the Tassafaronga area. *I-17* sighted an enemy boat at a point thirty miles off the coast and withdrew, submerging once. Then she appeared off Camimbo at 1730, but landing craft failed to come to meet her. She only saw blinking lights ashore and had to leave without attaining her mission.

On the other hand, the chief of staff, Seventeenth Army, at Guadalcanal sent in an urgent request for reinforcements. Everything was going wrong. When shall we be able to have smooth sailing after overcoming many difficulties?

[*On 25 November, destroyer* McCalla *inflicted considerable damage on Japanese landing barges off Tassafaronga.*][48]

Thursday, 26 November 1942. Rain, later cloudy. A submarine transportation was carried out last night. While approaching the beach at Camimbo, despite the continued patrol by enemy planes, the submarine touched the reef but could unload only eleven tons of materials.

On the other hand, the enemy is sending in about two transports daily under the escort of cruisers or destroyers. The enemy foothold is thus being strengthened day by day. A foreign broadcast stated that Guadalcanal had been secured. If things go on at this rate, we'll soon be unable to do anything about the situation. It seems a better policy to devise a new idea now to limit the attrition of our fighting strength.

Though strategically New Guinea is more important, its immediate reinforcement is impossible. It seems to be hopeless on all sides. However, one of my greatest duties is not to miss an opportunity to make a big change by observing the overall situation. The army is sticking to Guadalcanal alone, but we should have foresight not to be dragged into the bottomless mire by the army and lose everything in the end.

Rear Admiral Tokunaga, newly assigned as Eighth Naval Base Force commander from chief of the Education Bureau, Rear Admiral [Yasuo] Yasuba, who came here to investigate the problem of self-explosion of torpedoes, and Rear Admiral Nakazawa, slated to be the new chief of the Personnel Bureau, arrived from Tokyo by plane today. I conferred with Rear Admiral Nakazawa about the problem of personnel until 1900. Though he has not yet taken up his new post, he already has ideas of his own. Thinking him quite suitable for that important position in wartime, we placed much expectation on his performance.

[The Naval General Staff sent in an intelligence report concerning the

Allies' North African operation, and projected that they would next "land on the French Mediterranean coast." Simultaneously, they would "start a great offensive in Burma." Ugaki saw the first possibility as "getting ready for a pincers offensive against Germany." He thought the projection of a Burma offensive unlikely. Nevertheless, "Contemplating this and that, I couldn't help considering that the Axis powers were facing an extreme crisis."]

A great change, the strategic policy for abandoning Guadalcanal and securing Eastern New Guinea, won't be easy because of the army's stubbornness. Nevertheless, if any more useless attritions are added up after repeating desperate struggles, some break will surely take place elsewhere in our national defense. So I requested the senior staff officer to determine the limit of terms beyond which the recapture of Guadalcanal would be impossible, with the aim of taking necessary timely steps.

I wondered how far the high command was discussing this important matter. At present we are carrying out operations in accordance with the central agreement between the army and navy, but this delicate change should be made under present understanding of both those at the front and the high command. I think we must ask the high command to send the chief of the Operations Bureau to discuss the matter with us.

Friday, 27 November 1942. Fair. The enemy transports unloaded off Lunga as usual. A patrol plane on its routine flight sighted a destroyer and a transport at a point about 140 miles bearing 100° of Guadalcanal.

On our side, last night we succeeded in landing twenty tons of material by a submarine at Camimbo. The chief of staff, Seventeenth Army, sent us a telegram of gratitude even for the eleven tons of the night before last. The plight they are facing must be worse than imagined.

About five hundred of the naval landing party and a few hundred of a battalion commanded by a regimental commander were said to be still holding the airfield at Buna. They are worthy of commendation. But how are we going to reinforce them?

The enemy attacked a midget sub base at Camimbo with light machine guns but was repulsed. The enemy was to the south of the spot.

The younger staff officers have been longing for a gay party for some time, but there has been little time to spare for that purpose because of busy operations. As they were suffering, I told the fleet secretary to hold a party at a newly opened lively house at Truk tonight. Though the fleet engineer, surgeon, and paymaster attended, the commander in chief and I didn't go. The place was said to be too humble, and I was not brave enough to conform to "do as the Romans do." Besides, it was due to something else I was thinking of.

Under the strained condition of the adverse situation, the commander in chief became a bit too sensitive and sometimes mentioned trifling matters. But I took them all as my responsibility and passed them off.

Saturday, 28 November 1942. Fair. Three enemy transports entered off Lunga, escorted by destroyers. Last night's submarine transport seems to have succeeded.

Upon receipt of a report of three enemy landing craft proceeding from the east to the Buna area, torpedo bombers sortied but apparently have turned back.

The land-based air force has been fairly active in cooperating with the land warfare and attacks on enemy airfields.

We picked up a local order calling for transporting army troops, foodstuff, and ammunition to Buna with four destroyers beginning tomorrow. Not only have we no knowledge at all about what strength they are going to transport and under what policy, we have not yet decided our policy to direct such operations. Fearing the transportation by destroyers would only increase our losses, we inquired about the army's policy and what strength they were going to employ in that attempt.

Monday, 29 November 1942. Fair with winds. The movement of a transport convoy to the new airfield at Munda generally succeeded despite enemy attacks by plane and submarine. Captain Iwabuchi arrived on the spot yesterday to take up the command.

Today six B-17s attacked the Tenth Destroyer Division on the transportation mission to Buna while heading west after passing north of the Bismarck Islands. A bomb hit destroyer *Shiratsuyu* on her fore part and she flooded. Though she was able to make 10 knots, it was said there was a fear of her fore part breaking off.

Destroyer *Makigumo*'s No. 2 boiler room was set on fire and was under emergency repair. The whole division turned back. Since they will be able to reach within one hundred miles of Rabaul tomorrow morning, they should escape from danger somehow.

It was just as I predicted last night. I instructed the staff, though belatedly, to carry it out skillfully by a steady method or with fighter escort provided.

[Nakazawa returned from Rabaul and he and Ugaki "had an intimate talk" on personnel matters.

[The chief of staff, Southern Army, sent in a long reply to the fleet's inquiry of the previous night. The Eighth Area Army's tentative operational policy was "to promptly reinforce the Twenty-first Brigade and secure Buna, and then destroy the U.S. Army coming from Buna along the coast after first destroying an Australian army coming over the Stanley range." They had repeatedly warned the local army that, unless they recaptured the airfields around Buna, "another Guadalcanal would be repeated there." The local force was not optimistic and even opposed reinforcements as only doubling the transport difficulties. The Eighth Area Army pointed out that securing the airfields would alleviate the supply difficulty and requested their "prompt capture." This was generally in accord with the fleet's view.

[The Operations Bureau, Imperial headquarters, Naval Section, also sent in a telegram that the army command had been instructed to study a plan to capture the U.S. airfield south of Buna using the Sixty-fifth Brigade or the Twenty-first Independent Mixed Brigade.]

According to this, it was apparent that the army was still holding the Guadalcanal center principle, and the intent of the Naval Section in relaying this telegram seemed to be understandable and in some respects not understandable.

Monday, 30 November 1942. Fair and hot. I couldn't think of anything else but how to deal with the present plight. I scolded myself, saying, "This will never do!"

Yesterday I wrote to Fukudome, chief of the Operations Bureau, about my idea of what to do under the present circumstances. Far from being bearish, I just asked the high command's consideration with somewhat tentative wording.

An immediate step we wished the high command to take was to secure the Buna area and employ the Fifty-first Division in that area. The Guadalcanal issue and a change of operational policy might be put aside for a while.

This morning I added this point to my letter and also stated that if the chief of the First Bureau couldn't come here, I would send my senior staff officer to Tokyo. The letter was entrusted to Rear Admiral Nakazawa and would reach him the day after tomorrow.

Really, the fleet shouldn't ask for this sort of thing, but the high command in Tokyo should see the plight the fleet is confronting and give instructions in advance, well foreseeing the future.

Suppose that the Fifty-first Division will be sent to Buna to strengthen our forces and capture Emo field, how to transport it, as well as its strength and the army's confidence, were considered basic factors in determining future policy. But we requested the Eleventh Air Fleet to let us know about them.

After nightfall, the chief of the Operations Bureau informed us that the Fifty-first Division would be advanced to Rabaul, after calling off the original plan of having it await orders at Palau. The high command seemed to realize our plight.

An army unit staying at the coast in the Buna area sent in an SOS the night before last and reportedly has not been heard from since then. Enemy supply ships of over five thousand tons were seen near Cape Nelson. The enemy appears to be attempting to transfer cargoes to smaller landing craft there.

Night raids were carried out on Moresby by a small number of planes each night for three or four nights, taking advantage of the moonlight. This is worthy of congratulations.

Starting tonight the new transportation attempt to send foodstuffs packed in drums by destroyers began. Though they took the north detour route, enemy planes spotted them. Fortunately, however, they proceeded without being bombed. But the enemy encountered them at 2100 near Savo Island as anticipated. In the ensuing night battle between over a dozen enemy battleships, heavy cruisers and destroyers, and eight destroyers of the Second Destroyer Squadron, our forces sank one battleship, one heavy cruiser, and two destroyers. Our destroyer *Takanami* has not been heard from.

[*This was the battle of Tassafaronga. U.S. forces consisted of Task Force 67, under Rear Admiral Carleton H. "Bosco" Wright, who had replaced Kinkaid only the day before. His ships were heavy cruisers* Minneapolis, New Orleans, Pensacola *and* Northampton, *light cruiser* Honolulu, *and four destroyers. Just before the battle began, Halsey (newly promoted to full admiral) ordered two other destroyers, currently with a transport group, to join Wright. The Japanese forces consisted of the Second Destroyer Squadron under Tanaka, with eight destroyers. Tanaka was on a supply run, using the new technique of transporting food in drums which the destroyers would drop off near enough to shore for small craft to dart out and secure. Tanaka lost one destroyer—*Takanami—*and inflicted terrible punishment upon the Americans, although only one ship—heavy cruiser* Northampton—*was lost.* Minneapolis, New Orleans, *and* Pensacola *suffered severe damage.*[49]

[Ugaki received a list of the commodities landed at Guadalcanal from the 25th to the 28th, noting gloomily, "This must have been just chicken feed for thirty thousand men."]

Tuesday, 1 December 1942. Fair, hot outside. We don't feel at all like December. Though some time has elapsed since we sortied from home waters, it has been hot all the time.

We haven't yet received a detailed report of the night battle fought near Savo Island last night, but destroyer *Takanami* seems to have sunk at a point six miles south of the island. This could be surmised from the fact that her gunnery officer, one sailor and one soldier landed on Guadalcanal Island.

Today the transportation attempt to Buna was resumed with destroyers of the Eighth Destroyer Division, as there is no other way. Enemy planes continually shadowed and attacked them. Even after nightfall they were contacted with parachute flares. It's quite doubtful whether they can unload.

[*The struggle for Buna continued throughout December, with heavy losses on both sides, amid miserably unhealthy conditions.*][50]

Since 16 November of last year, Captain Miwa has served as deputy senior staff officer and greatly contributed to our command. But now we have to give him away as senior staff officer of the Eleventh Air Fleet, and he left the ship at 1430. I thanked him for his services and wished [him success in] his further efforts in a more difficult position. I also gave him my ideas about considerations toward the army under the current circumstances and other important matters.

As Staff Officer Watanabe was going to Rabaul by the same plane tomorrow, we discussed the draft of a local agreement and that of a transportation plan. I also gave him the same instructions regarding the army as I gave Captain Miwa.

Italian information dated the 25th reported that the British Far East Fleet, consisting of three battleships, one CV, six cruisers, and fifteen destroyers left Ceylon. Where were they heading? Were they going to start an offensive against our occupied districts in the Indian Ocean area, or were they going to be used in this area via Australia?

[Ugaki also learned that the Germans had entered Toulon in previously unoccupied France, and the French had scuttled most of their fleet. He did not have the exact figures, but they totaled sixty-one, including ten cruisers, twenty-eight destroyers, and fourteen submarines. Ugaki was indignant at this "unmanly action" and decided that France was "unworthy of being trusted as one of the Axis."]

Light cruiser *Agano*, newly completed as flagship of a destroyer squadron and now flagship of the Tenth Destroyer Squadron, arrived in port this afternoon accompanied by a destroyer. When the plan to build her was discussed, I attended the conference as chief of the Operations Bureau. Can she really meet the present requirements? If a bomb is enough to finish her off, I'm afraid she'll be no better than any light cruiser. I must inspect her when I have time.

Wednesday, 2 December 1942. Fair. Enemy planes constantly shadowed and attacked the Eighth Battleship Division, which headed for the Buna area last night, and it could not carry out landing. Only a part of the army troops was landed near the mouth of the Kumuai River. Though our fighters tried to cover it, we could do nothing about their continual shadowing on a dark, moonless night. In the end, we were the loser, as we failed to attain our objective.

As ammunition was running out in that area, the garrison commander sent in a request to chute it from planes. This was quite natural, and should have been done from the beginning. But instead they've been repeating the same old thing. Isn't there anyone with brains?

Two enemy transports again entered Guadalcanal under destroyer escort today and commenced unloading.

An overall report of the battle fought the night before last came in from the commander, Second Destroyer Squadron. Eight destroyers closed in Guadalcanal, expecting to meet twelve enemy destroyers which had been reported. At 2100 an enemy formation with a *Washington* type battleship in the center and four heavy cruisers and twelve destroyers was sighted. Four enemy planes were guarding them. Then they [the Japanese] charged in and fired twenty-six torpedoes against the battleship and ten against the heavy cruisers. One battleship, one heavy cruiser, and one destroyer were sunk and three destroyers were set afire, one of which sank later.

On our side, destroyer *Takanami* was sunk. As they had no spare torpedoes, they withdrew at 2130 without unloading. They attained a good result and proved worthy of being our destroyers. Regrettably, however, the important supply mission wasn't fulfilled. Presently we received a request from the Seventeenth Army to resume it by any means.

Self-explosion of torpedoes occurred every time a night battle was fought. Three explosions took place on destroyer *Kuroshio* in the last battle. Was it a defect of Type 93 torpedoes? Or was it still due to too much sensitivity of the exploder on warheads?

[Ugaki heard that some "small British warships" had left the Iran-Iraq area, ostensibly headed for Burma. This made Ugaki rather nervous, for he considered Burma Japan's current "weak point," and felt that it would constitute a suitable base for Allied operations to the west as well as a good base to fly material into China.

[The commander in chief, Fourth Fleet, and his chief of staff returned from inspecting the Marshall area. They asked for a reinforcement of one destroyer division "and an air arm to that district. These were the things most wanted elsewhere."

[Ugaki received a bonus of two month's pay, but, noting that "money has no use here," he sent some to Japan for savings, the rest to his brother one-third of which he used for "religious services for my ancestors," two-thirds to be given to two schools "as funds for moral training."]

Tuesday, 3 December 1942. Fair. Three enemy transports and six destroyers were off Lunga.

A midget submarine discharged last night penetrated the Lunga Roads early this morning and attacked an enemy transport between capes Lunga and Cori. After confirming two torpedoes hit, it withdrew, submerging deep, and eventually came back to the base at Camimbo, detouring Cape Esperance, after being attacked with depth charges for one and a half hours. Its crew was all safe, but the boat sank from leaking at 1430.

Ten destroyers under the command of the Second Destroyer Squadron commander undertook a transportation mission tonight. Enemy planes shadowed them at 1320 and twenty carrier bombers attacked them at 1630. But they proceeded without mishap since they were provided with float plane escorts. They jettisoned fifteen hundred drums filled with foodstuff off the landing point and headed back at 2300.

[*Fifteen bombers and torpedo planes with fighter escort, from Henderson, attacked the Tanaka force. But because of Tanaka's air cover, the Americans scored only damage to destroyer* Makinami *at a cost of two aircraft lost.*]⁵¹

We received a request from the chief of the Operations Bureau to dispatch a staff officer to Tokyo for a conference to plan transportation of army troops. The telegram seems to have been sent before my letter reached him.

I don't feel well because of a toothache. Though the fleet adjutant recommended that I take a walk ashore, I don't feel like going ashore under the present war situation. I don't think I'll collapse yet! I wrote ten letters in the afternoon.

Friday, 4 December 1942. Cloudy. According to the report from a staff officer on the spot, last night's transport attempt by the Second Destroyer Squadron succeeded in landing one-third of the load. The rest were still floating, due to the towing ropes breaking. Supposedly they made every effort to recover them by boat. Anyhow, the first attempt at this kind of transportation should be considered to have succeeded somehow. The enemy might mistake the floating cans for mines when he finds them.

A report from the Eleventh Air Fleet stated that the last transportation by destroyers was going to be carried out on the 5th, and the Eighteenth Army Command was determined to advance to Buna and take command at the front. The staff then wanted to send a vaguely worded telegram to stop it, but I couldn't approve that idea. We had already warned them of the recklessness of advancing the army command to the front too soon. Staff Officer Watanabe must have conferred with them yesterday. We shouldn't discourage them without any reason when they have already made up their mind to advance the command to the front. Moreover, to secure the Buna area was their particular responsibility and we had urged them so far.

In view of the result of the recent transportation by destroyers and the fact that enemy planes patrol the coast every night, this attempt can't be thought to have completed its mission.

Unless we show them a definite policy, is there any other way but to leave it to those on the spot, who know the situation best and are responsible for its execution? And we should be responsible, too, for the outcome.

[Tokyo warned the fleet that "the enemy appears to be planning a positive air offensive all around our country on 8 December, the anniversary of the outbreak of the war." Ugaki thought precautions should be taken "against a possible enemy surprise landing from submarines in revenge for the Pearl Harbor attack." Also, news from New York strongly hinted that the United States was aware of Japan's shortage of air power in the Solomon area. Ugaki feared that, unless the Japanese destroyed the enemy air arm to the fullest extent possible, "I fear the enemy will get more conceited and eventually we'll be overwhelmed by the enemy air might."]

The enemy doesn't care about losing battleships, cruisers, and destroyers, and is trying to beat us with its overwhelming air power.

Rear Admiral Ota, the newly established Eighth Naval Special Landing Force commander, arrived with his two staff officers, preceding his force. They came on board to visit us. The force was going to be equipped with 14-cm and 12-cm cannon, which was so far so good. But how to transport and land them would be a prerequisite.

I had a headache coming from the toothache all day today. It was extremely unpleasant.

[On Saturday, 5 December, several staff officers from the Eighth Area Army, the Army General Staff, the Naval General Staff, and the Eleventh Air Fleet met aboard *Yamato* to discuss the everpresent problem of the army's actions in the Buna and Guadalcanal areas. Staff Officer Yamamoto of the Naval General Staff advised that the Army General Staff had approved sending the Sixty-fifth Brigade and a regiment of the Fifty-first Division to Buna, "and also that if the Eighth Area Army still stuck to Guadalcanal alone, a proper directive would be sent from Tokyo." This was very satisfactory to Ugaki, indicating that "the immediate aim" set forth in his recent letter to Tokyo had been "fulfilled." Moreover, the Twentieth and Forty-first divisions "had been prepared as reserves, to embark respectively at Pusan and Tsingtao," so the army needed the navy's cooperation in transportation. Ugaki of course agreed, and "also urged them to prepare about three more divisions."

[The fleet received a message from Tokyo that the chief of the Operations Bureau would be coming down for liaison around the end of the month. It asked that the fleet not "worry too much. If such an atmosphere was revealed to our subordinate units, a serious consequence would come."]

My toothache has been terrible since this morning. But after a minor operation by a dentist and a discharge, I forgot the pain at once and was able to engage in negotiations.

At 1030 a U.S. submarine approached to three thousand meters of Nauru Island and fired seven rounds. Counterattacks from shore repulsed it. Was this because they wanted to publish the fact of the bombardment, or was it made to scout our countermeasures so as to plan a surprise attack in the future?

As the anniversary of starting the war is getting near, we issued a general warning anticipating enemy counterattacks.

Sunday, 6 December 1942. Fair. The Ninth Light Cruiser Division returned here at 0700 after completing its transportation mission. Its commander, Kishi, came on board to make his report.

The Sixty-fifth Brigade was said to consist of the heroes of Bataan, but actually most of them were recruits over thirty years old. Its commander was appointed from Mongolia and got on board after postponing the convoy's departure. Besides, there was no military academy graduate among the officers except a lieutenant colonel battalion commander. After a great loss sustained in the early stages of the Bataan invasion, they were replenished, and their equipment was third rate, too.

In addition, they came from Manila where they had spent days in easygoing ways, as if the war were over. I can't but be astounded at the great difference between what I had been informed and the reality. I had expected so much of them, as I heard they were picked soldiers. Even the Second Division, upon which much hope was placed, failed, as seen in the last futile attempt. Such a force as this would only consume provisions, contributing nothing to the current crisis, however much reinforced in the attempt to reach full strength. I wish the high command in Tokyo would take this into consideration.

Surgeon Captain [Shokichi] Odajima, chief of the Second Section of the Medical Affairs Bureau, came to visit us on his way back from the inspection tour of the Rabaul and the Buin area. He said he had never expected to see such a tragic situation at the front. Of course, insufficient provisions and bad living conditions may have contributed to the tragedy, but, at the same time, I would like to see tropical diseases like malaria, dengue fever, and ailments of the digestive organs cured with medicine so as to maintain fighting strength.

We received a congratulatory telegram signed by the chief of the Naval General Staff and the navy minister yesterday. Although we sent a reply, I didn't feel a bit happy. I felt rather like I had been ticked off.

Monday, 7 December 1942. Enemy planes are rampant over our positions in the Buna area. We found small enemy transports near Cape Nelson and sank two of them.

The enemy sends two or three transports into Guadalcanal daily and unload under destroyer escort. So frequent are they that it is rather too much trouble to make note of them.

A patrol plane found four enemy transports (two ten-thousand-and two five-thousand-tonners) at a point two hundred miles south of Guadalcanal. They were said to be escorted by one cruiser and three destroyers.

The transport attempt with eleven destroyers under the Fifteenth Destroyer Division commander was carried out today, but fourteen carrier bombers and forty fighters attacked them at 1640. Destroyer *Nowake* was hit and became unnavigable as her engine room was flooded, while destroyer *Arashi* was damaged in her boiler room. [*The near miss that flooded* Nowake's *engine room also killed seventeen men.*][52] Destroyer *Naganami* took the former in tow and headed back to Shortland, escorted by the latter. As one of the float plane screen made a forced landing, destroyer *Ariake* engaged in its rescue and then joined the above group. So the remaining seven ships continued on their mission.

[Ugaki noted that the Allied "counteroffensive against Burma, which had been feared for some time, finally commenced," with some forty transports with cruiser escort appearing off Chitagong. Japanese air forces in Burma were said "to have inflicted great damage and frustrated the enemy project." But, realizing the importance of Burma, "No doubt the enemy will repeat this attempt."

[Ugaki did not know this important piece of news until he read it in "the morning edition of the ship's paper. Why didn't the army on the spot try to give such important information promptly to the navy? In such a way, things never will be done in time!"]

Our judgment on the current situation and the future operational plan for the Southeast Area has been completed. A great duty of the Combined Fleet Command is to clarify the principle of directing operations without losing time and make those under its command concentrate in accordance with it. But we should pay much more attention to this point, as we have a trend of delaying to do so and also of often failing to clarify it.

As the senior staff officer was going up to Tokyo tomorrow, I entrusted the following to him:

1. As our offensive stopped and enemy preparations progressed, their will to counteroffensives became strong. Apparently they were aiming to recover the lost territories, mainly with their overwhelming strength in heavy planes, and encircle our homeland.

It was urgent to complete the defense of important places, to replenish planes and build destroyers. The number of destroyers available at present is the lowest limit for the movements of the fighting strength for the decisive battle.

2. It would be better for the chief of the Operations Bureau to come over here early in January. Half of our demand has already been fulfilled and the senior staff officer is going there, too.

3. We were quite reassured in hearing that we need not worry too much, as the high command was going to tackle the crisis with full responsibility. But the relationship with the army is very delicate now and we are racking our brains on this point, so it is essential not to have any discrepancy between the high command and the front command. The reason for asking the chief of the Operations Bureau to come over also lies in this. Our reasoning is listed below:

a. The root of Guadalcanal must be traced to the navy's unpreparedness.

b. We pushed the army pretty hard in the first, second, and third futile general offensives. Sometimes we pushed and induced them, while at other times we let them bear the responsibility. Of course the army was responsible for the failure, but we were also responsible because we failed to complete the supply and transportation.

c. The fleet had some success in fleet engagements which occurred on the occasions of our attempts to recapture Guadalcanal. But the aim of supply and transportation to the front has not been even half-filled each time, and the present plight was brought about. It led those on the verge of death to be extremely skeptical about the navy, with misguided notions of the fleet. They considered it selfish, only seeking its own ends at the sacrifice of the army, using the latter as its decoy.

d. When the army is enduring every hardship to prepare sufficient strength for its last attempt to recapture the island, can we tell them that the navy is unable to continue operations?

e. Even if we pushed the reluctant area army to send the Sixty-fifth Brigade and Fifty-first Divisions into the hard-pressed Buna area, much doubt had to be placed on their chance of success. If both Guadalcanal and Buna happened to turn out in our favor, it would be all right. But otherwise the Eighth Area Army would blame the fleet for its failure of transportation and its lack of a definite policy. The Seventeenth Army also would claim that dividing its strength in two had brought about the failure.

f. If an evacuation of Guadalcanal became unavoidable under these conditions, the Eighth Area Army would hold a grudge against the fleet, even if an Imperial Headquarters order was issued. Its influence would also affect the Seventeenth Army. In desperation they might aimlessly charge into the enemy or commit suicide, thus ruining the carefully planned evacuation operation.

g. In the event things turned out in such a way, not only would we be unable to apologize to His Majesty, but it would leave a source of evils for the Imperial armed forces. Furthermore, it would result in ruining the execution of this war, thus spoiling our glorious national history.

h. Considering the worst case, the utmost care should be taken for that eventuality from now on. Deeming wrong as wrong and impossible as impossible, and without being obstinate because of face-savings or without coaxing others, we should deal with this important matter with the utmost frankness.

i. In the light of past developments, we on the fleet side cannot say that the Guadalcanal campaign should be discontinued. Whether it be a transfer of the Fifty-first Division or an evacuation problem, a forceful push should be avoided by all means in negotiating with the army. It is essential to let them realize its inevitability by themselves.

Also it is essential that the high command take the lead at a proper time, well realizing the circumstances the lead command is facing. In order to do this, perfect accord should be maintained between the high command and our command. This worries me most these days, and I express my view to the commander in chief and the staff at every chance. The senior staff officer seems to have been thinking about it since the night before last, and he has now come to share my view completely.

4. Your warning that this command's concern should not be reflected on our subordinates is understandable. But we have never spoken of this sort of thing to them, and in fact we have taken especial care against it.

On the contrary, the commanders in chief of the Eleventh Air Fleet and Eighth Fleet revealed little confidence in continuing operations. Some division commanders engaged in operations in that area asked us if operations were still to be continued. Some of them even suggested the wisdom of strengthening the defense of Truk Island. To those inquiries, I used to reply that our operations were not to be discontinued. I prepared for it only in my mind. It is absolutely necessary for a command directing operations to foresee the future and make up its mind.

5. Each time members of the Naval or Army General Staffs came here, or at every chance of sending mail, we have urged the need of promptly preparing sufficient strength. But I regret to say that the forces prepared this time were not sufficient, either, and moreover not in time.

Since the Solomons and New Guinea are considered strategically important, preparations for a major reinforcement of over five divisions should be ordered promptly. Troop strength cannot be counted only by its number. They should be picked units, well equipped with firearms, and mechanized. Such a troop as the Sixty-fifth Brigade is nothing but a mere garrison force.

6. I have been feeling quite regretful that most of the Combined Fleet has been pinned down in this district and unable to promptly meet developments in other theatres. I would like to ask the high command to take steps to speed up the repairs on damaged ships staying in the homeland and properly arrange the supply of necessary materials, thus making us amply prepared.

7. Timor and Aru islands constitute the weakest point. It is reassuring to see that army forces are gradually being sent there after revising the army-navy agreement, but I would like to ask the high command to push the army to send more strength.

As I also fear that we will be forced to be more inactive in the Aleutian area with the completion of a highway in Alaska, proper measures to prevent such a plight in that district are urgently requested.

8. Many things cannot be made clear from this remote place. So we request that necessary information and warnings regarding enemy intentions, etc., be sent from the high command promptly.

From 0800 the fleet was alerted with two duty shifts.

While we are pinned down in this area, the stage of activities is now changing, for the enemy seems to be contemplating a new move, regarding the Solomons and New Guinea as already settled. So I warned the staff never to relax preparations and to watch the overall situation.

Tuesday, 8 December 1942. Fair at Truk. Beginning today, we entered the second year of the Great East Asia War. In looking back over the past year, I regret that we have not gained what we wished. I pledge myself to accomplish our war aims by good planning and hard fighting in the future.

I respectfully paid tribute to the 14,802 officers and men dead as of 20 November, a figure compiled by the Combined Fleet. We prepared an altar and a service was held at 0700. I'm not going to follow them in a hurry. I must make every effort possible until the last in order to break through this national crisis.

The U.S. Navy at last released its loss sustained at Pearl Harbor on this day last year and urged the people to stand up. The loss of U.S. Navy personnel up to the middle of November was said to be over seventeen thousand. This was two thousand more than ours.

War damage given for this one year (Imperial Headquarters announcement):

Army:	omitted	
Navy:	Battleships	11 sunk, 9 damaged
	Carriers	11 sunk, 4 damaged
	Cruisers	46 sunk, 19 damaged
	Destroyers	48 sunk, 23 damaged
	Submarines	93 sunk, 58 damaged
	Minelayers	5 sunk, 2 damaged
	Special transports	4 sunk, 2 damaged
	Minesweepers	5 sunk, 2 damaged
	Gunboats	8 sunk, 6 damaged
	Others	28 sunk, 29 damaged
	Vessels sunk [merchantmen & other misc. ships]	416
	Vessels captured	403
	Aircraft shot down or destroyed	3,798

[*Obviously he exaggerates.*]

Even if admitting some errors, this represents a considerable amount. In addition, we must count to our credit the captured territories and the secured resources. But we must anticipate that the next year won't be as easygoing as this.

Despite enemy air attacks, seven destroyers proceeded toward Guadalcanal for the transport mission last night. Repulsing enemy PT boats near the island, they kept on going, but finally had to turn back because of attacks by enemy PT boats and planes. Thus the transport attempt by destroyers has become hopeless, too.

[Tanaka *changed course once, then tried again, facing such an aggressive attack by four motor torpedo boats that he retired.*]⁵³

The Seventeenth Army reported enemy transports, four cruisers and four destroyers entered near Cape Cori today.

On the other hand, the last transportation attempt to Buna left Rabaul under cover of direct screen planes, but enemy aircraft attacked them after they had sailed about a hundred miles from Rabaul. Destroyer *Asashio's* Nos. 3 and 4 guns were damaged, and many holes were drilled in her stern above the waterline. They put about on orders. Destroyer *Isonami* was also damaged slightly on the way back.

Thus sea communications in both directions are severed. Only air and underwater are left. I hope the time won't eventually come when we cannot do anything.

Yesterday's enemy attack killed company commanders and section leaders of the Buna garrison force. Today's enemy air attack reduced available antiaircraft guns to only one. Basabua was captured. They are now gradually being pressed, unable to hold their positions any longer.

[*B-26s of the Fifth Air Force attacked the Buna area and Australian troops captured Gona in hand-to-hand combat.*⁵⁴

[Watanabe, with Yamamoto of the Naval General Staff and Major Hayashi returned from Rabaul. That evening Hayashi briefed the staff "on the situation at Guadalcanal, together with his views." He left no doubt that the island would have to be given up, and the fleet command decided "to plan the necessary steps."

[*On this date, Major General Alexander M. Patch, USA, replaced Major General Alexander A. Vandegrift, USMC, as commander on Guadalcanal, and the veteran marines began to be replaced. Certain marine units remained and others would arrive, but from this point on the defense of Guadalcanal was increasingly in the hands of the United States Army.*]⁵⁵

In view of the army's strong demand, it was arranged to carry out one more transport attempt to Guadalcanal with destroyers, with the aim of supporting our forces there, by the end of this month, together with transports to be made with submarines. This was formally decided yesterday between the commander in chief, Eleventh Air Fleet, and the Eighth Area Army commander. It was also decided to carry out one more transportation of only provisions and ammunition to Buna with destroyers on account of bad weather.

[Ugaki noted that the relationship between the Eighth Area Army command and the Eleventh Air Fleet had been "strained a good deal." Both has sent "serious telegrams" to Yamamoto concerning transportation by destroyer. "Some measure should be taken right now."]

As even destroyer transportation has now become impossible, the situation has undergone a sudden change. So the time for changing the future policy might come sooner than expected. Its necessity has now been keenly felt, especially so when the situation at Guadalcanal is as hopeless as described below, as Staff Officer Hayashi told us:

Out of 3,000 men of one regiment, now only 60 to 70 remain capable of continuing to fight. The present strength fit to fight is only 4,200 altogether. About 1,500 men a month are being lost.

They are putting up a gallant fight in position, but they are suffering forty to fifty casualties daily due to enemy bombing and gunfire. Less than one-third are fit for combat, while the rest are sick and wounded. Most of them are suffering from beriberi and malaria, and the losses due to those diseases reach two to three times those by enemy bombing and bombardment.

About sixty serious patients have been left in the jungle west of Mt. Austen. As three hundred stretcher bearers are needed to remove them, they were left there lest fighting strength might be lost in so doing.

By the other day's convoy transportation, sixty to seventy percent of the personnel were landed, but only one-fifth of the ammunition was unloaded. The provisions on hand could support them only twenty-two days on half rations. With an enemy offensive anticipated, it is very doubtful whether they could stand until the end of this month. Undoubtedly it is impossible to hold out until a convoy transport, to be carried out late in January, reaches there.

As to future operations, it is necessary to send one division first to recapture the western position and another division one month later, together with sufficient attached units, arms, and ammunition.

The known losses up to now are: 2,200 killed; 2,400 wounded, and 900 missing. Besides, there were many sick and dead.

If we give up future offensives and withdraw to the west for survival, there are some ways left. Extravagant as they [the Americans] are, they would not pursue our force right away.

An enemy patrol usually consists of ten to one hundred men. When they approach us, we used to stay still in position, as our ammunition is scarce, until they closed enough for us to charge them suddenly. They usually run away with loud cries. Their individual fighting power is not good at all, but we can hardly stand their firepower.

Since a revision of the operational policy regarding Guadalcanal is urgent, these two staff officers should report to Tokyo as quickly as possible, so a special plane was arranged for them to leave here tomorrow. We also instructed our senior staff officer, now staying in Tokyo, to return after finishing a conference to be held upon Captain Yamamoto's arrival in Tokyo.

Battleship *Yamato* spread her torpedo net. She is now safe from enemy torpedoes.

Thursday, 10 December 1942. Fair with rain squall. In these days, about ten fighters patrol the sky over Buna. But our attempt to chute materials there succeeded yesterday.

When *I-3* entered Camimbo last night and surfaced to lower a motor launch, two PT boats attacked her and hit her stern. She has not been heard from since. Her crewmen who landed ashore reported this. The enemy has also realized that we are attempting transportation with submarines.

[*According to U.S. records, there was only one Japanese survivor of* I-3, *an ensign who swam ashore.*][56]

Thus, even underwater transportation has met with great difficulty. The only ways left for us now are either to fire materials packed in waterproof bags from torpedo tubes while submerged or to chute them from planes.

How to rescue twenty-five thousand men at Guadalcanal has turned out to be the most urgent matter. On the part of the fleet, we couldn't do anything but await a change of policy to be made by the high command.

Over ten enemy planes raided Shortland, inflicting some damage. The new base at Munda was bombed yesterday. Though the loss of personnel was slight, eight of the eleven all-important motor rollers were damaged. I couldn't help but admire the enemy's selecting this good target. We could hardly carry out such an attack. Their skill and cleverness should be commended and followed as an example. I once warned Captain Iwabushi, now fighting at Munda, to hide at daylight when attacked by enemy planes and work at night. I did so anticipating such a clever attack as that.

[*Munda in New Georgia was important to the Japanese because its airstrip put Henderson Field and other targets on Guadalcanal within easy fighter range and enabled bombers to carry heavier payloads. Work on the airfield commenced on 24 November. United States aerial reconnaissance soon found it, and Munda became an almost daily target. The attack of 9 December came from eighteen B-17s. But the Japanese were as determined to keep the field operational as the Americans were to destroy it.*][57]

Those crippled ships which needed to be towed back from Rabaul and Shortland reached a pretty large number.

The Eleventh Air Fleet drafted an operational policy for New Guinea and submitted it to our command. Though its general idea was agreeable, it seemed to me that their plan for the invasion of Madang and Wewak wasn't minute. When our invasion vessels appear there, enemy planes will immediately come from Moresby to attack them. Fighter cover should be provided them all day long. Were they really prepared for it? We decided to have our staff keep in further touch with them.

[As Watanabe was to visit Rabaul for liaison the next day, Ugaki "gave him instructions on various matters." He was very much concerned that the Eleventh Air Fleet and Eighth Fleet "get through this crisis with broad minds . . . I believe such matters as individual feelings and putting blame on a local command should be cautiously avoided."

[As there had been no major American move around 8 December, as anticipated, the fleet headquarters resumed normal stations.

[According to a survey by the fleet surgeon, casualties sustained to 7 November were 15,656 killed and 7,080 wounded, "showing a great increase over the last time."]

Friday, 11 December 1942. Fair. Buna has requested prompt transport of ammunition, as only 150 rounds remained for two antiaircraft guns there. Of those two hundred soldiers who tried to reach Buna from Basabua the other day, only nine managed to reach the airfield next morning. Their plight could easily be imagined.

I ordered all ways and means devised for the last transportation with destroyers to Guadalcanal in order to make it a success because we are placing a good deal of expectation on it. They left port in the afternoon today and sailed down to reach 180 miles from Guadalcanal at sunset. Though an enemy plane found them once after sunset, so far they're proceeding without being attacked.

Saturday, 12 December 1942. Fair with squall. Last night's transportation to Guadalcanal progressed without hitch in spite of bad weather. When they reached the landing point, however, enemy PT boats harassed them. Destroyer *Terutsuki* was hit and rendered unnavigable. Two PT boats were sunk and one damaged. The commander, Second Destroyer Squadron, moved to destroyer *Naganami,* while half of her [*Terutsuki*'s] crew of 140 were rescued and the remaining fifty put ashore. The ship was sunk by our own hand at about 2345. Twelve hundred cases of provisions were said to have been landed on shore, but I wondered how many cases were actually landed.

[*On this occasion, U.S. aircraft failed to hit any of Tanaka's ships, but three PT boats attacked the column and sent two torpedoes into* Terutsuki, *and Tanaka promptly headed back. A fourth boat, PT-44, encountered the Japanese column and was sunk by shells from a destroyer. One of the original three PTs ran aground and was towed off early the next morning.*][58]

The Guadalcanal garrison reported two ships turning to the east and west of Savo Island after a battle took place. One of them seems to have sunk during the night.

All but destroyer *Terutsuki* returned to Shortland. Now we can hope that our forces on the island will be supported for some time. How hard it was! We must think of some ways to take revenge on those troublesome PT boats.

At 0910, an enemy submarine attacked CVL *Ryuho*, formerly submarine tender *Taigei,* engaged in transporting twenty army light bombers, personnel, etc., from Yokosuka at a point 160 miles east of Hachijojima. A torpedo hit her starboard amidship and she had to turn back to Yokosuka, accompanied by escorting destroyer *Tokitsukaze.*

Henceforth army planes should be sent to New Guinea by flying from base to base. Furthermore, a patrol boat reported the sighting of an unidentified plane on the sea six hundred miles east of Tokyo.

A telegram reporting developments in Tokyo arrived from the senior staff officer. It said that the Naval General Staff was completely agreeable to our proposition, while the army also generally shared our view and started a serious study of the issue. I was also glad to hear that the army was preparing to send the Forty-first and Twenty-first Divisions promptly, besides the Fifty-first and Sixth Divisions.

The Eleventh Air Fleet sent in a request to have CV *Junyo* cooperate with the invasion of Wewak slated to take place on the 18th. As this seemed reasonable, we ordered its preparation in advance. She recovered her planes today. This was done to make room at the airstrip here for the army planes supposed to be unloaded here soon.

Sunday, 13 December 1942. Rain. It rained all day. This was due to a low pressure, but is quite a rare phenomenon here.

Five destroyers under the Tenth Destroyer commander left Admiralty Island yesterday after refueling. They sailed southward to engage in the last transport to Buna. From about 1100 today enemy B-17s shadowed them from a point northeast of Madang and several planes attacked twice. No damage was sustained except for a leading medium bomber being set afire and making a forced landing at sea. Its crew was rescued. This was due to the effectiveness of the fighter screen provided them.

They're carrying eight hundred soldiers, ammunition, and provisions. I hope they'll succeed in tonight's landing. We've been waiting for bad weather to carry out this transportation, but the season in this area appears to be about one month late and the rainy season with the northeast monsoon hasn't come yet. And we had to carry it out today.

Carrier *Unyo* arrived early this morning from Surabaja carrying fifty army fighters. They were unloaded on the new airfield on Haru Jima and scheduled to fly to Rabaul after the 16th.

Lieutenant [Masatoshi] Funahashi, who had been sent to Guadalcanal from *Yamato* as a spotting officer, returned today and brought back a visiting card entrusted by Captain Kanae Monzen, the naval garrison force commander there. The following was written on it in pencil: "Hardships and shortages have reached beyond the limit this time. We have all experienced no wine, no smoking, reduced rationing, no tea, no salt—everything. But fortunately I am fine and burning with the spirit of revenge."

[Ugaki was impressed that such words could come from a "captain who was noted for his perseverance." Evidently the case of sake which Ugaki had sent him failed to reach him. Monzen was due for transfer to the rear soon. "If he is lucky enough to get on board a submarine on her way back, I may have a chance to hear about their hardships from him directly."]

Staff Officer [Commander Kurio] Toibana returned from Rabaul this morning. Judging from an air photo taken by an army plane which he brought back, there are six airstrips at Guadalcanal, and their installations seem to be gradually expanding to the east from Cape Cori. That is why they needed six transports, as seen today.

Now the time has come when we can't see any chance of recovering it. Nothing can be done.

According to information from the chief of the Operations Bureau, a warning was issued that there was a possibility of American planes air raiding Formosa and Kyushu from China today. Though the weather wasn't bad, nothing happened.

Monday, 14 December 1942. Partly fair. The Tenth Destroyer Division on the transportation mission reached Manbale, a few dozen miles north of Buna, early this morning. After unloading, it returned to Rabaul without mishap despite enemy bombings on the way back. Small craft are going to move the personnel and material landed there to the vicinity of Buna.

Enemy planes raided the new airfield at Buin several times, and it was quite trying, so its base force commander reported. Unless we beat them down once, they'll get very arrogant. It's really unbearable to be thus pressed.

The chief of the Communications Bureau of Imperial Headquarters, Naval Section, sent in a warning that enemy activities in this area have increased. But we can do nothing about it for the time being except take precautions.

Tuesday, 15 December 1942. Cloudy with squall. Though the transportation carried out on the 13th with the sacrifice of destroyer *Terutsuki* reported twelve hundred drums were jettisoned at sea and the towing hawser handed to a motor launch, those actually received were only 220. So they can't be supported after the 17th. The transportation by submarines was to be withheld until about the 25th on account of moonlit nights, and they were instead to be employed for the transportation mission to Buna. How to support our forces at Guadalcanal in the meantime came to the fore. The Eighth Army still insists on a transportation by destroyers, to be supplemented with planes and submarines.

It's doubtful whether those actually received were only 220. Wasn't it because of hiding or monopolizing some other drums, a phenomenon often seen among the army's lower rank units? In any case, it was a troublesome problem.

On the other hand, in these days the enemy had eight transports enter the road and unload under the protection of over a dozen destroyers and patrol boats. What a difference between them and us!

Landing tests at Munda base with both fighters and carrier bombers proved all right. But the actual advance of planes there was said to be around the 22nd. Why, then, all the hurry with desperate efforts to complete it? It might be because of an idea that if they were moved there too soon before its defense was completed, they would only become the enemy's prey.

[Accompanied by "the officer in charge of clerical work," Ugaki took his first shore break since the 10th, leaving the ship at 0430. They strolled along the coast and hills, inspected the reservoir, and shot quite a good bag. They were back aboard at 1040. That night the staff "enjoyed duck soup and grilled snipe."]

Wednesday, 16 December 1942. Fair, temperature rises. The invasion forces of Wewak and Madang sortied from Rabaul today. The former consisted of one battalion and the latter of two battalions. They are going to make surprise attacks the evening of the 18th on both places and finish landing during the night. Judging from the words of Staff Officer Watanabe, who came back from Rabaul today, I wondered if the surprise attack could really be made, as I saw some contradictory points in the plan. I hope they'll attain the objective without mishap. Moreover, in spite of the fact that there seemed to be a fairly strong enemy at Madang, as I said before, the plan lacked a definite scheme on how to enforce the landing when enemy resistance was met. So I felt I couldn't trust them.

The Tenth Destroyer Squadron with three destroyers sortied at 1015 in order to cooperate with this landing operation and the Second CV Division at 1300 to support the Wewak invasion force.

The senior staff and navigation officers returned from Tokyo, and Staff Officer Watanabe from Rabaul. We heard their reports after dinner.

An understanding seems to have been reached between two branches of the high command with regard to Guadalcanal. A revision of the operational policy, however, didn't seem likely to be made soon, and it would take some time.

While they wavered, I feared we would be driven to the wall and forced to give up both front operations. We couldn't solely depend on the message from Fukudome, chief of the Operations Bureau.

Thursday, 17 December 1942. Fair. The landing on Tuluvu, the southwestern end of New Britain, with destroyer *Tachikaze* and patrol boats succeeded without enemy opposition.

On the other hand, a B-17 was shadowing a ten-thousand-ton transport and three destroyers of the Wewak invasion force heading west toward the north of Admiralty through nightfall. An enemy attack should be anticipated tomorrow, when they proceed southward to their target.

We saw a newsreel and movies of the Hawaii sea battle and the sea battle off Malaya from 1730. Both were splendid pictures and enough to rouse men's minds, reminding them of the 8th and 10th of last December.

Friday, 18 December 1942. Fair. At 0915 Captain [Chiaki] Matsuda took over command of *Yamato* and Rear Admiral Takayanagi, the outgoing skipper, left the ship. The army's light bomber group commander, Colonel [Jyoichiro] Sanada, the new chief of the Operations Section of the Army General Staff, and two other staff officers arrived by flying boat today.

Major General [Shinichi] Tanaka, chief of the Operations Bureau of the Army General Staff, was transferred from the post, as he bitterly criticized the army vice minister about the shipping problem the other day. Colonel Hattori, chief of its Operations Section, was also said to be transferred on account of it.

When our senior staff officer returned from Tokyo, he reported that army and navy operations section chiefs would come over here with a revised central agreement with them. But, in fact, Colonel Sanada seemed to bring nothing with him. He said only that he came down here as he didn't know anything, being new to the post. Then everything will be delayed a great deal. I didn't say anything to him.

While yesterday the enemy sighted the Wewak invasion force, since this morning enemy planes have been shadowing the Madang invasion force, and finally attacked after 1700. Though a small fire broke out on board *Gokoku Maru,* it was brought under control, and they are proceeding toward the target. The former succeeded in landing on Wewak after 1900, but the problem was that of the latter.

Army fighters in two echelons took off from Truk's Haru Jima airstrip at 0700. Six naval planes, including preceding weather observation planes, led them. Except for one of them putting about from the way, they seem to have reached Rabaul safely. Very good indeed!

Saturday, 19 December 1942. Fair. The Madang Force entered the roads at 2100 and succeeded in landing. But an enemy submarine [U.S.S. *Albacore*][59] torpedoed light cruiser *Tenryu* and hit her in her stern with commander, Light Cruiser Division, aboard, at a point about eight miles off Madang. Her steering gear was rendered unusable and her stern gradually sank. After transferring the crew to destroyer *Sawakaze* and efforts to tow her by destroyer *Suzukaze,* she finally slipped into the sea at 2320, more than two hours after she was hit. When we escaped from the planes, the underwater enemy was waiting for us.

The Eighth Destroyer Division, which closed in Finschhafen, had to turn back on account of persistent enemy shadowing and attacks. But with an order to carry out the landing by all means, they resumed and succeeded in landing with a little loss. Enemy planes have continually shadowed them since this morning.

The Wewak Invasion Force attained its objective without mishap. As I had worried about the landing operations on those three places, I was all the more glad to hear of the success.

The enemy in the Buna area launched fierce attacks with ten tanks yesterday. In spite of our defenders' good fight, destroying half of their tanks, our side was also put into confusion, and carried out a change of disposition last night. So the airfield front was opened to the enemy, and the danger is increasing every minute, with losses mounting every day.

A chain of bases for small transports has been prepared along the south coast of New Britain to Lae; therefore, I hoped a connection would be made with Buna, so that we might extend a rescuing hand to those comrades there.

It appeared that no big enemy force was at Madang except a handful of radio and intelligence personnel. An airstrip there was reported to be 1,200 meters by 30, and immediately available for fighters. This is a matter for congratulations.

A patrol plane sighted an enemy main force, reportedly consisting of two battleships or transports, or three battleships, according to the afternoon reconnaissance, and two cruisers and four destroyers, sailing on a southeasterly, then northeasterly, course with 18 knots to the south of

Louisiade Island. The Eleventh Air Fleet dispatched contact planes successively and ordered them to stand by for an attack. But later it was called off, as the enemy went south. They appear to be supporting a transportation attempt to the Rabi area.

[That morning, "last-stage work" began on salvaging *I-33*. Her bow arose, "to the great joy and applause of everybody present," but three minutes later she sank again. Air pressure from the inner hull had blown off the manhole cover. Ugaki anticipated success in a few days and told the salvagers "that they should consider it a rehearsal."]

Rear Admiral Nakahara was attached to the Combined Fleet command from chief of the Personnel Bureau, as he was slated to be chief of staff of the Southeast Area Fleet, which will be organized on or about the 24th. He arrived here today by flying boat. Since he was leaving for Rabaul tomorrow, I told him about pertinent matters and wished him good luck for his future activities.

Two transport forces were organized to cooperate with the army in transporting army divisions to this area by naval vessels. The Ninth Light Cruiser Division, two destroyers, and many converted cruisers and transports of the Combined Fleet were included in them. Each force was to transport a half division.

Sunday, 20 December 1942. Fair, squall in early morning. The enemy fleet found to the south of Louisiade yesterday was said to be one group, while some said two groups. I told the staff to find out the truth and make clear its aim, but they got nowhere.

At 0725 two battleships and one cruiser with one small plane were sighted on course of 50° at a point three hundred miles bearing 164° of Guadalcanal. Another flying boat also reported sighting one battleship, two cruisers, one carrier, two destroyers, and one transport at 1023. It wasn't clear whether the enemy meant to prepare for our concentration or had some positive intention.

Based upon various information, the chief of the Operations Bureau sent in a warning that the enemy apparently intended to invade Isabel and New Georgia islands, so an alert should be taken.

The Eleventh Air Fleet was ordered to shadow and night-attack this enemy at an opportune moment, but I wondered if the force could meet the oncoming enemy alone. If support should be given from here, we need some preparations. But little preparation has been made, so I warned the staff.

The enemy in the Buna area seems to have commenced a general offensive since the 18th. Their attacks were fierce under cooperation between air and land forces. Consequently our loss was increasing. Its commander,

Captain Yasuda, never revealed any weakness. He was a really gallant fighter.

Starting from tonight, we're going to commence chuting materials on Guadalcanal on moonlit nights. Apart from how many planes can carry how much, we must carry out what should be done. Those in the first line at Guadalcanal cried that they would rather charge into the enemy position than starve to death. This was understandable. We have tried to prevent such an eventuality, but the tide has hardly been stemmed.

Monday, 21 December 1942. Fair. Today's search found no enemy. I would like to ask him if he hasn't any special intention. On the other hand, however, a search plane sighted an enemy fleet at a point three hundred miles bearing 190° of Guadalcanal, though the time was not clear.

[In Ugaki's opinion, "there were some obscure points" in regard to current operations, so he ordered the staff to revise the draft it had given him the previous night.]

Tuesday, 22 December 1942. Fair. We received a report that our forces at Guadalcanal got forty packages of provisions chuted by planes on the night of the 20th and they were deeply moved.

On the other hand, submarines unloaded twenty tons of materials near Buna on both nights, the 19th and 20th. But something like PT boats were patrolling the landing point. Unless there was a prospect of sending those materials from there to the front, the transportation would be of no use. So we asked the Eleventh Air Fleet to send back [a report of] the situation together with the policy of directing operations in that area.

Headquarters of the army regiment and the naval landing party at Buna were under concentrated enemy fire. They destroyed all confidential papers except one code book. The crisis is now really at hand. It's most deplorable to see that no air support was given to our forces, while the enemy air arm was rampant there.

Unless we open our eyes wider and take proper measures as we should, it's apparent that we'll miss the time. Army fighters arrived at Rabaul on the 18th. The Wewak and Madang operations were completed some time ago. It's most regrettable indeed that the navy's planes still remained inactive, though they were believed to have been relieved from such missions.

Wednesday, 23 December 1942. Fair. The coast of Buna was finally captured yesterday by five enemy tanks and fierce bombardments. Now our forces were about to be chased from the northwestern direction of the airfield.

As our air force still gave no cooperation even in this crisis, I couldn't but feel angry and called their attention to it at breakfast. However, I felt a little relieved after seeing in the afternoon a telegram stating that the Eleventh Air Fleet has ordered an attack on enemy positions tonight. It's necessary to force them not only into night attacks but daylight cooperation every day from now on.

The chief of staff, Eleventh Air Fleet, sent in the intentions of the Eighth Area Army, together with the subsequent development of negotiations, while at the same time asking our views. Contrary to the opinion of the staff, who thought it was hopeless, the heads of the Eighth Area Army were still holding the policy of carrying it through. It seems that they have been instructed by the high command to resume the offensive.

On the other hand, Colonel Sanada, chief of the Operations Section of the Army General Staff, and Major [Ryuzu] Sejima, its staff officer, came back from Rabaul. They said that the situation was more serious than they thought in Tokyo. They also disclosed a likely policy of sending ten thousand men with convoys as replenishment in January and also attempting to recapture the island with two divisions in February.

["But," mused Ugaki, "the problem was how to send them." The fleet could not guarantee anything beyond half the troop strength reaching the island, with another third left after landing. They could not deploy after landing without air support, and the naval air arm could not "afford it fully." So he urged the army representatives of "the need to make a decision from the overall standpoint. Furthermore, I had three of our staff talk with them ashore after dinner."]

Thursday, 24 December 1942. Partly fair, windy. The garrison commander at Buna sent in a report that they were facing the last stage, but were still going to make a last effort. Their spirit could not be beaten down, and their fighting was worthy of commendation. The commander in chief sent an encouraging reply with our appreciation, telling them that the navy and army were making every effort to rescue them.

[*On this day,* PT-114 *and* PT-121 *sank two barges carrying troops to Buna.*][60]

Whether they could hold out until a rescue team reached them or they were going to be annihilated, with this message as their last one, will become the turning point in the course of the war. Medium bombers attacked enemy positions and Dobodura airfield last night. Two attacks should have been made with army fighters this morning.

The chuting operation to Guadalcanal was suspended the night before last due to bad weather. Twenty-four fighters advanced to the new base at Munda for the first time. With this step, that area has been somewhat reassured, but we're still unable to take positive offenses against the enemy until Balale base is completed, so that medium bombers can be forwarded there.

B-17s raided Wake Island between 2115 and 2140 last night. Damage was slight. Four of them were shot down, while six others were set on fire. Judging from the fact that they withdrew to the direction of 60°, the enemy seems to have come from Midway.

This was also considered to be the start of a continuous air raid on Japan which the U.S. air secretary announced on about the 12th. Did they carry it out last night hoping to make it a Christmas present for us? Last year we specifically ordered that our submarine on the West Coast of the States withhold bombardment on Christmas Eve. If they're going to treat us in such a way, we'll treat them in the same way.

The Southeast Area Fleet was organized with the Eleventh Air Fleet and Eighth Fleet today. The Third Destroyer Division was transferred from the Second Fleet to the Third Fleet.

Friday, 25 December 1942. Partly fair. Our planes attacked enemy positions and the airfield at Buna the night before last. Army fighters cooperated in attacks twice yesterday morning, though whether they were actually carried out wasn't ascertained. Navy planes also made attacks there last night. And yet no response came from Buna, making us wonder whether radio transmitters there might have been destroyed.

In the evening a report came in from there at last, saying that six enemy fighters were flying over and enemy bombardments were terrible. I was glad to learn they still kept on fighting. The chief of the Naval General Staff sent in a message of commendation for the gallant fighting of the landing party there. All we can give them now is a word of hope for their good fight.

[*On 25 December, General Imamura ordered Buna evacuated, but had no way to get his men out.*][61]

Today enemy B-17s attacked ship bases extending along the south coast of New Britain and, plying small transports, were seriously damaged. Unless the air defense facility of those bases is completed, even the plying of small transports using those bases will be impossible.

According to the words of the staff officer who had a talk with the chief of the Operations Section of the Army General Staff and others the night before last, they considered New Guinea more important and intended to report it possible to change the policy concerning Guadalcanal. If so, that would be all right. Also, they were reportedly bringing back with them the words of the commander, Eighth Area Army, Imamura. To what extent will the Central Agreement be changed? Anyway, it will be made on about the 10th of January.

Nankai Maru and her escort destroyer *Uzuki* left Rabaul to transport a construction corps to Munda. While evading an enemy submarine attack on the way, both collided with each other and destroyer *Uzuki* sustained damage.

The tanker *Fujisan Maru,* which enemy planes at Shortland had attacked and damaged her stern, reached here today for repairs.

Two unidentified planes flew over Jaluit Island last night and dropped parachute flares. Though that district was alerted, nothing happened.

Saturday, 26 December 1942. Partly fair. Two torpedoes hit *Nankai Maru* in her fore part and Nos. 2 and 3 holds were flooded with increased draught. She came into the bay there once, but soon afterward left for Rabaul, escorted by destroyer *Uzuki*. Destroyer *Uzuki* collided with *Nankai Maru*'s bow with her midship and was flooded. Though capable of making 6 knots, she was towed by destroyer *Ariake*. That morning, enemy planes attacked them. A near miss damaged destroyer *Ariake*'s steering gear and she gave up towing. She headed back for Rabaul with emergency manual steering.

That should be called a case of going into the forest to cut wood and coming home shorn. This resulted in delaying the construction of the new air base at Munda.

The Buna area was still holding positions despite terrible enemy bombardments.

Samejima, commander in chief, Fourth Fleet, came to visit in the morning and Kondo, commander in chief, Second Fleet, in the afternoon. Rear Admiral Kameda, who was designated commander of the newly established Second Naval Base Force and concurrently of the Construction Corps, arrived here by today's plane and came to report his new assignment. He's leaving for Rabaul tomorrow. He's going to take charge of the Wewak and Madang area.

The Twenty-fourth Naval Base Force landed a landing party with light cruiser *Natori* and the minesweeper *Itsukushima* at Hollandia last night and captured it without opposition.

Sunday, 27 December 1942. Fair. An enemy force of three hundred finally overran an antiaircraft position at Buna. The fact that it was overwhelmed by only three hundred of the enemy well illustrated how our forces there had been weakened after the long, bitter fighting.

Last night a transport attempt to Camimbo by a submarine was accomplished without mishap, while chuting materials to the mouth of Shimi River with eight medium bombers was also done successfully.

Under date of the 24th, the chief of staff, Seventeenth Army, requested a priority supply, appealing that the shortage of foodstuff was so acute that they were only keeping themselves alive by eating tree buds, coconuts, and seaweed. Not only were they unable to dispatch even one soldier for patrol, but they could do nothing by themselves about an enemy threat from the rear. We certainly didn't think his request was unreasonable.

Construction work at Munda airfield made little progress, due to frequent enemy air attacks. Only the loss added up. The advance of at least two squadrons of fighters there is imperative. The landing of patrol boats today had to be postponed indefinitely, due to the loss of fighters mentioned above. It's deplorable indeed that everything is on the way of retreat due to the inferiority of our air power.

Maybe because the army's small transports were going to the island tomorrow morning, a transportation by submarines was put off by two days, and the chuting of materials by planes ended with last night's attempt. That seems to be too cautious, at a time when we still feel shortages even if every step is taken. However, there may be good reasons for that, too.

[Rear Admiral Matsuyama, former commander, Eighteenth Light Cruiser Division, visited *Yamato* on his way to Japan for reassignment. When his flagship, *Tenryu,* sank, that division, in Ugaki's words, "lost the meaning of its existence." Matsuyama had lost "half of his personal effects" when *Tenryu* sank, so Ugaki gave him some new underwear. He was to become commandant of Tateyama Gunnery school.]

B-17s obstinately attacked Rabaul last night, and an army transport was sunk, destroyer *Tachikaze* seriously damaged. At Munda our fighters were attacked right after their landing. Five of them were set on fire while ten were damaged. They were mercilessly beaten up.

For some time we've keenly felt the need of devising some effective countermeasures against B-17s. Against their tactics of coming to attack at daytime without being discovered, or attacking at night, dropping parachute flares, we hardly could do more than fold our arms. If our losses add up in this way, finally we would be unable to do anything but live in caves, or retreat. Now we must study this hard.

Monday, 28 December 1942. Fair. A telegram of yesterday from Buna stated the enemy continued bombardments day and night, spending a thousand rounds per day and concentrated two thousand rounds in thirty minutes before an attack. It was considered essential to cut the enemy's rear in future operations, it also advised. Furthermore, the following telegram was received from the garrison commander at Buna, dispatched at 0530 on the 28th:

Concentrated enemy fire has gradually destroyed our positions, but our men tenaciously fought back and inflicted heavy damage upon the enemy by charging into the enemy from time to time. Judging from the overall battle situation, however, we cannot help admitting that we will face doom today or tomorrow.

In the past over forty days of fighting, everyone, no matter he be a serviceman or civilian, has done his duty well. I am very grateful for the directions of the higher commands, the cooperation of the air forces and the army. Wishing future prosperity for the empire and good luck for all.

This was most tragic and extremely regrettable!

Flying boats raided Kavieng last night, attacking there three times. Many planes were damaged. Also two torpedoes were fired at a patrol boat near the north entrance. How can we allow the enemy to take such arrogant actions?

In the afternoon the Eighth Fleet command ordered the naval force at Buna to evacuate in cooperation with the army force there and move to the Giruwa area to defend it. Three companies of army forces under Major General Yamagata were said to go east to receive evacuating comrades. Giruwa is located on the coast, five kilometers away from Buna. Can they evacuate and join the friendly force? I regret the opportunity offered was too late. More than two thousand sick and wounded were surrounded at a place two kilometers south of North Buna. Their fate depends on how the Yamagata force fights.

Tuesday, 29 December 1942. Fair. In the evening a telegram came in from Buna which said, "Four enemy tanks are attacking the headquarters landing party and we are burning the code book." Another one followed that "we are destroying the radio sets at 1710." The rescue party from Giruwa will not reach there before tonight. I hoped they would succeed, but I thought it extremely difficult.

From now on we have to rely on the army radio in that area. In this connection, it should be noted that so far no information was received with regard to the army's transport attempt with small craft. The Southeast Area Fleet should be instructed to report the situation after getting in touch with the army.

Heavy cruiser *Maya* and destroyer *Umikaze* were going to sail for Yokosuka for repairs tomorrow afternoon.

Several views of mine on directing operations:

1. A revised Central Agreement anticipated to be made shortly will place

importance on New Guinea, but with regard to Guadalcanal it will not go beyond an indecisive policy. So operations will be stalemated.

2. Although the concentration of the air arm reinforcement will be completed by the middle of January, their loss is ever increasing due to incessant enemy positive actions. So we cannot expect much of the land-based air force partly because of a passive atmosphere among them. A positive operation cannot be sought with them.

3. The enemy air arm is being focused on both the Solomon and eastern New Guinea areas. At a time when there is little hope of completely beating down this enemy with our land-based air force, an employment of great strength of our fleet would only increase our losses and please the enemy. It should be left to the activities of the land-based aircraft, submarines, and small craft, while an enemy invasion attempt should be repulsed with our local defense force.

4. Two carriers of the Third Fleet will be completed by the middle of January and their crews will also be trained to some extent. Excluding those under repair, our destroyer strength will be ten for the Eighth Fleet, eight for the Second Fleet, and about twelve for the Third Fleet by the end of January. It will not be a good policy to keep all this strength at Truk. It will only result in lowering morale.

5. The main mission of the Combined Fleet is to destroy the enemy, swiftly maneuvering as the situation warrants, without sticking to a stalemated local campaign. Flexibility is essential in battle. If we can surprise an enemy's weak point at this stage, not only would it menace the enemy by showing him the existence of our fighting strength, but it would also result in diverging the enemy from this district. I believe it's necessary to plan for it promptly. However, care should be taken not to give an impression of neglecting the eastern New Guinea and Guadalcanal operations now at the crisis stage, especially to the army.

Wednesday, 30 December 1942. Squalls. Good news or bad—nothing came from the Buna area.

On the other hand, an army force with a naval antiaircraft unit, which landed on Wickham on the southern tip of New Georgia in the night of the 27th, was bombed on both the 28th and 29th. Both of the two small transports were sunk with two antiaircraft guns, most of the ammunition and all provisions. It was fortunate that no personnel were lost, but the food problem was urgent and another trouble was added. It was just as predicted. In the light of this, such an attempt as capturing Russell Island should be called reckless.

However, if convoy transportation to Guadalcanal was no longer possible, there was no other way but to send small craft stealthily along the chain of isles. These islands would be valuable as temporary bases, but they couldn't be held permanently.

Rear Admiral Sakamaki, former chief of staff, Eleventh Air Fleet, arrived from Rabaul on a medium bomber after a troubled flight. We had a long talk and exchanged views. Salient points of his talk are listed below:

1. The basic cause of the current plight is the decline of our aviation skill. They blame the weather, etc., but it boils down to this after all.

Their present skill cannot be regarded as more than one-third of that of the past. In a newly arrived fighter group, forty-four pilots out of sixty have had no experience with the Zero fighter. Most of them are only trained in the Type 96 fighters, so they have to be trained again after their arrival.

When superior quality pilots sortied for Munda some time ago, the enemy came to raid Buin, where inferior pilots took off to intercept them, but were miserably beaten down. Statistics showed:

Damage Inflicted on the Enemy			
From 7 August to end of October	307 (besides 83 not sure)	Our loss (including those 233 damaged in the group)	
From 1 November to 24 December	125 (besides 35 not sure)	159	

Especially, in the recent Madang operation, a total of thirty-six fighters were employed to cover our force. Thirty-three enemy planes (B-17s and B-26s) came to attack it and only two and a half enemy planes were shot down. We lost two planes. I was very much disappointed with this result.

2. Morale is high. This is because those who were in the positions to lead men were transferred elsewhere in late September, when morale was about to go down. When an enemy fleet was sighted a short while ago, a flight commander and his squadron leader had a heated discussion with regard to who should lead a torpedo unit against it. We need never worry about their morale.

3. There is no way of breaking through the present deadlock, if we leave things as they are today. It is not good at all to try to destroy the oncoming enemy at a front; we should strike them at their base. We should carry it out when the number of our fighters reaches one hundred. At present, there are only twenty of them at Rabaul and Tinian.

4. Guadalcanal is now hopeless. But a transport attempt with small craft, hopping bases along the chain of islands, and an attempt to cut off the enemy's rear should be made. How effective they might be is another question. I interpreted the Combined Fleet order of the other day in this sense.

5. In case we are not going to recapture Guadalcanal, whether we could hold the present line after all depends on our capability of continuing the air operation. Is there any hope for it? I want to ask the high command about it.

6. We need many small vessels.

7. They are trying to dig in underground, but unless air power is maintained the place eventually will be invaded.

8. Further efforts should be made to display air might. I hear I am scheduled to be an air flotilla commander in this area, so I shall do my best.

9. Lack of air defense ability.

[In exchange for these views of Sakamaki, Ugaki told him his own views "about an expected enemy operational intention, hoping to give him some help."

[Commander Miyo visited *Yamato* on his way from the Naval General Staff to his new post with the Southeast Area Fleet.

[Ugaki noted that "the atmosphere in Tokyo is said to have taken quite a change." At the liaison conference, the army had proposed the evacuation of Guadalcanal. "This was fine news so far. But they should know how difficult the evacuation will be."]

Thursday, 31 December 1942. Cloudy. The radio intelligence section of the General Staff warned that something was going to happen, judging from the condition of enemy communications. If so, what should be done? That's the trouble.

According to army information, the army force in Buna joined the naval landing party and was securing the line from the west end of the airfield to Buna village. Another army unit which had landed on Manbale arrived at Giruwa by small boats, and 450 of them were advancing toward Buna to the rescue. But I'm afraid this report is out of date.

We were informed that the chief of the Operations Bureau of the Naval General Staff was coming here on the 3rd, together with the chief of the Operations Bureau of the Army General Staff. The chiefs of staff of the Southeast Area and Eighth Fleet were going to be called in as they were requested.

The Eighth Area Army was said to have asked the reason for its receiving the directive to withdraw our positions at Guadalcanal in order to get ready for the next operation. What a slow perception they had! Or were they trying to ask it, although knowing it [the answer], before the arrival of the chief of the Operations Bureau?

In any case, the general trend of the future is now clear. When thinking of the withdrawal, I realized its difficulties more than ever. Skilled cooperation is essential.

It's regrettable that the loss of our naval vessels and others by enemy submarines in this area has been so frequent these days.

The year 1942 is going to pass tonight. How brilliant was the first-stage operation up to April! And what miserable setbacks since Midway in June! The invasions of Hawaii, Fiji, Samoa, and New Caledonia, liberation of India and destruction of the British Far Eastern Fleet have all scattered like dreams. Meanwhile, not to speak of capturing Port Moresby, but the recovery of Guadalcanal itself turned out to be impossible.

Looking back over all these, my mind was filled with deep feelings. Though it's the fortunes of war, it's most regrettable.

For the hardships endured by our men in bitter fighting up to the present, I tender my deep gratitude, and, at the same time, pay my hearty tribute to those many brave officers and men who fell for the country.

[*Most unfortunately, Ugaki's entries for 1943 before 3 April were lost during the early postwar period. See introduction to this section.*]

Saturday, 3 April 1943. Fair. First day in Rabaul. At 0705 a ceremony was held on the occasion of the anniversary of the decease of Emperor Jimmu, the first emperor of Japan.

Leaving the ship at 0715 we, the commander in chief, chief of staff, staff officers Kuroshima, Watanabe, and Muroi, the chief weather officer and chief code officer boarded two flying boats.

[*When traveling by air with a number of his staff officers, it was Yamamoto's custom to split the party between two planes, with himself in one and his chief of staff in the other.*][62]

The chief of staff of the Eighth Area Army and other army officers came aboard, too. We took off at 0800 and flew south. Three fighters escorted us from over Kavieng, and we arrived at Rabaul at 1340. We entered headquarters of the Southeast Area Fleet and broke the admiral's flag there temporarily. The senior air officer and the communications staff officer had already been there.

[*Yamamoto established his headquarters temporarily at Rabaul to take charge of Operation I (I-Go), the heavy aerial offensive he had planned to destroy Allied advanced bases, delay the Allied spring offensive, and give the Japanese more time to defend the Bismarcks.*][63]

We talked with Kusaka, Ozawa, and Mikawa, commanders in chief of the Southeast Area, Third, and Eighth fleets, respectively. We also received a visit by Imamura, Eighth Area Army commander. After being briefed on plans and preparations for Operation I, we dined with the above-menioned commanders in chief and their chiefs of staff from 1630.

Commander in Chief Yamamoto looked a bit tired. At 1930 we went up to the hilltop quarters of the commander in chief, Eighth Fleet, and slept there. Thunder on top of the hill broke the silence, but a rain squall served to protect our concentrated planes from an enemy attack.

Enemy aircraft raided Kavieng at 0300. Heavy cruiser *Aoba* was hit in her engine room and rendered unnavigable. Light cruiser *Sendai* took her in tow, but when she was about to be moved under escort her leakage increased, so that it became necessary to send a repair ship down there. *Aoba* had only just come back to this theater after completion of her repairs. Before doing anything, she was seriously damaged again. As an enemy plane flew there for reconnaissance yesterday, the Eighth Fleet anticipated danger and urged her to change anchorage, but *Aoba* did not listen to this suggestion and met with this misfortune.

[Aoba *had been badly damaged at the battle of Cape Esperance. In addition to the added severe damage to* Aoba *on this occasion, a near miss flooded the boiler room of destroyer* Fumitsuki, *and* Florida Maru *was sunk.*][64]

Increased danger is expected in the future to vessels at anchor in Rabaul port. Though the number of these ships has decreased recently, quite a lot are still there. They must be on the alert at all times.

When we decided to come down south to take direct command of operations, we of the Combined Fleet Command made an important resolution: If and when this attempt fails to achieve a satisfactory result, there will be no hope of future success in this area. I wonder if this has been fully brought home to those concerned with operations.

I can't help regretting to see that our commanders have hitherto been a little bit reluctant to go to the front line to command and encourage their subordinates. So I expressed my wish to go not only to Buna, Buin, and Shortland but as far as Kolombangara and Munda in this expedition. The staff officers seemed quite surprised.

As the commander in chief has already advanced here, matters awaiting my decision are limited to air warfare only. By all means, I should go to the foremost front line on this occasion. Risk cannot be avoided wherever we are, and this should be taken for granted, as this is war.

[Ugaki felt that he had on obligation to visit the Seventeenth Army. If the Japanese did not "get through this crisis, how could we answer to the souls of twenty thousand brave men who have fallen." If Ugaki's own death could "bring home to the general public the gravity of the situation in this area, and make the army and navy get together to display their real quality more than ever, I believe that it would settle everything and make the future prosperous."

[Having had "an unexpected opportunity to go Tokyo," Ugaki had settled some business there. He was satisfied that his son Hiromitsu's future as a naval surgeon had been determined and arranged for ceremonies for the third anniversary of Tomoko's death. Before leaving Truk that morning, Ugaki wrote a poem in his deceased wife's honor to be sent to his home.]

Sunday, 4 April 1943. Second day in Rabaul. There was a terrific rain squall since before dawn this morning. By the time I left the billet at 0745, it became light rain at last.

After descending the hill, we visited headquarters, Eighth Area Army, and met the Area Army Commander Imamura and his Chief of Staff Kato. Its headquarters building was the one formerly used by the Seventeenth Army and an annex was attached. Even in the army, the one who comes late lives in poor quarters. I returned to our place where the admiral's flag was hoisted.

Yesterday the chief of the Operations Bureau of the Naval General Staff issued a warning to the mainland and Formosa against enemy air raids. So far, however, no indication of such has been observed. Though enemy communications traffic became active in the Solomons area yesterday, we couldn't decide if the enemy had suspected our project.

The fierce rain squall since last night wasn't merely local; it extended to the north of the Solomons. Seeing that tomorrow's air attack would be impossible, we decided to postpone the date of launching a general air offensive on Guadalcanal by one day, that is, to the 6th.

By 1005, the time this order was issued, some of the planes at the east and west strips had completed preparations for the attack. But considering the difficulties expected on the way and the unavoidable losses prior to the attack, calling off the attack was inevitable.

[Yamamoto and Ugaki spent the afternoon hearing reports and talking with Kusaka and Ozawa. They left the office and returned to their hilltop at 1630. "The starlit night was quiet and fireflies were flying around." Ugaki noticed some natives playing football, "wearing fresh red and white loincloths."]

Monday, 5 April 1943. Cloudy with squalls. At 0800 visited the Eighth Naval Hospital next to our billet. When I visited there last September it could accommodate about three hundred persons, but was later expanded so that now it accommodates six hundred persons. I'm pleased to see its facilities much improved. Half the patients in that hospital are military, the rest civilians employed by the navy. Among them are natives of Formosa who went as far as Kokoda, crossing the Stanley Mountains as a road construction unit. They're pure-minded and well disciplined, I was told. They are worthy of praise.

The weather remaining unstable, there seemed little hope of launching an air attack tomorrow. So again we put off the date of the attack, to the

7th. At the same time, I ordered the staff to study the feasibility of shifting tomorrow's attack to Port Moresby. As I said often, my staff's plans are usually simple and lacking in flexibility. Only after confronting a wall do they think of a change in the plan. This time was no exception.

In the evening, they came to report that we could switch the attack to Moresby if we so ordered before the evening of the day before. But they said it was necessary to assemble those concerned tomorrow to make arrangements. Had we had an alternative plan in advance, we could have finished the necessary arrangements at the operational briefing held on the 3rd, so that we might be able to switch tomorrow's attack to Moresby on short notice when the weather in the Solomons area was considered unfavorable.

[Ugaki talked with Kusaka about his conviction of the "essential duties" of high ranking officers. They were responsible for calculating the risks in their preparations, even should they "be disliked or considered troublesome, or criticized as being nervous or even cowardly." Experience had its value.]

As of yesterday, communications traffic in Hawaii, Midway, and the Solomons area had returned to normal, and no sign of a new large-scale offensive was seen. Since we detected activities of enemy cruisers and night reconnaissance planes in the Solomons after nightfall, we issued a warning.

According to a report from (Captain Chusaburo) Yamazumi, chief of staff, Eighth Fleet, who had investigated the condition of *Aoba*, she was listing 6° to port and aground. With the arrival of the repair ship *Yamabiko Maru*, pumping out of water was making progress and her stern was being floated little by little. The pumping will take a week, and morale of her crew is said to be high. The immediate problem is how to provide her with air defense while making preparations for towing.

Tuesday, 6 April 1943. Fair, later cloudy and a heavy squall. At 0805 we inspected the workshops. These are government-owned and private works at Rabaul, both of which were captured without damage. But the scale of both is extremely small, and no machinery has been added so far. It's said that the workmen will be increased to 250. However, I felt like I was in a junk shop. They have a future plan for it, but their plan doesn't take air defense into consideration.

Thirty-five enemy vessels using different radio waves were suspected in the sea near Guadalcanal. A fairly large number of vessels seems to have entered there yesterday. Their activities are unusually brisk. The weather broadcast reports fine weather in Guadalcanal, also fair in the northern Solomons; only in New Britain some showers remain. Generally the same is predicted for tomorrow, too, but the weather at Guadalcanal appeared to worsen; nevertheless, we decided to carry out the attack as scheduled.

At 1045 we went to the east airfield and inspected the fighter and bomber crews of CV *Zuikaku*. Then we saw off twenty-eight fighters. After lunch at the headquarters, we went to the west airfield.

While we were still on our way, a pouring rain came in. Since the field was flooded with dirty water, I was worried a great deal. The rain subsided a little, so Vice Admiral Kakuta, commander, Second Carrier Division, ordered immediate takeoff. Forty-five of its fighters took off bravely at 1430, splashing water. Three of them failed to take off, owing to landing gear troubles.

Had today's advance been delayed, tomorrow's attack plan would have been greatly affected. So we were much relieved and went to the command post of the 705th Air Group. While we were briefed by its commander, [Captain Yukie] Konishi, on the airfield and being shown around, formations of fighters came back and landed one after another. They couldn't get through near the north end of New Britain, as the weather was bad.

Though it was necessary to change tomorrow's plan accordingly, a telephone cable was found out of order. Thinking we had better go down the hill, we returned to the temporary headquarters at 1730, braving the bad road. As a result of a study made at Third Fleet Headquarters, it was decided to dispatch the Second Carrier Division's filters early tomorrow morning, and refuel them at Balale base, and also to postpone the attack by an hour. There was no alternative.

Vice Admirals Mikawa and Samejima, the outgoing and incoming commanders in chief, Eighth Fleet, came to report their change of command. I expressed appreciation to Mikawa for his efforts in difficult situations and wished Samejima good fighting from now on.

At 1900 I got a telephone message on the hilltop about the new enemy situation. The reconnaissance report of a medium bomber of the 703rd Air Group: "At 1830, three cruisers, six destroyers sighted near Flak Island northwest of Russell Island, course 300°, speed 20 knots." Apparently they intend to bombard Munda or Kolombangara tonight. Anyway, they would be good prey for our attack tomorrow. They might boast tonight, but they're doomed.

Wednesday, 7 April 1943. Fair. In the morning inspected the 108th Air Depot and Supply Depot.

Fighter and carrier bomber squadrons left here early this morning as scheduled and carried out a combined attack with planes from Buin and Balale.

According to last night's radio intelligence, thirty-one ships were detected in the Guadalcanal area. At 0800 a reconnaissance sighted four cruisers, of which two were *Portland* and two others *Omaha* types, and seven destroyers in the Tulagi area, and about the same number of transports, big and small, in the Lunga area. Now a good prey seems to be setting itself up.

[*Rear Admiral W. L. "Pug" Ainsworth's task force of three cruisers*—Helena, Honolulu, *and* St. Louis—*and six destroyers were sortieing from Tulagi harbor when a warning from Guadalcanal gave them time to escape. But much lesser shipping remained.*][65]

Though there were scattered clouds, the weather at Guadalcanal seemed to be fair. Of the 157 fighters and 71 carrier bombers, the first challenging group entered the sky over the target from the direction of Russell Island and the rest from east of the island. At 1253 they charged in.

According to a report from a returned reconnaissance plane which was especially dispatched to confirm the battle result, one cruiser or transport off Tulagi and one transport off Lunga were burning, while three cruisers and six destroyers were cruising to the east of Tulagi and a fair amount of ships were found off Cape Cori.

The result seemed small, according to this report, but other reports gradually came in by nightfall. The accumulated battle report was as follows: one cruiser and one destroyer sunk; two large, six medium, and two small transports sunk; one big and one small transport slightly damaged; thirty-six planes shot down, of which twelve were uncertain. Our loss: twelve fighters and eight dive bombers lost.

[*Actual Allied losses were the U.S. destroyer* Aaron Ward, *tanker* Kanawha, *and New Zealand corvette* Moa, *and seven marine fighter planes. Ugaki's figures for Japanese losses—twelve fighters and eight dive bombers—almost exactly matches, in reverse, postwar Japanese figures of nine fighters and twelve dive bombers. Eventually the United States credited itself with twenty-seven Zeros and twelve dive bombers.*][66]

The RAAF changed its radio waves yesterday. They usually do this prior to a large-scale air raid on the Rabaul area. The probability of their coming to attack here soon was considered very great.

Thursday, 8 April 1943. Fair. As Takada, senior staff officer of the Third Fleet, came back from the Buin area, the detailed account of the attack and its results were made fairly clear. So we reported it to Imperial headquarters.

Due to bad weather in the northern Solomons area this morning, about half of the planes slated to return here failed to come back.

Lieutenant General Adachi, Eighteenth Army commander, returned on board a submarine the day before yesterday after an inspection tour in the

Lae and Salamaua area and came to see us this afternoon. We heard about the situation and his views for the future. He asserted that if we could send two battalions there, they could deal with the land warfare. He also said roads for automobiles could be constructed between Finschhafen and Lae in one week and between Madang and Lae in twenty days with two thousand men. What he said was generally optimistic. In the light of past experience, we can't trust his words entirely.

Staff Officer Ohmae of the Southeast Area Fleet also returned from the same area by a submarine today, and we heard his report at night. Supply would be sufficient if six hundred tons per month were sent there by submarines. That area could hold out if three thousand men on the sick list at present were replaced by the same number of fresh troops—two battalions now at Finschhafen and Tuluvu.

Unlike that of Guadalcanal, the general atmosphere there was more cheerful, but he complained of inactivity and lack of fighting spirit on the part of the army. Their easygoing behavior and feelings seemed to be the same everywhere. Why is this? They don't seem to realize what war is and how grave the present situation here is.

We had native cooking for dinner. Taro, tapioca, coconuts, and buds and vine of squash were quite tasty. We must encourage the local self-supply policy more than ever.

Friday, 9 April 1943. Cloudy. From 0840 I attended a briefing conference for aerial operations against southeast New Guinea. This operation, designated "Y," was of no comparison with those in the Solomons because of complicated topography, numerous enemy bases, and changeable weather. I hope for sound preparations and daring execution under a flexible plan.

According to the weather forecast in the evening, the bad weather zone over the Solomons area since yesterday will move westward gradually and cover the area south of New Britain tomorrow. Dense clouds were also expected on the Stanley range, so it would be difficult to cross it. Thereupon, we ordered the forces concentrated for Operation Y to get ready for the execution of Operations Y-1 and Y-2. However, as there was little hope for good weather and both the land-based air force and carrier air force wanted to have more time to make ready, we decided to cancel tomorrow's attack.

Four weather doctors of the Combined Fleet, Third Fleet, Southeast Area Fleet, and Eighth Meteorological Corps are here, and it's said that their diagnosis concurred today. Are they really right? I'll judge their skill tomorrow on seeing the result.

[Yamamoto permitted Ugaki to examine his calligraphy book, in which he wrote "with minute letters" famous old poems and a number of his own, dating from 4 December 1941 to 1 January 1943. "The merits of subordinates and their deaths, and a few words clarifying his position and resolution, many Chinese phrases and characters were included in it." Ugaki was immensely impressed that Yamamoto had written all this during January and resolved to borrow the book so that he might copy those not in his own book of calligraphy.]

A telegram was received from the chief of the Naval General Staff to the effect that when he reported the battle of the 7th to the throne, His Majesty seemed quite satisfied.

Saturday, 10 April 1943. Fair. From 0800 I visited the headquarters of the Twenty-first and Twenty-sixth air flotillas, where I had a chat with their respective commanders, [Rear Admiral Rinosuke] Ichimaru and Kosaka. Then I inspected the harbor master's office. Half of the pier was not usable and I felt sorry, as they had only a few vessels for their operations.

Then I visited the Eighty-first Garrison [Force] headquarters and heard the report of its commander, [Captain] Tatsuo Kiyama, who came from the same prefecture as mine. He was transferred to this post from chief instructor of the Tateyama Gunnery School and was taking care of the defense of New Britain with two thousand men. It was quite hard work.

Judging from a report of a weather observation plane leaving here at 1000 and conditions at various places, the weather in the Solomons area seemed to be generally fair, but that in the south of New Britain bad. Since the good weather zone was gradually moving to the west, it should be fair in eastern New Guinea tomorrow.

Two destroyers on transport mission for Finschhafen and another two for Tuluvu left here in the afternoon. They're taking separate courses, north and south. Maybe because of the foul weather, so far they're proceeding without being discovered by enemy planes. We might expect their success.

The land-based air force attack will not be made tomorrow in order to provide a fighter cover to them on their way back, and only the carrier air force is going to carry out Operation Y-1.

[After dinner, three explosions sounded at close range. Ugaki was rather upset because no one ordered an investigation. It turned out "that a fighter lost its position while undergoing training at high altitude, and fired some machine-gun incendiary bullets as it delayed its landing."]

Sunday, 11 April 1943. Fine, the first day of fever. At 2030, the enemy discovered the transportation attempt by destroyers for Finschhafen last night in the south of Surumi, and it was forced to put about, as parachute flares were dropped. Two destroyers on the north course gave up going to Finschhafen, instead entered Tuluvu together with the other two and carried out unloading there. Even Tuluvu will do!

Operation Y-1 was carried out with the air strength of the Third Fleet. Seventy-three fighters and twenty-seven carrier bombers attacked the Oro Bay area. [*Operation Y-1 sank one merchantman, beached a second, and damaged an Australian minesweeper at a cost of six aircraft shot down.*][67]

Good weather being expected in the Moresby area tomorrow and heavy clouds later, at 1600 we ordered the date of Y-Day set for the 12th.

At 0800 Lieutenant General Hyakutake, the Seventeenth Army commander, paid us a call on the occasion of his coming up from Shortland for a commanders' conference. This was a reunion since September last before the second general offensive was made. He was far from nervous and made a favorable impression. A commander should be like this.

In the afternoon I returned the call to Adachi, the Eighteenth Army commander and Hyakutake, the Seventeenth Army commander.

I had a little fever since morning and felt languid all over. Not only did my throat hurt, but all the symptoms resembled those of what people call dengue fever. I won't be beaten by dengue or whatever it might be!

Monday, 12 April 1943. Second day of fever, at sick bed. When I got back to my quarters last night, my temperature was found to be 101.3° and I felt quite sick. I got into bed right away.

An air raid alert sounded at 0340. Thinking that I should go while I could move, I went out as far as the corridor, but I felt like vomiting. As my temperature was the same as last night, I decided to rest for the time being.

Commander in chief left the billet at 0430 for the west airfield to send off the medium bomber squadron. Just before 0500, many sounds of explosions and gunfire were heard. One of the enemy planes that raided the east airfield flew low over our heads and dropped bombs on a side of the highest peak. There were three B-17s, and several of our planes were set on fire. Though they were clearly seen in the morning sky at an altitude of about three thousand meters, our shells reached far behind them, to my regret.

In the morning, the area fleet surgeon came to examine me. His diagnosis was also dengue fever and he recommended hospitalization. As it was the same whether I was here or in the hospital, I let myself be led to a sick room for a captain and above. It had never been occupied before.

The commander in chief dropped in to see me on his way back to his billet and told me about the result of today's attack. I was very grateful for his kindness.

[*The massive strike on Port Moresby by 131 fighters and 43 medium bombers achieved far from spectacular results. No ships were hit; a few small craft in the harbor and planes on the airstrip were damaged, and two Allied fighters were shot down at a cost of five Japanese aircraft.*][68]

[On Tuesday, 13 April, Ugaki's fever returned to normal, and he "would be all right again when my diarrhea stops." This was his first experience in a hospital and he was quite proud that obviously he had "never suffered from serious sickness." His room had a beautiful view of the valley and he watched the big bats which flew about "freely in the evenings."

[The next day Ugaki was able to leave the hospital, although there was no hurry, for a scheduled trip to Shortland on the 15th had been rescheduled for the 18th. "After heartily thanking the hospital chief and nurses," Ugaki returned to duty.]

Today's operations of Y-1 and Y-2 a great success. Congratulations! But at the same time our losses gradually increased too. This was natural. A telegram from the chief of the Naval General Staff stated that when he reported the result of Operations Y-1 and Y-2 to the emperor, His Majesty gave the following words: "Please convey my satisfaction to the commander in chief, Combined Fleet, and tell him to enlarge the war result more than ever."

[*In fact, the operation of 14 April netted a very poor bag—a Dutch transport sunk, a British motorship hit but salvaged, a gasoline dump set on fire, and three U.S. aircraft shot down. The Japanese lost seven planes.*][69]

Thursday, 15 April 1943. Rain. An air raid alarm was sounded at 0300. Enemy planes circled over the clouds and dropped four bombs but did no damage.

It was decided to spend all day today in readying the planes and to carry out Operation Y-2 with only fighters, but part of them were assigned to dive bomb with 60-kg bombs, and also attempt to attack enemy aircraft in the Buna area with fighters of the land-based air force tomorrow.

Friday, 16 April 1943. Fair. A reconnaissance plane leaving at 0430 did not find any game on the northeast coast of New Guinea. Accordingly we called off the attack ordered yesterday. The end of Operation I-Go was then ordered, and we made reports of its results, etc.

[On Saturday, 17 April, Ugaki presided over a study conference of Operation I-Go held at Eighth Base Force headquarters. He "praised the result," but stressed "that lack of air power was the main cause of our present plight," and they could not expect "its swift reinforcement." So he urged everyone to exert his "very best efforts." He also stressed the need for better reconnaissance, countermeasures against large aircraft, and new attack methods.

[This meeting was over at noon, and Ugaki moved on to preside over another conference in the same location, concerned with policies and principles. A number of reports were delivered on future plans, requirements, repair of air bases, "and epidemic prevention." Something he said irritated Kusaka, the area fleet commander in chief, who evidently took it "as an insult to his men." Ugaki did not specify what the source of irritation was, noting only that Kusaka shouted at him after they returned to fleet headquarters.]

Eruptions have broken out all over my body since this morning and proved that I had really suffered from dengue fever. It was just a week from the beginning. I felt like myself, but I haven't enough appetite yet.

Results and Losses of Operation I-Go*

Operations (Dates of Execution)	Planes participated	Vessels	Airfields	Planes shot down	Losses
X Apr.	157 fighters 67 bombers	2 lg., 6 med., 2 sm. transports, 1 cruiser, 1 DD sunk. 1 med., 1 sm. transport seriously damaged. 1 lg. transport slightly damaged.		41 (31)	12 fighters 9 bombers
Y-2 11 Apr.	71 fighters 21 bombers	2 med., 1 sm. transports, 1 DD sunk.		21 (9)	2 fighters 4 bombers
Y 12 Apr.	131 fighters 43 med. bombers	1 lg. transport sunk.	11 places afire at Moresby (3 big explosions included)	28 (7)	2 fighters 6 med. bombers
Y-1 14 Apr.	52 fighters 37 bombers	1 lg., 1 med. transports sunk. 2 to 3 sm. transports damaged.	5 places afire at Rabi	27 (6)	3 med. bombers
Y-2 14 Apr.	75 fighters 23 bombers	2 lg., 1 med. transports sunk. 2 lg., 3 med., 1 sm. transports seriously damaged. Several other ships damaged.		17 (3)	2 fighters 3 bombers

Condition of Planes Expended

Classifications	Planes prepared	Planes lost	Percent
Carrier fighters	206	25	12%
Carrier bombers	81	21	26%
Land medium bombers	83	15	18%

*[These figures, based upon the fliers' reports, are grossly exaggerated.]

Sunday, 18 April 1943. [*Ugaki dictated this and the remaining entries of April 1943 to Ensign Kenzo Ebima, retrospectively, on the first anniversary of the tragic events of 18 April 1943.*][70] At 0610 left Rabaul aboard two medium bombers from the east strip. Six fighters escorted us. The weather was fine with intermittent cumulus.

[*Yamamoto had decided to visit various forward areas to inspect them and to boost morale.*][71]

At 0730 twenty-four enemy P-38s encountered us northwest of Moele Point. Two enemy planes were shot down but one bomber (commander in chief, chief medical officer, senior air staff officer and aide aboard) was set aflame and shot down in the jungle about six kilometers from the coastline, while another bomber (chief of staff, chief paymaster, chief meteorologist, communications staff officer, and junior air staff officer aboard) was shot down about 150 meters from the coast near Moele Point. Only the chief of staff and chief paymaster survived and received first aid treatment at the lookout post of Moele Point.

[*For Ugaki's full eyewitness account of these events, see his entry for 18 April 1944. Through communications intelligence, the United States learned of Yamamoto's projected flight and even his exact schedule. Sixteen P-38s of the 339th Fighter Squadron at Henderson Field were assigned to ambush the two Japanese planes. Yamamoto's was shot down by Lieutenant Thomas G. Lanphier, Jr., Ugaki's by Lieutenant Rex T. Barber.*][72]

Then a subchaser brought them to Buin. After treatment at the Seventh Base Force Headquarters we stayed there. Commanders of the First Base Force and Twenty-sixth Air Flotilla came. According to their story, at about 1400 a search party saw the commander in chief's plane with both wings burnt out but no one around it. Beginning that evening, enemy planes repeatedly came to attack here so that they stayed the whole night in the air raid shelter.

[On Monday, 19 April, Ugaki conferred with various officers who visited him and received treatment from "the chief medical officer of the Eighth Fleet." Watanabe, with two chief medical officers, one each from the Southeast Area Fleet and Eighth Fleet, boarded a subchaser "to go to the place where the commander in chief's plane was shot down." The next day the subchaser returned with the bodies of Yamamoto and those who had accompanied him. On Wednesday, 21 April, the bodies were burned.]

Thursday, 22 April 1943. In the morning received the last treatment here. On account of foul weather, departure was postponed for a while. In the meantime, enemy planes came to attack and a duel took place right over the air base. At about 1400 we boarded two medium bombers with the ashes and took off from the base. Seventeen fighters escorted us and, due to bad weather, passed over Kieta. At 1600 we arrived in Rabaul East base and entered the former Third Fleet's headquarters for security reasons. Conferred with commander, chief of staff, and other staff officers of the Southeast Area Fleet.

Friday, 23 April 1943. At 0830 left Rabaul East strip aboard two medium bombers with the ashes of the commander in chief and others. In order to avoid attention, only the commander in chief of the Southeast Area Fleet came to see us off. At 1345 we arrived in the Takeshima base, Truk, and immediately returned to the flagship. [*The flagship was now* Musashi, *Yamamoto having transfered his flag from* Yamato *on 12 February 1943.*][73] Vice Admiral Kondo, acting commander of the Combined Fleet, and commander in chief of the Third Fleet, came aboard to pay their respects to the ashes of the admiral. After that I conferred with them.

Sunday, 25 April 1943. [Admiral Mineichi] Koga, the new commander in chief of the Combined Fleet, left Tokyo today and arrived at the flagship via Saipan at 1430. In the evening the new commander in chief came to see me and I conferred with him.

[*Yamamoto had designated Koga to be his successor.*][74]

[Musashi *arrived in Tokyo on the 22nd, and Ugaki was sent to the Tokyo Naval Hospital. On 21 May, Admirl Fukudome replaced him as chief of staff, Combined Fleet.*][75]

[*According to Watanabe, who knew him well, Ugaki always considered himself responsible for Yamamoto's death. The rumors in the Japanese Navy said that admirals Nagano and Shimada agreed with him. The diary gives no definite reason for this belief, but possibly Ugaki felt that his eagerness to visit the front lines might have influenced Yamamoto.*][76]

[*Ugaki kept up his diary while convalescing, but his son and later his son's widow were unwilling for these entries to be published on the ground that they were personal and of no historical interest. See introduction to this section.*]

7

Time Is Running Out

22 February–31 May 1944

FROM 17 TO 18 *February 1944,*
U.S. forces blasted Truk so effectively that the Combined Fleet no longer
could use it as an operational base and had to retreat to the west. Premier
Tojo concurrently assumed duty as chief, Army General Staff. Likewise,
Shimada became chief, Naval General Staff, to serve concurrently as navy
minister.

Such was the unpromising background for Ugaki's return to active service on
22 February in command of the First Battleship Division. He had expected
something a little higher up, but accepted with good grace, glad to be useful
again. After touching base with several navy VIPs, he flew to Lingga Anchorage
near Singapore and arrived on 6 March.

The Combined Fleet ordered preparation for Operation Z—the concentra-
tion of Japanese naval power and reinforcement of the Marshalls and Carolines
with troops from Manchuria. Ugaki plunged into training, feeling the weight of
command responsibility toward his men.

In an incident remarkably similar to that which cost Yamamoto his life and
sent Ugaki to the hospital, the aircraft carrying Koga to his new headquarters at
Davao via Saipan disappeared; the one transporting chief of staff Fukudome
and others came down near Cebu. Fukudome was a classmate and one of
Ugaki's best friends, so he was overjoyed when Fukudome turned up alive and
well after two weeks of captivity by Filipinos.

On 18 April Ugaki made two entries, one the usual record, the other a minute
description of the events of 18 April 1943. This is one of the most historically
important as well as one of the most interesting portions of the diary.

As for the current situation, Ugaki was caught up in training and preparing
his battleships for a "decisive battle"—a strategy that Ugaki increasingly ques-
tioned. Why was the Japanese Navy wedded to the "decisive battle" concept, which
meant waiting to engage a major American fleet instead of attacking smaller
enemy groups whenever and wherever they presented themselves? He knew
Japan's strength was dwindling. Oil was frighteningly scarce, and U.S. radar
and night-flying aircraft had rendered Japan's tactical specialty, the night

332

attack, "almost useless." How to die honorably constantly occupied his mind.

Much action was taking place around Truk and, although Ugaki's battle-ships were not engaged, he recorded the usual exaggerated claims. Then on 11 May the fleet left Lingga for Tawi Tawi in the Sulu Sea off northeast Borneo in anticipation of Operation A (A-Go)—an all-out battle near Palau in the West Carolines. The plan was activated on 20 May. Ugaki was troubled about how to supply the fleet; the condition of the supply ships "appalled" him. Submarines also continued to worry him, not only because of the danger to Japanese ships but because the submarines could locate Japanese positions, making secrecy impossible.

The U.S. attack on Biak in the Schouten Islands gave Ugaki the opportunity to play an active part. He promptly grasped the fact that American occupation of this island would throw any number of monkey wrenches into Japan's strategic machinery, including making A-Go impossible. Thus, he presented his ideas vigorously, and the Combined Fleet decided to relieve Biak, an action designated "Kon," to be activated early in June. One cannot be certain that Ugaki's eloquence directly resulted in Kon, but very likely it was a factor.

Tuesday, 22 February 1944. I went to the Navy Ministry in the morning in accordance with a telephone call received yesterday from the chief of the Personnel Bureau. With the disbanding of the First Fleet, the task fleet has been newly organized with the Second and Third Fleets. The First Battleship Division is to be commanded by a flag officer, to which post I am going to be appointed. This isn't exactly what I expected, but I'll gladly take it up and serve the country again. I saw both the vice chief and the chief of the Operations Bureau of the Naval General Staff.

Wednesday, 23 February 1944. I got in touch with Lieutenant Commander Yoshio Yaguchi, who has just graduated from the War College and is to be one of my staff officers in charge of engineering. I began preparations to leave for the new assignment.

Thursday, 24 February 1944. Light rain. At 1000 I visited Fleet Admiral Nagano in his private home and heard about the delicate circumstances under which he had to resign as chief of the Naval General Staff. Then I called on General Kazunari Ugaki, talked about recent developments, and stayed to dinner.

[From 17 to 18 February 1944, U.S. carrier-based planes blasted Truk, destroying some 275 Japanese aircraft and sinking 200,000 tons of merchant shipping. Although Koga had managed to get most of his warships out of harbor before the raid began, the United States destroyed two light cruisers and a

destroyer. Light cruiser Agano *fell to the U.S. submarine* Skate; *light cruiser* Katori *and destroyer* Maikaze *fell to the guns of the U.S. support forces under Vice Admiral Raymond A. Spruance, commander, Fifth Fleet. These raids made Truk untenable as the headquarters base for the commander in chief, Combined Fleet.*

[As a result of this setback, Tojo reorganized his cabinet and designated Shimada to succeed Nagano as chief of the Naval General Staff and to serve concurrently as navy minister.][1]

Friday, 25 February 1944. Rear Admiral Nakazawa, chief of the Operations Bureau, told me his operational intentions. My assignment as commander, First Battleship Division, has been formally issued with today's date.

Saturday, 26 February 1944. At 1230 I saw Mr. [Shu] Yabe at the Navy Club. [*Shu Yabe was confidential secretary to General "Issei" Ugaki, a distant connection of the admiral.*][2] The recent political situation has been getting more muddled and the pigheaded Tojo may find himself facing a dead end yet. [*In his cabinet shake-up, Tojo took over as chief, Army General Staff, as a concurrent duty, succeeding General Gen Sugiyama, a move not universally popular in Japan.*][3]

[Ugaki spent the rest of the day paying his respects to various VIPs, including Shimada, and paid his respects to Yamamoto's "Buddhist tablet."]

Sunday, 27 February 1944. I sent some baggage to go by air with Lieutenant Commander Yaguchi and spent the afternoon writing some calligraphy and also getting some political information from Mr. Yabe. In the evening I invited a few neighbors to a farewell dinner.

Monday, 28 February 1944. Fair, later cloudy. I had a photo taken at Denen Studio to leave behind. After saying a prayer at a nearby shrine and bidding farewell to the neighbors, I left home at 1330, having said another prayer at the family altar. I was grateful to those who came to see me off at the station. At 1430 I left Tokyo on my trip heading west.

[The morning's fine weather became "a bit threatening," and Ugaki wondered if this might "signify difficulties lying ahead." Later, it cleared up again, and Ugaki celebrated his departure for the front with one of his two-line poems.]

Tuesday, 29 February 1944. Fair. At 0820 I arrived at Kure, and after breakfasting at a hotel I inspected *Yamato,* placed under my command, which was just then in drydock. She's going to be completed in April. [*On 25 December 1943, a torpedo from* Skate—*the same submarine that sank* Agano—*had damaged* Yamato.]+ What an added power she'll be to the division and what an assurance! I visited Vice Admiral Nomura, commander in chief of the Naval Station there, at 1120 and was invited to lunch with him and Mrs. Nomura.

[On Wednesday, 1 March, Ugaki left Kure by train at 0830, arriving at Hakata at 1700. There Ugaki put up for the night at a hotel.]

Thursday, 2 March 1944. Fair. At 0620 I arrived at Japan Air Line's office and went to the airfield. Commanders of the local naval establishment were there to greet [Vice Admiral Toshibejin] Nakamura, aide-de-camp to His Imperial Majesty the Emperor, who was going to Southeast Asia and happened to go most of the way with me. We took off at 0900. The weather was fine and on the plane I wrote a letter to my son to be posted in Japan tomorrow.

About 1330 I arrived at Shanghai and had a little rest while the plane was refueled. I left my visiting cards with the commander in chief of the China Fleet and my cousin, [Vice Admiral] Kanji Ugaki, the chief of staff. At 1700 landed at Taihoku, Formosa. Aide-de-camp Nakamura was received quite ceremoniously, although his trip wasn't a formal one. Such treatment was quite imaginable in a colonial place like Formosa.

Later we went together to pay a visit to the governor general, Admiral [Kiyoshi] Hasegawa. At 1945 attended [an entertainment] at the invitation of the governor general. Banquets, restaurants, and geishas have been banned, as in Japan proper, but the governor general still seemed as full of life as before. [*On 25 February 1944, Japan instituted a stringent "simplification of the national livelihood," which included, among other measures, the closing of geisha houses and other places of amusement.*]⁵

[Ugaki mentioned that the climate was good and "like early summer already." Although the previous night he had to take a hot water bottle to bed, on this night he needed a mosquito net, a fact which moved him to one of his two-line poems.

[On Friday, 3 March and Saturday, 4 March, Ugaki was in transit to Singapore by way of Hainan Island and Saigon. His communications staff officer, Lieutenant Commander Torao Suematsu, met him at the Singapore commercial airport "and took care of everything." That evening Rear Admiral Susumu Imamura, commander, Nineteenth Naval Base, picked Ugaki up at the Navy Club and took him to his quarters.

[On Sunday, 5 March, Ugaki acquainted himself with his new area, taking an early walk "on the grass still wet with morning dew" and later visiting Shonan Shrine. Between these expeditions, he visited Vice Admirals Tayui, commander in chief, First Southern Expeditionary Fleet, and Ozawa, commander in chief, Third Fleet (task fleet), as well as an old friend, Field Marshal Terauchi.]

Monday, 6 March 1944. Fair. At 1000 I boarded destroyer *Tanikaze* and left Seleter harbor. While inspecting the coast from the sea, speed was increased to 21 knots outside the channel heading south. Arrived at Lingga anchorage [near Singapore] at 1645.

Then I boarded *Nagato* and my vice admiral's flag was hoisted, thus making this ship my place of death. [*This curious phrase plainly indicates that if* Nagato *should be sunk, Ugaki intended to go down with her.*] This is the fourth time I have served on *Nagato*. If she had a heart, she would be glad of my coming on board her. For my part, too, I'm glad to see her well, and grateful for her gallant fighting up to now. Her skipper is Captain Yuji Kobe, who was a midshipman in my days with the training squadron. The ships at anchor here are *Fuso* (under my operational command), *Shokaku*, *Kumano* (flagship, Seventh Heavy Cruiser Division), *Yahagi* (flagship, Tenth Destroyer Squadron), and the Sixty-first Destroyer Division. On account of the commander in chief's absence, I, as the senior commander, take charge of the forces' readiness and training.

Tuesday, 7 March 1944. Fair. The ensign is hoisted here at 1000. There is about two hours' time difference from that of home waters. From 1015 briefly inspected *Nagato*. At 1800 [Rear Admiral Masafuku] Kimura, Tenth Destroyer Squadron commander, and later Nishimura, Seventh Heavy Cruiser Division commander, came to see me. Talked about things since we parted.

Wednesday, 8 March 1944. Fair. In the morning, received reports from the staff officers concerning their respective assignments. The engineer staff officer was sent to Singapore on board *Yahagi* to arrange for docking.

On 5 March, the Combined Fleet headquarters issued an order calling for concentrating our war strength by the end of March in order to meet an enemy offensive against the line of the Carolines and Marianas. This change was made because we couldn't possibly put off the showdown until May, when it would be more favorable to us. This step should be called very natural. [*This was Operation Z to concentrate Japanese naval power and reinforce the Marianas and Carolines with troops from Manchuria.*][6]

Thursday, 9 March 1944. Fair. At breakfast (0830) I noticed the staff officers were missing. While I was wondering what was up, a message came in, relayed by the Tenth Communications Corps, which said that "at 0120 lost sight of something like an unidentified submarine to the south; its course west." Though its transmitter origin wasn't determined, it was roughly estimated to have been sent from the south of Berbara Channel. Accordingly, I ordered No. 2 antisub stations. While making patrols with planes and boats, I sent the Sixty-first Destroyer Division to the outer position and destroyer *Akitsuki* separately to Berbara to investigate there. The original transmitter turned out to be the lookout post there, as we thought. When we contacted it, it repeated the same signal.

While preparing to change anchorage, a false report by *Kumano* about finding a submarine caused confusion. Under such circumstances as these, it's apparent that, if one thing goes wrong, everything tends to go haywire. This has been proved in the fleet anchorages at the Inland Sea and Truk. Unless and until we get counterevidence of its being other than a submarine, we shall never be free from worry like this.

At 1630 I decided as the senior commander to shift the fleet anchorage to No. 3 and so ordered. Other ships left some launches and boats in our care, besides our own patrol boats to be hoisted. Reports that 16 knots instant notice had been completed only meant that their engines were ready; *Nagato* alone was ready to weigh anchor. All the rest were delayed by hoisting the boats, etc., arranging to send them under their own power to the new anchorage. On the way north, a towboat of five hundred or six hundred tons and barges were sighted to the left in the evening light. A destroyer was dispatched to investigate them.

At 2015 we arrived at anchorage No. 3 in moonlight. *Shokaku* was a little late because of raising her boats. According to the dispatched destroyer's report, the towboat was an army oil transport heading to Singapore from Palembang with about five hundred tons of oil. She passed Berbara at about 0300. Now that the cat was out of the bag, we were relieved at last. So the alert was resumed to No. 3 stations, and I went to bed.

According to this instance as well as air reconnaissance, evidently other vessels towing lumber, etc., ply through the channel freely. In view of this, I consider it necessary to restrict their passage to daytime only, if we can't stop them altogether, and at least put patrol boats at Berbara to check anything suspicious. Those lookouts are dispatched by the First Southern Expeditionary Fleet, and they don't seem to be supervised properly. To find out the real situation, fleet headquarters should investigate at a proper time.

Friday, 10 March 1944. Fair. Many shoals are in No. 3 anchorage to the north, and both entrances to the south and southwest are wide open, contrary to the chart. Moreover, its depth is a little deeper than No. 1

anchorage, with strong current. In addition, it has a security disadvantage of a good deal of sailing boat traffic. It seems a good policy to change the anchorage from time to time and to stay there for a few days. However, as we have firing practice for the First Battleship Division, I have decided to go back to anchorage No. 1 tomorrow.

Saturday, 11 March 1944. Fair. At 2230 sailed into the anchorage through Rio Channel. The watch post reported detection of a ship by the guard loop but not by visual observation. But at night I ordered No. 2 alert stations, increased the patrol boats, and made the destroyers stand by, as we had to do something, though we found nothing unusual. CV *Shokaku* caused another disturbance by mistaking a piece of driftwood for a submarine. The fleet returned to anchorage No. 1, practicing some training on the way.

The First Battleship Division sailed out at 1300 and trained against destroyer attacks, practice firing of main and secondary batteries, formation maneuvers, shrapnel firing, searchlight practice, and non-searchlight secondary battery firing. It returned to anchorage No. 1 at 2345. Everything went smoothly without a hitch. The equator lies four miles to the south of *Nagato*'s roads, so we crossed it twice today.

Sunday, 12 March 1944. Fair. The engineer staff officer returned in the afternoon by one of our planes. This ship's docking was generally scheduled from 2 to 8 April. *Yahagi* returned in the evening. It became quite cool at night under the Milky Way and reminded me of summer at home.

A movie show was held tonight and the quarterdeck after the No. 3 turret was filled with men. Looking at all those men, the loyal sons of His Majesty, and thinking that they would all gladly live or die together at my command, I couldn't help feeling the weight of responsibility resting on my shoulders. Human life is precious, yet we must not avoid sacrifices to win the war. It's no easy matter to be a commander. In the meantime, the moon has risen.

[On Monday, 13 March, Ugaki was host to the imperial aide-de-camp who conducted an inspection of *Nagato* and heard Ugaki's report "on the local situation and the present state of training." Ugaki invited his key officers to lunch with them. He was grateful to the emperor for "sending his proxy to such a faraway place as here." This was the second time Ugaki had received an Imperial emissary. "Considering that I received an Imperial gift of crested pastries while I was hospitalized, I think I must be an extraordinarily lucky man."]

Tuesday, 14 March 1944. Fair. *Nagato* put out to sea in the morning and *Fuso* in the afternoon to carry out individual training. The tanker *Hayatomo,* unable to navigate by herself because of a broken engine, made port from Singapore in tow after three days of sailing. She'll be used only as a supply tank here. Her commander came to see me and I appreciated his hard efforts.

[Around midnight, there was another submarine scare, but nothing came of it. On the morning of Wednesday, 15 March, Ugaki and his officers "held a conference to study recent training operations." The admiral regretted that his force was "not satisfactory in some points" yet.

[That afternoon, *Nagato* held "an equator festival," which Ugaki viewed with mixed feelings. "It was good to relax and bolster up morale. But seeing that they had lots of theatrical props I couldn't help wondering whether they were really ready for a battle, too." But part of their dialogue expressed regret at having missed past battles and concerned their expectations for the future. Ugaki could "appreciate their feeling; so would Neptune."

[Accompanied by a destroyer division, the Third Battleship Division arrived at Lingga from home waters, and its commander, Rear Admiral Yoshio Suzuki, came to see Ugaki. The two had been Eta Jima classmates.]

Thursday, 16 March 1944. Fair. Rain has not come in spite of growing signs of it. I dispatched a gunboat each to Berbara and Pengelap for guard duties.

Since the evacuation of our planes from Rabaul, enemy aircraft have mercilessly devastated the whole town area, jetty, and, further, attacked the cave area and dispersed storage dumps. Admiralty Island also fell.

[*The aircraft blasting Rabaul came from the Thirteenth Air Force. U.S. forces, with MacArthur present, began the occupation of the Admiralty Islands on 29 February 1944.*][7]

The only bright spot was the Seventeenth Army's offensive, seemingly the last, against the Torokina area on Bougainville Island. Even this can give little future hope, in view of little air support for it and the recent arrival of big enemy reinforcements in the Guadalcanal area. A type *Ro* submarine has reported a big group of fifty ships seventy miles northwest of Mille, its course being 180° to 230°. Are they heading for Ponape? Wherever it may be heading, odds are completely against us. But something must be done anyhow.

> After leaving matters to the army for a while,
> Alas! We face today's ebb tide!

[For Friday, 17 March, Ugaki made no notation beyond the weather, which was "Fair." On Saturday, 18 March, three ship captains came to pay their respects, including Captain Kazutake Shigenada of *Haruna*. On Sunday, 19 March, Ugaki complained about the weather. "During the northeast monsoon the sun blazes mercilessly on the port side only." He added, "Movies in the evening prove to be a cooling tonic at times."]

Monday, 20 March 1944. Fair. *Zuikaku* came in from the homeland via Singapore, and her captain came to see me. With the arrival of various ships, the anchorage has begun to look alive.

This morning we held a conference to discuss training at sea. But I regret that it lacks any distinct characteristic of wartime, especially at a time when the sand is running out quickly. It looks very much like that of peacetime training. Though their desire to fight is quite recognizable, are they not lacking in earnestness? Should this, too, be blamed on "big ship mentality"?

The enemy landed on the southeast part of Kavieng, making the assault with naval vessels. Again, considerable damage was sustained. (This later proved to be a false report.) [*The U.S. had decided to by-pass Kavieng.*][8]

On the other hand, our shipping losses have so mounted that there is scarcely any oil storage left in Japan. As a result, a conference to study the escort system was held in the Imperial Palace, and the chief of the Naval General Staff conveyed to us the words of the emperor. By the time one bottleneck has been solved after concentrated efforts, another one has come to the fore to make it difficult to display our fighting strength fully. Those who serve as the central authorities should not be caught by a narrow vision and should study matters carefully from all conceivable angles so as not to cause a bottleneck. Since this is a war between the rich and the poor, the poor should devise and contrive with the utmost effort.

[On Tuesday, 21 March, Ugaki's ships held a ceremony to celebrate the vernal equinox, saluting in the direction of Tokyo. "The sun was directly above the equator. A junior officer of the deck made an orderly stand on deck at about 1400 and looked for his shadow."]

Wednesday, 22 March 1944. Fair. My inside doesn't feel well. It's best to eat less. Under the present circumstances, our food is too much of a luxury. It might still be all right if no home product is included. But this isn't so, depending on commodities. If we can't be self-sufficient even in such a faraway place as this, it's certain the homeland people will suffer more and more. We must be considerate!

[On Thursday, 23 March, a "long-awaited squall" came, and Ugaki had orderlies bring the potted plants on deck, but the squall passed without giving them enough water. So the orderlies returned the plants below deck and watered them.]

In the evening *Tone, Chikuma, Shokaku, Zuikaku,* and later *Suzuya* and *Mogami* returned to the roads. *Tone* and *Chikuma* now belong to the Seventh Heavy Cruiser Division. I can't but think about those days back in 1941 when I commanded them for some three months. I'm very happy to meet these fresh ships from the Maizuru Naval Base again, with hardly any damage inflicted upon either of them except a bomb hit on the bridge of *Chikuma,* in spite of their brilliant records since the outbreak of the war.

[That evening Ugaki and his staff dined on a wild boar that an officer had shot. On Friday, 24 March, the First Battleship Division "carried out preliminary battle practices" at sea.]

Saturday, 25 March 1944. Rain. It started to rain from about 1100 with wind from north to west, then the wind turned to the south and, for the first time, the rain was quite heavy and the waves got fairly big. It cleared up at 1600.

The Third Fleet flag and his staff officers returned here aboard a destroyer from Singapore, and hoisted his flag on *Shokaku.* After sunset I went to see Vice Admiral Ozawa to report to him on matters which occurred while he was absent.

A closing ceremony of the Diet was held in Tokyo. The Diet is necessary, of course, but it doesn't seem to do anything at all. I can't help feeling that that might be its real function!

In its offensive, presumably the last one, at Torokina, Bougainville, the Seventeenth Army fared not so badly in the beginning, but having no aerial support or supply they failed to recover the air strip after all. Abandoned enemy corpses amount to thirty-some hundred and many prisoners, while our losses reached over five thousand dead and wounded. As they could not stand losing more able men, the offensive had to be suspended. This is just as I expected, although I admire their courage. My deepest sympathy should go again to the Seventeenth Army, which had to carry out such a stand against odds.

[*In March 1944 the Seventeenth Army under General Hyakutake made three determined efforts to dislodge the Allies from Bougainville. According to U.S. records, Japanese losses were twenty to one U.S.*][9]

[On Sunday, 26 March, Ugaki held a conference to discuss the "preliminary battle practices." He was "glad to notice a little more enthusiasm," but there was "much room for improvement in the firing skill." On Monday, 27 March, Ugaki had nothing to say beyond "Fair, very hot."

Training at sea took place again on Tuesday, 28 March. "*Nagato* assumed the position of direct screen for carriers, perhaps an unprecedented step." That evening they carried out "antisub practice for the anchorage." Again Ugaki's ships went to sea on Wednesday, 29 March, for antisubmarine training. That afternoon he went ashore and for the first time in almost a year took along his shotgun, but his bag was small.]

Headquarters, Combined Fleet warned yesterday that according to radio intelligence an enemy task force has been maneuvering between New Guinea and the Carolines. Today two CVs, two battleships, and about a dozen others were spotted at 490 miles southeast of Palau. Ships in Palau harbor were ordered to get out of the harbor, while Combined Fleet headquarters was moved ashore and *Musashi* was ordered to join the mobile force. According to a top secret signal issued at about 2000, *Musashi* was ordered to go to Kure, escorted by three destroyers. I wonder whether they want to have her refitted in a hurry at this moment, or if she sustained some damage from enemy sub attacks in the waters near Palau. [Musashi *had indeed sustained minor damage from the U.S. submarine* Tunny.][10]

In any case, it's now apparent that I shan't be able to get her under my command, after the Combined Fleet changes its flag to light cruiser *Oyodo* upon completion of her refitting, and together with *Yamato* do some great work as I anticipated. Another group of two converted carriers was also sighted to the north of New Ireland, while B-24s raided Truk.

[*On 29 March B-24s of the 307th Bomb Group conducted the first daylight raid of Truk Atoll. They claimed to have destroyed thirty-one Japanese interceptors plus some fifty aircraft on the ground, at a cost of two B-24s*][11]

The 601st Air Group of the Third Fleet has been ordered to prepare to move to the Davao district. Some planes attacked the enemy this evening but without much result.

Thursday, 30 March 1944. Cloudy, squall. At 0900 *Nagato* sailed for Singapore and on the way saw the Sixteenth Heavy Cruiser Division under the command of Rear Admiral [Naomasa] Sakonju. We arrived at Seleter at 1615. This is probably the first time a capital ship visited this port.

At 0800 today, commander in chief, Combined Fleet, ordered Operation Hei Method No. 6 and alerted for Operation Tei. The 601st Air Group was also to go to Davao.

An enemy task force appeared at ninety miles south of Palau and they have been repeating attacks since this morning. Judging from the great number of planes, they're estimated to consist of about eight carriers. But what makes me mad is their insolent attitude of doing whatever they like and completely disregarding us. If we don't crush the whole lot of them and stop their spearhead at this stage, there will be no end to their reckless onslaughts with serious effects on the future.

[*Task Force 58 attacked Palau Islands in force on 30 and 31 March 1944, during which aircraft from* Bunker Hill, Lexington, *and* Hornet *mined the passages to the harbor. A total of thirty-six Japanese vessels were destroyed in this raid at no cost to Task Force 58's ships.*][12]

Friday, 31 March 1944. Fair, squall. Late midnight, Combined Fleet ordered Operation Hei Method No. 6 and stood for Operation Tei. Except the First CV Division, all units at Lingga were also ordered to prepare for sortie.

Early morning the task fleet order came in. Accordingly, preparation for docking was suspended and that for sortie was ordered instead. At 1100, *Nagato* went alongside the wharf and loaded fuel and victuals. At 1830 she left the wharf and returned to the anchorage outside the floating dock. At 1100 *Shokaku* arrived in front of the airstrip, and in the afternoon *Kongo* neared us. *Chikuma* and *Tone* were also moored to the wharf and started loading materials for the 601st Air Group.

The task fleet issued Forces Disposition Otsu, under which order I was slated to lead the First Battleship Division (plus *Fuso*), Third Battleship Division, Seventh Heavy Cruiser Division, and Tenth Destroyer Squadron as the Second Mobile Force commander, and advance to Tawi Tawi upon an order to sortie. The task fleet commander, on the other hand, has decided to go to Davao with the 601st Air Group the day after tomorrow. Regardless of whether a sortie order will be issued after all, I'll be slated to remain in this Lingga Roads to take command of a considerably strong force. I'm quite determined and ready to tackle any hardship to execute my duty, but I worry for my staff officers because I have only three of them as a division headquarters.

The enemy forces which attacked Palau consisted of ten carriers, eight battleships, and many cruisers and destroyers. They launched eleven series of attacks from early morning to the evening with total number of attacking planes reaching 456. Except the one group found earlier, all the rest of the enemy were discovered after the air raids. In light of such insufficient reconnaissance ability as this, it's extremely difficult to beat the enemy with an inferior force. We must pay due consideration to this defect in planning the mobile force operations.

Since this morning the enemy has moved to the northeast direction and attacked Yap and Kusaie. Counterattacks by our land-based air forces appear to have achieved little, if anything, which drives me crazy. Though the enemy doesn't plan an immediate landing at present, he'll be so reckless as to lick all the important places. This is really what is called a "licking"! [*The attack on Yap came from Rear Admiral John W. Reeves's Carrier Division 3.*][13]

Our damages sustained at Palau are pretty heavy, including *Akashi, Uragami Maru, Ose,* etc. Headquarters Combined Fleet seemingly took it to be intolerable and tried to flee to Davao via Saipan on board flying boats that very night. It's only natural that they can't possibly take overall command of the situation stationed in the very place where the enemy attack hit.

[*As had Yamamoto and Ugaki, Koga and Fukudome took off in separate aircraft. Koga's plane disappeared forever, probably lost in an accident, for there is no U.S. record of its being shot down. Fukudome's plane came down off Cebu in the Philippines, and he spent two weeks in captivity by the natives. The Japanese freed him at the end of that period.*][14]

Musashi was due to go to Kure accompanied by three destroyers, as stated before. If the reason were due to her hasty refitting, she could have been so informed sooner. In view of the fact that a change was made all of a sudden, the signal was labeled top secret, and she'll reach Okinoshima on 3 April maintaining 17.5 knots. It must be considered very likely that she was hit by enemy submarine torpedoes out of Palau harbor.

Saturday, 1 April 1944. Squall. The Second Mobile Force finished its preparations to sail at 0900 when *Kongo* completed her loading of fuel, so I reported accordingly. Leaving the ship at 1030, I visited Commander in Chief Ozawa aboard *Shokaku* anchoring off Seleter airfield and talked about the force's future arrangements. Its chief of staff was out. The headquarters is going to leave for Davao tomorrow morning.

In the afternoon the Sixteenth Heavy Cruiser Division commander, Rear Admiral Sakonju, one of my classmates, came to see me. In order to leave here to transport materials to the Dutch East Indies tomorrow, he returned here soon after he had left. The Seventh Heavy Cruiser Division commander, Shiraishi, also came to see me. He left for Davao at 1630 leading *Chikuma, Tone,* and two destroyers to transport base materials of the 601st Air Group.

At 1645 I went ashore for the first time here and visited the local naval base commander, the First Southern Expeditionary Fleet chief of staff at his headquarters (commander in chief was out for golf), and chiefs of the Engineering and Supply Depots. It was cooler in the buildings, and all of them were so finely built that I thought the Japanese could hardly build such good ones.

From 0600 to 1100, the enemy raided Meleyon [Woleai Atoll] with a total of two hundred planes, inflicting considerable damage. I regret that we couldn't cope with it effectively. The Combined Fleet headquarters left for Davao via Saipan last night on board three flying boats. [*Three U.S. carrier groups struck Woleai on 1 April. Results were minimal from the American standpoint, as very few Japanese aircraft were stationed there.*][15]

Sunday, 2 April 1944. Fair. A great force was reported at 270 miles south of Tinian Island last evening, but later it proved a false report, having mistaken friendly ships [for hostile ones]. Nothing else has been heard about the enemy since yesterday. I think it's about time for them to withdraw as they recklessly attacked all over as they liked.

[*Ugaki was correct. The carrier groups that attacked Woleai on 1 April had retired and on 6 April entered the harbor at Majuro.*][16]

I've been worrying about *Musashi* a great deal. Her captain's report came in today. A torpedo struck her on her port side beam No. 27, six meters under the water line. A hole extending beam Nos. 12–40 was inflicted, while all of the windlass machineries were rendered inoperable, with minor damage to others.

After the Combined Fleet headquarters left Palau on board flying boats, nothing was heard at Saipan about their arrival. In addition, the alert hasn't yet been cleared, although the enemy retreated. Also, telegrams were received advising of the nonarrival of the flying boats. All these added up to my deepest worry this evening, when the following dreadful news came in:

Issued at 2150 of the 1st by [Commander Chikataka] Nakajima, Combined Fleet staff officer. Type II flying boats, one each from the 802nd and 851st air groups, with commander in chief, Combined Fleet and most of his staff aboard, left Palau at 2200 the 31st for Davao, but have not yet arrived at the destination as of 0955. 802nd Air Group's flying boat (chief of staff on board) made a forced landing off Fernando to the southeast of Cebu at 0300. It was destroyed and burned, with the fate of passengers unknown except that of crew. Ask to relay this to vice chief of staff, Combined Fleet, from headquarters, Fourth Southern Expeditionary Fleet. Addressed to the navy minister, chief of Naval General Staff.

Today the vice chief of the Naval General Staff requested the commander in chief, Southwest Area Fleet, to take command of the Combined Fleet for the time being and let commander in chief, Central Pacific Fleet, take command of all fleets other than the Southwest Area Fleet and Northeast Area Fleet.

What rotten luck at a critical time like this! It looks like God is testing the Imperial Navy. As I've had a similar experience, having already been through the death line, it doesn't affect me so much. But its effect upon the general public will be tremendous.

I hope that the commander in chief's plane managed to land somewhere and he's safe on one of the isles. However, the fate of Fukudome, his chief of staff, seems to be hopeless. He was one of the most intimate friends among our classmates. He has followed me successively as chief of the Operations Bureau and chief of staff, Combined Fleet. His death should be called a great loss to the nation. April seems to be a bad month.

The commander in chief, Northeast Area Fleet, alerted the Kurile Island district. This was said to be because radio intelligence picked up brisk enemy activities in that district, and enemy reconnaissance by a plane and a submarine was made at Kakumabetsu Island. Getting busy both in north and south.

Monday, 3 April 1944. Partly fair. At 1005, all hands on deck to pay respects on the memorial day for the Emperor Jimmu. I brooded over the troubles and hardships he had to overcome during his subjugation of eastern Japan, comparing them to the present situation.

The enemy task force has withdrawn, and it will be some time before it comes back again. At this moment it's considered necessary to release the Second Mobile Force from short-notice readiness to finish the docking of *Nagato* and *Fuso* as soon as possible and train to increase its fighting ability. So since last night I've pushed them to hurry their preparations for docking. In the morning I received an order from the commander in chief, task fleet, that cancelled "Force Disposition Otsu" and "Notice to sail." At the same time, he ordered the Seventh Heavy Cruiser Division to return to Singapore and also the 601st Air Group to concentrate at Singapore.

On the other hand, the commander in chief, Southwest Area Fleet, taking command of the Combined Fleet, has ordered this *Asahi* force to proceed to the southern part of the Philippines by the 20th. The chief of staff, task fleet, notified us to fix the date of sailing as the 15th.

Tuesday, 4 April 1944. Fair. Preparations to dock were made, and unloading fuel oil took considerable time. At 1000 shoved off the wharf and docked. This is the first time a battleship ever docked here, and those concerned with both the harbormaster and the yard did their utmost.

To which direction the enemy task force of the other day withdrew couldn't be determined, so the chief of the Naval General Staff, thinking that there might be a possibility of their being in the sea south of Japan, instructed naval stations and fleets to carry out searches for them on both the 4th and 5th. But I think that they are not there, and instead have gone south, intending to come back again later. [*As previously noted, Ugaki's estimate was correct.*] Upon my suggestion, both the General Staff and the local authorities have become much concerned about the status of Tawi Tawi advance base. The Second Fleet also is coming down to Lingga for consultation and training since it considers it unwise to stay longer at Davao.

We had a party with the staff officers tonight at a restaurant ashore. We brought our own sake with us, as only watery beer was available on shore. I returned on board at 2300.

Wednesday, 5 April 1944. Fair. *Nagato's* repair is going well, and she'll be out of the dock by the 13th after changing the lignum vitae.

CV *Taiho* arrived from home waters bringing mail. I got letters for the first time since coming on board this ship. Though I came on board only recently, I was told that it was the first time for others to receive mail since the end of January.

[The next week was almost entirely routine for Ugaki. On Tuesday the 6th he went shooting but bagged nothing but a pigeon. The next day he had a rather sad encounter with a former classmate, currently skipper of the tanker *Kyokuto Maru*. He explained that those of their class who had not reached flag rank had been retired, then recalled to duty to command such ships as transports, "thus meeting their sad fate." Saturday the 8th found Ugaki trying his luck again, this time with the engineer staff officer, and they got ten pigeons between them. These birds formed the *pièce de résistance* at Sunday's dinner. Monday the 10th he invited two ship captains to a restaurant and on Tuesday and Wednesday again went shooting.]

Thursday, 13 April 1944. Fair. At 0830 *Nagato* left the dock and *Fuso* entered the dock. The docking business seems to be quite flourishing.

According to yesterday's telegram from a Third Southern Expeditionary Fleet staff officer, army units are still fighting on Cebu Island, but the survivors of the accident Otsu (that of headquarters, Combined Fleet), nine in all, have been brought down the hill, and Vice Admiral Fukudome and others are safe. This must be really a miracle. Those for whom we had given up hope are still alive and brought down safe! Congratulations to them.

[On Friday, 14 April, Ugaki and his staff vacated their shore quarters, saying farewell "to the commander in chief and others." He wondered when and if he would see them again. This would be his first night on shipboard "after a pretty long time."]

Early this morning, the Berbara watch post reported the passing of a submarine, and Lingga units have been quite alerted. As *Nagato* is going there tomorrow and it takes so much time to communicate, I made an inquiry in advance.

Saturday, 15 April 1944. Fair. Sailing to Lingga. This morning the Tenth Destroyer Squadron asked my permission to load 150 depth charges. In spite of much hurry, we were delayed about two and a half hours behind schedule. *Nagato* sailed out of Seleter at 1225 and, sailing at a speed of 18 knots, arrived at Lingga at 1725. On the way we met *I-166* going north.

The anchorage has become very brisk, with the Fourth and Fifth Heavy Cruiser Divisions, *Taiho,* and others joining. After sunset I called on the commander in chief, Second Fleet, Kurita, aboard *Atago* and had a talk with him and his chief of staff. I was told that the vice chief, Naval General Staff, came here for a short while yesterday and left for Singapore after visiting headquarters, task fleet.

The details of the accident Otsu were not yet made quite clear, but Admiral Soemu Toyoda, commander in chief, Yokosuka Naval Base, was appointed commander in chief, Combined Fleet, and Rear Admiral Ryunosuke Kusaka, chief of staff, Southeast Area Fleet, his chief of staff. Now that Vice Admiral Fukudome has been found to be alive, Kusaka will need a new assignment. Should headquarters, Combined Fleet, function from Tokyo from now on?

Regarding the submarine fuss since yesterday, a reconnaissance seaplane reportedly sighted a submerged submarine eleven miles south of Rusu-kubuya and bombed it. It went north trailing oil under half-submerged conditions and a destroyer depth-charted it. It was also reported that attacks still continued today, floating oil being sighted at the same spot. A report also said that sweeping caught something like a submarine, and an order to try to get important documents from it was intercepted. As it turned out, however, it was nothing but a sunken vessel drifting with a 2-knots current, which they mistook for a submerged submarine. This is the low-down. It's always the same—foolish stories that annoy us. But can't such be helped with different men at different places under differ-ent circumstances?

Sunday, 16 April 1944. Rain, later fair. The wind started to blow before dawn, and the rain came. It's a disadvantage of this anchorage that it develops fairly big waves when the wind blows from the south. Most of the ships were out participating in aerial battle practice, but *Nagato* remained to dispose of things transported for others.

Commander Arima, an operations staff officer of the task fleet, came to see me and I told him my views on impending operations as follows:

The operational policies of both the Combined Fleet and the First Task

Fleet are not bad, but their past operations were not executed in accordance with them. The present status is such that, when those policies are followed, in most cases they result in our defeat because we haven't sufficient strength. If something is insufficient, an impending operation must be planned based on this condition—we must definitely decide how to cope with the present operational situation and carry it through. We must not go on without a prospect of success inspired by idealism.

In order to turn the extremely unfavorable tide of the war situation today, we must seek to replenish our air power by all means. The number of planes the First Air Fleet (land-based) possesses amounts to only 250 against the expected number of 700. In addition, they haven't been sufficiently trained. [*According to its senior staff officer, Commander Mitsuo Fuchida, the land-based First Air Fleet, under the command of Admiral Kakuta, was committed prematurely after the U.S. carrier raid on Truk in February 1944. It established headquarters on Tinian on 20 February and took a fearful beating from Vice Admiral Marc A. Mitscher's carrier aircraft on 23 February.*][17] Though those planes of the task fleet are undergoing hard training day and night, they're still bothered by successive accidents in landing on and taking off the carriers; therefore, it will probably be some time before they can be available for task force duty at sea.

Furthermore, neither the fleet advance bases at Tawi Tawi nor those at Gimaras are completely prepared. And with only four tankers available for the task fleet, it's almost impossible for the fleet to make any attack or other moves; the only possible consequence is to become an easy prey to enemy planes and submarines. The further we venture out, the more we shall be beaten. It's like one can't help getting soaked if one goes out in the rain without a coat or umbrella.

It's essential never to be led on by the enemy's initiatives, rationalizing that it's not our turn and just remain quiet until our turn comes when we'll be ready again. Certainly the general trend advocates that we be passive, but if so we must take advantage of the merit of passivity. It's an advantage of passive controls.

Enemy air raids will be intense and frequent, but when we expect and prepare for them our damage won't be so great. (As they lacked preparedness and resolution, they suffered such a miserable loss at Palau Island.) [*Ugaki referred to the attack on Palau of 30–31 March by Task Force 58, in which the Japanese lost thirty-six miscellaneous ships.*][18] In the meantime, various preparations will be promoted to wait for an enemy to come into a certain area. Thus, a definite plan of how to destroy the enemy once he gets in this area will be established, and all forces should encounter the enemy with this conviction and determination. In order to do this, the deficiency of our reconnaissance and patrol, constituting the basic defect of our forces, must be remedied so as to get a clear picture of the enemy situation at all times, thus avoiding being tricked in trying to trick him.

Also essential are freely interchangeable planes as well as free concentration and movement of air forces. For this purpose, properly controlled preparations of men and materials must be established at every base. In other words, preparations must be made to make full use of land-based air forces together with carrier-borne air forces at the designated defense front.

Now we have only thirty-six submarines in the Sixth Fleet. In connection with this, some are suggesting that its headquarters should be withdrawn to the Inland Sea, since it's no longer possible for it to stay in Truk. However, look how vainly they have been employed, after having been sent to the east or to the west as they saw some possibility of enemy onslaught, only to be completely exhausted! A steadier and more efficient method of using them must be found.

While the general trend indicates our passivity by encountering an enemy in a designated area, we must always study, plan, and execute attempts to diminish enemy strength or disturb and intercept enemy attempts, as long as our own loss is tolerable. We must never sit idle doing nothing, only blaming the shortage of air power.

The night raid on Brown (Eniwetok Atoll) and the attack upon Admiralty were all very good. It's no use getting impatient when one is out of luck. When one awaits a favorable turn of events after preparing for it, everything will come out all right again. One mustn't cut off an opening bud of good luck after being dragged down by local affairs.

[On Monday, 17 April, Ugaki went hunting again, but he and his comrades found only "two sets of wild boar's trails" and snipe which "seemed to be the world champions for getting away." Reminding himself that the next day would be "the anniversary of the day I was supposed to have died," perhaps it was only natural that he could not "kill anything on the eve of the Buddhist ritual." Back aboard *Nagato*, on her deck, he looked up "at the galaxy of stars in the sky" and "was reminded of the enormous expanse of the universe and the smallness of human beings whose affairs are certainly much smaller than a tempest in a teacup."

[At midnight there was another submarine report, but it could not be confirmed. Ugaki had his ideas about repairing *Musashi's* damage and increasing her antiaircraft fire, but since the fleet intended to concentrate all forces by 10 May, he "decided to end the work on 5 May and sent a signal to that effect to the task fleet headquarters."]

Tuesday, 18 April 1944. Fair. [*This is a special entry giving Ugaki's recollections of the events of 18 April 1943, when Yamamoto was killed and Ugaki* *wounded. The regular entry for 18 April 1944 follows.*] The first anniversary of the tragic event came to greet me on board a battleship. As usual, I went up on the weather deck after saluting their majesties' portraits in my cabin. Facing the rising sun, I prayed for the souls of Admiral Yamamoto and six others who were killed on this day last year and pledged myself to revenge them.

I dictated all the entries in my diary for six months since that day. Specifically, those portions up to my hospitalization were written by Ensign Ebima, to whom I dictated. At that time I dictated only the outline, intending to supplement it some time later. But so far I have failed to do so. On this day of the first anniversary, I'm going to write the account in more detail, retracing my memories.

PREFACE

1. The course of events leading to the advance of the Combined Fleet command to Rabaul and the inspection trip is omitted here, as I dictated it upon my return to the homeland after the event and submitted it to the vice chief of the Naval General Staff and vice minister of the navy.

2. The aerial offensive with the carrier air strengths of the Third Fleet and the land-based air force had been completed with a great result after about two weeks' operations. The Eighteenth Army commander, who had returned from an inspection tour of the New Guinea front, also presented a favorable view that if another battalion could be sent there, we would be able to hold on there. So we, from the commander in chief on down, felt somewhat relieved, though not entirely. And we intended to inspect future important points and the front line to encourage our men and also pay our debts by visiting the Seventeenth Army Command at Shortland before returning to Truk.

3. With regard to maintaining alert, I, as chief of staff, had taken every step possible, so I had nothing to worry about, leaving it to the local command.

4. Before we left Truk for Rabaul, it was decided to take along only those concerned with the operation, as we were temporarily moving our command post to Rabaul. I told the fleet engineer, surgeon, and paymaster not to come this time because accommodations there wouldn't be sufficient.

So I was surprised when the fleet adjutant reported the arrival of the fleet surgeon and paymaster on the day I contracted dengue fever around the 13th. Since they had already come over, I could do nothing about it, so I left the matter without interfering. Only the fleet engineer, who seemed to have a little cold, didn't come down, respecting my words. He said he wouldn't come as long as he wasn't needed for operational reasons.

On the trip to Shortland, it was decided to accompany only the necessary staff officers in two medium torpedo bombers. Though I repeatedly asked the fleet adjutant who was going with us, his answer was vague, except that he asked my approval for two other officers to be taken aboard the same plane. The fleet adjutant had been suffering from dengue fever at that time. He was so sick that Admiral Yamamoto told him in a car that he had better not come, as other staff officers were coming.

5. In a car the day before the event, a discussion centered on whether white open-neck shirts might be worn during the trip. The general opinion seemed to favor wearing them. But I asserted that it wouldn't be very hot, as we were going to go and return by plane, and, moreover, it wouldn't be proper for the commander in chief of the Combined Fleet and his staff officers to visit officers and men at the front wearing unofficial uniforms. After we got back to the billet, therefore, I had the fleet adjutant telephone them to wear the regular khaki shirts during the trip.

I further told him to arrange for a snapshot of the commander in chief in khaki uniform as he might not have a chance of wearing it again. But this failed to materialize. Consequently, the last picture was the one taken with the commander in chief, Mikawa, and others on the occasion of our visit to the Eighth Fleet Command on the day after we arrived at Rabaul. Others were only those taken by press photographers when he [Yamamoto] was seeing off departing planes.

6. As I had made up my mind to inspect the front line, I prepared a khaki uniform, boots, and a pair of leather leggings before the trip. But the commander in chief and others decided to wear airmen's boots. On the morning of leaving the ship, after contemplation, I changed my mind and had the same kind of boots on as the others did. They were easy to put on and off and quite comfortable. And that fact eventually turned out to help me survive.

NARRATIVE

1. As we were going to take off at 0600, I got up earlier than usual. The sky was quite clear and the early birds sang pleasantly in the trees. I ate breakfast at about 0530 and prepared for the trip. In khaki uniform, I looked gallant. As we were slated to come back on the same day, I brought only a pocket diary, spectacles, cigarettes, and handkerchiefs in my pockets.

2. We left the billet at 0550. I saw the commander in chief in khaki uniform for the first time. It suited him fairly well, but looked a bit strange, perhaps because we were not accustomed to seeing him in such uniform. I myself might have been more so, but I thought I looked all right. We reached the east airfield at 0600.

Then, both air staff officers and others who were to accompany us came from the direction of the field post. I noticed two among them in white uniform. While I wondered what this was all about, eventually they turned out to be the fleet surgeon and paymaster. Though the commander in chief thought it rather awkward, too, we couldn't do anything then. We left the car and got on the planes immediately. Since I followed the commander in chief and proceeded to the second plane, I didn't talk to them.

The first medium torpedo bomber: the commander in chief, the Adjutant [Commander Noboru] Fukuzaki, Fleet Surgeon [Rear Admiral Rokuro] Takata, Staff Officer Toibana.

The second medium torpedo bomber: the chief of staff, Fleet Paymaster [Captain Gen] Kitamura, staff officers [Commander Kaoru] Imanaka, Muroi, and Weather Officer [Commander Jyunji] Unno.

3. After we enplaned, the communications staff and the weather officers greeted me. I sat on the skipper's seat. I took off my sword, leaving the belt on, and handed it to Staff Officer Muroi, who put it behind out of the way. Both planes then started to roar, taxied to the end of the runway, and took off in the order of first and second plane. Looking down on the volcano at the mouth of the bay, the planes flew in formation heading south-southeast.

The weather was fine, visibility good. From time to time three fighters each were seen escorting to the right and left in the rear above. I remember our altitude was about 1,500 meters.

4. The second plane was flying in tandem with the first aircraft at its left side rear in perfect formation, so I feared their wing tips might touch. I could clearly see the profile of the commander in chief in the skipper's seat and other people moving in the first plane. I enjoyed a pleasant flight as I followed the explanation of the topography down below with an aviation map.

5. When we reached the west side of Bougainville and were passing straight over the jungle with altitude lowered to seven hundred or eight hundred meters, the skipper handed me a piece of paper on which was written, "Expect to arrive at Balale at 0745." I looked at my wrist watch; it was just 0730 and I thought it would be fifteen minutes more before we landed.

At this point the plane suddenly started to dive, following the first plane, and went down to fifty meters. We all wondered what happened! I asked the skipper, an air warrant officer, who was in the passage, "What's the matter?" "May be some mistake," he answered. But it was a great mistake to say so and he was most careless.

One of our fighters flying over us had sighted a group of twenty-four enemy fighters coming after turning back from their southward flight. While it was coming down to warn the medium bombers, our first plane also found the enemy and lost no time in diving to the level of the jungle treetops. This was learned later. Then for the first time the crews took up combat stations and opened gun ports to prepare for firing. It got noisy for a while with the handling of machine guns and the wind blowing in.

6. By the time we lowered altitude to treetop level, air combat had already been in progress between our escorting fighters and the enemy. Four times as many as our fighters, the enemy planes bore down mercilessly upon the bigger game of the two bombers. We made a quick turn of over 90° to evade them. Watching the sky above and noticing an enemy plane charging in, the skipper tapped the chief pilot's shoulder and directed him to turn left or right.

The first aircraft turned to the right and the second to the left. The distance between them increased.

After we had evaded about twice, I turned to the right to see how the first plane was evading. What I saw then was astounding. Lo! The first plane was staggering southward, just brushing the jungle top with reduced speed, emitting black smoke and flame. It was about four thousand meters away from us. I just said to myself, "My God!" I could think of nothing else. I grabbed the shoulder of Air Staff Officer Muroi, pointed to the first aircraft, and said, "Look at the commander in chief's plane!" This became my parting with him forever. All this happened in only about twenty seconds.

In the meantime, my plane turned again sharply to evade another enemy attack, and we lost sight of the commander in chief's aircraft. I waited impatiently for the plane to get back to the level while full of anxiety, though the result seemed apparent. The next glance revealed that the plane was no more to be seen, only a pall of black smoke rising to the sky from the jungle. Oh! Everything was over now!

7. At that moment our bomber was heading toward the direction of Cape Moira at full speed and soon came out over the sea. Enemy attacks were at first concentrated on the first plane. Looking back, I could see dogfights still going on.

Making a rising half-turn and then a quick turn, a P-38 came upon us at last. Here he comes! Our machine gun opened fire upon him desperately. Though it worked well, it didn't seem to hit him. The enemy P-38 rapidly closed in, taking advantage of his superior speed. His gunfire caught us splendidly, and oncoming bullets were seen on both sides of our plane. I felt them hitting our aircraft from time to time. Now we were hopeless, and I thought my end was very near at hand.

The sound of our machine-gun fire was reduced by this time, and the skipper could not be heard any more. I thought quite a number must have been killed in the plane.

Staff Officer Muroi was leaning on a table with his face down and arms outstretched. He must have already been killed. The paymaster later revealed this.

8. The chief pilot sitting in front of me felt bullets hitting the right wing and tried to get down to sea level with a down rudder in preparation for a crash landing. At this moment, our fighter above was said to notice our second plane also trailing dark smoke.

When the bomber was near the sea surface, the pilot lost control. He pulled back all the throttles at once, but it was no use. The ship ditched into the sea at full speed and rolled over to the left by more than 90°.

9. Preparing for an emergency, in case of either being shot down or making a crash landing, I had stiffened my limbs, so I didn't feel hurt by the impact. But when the ship crashed on the sea I was thrown off the skipper's seat and landed in the passage. I think I must have gotten most of my wounds at that moment.

Everything went black and I felt the sea water rushing all over my body with fair pressure. I could do absolutely nothing. I told myself, "This is the end of Ugaki." Since I thought all was over, my mind was a blank. I don't think I struggled or made any impatient effort, but that wasn't clear anyway. (I can't think I became unconscious; I didn't swallow any water. I suppose it must have been only a few seconds until the next moment.)

Right after I gave it all up, all of a sudden it lightened. When I opened my eyes, incredibly I found myself floating on the sea surface. What a miracle! The fuselage had already disappeared and the right wing was standing upside down in the sea right behind me and was still burning fiercely. I couldn't see any men around.

I thought it extremely dangerous to stay there. It was less than two hundred meters to the beach and, although I felt somewhat strange all over my body, I thought I could reach shore somehow. And I made up my mind to swim. But I warned myself that I shouldn't exhaust my strength by too much exertion; I wasn't young anymore.

10. I didn't have a cap on my head then and unknown to me the right boot had come off. As the remaining left boot was troublesome, I kicked in the water and it came off easily. My left leg usually got cramps and I often suffered from it when I was playing deck billiards or while hunting ashore. It was really sheer luck that it didn't happen then. Having rid myself of all this trouble, I now calmly swam with breast strokes toward the shore. I looked back from time to time; the plane continued burning. Nobody could be seen there, however. I felt I was the only survivor.

11. When I had advanced about seventy or eighty meters, I saw boxes

come floating toward me. Two of them were small and had a rough surface, while another was painted gray and actually was a gear locker. All of these must have come out of the plane. This was a heaven-sent rescue boat. I thought the bigger one would be better, so I grabbed the gray box with my right hand. But my right hand didn't work. I found it to be hanging from its wrist and blood was dripping. For the first time I realized that my right wrist was broken. Thinking the right hand wasn't enough, I put my left hand on the box, too. Whereupon, I had to propel myself only by legs.

Just then I found one of the crew members with a flying cap on swimming energetically before me, so I called to him "Hey!" in a medium voice. He turned around and noticed me, but kept on swimming toward the beach.

Now that I had hold of the box, I had enough freedom of mind to look around. I saw the wing still burning, but the rest had disappeared. I suppose a rapid current carried it away.

12. As I approached the shore, the current became stronger, seeming to be more than 2 knots. I was drifting with the current more than by pushing the box only by propelling with my legs. The tree I had chosen for a target passed at an angle. But I thought I had no need to hurry. If there was a current I could take advantage of it and should be able to reach shore sometime. I was enveloped in tranquility; I even felt like humming a song.

Meanwhile, four men looking like soldiers came running from the direction of Cape Moira along the boundary between the jungle and the sandy beach. I heard two rifle shots. My eyes seemed hazy and I couldn't distinguish clearly, but they must have been friendly ones as this was our occupied zone.

Thinking that if they were enemies I had no choice but to sink forever, I stared for a while. The crew member who swam preceding me then reached shore and they met him. He seemed to be telling them about me, pointing toward the sea. (I asked them about their behavior after I had recovered, but they remained silent. They seemed to be guards or captors for shot-down enemy fliers. As they didn't know anything about our planes, it might have been a proper step.)

13. One of the men took off his clothes leisurely, got into the water, and approached me. When he came about ten meters from me, he seemed to notice my aiguillette and shouted to the shore in a wild cry, "He's a staff officer!"

The man, who hitherto had approached cautiously, suddenly got lively and pushed my body. "Wait! I'm wounded. Push this box!" I told him, and he obeyed. Meanwhile, another man got into the sea and helped me reach shore.

14. Both planes ended in tragedies and the commander in chief and many capable staff officers were lost. I was the only survivor. Though I felt an urgent need to make contact with our friendly force as soon as possible, I couldn't help squatting down on the beach to rest for a while.

They told me it was only a fifteen minutes' walk to the barracks, so I stood up and started to walk on the sun-scorched sandy beach in drenched clothes without a cap, supported by them. I was feeling faint from the heat and fatigue when they brought a wooden door just in time. I was carried on this to a tin-roofed barracks in the shade of trees. I had my sleeve ripped open, exposing my right arm, and lay on a bed. I received first aid from an army medical orderly, who put a splint on my right hand. His treatment was quite proper.

While I was being treated, I ordered them to telephone the commander, First Base Force, and tell him that "report of this accident should be made by confidential telegram and be restricted as much as possible. This is from the chief of staff."

The chief pilot had only a little scratch on his head. When he came back after reporting the situation by telephone, I sent him again to the beach to confirm the position of the wreck in order to facilitate the future search for missing persons.

15. After first aid was completed, I felt thirsty. Though they said the water wasn't fit to drink, they brought something for me to drink. And it tasted just wonderful! Then I asked them for a cigarette; they lit some cheap brand and handed it to me. Being the first one since I left Rabaul, it tasted grand, too. I didn't care what brand it was!

I thought the chief pilot was the only survivor besides myself, but about this time someone told me the paymaster was alive, too. As to his wounds, I was told that both his eyes were blinded and he had a big hole in his throat. While I was thinking that his must be serious wounds, he was brought in beside me.

I couldn't get up, so I called to him from my bed, "Paymaster!" He only groaned "Oh!" I called to him again, "Pull yourself together!" Again he only groaned "Oh!" He was very downhearted. I even feared he might die if he bled too much.

16. The first report of this incident was made by one of the escorting fighters that developed engine trouble and landed at Balale or Buin. It claimed to have shot down several enemy planes. Then a report from Cape Moira apparently came in by telephone. The Base Force commander was at Balale base to greet the commander in chief and his entourage. The Base Force command immediately sent the chief surgeon and others to Cape Moira by a subchaser. They arrived there about forty or fifty minutes after

my emergency treatment. They properly treated my whole body. I was very grateful for their prompt assistance.

I asked them to take care of the paymaster first, but they started with me after all. While they were attending the paymaster after finishing with me, I asked the surgeon about his condition. Hearing that "neither eyes nor throat was anything serious," I was quite relieved.

17. On the other hand, the search for the plane wreck seemed to have started by this time, but I didn't know about the details.

My temporary treatment finished, I was put on a stretcher after a little rest and moved to a motor launch, which took me to a subchaser. The glaring sun shone overhead. Every time I was moved to another place, men peered at my face. Everybody seemed to be curious.

The subchaser went alongside a jetty in front of the Base Force command and then I was moved into an ambulance. Here I met [Captain Akira] Itagaki, the commander, Base Force, for the first time through the car window. I was moved to a small wooden room where I dressed in a hospital robe. Up to that time I wore nothing but a white cloth spread over my body.

After the broken part of my right hand was photographed with a portable X-ray apparatus, I was moved to the Base Force command. I got in the ambulance again and was placed on a collapsible bed in an officer's room in a coconut grove. As malaria was prevalent, I had to have a green mosquito net even in daytime.

The Base Group commander came and assured me that all efforts were being made to recover and search for both planes. He also urged me to go back to Rabaul for my treatment as well as to take care of various affairs concerning the incident. But I replied as follows:

> Necessary steps will be taken care of by the senior staff officer who remains there and also the Southeast Area Fleet command. I can't bear to return alone without settling affairs here after the incident, as I accompanied the commander in chief. So I shall stay here to await reports of rescue, though it may trouble you. Furthermore, I wish you to arrange to get my approval on any dispatch regarding the accident before it's sent out.

I received various shots this night. I had no appetite except for fruits.

18. My wounds were found to be as follows: four scratches on the top and back of the head; a small bruise in the left eye and the area around it was swollen; many bruises in the upper right part and around the mouth and clots of blood in spots on the face; some abrasions in the back and hip; right forearm sprained and compound fracture; some bruises on the left

shin; second rib from the bottom in the left back was broken (found after reaching the homeland).

Though I had so many as listed above, none proved fatal. How lucky I was!

EPILOGUE

1. During the same day, a search plane confirmed the point where the first plane crashed. It reported the burning of the aircraft, but saw no one around the wreck. A native swiftly reported the crashing of a plane to an army unit that was building a road on the west coast of Bougainville. The army at once dispatched a rescue party which reached the spot the next day. They recovered the bodies prior to the arrival of a naval team, which met the former on its way back.

The body of the commander in chief was found on the seat outside of the plane, still gripping his sword. It hadn't decomposed yet and was said to be in a state of great dignity. He must really have been superhuman.

A postmortem made while his body was being carried on a subchaser found two piercing machine-gun bullet wounds in his lower jaw and shoulder. Most probably he was killed instantly while in the air. The remains of the fleet surgeon were recognizable as his body was only half burned, but all the rest were difficult to identify as they were burned and decomposed.

The spot where the second plane crashed was about twenty meters deep. In spite of all efforts by divers, only wheels, motor, propeller, machine gun, and a sword were found scattered around, but not the fuselage itself. Two crew members' bodies washed up on the beach the next day and the day after.

2. Among those on both planes, the survivors were only myself, the paymaster, and the chief pilot of the second aircraft. Altogether twenty lives, including the commander in chief, staff officers, and the crew members were sacrificed. Though such was usual in war, it was in a way my fault, too.

According to what I heard afterwards, the enemy had employed fighter formations in its morning reconnaissance of that area since a few days before. It was quite a change compared with the enemy's past activities, but the report reached the Southeast Area Fleet as a summary report on the day after the incident took place. That was too late.

Had the report reached us in time, we could have called off the trip or changed its schedule and provided powerful escorts. Or we could have taken refuge in case of an enemy contact by maintaining close contact with the destination base. We should have thought of all these [things], as the trip was decided only with all deliberation. I can never cease to regret.

The enemy planes sighted us and turned back to attack us while they were already on their way south. Had there been a few minutes' difference, we would never have met with such an incident, and everything would have gone all right. It was just a turn of fate.

[*Of course, it was nothing of the sort. It is interesting to note that a full year after the incident, Ugaki still had no inkling that the American attack was a trap based on radio intelligence. He attributed it to sheer luck.*][19]

At the same time it's always essential to think of unexpected things that can take place in war, and we should always maintain a stricter alert than necessary.

3. The chief pilot had good reason to be saved. The paymaster was sitting at the work desk on the other side of me. Though he was hurt in his face with his spectacles, he should have been able to escape through the upper window when the ship rolled over to the left.

But as to myself, there was no clue to show how I could have been saved. Seeing that everything went black after I fell into the passage, I must have slid forward as far as under the pilot's seat. How I got out of danger can't be explained. Such aviation experts as air staff officers of the air fleet thought that the fore part of the plane must have broken open upon impact with the water and the opening happened to face outward, through which I might have been pushed out.

I wasn't hit by an enemy bullet in the air, and when the plane hit the water I rose to the surface from the worst situation without any effort. If this is not to be called a work of God, what else can it be? If and when I had been hit in vital parts when the ship crashed, it would have meant the end of my life. All the wounds were off the vital parts and not serious. That I wore airmen's Wellington half-boots instead of boots and leather leggings, that I handed over my sword soon after I boarded the plane, that I didn't get cramps when I got rid of the left boot, that the boxes came floating in front of me while I was swimming, that the spot where we crashed was in our occupied zone so that our force was garrisoned nearby, that the chief pilot reached shore ahead of me, that I could get first aid from the army medical orderly right after I was rescued, that I was given prompt and proper treatment by the chief surgeon of the Base Force, who was a great surgical specialist from my native place, and also that my right arm was able to be put in a clay cast three days after the incident took place—all these were a series of good luck I was given. I couldn't but think that God must have done everything he could to save me.

Contrary to my determination to sacrifice myself for the commander in chief, instead I lost him and survived. It was a completely unexpected event. I should be resigned to my fate, deeming it God's will, and do my best to live and serve to repay God by carrying out revenge.

Tuesday, 18 April 1944. Fair. [*Here the chronological diary resumes.*] The day on which I should have died has come round again aboard a warship at the front. After getting up, I paid my respects in front of His Majesty's portrait as usual and went up on deck. Then, observing the rising sun sideways to the right, I prayed for the departed souls of Fleet Admiral Yamamoto and the staff officers who died with him and pledged to revenge them.

Today last year the war situation didn't seem as bad as it does now! Last year we had to evacuate our forces from Guadalcanal, yet we could place the rest of the Solomons under our control, and we were convinced of holding the south of Lae and Salamaua for a considerable period.

As the days passed, however, the enemy's counteroffensive grew more and more furious. When I look back and think of our lost territories and the losses so far sustained, I can't but be surprised at the quick change that has taken place in the last months. The enemy has also been building themselves up, and the chief of Naval Operations said on the 15th that the personnel and materials of the U.S. Navy had reached their peak for the first time since the outbreak of the war, and the Japanese Navy would be made to realize it in a few months. This morning ten and twenty large-type planes raided Saipan and Meleyon [Woleai], respectively. Brisk activities of long-range planes are a sign of impending operations of brisk task forces and invasion forces.

[*Ugaki's foreboding was justified. In March the United States had set the target date to begin the invasion of Saipan as 15 June 1944*][20]

Time is running out for a once-for-all showdown. Even if we can inflict a certain amount of damage on the enemy by staking everything we have, our own strength will be a good deal exhausted. We must calculate how soon he can replenish his strength against our capacity to recover, but we must bear in mind "nothing ventured, nothing gained." Moreover, our doing nothing will only make the enemy swell-headed.

However, it seems to me that we are well absorbed in improving the fighting strength of individual ships only and have no room for studying how to improve the fighting ability of a fleet as a unit. It makes me shudder to wonder if we could successfully carry out the decisive battle, staking the fate of the empire in this way. So I have had my staff submit a suggestion to fleet headquarters.

Wednesday, 19 April 1944. Fair. A few dozen enemy fighters and carrier-borne bombers raided Kuta Raja and Sabang at the northern tip of Sumatra this morning, and an alert was issued for the Western Force. It was surmised that they came from British carriers, but that couldn't be confirmed. Air Defense Second Station was ordered at Lingga for an enemy attack coming from the south of Sumatra.

At another theater, an army plane sighted two groups centering around two converted carriers and accompanying transports to the south of Meleyon (West Caroline Islands). Whether they are going to the northern coast of New Guinea we can't tell. [*This was probably a portion of Task Force 58 which sortied from Majuro on 13 April for the projected assault on Hollandia.*][21]

Nothing has been heard about enemy task forces. But I think there is much fear of their coming to the central part of the Marianas from the east prior to their full-fledged offensive. Against this possibility, our present air strength on the eastern front totals only 250 planes, to my great horror.

It isn't hard to guess that the next enemy offensive will be made on a great and full scale. The attack on Sumatra must have been a coordinated operation from east and west. The day for the showdown is approaching quickly, and yet we can't be completely ready for it at this pace.

[On the morning of 20 April, the fleet was placed on air defense alert. That afternoon Ugaki attended a meeting aboard *Taiho* to study the Fourth and Fifth Aerial Warfare Practice. Later they saw "an American film concerning a study of aerophysiology taken at San Diego Base." Ugaki thought the Technicolor photography beautiful but could not understand the dialogue.]

A reconnaissance plane from Palau sighted an enemy task force consisting of four carriers, eight cruisers, and ten destroyers at a point five hundred miles to the southeast, its course being 290°, speed 16 knots. [*It isn't clear whether the sighting was of TG 58.1, TG 58.2 or 58.3, each of which had four carriers with their support vessels.*][22]

[On Friday *Nagato* participated in aerial warfare practice, and she had trouble maintaining the speed of 24 knots. "As a precaution against an air raid, the whole fleet entered Anchorage No. 3 to the north."]

Though no definite information on the enemy has been obtained by today's search, commander in chief, Combined Fleet, ordered "Stand by for Operation Z-1" at 0100 today. At 0430 various kinds of enemy fighters raided Wakde on New Guinea, and the Combined Fleet ordered the "start" of Operation Z-1 at 1624.

Saturday, 22 April 1944. Fair, later squall. War situation: At 1700 yesterday off Hollandia, four carriers, two cruisers, twenty destroyers. At 0500 the 22nd, at Aitape Bay, two cruisers, ten destroyers, and many transports.

It seems that the enemy landed at Hollandia after inflicting considerable damage there.

Air reconnaissance report by submarine *I-6:* at Majuro, three battle-ships, eleven carriers, three merchant ships, and two others.

Expecting a possibility that an enemy might make a leap, landing at Geelvink Bay, Combined Fleet ordered the 601st Air Group of the task fleet to prepare for sortie from Kendari.

Sunday, 23 April 1944. Fair. In the evening a movie was shown after a long time, and the men were very much pleased.

War situation:

1. At 0400 large-type vessels, including carriers and battleships, etc., ten in all, and fifty other vessels were passing west at the eastern tip of Wewak. (Army plane's report).

2. At 1720 four carriers and others were at a point twenty miles bearing 310° from Hollandia heading northeast. (Reconnaissance plane).

3. Following the above, three carriers, two battleships, five cruisers, approximately ten destroyers were sighted at a point sixty miles bearing 10° from Wakde Island. (Reconnaissance plane). The enemy reported in No. 1 seems to be different from those in No. 2 and No. 3. I wonder how we are going to deal with them?

Monday, 24 April 1944. Fair. A conference to study *Nagato*'s past train-ing was held from 1000 and continued until 1800.

The Combined Fleet has issued successive orders against the enemy to the north of New Guinea. But only a few planes sortied; about a dozen land-based medium bombers which went out to attack could not attack at dusk on account of poor contact with shadowing planes. All noise and nothing done!

The swiftness of the enemy offensives are making all our sluggish coun-termeasures abortive, thus leaving our garrison forces idle, which were stationed in various places only by arduous efforts. And our transports were either forced to go aground, set on fire, or sunk, only adding more to the already heavy damage lists. On the other hand, the enemy is killing two birds with one stone, without losing even a ship or a plane. Nothing is more deplorable than this.

The enemy's present strength is just like a raging fire, so irresistible that a small amount of water can hardly put it out. The only way, I think, is to pull down houses along a road far enough distant from the fire, thus making it a line of resistance to stop the fire, just like I felt at the time of the great earthquake.

[In the morning of Tuesday, 25 April, the fleet moved to Anchorage No. 1. On the way *Nagato* carried out "spotting training with the Third

Battleship Division." At 1005 they celebrated "the Memorial Day of Yasukuni Shrine."]

War situation (yesterday's summary):

1. At 0855, a large force including carriers, 120 miles north of Hollandia.

2. At 0915, two carriers, one battleship, five cruisers, six destroyers, twelve transports (full load), 195 miles northeast of Hollandia, course 270°, speed 16 knots.

3. At 1735, four carriers, over ten others, sixty miles, bearing 335° from Hollandia.

All these add up to show that the enemy task force and invasion force are still active in that area. The Combined Fleet seemingly grew impatient and ordered repeated attacks, but nothing much was actually carried out. Naturally, little results were obtained, only adding to our losses.

Today the following dispatch was sent to the commander in chief, Combined Fleet, over the name of the vice chief of the Naval General Staff:

> It can hardly be hoped to check the enemy's offensive in general by the middle of May, when the strength of the First Task Force will be completed. In the meantime, operations on the part of the base air forces without confidence only result in exhausting their own strength in noncombat missions, thus making them unable to cooperate with the task force when the latter will be ready for action. Therefore, let the enemy get on with their crude activities for the time being, and guide your command forces not to go beyond launching surprise attacks with those well-trained forces.

That the newly staffed headquarters, Combined Fleet, can't sit idle may well be appreciated, but a war can't be fought with orders only. So I completely agree with this instruction by the vice chief and only hope that headquarters, Combined Fleet, on receiving this, won't get peevish and take up an attitude of *laissez-aller*. After all, it's most important to have capable men at the supreme headquarters.

Wednesday, 26 April 1944. Fair. Today is the day on which four years ago the death of Tomoko, my wife, took place. Early in the morning I prayed for her happiness and told her spirit of my determination. It's my firm belief that I owe her soul a great deal for my being able to do my duty today like this. No service will be held at my home today, but a sincere service for the fifth anniversary of her death will be held today of next year, if and when I can reach that day alive.

[Ugaki attended the task fleet's table maneuvers aboard *Taiho*. He noted that the war situation showed little change.

[Apparently the combination of the unpromising war situation and reflections upon the death of his wife turned Ugaki's thoughts to how "to die in an honorable way," a subject never far from his mind. "To fight so gallantly that one's name goes down in history, and commit hara kiri when nothing is left to one will be best, I think." Still, any deaths in the service of the country "should be regarded as honorable ones." He remembered one of Yamamoto's brief poems: "Mikado's shield I always strive to be, / Never caring for my fame or life."

Thursday, 27 April 1944. Fair. A study of the table maneuvers was held on board *Taiho* in the afternoon and I went to attend it. I have my own opinion, but decided to remain as an observer for the present. At this table maneuver upon which our fate is resting, developments too favorable to the "Blue" (Japanese) forces took place, to which the supervisors must give serious consideration. I wonder why they don't give enough consideration to attacking enemy elements easy to destroy, instead of always seeking a decisive battle. It wouldn't be a policy worth adopting at this hour, unless it has been reached as a conclusion after losing confidence as a result of having gone through all kinds of difficulties and hardships.

The enemy task force seems to be still operating off the northern coast of New Guinea. But our land-based medium bombers on reconnaissance missions were lost so often that even reconnaissance could barely be maintained. It's regrettable indeed to see that the number of operational planes the First Air Fleet possesses now come to only thirty-two. Upon receipt of the Imperial General Staff's instruction, the Combined Fleet has changed its plan to refrain from launching reckless attacks.

Friday, 28 April 1944. Fair. *Yamato,* under my command, which left Kure on the 21st and sortied from Okinoshima on the 22nd, accompanied by heavy cruiser *Maya* and two destroyers, arrived at Manila on the 26th with a full load of personnel and material. After unloading part of her load, she left there at 0800 this morning heading here. I thought of her captain's troubles and prayed for her safety.

[The 601st Air Group practiced bombing against the target ship *Namikatsu,* and Ugaki noted that "their skill seems to have improved to a certain extent." That afternoon *Nagato* sailed out to participate in training and "a night battle practice" in which Ugaki commanded the Otsu force. He thought it was important that the night battle practice demonstrated that "basic training on a fair scale can be carried out in an inland sea."

[Saturday, 29 April was the emperor's birthday and *Nagato* held a suitable ceremony. Despite the "terrible" heat in the wardroom, Ugaki addressed his officers because he was soon to change flagships.]

While the Naval General Staff wants to fix the date of the First Task Force sortie as 20 May on account of preparations for replenishing materials and forwarding tankers, etc., the Combined Fleet says that if they wait so long they'll lose the chance of battle. I wish they would settle it one way or the other quickly, as ten days' difference would affect the situation pretty heavily. At 1030 today, two carriers, three battleships, seven cruisers, and a few transports were sighted at a point 450 miles, bearing 205° from Truk, with its course 310° and speed 18 knots. They'll come to the East Caroline area tomorrow morning. [*Task Force 58 attacked Truk in force following the Hollandia operation.*][23]

U.S. Secretary of the Navy Knox died of a heart attack yesterday.

Sunday, 30 April 1944. Fair, later cloudy. Since 0500 this morning, ninety enemy planes, sixty in the second wave and some in the third wave, raided Truk. A fair number of them were shot down. As I wrote before, we don't receive heavy damage, as in today's case, if and when we expect it and are prepared for it.

The Combined Fleet finally gave in and agreed to make the date of the First Task Force's sortie on the 20th. This gives us some more time. *Yamato* and her group passed Great Natuna Island this evening, and I pray for their safety.

Monday, 1 May 1944. Fair, later cloudy. April, not of cherry blossoms but of heat, has gone and May is here in this land of eternal summer. Both *Nagato* and *Fuso* carried out damage-control training at anchor in the morning and afternoon, respectively. The *Yamato* and *Maya* groups arrived at 1900. Congratulated the safe arrival of sixteen hundred personnel and two thousand tons of transported materials. My deep appreciation should go to those concerned for the hardships and troubles they've gone through. The captains came at night and brought with them cherry blossoms from home, having preserved them with great care. I also received a box of cigars from the commander in chief, Third Southern Expeditionary Fleet, in Manila. I was very grateful.

Truk was air raided again this morning, and seventeen vessels including battleships approached Ponape from the southwest. They seem to be trying an invasion of the island.

[*Despite the heavy bombardment by Vice Admiral "Ching" Lee's six battleships*—Alabama, Iowa, Massachusetts, New Jersey, North Carolina, *and* South Dakota—*with support by carriers under Rear Admiral J. J. Clark, the Americans did not plan to invade Ponape.*][24]

[*Yamato's* arrival relieved Ugaki of worry, so on Tuesday, 2 May, he went shooting and bagged a few pigeons. He returned aboard ship at 1020, received new midshipmen, and studied the results of *Nagato's* and *Fuso's* training. He warned those concerned that *Fuso,* being old, had "revealed many points insufficient in her preparation and training for damage control."]

Yesterday, an enemy force with seven carriers and six battleships as nucleus maneuvered in two groups at a point sixty miles bearing 150° from Kaedeshima at Truk. Three hundred planes buzzed over from morning until afternoon, but our damage was quite small. On both days of the 30th and the 1st, seventy-five were shot down and twenty-five damaged by our ground fire.

[*Actually, Task Force 58 lost twenty-six planes shot down and nine to other causes. More than half the airmen shot down were rescued.*][25]

On the other hand, three battleships, two cruisers, six destroyers, and five unidentified ships appeared at a point eight kilometers bearing 220° from the south channel of Ponape and bombarded there from 1225 to 1540.

Wednesday, 3 May 1944. Cloudy, squall. From 1015 a meeting was held aboard *Taiho* to study operations; it lasted until afternoon.

Admiral Soemu Toyoda has been appointed commander in chief, Combined Fleet, and has taken command, according to a telegram we received.

[On Thursday, 4 May, Ugaki devoted most of the day to training problems. He attended a meeting aboard *Atago,* discovering that there were "not a few points to discuss even in a very simple training." He particularly worried over the fact that Japan's specialty, night engagements, had been "rendered almost useless by the enemy's radar and his use of planes at night. Furthermore, with the diminished number of our destroyers and the enemy's increased speed, isn't it almost hopeless to wage night engagements? Then how are we going to win? We must find other specialties."]

At 1700 I left the accustomed *Nagato* to shift my flag to *Yamato.* This ship was the flagship of the Combined Fleet from 11 February 1942 to the same date in 1943, and memories of the Midway and Solomon operations in connection with her are still fresh in my mind.

Now the secondary battery turrets on both sides have been removed and new power added by installing antiaircraft guns and machine guns in their places. Enemy planes need not be feared, so she'll be the pride of the navy among the new capital ships. I feel it a great honor to make her my flagship and to live in the cabin where Fleet Admiral Yamamoto used to live. I shall make her my death place and devote myself to accomplishing my duty.

[On Friday 5 May, Ugaki's battleships trained at sea. He was not satisfied: "It looked quite imposing at first, but as the training went on various defects and the lack of training were exposed." He noted that the death of Koga had been made public in Tokyo that day and thought reaction would be less shocked "because this is the second time of similar mishaps and, moreover, the country is now under emergency status."]

Saturday, 6 May 1944. Fair. Table maneuvers of the staff work from the time of sortie up to the attack by surface units (in the coming theater) were held on board *Taiho*. I attended both in the morning and afternoon and expressed some of my views at a conference. In general, headquarters, task fleet, seems self-centered. War is no childs' play; there is an enemy to be coped with. More caution must be taken.

Furthermore, they only think of one decisive battle and seldom think of an easy way to destroy elements of an enemy with all our force, thus overlooking the fact that the enemy has made one onslaught after another in a successive wave of decisive battles. The consequence is that sufficient determination and preparation can't be made. At night I sent for the captain and navigation officer and studied yesterday's training to prepare for tomorrow.

Admiral Koga was posthumously promoted to fleet admiral and decorated with the First Class Order of the Golden Kite and also of the Order of Paulownia. May his soul rest in peace! He was a close friend of mine and I shall take care of the affairs which he left behind.

[On Sunday, 7 May, Ugaki's division sailed out for further training. This time, "everything went fairly smoothly." The next day, Monday, 8 May, *Yamato* went out alone to conduct antiaircraft firing. Ugaki remarked, "No matter how many guns and planes we may have it's like casting pearls before swine unless your skill is good."]

Tuesday, 9 May 1944. Fair. Originally we were to leave here today for the advance base, but the task fleet's movement was put off two days as the First Air Fleet's concentration was delayed.

A table maneuver of the staff work was held in the Second Fleet and its studying conference in the afternoon. I frankly expressed my views, as the fate of our country rested on that operation. Unlike the time of the battle of the Japan Sea, in which we were well prepared for the oncoming enemy, there is hardly anything, if any, in which we can have confidence as at the time of the outbreak of the war. Naturally, I can't help wondering if a decisive battle can be waged in such a situation. However, at the same time the enemy, too, may not be as good as we think. It may turn out all right, if and when we fight with them.

The commander in chief, Second Fleet, gave a reception. That is rather unusual. Is this an advance celebration, or a farewell?

[The morning of Wednesday, 10 May, was occupied with another conference to study training. Ugaki was uneasy because "the headquarters, as well as each ship, seems to have lots of things which need further study." This was the last day of their stay in Lingga anchorage, and that evening Ugaki "said a reluctant farewell to the quickly fading isles."]

The following was received from the chief of the Intelligence Bureau of the Naval General Staff:

An estimate of U.S. main forces to be directed against Japan as of 1 June (ground forces not included):

1. Naval vessels (including those under repair, with their number undetermined): Battleships: new type, eight; old type, eight. Carriers: regular type, ten; converted carriers, approximately ten; auxiliary, approximately twenty. Super cruiser, one. Heavy and light cruisers, twenty-five. *Omaha* class: some. Destroyers: two hundred. Submarines: ninety-five.

2. First line planes: army and navy combined, approximately eight thousand. Regular and converted carrier-borne planes: twelve hundred.

I don't think all of them are coming to attack us, but anyway they can be a tough enemy. One feels happy when he anticipates a big game, and I think it won't be far off that my hunting instinct is satisfied.

Now I shall close this chapter of the reassignment and the decisive battle preparations, and I shall start a new chapter on the decisive battle.

Thursday, 11 May 1944. Squall and partly fair. The Mobile Force, except the Fifth Heavy Cruiser Division, was to sail off today from Lingga to the advanced base.

After two months of training, our fighting ability has been improved a good deal, and the time for the showdown is close at hand.

At 0300, taking advantage of the moonlight, the fleet left the anchorage in order of Second Destroyer Squadron (which left earlier), Fourth Heavy Cruiser Division, Seventh Heavy Cruiser Division, Third Battleship Division, and First Battleship Division. First CV Division, Fifth Heavy Cruiser Division, and Tenth Destroyer Squadron remained behind. Proceeded at 16 knots until passing Pengelap. Then on an easterly course speed was increased to 20 knots, under the alert formation. The first course passing north between the Anambas Islands and Great Natuna Island was then followed. It was quite dark until 2250, when the moon came up.

I read the Combined Fleet's orders regarding Operation A. I think it would be wonderful, if such could be carried out as instructed. [*The plan for Operation A (A-Go) was issued on 3 May in anticipation of an all-out battle near Palau in the West Carolines.*][26]

Friday, 12 May 1944. Many squalls, partly fine after nightfall. From a point north of Great Natuna, course was set to 55° and again altered to 85° in the evening. Mostly speed was set at 18 knots.

Fleet deployment practice, daylight formation firing practice, spotting practice, night warfare practice, etc., were carried out. Probably this will be the last training as a fleet.

The area we were passing through was wide and open, so we thought danger from enemy submarines would be comparatively small. But after nightfall we detected enemy radar, wave sensitivity degree 5 and radio telephone, sensitivity degree 2. So the existence of two of them in this district was suspected.

In night warfare training I commanded one side force, but, failing to confirm *Atago*'s instruction to end that practice, we kept on training without an enemy for forty minutes. It wasn't before 0400 that we were able to join the rest. It could be called rather humorous, but we must learn that uncertain communication can spoil operations.

From the 5th to the 8th, brisk enemy radio activities were observed in the Marshall district. In addition, briskness was noted in the Hawaii commander's radio activities and Midway's airplane alert. The Naval General Staff sent in a warning that it considered these indicative of a powerful enemy force operating at sea.

Saturday, 13 May 1944. Partly fair. We crossed toward the Shinnan Islands and the north of Borneo. At 1830 we entered Balabac Channel. We sailed in a long line of columns. On the first day, two reconnaissance seaplanes cooperated with us in guarding from Singapore. Yesterday we didn't dispatch any of our own aircraft. Today we saw an army plane cooperating with us just outside the channel. Apart from the extent to which it could help us, I was pleased to see they have come to cooperate with us at sea. After passing through the Balabac main channel, we took the northerly course, avoiding shoals. Fleet training wasn't executed today. The sensitivity of enemy submarines' telephones has become stronger after entering the Sulu Sea.

Sunday, 14 May 1944. Fair. At 0120 course was altered to the south and the formation drew in. When we were preparing for antiaircraft firing in the afternoon, the following telegram came in: "At 0400 this morning an enemy submarine [*Bonefish*][27] fired a torpedo off the western coast of Borneo and west of Tawi Tawi. Later the destroyer *Inazuma* was torpedoed and sunk at a point thirty miles west of the island, and another merchant ship was torpedoed fifteen miles west of the island."

Accordingly, we canceled firing practice and proceeded south, taking precautions. The Third Battleship Division twice sighted something like a periscope at the northern sea of Tawi Tawi and each time we changed course to the south. A considerable number of seaplanes were also employed, but no submarine was sighted. Passing the new defense installations at the entrance at 1600, we dropped anchor at 1650. I'm very glad that we've been able to advance to this Tawi Tawi Base safely. Fish are leaping and birds are flying; it makes us feel nearer to the Inner South Sea than at Lingga.

Monday, 15 May 1944. Fair. At 1030 all commanders assembled aboard *Atago*. I hadn't much to report. Just then the Third Fleet appeared at the entrance, much ahead of schedule. I'm glad they have arrived safely too. Now I pray for the safe arrival of the Second and Third CV Divisions and *Musashi* tomorrow.

[On Tuesday, 16 May, Ugaki took his gun ashore to try his luck. He visited the "local Thirty-third Garrison Force commander," who gave him an orderly and "two armed men to act as guides." Much of the scenery was new and interesting to Ugaki. Rice stood about a foot high. "We saw macaws, pigeons, and occasionally a few pheasants." The men got about fifteen birds to take back to the ship.]

At 1915, before dusk, *Musashi*, the Second and Third CV Divisions arrived safely. With them, the whole force has been concentrated and I'm greatly relieved. At 2100 Rear Admiral [Bunji] Asakura (promoted in May), Captain of *Musashi*, came to report and we held a conference.

The aircraft fuel tanker *Sunosaki* came alongside.

Wednesday, 17 May 1944. Fair. I was appointed controlling officer for unloading unnecessary materials and boats ashore before the sortie.

This morning ten enemy planes raided Surabaja. The deployment of the First Air Fleet will begin on the 18th and be completed on the 26th. And their preparations for the operation will be finished by the end of the month. Accordingly, the sortie of the task fleet will be on or about the 25th.

[On Thursday, 18 May, Ugaki inspected *Musashi*, then addressed all her officers "above the rank of warrant officer." He expressed his great pleasure at being reunited with *Musashi* and reminded them that the war situation was not going well. Once-occupied areas had been recaptured;

enemy submarines were "rampant in a vast area. . . . Our loss of ships is far exceeding our capacity to rebuild them."

He gave his estimate of enemy intentions—increase in submarine warfare, "a westward advance along the northern coast of New Guinea, and an attempt to recapture the Philippines, with the final goal of reaching China" from which the Allies would attack Japan proper and cut their connection with "the southwest resources area." To accomplish this, the enemy would attack Palau, Yap, and Saipan. If matters remained as they were, Japan would be in sore straits. "No longer would our self-existence or self-defense be possible, and beyond that it would mean an end of the empire. We're now being pressed against a wall; we can't fall back any more. Unless the main enemy force is destroyed by any means, our future will be doomed."

[He outlined the strategy for the anticipated decisive battle. First the air force, as the main body, would attack, whereupon the battle would "develop into a chase or an attack on an invading fleet and convoy." Then the surface force would "play a main role." Giving the current estimate of Allied strength, he warned that the task would be by no means easy. But, "however hard or however difficult it may be, this is the one battle we must win by all means." Nothing must happen to *Musashi;* they must "fight with all our might . . . until we attain our objective"; they must not relax after victory. "Though I do not worry since I trust you, many excellent veterans, I wish you to make efforts in studying and training so that you'll have nothing to regret afterwards." And he wished them all "the best of luck."

[That day a telegram came in from the chief of the Intelligence Bureau, Naval General Staff, giving the estimate of British strength that could be directed toward Japan. Ugaki made no comment upon it.]

The enemy planes that raided Surabaja yesterday were surmised to have come from an enemy task force. Summing up army reports, approximately 110 planes came from the south coast of Java Island at 0830, and about sixty raided Malang and about thirty Surabaja. Seventeen planes were set on fire at Malang and an oil refinery badly damaged at Wonokoromo, while others were damaged, too. It seems to me that the enemy has started a diversionary attack from the west, and its imminence was felt on the eastern front. [*These were probably raids by the British Eastern Fleet's carrier force. Only seven U.S. planes—B-24s of the 531st Squadron—struck Surabaja on the night of 17–18 May 1944.*][28]

From 1400 a practice of those concerned with the main battery firing (aerial communication included) was held on board *Yamato.* Various problems had to be settled. The young men seemed impatient with regard to the fire-opening range of *Yamato* and *Musashi.*

In one chapter of the *Words and Deeds of Famous Leaders,* I read the following: A hawker told that holding back a hawk for a while when it gets excited at finding a prey would result eventually in stimulating it a great deal when it finally was released. A warlord praised him very much, saying, "I have learned how to handle men by listening to your story of how to handle your hawk!"

This subtle psychology and the knack of handling men can only be understood by higher commanders, and it's hard to explain, too. So I just told them something else and asked them to trust their commanders and leave it to them.

The First and Second CV divisions sailed out for training today. If destroyer escorts are available, this division must carry out formation training, too.

Friday, 19 May 1944. Partly fair. At 0930, Commander in Chief Ozawa on board *Taiho* delivered an address to all commanders on the occasion of the concentration of the task fleet at Tawi Tawi. Afterwards a briefing on Operation A and an address by the chief of staff were held. I invited their attention to a few points in the form of questions because I believe that we must not criticize an order once it has been issued, even if it's too optimistic and self-centered—a plan which intentionally overlooked a possibility of the enemy main offensive line attacking our most vulnerable point. Only we have to be prepared for a case in which our planning fails.

Finally, the following three points which the commander in chief stressed in his speech were enough to encourage my views:

1. We don't consider our losses.

2. If and when necessary for the sake of the main issue, an element will be sacrificed.

3. In case communications and liaisons go wrong, a commander must act as he sees fit.

A patrol boat sent outside of the reef found a submarine and depth-charged it last night. Planes and destroyers have searched the suspected area since this morning, but in vain.

For the past three days the army has been reporting movements of enemy battleships, cruisers, destroyers, and others off Hollandia, the north coast of New Guinea. While the navy failed to do anything directly about them, it was learned through enemy broadcasts that Wakde Island had been occupied. The time when the enemy swarms en masse toward the western part of New Guinea isn't far off. But we sit idle doing nothing! [*Wakde Island was occupied on 18 May in the face of determined Japanese fire. By 21 May the airstrip was operational and remained an important Allied air base for the remainder of 1944.*][29]

Saturday, 20 May 1944. Cloudy, squall. It was cloudy all day long with squalls, as a discontinuous line ran east to west. It was cool, too. At 0000 the Combined Fleet ordered the commencement of Operation A, and the task force was ordered to be ready to sail at six-hours' notice.

At 0415, enemy planes raided Marcus Island. At 1105 a reconnaissance aircraft from Saipan sighted two carriers, four battleships, eight others, course southeast, speed 5 knots, at a point six hundred miles bearing 43° from Pagan (eighty miles northwest of Marcus Island). As anticipated, they have started a diversion in this area. [*Ugaki correctly identified the raid of 20 May on Marcus as diversionary.*][30] Anyway, I feel the showdown is approaching day by day. A table-top antiaircraft firing practice was held in the afternoon. Even this did us some good. I told them not to be afraid of enemy planes.

[On Sunday, 21 May, staff work practice was conducted aboard *Taiho*. "Each time the same thing is practiced, but still some problems always crop up," lamented Ugaki.]

How to supply is a great question. One is appalled at the condition of supply ships. The enemy task force that attacked Marcus Island yesterday came back again to attack from the northeast direction this morning. There are signs that an enemy force intending to attack the Kurile district left Hawaii on about the 15th. An outpost scuffle of a surprise attack on eastern Japan and the Bonins has already been started at Marcus Island. Nevertheless, the enemy's main operation is believed to be directed toward the Philippines via New Guinea and the West Carolines.

Monday, 22 May 1944. Fair. Though I was rather skeptical of a report that an enemy submarine had appeared outside the channel before dawn yesterday, *Musashi's* patrol boat was attacked twice with two torpedoes each after sighting something like a periscope quite close to the reef late last night, and the boat depth-charged her. Planes and destroyers searched since this morning, but in vain.

Then *Chitose* of the Third CV Division, which left the anchorage for training, was attacked with six torpedoes from four thousand meters astern while launching planes. One of them passed ahead of her and exploded near a destroyer in the front screen. Fortunately both escaped unscathed. So we have no choice but to postpone tomorrow's training of this division's first section. The enemy already knows that we're staying here. Next he'll attempt to find out our strength and attack us when we sortie. He may also seek an opportunity of sneaking into the reef, so we mustn't relax. From now on, enemy submarines will concentrate more in this area and seek a chance to attack us, while scouting our movements. Moreover, we must expect a considerable number of enemy submarines to come to those places where our forces are to be deployed, so the secrecy of our movements no longer can be maintained, thus rendering Operation A impracticable. More than that, there is much possibility of the enemy defeating our plan.

We must hunt enemy submarines now. After all, if staff officers get up about breakfast time to figure out how to catch the submarines found the preceding midnight, it will be impossible to destroy them. In view of the fact that we're permitting rampant activity of enemy subs in spite of our overwhelming strength, we can imagine how it will be in the future.

Those oilers that have finished their refueling are going to leave here for oil-producing areas early tomorrow morning. It's apparent that, if one or two of them get hurt, it will directly affect the operation badly. Yesterday I called the attention of Arima, staff officer of the task fleet, to the probable occurrence of various unexpected things before the commencement of an aerial attack, thus preventing us from carrying out operations as expected. The events that happened right after I warned him are good examples.

Tuesday, 23 May 1944. Cloudy with occasional squall. A briefing of the advance force was held on board *Atago* at 0930. With the Third Carrier Division, a newcomer, joining us, there were many problems. From 1530 another conference of Group 11 was held aboard *Yamato*. As we're going into actual battle without practicing the ring formation even once, we had many things to think about.

At about 1215 a patrolling plane found a submarine in the vicinity where *Chitose* was attacked yesterday, and a destroyer threw over sixty depth charges on her, but without much result. Twenty minutes after sunset the submarine surfaced at a point 1800 meters south of the channel. Two submarines had just fooled us.

[On Wednesday, 24 May, *Yamato* and *Musashi* held damage control practice. At 1600 Ugaki went ashore to go hunting. He was surprised to see "huge piles of things" which had been unloaded from various ships.]

Two whales were found today in the vicinity where planes and destroyers attacked after sighting a submarine yesterday. The submarines might have been these whales. This reminded me of a false report sent from this district just after the outbreak of war which said about fifteen submarines were sailing at ten-mile intervals.

The enemy task force that attacked Marcus Island attacked Wake Island today. Though it inflicted a fair amount of damage, we shot down thirty of them, too. [*This, too, was a diversionary attack. As yet, however, the Japanese seemingly did not anticipate a major strike in the Marianas.*][31]

Thursday, 25 May 1944. Fair. Two torpedoes from an enemy submarine struck *Tatekawa Maru*, an oiler of the task fleet which was to reoil to the advance force in Davao Bay. Her hull broke in two and she sank.

Headquarters, Second Fleet, wanted to have some good ideas about submarine hunting, so I ordered the ships under my command to submit them. But I was disappointed to hear that there were no new ideas.

I have decided to find some measures to cope with various damages, while engaging action in ring formation.

[Ugaki made no entry for Friday, 26 May, beyond noting the weather. Saturday, 27 May, was Japan's Navy Day, and Ugaki was "filled with a feeling of remorse . . . the Rising Sun ensign is still gleaming as before and the vice admiral's flag is on the masthead. Yet I wonder whether we are really fulfilling our duty."]

Since the 21st, small enemy vessels have been maneuvering in the vicinity of Biak Island, making us suspect the overture to an invasion of the [Schouten] Islands. From 0500 to 0615, three battleships, two cruisers, and fourteen destroyers came to bombard the shore, while at the same time twenty B-24s bombed airfields there. Eight large and small transports, together with thirty small craft were seen off the coast of Bosnik. At 0700, two battleships, two carriers, four cruisers, and four destroyers were also in the Bosnik area, and the enemy reportedly started landing operations at last.

[*The U.S. ground forces attacking Biak were under the command of Major General Horace A. Fuller, U.S.A., the naval operations under Rear Admiral W. M. Fechteler, commanding the VII Amphibian force. The B-24s came from the XIII A.A.F. Col Naoyuki Kuzume commanded a numerous, excellent defense force and kept the Americans away from Biak's airfields for almost a month.*][32]

For this new development the Combined Fleet ordered two fighter squadrons and one carrier-bomber squadron to move. On the other hand, the Fourth Southern Expeditionary Fleet, responsible for the defense of that area, showed a tame attitude of avoiding dissipation of fighting strength, only requesting a reinforcement of air strength to prevent enemy invasion of that strategically important island.

The enemy's steady advance toward the west along the northern coast of New Guinea, as I predicted, is most painful to us. Many airstrips can be built on Biak Island, and then it will be very hard for us to maintain airstrips on the western end of New Guinea. Palau will also be within his striking range, so movements of the task fleet east of Mindanao will be impossible. Finally, Operation A will be made impracticable. Therefore, Biak Island is the most critical crossroad of the war.

[Despite Biak's importance, the Japanese Army had recently moved the defense line to Sorong and Halmahera, thus leaving Biak in the position of an abandoned last ditch.][33]

If something isn't done right away, it will be too late to do anything. As I couldn't stop worrying, at 0030 I ordered a motor launch to go to *Taiho*. I saw the commander in chief and chief of staff, both of whom had already gone to bed, and told them my views, the gist of which were as follows:

1. As it is absolutely necessary to hold Biak Island, reinforcement of air power to there is most urgent. In preventing the enemy from landing there by force, we can produce a chance for the decisive battle.

2. The present plan for Operation A is too optimistic. In an encountering operation we cannot take the initiative. Therefore, we must have a plan, together with its preparation, to be able to operate with forces of the task fleet against an enemy advancing west along New Guinea.

The commander in chief understood me and I got back at 0130. If it does any good, this will be another memorial day. [*Ugaki referred to this date being Japan's Navy Day.*]

A fleet Sumo contest was held on board *Yamato* today. *Kongo* seemed to overwhelm the rest of the ships with her strong team.

Sunday, 28 May 1944. Cloudy, partly rain. At 0900 a table maneuver was held aboard *Taiho* under the commander in chief's supervision. With regard to my suggestion of last night, the chief of staff revealed that a suggestion to reinforce Biak would be made to the higher command, pending the result of a dauntless reconnaissance to be carried out today and tomorrow. But he also added that he wasn't entirely agreeable to the idea of throwing the task fleet into that area because of the present state of its fighting ability and also the resultant consumption of forces. Commander in Chief Ozawa also told me that he was afraid the Combined Fleet hadn't an idea in mind of using his fleet's air power as reinforcement, when necessary.

Anyway, I was glad that there were reactions to my suggestion. It isn't fame I seek, but at a time like this, when the fate of a nation is at stake, one should express his views without hesitation as he believes. [*It is possible that Ugaki's strong recommendations contributed to the Combined Fleet's decision to relieve Biak.*] Even if it is not accepted entirely, I shall be satisfied if it can serve to help them reflect and contemplate. Moreover, it isn't my thought alone, but every thoughtful person who worries about the future shares it.

The enemy landed on Biak one division strong, its main force at Bosnik and two companies with ten amphibious tanks east of Mokmer at 1530. Since last night our army garrison has been continuing attacks on the enemy main force and is reported to have checked an enemy advance to the airstrip. The navy garrison force is said to be cooperating with the army guarding the airstrip area. But we have had many examples like this, and its outcome is only too obvious.

Monday, 29 May 1944. Cloudy, later rain and partly fine. A conference to study yesterday's practice was held aboard *Taiho* from 0930. Discussions centered on the necessity of antiair defense of this anchorage, supply needed at the time of the fleet's sortie, importance of Biak, faint possibility of materializing Operation A, and the employment of this fleet in this district. Many points were in accord with my suggestion.

From 1400 a conference to study antisubmarine measures took place until nearly sunset. If matters are carried out with the enthusiasm and tenacity shown at a conference table, there's no doubt of destroying enemy submarines. But why is it that so many things contrary to this actually happen?

The Combined Fleet seems to be well aware of Biak's importance, and sent a telegram encouraging the air forces.

Tuesday, 30 May 1944. Fair. Yesterday the Southeast Area Fleet twice sent its suggestion of launching a counter landing at Biak to the Combined Fleet. At about noon, the latter finally ordered its preparation by Telegram Operational Order No. 102, which was dated as of 2342 of the 29th. It said as follows:

The Combined Fleet plans to rapidly transport the Second Sea Mobile Brigade at Zamboanga with a part of its forces to Biak with the aim of securing the island, thus intending to seek an opportunity for Operation A by carrying out this operation and inducing the enemy task force to come out.

This operation will be named Operation Kon and its participating forces the Kon Force.

1. The day (X-Day) to penetrate into Biak is set at 3 June. (The assemblage at Davao will be made by 31 May).

2. The Sixteenth Heavy Cruiser Division commander (Sakonju) will command the force, which consists of the transporting unit (*Aoba, Kinu, Uranami, Shikinami,* and *Itsukushima*), escort unit (Fifth Heavy Cruiser Division), and indirect escorts unit (*Fuso,* two destroyers).

3. The Third Air Force will support the operation by attacking the north coast of New Guinea.

4. The Southwest Area Fleet will swiftly transport an army force stationed at Sorong to Manukwari.

5. The Operation A forces will give necessary support to Operation Kon, while keeping a sharp watch on developments.

6. With an order of "stand by" for the decisive battle, the escort and the indirect escort forces will return to the original units.

In accordance with this order, the task fleet ordered the First Disposition Alternative at 0130. So the diversion force is to engage in a more effective attempt to lure the enemy out, though under a different name. However, we haven't yet a definite plan of attacking this lured-out enemy. We're only going to "keep a sharp watch on its development" and nothing beyond that.

An hour after the departure of destroyers at 1100, the Fifth Heavy Cruiser Division and *Fuso* sailed out. We sent them off by "manning the ships," praying for their good luck.

At 1400, a *Musashi* plane, which had been guarding the departing force to the south of this anchorage, sighted an enemy submarine just trying to fire torpedoes at a point three kilometers, 20° to the right of the Fifth Heavy Cruiser Division and bombed it right away, marking a near miss of five meters. Then it led destroyers to make over twenty depth charges. A narrow escape from danger indeed! The *Musashi* plane's merit was worth a citation.

Situation at Biak:

Before dawn yesterday, navy medium torpedo bombers carried out an attack, with two keeping contact, four dropping flares, and ten torpedoing. One enemy cruiser and one medium ship were sunk instantly. A torpedo hit one large merchant ship and one unidentified vessel while six planes failed to return due to bad weather and other reasons.

The army garrison force also carried out a night attack and repulsed an enemy on the road running from Mokmer to Solido airstrip, after giving them considerable damage. But most of their ten tanks have been out of order and no friendly planes cooperated with them in the daytime. They're only grinding their teeth at arrogant enemy attacks by planes and ships. How it will come out is already obvious.

[That day, the First Battleship Division held night firing practice. Ugaki was surprised to discover many things remained to teach them; he had thought "there would be nothing more to say."]

Wednesday, 31 May 1944. Fair. After breakfasting in a hurry, I went to the flagship *Junyo* to see today's training of the Second Carrier Division. The ship sailed out at 0800.

Takeoffs were generally pretty well done, but landings needed much more training. While training, *Junyo* damaged two planes and *Hiyo* one. One of the pilots whispered, "This is self-destruction air warfare." With this type carrier's inferior speed of 24 knots, it's impossible to use the new type planes, *Tenzan* and *Suisei,* unless favored by a wind over five meters per second. Further study is needed on how to allocate the kinds of planes and also how to use them in operations.

[Ugaki had a few ideas, including use of carrier-borne bomber crews to man fighters and carry out attacks with 250-kg bombs, and to practice "barrage firing against dive-bombers with flare shells as targets." He noted "little confusion" among the screening destroyers, although sometimes they maneuvered simultaneously and other times in groups.]

In today's training many destroyers were employed, with hunting enemy submarines as the secondary purpose. But none of them appeared. Bad luck! We got back to the anchorage at 1930 after sunset. I've learned a lot by a day's observation and appreciate the painstaking efforts of its commander [Rear Admiral Takatsugu] Jyojima and his subordinates.

The Fifth Heavy Cruiser Division and *Fuso* arrived at Davao today. Since they couldn't accommodate the whole strength of the Second Mobile Brigade, 5,500 men in all, *Tsugaru* of the Third Southern Expeditionary Force was quickly added to them.

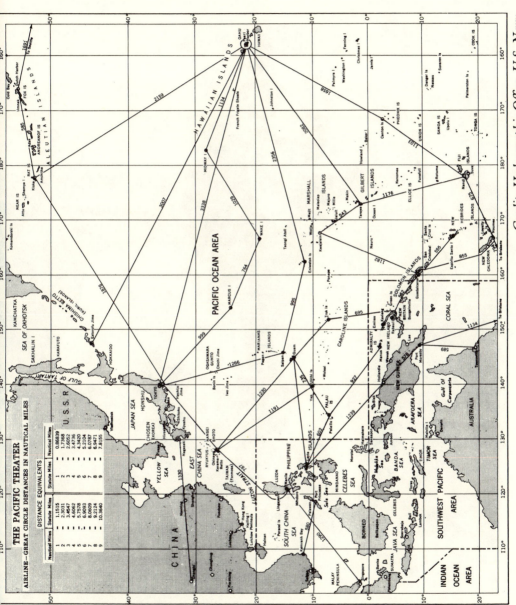

Credit: *Hydrographic Office, U.S. Navy*

His Imperial Majesty Hirohito, Emperor of Japan. (UPI Photo)

Ugaki's family in 1936, when he was a captain. To his left is his wife Tomoko. Hiromitsu, his son, stands behind Ugaki. The seated young man is unidentified. (Courtesy of Masataka Chihaya)

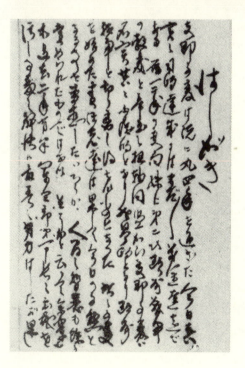

Portion of Ugaki's preface to his diary. (Courtesy of Masataka Chihaya)

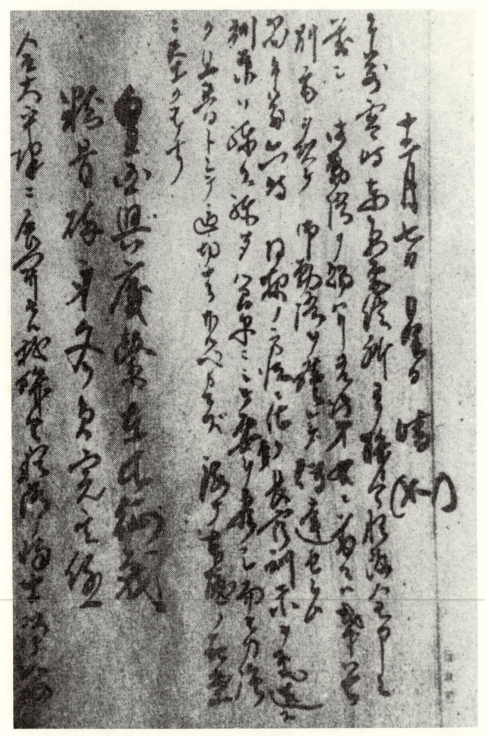

Ugaki's entry for 7 December 1941.　(Courtesy of Masataka Chihaya)

Admiral Isoroku Yamamoto, Commander in Chief, Combined Fleet. (Gordon W. Prange collection; U.S. Navy)

*Admiral Yamamoto with members of the Combined Fleet staff and the subordi-
nate fleet commanders. First row, sitting: VADM Mitsumi Shimizu, VADM
Hosokaya, VADM Nobutake Kondo, Adm. Yamamoto, VADM Shira
Takasu, VADM Chuichi Nagumo, VADM Nishizo Tsukahara, VADM
Shigeyoshi Inouye.   (Gordon W. Prange collection)*

*Rear Admiral Takijiro Oni-
shi, founder of the kamikaze
special attack force.
(U.S. Navy)*

Vice Admiral Chuichi Nagumo, commander in chief of Pearl Harbor Task Force. (Gordon W. Prange collection)

Capt. Shiegnori Kami, staff officer, Naval General Staff. (Gordon W. Prange collection)

Rear Admiral Ryunosuke Kusaka. (Gordon W. Prange collection)

Admiral Yamamoto (seated fifth from the right) and staff of Combined Fleet. Ugaki is seated to Yamamoto's right. (Gordon W. Prange collection)

*Vice Admiral Jisaburo Ozawa, commander, Southern Expedition-
ary Fleet; later commander in chief, Third Fleet   (U.S. Navy)*

*Admiral Osami Nagano, chief, Naval
General Staff.   (U.S. Navy)*

*Rear Admiral Takeo Kurita
(Gordon W. Prange collection)*

Vice Admiral Mitsumi Shimizu.
(Gordon W. Prange collection)

Rear Admiral Tamon Yamaguchi, com-
mander in chief, Second Carrier Division.
(Gordon W. Prange collection)

Captain Yasuji Watanabe, plans officer,
Combined Fleet. (Gordon W. Prange
collection)

Admiral Teijiro Toyoda, foreign minis-
ter, Third Konoye Cabinet. (Gordon W.
Prange collection)

Admiral Soemu Toyoda, commander in chief, Combined Fleet, in the later years of the war. (Gordon W. Prange collection)

Captain (Baron) Sadatoshi Tomioka, chief, First Section, Naval General Staff. (Gordon W. Prange collection)

Type 97 attack plane of the second wave pulls up and away from Shokaku's flight deck in the early morning light of 7 December 1941.   (U.S. Navy)

Admiral C. W. Nimitz assumes command of commander in chief, Pacific Fleet, 31 December 1941.   (U.S. Navy)

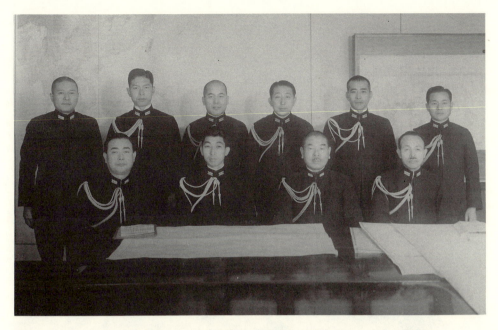

Operations Section, Naval General Staff, 11 December 1941. Front row: Capt. Sadatoshi Tomioka, Cmdr. HIH Prince Nobuhito Takamatsu, RADM Shigeru Fukudome, Capt. Shigenori Kami. Back row: Cmdr. Nasatomo Nakano, Cmdr. Shigeshi Uchida, Cmdr. Sadamu Sanagi, Lt. Cmdr. Marquis Hironobu Katcho, Cmdr. Yuji Yamamoto, Cmdr. Tatsukichi Miyo. (Gordon W. Prange collection)

Rear Admiral Frank J. Fletcher, Commander, U.S. Task Force 17. (U.S. Navy)

Rear Admiral Raymond A. Spruance, Commander, U.S. Task Force 16. (U.S. Navy)

Torpedo hit on Yorktown. *(U.S. Navy)*

Yorktown *sinking, January 1942.* *(U.S. Navy)*

Burning oil tanks on Midway Island after they were hit by Japanese bombs, 4-6 June 1942. (Defense Dept. Photo, Marine Corps)

USS Enterprise. *(U.S. Navy)*

Japanese heavy cruiser knocked out by carrier planes in the battle of Midway, June 1942. (U.S. Navy)

Japanese fleet under attack by carrier-based aircraft west of the Marianas, 19 June 1944. (U.S. Navy)

Japanese carrier bombed and torpedoed by U.S. Navy planes, 24 October 1944. (U.S. Navy)

Japanese submarine I-55. *(U.S. Navy)*

Zuikaku *claimed more battle honors than any other Japanese carrier. With the exception of the battle of Midway, she participated in nearly every major carrier action of the war. She was sunk on 25 October 1944 at the battle of Cape Engaêo. (U.S. Navy)*

Close-up of Japanese kamikaze just before crashing on USS Essex, *25 November 1944. (U.S. Navy)*

Shokaku, *Japanese aircraft carrier.   (Naval History Photo)*

Yamato.   *(Gordon W. Prange collection)*

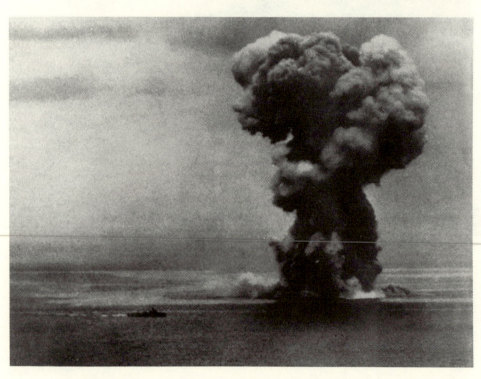

The battleship Yamato *sunk by U.S. Navy planes in the East China Sea, 17 April 1945.   (U.S. Navy)*

The USS Bunker Hill *takes two kamikazes in thirty seconds, 11 May 1945.*
(U.S. Navy)

Ugaki addressing kamikaze pilots at Oita, 15 August 1945. (Courtesy of Masataka Chihaya)

Ugaki stripping his rank from his uniform before his last flight. (Courtesy of Masataka Chihaya)

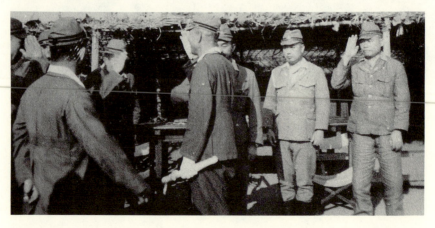

Ugaki says good-bye to his staff at Oita before his final flight. Note sword in his left hand, given to him by Admiral Yamamoto. (Courtesy of Masataka Chihaya)

Ugaki standing before his plane prior to his final flight. (Courtesy of Masataka Chihaya)

Last known photo of Ugaki as his plane leaves from Oita. (Courtesy of Masataka Chihaya)

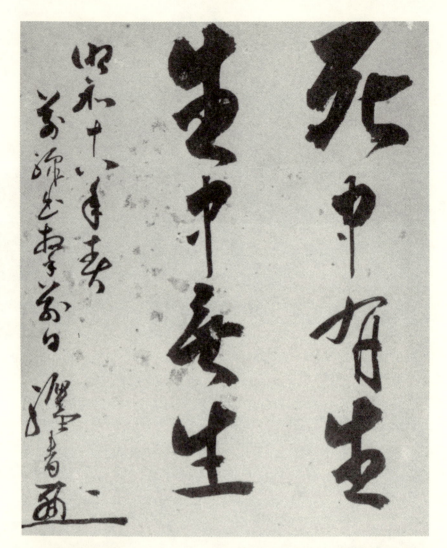

Ugaki's writing on the eve of leaving for Rabaul on 2 April 1943. "Life exists in death / Life doesn't exist in life. April of 1943, on the eve of going to the front line. Written Matome." (Courtesy of Masataka Chihaya)

Rare photograph of Ugaki relaxing before his final flight. (Courtesy of Masataka Chihaya)

8

Awakened from a Dream of Victory

June–August 1944

FOR THE FIRST *weeks of June, Ugaki kept close to the Biak problem. He feared that the Kon plan lacked flexibility, and if it did not "lure" the U.S. fleet to Palau, as planned, Japan would have wasted "precious fighting power." The Combined Fleet canceled Kon, then restored it the same day. On 10 June Ugaki received word that his First Battleship Division would become part of the Kon Force, and he would assume command. His mission was to destroy the U.S. task force in the Biak area, bombard U.S. landing parties there, transport Japanese troops to Biak, and try to entice the United States into the "decisive battle." Ugaki was surprised and delighted with this formidable assignment, and his ships sailed out that very afternoon. He wrote that his only real worry was the shortage of air power.*

He had other, more generalized, worries, however. The Allies had landed in France, and he was pessimistic about Germany's chances. But he reflected that in Asia Japan could still turn the tide if only she could secure enough aircraft. And why couldn't Japan turn out planes that were virtually impossible to shoot down, such as the big Boeing bombers? Palau was now within United States attack range. Yet when a reconnaissance aircraft reported the U.S. task force had left Majuro anchorage, Ugaki's old boastful confidence returned. Let them sail west "right into our net of Operation A," he wrote.

While the Kon force was en route to Biak, U.S. forces raided the Marianas, inflicting heavy damage, much to Ugaki's frustration. Kon was canceled, and Ugaki's ships hurried toward the projected scene of the "decisive" battle estimated to take place on 19 June. Meanwhile, the United States commenced landing on Saipan.

Ugaki asked himself if Japan could possibly lose with such a mighty fleet as was moving toward the enemy. "No! It can't be!" His confidence was misplaced. The Combined Fleet got the decisive battle it had anticipated, but the results were not exactly as planned. Under the overall command of Admiral Spruance, victor at Midway, U.S. naval airmen shot down their Japanese counterparts so devastatingly and at such small cost to themselves that the Americans called the engagement "The Great Marianas Turkey Shoot." For all intents and purposes, Japanese naval air power was no longer a major factor in the war.

Ugaki's force was ordered to the Inland Sea to prepare for the next sortie. En route, he wrote his usual assessment of the reasons for the disaster. Shortly after his arrival in the homeland, the Combined Fleet ordered him to take Yamato *and* Musashi *to Kure and there load army troops for transport to Singapore. They reached Lingga Anchorage on 16 July, and Ugaki set about training his force in submarine detection, night warfare, refueling, and gunnery.*

All the while, he was "in agony" trying to figure out a way to win through to victory. Loss of Saipan had resulted in the fall of the Tojo cabinet; B-29s were raiding the oil refineries in the Palembang area; Guam once again came under the U.S. flag; Ugaki's staff officers produced only conventional ideas for maneuvers. Ugaki finally decided that he should confine himself to his own First Battleship Division and accept the fact that all other problems were none of his business.

He received a psychological boost with the arrival of orders for Operation Sho. According to this script, Ozawa's carriers were to decoy Halsey's Third Fleet northward, while the A Force, of which Ugaki's division was a part, and the C Force caught U.S. ships in Leyte Gulf in a pincers movement. Whether adequate or not, Sho at least gave Ugaki a constructive goal to occupy his energies.

Thursday, 1 June 1944. Fair. At Biak, the army unit drove back the enemy from Mokmer in Bosnik by a night attack, and a part of the enemy seems to have escaped to Owi Island. Enemy artillery on the latter island bombarded Biak. Two battleships and others are maneuvering northeast of Biak.

On the other hand, at 1205 an army reconnaissance plane sighted, from altitude nine thousand meters, a large enemy force with eight carriers (most probably large transports) as its nucleus and accompanied by two heavy cruisers, two light cruisers, and more than ten destroyers, sailing on course 270, speed 20 knots at a point sixty miles due north of d'Urville Cape. [*The eight "large transports" were probably the eight U.S. LSTs on the way to Biak from Hollandia with reinforcements.*][1] The Third Air Force sent a carrier-borne reconnaissance aircraft to confirm it. Anyway, they'll come sooner or later. Only from now on it will get more serious. And it's also quite evident from past cases that the initial activity of a garrison at an early stage doesn't last long. How will the counterlanding on 4 June come out? There seems to me a good chance of both sides' landing forces fighting at sea.

[On Friday, 2 June, *Yamato* and *Musashi* maneuvered and practiced firing, then refueled from the oiler *Genyo Maru*.]

At the Biak area, two enemy transports seem to have been sunk by the medium bomber attack the night of the 31st.

The Kon force's landing point has been fixed, with Wardo as the first choice and Korim as the second. The Third Air Force transfered its command force to Wasile, Babo, Nabire, Moemi, and Kaoe.

Commander in chief, Combined Fleet, sent a telegram order to all commanders in chief and commanders, the gist of which is as follows:

> In view of the dauntless reconnaissance, communications intelligence, and the war situation at Biak, the major part of the enemy task force seems to be coming to the West Carolines and there is a good possibility of the first decisive battle taking place at the West Carolines on the 3rd, 4th, 5th, and 6th. Under this order, "Stand by for the decisive battle of Operation A," the screening and escort forces of the Kon Force will maneuver so as to lure the enemy to Palau in case of being discovered by the enemy or specifically ordered. The task force will promptly advance to the east of the Philippines, preferably taking the third course.

Summing up the dauntless reconnaissance recently carried out, enemy regular carriers are six and battleships the same number, both of which are dispersed. Although many transports are seen at various places, they aren't an invading force. I can't see any indication at all of the enemy's readiness for a large-scale, determined offensive.

The Combined Fleet seems to be getting too nervous and is exaggerating things too much as a result of concentrating on communications intelligence, etc. It has dogmatically concluded that the enemy will come to Palau, sticking to its own planning. The greater the resistance at Biak, the more chance there will be of the enemy creating some diversion elsewhere, but still it's quite natural to believe that his concentration will be directed toward the Bird's Head [Vogelkop], the western end of New Guinea.

If another provoking event takes place, I'm quite sure that the task force will be ordered out. If we go out and the enemy comes to the West Carolines on a large scale, we shall be able to attain our object. But against a possibility that he'll stick to the Bird's Head and go on with a gradual invasion of the district, we have no plan at all to employ our task fleet at an opportune moment. Our plan is too rigid and lacks flexibility, so I'm afraid of only vainly expending precious fighting power and materials in thus maneuvering.

For the first time, the chief of staff of the task fleet wired the chief of staff of the Combined Fleet the following view:

> In view of the great probability of the enemy throwing his task force against Western New Guinea and Halmahera as a diversion to break the stalemate at Biak, it is necessary to expect a decisive battle, in connection with Operation Kon, in the vicinity of point "A" (180 miles southwest of Palau). In order to meet this probability it is considered necessary to prepare to concentrate most of the Fifth Land-Based Air Force's attack groups at an appropriate time, to be able to cooperate with the task force's operation.

The above view is in accord with what I have often said. I'm glad to see that the general public has gradually come to take the war situation at the north coast of New Guinea seriously and that the expected place for a decisive battle is moving down south.

But I think this isn't enough, and we should further expand an area to the southeast as far as Helen Reef [*about two hundred miles north of Vogelkop*] rather than point A, because when most enemy forces are operating in the Biak area, our task force can advance as far as Helen Reef, taking the same route as in Operation A, launch all attacking planes and withdraw immediately, while all planes promptly return to their mother carriers via our land bases after the attack. In this way, our task force can destroy the enemy task force without much risk. Once our object of destroying an enemy is obtained, it will make no difference whether it's at Palau or New Guinea. Then developments will take their natural course and settle down eventually.

The following is the summary of enemy forces sighted by our dauntless reconnaissance and appearing since 27 May:

(As of 2 June)

	Central Pacific Inner South Sea Islands	Solomon Islands Area	Western New Guinea	Total	
Carriers	5	1	1	6	(7)
Converted	5	2		7	*
Battleships	3	2	4	8	(9)
Cruisers	3	3	7 (9)	12	(15)
Destroyers	21 (24)	3	19 (28)	43	(52)
Transports	29	29	60 (68)	118	(126)
Small craft	9	80	120 (160)	209	(249)

Note: Figures in parentheses are total numbers; others are estimated ones.
*Among them 3 CVLs

[On Saturday 3 June, a conference to study the firing practice of 2 June was held. Ugaki was very disappointed with *Yamato*'s salvo spread of some eight hundred meters at thirty-five kilometers.]

Two B-24s shadowed the Kon force which left Davao yesterday in the order of the screening force, transporting Main Force and escort force at a point 330 miles southeast of Davao about noon today. The enemy planes repeatedly sent "R." An enemy submarine seems to have detected our plan after the Fifth Heavy Cruiser Division and *Fuso* left here, and it is no longer possible to conceal our movement. [*According to U.S. records, a Seventh Fleet B-24 out of Wakde sighted this Japanese force. The submarine sighting is not identified.*][2] If air support on this force is insufficient tomorrow, the Kon force will find itself in a very tough position before it reaches its destination. Also, the screening force commander can hardly stand to leave the transport force alone and operate in the Palau area. Anyway, we should watch tomorrow's development with keen interest.

The Second Tanker Train, consisting of *Genyo Maru* and *Azusa Maru,* which had been here, sailed out early this morning under orders. Escorted by two destroyers, it headed for point "I," 130 miles east of the northern part of Mindanao, passing the third route. Whether one likes it or not, the time for the battle upon which the rise or fall of the empire depends is thus ripening.

By Operational Telegram Order No. 114 the commander in chief, Combined Fleet, ordered the Fifth Land-Based Air Force commander to concentrate the Second Attack Group under his direct command at the West New Guinea and Halmahera areas.

Advanced bases were to be prepared at Sorong and Babo, with rear bases at Wasile and Kaoe. This is a bit late but is in accord with what I suggested to the commander in chief of the task force on the 27th. With this new arrangement, we can now inflict damage on the enemy. It will even become possible to reinforce an army force to Biak.

Sunday, 4 June 1944. Partly fair, squall. No work today and a movie was shown in the evening. The men of the fleet are relaxed.

At 2200 yesterday, the Combined Fleet suspended Operation Kon against the wish of the army and ordered the Fifth Heavy Cruiser Division and *Fuso* to return to their original units. The transport force was also ordered to disembark the troops either at Sorong or Manukwari and withdraw to Ambon. This, I surmise, is because of a radio intelligence report of an enemy task force movement detected to the south of Meleyon [Woleai] and also of yesterday's shadowing by enemy B-24s. [*The report of a carrier force off Biak was false.*][3]

The task force had previously ordered the Fifth Heavy Cruiser Division and *Fuso* to await orders at Davao, but today the Combined Fleet ordered them to go to Palau as a diversionary force. At 1130 an army reconnaissance plane reported an enemy task force of two CVs, two battleships, and ten destroyers in a ring formation accompanied by three groups of two fighters, sailing on course 270° at 20 knots, at a point fifty-five miles bearing 30° of Cape d'Urville. This report caused quite a fuss. The Combined Fleet ordered all vessels in the western part of New Guinea and Halmahera area to take refuge. However, at 2013 it was learned from a navy plane's contact that they were actually two *Portland*-type and *Omaha*-type cruisers and eight destroyers. [*Probably Rear Admiral V. A. C. Crutchley's force of the cruisers* Australia, Boise, Nashville, Phoenix, *and fourteen destroyers which a Japanese reconnaissance plane spotted around noon on 4 June.*]⁴

At 2210 the Combined Fleet ordered resumption of Operation Kon. In light of the confusion and fuss since yesterday, their command of force can't be called perfect. My sympathy goes to those forces concerned, which found themselves at a loss on how to follow instructions.

Monday, 5 June 1944. Cloudy. The task fleet ordered the Second Tanker Train to await orders in the vicinity of point "J" (Surigao anchorage). They will find themselves with nothing to do, since sortie of the fleet has been suspended.

The Kon Force commander suggested to the Combined Fleet that, even if the operation is resumed, there will be little chance of success in transporting troops by destroyers alone to Biak, where there is no pier facility and few boats available for landing, in addition to interceptions by enemy planes and ships. On the other hand, the chief of staff, Southern Area Army, has begun demanding that the Second Mobile Army Corps be landed at Biak promptly. During the night of the 3rd, several medium bombers attacked an enemy on the south coast of Biak, destroying one cruiser and one destroyer. [*This attack by ten Fourth Army bombers from Samate, nine navy bombers, and twenty-two Zeros of the Twenty-third Air Flotilla, actually sank nothing. They inflicted minor damage on destroyer* Reid, *which lost one man killed and five wounded, and wounded two men aboard* LCT 248, *at a cost of eleven Japanese aircraft. However, on the evening of 4 June the Twenty-third Air Flotilla attacked Crutchley's group and a near miss slightly damaged* Nashville.]⁵ While the air strength deployed at western New Guinea is dwindling, the Second Attacking Group of the Fifth Land-Based Air Force, which was about to move into that district, was ordered to come under the direct command of the commander in chief, and its use before the showdown was to be made by special order.

[Ugaki was sure that eventually lack of air power would "bring about an adverse situation," and it was useless to keep throwing in "piecemeal reinforcements." He had been afraid the United States would begin building airstrips "elsewhere other than at Biak," and, in actuality, one had begun near Bosnik.]

At 1050 today enemy submarines torpedoed the convoy including *Takasaki* at a point 6° 33′ N, 120° 13′ and *Takasaki* and *Ashizuri* were sunk. [*Tankers* Ashizuri *and* Takasaki *fell to the U.S. submarine* Puffer.][6] We sent a reconnaissance seaplane from here to cooperate in guarding the force and sweeping enemy submarines at night. *Takaoka Maru* and *Kumihime Maru* were also sunk at a point 170 miles east of Pagan in the Mariana Islands. The rampant activity of enemy submarines is spreading day by day, adding to our worries. In sharp contrast to this, our two submarines transporting supplies to Buin in the Solomons are missing. Therefore, the Combined Fleet suspended the transport operation by submarines in that area as well as in the Rabaul area.

[Tuesday, 6 June, began with *Yamato* carrying out damage control training in the morning, *Musashi* in the afternoon.]

The Second Air Force carried out reconnaissance over Majuro in the Marshalls at altitude 8,500 meters. Quite a number of ships are assembled there as follows: six CVs (*Essex* or *Enterprise* type), six battleships (two *Iowa* Type), over eight cruisers, over eighteen destroyers, four tankers (one of which was refueling a CV), ten large transports, and ten medium ones. There is strong indication of their going out shortly. [*Vice Admiral M. A. Mitscher's Task Force 58 actually sortied from Majuro on 6 June.*][7]

Another fighter reconnoitering the Admiralty Islands reported one CV, two battleships or large heavy cruisers, and three destroyers at Seeadler. [*The escort carrier* Hoggatt Bay *and four destroyers were stationed at Seeadler at this time.*][8] The Combined Fleet sent word of praise for those brave missions and ordered them to fix their planes tomorrow to be ready for use from the day after tomorrow.

At 0925 a reconnaissance plane from Meleyon [Woleai] sighted four ships including CVs, with course 305° and speed 18 knots at a point 470 miles bearing 160° from there. In the evening it was also reported to consist of one CV, one battleship, and four destroyers sailing east at 10 knots. I wonder what idea they have. Are they waiting for others?

The chief of staff of the Area Army has asked the chief of staff, Combined Fleet, to carry out Operation Kon, though in elaborate wording. Maybe because of this the chief of staff, Combined Fleet, ordered the Kon Force commander to carry out the operation promptly while on the other hand sending an explanatory wire to the army. What a weak attitude! Moreover, he confessed that Operation Kon was a diversion to be carried out with an element force simultaneously with Operation A. This revealed a great mistake in his basic thinking. I rather pity him. If nobody questions his ability, he'll be lucky.

My staff officers urged launching a surprise attack with medium bombers or *Ginga* upon the main enemy force at Majuro. Good! Very good! I told them I had better make them staff officers of the Combined Fleet. [*The* Ginga *was a twin-engined medium bomber developed in 1944 which could dive bomb. The United States code-named it Frances.*]⁹ According to a telegram sent from the commander, Sixteenth Heavy Cruiser Division, and brought to me at 2300, the Kon Force (*Aoba*) was fighting with eleven B-24s at Kabare Bay, Waigeo Island (western end of the Bird's Head), at 1617. [*This B-24 attack of the 380th Group was unsuccessful.*]¹⁰ The enemy seems to overlook nothing and to be quite diligent. I can really appreciate the hard time the Kon Force commander must be having.

Wednesday, 7 June 1944. Fair. At 2345 last night, destroyer *Minatsuki* went to attack a surfaced submarine while escorting *Okikawa Maru,* and has been missing after she counterattacked her. Since this morning planes and destroyers have been sent to the scene. And we had another misfortune, losing destroyer *Hayanami,* torpedoed and sunk at a point forty-five miles bearing 203° from Tawi Tawi at 1230. Only forty-five, including one officer, the navigator, survived. [*Both* Minatsuki *and* Hayanami *fell to the U.S. submarine* Harder.]¹¹

These bring to three the losses of destroyers sustained south of the anchorage. It's most regrettable that we can't sink enemy submarines shortly after their attacks. They might have been employing some special measures.

The vice navy minister and the vice chief of the Naval General Staff jointly issued a warning that our ship loss by enemy submarines in May amounted to over 210,000 tons, to their deepest concern. Isn't it necessary to review countermeasures fundamentally?

No news has been received about *Aoba*, which enemy planes bombed yesterday, but as its flag commander shifted his flag to a destroyer, her fate isn't hard to picture. It was later learned that he shifted his flag to destroyer *Shikinami* to continue his command. [*Ugaki was unduly pessimistic.* Aoba *and* Kinu *rendezvoused with six destroyers off Misool Island, and Sakonju transferred his flag to* Shikinami *while the cruisers went to Ambon to be replenished.*]¹²

The Combined Fleet added the Fifth Heavy Cruiser Division and two destroyers to the Kon Force.

The army desires to transport troops by cruisers as far as Manokwari from there shuttling to Biak by destroyers. But Manokwari and Babo are under frequent enemy raids, installations and small craft greatly damaged. Moreover, Korim, a landing point on the north coast of Biak, is also under strict enemy vigilance, so counterlanding will be no easy task. It has been reported that the enemy penetrated Solido's No. 3 airstrip in Biak. Dangerous! But this is no wonder as it's the twelfth day since they came to attack the island.

As an additional order of Operation A, the task fleet has issued its plans to attack the enemy task force with its whole fleet when the latter sticks to the northern coast of New Guinea, and also of attempting to lure them out with its elements. This is almost what I suggested before. This step may be considered quite daring, as the task fleet has taken it without consulting the Combined Fleet. But I think that, as the commander in chief commanding the whole task force, he should always be mentally prepared to have a better judgment than that of the present Combined Fleet.

[General Dwight D.] Eisenhower announced that the Allied force landed on the north coast of France. Now the second front in Europe has commenced. In spite of the German boasting of the completeness of her defense, we cannot but conclude, hearing this announcement, that the Allied forces have made favorable progress. If Germany can't cope with this crisis, the Axis powers both in the East and West will be doomed. We must watch developments attentively.

Thursday, 8 June 1944. Partly fair. The Fifth Heavy Cruiser Division of the Kon Force sailed out for Western New Guinea by order of its commander, but at 0330 yesterday destroyer *Kazagumo* was torpedoed and made unable to navigate in Davao harbor entrance. [*The U.S. submarine* Hake *sank* Kazagumo.][13]

At 1245 today, ten B-24s and seven P-38s attacked and sank destroyer *Harusame* at a point eighty miles bearing 320° of Manokwari, while she was engaged in transporting troops. A near miss at 1317 also partially flooded destroyer *Shiratsuyu* and her oil was leaking. It's apparent that more destroyers will be lost in carrying out operational transport to the Biak area. Nothing can be done without replacements. [*The attack came from ten B-25s of the Seventeenth Reconnaissance Squadron—all the 310th Bombardment Wing could spare after a damaging Japanese air strike on Wakde on the night of 5–6 June—with P-38 escort. They sank* Harusame *and damaged* Shiratsuyu, Shikinami, *and* Samidare. *The AAF paid dearly for this success, losing three crews, including that of the squadron commander. The other B-25s were so badly damaged that the entire squadron had to be reorganized at Finschhafen.*][14]

Yesterday an army reconnaissance reported fourteen enemy vessels at 1300 and five transports including battleships and twenty small craft at 1515, both sailing west near Wakde. A naval reconnaissance plane also sighted four battleships, four cruisers, and eight destroyers at a point 366 miles bearing 83° from Sorong at 1342 today. [*This was Crutchley again, with heavy cruiser* Australia, *light cruisers* Boise *and* Phoenix, *and fourteen destroyers sailing to a position off Korim Bay.*][15] The enemy has no carrier and seems to intend to bombard with battleship's firepower under cover of superior land-based air power.

Against this, our Third Air Force has only thirteen Zero fighters, eighteen Type I fighters, and seven carrier-borne *Suisei* bombers. With this small strength we must meet more than three hundred enemy planes deployed west of Hollandia. This is worse than sweeping back the sea with a broom.

When a miser tries to be more stingy, he loses everything in the end. However many times he may dole out in small portions, it will be just the same. Not only is the enemy's supply line exceedingly stretched, but his advance line is limited to only one route along the north coast of New Guinea at this very time.

Against this line of enemy advance, we have several bases forming a letter T to it. If only our planes could be replenished, it wouldn't be impossible to turn the tide of war. What do they think of the present plight, those responsible men in Tokyo who promised that so many planes would be produced by May? Shame on them! Thus the loss of western New Guinea will spell a direct cause for defeat in this war. Even if Operation A can be materialized to attain some success, we can't think we would thus be able to stop the enemy advance at western New Guinea. These two have connections with each other, of course, but it's also necessary to consider them separately; much more so when the chance of Operation A preceding western New Guinea is small. My feelings are expressed in a Chinese poem:

> In land of the south where green trees cover isles
> Lies an armada impatient to go to sea.
> Time for the showdown is close at hand,
> At a loss who is to do with Operation "Fool."

[*Ugaki was making a bitter pun.* Aho *means "damn fool" and Ugaki used it to criticize* A-go.]

[After lunch on Friday, 9 June, Ugaki went to the wardroom to see a movie "which would not have been suitable for the men." Later he and the engineer staff officer went shooting and bagged enough pigeons for Ugaki to plan "a reunion of classmates" for the next day. Both time and "small bullet ammunition" were running out, so this would perhaps be their last chance for such a get-together.]

At about 2230 last night, the Kon Force, which has shifted to transportation by destroyers, found an ambushing enemy of one battleship, three cruisers, and eight destroyers off Korim and immediately turned about. Fire was concentrated on destroyer *Shiratsuyu* and destroyer *Samidare,* and they fired torpedoes against ten pursuing enemy ships. At one time, the Sixteenth Heavy Cruiser Division sent back that they were withdrawing toward Palau, but they finally escaped the danger and headed for Batchian anchorage in Halmahera.

[*In effect, Sakonju declined battle with Crutchley, casting off the barges the destroyers were towing and retiring after firing torpedoes.*][16]

At breakfast this morning, I thought that we had no choice but to give up Biak. Further attempts to hold it against odds would only add to our losses. If the army insists on sending reinforcements, there is no other means but to make shuttling transport from Manokwari at night by small craft. Even if we can send more ground troops, they wouldn't be any good without air protection. Instead, we must firmly defend the Bird's Head and neck of New Guinea, and concentrate every available plane at bases there. This is the only way I can see; there is no alternative.

On the other hand, four B-24s attacked Peleliu base in Palau with small bombs and three staff officers were said to be injured. It's deplorable that we have to admit that Palau itself has been brought within enemy attack range. The only comfort is that we have been raiding the enemy airfield at Wakde from time to time, taking advantage of the moonlight, and have set fires there, damaging enemy planes. As we can hardly shoot down those big Boeing planes in air fights even if making them emit white smoke, is there any other means but to destroy them on the ground? Why can't we get planes that can't be shot down?

Enemy planes raiding Kusaie Island dropped a propaganda pamphlet in some San Francisco-made beer bottles, saying, "Where is the Imperial Navy which can't recover?" It's ridiculous! My answer is, "Here we are!"

As a result of the third reconnaissance on Majuro, carried out at 0937 today, it was learned that many CVs and battleships which the last reconnaissance spotted there were all gone. Well, where did they go? I tell them, "Don't hesitate about where to go but come west, right into our net of Operation A." At last the Combined Fleet has hurried up planning a night attack on enemy ships there by medium bombers with a suggestion of others, but that won't be any good after the birds have flown away.

At 2225, enemy submarines twice struck destroyer *Tanikaze* while she was searching for submarines at a point nine miles bearing 229° from this anchorage. She sank at once; 126 survivors were picked up. [Tanikaze *and another destroyer were after* Harder, *which instead sank* Tanikaze.][17]

[On Saturday, 10 June, Ugaki had to cancel his projected reunion of classmates, for he had received a very important message, Combined Fleet Telegram Operational Order No. 127.]

The gist of the Combined Fleet Order:

1. First Battleship Division (*Yamato, Musashi*) and Second Destroyer Squadron (*Noshiro*, two destroyers) will be included in the Kon Force. Commander, First Battleship Division, will command the force.

2. The Kon Force will continue Operation Kon in accordance with the following:

a. To destroy the enemy task force and enemy reinforcements in the Biak area as well as to bombard enemy landing forces on Biak and Owi Islands.

b. To transport the Second Mobile Brigade to Biak at an opportune moment. Unless otherwise ordered, to continue Operation Kon even if an order to "Stand By for Operation A" is given and to act so as to lure the enemy task force to the decisive battle scene according to the enemy situation.

I never expected that I, who have had nothing to do except criticize operational plans, would be appointed commander of this operation in which much trouble is anticipated. I've made up my mind to accomplish this operation with all my efforts, just as if I were commander in chief of the mobile force, for I shall have under my command flags of the Fifth Heavy Cruiser Division, Second Destroyer Squadron, and Sixteenth Heavy Cruiser Division, as well as many ships and forces.

I've also decided to start preparations right away and proceed to Batchian anchorage in Halmahera, where the force under my command will assemble for briefing, and then commence the operation. As refueling was the first thing to be done, we brought *Tone* alongside *Yamato* and *Chikuma* to *Musashi* and took fuel from them. At 1400 commanders and staff assembled for a briefing on the sortie. From 1500 I made farewell calls on both commanders in chief on board *Taiho* and *Atago*, respectively.

At 1600 we sailed out in order of the Second Destroyer Squadron (two destroyers of the Tenth Destroyer Squadron added) and First Battleship Division through manned ships at Tawi Tawi, where we've stayed nearly a month. In the morning, Third Battleship Division Commander Suzuki and Seventh Heavy Cruiser Division Commander Shiraishi came to bid farewell. I was very grateful to them.

After leaving the reef, speed was increased to 22 knots and zigzag movements began under First Alert Disposition. Planes of the Second Fleet escorted us until dusk.

Before 1800, soon after we changed course from 180° to 130°, a periscope was seen eight thousand meters port abeam and destroyer *Okinami* in the screen promptly attacked it. The enemy submarine fired two torpedoes against her, surfacing her periscope several times, but the torpedoes passed parallel to her at a close distance and did no harm. The destroyer dropped depth charges near the periscope, and at the second attack a bubble of a hundred meters diameter, then fuel oil, gushed out over an extensive area. It was certain that she was sunk.

In the briefing before the sortie, the Second Destroyer Squadron commander suggested that destroyer attacks upon enemy subs were considered to be of little effect but risky, so it would be better to avoid them. But it was decided to carry out attacks in accordance with orders, and it was a good omen to have this good result on the first leg of our voyage. I couldn't but say that it was the usual thing to see a fuss arise about seeing periscopes here and there.

Although I have nothing else to be afraid of in carrying out the coming operation, the shortage of our air power that can cooperate with us is the most important problem, about which I am worried. The Third Air Force and the front line as well have several times urged the urgent need of its reinforcement. But the Combined Fleet has not yielded to the use of the Second Attack Group, which has already been sent there, except for some fighters. I think that to reach the front line itself without air cover is awfully difficult, but I won't grumble about it now. I shall do all that is humanly possible.

[That afternoon Ugaki received a telegram of advice from the Combined Fleet, another of appreciation from Field Marshal Terauchi, and one from the Second Area Army which "seemed quite nervous." But Ugaki decided that he would rely on himself as to what to do.

[Sunday, 11 June, found the Kon Force proceeding on its way, crossing the Celebes Sea, and using its own planes as escorts. Receiving word that Captain Inako Otani, a staff officer of the Southwest Area Fleet, was flying to Tawi Tawi for a liaison mission, Ugaki sent a plane to catch him at Menado and bring him to Batchian. At 2000 the force altered course, making an evasive movement because of a false submarine report. Two of his ships nearly collided, to Ugaki's disgust.]

While we were talking about reinforcing our eastern reconnaissance planes to search for the enemy task force, which hasn't been found since its departure from Majuro, they appeared in the Marianas. In the early morning today, our patrol plane sighted enemy carrier-borne aircraft at a point more than three hundred miles east of Guam, at 1000 its surface forces, then its carrier force at about 170 miles. The enemy repeatedly attacked Rota, Saipan, Guam, Tinian and approached as near as eighty miles. His arrogant attitude makes me mad, yet we're not even able to get a clear picture of his whole force. An order has been issued to contact the enemy tonight and carry out night and dawn attacks, but I wonder how effective they could be.

Enemy planes attacked Saipan in two waves of fifty planes each, but it was good to learn that our navy and army shot down forty of them and our damage was small. [*Four task groups were involved—TG 58.1 under Rear Admiral J. J. Clark with* Hornet, Yorktown, Bataan, Belleau Wood; *TG 58.2 under Rear Admiral A. E. Montgomery with* Bunker Hill, Monterey, Wasp, Cabot; *TG 58.3 under Rear Admiral J. W. Reeves with* Enterprise, Lexington, Princeton, San Jacinto; *and TG 58.5 under Rear Admiral W. K. Harrill with* Essex, Langley, *and* Cowpens. *These carriers, with supporting battleships, cruisers, and destroyers, attacked Tinian, Saipan, and Guam. One Japanese source estimated that thirty-six Japanese planes were destroyed that day. Early in the morning of 12 June, ten bombers from Truk attacked the northern groups—TG 58.1 had sailed on toward Guam—but inflicted no damage.*][18] This seemed to confuse the Combined Fleet, which ordered the Second Attack Group to shift back to the first attack position (Tinian area). Why did they order its advance and then call it back? They'll be exhausted going back and forth and become unable to operate after all. This also made the execution of our Operation Kon more difficult.

Just before destroyer *Yamagumo* and *Nowake* of the Tenth Destroyer Squadron, which had been in the direct screen by 1500, were going to depart to head back to Tawi Tawi, we fortunately received an order putting them under my command, replacing the damaged Twenty-seventh Destroyer Division.

From 2000 we changed course suddenly and sailed south to the southwest of Halmahera. Enemy telephone registered sensitivity 5, but we didn't see him.

Monday, 12 June 1944. Fair. At 0530 we reached the north of Batarata Island of the Batchian Anchorage in Halmahera (a few miles error was observed in the chart.) Under guidance of a destroyer accompanying the Fifth Heavy Cruiser Division, we dropped anchor at 0° 25′ S, 127° 10′ E. The time was just 0800. Two cruisers of the Fifth Heavy Cruiser Division and *Aoba* and *Kinu* of the Sixteenth Heavy Cruiser Division were already there. Most of the Kon Force (*Itsukushima, Tsugaru* of the transport force and the escorting ships were operating from Kaoe area to Sorong) has thus completed assemblage. The south and north channels leading to this anchorage are narrow and the road itself isn't so wide. So it's quite suitable for a temporary shelter anchorage. I think the enemy hasn't yet found this.

[There Ugaki had a "friendly talk" with Sakonju and attended a briefing.

He told them that the operation would require "a firm determination of never yielding" and to make preparations for "a close night fighting."]

In view of the past experience of being forced to abandon all landing craft towed by destroyers when encountered by an enemy before reaching the destination, I have arranged to carry ten landing craft brought here by the army on board ship—two each by *Yamato* and *Musashi* and one each by six destroyers. Necessary work to load them on board a destroyer was started immediately. This has settled one problem. But everybody believes that the weakness of the air force that is to cooperate with us should be the first consideration. The commander in chief, Fourth Southern Expeditionary Fleet (Vice Admiral Yamagata), also wired to Tokyo on the 9th urging the absolute necessity of it in order to hold Biak and send troops there. He asked me to do the same. In view of the general situation, I thought his suggestion agreeable, so I prepared a plan.

But from early morning today the enemy task force moving to the east of the Marianas the same as yesterday made repeated air raids upon various places there. The Combined Fleet has been impatient to get the complete picture of the enemy, but that's no easy matter. According to papers a POW had, they seem to be fifteen ships, including converted carriers. But summing up past reconnaissances, it's certain that there were twelve ships. [*The count of fifteen carriers, including converted ones, was correct.*][19]

In the evening the Combined Fleet sent in operational intentions that either "when it becomes apparent that the enemy is planning an invasion of the Marianas" or "when the enemy task force advances to the west of the line of the Marianas," the decisive battle would be sought. Instead, if it moves up north as a mere independent operation or withdraws, we shall continue present operations with the present disposition while tenaciously carrying out Operation Kon in cooperation with fighters of the Second Attacking Group.

[This convinced Ugaki that the Combined Fleet "well realized the need of reinforcing fighter strength to carry out Operation Kon," so he decided not to send in his plan. The ships that came into harbor that day received a quick refueling from *Eiyo Maru*, which bumped into *Musashi*, inflicting slight damage. Ugaki entertained all commanders at lunch, and several staff officers came aboard "for liaison missions."]

Tuesday, 13 June 1944. Fair. The First Air Fleet gave a summarized report on the enemy situation as follows at 1943 on the 12th:

Summing up several reconnaissances since the 11th and photos taken and observations by a *Saiun* reconnaissance plane, it is judged that the whole enemy force consists of a total of four groups (eleven carriers in all), of which three groups (nine carriers in all) are on the sea close to the Marianas, and one group (two carriers) is 159 to 200 miles east of the first groups.

So far no landing force has been found. So it seems to be a mere task operation, but this might be because of our failure to discover enemy landing forces.

Many planes have raided the Mariana area since early this morning. The first enemy group consisted of four carriers, eight battleships, six cruisers, and four destroyers, and the second group two or three carriers and nine or ten others. They moved to the west of the Marianas, and, at 0830, two battleships, six heavy cruisers, and seventeen destroyers approached Tinian from the north and started bombardment from 0940. It makes me grind my teeth to think we can do nothing against this ferocity.

[*Raids of the 12th and 13th decimated Japanese air power in the area.*][20]

A Zero fighter's reconnaissance report on the Seeadler area made at 1530 to 1615 on the 12th:

1. Two carriers, five new battleships, ten cruisers, thirty transports (over medium type) at a point seventy miles bearing 260° from Kabieng, its course west, speed 18 to 20 knots.

2. Five battleships, ten destroyers, ten transports at a point thirty miles bearing 45° from the entrance to Seeadler harbor heading toward it.

3. Two CVs, two medium carriers, five battleships, nineteen cruisers, fifty transports (over medium type) in port.

Total: six carriers, fifteen battleships, twenty cruisers, ten destroyers, ninety transports.

That should be called a great force indeed. Where are they heading? [*Probably units of Task Force 51 Joint Expeditionary Force of Operation Forager, the capture of Saipan and Tinian.*][21] Anyway, I feel the time for the showdown is close at hand at last. Unless Operation Kon is carried out soon, we'll be at a disadvantage.

Our ordered mission calls for an attack and a transport; these can't be carried out simultaneously without affecting both. Therefore, I've decided to carry them out separately as follows and have ordered plans made accordingly:

In view of the fact that we have to carry landing craft on board battleships and destroyers, and there is no better landing point than Korim, the first attempt shall be carried out to the north coast with transportation as its main object. Then, from the second time on, we shall have nothing to encumber us so shall attack (including shore bombardment) mainly on the south coast with the attacking force alone.

A signal from the Central Pacific Area Fleet at Saipan received at about

1600 stated, "The enemy bombarded our batteries and coastal positions, and destroyers are minesweeping the roads." [*These bombardments, by battleships which had no practice in this technique, were unproductive.*][22] At the same time, the Combined Fleet ordered that we seek an enemy landing force in earnest. Maybe they've already lost almost all of their reconnaissance planes, and our chronically poor reconnaissance has been fully displayed, rendering the overall command impossible.

Considering that the enemy's minesweeping meant an impending landing developing into a decisive battle, I decided this wasn't the time for a minor operation like Kon and suspended the loading of landing craft on board. Besides, I determined not to send a request for urgent reinforcement of fighter power for the Second Attacking Group, a request which I had drafted to submit to chief of staff, Combined Fleet. Unless otherise ordered, I was instructed to continue Operation Kon in case an order to "Stand by for Operation A" was given, but I've made up my mind to go up north commanding reinforcing forces, depending upon my own judgment in a case like that.

After lowering the ensign, I received an emergency telegram, "Stand by for Operation A," so immediately ordered preparations for sortie. About fifteen minutes later another order was received, suspending Operation Kon and changing the reinforcement from the task force back to the original units. Thus everything was settled and I was saved from acting contrary to orders.

I hastily drafted a plan for rushing to the decisive battle scene, and at 2045 assembled all commanders and staff officers for briefing. However hard we might try to get ready quickly, patrol boats had to be recalled and landing craft returned to the Sixteenth Heavy Cruiser Division, and they returned our cutters. Besides, lights had to be lit at the narrow north entrance. We left at 2200.

I unexpectedly met Rear Admiral Sakonju, a classmate, but we had to part again after I returned the command to him. Those who meet must part again. I commanded the Kon Force for only four days, yet I have no regrets at all because I did my best for its success. I only think the army must have been very much disappointed.

At 2200 in the moonlight we left the anchorage in order of the Second Destroyer Squadron, First Battleship Division, and Fifth Heavy Cruiser Division, formed an alert formation and sped along the west coast of Halmahera at 20 knots. We had information about a submarine fifty miles north of Batchian Island yesterday, but nothing happened. At about 1100, we sighted an unidentified large-type plane at a long distance. There is a good probability of its being an enemy patrol plane.

[A typhoon developed west of the Marianas, and Ugaki facetiously wished they had some way of directing it to the enemy. He received rendezvous point orders for the morning of the 16th and wondered if the enemy would stay until the 19th, "when the decisive battle is slated to take place."]

Wednesday, 14 June 1944. Fair. At 0700 we altered course to 20° from the south of Taraud Island. In the morning we reduced speed to 18 knots for a while, but made it back again to 20 knots.

There seemed nothing conclusive about the general situation this morning. But the Central Pacific Fleet suddenly reported the commencement of the enemy landing. This upset me, for I thought, if so, a showdown slated on the 19th would be too late.

Realizing the need for refueling smaller vessels to full capacity as soon as possible, I decided to carry out refueling tomorrow afternoon and the day after tomorrow. A tanker force apparently will reach the designated A point tomorrow evening, though the original plan calls for refueling from the morning of the day after tomorrow.

Seeing one large and six small planes passing from the west to the south at about 1300, I ordered an antiair alert, as I thought it might be good for training. But they were soon confirmed to be ours. However, at 1100 another ship sighted a large plane passing ahead of us to the west. It must have been a B-25, and I'm afraid it might have discovered our movement.

Today we employed two to four antisubmarine planes, and with a wind coming astern it was hard to lift them on board. The consequent loss of the run as a whole was considerable. Moreover, just before recovering them in the evening, destroyers depth charged, based on a false report. A *Musashi* plane overturned after landing on the sea, and a rescue boat didn't move. It took quite a while before we could resume our movement. What trying children they are! I thought.

A summary of the battle situation in the Marianas area sent from the First Air Fleet and Central Pacific Fleet commanders:

> Saipan area as of 1230 on the 14th: nine battleships (new and old), five heavy cruisers, and more than thirty destroyers were divided into four groups and bombarded all areas. Lowering high-speed landing craft, they carried out a forced reconnaissance on reef and shore. Fierce firing of shells like Type III shell, with about ten fighters flying at high altitude all the time, and one or two ship-borne observation planes at about one thousand meters. Five destroyers sweep Saipan channel.
>
> Pagan area as of 1430 on the 14th: battleships, cruisers, destroyers,

and minesweepers, forty in all, bombarded the air base successively
since this morning.

*[The bombardments of the 14th, by nine battleships, six heavy cruisers, five
light cruisers, and some twenty-six destroyers were much more successful than the
battleship attempt of the 13th, for these ships had practiced and had plans which
were carefully worked out.]*[23]

Neither included carriers but there must be several. Further, the Second
Air Force's report sent at 1510 on the 14th said: "An enemy which a patrol
plane discovered at a point 350 miles bearing 352° from Truk at 0615 includes six carriers (two with super-structures, four without), four battleships and cruisers, four destroyers, three tankers, and three 38,000-ton
transports (three hundred miles from Saipan]."

Based on these, the chief of staff, Combined Fleet, wired his judgement
of the situation to Operation A forces as follows at 1745:

> The enemy task force which has been raiding the Marianas since
> the 11th is nearly the whole strength of U.S. regular carriers. They
> made attacks with more than half of them on the 11th and 12th, and
> probably a part of them is being refueled in the rear on the 13th
> and 14th. In connection with enemy bombardments on Saipan and
> Tinian, and also with the Second Air Force's telegram No. 141510,
> an enemy invasion is considered imminent.

An army report from Rota Island also stated, "At 0900 eight carriers,
eight battleships, fourteen cruisers, and several others were sighted near
Rota Island."

The moon rises after 0100 tonight so until that time we shall proceed
straight at 20 knots.

We didn't hear any telephones of enemy submarines.

Thursday, 15 June 1944. Rainy and cloudy. First Air Fleet telegram at
0440, 15th: "About fifteen large-type transports and fifteen medium and
small ones are sighted off to the west of Saipan. Four carriers and other
surface craft about the same as seen yesterday are in sight off to the
west, too."

Central Pacific Fleet telegram at 0500, 15th: "At 0500, to the west of
Saipan, there are twenty-eight large-type transports, forty special transports, more than a dozen others including battleships in sight."

First Air Fleet telegram at 0522, 15th: "Seventy large-type landing craft,
approximately one hundred small and others, and it is considered that

simultaneous landing on Saipan and Tinian are going to be made."

First Air Fleet telegram at 0620, 15th: "The enemy has unloaded all landing craft and is awaiting orders to proceed to the shore."

First Air Fleet telegram at 0640, 15th: "Enemy landing craft are grouped into two, one heading for the west coast of Saipan and the other to the west of Tinian Airstrip No. 1."

First Air Fleet telegram at 0800, 15th: "All enemy landing craft are heading for Saipan harbor. No enemy craft seen in Aslete area."

Combined Fleet Telegram Operational Order No. 154 at 0717, 15th:

1. In the morning of the 15th, the enemy has commenced its landings in Saipan, Tinian areas with its powerful force.

2. The Combined Fleet will destroy the enemy task force which has come to the Marianas area, then annihilate its invasion force.

3. Decisive-battle Operation A will begin.

[*The landings were directly in charge of Vice Admiral R. K. Turner, under the overall command of Admiral Spruance.*][24]

Combined Fleet telegram at 0800, 15th addressed to all A forces: "The rise and fall of the empire depends on this one battle, so everyone is expected to exert further efforts."

The above are telegrams in the initial stage of the battle, and thus the long-awaited battle has started once for all. The scene in which a decisive battle is going to take place is far more favorable to us than the Palau area. Once they're committed to taking it, it's hard for them to break off, so that much good game will come into our hands one after another. We should exert ourselves all the more.

[Most of the day Ugaki's forces tried to rendezvous with the tanker force, but it was not at the prearranged position, and only with the help of a flying boat from Davao did they discover its location, finally meeting at 1800. But the tanker force could not understand Ugaki's instructions for the next day's "supply and movement." He thought of sending a destroyer with instructions, but, fearing enemy submarines, decided against this move.]

Last night a task force order temporarily placed the First Tanker Force under my command until the reunion. However, destroyer *Shiratsuyu*, on convoy escort duty, collided her port amidship against *Seiyo Maru*'s bow while making irregular movements through the convoy. This resulted in an explosion of depth charges which sank her in three minutes and killed her captain. It was quite regrettable. This incident delayed the movement of the force.

An enemy fleet [TG 58.1][25] approached and bombarded Guam.

Twenty enemy B-29s and B-24s attacked northern Kyushu coming from China on the continent and inflicted some damage. This is a new tactic. Everywhere there is nothing but a decisive battle. (Written at 0200 on the 16th).

[*Forty-seven B-29s of the Twentieth Bomber Command struck Japan with the Imperial Iron and Steel Works at Yawata as primary target. It was estimated that this installation turned out about twenty-four percent of Japan's annual production of rolled steel. This was the first air attack on the home islands since the Doolittle raid, and by coincidence one B-29 Wing was commanded by Brigadier General Laverne G. "Blondie" Saunders, who on 7 December 1941 had been able to get his B-17 airborne after the Pearl Harbor attack in a futile attempt to find the Nagumo task force. Damage to Imperial was minor, but this and subsequent raids in 1944 gave the Japanese press trouble in explaining why, if Japan was winning the war as claimed, the United States could send bombers over the home soil.*][26]

The Allied forces that landed in northern France were about 400,000 and sustained fairly great damage. German announcements sounded quite confident. Now decisive battles are going to take place in the east and the west.

The Combined Fleet ordered the Fifth Air Attack Group to commence attacks. Now at last they let go of the rein, but I wonder how much good the already-wounded steed can do.

[Friday, 16 June, opened with another unsuccessful attempt to find the tanker force. Eventually a medium bomber spotted it and rendezvous was made at 0900. According to Ugaki, "the tankers' movements were damn slow as usual." The damaged *Seiyo Maru* was able to refuel but soon dropped behind as Ugaki's ships headed for the task force, which they joined at 1600.

[Looking back, Ugaki wondered how they had been able to "accomplish our duty" with only a small division staff. "Now that we have come through one stage of operations with the reunion of our force with the Vanguard Force of the task force, I was able to relax for a while, for which I should be grateful for the help of God." From evening, the fleet proceeded through the night, "while refueling was continued with utmost efforts." By sunset all of Ugaki's cruisers and destroyers had completed refueling; then it was the Vanguard Force's destroyers' turn.]

Today the enemy was still maneuvering near Guam, and a report came in of witnessing the sinking of an *Iowa*-type battleship. It must have been the result of a submarine attack.

[*Actually, no battleship was sunk. Shore batteries on Tinian had hit one of Tennessee's gun mounts, killing eight men, wounding twenty-six, and inflict-*

ing minor material damage. They also killed one man and wounded nine aboard California.][27]

A part of the enemy task force went up north and air raided Iwo Jima and Chichi Jima, threatening places not far from our capital. [*Seven carriers of TG 58.1 and 58.4 under Clark conducted these raids.*][28] In preparation for an attack from the west, the western part of Honshu, the Southwest Islands, and Formosa are strictly alerted for an air raid.

We have inflicted some damage on transports and others in the Saipan area, but none of the carriers has been sunk. The chief of staff, Combined Fleet, therefore, strictly requested that we not go after such targets. Land-based planes must sink at least one-third of the enemy carriers before the decisive battle takes place.

About sixty enemy transports which are concentrated at Saipan seem to have established some bases there. The Central Pacific Fleet and the Base Force there had difficulty in maintaining outside contact and showed the urgency of the situation by burning code books.

Yesterday evening an enemy submarine transmitted an urgent message from Mindanao Sea, and a base post relayed it. This makes us suspect that our task force's movement might have been detected. [*The U.S. submarine* Flying Fish *had sighted Ozawa's force and* Seahorse *spotted Ugaki's within an hour of each other. These reports, indicating two major but widely separated forces approaching, were immensely valuable to Spruance, who postponed the invasion of Guam in consequence.*][29] On the other hand, other information reported detecting an enemy surface force at a point three hundred miles bearing 200° from Palau. This may indicate that an enemy will come to attack from the Admiralty Island district.

The Second Air Fleet was newly established yesterday, the 15th, and I was glad to see Vice Admiral Fukudome, a classmate of mine who has been awaiting orders since the accident last April, appointed its commander in chief.

Saturday, 17 June 1944. Fair. Enemy forces sighted yesterday are as follows:

1. East of the Marianas: Nine carriers (two converted ones included), four battleships, fourteen cruisers, about fifteen destroyers. (Among the battleships, one *Iowa*-type sunk, another one struck with two torpedoes.)

2. West of the Marianas: Three carriers, five battleships, twelve cruisers, thirty-eight destroyers, and eighty-seven transports.

3. North of Truk: Two carriers, one battleship, three cruisers, and others sailing west.

4. South of Truk (350 miles bearing 190°): Two carriers and over a dozen others sailing south.

5. North of the Marianas: Three carriers and more (within 150 miles southeast of Iwo Jima).

Total (except four): Seventeen carriers, over eight battleships, over thirty cruisers, over fifty-five destroyers, eighty transports.

Combined Fleet chief of staff telegram at 2220, 16th:

Judgment on enemy strength attacking the Marianas and its movements are as follows:

1. The invasion force consists of a task force centering around regular carriers, a supporting force of converted carriers, battleships, cruisers, and destroyers etc., and an invasion force. Most of the U.S. regular carriers seem to be involved.

2. Enemy task forces consist of four groups, which in turn are made up of two large-type carriers, three cruisers, and two battleships as a main body. (One of them includes one large-type carrier.) Three of them came to attack Saipan, Tinian, and Guam on the 11th, 12th, and 13th, while another one probably guarded a landing force at a point three hundred miles east of Saipan and refueled at the same time. Leaving one group near Saipan and Guam after the 14th, they air raided Iwo Jima and Chichi Jima with one or two groups on the 15th, 16th, while the other two or one group probably have been refueled preparing to meet our task force.

3. The supporting force appeared near Saipan since the 13th and bombarded Saipan and Tinian every day and also Guam on the 16th. It has quite a number of converted carriers which seem to have cooperated in the landing assault. It is also probable that a part of the battleships which have been with the task force until the 12th were added to this force.

4. One division plus of the landing force landed on Saipan, and more seem to be coming in succession from the Marshall area. (It is not entirely improbable that they might come from the Admiralty area.) There is a possibility that they will attempt to land on Guam on about the 17th.

5. There is a possibility that the enemy task force suspects the movement of our task force and is concentrating to make ready for us. Also, they might attempt to neutralize Yap and Palau on around the 18th.

Chief of staff, Combined Fleet, to task force at 1850 on the 16th:

1. The enemy in the Saipan area landed its large force near Charanca by 1000 on the 16th and established a beachhead there. So far, our

force has been unable to destroy them owing to fierce bombardments, but a further enemy advance is considered difficult.

2. At 1943 on the 19th an enemy submarine near Mindanao Sea sent two special urgent operational signals to the commander in chief, Pacific Fleet, and they were broadcast from Hawaii. They might have detected the movement of our task force.

3. In connection with paragraph 2, there is a probability that a decisive battle will take place on the sea west of the Marianas on about the 18th.

4. The land-based air force is going to intensify its reconnaissance with all its strength from the 18th. Forces other than the Combined Fleet will cooperate in reconnaissance as follows:

a. Within six hundred miles between bearings 90° to 130° from Koroku base at Okinawa.

b. Within seven hundred miles between bearings 90° to 120° from Toko base at Formosa.

c. Within six hundred miles between bearings 90° to 140° from Toizaki, Kyushu.

5. Identification of enemy regular and converted carrier groups is very difficult, so your attention is called to the following points:

a. Those operating near landing convoys are most likely converted types. So when regular ones are reported there, careful identification should be exercised against them.

b. Battleships so far appearing within sight from Saipan and Tinian are mostly old types. The enemy task force that attacked Palau last April is considered to have had no battleships. So whether battleships are included or not cannot necessarily be accounted as an identification factor.

c. Reference to Combined Fleet telegram No. 161828, and in view of a result of expected reconnaissance by the land-based air force on the 18th, the task force should have its own reconnaissance properly reported to thus get a clear picture of enemy regular carrier groups.

6. The enemy carrier-borne air strength has sustained considerable loss in actions since the 11th, and they are being replenished from converted carriers. Due to refueling, etc., however, their replenishment might be interrupted, thus offering the best chance for us to get them.

By 0400 *Yamato* loaded fourteen hundred tons of fuel to her full capacity. At dawn let go hawsers and she took position at the rear center of the Vanguard. At 0530 we turned about and headed for point E while refueling the cruisers. At about 1600 refueling was finished and we formed the Seventh Alert Formation. Then we took position in the Eleventh Group, the right-wing top of the Vanguard, when the commander in chief, task force, signaled as follows: "As of now the task force will advance to seek and destroy the enemy. Firmly believing in the grace of heaven, everyone shall exert himself."

When the main body was about to make formation, a submarine was definitely detected so we went south for a while, then we divided into three groups and made way on course 60° with speed of 20 knots. Soon the sun set.

Enemy planes attacked Guam and Tinian today. We intercepted enemy telephone exchanges talking about the shortage of ammunition at Saipan and sending of 60-mm ammunition by large craft after bursting through the reef. It seemed that U.S.S. *Cabot* (*Lexington II*) was damaged and listing to the east? [*the question mark is indicated in the original Ugaki diary*] of Guam, and an enemy convoy was also damaged by our bombers from Yap, but otherwise nothing much was done.

[*Probably the damaged ship was the escort carrier* Fanshaw Bay *which was hit, killing eleven men and necessitating her sailing to Eniwetok for repairs.*][30]

Chief of staff, First Task Fleet, telegram at 0845, 17th, to chiefs of staff, Combined Fleet, Central Pacific Fleet, and Fifth Land-Based Air Force:

After completing refueling at point E on the evening of the 17th, this fleet will advance to the west of Saipan by daybreak on the 19th via point C (15–0 N, 136–0 E), while paying attention to a possible enemy advance to the west, also a possible diversion from the north. And it will seek to destroy enemy regular carrier groups first, then will annihilate enemy task forces and invading forces with all its strength.

Regarding cooperation of the land-based air forces, your consideration is requested to be given to the following points:

1. To maintain contact with enemy regular carriers near the Marianas after the eve of the decisive battle. If this is possible, inform us without delay the disposition of enemy regular carriers at about noon.

2. Intensifying the sea patrol west of the Marianas from all bases the day before the decisive battle. Especially, much importance is attached to patrol sectors U-32 to U-42 from Iwo Jima.

3. In case the deployment of the Hachiman Unit (Yokosuka Air Group) is delayed we consider it inevitable to put off the decisive battle for one day, so inform us of this prospect immediately.

After nightfall we received a telegram from the Combined Fleet to the effect that four unidentified carrier-borne planes were sighted 360 miles west of Saipan today, and there's a good possibility of the decisive battle taking place tomorrow. Maybe on account of this the fleet changed course from 60° to 50°. However, the enemy seems to have advanced a little too far. Will it really happen tomorrow, I wonder? I had a haircut today and saved some of the hair to be left in case of my death. And I took a bath when I had time, so I'm well prepared for the worst as in past cases.

[Ugaki ended his entry for 17 June with a record of how many tons per hour his ships took in refueling. Sunday, 18 June, opened with a telegram from the Combined Fleet, dated 2119 the 17th, conveying His Imperial Majesty's hopes that "the operational forces will exert themselves" to secure a success comparable to the battle of the Japan Sea. Ugaki noted, "I was deeply moved and pledged myself to relieve His Majesty's anxiety."]

At 0500 reconnaissance planes were dispatched. There were fourteen lines covering from east-southeast to northeast with an advance of over 320 miles. Nearly at its farthest end, a plane on the center line sighted two shipborne planes flying east at altitude of one hundred meters. Probably they might be enemy ones, but they found nothing else. At 1130 aircraft were further dispatched mainly to the north as a precaution against an enemy which might flank us.

Information on enemy movements so far obtained by 1300 were only the following: At about 1400: four carriers, one hundred miles bearing 110° from Saipan; three carriers, forty miles bearing 150° from Saipan. (Among the above, four are converted carriers.)

Commander in chief, Central Pacific Fleet, telegram at 2125, 17th:

1. Night attacks have been carried out every night since the enemy landing, but so far in vain as the enemy position is strong. Enemy has directed its attack to airstrip No. 1.

2. According to transport service phones, the enemy finished landing today. The enemy strength which landed is considered to be three divisions.

3. Today we sighted five enemy flying boats alighting in the anchorage. The cooperation of enemy carrier-borne planes with the land fighting was less active.

4. We judge that the enemy is not going to land on Tinian and Guam at this stage. In view of the above, it seems that the enemy has finished first-stage landing operations on Saipan, and it is likely that most of its carriers have left this area. A delay in carrying out Operation A will not only make us miss the chance for a battle, but will also make it difficult for us to hold here.

The enemy started this invading operation on the 11th and made landings on the 13th. And our task force is going to fight a decisive battle tomorrow. In the meantime, the enemy has finished landing at least three divisions and is now approaching the airstrip with strong forces. If they take the airstrip, the matter will grow more difficult. We can't delay the task force's decisive battle any longer.

Though I was afraid that a big fish might have gotten away, fortunately reconnaissance seemed to find an enemy task force in the afternoon at a point 350 miles bearing 220° from Iwo Jima. But the details were not clear, since we didn't receive that telegram directly. Three groups, each consisting of two carriers and ten more ships, were also seen heading west at a point 160 miles west of Saipan. (It was later learned that its course was 200° and its speed 15 knots.) Accordingly, the task force turned about, setting course at 200°, aiming to attack first the enemy in the north tomorrow morning, then aim for the enemy in the south. Relative positions as of 1530 were as follows [*Ugaki's sketch of these positions is not available*].

A reconnaissance plane dispatched to the southeast met an enemy flying boat on the way. Five flying boats already arrived at Saipan anchorage yesterday, and the need to destroy them is urgent. The Combined Fleet as well as the First Air Fleet were determined to destroy them and attempted to attack them yesterday evening but without much result. So this morning a sudden attack was made upon them with fighters, but the enemy laid a white smoke screen to prevent our attacks. A splendid tactic indeed, even for the enemy!

Enemy dispositions deployed to the north and south suggest that they intend to counterattack us together with their submarines and flying boats, after suspecting the sortie of our task force.

Can it be that we'll fail to win with this mighty force? No! It can't be! However, seeing that our forces made all these discoveries of the enemy forces, I can't help regretting a great deal the land-based air force's insufficient reconnaissance. I want them to exert their utmost efforts to contact the enemy throughout tonight. If this alone can be done, there will be no room for doubt of our success.

As to the enemy in the Iwo Jima area, no reconnaissance reports came in yet. Even within the Eleventh Group, some asked me about that. As that information was necessary for tomorrow morning's search, I inquired about that when we approached *Taiho* in the evening. A short while afterwards an answer came in saying that it was a mistake; the task force was going to attack an enemy west of Saipan tomorrow morning. It isn't known how this mistake was made. Anyway, it was lucky we discovered it early.

Since early morning a ring formation of the Fourth Alert Formation was made. The radius of three kilometers was later shortened to two kilometers by order of the Vanguard Force. As this was the first time for both the flag commands and individual ships to maneuver in such formation, they lacked mutual understanding and committed errors in maneuvering, so I was never free from a feeling of danger. The Eleventh Group commander also seemed to have much trouble with the vulnerable *Zuiho*, the third ship of the Third Carrier Division, right in the center.

The seventeenth line reconnaissance plane, which went out for the second time to search and reconnoiter an enemy situation, failed to return by dusk, probably due to trying to maintain contact with the enemy. A smoke screen was laid from time to time and searchlights lit skyward in the Main Body Force because the plane itself requested by telegram of about 1900 that searchlights be lit. But it does not seem to have returned after all.

Monday, 19 June 1944. Fair, but partly cloudy and occasional small squall. At 2200 last night we changed course to east, and Groups A and B widened the distance from the Vanguard to take a deeper disposition. [*The A Force, under Mobile Fleet Commander Vice Admiral Jisaburo Ozawa, consisted of the First CV Division—CVs* Taiho, Shokaku, Zuikaku; *Fifth Heavy Cruiser Division—*Myoko, Haguro—*and nine destroyers. The B Force under Rear Admiral Takaji Joshima consisted of the Second Carrier Division—CVs* Junyo, Hiyo, *CVL* Ryuho, *battleship* Nagato, *heavy cruiser* Mogami, *and ten destroyers. The Vanguard Force under Vice Admiral Takeo Kurita consisted of the Third Carrier Division—CVLs* Chitose, Chiyoda, *and* Zuiho; *Ugaki's First Battleship Division of* Yamato *and* Musashi; *the Third Battleship Division of* Haruna *and* Kongo; *and nine destroyers.*][31] At 0340 the Vanguard started the first stage search with its dozen seaplanes. As it was one and a half hours before sunrise, second stage search planes were also dispatched from the Third Carrier Division at 0415. All this was done in the dark. Some of those planes met enemy aircraft on their way and others engaged in combat.

At 0638 the ninth-line plane of the first stage search issued the following first report: "Enemy force sighted, existence of carriers not confirmed, position 14°–40' N, 143°–10' E." The seventh line plane reported at 0635 (received at 0653): "Enemy force including carriers sighted, number of carriers unknown. Position 14°–40' N, 143°–10' E, sailing SW." (While I was writing the above on the 20th, I was called up to the bridge suddenly and couldn't take up a pen until the 22nd. So I shall write just the outline hereafter.)

At this stage, the Third Carrier Division dispatched specially organized fighter-bomber units, carrying many expectations. Then the enemy condition gradually became clear. The summing-up picture of the enemy as of 1030 was as follows:

The first group as of 1005: four to five large carriers, four battleships, and ten others, heading west.

The second group as of 0900: one large carrier, two small carriers, one battleship, and five others.

The third group as of 0845: three large carriers, five battleships, and ten others, its course 240°.

There were eleven carriers, ten battleships, and twenty-five others altogether, and I thought they were just enough and in some respects too much for game, and yet felt our success would be sure.

Our attacking planes took off one after another, but our two groups were situated far away, so their movements couldn't be made known to us.

After 0800 a large group of about one hundred planes was sighted to the west. They approached the Eleventh Group at an altitude of about three thousand meters. *Takao* of the Tenth Group fired four rounds from an antiaircraft gun to indicate the direction, while the Vanguard commander also issued an alert radio signal. However, their identification was not possible, even though they approached nearer. So we increased our speed and made preparatory movements for evasive maneuvers.

At this very moment, cruisers started firing against them, and then carriers and destroyers all raced to shoot at them. Noticing shells bursting ahead of them, they banked at fifteen kilometers from us. We immediately telephoned the order "cease fire," but it took quite a time for them to understand it, and two of them were shot down, to our great regret. Later we received a telegram sent from the third wave attack saying, "We are being attacked by our Vanguard."

[*These planes were from Ozawa's First CV Division. His carriers launched fifty-three dive bombers, twenty-seven torpedo bombers, and forty-eight Zero fighters. Of these, one was lost when the pilot dove for a torpedo from U.S.S. Albacore in an unsuccessful attempt to save CV Taiho. Eight had to turn back because of engine trouble. The remainder, headed for Task Force 58, flew over the Vanguard Force, which opened fire and, as Ugaki noted, shot down two. Another eight were damaged and had to turn back. The Americans called this Raid II. Of the 128 launched, 97 were lost.*][32]

It might have served them right, because they came in with great strength at high altitude without any identification at a time when we all were prepared to meet enemy attacks. But a warning was issued to be careful about identification, as Groups A and B were to the west.

We waited impatiently to hear the result of the fighter-bomber attack, but it didn't come in soon. Later, we learned that they approached the enemy at about 1035, but enemy fighters seemed to have intercepted them about twenty miles short of the target, so they only succeeded in causing four carriers to emit black smoke. [*Ugaki probably referred to the fact that Raid II aircraft attacked* Wasp, Enterprise, Princeton, *and* Bunker Hill, *a near miss damaging the latter. Japanese fliers erroneously reported at least four U.S. carriers sinking and six covered with black smoke. The only hit of the day came when an aircraft of Raid I, consisting of sixty-one Zeros, forty-five of them armed with bombs, and eight torpedo planes, hit South Dakota. The hit killed twenty-seven men and wounded twenty-three, but did not affect the battleship's efficiency.*][33] The second wave, supposed to be a great force, said that it was returning as it didn't see an enemy. What a shame!

[*This occurred during Raid III of forty Zeros, twenty-five carrying bombs, and seven torpedo bombers from the Second Carrier Division. They failed to receive orders to divert from their original target and, although intercepted, most of these aircraft returned to their carriers.*][34]

On the other hand, First Air Fleet Telegram at 1335 clarified the whole picture of the enemy as follows:

> Positions of the enemy task force as of 1000 (Cardinal point, Guam):
> Group I: 322°, 150 miles: three large carriers, two special carriers, one battleship.
> Group II: 282°, 95 miles: four large carriers, four battleships.
> Group III: 226°, 80 miles: three carriers, four battleships, nine cruisers.
> Group IV: 320°, 47 miles: eight carriers (probably converted ones), ten heavy cruisers.
> Group V: 300°, 100 miles: three carriers (converted)
> Total: ten regular carriers, thirteen converted carriers, twelve battleships, nineteen cruisers.

The Vanguard maneuvered north and south so as not to approach within three hundred miles (mostly 350 miles) of the enemy while recovering seaplanes and carrier-borne planes which came back one after the other. I thought that the movement of the Main Force would be the same.

At 1400, all of a sudden *Yahagi* sent in "*Shokaku* sunk, and we are rescuing survivors." I thought that a submarine must have attacked her and took up a stricter antisub alert. Then at about 1600 *Haguro* sent in, "We are taking charge of *Taiho*'s communications." Has *Taiho* met the same fate as *Shokaku*?

[*The submarine* Cavalla *hit* Shokaku *at 1215;* Albacore *hit* Taiho *at 0910.* Shokaku *sank at about 1500 when one of her bombs exploded. Normally* Taiho*'s torpedo damage would have been minor, but poor damage control measures made her exceedingly flammable, and she exploded within an hour of* Shokaku*'s loss.*][35]

Also from *Haguro* came in, "The task force commander has moved aboard this ship and we are recovering crews." Soon after commander in chief sent in, "I am commanding the operation aboard *Haguro*." Then it was followed by, "All planes of the First Carrier Division will be recovered on board the Second Carrier Division and *Zuikaku*." I can scarcely imagine how hard it will be to continue the operations now under way, after losing two powerful ships at this very moment.

Enemy submarines have come after us all the time, reported our movements by urgent telegrams, and finally sank two of our ships. Furthermore, they sank them just when they were recovering planes. This must be called extremely skillful.

On the other hand, the number of planes raiding Guam has greatly increased since this morning, and when our Second Carrier Division's attack aircraft arrived there they were forced to engage in a dogfight over the base. As a result, after the battle only one plane was left still operable out of fifty planes.

It was just the same at Rota, where we lost over twenty aircraft. Out of over ten seaplanes of the Vanguard we used today, nine were lost. Since this morning we had been waiting for a chance to become an attack force, but now we have to admit that, to say nothing of chasing an enemy, not only did we fail to inflict damage on an enemy, but we sustained heavy damage. Is it that heaven still doesn't side with us? Since the Vanguard withdrew to the northwest and Groups A and B came up north, we could see the lonely *Zuikaku* approaching us. Thus the fateful day has passed.

Commander in chief, task force, issued an order to air screen for tomorrow the 20th. It only called for searching the area of movements with seaplanes as specified by commander in chief, Second Fleet, an antisubmarine patrol and a ready-for-emergency with carrier-borne planes of the Second and Third Carrier Divisions and *Zuikaku* as specified by commander, Second Carrier Division. It has become all too passive.

Then at 2010 and 2245 came in, "The First and Second Tanker Units will go to a point 15–20 W, 134–40 E. The task force will proceed to northwest immediately and move so as to refuel on the 21st."

In reply to the Central Pacific Fleet's last request, the Combined Fleet said that, as they were going to rescue it with their whole forces after the decisive battle, it was requested to concentrate its forces and secure airstrips instead of falling into passive defense only. Will the Combined Fleet be able to keep their word?

Combined Fleet Telegram No. 192257, from chief of staff to Force A:

> We intend to conduct pursuit of the enemy from this headquarters, depending upon the situation prevailing after regrouping our forces.
> 1. Base Air Force
>   a. Pending the enemy condition, the Hachiman Force will ad-

vance to Iwo Jima speedily, and the Third Air Force and Eighth Air Force to Peleliu.

b. On the 21st, reconnaissance will be made, while the attack force will be concentrated at the Marianas.

c. On the 22nd, seek and attack enemy task forces with the forces concentrated at the Marianas. Then continue operations to hold air supremacy over the area.

2. Task Force

a. On the 21st, carry out refueling and regrouping of the forces, and send home the damaged ships, while a part of the carriers will be sent to the training site. (Lingayen)

b. On the 22nd, pending the situation, advance and attack enemy task force in cooperation with base air force. Then send air units to land bases to continue operations under the commander, Fifth Base Air Force, and send carriers to the training site.

c. After the 22nd, depending on the situation, carry out sweeping attacks on Saipan with most of the surface craft.

The above is considered a good idea, if the loss of the task force air power is small enough to continue further operations. The number of planes returned to the carriers this evening, as we learned later, is as follows: Torpedo bombers—30; dive bombers—11, fighters—44; bomber-fighters—17. Total—102.

[*Japanese aircraft losses on 19 June alone totaled 330 of 430 carrier planes and sixteen of forty-three float planes, which is why the Americans called this day's action "The Great Marianas Turkey Shoot." The U.S. lost thirty aircraft and twenty-seven fliers on this day.*][36]

Tuesday, 20 June 1944. Fair with clouds, small squalls. After dawn, everything within vision came in sight. Five tankers sailing east were seen to the north. They didn't know about last night's wire. Why were they approaching the enemy like that? It's extremely dangerous. Then I noticed a ship like *Taiho* to the west. A staff officer told me she didn't sink but couldn't make high speed. I was pleased that she was saved.

Groups A and B, the Vanguard Force, supply unit, and others all met at a place in the early morning. Some confusion ensued in taking positions of the Eighth Alert Formation. It's awfully hard to maneuver ships skillfully after getting in too close. Young men, be careful!

The task force commander ordered refueling started after distributing tankers at 1119. (Position, 15–27 W, 134–52 E). Tankers were approaching the Vanguard from the starboard and *Yamato* and *Musashi* were ordered to take up positions behind the Fourth Heavy Cruiser Division when at

1044 we received the following wire from a patrol plane, reconnaissance on Area P: "Enemy force with carriers sighted; these are two carriers, two battleships, one cruiser, several destroyers, position five hundred miles bearing 20° from Peleliu."

The above position was only 280 miles bearing 95° from our fleet, so near that the radio room did not dare broadcast it by teletalk. The Vanguard commander issued an alert promptly and signaled *Haguro,* then sailing ahead to the starboard, to close in. At this moment, that is, 1200, commander in chief, task fleet, was in the midst of changing his flag to *Zuikaku,* and didn't pay attention to a suggestion that he suspend refueling and withdraw to the west. He only wired, "This force is refueling at a point five hundred miles bearing 5° from Peleliu, so the enemy found on P04 line is considered to be this force," and didn't take any emergency step.

On the other hand, in view of the fact that two planes dispatched to that area failed to return, and enemy planes were discovered, the Second Fleet again advised the need to withdraw, and at the same time ordered the Vanguard to proceed to the northwest as far as possible. After all this, refueling was suspended and course set at 270° and speed 26 knots.

In the meantime, Force B, unaware of anything, had moved slowly ahead of us, while the tanker unit was left behind, seemingly without knowing even what it was all about. Yet we couldn't very well order or instruct them; we had to be content with only relaying fleet signals to them.

It was extremely unfortunate that the flagship of the supreme commander was shifted twice at the most critical time of war. At a time like this I thought it might be better to transfer the command temporarily to the next number while changing the flag.

While the Vanguard could speed to the west, Groups A and B had to face the enemy, owing to the wind direction when taking off and recovering planes. Consequently, the Vanguard was placed farther away from the enemy than the Main Force.

At 1645 one of the second-stage reconnaissance planes dispatched ahead reported the certain existence of one carrier, two battleships, and more than several others at 14–10 N, 138–20 E. Thereupon, movements against this enemy were taken up seriously, and "Stand by for all-out attacks" was issued. Meanwhile, enemy shadowing planes, which came to us in the morning, seemed to be increased by two or three in the afternoon, as the sensitivity of their telephones became extremely great.

[*No U.S. planes sighted the Japanese the morning of 20 June. The first sighting came at 1540 from an* Enterprise *pilot.*][37]

Yamato's radar worked quite well too, for it picked up reactions from about ninety kilometers away.

Prior to this, our planes reported a large group of enemy aircraft flying west. While we awaited their coming, at 1747 twenty enemy planes came to our Twelfth Group at our southern end, and carried out slow dive bombings, strafing, and torpedo-firings of twelve tubes. Though it was sailing some distance away from our Eleventh Group, we opened fire with our main batteries first, then with all our secondary batteries and antiaircraft guns. Black smoke arose from *Chiyoda's* stern. She seemed to be hit. [Chiyoda *had been hit but not sunk.*][38] At about 1810 we fired at another group passing in the south, but the enemy flew to the direction of Group B and did not come to us directly. Following gunfire and aerial combat, we saw two columns of black smoke rising in the distance.

The Fourth Force Disposition was ordered effective 1700, and another task force order was also given calling for the attack force to advance promptly and attack an enemy in cooperation with an air attack to be carried out at dusk.

When we disbanded the ring formation and regrouped into the night-attack disposition, all units started fierce M/G fire and a considerable number of shells came near the First Division, so we had to evade them for a while. As a flare was dropped over us, there might have been enemy planes, but most of the fire was aimed at stars. Even within a single ship, orders were hard to deliver. Firing couldn't be stopped easily.

The Fifth Heavy Cruiser Division, Tenth Destroyer Squadron, and *Mogami* joined the attack force, but *Nagato* didn't join us because she followed the Main Body, then was grouped into Group B. The attack force sailed east at 24 knots. On the way *Seiyo Maru* on fire was seen twenty kilometers to the south. [*The tankers* Genyo Maru *and* Seiyo Maru *were hit early in the day's action and were damaged so severely they had to be scuttled.*][39]

While it was unknown whether night reconnaissance aircraft made contact, torpedo planes were ordered to deploy. So I thought they would be able to get the enemy tonight, but since then nothing has been heard. And finally a dispiriting telegram came in, "No enemy sighted, so I shall return."

As it became apparent that there was little hope for a night attack, at 2100 we turned back, changing direction by columns and set course at 340° to 320° to withdraw from the enemy. Just before this, we received an order from the task force calling for turning back in case there was little hope for a night attack. The Combined Fleet also ordered by Telegram No. 2220, "Task force will make a timely withdrawal depending upon the local situation, and move as its commander considers fit." During this movement enemy planes seemed to have contacted us, but this was not clear.

[*20 June ended with only thirty-five operational carrier aircraft remaining to Ozawa. U.S. plane losses were higher than on the 19th, but thanks to excellent rescue work personnel losses were confined to ten pilots and thirty-three crewmen.*][40]

Wednesday, 21 June 1944. Fair. At 0100 the Fourth Heavy Cruiser Division, sailing behind us, issued an order altering course to 300° and soon after canceled it. The Third Battleship Division positioned in the middle sailed on course 300° and replied to us that "the ordered course was 300°." So we sailed on course 300°, feeling uncertain about it, but when the dawn came we found no other forces in our vicinity except the Third Battleship Division. Thereupon we increased speed to 26 knots and set course at 350° heading in a likely direction, while reporting our position and movement to the attack force commander by medium wave telephone. Soon we found the Fourth Heavy Cruiser Division and others and joined them. It was fortunate that we didn't affect the operation except for becoming a lost child due to faulty communications.

[As the force moved on, two enemy planes shadowed them and Ugaki noted uneasily that "their reports of our position, course, and speed were very accurate." They expected an attack this morning, and made preparations. Ugaki's battleships joined in protecting the Third CV Division.]

Reconnaissance planes dispatched to our rear by the Third Carrier Division early this morning reported our attack force as an enemy soon after its departure and also reported an enemy again on the way back. The enemy's position was still two hundred miles to our rear, so we were under a possible enemy air attack, which made us feel like a fugitive. The feeling of being chased by an enemy without having any means of counterattacking is most unpleasant. However, in the afternoon we learned that the report was false, and the enemy shadowing planes also left at about 1000. We could feel we were at last free from danger of an enemy pursuing us.

Today the task force ordered the Main Force to go to Chujo Bay at Okinawa and the attack force to Gimaras, and also gave instructions to the tanker units.

Now I had a little time to ponder and I composed the following on the bridge:

> Utterly awakened from the dream of victory,
> Found the sky rainy and gloomy.
> Rainy clouds will not clear up,
> My heart is the same
> When the time for the battle's up.

It's the rainy season at home but here it's fine. Yet what isn't fine is my heart. The result of the decisive battle on which we staked so much was extremely miserable. Not only was our loss great, but we couldn't save Saipan from peril. Enemy planes began landing at airstrips and are also raiding Pagan Island. It will be extremely difficult to recover from this disaster and rise again. When I think the prospect of a victory is fading out gradually, it's only natural that my heart becomes as gloomy as the sky of the rainy season.

Some of the destroyers had less than thirty percent of fuel by this morning, while battleships had fifty percent and cruisers twenty-five to forty percent. As waves made refueling at sea difficult, the attack force commander decided to refuel hurriedly at Chujo Bay and then come to Gimaras. So, setting course to 340°, we headed for Chujo Bay at 20 knots in the evening, leaving the Third Carrier Division behind. After making formation, burials at sea were performed on board two ships for those killed in action, and I prayed for them.

[Thursday, 22 June began with rain, high waves, and strong winds. Ugaki's force sighted Okinawa at 1100, and dropped anchor at 1300. At 1600 Ugaki went on board *Zuikaku* to meet with the commander in chief. After the commanders had reported, they "drank a toast, not of victory."]

The commander in chief and others did not seem so much worried and were in high spirits, which quite reassured us, and we promised ourselves a comeback.

Our damages sustained were roughly as follows:

1. At about 1000, a torpedo hit *Taiho* on her port side near the bow and flooded a little, but she was still able to make 30 knots. But the fore lift struck before fully up on top, for which they made an extraordinary effort to build an emergency deck. When this was just about to be completed, gasoline inside exploded and the flight deck was bent. She sank from her port side almost horizontally.

2. *Shokaku* was torpedoed and sank at 1400.

3. One torpedo struck *Hiyo* on her stern at the time of the air raid. She was rendered incapable of navigation and was struck again with one bomb, set on fire, and sunk. [*The Japanese believed a torpedo from a submarine struck and sank* Hiyo *after the initial aircraft hit. Actually she took a confirmed one, probably two, aerial torpedoes from* Belleau Wood *and sank two hours later.*][41]

4. *Junyo* was hit by one bomb near her funnel.

5. *Zuikaku*. Two were dead and wounded beside the commander in chief on the bridge by splinters from a near miss.

6. *Chiyoda*. One small bomb on her stern deck.

7. *Haruna.* One bomb exploded on her steering machine room, and steering became out of order.

8. *Maya* was damaged by a near miss and needs to be docked.

According to today's reconnaissance, the enemy task force has stayed at almost the same place since the day before yesterday. We also learned from communications intelligence that the enemy was to some extent taking positions to the west of the Marianas line. Since long-distance reconnoitering has already been carried out from Saipan, we will no longer be able to maneuver skillfully in that battle area. And I'm afraid lest the enemy be allowed to reach China, for they have planes and established air bases there.

Friday, 23 June 1944. Cloudy, later partly fair. After I got up, I read signals which said that, quite different from yesterday's briefing, the attack force and the Main Force were to go to the western part of the Inland Sea and prepare for the next sortie promptly.

At 0815 I asked the captain of *Nagato* to come on board and heard his report of the battle. *Nagato*, in the center of Group B, displayed her defense gunfire a great deal against enemy planes swarming on the three carriers around her, while avoiding torpedoes. She fought quite well.

At 1015, we left Chujo Bay in the order of the Second Destroyer Squadron, Fifth Heavy Cruiser Division, Third Battleship Division, and First Battleship Division, and sailed north, taking strict antisubmarine precautions. The Seventh Heavy Cruiser Division was to move separately after refueling to destroyers.

A northeast gale blew fairly strong and it became cooler. We changed to summer uniform. I was coming home without any merit and I felt not so happy. At 1900 we changed course from 50° to 40°. According to advice from Sasebo Naval Base, it was considered safer to navigate between fifty to sixty miles off the coast. Also, it will be easier for escort planes, disposed at various places as antisub measures are strengthened, to cooperate with us.

Saturday, 24 June 1944. Fair. It is essential that a correct judgment be based on sufficient materials, and my views upon the causes of the failure of the last decisive battle, thus casting a dark shadow over the future of the war, are as follows:

1. Judgment of the situation and operational planning

   a. Unlike offensive operations, encountering operations are up to the enemy's initiative. Therefore, all eventualities should be taken into account. This especially should be more stressed in the present stage of war in which encountering operations have a close connection with the defense of strategic points and more importance attached, instead of encountering an enemy far away at sea.

As there was a surprise attack on Palau Island before the planning of Operation A, it was taken for granted that the enemy would come to that area, which was also considered a favorable decisive battle scene for us. And even an attempt to lure the enemy to that area was planned. On the other hand, little consideration was given to possible enemy invasions of the Marianas and the western part of New Guinea, thus the planning lacked flexibility. (As a general rule, it was planned not to send our task force to the Marianas, for only diversionary enemy movements were anticipated there.)

Of course, it's undoubtedly impossible to be ready for every eventuality with an inferior force, but, as I have often urged, it's also essential to set up a policy of fighting a decisive battle with its own initiatives, even though pressed to remain passive. However, it could definitely be said that from its very start Operation A was too optimistic and self-centered as well as too limited.

b. One of the fundamental principles of war is to win an easy victory by destroying enemy components one by one with our whole strength. To fear that invaluable and irreplaceable strength would thus be expended is wrong. On the contrary, it's usually possible to damage an enemy heavily with a small loss of our own. It must be called reckless to try to beat the enemy's huge force by one stroke, only calling for a decisive battle without reflecting on our own power and skill. The fact remains that in the Russo-Japanese War they tried hard to capture Port Arthur and destroy the Far Eastern fleet before the arrival of the Baltic fleet. In general, this was in accord with a great policy of destroying enemy components.

Also, the failure at the battle of the Yellow Sea on 10 August, which took place for this purpose, taught an invaluable lesson for the victory at the battle of the Japan Sea. No greater training can be gained than in participating in actual battle. The second time one improves over the first, and the third time one is far more skillful than in the second. Great caution should be paid to the wisdom of waging a once-for-all decisive battle, on which the fate of the country depends, with those of whom only a few have some little experience.

This is also what I have often urged, either at conferences of the task force or directly to the commander in chief and his chief of staff.

c. In relation to (a), if we have to encounter an enemy in one area and defend other points, it's most essential at this time to defend the Marianas. Preparations and sufficient strength at least to destroy an enemy landing at the beach and hold airstrips should have been made. I can't but conclude that there were some defects in its defense. It was also a fault of judging the enemy would come to Palau and not to the Marianas.

2. Execution of the operation

a. An operation starts with knowing its enemy. It was good that a dauntless reconnaissance of the Marshalls area found a large concentration of the enemy at Majuro, and planes and submarines detected its departure, but nothing was heard of it thereafter. While we were preparing for an attack on the southeastern coast of the homeland and were talking about reinforcing the reconnaissance strength there, an enemy suddenly attacked Saipan on the morning of the 11th. What loose reconnaissance!

Moreover, the convoy of the enemy invasion force had not been discovered until the very day of landing, the 14th. As a result, starting the overall operation was delayed. After the task force sortie, much was hoped for from the land-based air force reconnaissance. Although the scarcity of reconnaissance air strength must be held accountable, the lack of a sense of reconnaissance must be the cancer of our system.

b. Partly due to the faulty reconnaissance mentioned above, the Combined Fleet ordered "stand by for decisive battle" on the evening of the 13th, only after receiving a report of the enemy beginning to minesweep at the Saipan channel that morning. This should be called too late, and a chance was lost. In spite of its [the enemy's] usual custom of carrying out its simple attack for two days, he repeated his attacks this time on the 11th, 12th, and 13th. Its strength was powerful, too. In view of the importance of Saipan, that order should have been issued after the air raid the morning of the 13th at the latest. Unless we destroy enemy invasion forces before they have dug in, it's very hard to destroy them afterward on account of their manpower, equipment, and mechanical power.

It's preposterous to think that we can let him dig in a little, making it hard for him to pull himself out again, thus we can destroy his reinforcements as they come. I once advocated such an idea, though didn't try it, but it's absolutely no good. The loud cries of the Germans about the second front in Europe must also be regarded as another case of being a bad loser.

Contrary to the above thinking, the Combined Fleet least expected an enemy invasion of the Marianas. In view of the enemy concentration at the Admiralty area, they thought that the Marianas were a mere attack target and the enemy's main aim was the capture of Palau. I can't help but conclude that thus they were caught by their self-centered Operation A, and took precautions against premature actions.

Of course, Operation A was large-scale, employing most of our forces. Though I can see that, once started, it was very hard to pull back, I have to admit that measures the Combined Fleet took to prevent enemy invasion of that important position were very slow. Here again, I can't but criticize that they must have been daydreaming a pleasant dream of destroying the enemy in one decisive battle. But I think that steps and instructions the Combined Fleet took at the time of the task force sortie were generally appropriate.

c. The task force movements lacked speed. In spite of the fact that the operation began on the 13th, and the enemy landing on the 14th, it couldn't be ready for the decisive battle before the 19th. It must be called a very slow-moving force.

If this was partly due to the fact that it had to move further toward the east than the expected decisive battle scene, selection of the standby point should have been made more carefully.

Although I wasn't quite clear about the situation during those days, as I was taking part in Operation Kon, I thought it extremely slow when I was informed of that plan, while joining the other force. The situation at Saipan seemed to be doomed to some extent, so I thought that steps should be taken immediately, and I even planned to expedite refueling on the way to meet a sudden change of plan. Refueling was a troublesome problem involved in movements of the task force, and tankers had to be dispatched from specified points in advance. But I think we can continue operations by refueling to destroyers from battleships, in case of being content to deliver a blow with air forces at an opportune moment and seek another one, unless we attempt a decisive battle with the whole strength.

d. An important question to be decided was from what direction attacks should be made, when the whole picture of the enemy became clear on the 18th. We attacked straight to the front of the enemy's deployed great forces. And the enemy seemed to have encountered our attack forces. In such a case, I think it would have been better, in view of our strength, to approach the enemy from the north to attack its flank. This might have the disadvantage of increasing the distance from Guam, where bases could be used, but it would afford us a chance to destroy enemies separately when a pursuit attack could be made upon them. In addition, it would be advantageous in such a case as occurred on the 20th, when the enemy task force was found suddenly approaching us.

e. After the attack planes took off, the strictest precautions should have been taken against enemy subs because both the Vanguard and the Main Body had to sail back and forth to the north and south in order to facilitate the recovery of those planes and also to keep the distance from the enemy at about three hundred miles. On the 19th, all seaplanes and carrier-borne aircraft were employed in reconnaissance, shadowing, and attacks, leaving no planes at all for antisubmarine purposes. Since that morning, I had been concerned about this, and, sure enough, we had a great misfortune, losing *Taiho* and *Shokaku* within a few hours in the same area. Not only was the spirit of our men greatly affected, but considerable confusion ensued in recovering returning planes, refitting them, and preparing another attack. Furthermore, the supreme commander in this area had to change his flagship twice, which resulted in great disadvantages in collecting information, judging the situation, overall command, and communications. Substitute flagship facilities to meet such a case as this should have been arranged on *Mogami,* which was attached to the task force, and she should have been kept nearby during the battle. By what mistake I don't know, *Mogami* was included in Group B. (I had warned the commander in chief of this before he changed his flag to *Taiho.*)

f. On the 20th, the refueling point was set too near the enemy. If we had had a sufficient result on the 19th, it would have been all right. But under such a situation, when we had no certain report of the result, we should have withdrawn farther away and refueled on the 31st. At dawn on the 20th, when I saw the tanker units near and, moreover, sailing east, I couldn't help saying to myself that it was dangerous. Just as I thought, a superior enemy force moved up to the north of Palau and threw us into great confusion by sinking *Hiyo* and inflicting a good deal of damage to other ships. On the other hand, we couldn't retaliate on them at all.

g. The skill of the flying crews must be improved more and more and at the same time the number of fighters on board carriers should be increased. I placed great expectations on the results of suicide attacks by fighter-bomber squadrons on the 19th, but powerful fighters counterattacked them at a point twenty miles short of the enemy, and only about ten of them seemed to succeed in crashing on the enemy. Also some attack planes returned without seeing the enemy. It was most regrettable under such weather and visibility as on that day. Several dozen planes that went to Rota and Guam were annihilated by enemy fighters above bases.

A reconnaissance plane which sighted and shadowed the southern enemy group made a mistake of thirty to fifty miles in reporting the enemy position, so the attack planes which headed for it failed to find it. The attack aircraft of the First CV Division went for the center group and attacked carriers and battleships. For the rest, only a suicide force of the Third Carrier Division attacked the northern group.

On the 20th, first-stage reconnaissance planes failed to find an enemy task force quite near within range, thus causing a great disadvantage to us. (I don't know whether or not they were suddenly attacked by enemy planes and shot down.) On the other hand, on the following, 21st, some crews using the same chart as was used yesterday erroneously sent in a report "enemy sighted," when it was not actually there. Moreover, they mistook our Vanguard for an enemy and inconvenienced our movements.

In the evening of the 20th, in spite of a shadowing aircraft's sending long-wave transmitter guidance, the torpedo-attacking planes failed to find the enemy and made it impossible for the attack force to wage a night attack upon the enemy.

Among other things, though we took a favorable position and sighted the enemy timely on the morning of the 19th, we couldn't damage the enemy severely. I can't help concluding that our failure was due to the fact that it was a daylight attack and we couldn't provide sufficient fighter escort and also to inferior skill of our crews in general. (Counting carrier planes only, we had 450 planes at that time.)

3. Enemy strategy

The enemy who has experienced several invasions, whether it be [Lieutenant General Joseph "Vinegar Joe"] Stillwell or [Admiral William F.] Halsey, has become ever confident. Together with thorough reconnaissance, they carried out the Saipan operation with powerful task and invasion forces against our inferior strength and successfully attained their objective. Though his land-based air power couldn't cooperate more than to search a small part of the area, the enemy well detected the movement of our task force by disposing submarines and going after us with them. On the 19th, he was prepared to encounter our attack and took positions anticipating a decisive battle while on the one hand supporting the invasion of Saipan.

His movement of dispatching a high-speed task force quite near to the east of us on the 21st was quite reasonable, and he is no mean adversary. His striking range isn't limited to two hundred miles; he attacks from three hundred miles away as seen this evening. Their shadowing and reconnaissance, whether day or night, are skillful and their reports very accurate. They seem to be quite confident in taking off and landing planes and operational flights at night. Battleships are used in a ring formation while a CV group is situated in its rear. So when our planes dove into the battleship group first and didn't realize the existence of CVs, it was too late. Fighters were placed fifty to sixty miles outside of the battleship group, and after passing that line almost no interference was met.

Their diving was mild. Simultaneous attack of strafing by fighters and a small number of torpedo planes also seemed to be planned. Many kinds of bombs were used, too. Those who came to attack the Main Body were said to have dove sharply. The skill of torpedo planes was poor but the timing of attack was good. The hit rate of bombing was less than ours. Those who attacked the Twelfth Group were said to have had two fighters (about half of them loaded with bombs) accompany each bomber. The enemy task force displaying its 32 knots is surely a tough customer.

At about 1140 Okinoshima was sighted to port, and we entered Bungo Strait from the eastern swept channel at 1230. The attack force, without the First Battleship Division, sailed through Nuwajima channel. After parting from them, we went through Kudako channel. As it was just the time of no current at all, we had a rare chance of passing through the channel with no current. *Zuikaku* overtook us in her hurry.

At about 2030, in gathering darkness, we dropped anchor in Hashira Jima anchorage in the vicinity of the commander in chief, Combined Fleet's, flagship, *Oyodo*. The purpose of this voyage to the western part of the Inland Sea was to prepare for a quick sortie. So damaged ships were ordered to Sasebo and Yokosuka on the way.

For me it has been a long time since I left here in August 1942 and I was reminded of many things. But it's regrettable indeed to see a red buoy indicating the sunken *Mutsu*.

[On Sunday, 25 June, various fleet headquarters "were busy with conferences" but those on a lower level were idle and "had a picture show in the evening." Ugaki felt this was not quite right, in view of the situation on Saipan, but he realized they could do nothing for the defenders.]

On the 24th, an enemy force including converted carriers appeared to the south of Iwo Jima and raided the island.

[*This was Clark's group of* Hornet, Yorktown, Bataan, *and* Belleau Wood *with their escort. Clark had requested and received Mitscher's permission to strike Iwo Jima before retiring to Eniwetok. The Twenty-seventh Air Flotilla gave battle and lost sixty-six aircraft.*[42]

[Monday, 26 June, was a day of meetings and study. Ugaki noted, "There were many things which only endorsed what I wrote in the entry of the 24th and nothing else worthy to write for future reference."]

Tuesday, 27 June 1944. Cloudy, but occasionally clear. *Atago* sailed to Kure in the morning and *Nagato* in the afternoon. *Kongo* also received an order to go there on the 29th, but nothing was said about *Yamato* and *Musashi*. *Oyodo* was to sail for Kisarazu in Tokyo Bay tomorrow morning. Do they need to effect liaison with Tokyo?

In the afternoon I went to see *Hyuga,* flagship of the newly established Fourth Carrier Division. Rear Admiral Chiaki Matsuda, Captain [Tomekichi] Nomura, her skipper, Captain [Michinori] Yoshii, the senior staff officer, and others welcomed me and showed me around the converted afterdeck. After that we talked about the battle and affairs at home which seemed neverending and I left her after about two hours' stay.

I thought of the time when I was her captain. She looked entirely different now, after having been converted to accommodate thirteen carrier-borne dive bomber *Suiseis* and nine *Zuiuns* by widening the afterdeck, removing turrets No. 4 and 5, installing a hangar and M/Gs on projecting side decks. How to use this division will be rather a difficult proposition, but I think there will be some. I wish her good luck.

[On Wednesday, 28 June, Ugaki went aboard *Oyodo* to report on Kon and other matters, including his "views on the last operation."]

Special points of note among what they said were as follows:

1. Commander in chief sounded rather like grumbling that everything seemed to be controlled by the Naval General Staff and the Combined Fleet seemed to be just nominal. (There were some problems regarding reestablishment of Combined Fleet headquarters. A plan to absorb it into the General Staff was once considered, but Chief of the General Staff Shimada, who wished to leave it unchanged, ruled it out.)

2. The General Staff considered it wise to hold the issuance of "Stand by for decisive battle" one or two days. Had the battle been fought two days earlier, it would have been more favorable. (Commander in chief)

Looking back from now, it appears that we were given the fixed plan of Operation A and only carried it out. But the plan seemed to be based upon too optimistic thinking. (Commander in chief)

3. Regarding the defense of the Marianas, the army had been boasting that it could hold the islands for a few months, while in the meantime wanting the navy to destroy the enemy. And the central authorities be-

lieved it too much. We never could trust the army since the outbreak of the war. (Commander in chief) [The following was written in the margin of paragraph 3: "When the enemy came to Saipan, the army was said to be even pleased to think that their planning was right, even saying, 'Now they come where we have been waiting.'"]

4. The present organization seems defective as regards the air forces, but the Combined Fleet has little intention of changing it. (Commander in chief.) (I told him that I agree with him, and though this kind of talk comes up from time to time, we're now making all our efforts on how to display our air strength fully. The organization of the task fleet has few defects, and this can be proved by past experiences of having no trouble at all.)

A disadvantage of checking commanders, a blind judgment of the army—I can see various fundamental causes for the adversity of the war.

I heard that the vice chief of the General Staff, Ito, came on aboard on the 25th and returned after attending the fleet conference on the 26th. The General Staff had to realize their responsibility was not light.

I left the matter of *Yamato* and *Musashi* going to Kure to the decision of my superior and have heard nothing about it since. But at 1600 I received a task force order to go to Kure tomorrow. As I don't know anything about the future, I hurriedly went on board *Zuikaku* to see the commander in chief and Chief of Staff Komura. We were to load army troops at Kure on the 5th and 6th and transport them to Singapore, from where we proceed to Lingga to undertake training and await orders.

Neither the Third nor Fourth CV divisions will be ready until the end of July, while as to the First and Second CV divisions, no definite plan can be made. It doesn't seem likely that we'll be able to get through the present crisis under such circumstances as this. Nothing is more deplorable. At what point do those in Tokyo expect to get a chance to win from now on?

On the 24th four ships in a convoy were sunk simultaneously, and one each was sunk on the west coast of Luzon and in Luzon Strait. Among them were tankers. A country with no oil and a navy without fuel, how can we do [anything] with this? We have been stuck in every respect, and we can't help being gloomy. This visit to Kure should be considered the last one in the homeland.

[Thursday, 29 June, saw Ugaki under way for Kure with *Yamato* and *Musashi* under his command. The weather was hot: "The heat seems to follow me everywhere I go." At Kure he paid his respects to local navy brass and went to a hotel. "I noticed civilians were becoming aware of the gravity and becoming more sympathetic as the situation became serious."

[The next day, Friday, 30 June, Ugaki received a number of letters, including one from Hiromitsu, his son. He had graduated and would join the navy in mid-July "as an apprentice naval medical officer." Ugaki almost burst with pride that "from now on we, father and son, will serve in the navy hand in hand." That night Ugaki and a number of his colleagues attended a party. "geisha girls I met after a long time were now calling themselves Hanazono Service Corps, and worked on sewing buttons in the daytime and offering services at night." Ugaki returned to his hotel early, where some of his classmates joined him, "making merry for a while."

[The first three days of July were routine for Ugaki. On Saturday the 1st he attended the monthly festival of *Yamato* shrine aboard the battleship, where a plan "to transport army and navy personnel and materials by the attack force" was under way. The next day he visited colleagues in the Kure Naval Hospital. Monday the 3rd he called on two geisha girls who had asked him to see examples of Yamamoto's calligraphy. "Both were very good and reminded me of him." That evening he invited "the skippers and staff officers" of his command to a party, which "was not so gay."]

Tuesday, 4 July 1944. Fair. About one hour after I got back to the ship, Kure Naval Base issued an air raid warning, as enemy task forces were reported five hundred miles bearing 145° from Yokohama and also on the sea northeast of Iwo Jima.

More than one hundred enemy carrier-borne planes attacked Chichi Jima from 0345 and Iwo Jima from 0425. Furthermore, in the afternoon, six battleships and six cruisers appeared off Iwo Jima and cruisers and destroyers began bombarding the airstrip at 1400. [*TG 58.1 and 58.2 conducted these raids.*]⁴³

Chief of the Munitions Department, [Captain Tojiro] Shimada, came to visit me. He should, for there are many things we're going to transport at his request. I told him I would have liked to transport all of them, but I was afraid the present situation wouldn't allow us to do so.

After that I went to *Atago* after 1500 and heard about the situation from the chief of staff who returned last night. He said that responsible people in Tokyo were in a turmoil so he couldn't get any essential thing settled, and no future policy was made clear to him. The Combined Fleet was rather optimistic, stating that they're going to shift to guerrilla warfare from now on. And he couldn't get their approval for changing the Second Fleet's flag to *Yamato* or *Musashi*.

So I told him my opinion as follows: "Isn't it unwise under the present circumstances for the attack force to engage in a transport mission as far as Singapore, because it takes nearly twenty days only to get there and back and unload? The reason why the enemy rather hesitates to advance to the west in the New Guinea area is that he has found the Marianas area rather weak. Taking this opportunity of having inflicted severe damage upon our Combined Fleet, he might dash right into our bosom with his four fleets. I think we must prepare for this eventuality. It will take a long time before the task force's carrier strength is ready. In the meantime, if and when the attack force operates with the cooperation of the land-based air force, we can expect a fair result. Of course, we must take the fuel problem into account, but this is worth thinking about." I told the same to the commander in chief, but there was no reaction at all. I was rather exasperated.

But soon after I returned on board my ship an order was issued to suspend loading and filling up the fuel to full capacity after consulting with the Combined Fleet. In the evening the chief of staff, Combined Fleet, telegraphed requesting that "preparations be made as the attack force might be ordered to sortie in case of an enemy invasion attempt on the Bonin Island area."

It will take twenty-four hours to unload the things we have taken on board during the last three days. If the enemy's action was only to support the Marianas, there wouldn't be much of a problem, but if it was a case of invasion, we should start our actions very early, otherwise the fate will be the same as in Saipan.

Operation Togo was started to prepare the homeland forces for an enemy attack.

Because we might again have to unload all the things we had worked hard to load, I ordered to be ready for it.

Wednesday, 5 July 1944. Light rain, later cloudy. Following yesterday's wire, the chief of staff, Combined Fleet, sent one in about the way of the attack forces operations and asked the task force to place *Zuiho* under the attack force after interceptors were rapidly loaded on board her. It was moving on almost the same line as I envisaged. However, it seemed to me that the Second Fleet was rather reluctant to make plans and preparations for taking the initiative in operations.

At about 1100 the Combined Fleet canceled all those telegrams sent in as of yesterday and ordered the attack force to resume loading. Stacks of miscellaneous things were piled up on deck.

Though we might have escaped danger once, it's quite clear that should the enemy come up north again, when the attack force sails southwest on a transport mission, no force will be left in immediate readiness. It will be lucky if the enemy doesn't make them jump by setting a fire right under their noses.

The loading of army materials has begun and a colonel commanding Wolf 18702 Unit paid me a visit.

Thursday, 6 July 1944. Cloudy. Except for *Nagato,* we finished loading army materials in the morning. Admiral Nomura with his staff inspected the loading work and I attended too.

We received a signal dated the 4th from the commander in chief, Central Pacific Fleet, after a pretty long silence:

1. Before dawn on 30 June, we moved the combined battle command post inside a ravine one and a half kilometers south of Matansa. Enemy bombings have been fierce since early morning of the 4th.

2. We carried out regrouping of miscellaneous units and forces, strengthening forces, constructing field positions, and recovering personnel under the most difficult conditions.

3. A general attack will be carried out on the 5th mobilizing all the army, navy, and civilians in order to display the traditional spirit of the Imperial Forces. If we can obtain cooperation of air forces after dusk on the 5th, it will be extremely effective.

The commander in chief, Sixth Fleet, further, sent in the following telegram at 1800 to the commander in chief, Combined Fleet, and the rest of the fleet: "I am pleased to have defended Saipan to the death and eyewitnessed the brilliant achievements of the submarines under my command. Commanding all Sixth Fleet personnel remaining and . . . [an omission here appears in the diary] I am going to charge into an enemy position. Banzai!"

[*On the night of 6–7 July, some three thousand Japanese on Saipan staged a mass banzai attack on the U.S. Twenty-seventh Division at the Tanapang plain. Despite advance warning, the Twenty-seventh was caught by surprise. The United States lost 406 dead, but all the attackers perished.*]++

The end of Saipan is near at hand. How tragic! Bad strategy and tactics and scarcity of fighting power brought about this doom. Nothing is more deplorable.

[The commander in chief, Central Pacific Fleet, received a joint telegram from the chiefs of the Naval and Army General Staffs conveying their respects for the fighting men at Saipan, including a message from the emperor: "I am satisfied with the way the officers and men at Saipan are fighting with all their strength. The present situation of Saipan is extremely regrettable, but I am deeply grateful for the fighting of the surprise-attack force." The chiefs continued with the hope that the officers and men in the Central Pacific district would continue fighting to "reduce the enemy fighting strength." Ugaki, as usual, was impressed with the emperor's words, but saw all too clearly that "this was a requiem of farewell." How to revenge Saipan would be the duty of those "left alive."

[That evening Ugaki went ashore to dine with his classmate, Vice Admiral Suzuki. "But the crisis in the war was not a little reflected in the taste of the wine."

[On Friday, 7 July, Ugaki "bade farewell to Kure" and boarded his ship. The army force to be transported had embarked; its regimental commander and other officers reported to Ugaki, who noted in passing that this was the eighth anniversary of the China Incident.]

The commander at Saipan sent the last message last night at midnight, saying that he was burning code books and severing communications thereafter. In light of nearby air forces being ordered to cooperate in land battles with its whole strength from this evening, Z-Day must be today, and the last desperate fight will begin from this evening. If so, today will become another sad memorial day, too.

[*The army commander on Saipan, Lieutenant General Yoshitsugu Saito, and the ranking naval commander, Vice Admiral Chuichi Nagumo of Pearl Harbor fame, committed suicide.*[45]

[That afternoon Ugaki, with all the skippers under his command, dined at a villa in the suburbs of Kure, returning to the ship by sea after "a nice refreshment."]

Saturday, 8 July 1944. Partly cloudy. At 0100 the naval base issued an air raid warning, followed by an air raid alert at 0130. Because a warning of "enemy planes coming" was received from Saishu Island off Korea, it became necessary to alert Kyushu and the Kominase Chugoku area. "The enemy bombed in the sea at Cape Nobozaki," "Yawata." "Moji, number unknown, direction north," etc., came in succession from the naval base. It seemed two enemy groups were attacking Nagasaki, the Sasebo district, and Yawata, Moji area, but the damage was not great.

[*B-29s of the Twentieth Bomber Command attacked various targets on Kyushu with minor results.*][46]

Ready to sail at instant notice at 16 knots, recalling the crews on shore leave and returning the landing craft were all carried out fairly well even though at night. Maybe it was because of the full moon.

The attack force left Kure in two groups this morning.

At 0845 I left port with *Yamato* and *Musashi* under my command. It took a long time to turn the ship, for the trimming was bad due to the unusual load. We passed Kudako Strait at 1230, and carried out antisub training from Kominase Island, using three submarines. As before, the underwater sound detector didn't work well. All units entered Usuki Bay at 1830. At 2000 I went on board *Atago* where the chief of staff briefed me with other commanders about the policies of the General Staff and the Combined Fleet on the coming operations.

I wonder if the enemy will come out as we hope. I urgently felt the need to establish an operational plan to destroy the enemy with mainly the attack force and the land-based air forces, as well as preparations and training for it.

According to air reconnaissance of Saipan last night, its western section became inactive. The end of the courageous men could thus be imagined.

The Thirty-first Army and Chichi Jima area force were placed under the direct command of the commander in chief, Combined Fleet.

Sunday, 9 July 1944. Partly fair with mist. We sailed out of Usuki Bay at 0400 in the dawning light. Passing through the swept channel, we bounced into the open sea off Okinoshima at 0730 and bade farewell to the homeland. We were quite familiar with such an occasion, but the army people on board our ships must have some sensations. We made way south on a calm sea like a mirror on course 180° with 20 knots, then on 205° with 18 knots. Seaplanes and flying boats cooperated in escorting us throughout the day.

Bombardments on Guam were quite fierce. Coupled with statements of POWs captured at Chichi Jima, this indicates a strong possibility of the enemy's next invasion being directed to that island.

Monday, 10 July 1944. Partly fair. From early morning the course was changed to 240° and we sailed close to Okinawa. At 1430 we entered Chujo Bay, where four destroyers refueled. At 1900 Group A left, headed for Singapore and Lingga with course 200° and speed 18 knots. Group B (*Kongo, Nagato, Mogami,* and the Tenth Destroyer Squadron) will disembark army troops here and leave the day after tomorrow heading for Manila, where materials will be unloaded. Then it will come down to Lingga.

Tuesday, 11 July 1944. Partly fair, light squall. The southeast wind blew in and splashes coming on board wet the soldiers' uniforms. From 0830 we widened the interval distance, carried out radar spotting practice, and made adjustments of range-finders, etc.

At 1000 *Yahagi* at the top of the first group detected an underwater signal of an enemy submarine to 260° and avoided it. This was south of the Miyako Islands. In view of many enemy submarines gathering in Luzon Strait, we changed our course to 220° and also changed a plan in order to go through Balintang Strait at night.

Vice Admiral Shunichi Kira was appointed commander in chief of the newly organized Third Air Fleet.

Wednesday, 12 July. Partly fair, later cloudy, squall. At 0100 speed was increased to 20 knots, course set at 270° at 0150, and we passed through

Balintang Strait under the light of the moon, which rose past midnight. I stayed on the bridge all the time, but nothing happened. However, since last night, we have detected enemy phones several times.

Group B left Chujo Bay early this morning, but an enemy submarine sent in an urgent signal after 0700. They seem to have been discovered.

Thursday, 13 July 1944. Squall all day. We sailed down west of the Philippines. At 1250 course was altered to 230° and we headed for west of Pratas Island from a point 250 miles west of Manila.

The southwest wind became gradually stronger. Squalls came and went all day long. An order "All hands on deck for squall bathing" seemed strange to the soldiers. After sunset we heard enemy phones as usual. From 1500 to 1700 we carried out usual radar and range-finder practices.

[Ugaki was not at all happy with the effectiveness of these exercises. He was equally displeased the next morning, 14 July, when destroyer *Samidare* in *Musashi*'s screen turned up missing. Fleet speed had to be reduced, and the heavy cruiser *Tone* with a destroyer sent to hunt for her. *Tone* found *Samidare* none the worse. "She must have dropped behind because of the big waves together with poor visibility. Anyway, she must be blamed for being chicken-hearted."

[On Saturday, 15 July, the fleet changed course and again checked our range-finders. They passed between Great Natuna and Anambas Islands. That night, the sight of both the Southern Cross and the Great Bear inspired Ugaki to another of his short poems.]

Sunday, 16 July 1944. Fair. At 0530, while it was still dark, the Fourth Heavy Cruiser Division, Seventh Heavy Cruiser Division and Second Destroyer Squadron parted from us heading for Singapore, while the First Battleship Division with *Shigure, Samidare,* and *Shimakaze* headed for Lingga. After passing the dangerous Pengelap Channel at 1300, we reached the First Alert Anchorage at 1610. Two army transports, four motor schooners, and ten landing craft have been there since this morning to unload the personnel and materials we brought there. We brought them alongside immediately and began unloading a tremendous amount of materials. Sunset was after 2000. We celebrated our safe arrival, the regimental commander joining us.

Monday, 17 July 1944. Fair, later cloudy. *Yamato* unloaded mainly materials to *Shinsei Maru* No. 17, *Musashi* army materials to *Zuisho Maru*. Although we tried to supplement unloading by using ten landing craft, we couldn't finish today. In addition to this, each ship found difficulties in unloading six landing craft due to insufficient derrick capacity.

At 1030 a report came in that fifteen enemy vessels and seventeen large transports were nearing Tinian Island. It wasn't yet clear whether they were a new attempt at landing there or reinforcements to Saipan.

[*Invasion of Tinian was planned and preliminary softening up had been almost continuous from mid-June.*[47]

[By chance Ugaki heard over the radio that Shimada had resigned as navy minister and Vice Admiral Naokuni Nomura was appointed in his place. "This was some shuffle!"]

We finished unloading in the morning. At 1330 the regimental commander left with his regimental color to embark *Zuisho Maru*. He sincerely thanked us for our hospitality rendered to them during the voyage and pledged that he would repay it on a battlefield. I wished him good luck. Three ships left for Singapore at 1730. The remnant of about three hundred are to leave tomorrow morning.

The army tanker *Kokki Maru* has been refueling the First Battleship Division since yesterday. This was far more effective than transporting fuel in a barge.

Rear Admiral Imamura, Commander, Tenth Base Force, sent me a basket of papayas in return for a case of home-produced fruits I sent him yesterday. Friendship among classmates is special.

Concentration of enemy vessels and transports in the Guam area was fairly big. Are they planning a landing there? Whatever they do, we can't do anything against them.

[*Guam was under heavy bombardment. On 20 July, Spruance's flagship* Indianapolis, *with the admiral aboard, took part. Landing began on the 21st.*[48]

[Wednesday, 19 July, passed in preparation for night warfare practice that night. As usual, Ugaki was not entirely satisfied, but saw his own duty clear: "Unless a commander leads the rest in devising, utilizing new weapons, and contemplating new ideas by making use of past battle lessons and in repeating earnest training, I firmly believe that, in the end, it will be impossible to recover from our present plight."]

Imperial headquarters announced the deplorable event at Saipan at 1700 on the 18th. Premier Tojo and the chief of the Naval Information Department also made announcements. It was no use saying anything now. I think it would be better to make clear the responsibility for it.

Thursday, 20 July 1944. Fair. At 1000 I went on board *Takao* (temporary flagship) to pay a visit to the commander in chief, Second Fleet. After making my report, I had a talk with the commander in chief. *Takao* put out at night and we carried out radar spotting training.

Group B arrived at 1630 and the captain of *Nagato* came on board to see me. He told me that an enemy submarine, which seemed to have sunk *Oi* north of Pratus Island, fired four torpedoes against *Kongo* at midnight, but a destroyer in the direct screen dashed for it, so no harm was done to either of them.

In the Philippines public order is not maintained well. Prices have skyrocketed, thieves have increased, and no one but [Jose] Laurel seems to be really cooperating with the Japanese.

[*Laurel was president of the Philippines. Originally ordered by then President Manuel Quezon to remain in Manila to act as a buffer between the Japanese and the Filipino people, in time he became an enthusiastic collaborator.*]⁴⁹

The army was determined to hold that area and continued transportation to pour five divisions in there. Enemy submarines are said to have already destroyed some of them.

[A telegram came in from the navy minister that Nomura had resigned with the rest of the cabinet on the 18th. Ugaki waxed sardonic: "He took up the post on the 17th, issued a message to the navy on the 18th, and submitted his resignation on the same day!"]

Considering that the end of Saipan was announced on the 18th by the Imperial headquarters I think the present cabinet, which has long been criticized, was forced to give up on this occasion.

The army appointed General Umezu, commander of the Kwantung Army, to be full-time chief of the Army General Staff on the 17th, in order to have him devote himself to operations, while appointing General Otozo Yamada, the inspector general, in his place and Field Marshal [Gen.] Sugiyama in Yamada's place. On the same day, the navy appointed a full-time navy minister and Admiral Shimada remained as chief of the Naval General Staff. At his first press interview the new minister, Nomura, said that it was decided to appoint a chief of the General Staff and minister respectively, as the present war situation warranted this step in order to establish firmly an authority to supervise execution of the war. Together with the army action, these words show that the past change and renovation were not proper. Who is to blame for such a blunder committed at a critical stage in the execution of the war? A proper step for Tojo to take is to resign from the post of chief of the General Staff first, then also as premier and as war minister.

[*Dissatisfaction with the Tojo cabinet, especially among the emperor's senior advisers, had been growing for some time. The loss of Saipan brought matters to a head.*⁵⁰

[Ugaki had a few thoughts about this cabinet shuffle, but ended resignedly, "Upon whom the order to organize the next cabinet falls is no concern of mine. But may he be the one who knows how to govern and to deal with the present situation and be able to uphold the war strength forcefully!"

[Friday, 21 July 1944, opened with more antisubmarine training with

Ugaki as supervisor. "Those who were good proved good and the bad were bad indeed."]

An urgent telegram from Guam stated that sixty-four enemy transports, four battleships, two cruisers, several destroyers, and forty minesweepers approached early this morning and were lowering boats. Another from the chief of staff, Thirty-first Army, said that they were all prepared to meet an invasion force, expecting to perish.

[*The forces invading Guam were Task Force 53, Southern Attack Force, under Rear Admiral Richard L. Conolly, and the southern troops and landing force under Major General Roy S. Geiger, USMC.*][51]

Headquarters, Thirty-first Army, had wanted to move to Palau to facilitate its general command, but was stopped by the Combined Fleet and now met this fate. We must expect this will be another Saipan soon.

The cabinet-organizing headquarters announced yesterday that General Kuniaki Koiso and Admiral Mitsumasa Yonai received His Majesty's order to cooperate with each other to establish a cabinet. It doesn't make any difference to us who is chosen; I only want somebody who can deal with this crisis. Now that the heads have been determined, I hope they will gather capable men and quickly attain their object of forming a cabinet.

[*Yonai's appointment was especially significant. When premier, he had opposed trouble with the United States. A high court official stated that "Admiral Yonai was chosen because he had the trust of the emperor and also because the emperor knew that he entertained thoughts of peace."*][52]

Saturday, 22 July 1944. Fair. From 1015, a meeting to study a joint night gunfire of battleship and cruiser divisions was held on board *Chokai*, and I was appointed its chairman. We made studies using our plan prepared by my staff officers as a basis.

The enemy started landing at Guam since yesterday morning with many tanks, etc. His strength seemed to be two divisions. Casualties given to the enemy up to now amounted to 4,300, and they seemed to be fighting hard. The commander in chief, Combined Fleet, wired the commander, Thirty-first Army, that he could do nothing to help him from a general standpoint, though it was intolerable to him personally. The outcome is apparent.

[The investiture of the new cabinet was held at 1430 on the 22nd. Yonai issued a message to the navy, and Ugaki noted rather nastily, "What he said is almost the same as that of Mr. Nomura. It is only natural, as probably the same man prepared it."]

Monday, 24 July 1944. Partly fair. Since this evening the enemy landed on the west side of the first airstrip at Tinian and on its port. A fierce battle is going on, with level batteries doing some damage to the enemy vessels.

[*Destroyer* Norman Scott *took six hits, which damaged her and killed her skipper and eighteen men. Battleship* Colorado *was hit no less than twenty-two times and damaged, losing forty-three officers and men killed, with ninety-seven badly wounded. However,* Colorado *was not disabled.*][53]

The First Air Fleet with its officers, many pilots, and crews couldn't be evacuated to Davao and met this fate. Vice Admiral Kakuta, its commander in chief, wired his determination to hold his hilly position to the last, and transfered command of the fleet to the commander, West Forty-first Force. Tragedies in succession! I feel rather hesitant to take up my pen for the everyday record.

Tuesday, 25 July 1944. Partly fair. We sailed out at 0930 and carried out a full-fledged training program. The effective range of flare shells for secondary batteries is insufficient for firing, beings only sixteen kilometers. Other ships' firing flares can't attain the accuracy of the searchlights. We returned at 0100.

At 0830 a total of twenty enemy planes raided Babang and a part of them attacked Kuta Raja. At 0930 four battleships, five cruisers, and nine destroyers (some of them flying French flags) approached from the northwest and bombarded from fifteen to sixteen kilometers away, while four destroyers entered the harbor, attacking with gun and torpedo fire. They withdrew to the west at 1130. The damage was fairly heavy. Sinking of a submarine by an army heavy bomber was almost certain, and they made hits on three destroyers. [*This was a British attack.*][54]

In the first report they related the existence of five transports, which made me think that, if the enemy really intended an invasion there, we no longer would be able to stay here to train. But fortunately it turned out to be a simple surprise attack. However, we should expect an enemy attack in that area for certain and prepare everything accordingly. The Eighth Air Force in this area concentrated promptly but their strength was only about ten fighters, five carrier torpedo bombers, and one *Tenzan*. They went out to seek and attack the enemy, but only sighted two carriers, two battleships, two cruisers, four destroyers, and one other sailing west at a point 150 miles bearing 280° from Kuta Raja.

On the other hand, an enemy task force raided the Yap district. [*TG 58.1 attacked Yap and other atolls in the Carolines 25 through 28 July.*][55]

The Thirty-first Army commander is determined to charge into the enemy in Guam tonight. The commander in chief, Combined Fleet, was moved deeply and wished the force to hold on as long as possible in order to gain time from the viewpoint of directing the war. And both chiefs of General Staffs conveyed the emperor's words as follows: "I am satisfied with the arduous efforts of those fighting at Guam and Tinian under difficult circumstances. I hope the navy and army jointly make a further effort and try to hold on longer."

Also at Tinian casualties sustained in the field battle were mounting, and the commander in chief, First Air Fleet, put off the last charge scheduled to be carried out on the night of the 25th for the sake of readjustment and liaison. On receipt of the above report of the urgent situation, the commander in chief, Combined Fleet, expressed his satisfaction with the good operational conduct by the commander in chief, First Air Fleet, since last spring and also with the gallant fighting by the army and naval forces, and wished them further brave fighting.

Together with the late Fleet Admiral Yamamoto, I bitterly experienced almost intolerable feelings of sorrow and regret at the time of the fall of Buna in Eastern New Guinea when I was chief of staff, Combined Fleet. Now important points are falling into enemy hands one after the other and capable commanders are perishing together with their staffs and men. I can imagine how bitterly the Combined Fleet headquarters is feeling about this.

I understand perfectly that it's only a matter of time that one dies sooner or later, and as long as one lives one must fight until the end. However, human feelings can't always be rational.

The gist of a telegram from the chief of the Operations Bureau, Naval General Staff: "King has conferred with Nimitz in Hawaii. [*Admiral Ernest J. King, commander in chief, U.S. Fleet, and Admiral Chester W. Nimitz, commander in chief, U.S. Pacific Fleet.*] The next enemy offensive will be directed to the Philippines and will be carried out shortly."

Wednesday, 26 July 1944. Overcast. A total of 120 fighters and bombers raided Yap yesterday. Four Zero fighters intercepted them and all were lost. Today the Palau area was raided several times. Will the enemy come straight to the Philippines, leaving the western Carolines untouched?

[Thursday, 27 July 1944, was another day of training and study. Ugaki asked his officers to think of what might "increase fighting power," and to "try to devise or invent a new idea about anything, either on ship, weapons, or engines." After this, they put to sea at 1600 for firing practice and later night warfare exercises, returning to the anchorage at 0015.]

It appears that the last charge was carried out at Guam on the 25th as scheduled, for there has been no further communication from there. From Tinian the First Air Fleet sent in battle lessons, etc. However, water is scarce there and, in addition, there is little rain these days, so how to secure the only water reservoir on the island is the key to how long they can hold out. And it's said that they can't hold more than ten days from now.

Saturday, 29 July 1944. Fair. A conference on the second and third night-raid practice was held on board *Chokai* in the morning, and I had a chance to see Rear Admiral Sakonju, a classmate and commander of the Sixteenth Heavy Cruiser Division. It reminded me of the time of Operation Kon.

I couldn't read without tears a telegram sent from the commander of the army and naval forces at Tinian to the ministers of War and Navy and the Minister of East Asian Affairs, with a copy to the chiefs of the Army and Naval General Staffs, which was dated the 28th:

> 1. Under the guidance of the local government and principal ci-vilians, 3,599 men of the ages from 16 to 45, out of 15,000 local Jap-anese people have been organized into a volunteer corps and are fully cooperating with the armed forces. The rest are old, women, and kids, most of whom had already been evacuated from the Caroline district.
>
> 2. The volunteer corps has been organized into six companies, which are attached to each unit of the armed forces. They are fighting gallantly, thus displaying the tradition of our nation to the fullest.
>
> 3. The acting governor, together with the representative local ci-vilians (25 words illegible) [*Ugaki's note*]. Women and old men have assembled together and are going to commit suicide by exploding explosives. The governor has not yet returned from a visit to Saipan, where he went before the enemy captured it.

[*On 11 and 12 July, hundreds of Japanese had killed themselves at the north-ern end of Saipan. A similar but smaller mass suicide took place on Tinian.*][56]

It's only to be expected that servicemen should be killed in action, but women, children, and old men in such large number prefer death to being taken prisoner by an enemy on a helpless, lonely island, and are going to blow themselves up en masse. What a tragedy! No people but the Yamato nation could do a thing like this. I think that if one hundred million Japanese people could have the same resolution as these facing this crisis, it wouldn't be difficult to find a way to victory.

Furthermore, we, the servicemen, shouldn't waste a single day in mak-ing sincere efforts for the services. We should accept the responsibility for having led the civilians to this plight.

Sunday, 30 July 1944. Fair. Guam is still continuing a gallant fight, Vice Admiral Kakuta, commander in chief, First Air Fleet, sent an apology to the throne and farewell to the commander in chief, Combined Fleet, at 0000 today, according to a delayed telegram. They seem to have perished today.

Monday, 31 July 1944. Fair, later cloudy. A meeting to study antisubmarine warfare was held on board *Chokai* in the morning. Now that the effect of acoustic and electronic detecting instruments has been more or less stabilized, it's important to adopt a measure to prevent enemy sub attacks and to destroy them by means of those instruments.

It has been decided to establish a seaplane base at Tempa Island, and the First Battleship Division has begun the work.

There has been some sign of an enemy landing somewhere between Manukwari and Sorong in Western New Guinea. And a task force and invasion force are nearing Rota, which makes us think a landing on that island is quite near, too.

[Ugaki ended July's entries by noting unhappily that the segment in which he had intended to cover the "decisive battle" had "become a collection of criticisms and sorrowful events." As he did not anticipate another "day of decisive battle in the near future," he closed "this chapter on the decisive battle with the departing month of July."]

[*Ugaki began a major division here entitled "Battle of the Philippine Sea."*]

[On Tuesday, 1 August, the First Battleship Division trained alone at sea, then held gunfire practice jointly with the Fourth Heavy Cruiser Division, returning to the anchorage at 2345. "Despite the bright moonlight of about the thirteenth lunar night, destroyer *Shikiname* . . . went aground near west of Roban Island." Ugaki could not blame the destroyer's skipper, "as the lone shoal was uncharted."

[Ugaki and his officers studied the previous day's training from the afternoon of Wednesday, 2 August, until nearly midnight. The spread of *Yamato*'s shells had "greatly shortened," but "*Musashi* showed no improvement from the last time and still presented a problem."]

With today's date, Admiral Oikawa was appointed chief of the Naval General Staff, Admirals Shimada and [Zengo] Yoshida members of the War Council, and Admiral Nomura commander in chief, Yokosuka Naval Base, and concurrently Maritime Escort Force commander. Frequent shuffles of the chief of the Naval General Staff are certainly not good. Has Admiral Shimada been forced to do so because of his responsibility to the public?

[The next three days were routine, with a study meeting held on Thursday, 3 August. *Shikinami* was refloated and navigable, but had sustained "fairly heavy damage." Ugaki's ships sailed out on Friday, August 4, for radar firing practice and testing of the direction finder and an emergency rudder. "Since this morning enemy carrier planes raided Iwo Jima twice and Chichi Jima three times." Ugaki made no note for Saturday, 5 August, beyond recording that the weather was fair.]

Sunday, 6 August 1944. Fair. I think that a human can't display his real strength, however hard he's urged to do so vaguely, when he can see little way to win. So I'm in agony trying to discover the way to win by all means.

[The damage control officer of *Nagato* sent Ugaki the leg of a wild boar he had shot. Ugaki had no desire to go hunting. "As the war situation is deteriorating and my health is not so good, I couldn't feel like going out to shoot. 'Thou shalt not kill' for me for a while."

[Ugaki suffered from an unpleasant rash and had two shots on Monday, 7 August, mitigated by several letters from Japan, including one from his son, Hiromitsu. The morning was spent studying the radar firing and emergency rudder tests. Ugaki was pleased to learn that a classmate, Vice Admiral Kimpei Teraoka, had been appointed commander in chief, First Air Fleet.]

Tuesday, 8 August 1944. Partly fair, the setting-in of fall. At 2230 last night we received word of detecting an enemy submarine at Belhara Channel to the Sumatra side. We got quite busy until 0200 in ordering second stations, ready for 16 knots with instant notice, dispatching a destroyer and patrol boats. I couldn't sleep the rest of the night as I was itchy and uncomfortable.

[Ugaki postponed sailing out until 0930 pending completion of the morning's air reconnaissance. Then they sortied and practiced refueling. *Musashi* held "secondary battery radar firing practice, with *Yamato* serving as observer from the flank."]

Wednesday, 9 August 1944. Fair, light squall. A meeting was held on board *Atago* in the morning to study gun and torpedo firing, using radar and sound detector. I supervised it as the chief of staff was in Manila attending table maneuvers. How to use radar is taking shape, but much is still desired in its capacity and accuracy. It's all right to utilize it for gun and torpedo firing, but to depend entirely and blindly on it should be limited to cases where no other means are available. I wish we could make some improvement in this useful weapon, in which we're so far behind.

Thursday, 19 August 1944. Cloudy, later fair. I had nothing to do especially today and read books. I looked back at the time of the battle of the Yellow Sea and thought we shouldn't get so downhearted; they had some hard times, too, during the Russo-Japanese War. As my assignment is commander, First Battleship Division, everything will be quite simple if I'm satisfied only with fulfilling the command of my division and fully training its fighting strength. If I consider the rest none of my business, I have nothing to worry about.

Friday, 11 August 1944. Rain, later cloudy. It was rather unusual lately to have rain all day long on account of a discontinuous line of weather. A typhoon has developed to the south of Honshu and is going up north. I hope it will go over to China. If it sweeps over Japan, essential foodstuff will be beaten down.

As there was considered to be a probability of the enemy attacking the west Caroline area about the 12th (communications intelligence), a warning has been issued in Palau and the Philippine area. Also, some enemy submarines were in the Ryukyus, east of Formosa or west of the Philippines which issued an urgent operational telegram. (Relaying continues.) Other information stated they might have some plans other than menacing our line of communications. Quiet is a sign of movement. We must be careful.

[*The intelligence estimate was correct. During 10 and 11 August, B-29s of the Twentieth Bomber Command flew two missions against land targets. One was against Nagasaki, with minor damage, the other against the Pladjoe refinery at Palembang, Sumatra. This was a major target, estimated to be producing twenty-two percent of Japan's fuel oil and seventy-eight percent of its aviation gas. Here again results were disappointing to the United States.*][57]

Saturday, 12 August 1944. Fair. No special work today, and sailors mended the sides of the ship. Due to tides we couldn't fully use the seaplane base at Tempa, which was built after all the trouble, and we had to withdraw from it yesterday.

The enemy didn't come to the Carolines area today. During a picture show at night, an air raid alert was issued in South Sumatra and a warning in the Singapore area. In case enemy large-type planes come more often, the fleet no longer will be able to stay here like this, not to mention the loss of the Palembang oil source. Where shall we be able to wait?

Sunday, 13 August 1944. Fair. A table maneuver gathering young reserve commanders of the division was held in the morning. It won't do much good if always conducted in an orthodox way, with nothing new. I was sorry to see that they were blind to methods of inducing progress and prejudiced by conventional ideas; there were few who contemplated their ideas basically.

An air raid alert was issued again in the Palembang area today. We don't know whether the enemy actually came there yesterday, for we have had no report about it. Are they becoming too nervous?

The shuffle of the skipper of *Musashi* was announced. Rear Admiral Bunji Asakura was assigned chief of staff, First Southern Expeditionary Fleet, and was succeeded by Captain Inoguchi, who arrived here yesterday from the post of senior instructor of the Naval Gunnery School. I've known Asakura well, and I thought his assignment as chief of staff was quite suitable at a time when this southwestern area was becoming serious, too. I wished him to strive greatly for its defense.

[Monday morning, 14 August, Ugaki's ships carried out training in antisubmarine warfare and radar firing. He noted that large planes had been raiding the Palembang area, and the army planes stationed there complained that they had trouble catching the enemy aircraft, "whose speed is over five hundred kilometers."]

Flares are still seen in Tinian and Guam at night, but judging from the fact that most of the enemy fleet were not in the vicinity it seemed an end has already come to them.

[*Guam was doomed when Lieutenant General Hideyoshi Obata's command post was captured on 12 August. All the Japanese present, including Obata, were either killed or committed suicide. But some nine thousand Japanese had taken to the jungle, and mopping-up continued for the duration of the war. Individual Japanese straggled out of the jungle for several years thereafter.*][58]

Roosevelt visited Attu and Hawaii and met with the commanders. The Pacific operation seems to have come to an end of one stage. Such enemy news such as there will be a big offensive against Japan shortly, etc., have been heard. The United Kingdom seems to be reinforcing her Far East Fleet, too. Come on! We shall fight you all!

[Tuesday, 15 August, was another day of training, in the afternoon practicing "antiaircraft firing in a close ring formation without carriers." At 1930 they moved into night warfare training, "attack and defense of a convoy at anchor."]

With today's date, Vice Admiral Mikawa, commander in chief, Southwest Area Fleet, has been appointed concurrently commander in chief, Southern Expeditionary Fleet. Was it because there was no need of a separate command for the Third Expeditionary Fleet because the Southwest Area Fleet is located in Manila? I wonder what would happen to Vice Admiral Oka, a classmate of mine.

[On Wednesday, 16 August, Ugaki held the usual meeting to study the previous day's training. "Training as a surface force seems to have made progress to some extent, yet far more remains to be accomplished." He noted that enemy attacks had inflicted some damage to the Palembang refinery. Ugaki was somewhat disgruntled because the army planes there "seem to be of no use."

[*Musashi* trained destroyers' gunnery officers on Thursday, 17 August. Ugaki noted that most of these officers were "young and inexperienced," and few had had advanced courses at technical school, so he didn't hope for too much skill on their part. Meanwhile, *Yamato* hosted "logistic practice for aircraft crews," and Ugaki went aboard *Atago* for a study of torpedo firing.]

Captain Shiki, senior staff officer of the Second Fleet, who had been in that position since January last year, left the fleet, as his successor, Captain Yuji Yamamoto, arrived.

The chief of staff came back, bringing with him a copy of the order for Operation Sho. [*Operation Sho was divided into four parts to cover possible U.S. invasion locales. The part activated and brought to Ugaki was Sho-1, postulating invasion of the Philippines. As originally planned, Sho aimed primarily at the destruction of manned U.S. troop transports. Sho-1 called for Ozawa to decoy Halseys' Third Fleet northward, while Kurita's A Force, which included Ugaki's* Musashi *and* Yamato, *and Nishimura's X Force caught U.S. ships in Leyte Gulf in a pincer.*][59] Now we have something to study. It's hard to ask us merely to keep on training when we have nothing to depend on as its basis. It's essential still to hope for victory, whatever difficulty one may be in, and endeavor to attain its object. In order to do this, it's necessary to make clear a concrete operational policy.

Now I feel I have already given vent to my pent-up feelings since Operation A. Whether the plan is adequate or not needs further study, but at the time when we have been driven into the last ditch we have no other choice, as the battle front has been narrowed so much. Well, let's bind ourselves together tightly for one object and seek the last decisive battle once for all.

[A meeting was held on board *Atago* in the morning of Friday, 18 August, to study the last training session.]

While engaging in transport from the Philippines to Palau, destroyer *Samidare* went aground at the west of Kulaangle Island due to an error in her estimated position, and her boiler room was flooded. Also, an enemy submarine attacked light cruiser *Natori* northwest of Palau and she was withdrawing at 7 knots. It seemed to be the last supply, and yet how unlucky they were! Thus fighting strength is gradually diminishing. *Musashi* went out alone today and carried out training.

Saturday, 19 August 1944. Fair, occasional squalls. At 0900 *Yamato* went out alone and carried out damage control practice while undertaking attached small gun firing practice and also antiair warfare and emergency engine practice. She returned at 1550.

I thought they [the men] might put off Saturday's usual picture show as they must have been tired out today. But no, they wouldn't go without recreation. They had four to five features from about 2140. Movies may be the only recreation, but I felt that was rather too long. However, I suppose the men wouldn't be satisfied with less. How to obtain films should be a job of the fleet adjutant to uplift the men's fighting spirit.

Sunday, 20 August 1944. Fair. A meeting to study radar firing was held in the morning. Firing exclusively by means of radar can never be successful. Its application to this type of ship with a small amount of ammunition is completely out of the question.

United States news relayed from Lisbon carried a story about the courageous end of the Japanese civilians on Saipan, and said the Japanese are a nation that prefers death to surrender. Well done, those people, and they displayed the real Japanese character! If any army or naval men do a shameful thing, they should be ashamed to face those women and children.

The enemy has established bridgeheads at Toulon and Marseilles in South France while U.S. forces are advancing toward Paris from three directions. The Vichy government has moved elsewhere, and it seems that Paris will fall into enemy hands soon. I think the Germans should put up more resistance.

It's regrettable for the Axis powers to see that we're having a bad time both in the west and east.

Monday, 21 August 1944. Fair. The fleet carried out antiair practice against our six planes for one hour this morning.

Radio activities in the Colombo area looked like those of their [the enemy's] last task force assault on Sabang. It seems to be fairly certain that the enemy will come shortly.

Last night an air raid warning to be directed to the mainland of Japan from the Nanking area was issued, and I wonder what happened. Air raids by B-29s flying 1,350 miles from the China continent (Sintain, west of Chengtu) are one of our troubles. However, if they come in piecemeal, they'll give the people back in the homeland necessary stimulation and training.

[*On 20 August B-29s of the Twentieth Bomber Command made two attacks on Yawata. These raids were proportionately more costly to the United States than to Japan—four B-29s were destroyed over the target, ten lost to other causes, with a total of ninety-five airmen killed or missing.]*[60]

Tuesday, 22 August 1944. Fair. I read reports on the European war situation, foreign information for June and July, Naval General Staff intelligence, etc. I can get some knowledge from them even if it might be a bit out of date. I can't get any other materials at present.

Having completed her repair work, *Haruna* arrived at Singapore yesterday and is now unloading materials, among which are some electric devices. The attack force will be divided into two groups, and starting tomorrow will go to Singapore to install these devices by 2 September. To help the work we are to send forty technicians. As *Yamato* and *Musashi* were unable to go to Singapore for security reasons, fleet headquarters suggested that we send liberty parties there in turn. But under such circumstances as our being urged to complete operational preparations and promote our strength by all means, and also because a strict alert should be maintained even while staying here, a responsible commander can hardly agree to interrupt training for six days and maintain alert with half crews. So I had my staff convey to headquarters my view that as a commander I wasn't agreeable to that suggestion and wouldn't let *Nagato* go either.

In fact, the present fleet headquarters is taking things too easy. When the day for a decisive battle is approaching day by day and the fate of the empire is staked on this battle, no operational plan has been completed yet, and none of the pending problems has been solved. I think that now is the very time when arrangements to improve skill should be decided promptly. We're not going to act as a part of the task force. Instead, we'll have to engage in a very difficult operation almost independently as a surface force. It would be fortunate if they didn't lack independent views and controlled practicability.

Wednesday, 23 August 1944. Fair. *Kongo* and others left early for Singapore for radar and other electrical work.

In spite of the effort of headquarters Maritime Escort Force in asking its subordinate forces to reduce losses, there seems to have been a loss of two or three ships according to today's telegram. Ship losses inflicted by German submarine warfare in June dropped greatly to only fifty thousand tons, a fact which apparently proves how difficult German submarine activities have been.

What's the basic reason why we, on the contrary, are suffering great losses, allowing the rampage of enemy submarines? It's because our antisubmarine policy isn't perfect. Even though the Pacific Ocean is vast, the routes and passages aren't unlimited. Can't we do something about it?

Thursday, 24 August 1944. Fair. The First Battleship Division went out at 0900 and after numerous battle practices returned at 0100 of the 25th. It's regrettable that night gunfire using flare shells hasn't been mastered. At 1000, twenty-eight enemy planes raided Padang and an air raid warning was issued including the Singapore area. At about 1500 radar detected a reflecting wave like an identification signal, so we took precautions against it for a while during training. We should be careful, as large-type planes might come to attack, though the northern coast of Sumatra would be a difficult target for carrier planes to reach.

[Ugaki and his officers carried out table maneuvers all day Friday, 25 August. The next day the Fourth Heavy Cruiser Division left for Singapore, leaving only the First Battleship Division, *Mogami,* and the Second Destroyer Squadron. "And I became a Triton among the minnows." On Sunday the 27th, Ugaki held gunfire practice and noted that the U.S. forces had entered Paris on the 25th. Flares were still being seen on Guam and Tinian, and Ugaki felt deeply "for the lone efforts of the still surviving units there."]

Monday, 28 August 1944. Rain, later fair. In the afternoon a meeting was held to study the last training. Some improvements have been seen, but the most important, level firing, especially using flare shells, is always the same. I wonder why.

I got a few letters. Hiromitsu seems to be all right after joining the school and being trained to be a naval officer.

[Ugaki spent Tuesday 29 August quietly, as he "had been suffering from piles lately." A friend sent him some dried vegetables, and he received a "comfort bag" from home. The next day he wrote twelve letters in reply to some received recently. The Fourth Heavy Cruiser Division returned from Singapore.]

Thursday, 31 August 1944. Partly fair. Following an information report on the enemy from the chief of Radio Intelligence, Naval General Staff, the chief of the Operations Bureau sent in the following judgment on the enemy situation:

1. Enemy preparations for wholesale offensive have been completed, and there is a great probability of its commencing invasion operations toward Davao, West Carolines (. . . illegible) within a

week. As of the 29th, the strength and dispositions of the enemy force to participate in the offensive are estimated as follows:

a. Main force of the task force (its element already at sea), at the Marshalls area.

b. Element of the task force and invasion force and follow-up forces, in the Admiralty area.

c. Most of the invasion force, in Western New Guinea.

d. Most of the submarines, moving to positions for watching, rescuing, and meeting an enemy.

2. There is a great probability that the enemy will carry out a coordinated operation from the Marianas, air raids on the mainland of Japan, and a diverting operation against the Kuriles in connection with the above operation.

[*There had been considerable top-level U.S. discussion as to the next campaign. In general, the navy wanted it directed at Formosa, thence to the Japanese home islands, bypassing the Philippines. MacArthur insisted upon liberating the Philippines at the earliest possible date. At the end of July a decision had been reached in favor of the latter strategy.*]

Against these, our plan is to do almost nothing except for the south of the Philippines. The enemy most probably will take advantage of our weak points, and the preparation of our First Attack Force for the operation isn't yet clear. In this way August has gone.

> Gone is the sun, and the mountain
> Of the clouds loses its color.

9
Another Complete Defeat
September–November 1944

In THE MIDST *of his problems, Ugaki characteristically took the time to deal with the case of a petty officer who, because of "lack of liaison," had been shunted around the Philippines for three months. A letter from a classmate, then in Berlin, set him to reflecting on the Tripartite Pact, which he had opposed. Another officer, back from Europe, reported that no one believed in a total German victory.*

Ugaki led his division through the usual training at sea and table maneuvers, frustrated that Japan seemed unable to counter U.S. landings on various islands. He was under the impression that the United States had two full fleets— the Fifth under Spruance, the Third under Halsey. Actually, it was the same fleet, changing numerical designation with change of commanders. The latest change occurred on 26 August when Halsey took over.

Ugaki still had his doubts about the wisdom of the decisive battle strategy, believing that the Japanese should attack at opportune moments instead. His division was alerted for Sho-go 1 and 2 (anticipated U.S. attempts at landing on Leyte and Formosa, respectively). Almost immediately, the United States struck Formosa heavily, destroying about one-third of Japan's fighter aircraft. In the engagement of 13 and 14 October, the Japanese slightly damaged one U.S. CV and heavily damaged one heavy cruiser. In reports to the homeland they promptly transmuted these figures into some eleven carriers and sundry other ships sunk. This fantasy was widely believed in Japan, touching off "victory" celebrations. Ugaki was somewhat skeptical—if the Americans had lost all those flattops, how could they still be conducting heavy carrier raids? Still, he was quite optimistic about Sho-go's chances for success.

About this time the Kamikaze Special Attack (or suicide) Corps was organized "to destroy enemy carriers without fail." Predictably, this concept moved Ugaki to exaltation: "Oh, what a noble spirit it is!" These kamikazes would prove to be a real trouble to the United States, although they never came near their goal of one plane for one ship.

On the way to the decisive battle scene, submarines sank heavy cruisers Atago,

Maya, and damaged Aoba—*an ominous beginning to the battle of Leyte Gulf, an engagement as devastating to Japan's surface fleet as the Marianas Turkey Shoot had been to the naval air arm. It might have been even worse had the Japanese diversionary movement of carriers not lured Halsey northward. The tactic cost Japan four carriers which, however, were almost denuded of planes. In the Leyte region, Ugaki lost* Musashi, *while* Yamato *and* Nagato *were damaged. Heavy cruiser* Chokai *had to be scuttled, heavy cruisers* Chikuma *and* Suzuya *and destroyer* Nowake *were sunk, and Admiral Nishimura lost every ship in his force except destroyer* Shigure.

Ugaki blamed the fact that Japan was "a loser all the time" upon the shortage of aircraft. He believed Japan would need five hundred planes in the pipeline at all times and thus was utterly shocked to learn that the entire navy would be able to muster only 828 aircraft of all types, including projected replacements, by the end of the month.

Soon, however, such concerns were of only academic interest to Ugaki. A major fleet reorganization on 15 November disbanded the First Battleship Division, leaving him temporarily without a job. His new orders merely assigned him to the Naval General Staff, which was purely for administrative convenience, and could mean anything. His beloved Yamato *was scheduled to return to the homeland for repairs, and Ugaki traveled aboard her, this time as a passenger.*

On the homeward voyage, a U.S. submarine sank the battleship Kongo *and destroyer* Urakaze. *Admiral Suzuki, commander of the Third Battleship Division and a good friend of Ugaki, went down with* Kongo. *Ugaki tried to ease his grief by writing a long, touching memorial to this fine officer.*

Yamato *arrived at Kure on 24 November and Ugaki, with his former staff officers, took leave of her and set out for Tokyo. November ended for Ugaki with an all-night B-29 raid.*

Friday, 1 September 1944. Cloudy, light rain, later cleared up. At 0930 I sailed out with *Yamato* and *Musashi* under my command. We carried out towing and towed practice between *Yamato* and *Musashi*, division gunfire practice with attached small guns at dusk, night warfare practice commanded by captains, night torpedo attacks with antiaircraft guns and M/G, and obtained respectable results.

Judging from intensified enemy raids on West New Guinea, about fifty large-type planes attacking Davao on a large scale for the first time, air raids with a few small carriers and bombardments by cruisers on Chichi Jima, and submarine dispositions in the east of the Philippines, it seems that a part of the major enemy offensive has already been started, as the Naval General Staff said. It's no exaggeration to say that none of our forces are ready for it. It's truly deplorable that the attack force isn't yet fully prepared, especially in planning.

[*CVs* Enterprise, Franklin, *CVL* San Jacinto, *two cruisers and their destroyer screen struck the Bonins on 1–2 September* Enterprise *attacked Chichi, Haha, and Ani Jimas.*][1]

Today is supposed to be the day on which a storm comes every year, but there is no typhoon around Japan. [*1 September was the anniversary of the Great Earthquake of 1923.*]

A petty officer [Petty Officer Second Class Yoichi Sato], who had been recalled on duty and ordered to *Musashi* from Yokosuka, arrived aboard only the day before yesterday after wandering around the Philippines on board a freighter since early June. But his vacancy has already been filled, and I was told that he was going to be sent to the Third Reserve Corps in Surabaja as soon as transportation was available. A lack of liaison has made an individual roam about for three months and will further give a bad shock to his morale. I think it might be better at this critical time before a decisive battle to keep a man like that on board as a fleet reserve, so I ordered that we negotiate accordingly.

Saturday, 2 September 1944. Partly fair, squall. Two cruisers and four destroyers approached Chichi Jima from the northwest and bombarded the airfield and radar [sites], etc. [*The two cruisers were heavy cruiser* New Orleans *and light cruiser* Biloxi *of the* Enterprise *force.*][2]

Nagato came back from Singapore at night.

I received a letter dated 1 April from Vice Admiral Katsuo Abe, a classmate of mine who is in Berlin now [*as Japan's Naval Attaché.*] He had heard about my being wounded from Commander [Kazuta] Oogi and asked after my health. Though he thought of asking for combat duty after having stayed there for three years and three months, he said he would not regard his personal wishes, intending to serve longer in view of the importance of the war. Of course, the Tripartite Alliance was an indirect cause of the war. In the fall of 1940, Germany sent Stahmer to Japan to sound out a cordial relation with her. Yosuke Matsuoka, foreign minister at that time, thought it a good chance to conclude the treaty, and after the cabinet had almost decided for it the navy minister secretly consulted with the Naval General Staff about it.

I, (then chief of the Operations Bureau) representing the Naval General Staff's opinion, opposed it. My reason was that the alliance with the Axis would antagonize the United States who would consider Japan as well as Germany her enemy, and as a result we would have to expect the worst. Though the Germans were winning on a large scale in Europe then, we never knew what might happen in the future. They wanted an alliance with us then, so we could choose our own time to accept it; it was too early for Japan to conclude it under the current situation. At that time Abe was chief of the Military Affairs Bureau and urged that, if we missed that chance, it would be impossible later on as the Germans would refuse. Besides, unless it was concluded, the cabinet would fall. Under the circumstance that no leader other than Premier Konoye was available, serious consideration should be given to the problem for the sake of the country. Thus, representing the Navy Ministry's view, he strongly advocated the treaty. I remember the navy minister was of the same opinion, too; therefore he should share some responsibility for the cause of this war. [*See Ugaki's preface for Ugaki's further comments on the Tripartite Pact.*]

[Ugaki recalled that Abe, with Naokuni Nomura, had been alliance liaison officers in Rome and later Berlin. He was sorry for Abe, stuck in a desk job for so long, but he would just "have to put up with it."]

Sunday, 3 September 1944. Partly fair. After a slightly delayed monthly rite of the Yamato Shrine, we had sports contests dedicated to the shrine.

Captain Sutejiro Onoda, who had been dispatched from the Naval General Staff to Europe (March of last year) and was appointed skipper of *Takao* after coming back on board a submarine last month, visited me and I heard about the European situation. Nobody thought Germany would win completely. The question was how long it would last, which depended on Hitler's ideas. Also there was no evidence of a separate peace with the Soviets, but deceitful Stalin, with an eye on German industry, might be up to anything, so there is still some hope.

[Fleet table maneuvers were held on board *Yamato* to study Operation Sho. Ugaki complained of "a slight temperature." The next day these maneuvers were suspended and a study of towing took place. *Atago* issued an air raid alert but the sighting proved to be Japanese float planes participating in a training exercise.]

A few dozen carrier aircraft raided Kaoe in West New Guinea today. Two small carriers were seen operating there. [*It is possible that Japanese intelligence reported erroneously on this raid. A B-25 force of the Far East Air Force—FEAF—struck Kaoe on this date.*][3]

[On Wednesday, 6 September, *Atago* hosted a meeting to study the table maneuvers, and in the evening all forces participated in night warfare practice. Ugaki noted that they were improving. Routine but intensive training continued on Thursday, 7 September.]

The opening ceremony of the Fiftieth Extraordinary Diet Session was held today, and the new premier delivered a policy speech. The war and navy ministers reported on the war situation.

A few dozen B-24s raided the Menado area, inflicting some damage.

Since the 6th, more than two enemy task forces have air raided Palau and Yap. More than five hundred planes (in total) attacked Palau.

[*Enterprise hit Yap on 6 September. Although defenses had been almost*

wiped out by the AAF, a few worthwhile targets remained. The Enterprise
*pilots encountered no Japanese aircraft, but antiaircraft fire shot down three
U.S. planes. On the 7th, they returned and devoted special attention to gun
emplacements.* New Orleans *and* Biloxi *bombarded from off shore.*]⁺

Friday, 8 September 1944. Fair. A meeting to study the last training was
held on board *Atago* in the morning.

The enemy task force attacking the west Carolines has not disclosed
transports yet, but they started exploding underwater obstacles at Yap. It
made us think an enemy invasion would be soon.

As I haven't been feeling well lately, after urine tests, etc., the diagnosis
showed that I was suffering from simple inflammation of the bladder.
Besides having a shot, I was cauterized with moxa.

Saturday, 9 September 1944. Cloudy, squall. We put off the second table
maneuver of today and tomorrow due to the war situation.

Since 0700 this morning, 280 enemy carrier planes have attacked three
places in the Davao area. They were the enemy task forces that attacked
Yap and the Palau area on the 7th and 8th, and now they came to attack
Mindanao.

[*From 9 to 13 September the* Enterprise *group conducted a strike a day
against Babelthuap, Peleliu, and Anguar. On 9 and 10 September Mitscher
conducted two heavy strikes against Mindanao. He found that the Fifth Air
Force had already flattened Japanese installations and few Japanese planes were
left, so he decided to switch targets to the central Philippines.*]⁵

As a result of the search in the afternoon, it was found to be as in the
following diagram:

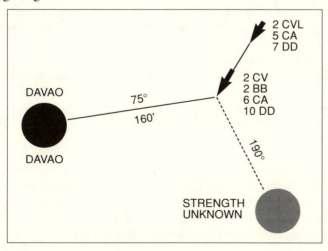

According to statements of POWs, *Enterprise, Bunker Hill, Hornet, Wasp,* and *Franklin* participated without accompanying transports while six *Independence* types, four heavy cruisers, and eight to ten destroyers cooperated with them.

The object of this attack seems to be support of an invasion of the Palau and Yap areas, but most of our air units have been withdrawn. As there is no strong resistance except the local antiair defense, no doubt the enemy did whatever he liked.

Sunday, 10 September 1944. Fair, later a little cloudy. While we were holding a meeting to study a division maneuver in the afternoon, a report came in of an enemy landing at Davao. The Combined Fleet issued "Alert for Operation Sho No. 1," and this attack force was prepared for 20 knots with four hours' notice.

At first it was suspected that an enemy landed on Samalanga Island. Then reports came in succession: Enemy landing craft were being concentrated on the east side of Samar Island. Amphibious tanks were landing at the Second Davao Air Base. All these partial reports were sent in one after another realistically, as they should be. Accordingly, the Combined Fleet issued an alert, ordered attacks on convoys and an urgent sortie of submarine forces. The task fleet also ordered the available strength of the Third and Fourth Carrier Divisions placed under the Second Attack Force, which, in turn, was ordered to assemble at Kure to be ready for sortie. The commander in chief, First Air Fleet, withdrew to the rear, transfering his command temporarily to commander, Twenty-sixth Air Flotilla, and attack orders of the Air Fleet were issued in close succession amid a great fuss.

Then at about 1700, the Fifth Air Assault Force of the First Air Fleet reported, "As a result of close investigation there is no evidence of enemy landing at the Davao area." Having been in constant fear since yesterday's air raid, they must have become so nervous that they just got frightened of a nonexistent thing. If so, it's a pitiable plight, and it shows that a faulty patrol system together with enemy bombings have wrought fear in their minds, so they're not entirely in a condition to meet an enemy. Still, it was lucky that the report was false. Had it been true, we might have been beaten already. We must be careful.

Monday, 11 September 1944. Slightly cloudy. Enemy carrier planes attacked the Davao area this morning, but it was learned that the concentration of landing craft reported yesterday at Samar was that of fishing boats and completely false because a careful search revealed no enemy force in that area. Therefore the Combined Fleet issued "all clear" at 0700, and the whole fleet regained its calm. Intercepting our torrent of urgent telegram exchanges, the enemy seemed to have left with a contemptuous smile.

As both headquarters, Thirty-second Base Force, and the garrison force at Samalanga carried out first-stage disposal of code books, the Southwest Area Fleet sent a staff officer to redistribute code books. This is no laughing matter at all. It's absolutely necessary to give serious thought in order to leave nothing to regret when it really happens. I want to call all the operational forces' attention to this incident in order to let this be a lesson to them and material for reflection.

Tuesday, 12 September 1944. Partly cloudy, squall. A few dozen enemy carrier planes raided Peleliu yesterday. At 0540 today, seven vessels approached the island from the directions of 100° and 270° and started bombardments, indicating a good possibility of an enemy landing. A total of 168 fighters and bombers also attacked Palau all day long.

At 0900 a lookout at Suluan Island sighted a big formation of medium-type planes flying west, another big formation of large planes heading east at 1057, and also an enemy fleet sailing north at a point seventy kilometers bearing 90° from there at 1200. At 0930 carrier planes raided Cebu and Tacloban.

On the other hand, a summary report of radio intelligence came in showing an enemy task force left Brown [Eniwetok] on the 10th, while on the 11th there was a probability of another task force at sea in the Marianas area.

Wednesday, 13 September 1944. Cloudy. It was decided to carry out no training at sea for a while and to engage in repair and fixing, with lectures and table maneuvers held in the meantime. This was also necessary from the viewpoint of keeping a full fuel load.

Damages sustained at the Cebu and Bacolod areas since 0920 yesterday are as follows:

Damages sustained by airplanes at Cebu (approximately 150 planes comprising the main strength of the First Air Fleet's attack forces) was serious. Damage to the army planes at Bacolod area isn't known yet, but seems to be fairly big. According to an army search plane, the enemy task force consisted of eight carriers and four others, its position being 140 miles bearing 90° from Tacloban base at 1210.

Furthermore, a big formation of enemy planes reportedly flew over Suluan and headed toward Surigao at 0635. There was also a report of the Legazpi and Cagayan areas being attacked at 0730.

Judging from an enemy announcement that "the Third Fleet under the command of Halsey attacked Mindanao," it seems that the Third Fleet has also the character of a task force besides the Fifth Fleet, a special task force under [Admiral Raymond A.] Spruance.

[*Ugaki's comment reflects the confusion engendered among the Japanese on this subject. Actually, the Third and Fifth Fleets were virtually identical, known as the Third when Halsey was in command and the Fifth when under Spruance. This particular change took place on 26 August. Halsey in his flagship* New Jersey *joined forces with Mitscher on 11 September.*

[*The Third Fleet attacked the central Philippines on 12 and 13 September. Halsey claimed 173 Japanese planes shot down, about 305 destroyed on the ground, 59 ships sunk with 58 probables, at a cost of nine aircraft and ten men.*][6]

"A" information based upon radio intelligence stated early this morning: The date the enemy will commence its invasion of the western Caroline area is considered to be in one or two days. Its attempt to invade the Halmahera area from New Guinea and the Solomons is also quite noticeable.

Nothing is more indicative of MacArthur's next advance from the Bird's Head to Halmahera than daily attacks on Menado by dozens of large planes. [*The attacks on the Menado area were by FEAF B-24s and B-25s.*][7] In the Colombo area considerable forces have assembled. In view of their carrying out a maneuver for the past few days, they probably will start action soon. Everywhere we turn, enemies surround us.

Thursday, 14 September 1944. Fair. The third table maneuver of the attack force was held on *Yamato,* and I was its chief judge. As planning was left to the chief judge this time, I hypothesized that the enemy would invade Yap, Palau, and Halmahera in September, toward the end of October land on strategic points in Mindanao as the first step, and finally attempt to recapture Luzon as the second stage after consolidating bases. This was the hardest situation for the "Blue" country (Japan) to grapple with and yet the most probable one.

Enemy carrier planes attacked the Legazpi, Cebu, Davao, Zamboanga, and Menado areas this morning. They are very persistent. [*The attacks of the 12th, 13th, and 14th were so successful and destroyed so many Japanese planes and so much shipping at so small a cost, that Halsey recommended that Mac-Arthur's planned landing in the Philippines be advanced from December to 20 October.*][8] According to radio intelligence, the enemy forces engaging in the present offensive seem to be on a very large scale. Therefore, there is some fear that they might attack the Philippines directly besides the cases listed in the above hypothesis. On the other hand, enemy vessels approached the Palau area yesterday and carried out minesweeping in two areas. Does this mean that after all they intend to invade the west Carolines and Halmahera first? Placed in a passive position, one tends to be harassed with various doubts, and it's indeed unpleasant. (In a telegram received later, the chief of staff, Combined Fleet, expressed the same idea of the enemy coming to the Philippines directly.)

The chief of staff, Combined Fleet, seems to have sent a strong warning to the chief of staff, First Air Fleet, not to be reckless in the midst of hostile natives, and not to overconcentrate its forces, thus inviting major damage.

Air raids in the Philippines, which became known today, are as follows:

Davao Area	0700–1430	117 planes
Cebu "	0810–1600	165 "
Legazpi "	0750–1340	37 "
Bacolod "	1300	50 "
San Pablo "	1200–1515	43 "
(South of Legazpi)		
Zamboanga Area	A.M. and 1535	a few dozen
Jolo	unknown	
Menado		a few

The enemy also bombarded the neighborhood of Cape San Augustine at 1135–1400.

Southwest Area Fleet's estimate of enemy situation:

1. The enemy task forces which have been at sea in the west Carolines and the east of the Philippines since 6 September are two groups, each containing two or three groups of carriers, with the total number of carriers reaching twenty. (I agree)

2. Their estimated positions by radio direction finding: The first group (most powerful), in the east of Samar. The second group, in close east of Cape San Augustine. In addition, some carriers in the Palau area.

Friday, 15 September 1944. Cloudy. We continued the table maneuver and finished at 1400. The reason why its development turned out more favorable to the Blue force than feared in the beginning was that the concentration of Red's offensive forces were insufficient and, relying too much on its superior strength, made widespread simultaneous attacks. It was also due to an ideal activity of Blue's base air forces. If it goes like this in reality, we shall have a chance to win and also be able to die satisfied even if we don't.

This morning the enemy began invasion operations simultaneously both in the Palau and Halmahera areas. The following telegram reached us while we were at the table maneuver. Though it was anticipated, it gave us a shock:

Forty-fifth Garrison Force (Palau) at 0708 of the 15th (decoded at 1120):

The enemy within sight of the Maracal lookout post at 0630 of the 15th:

1. Two battleships, three destroyers, and four large transports maneuvering off Peleliu bearing 250°.

2. Three carriers and five destroyers twenty-five kilometers off Maracal.

3. Two cruisers, one destroyer, and fifty transports (ten thousand tons) forty kilometers bearing 150° sailing south. Transports seem to be increasing. (Later they were reported to be lowering boats).

The Twenty-sixth Base Force at 0800 of the 15th (decoded at 1148): "The enemy began landing at Gotararamo, the southwest end of Morotai Island. (One battleship, eight cruisers, three submarines, and scores of transports, large and small.)"

Kairal Air Base, at 0630 (decoded at 1200): "A large enemy task force appeared off the southwest coast of Morotai, bombarded the island and entered Galela. Over one hundred vessels."

[*The United States wanted Morotai as a base to neutralize Halmahera. Vice Admiral Daniel E. Barbey's Seventh Amphibian Force was almost unopposed. The Third Amphibians under Vice Admiral Theodore S. Wilkinson and the First Marine Division, under Major General W. H. Rupertus, experienced much more difficulty landing on Peleliu. The Japanese were well entrenched in caves and had plenty of food and material. Peleliu was not secured for about a month.*][9]

According to the above, the commander, Southwest Area Force, activated Operation P.H. and wished the garrison force "Gan" to fight with their best. Among later telegrams: from the commander in chief, Southwest Area Fleet, at 1625, according to a report of an army reconnaissance, two carriers, two cruisers, and four destroyers were at a point 450 kilometers bearing 100° from Sandakan at 0830 of the 15th. If this is true, the enemy will ravage the Celebes Sea, and advance anchorage, fuel resources, and other strategic points will mean nothing to us.

[On Saturday, 16 September, Ugaki participated in two table maneuvers, one aboard *Atago*, the other on *Yamato*. He was chairman in both cases and duly thankful that by this time he had recovered his health.]

In the Palau area the enemy carried out minesweeping near Kossol Channel while two hundred landing craft and one hundred tanks approached the south end of Peleliu at 0630, but our army repulsed them out on the reef. The enemy attempted landing again in the afternoon, and twelve tanks with about three hundred men landed near the airfield. Despite a night attack last night, it was reported that enemy tanks and soldiers made some advance this morning.

On the other hand, in Halmahera many vessels are still staying near Morotai. The enemy that landed on the west side of the south end of the island yesterday started building airstrips. Four PT boats came into Kaoe Bay but were repelled with gunfire. It seems that they have not yet landed on the mainland of Halmahera. Though enemy task forces are operating in that area, no attack has been launched upon them, allowing them to go unmolested. Surprise attacks by submarines and planes should be carried out at a time like this.

According to a telegram sent in by the chief of the Operations Bureau yesterday informing us of the schedule for the organization change, *Nagato* was slated to be placed into the Second Battleship Division in late September. So I promptly contacted the Second Fleet, which sent a telegram asking to leave her as she is. Such a change is entirely inadequate at such a crucial time as this, and also it's not the way to let *Nagato* display her fighting power.

There has been an outbreak of TF-type dysentery in *Haruna* and *Musashi* recently, while a paratyphoid type A broke out in a destroyer today. We must be prepared against these enemies, too.

[On Sunday, 17 September, Ugaki heard briefings about conditions in the Philippines and on the European situation. He invited to lunch several officers who came from his prefecture and later attended a Sumo contest to commemorate the anniversary of the battle of the Yellow Sea in the Sino-Japanese War. Ugaki "enjoyed it very much," especially as a wrestler from *Yamato* won the contest. And that night's movie "was not bad."]

Since communications between Palau and Peleliu have been severed since yesterday, the situation there was not quite clear. But the enemy strength operating in the area was ten carriers, three battleships, fifteen cruisers, twenty-five destroyers, fifty transports. It was also reported that a cruiser sank instantly at a point thirty thousand meters north of Almondai gun position.

Two carriers, two battleships, eight cruisers, seventeen destroyers, and fifty transports were in Halmahera to the east of Morotai. Although the enemy seemed to be hesitating at points where he meets strong resistance, out of fear of losing human lives, we must be aware of the fact that his invasion is progressing methodically second by second.

Monday, 18 September 1944. Cloudy, squall. Reports on investigation date of local battles which each division conducted were reviewed on board *Atago*. They covered from the Philippines to Amamioshima, and yet no prospect of a victory could be seen. How can I answer to those comrades killed in action?

An explanation and briefing of the attack force's Operation Sho plan was held in the afternoon. Apart from Combined Fleet orders, how is it that the headquarters, attack force, which is going to fight a decisive battle actually commanding the surface force, has no definite idea about answers to basic questions?

The sound of gunfire was heard in Kossol Channel in the Palau area. Minesweeping in and out of the channel is progressing. About one division of enemy troops landed at Peleliu during the night of the 16th. Our army destroyed one hundred tanks and sixty landing craft, but our casualties were also fairly heavy. In the morning of the 18th, the enemy advanced to the edge of the airfield, and our air base force lost one-third of its strength. Enemy bombardments and bombings were so fierce that its fate is feared.

[There was "no special work" on Tuesday, 19 September, and Ugaki composed a short poem in honor of the light rain.]

The enemy at Morotai has roughly completed an airstrip at Cape Gils, and has begun to build another one. There were two carriers, nine cruisers, twenty to thirty destroyers, and twenty-four transports. Two transports arrived in Kossol Channel in Palau while forty flying boats seem to have arrived there. From now on, enemy air activities will be intensified using these places as bases. And yet we can do nothing about it.

[After considerable effort on Ugaki's part, the case of Petty Officer Sato was settled. Ugaki thought the current system of personnel assignments needed changing. "It was not for Sato alone that I took all the trouble, but for fulfilling *Nagato*'s fighting power and also for breaking the conventionalism regarding the complement of personnel. I admit it's still not enough, although I've gained my point."]

Wednesday, 20 September 1944. Fair. A rite to pay tribute to those who have been killed in action since 5 August last year was held from 1100 on board *Yamato*. When I thought of those changes in the war since then and saw the present plight, I felt ashamed of myself.

After the ceremony I discussed much about operations with Rear Admiral [Tomiji] Koyanagi [chief of staff], and Captain Yuji Yamamoto, senior staff officer. I advocated the wisdom, as an inferior force, of a policy of gradual reduction of the enemy strength, destroying enemy components with our local superior strength at an opportune moment, rather than a once-for-all decisive battle policy. I further urged them to seek a decisive battle of the surface force with enemy surface battle forces rather than with enemy convoys. Moreover, I told them other things I thought of. Though we couldn't exchange our views entirely, they said they would send suggestions to the Fleet Headquarters based upon the result of table maneuvers, etc., and also ask the Combined Fleet to dispatch a staff officer here.

One battleship, one cruiser, one cable layer, and one transport entered Kossol Channel in Palau yesterday, and a total of two hundred fighters and bombers raided all day, while fighting continued on Peleliu. On the 16th one cruiser sank instantly at Kossol Channel, then another ship of unknown description. If this was due to our mines, it shows that mines laid in an area like this are quite effective.

At Angaur our garrison destroyed enemy landing craft on the 17th, but reinforcements in great numbers arrived there from Peleliu, so finally about one thousand enemy succeeded in landing. Fierce fighting still continued. [*On 17 September Major General Paul J. Mueller's Eighty-first Infantry Division landed on Angaur and subdued the island within three days.*][10]

[Ugaki went shooting for the first time in three months, landing on Tempa Island. "Though I got all wet, the bag was small." But he enjoyed the exercise. That day the Sixteenth Heavy Cruiser Division entered port and two of its officers sent Ugaki a basket of fruit and "six mangrove crabs," which he saved "for a class reunion."]

Thursday, 21 September 1944. Partly fair. The Second Air Fleet ordered Second Alert Disposition in light of the fact that its search plane met enemy fighters at sea the day before yesterday. The Southwest Area Fleet also issued a warning yesterday, which made us anticipate an air raid today.

Sure enough, at about 1100 the Thirty-first Communications Corps sent out an emergency signal to the effect that 200 and 150 carrier planes were attacking Manila and Clark Field, respectively. Then at 1020 to 1040, the second wave of 120 fighters and bombers combined attacked ships and army airfields, and two ships were sunk and one set on fire. At 0905 a floatplane searcher found an enemy task force of 52 vessels on course of 90° at a point 153 miles bearing 60° from Manila. [*Halsey's carrier-borne aircraft conducted four strikes on Manila on 21 September.*][11]

The First Air Fleet decided to attack the enemy task force with all its strength at 1128. It should do so. If it adheres to a policy of preservation, in the end all its planes will be annihilated on the ground. If they flee without attacking, they had better be sent back to Japan. If the planes are to be expended anyway, attack the enemy and perish! The lack of training may be one of the causes, but not a little is due to the basic operational policy of the Combined Fleet. It urges them to preserve their strength until the so-called decisive battle and avoid its gradual expenditure, thus giving rise to a tendency to restrain an active offensive at an opportune moment.

If we only had an active intention to destroy an oncoming enemy, search and patrol would be more minute, and it would also be possible to seize and develop an opportunity. Then the result would be greater, while the loss would be less. On the other hand, once we fall into passivity, we won't be able to do anything, and the enemy will fool us. As I told the chief of staff yesterday, we lacked a fundamental policy of attacking an enemy component at an opportune moment. In Operation A we intended to destroy the enemy at one stroke, but, on the contrary, we were rendered incapable of continuing the battle. In addition, Saipan was captured.

In Operation Sho, too, our planning is to encounter the whole strength of the enemy with our inferior force when they come to invade the Philippines and north thereof, thus waging a decisive battle. Though they are vulnerable when engaging in a landing operation, their strength is still formidable. It was also certain that enemy forces would come to the east, west, and south either as a main attack or a diversion. Under such circumstances, there was little chance of winning a victory with an inferior force, no matter how many were mobilized. Even if we could destroy their elements, they would succeed in landing somewhere else.

Watching a Sumo wrestler beating five men in a row, I realized that one couldn't win if one grappled and exerted too much effort with each of the five. One had to win four out of five by just pushing them out or outwitting them. A case where he was really matched in earnest occurred only once or twice. In the same way, in order to destroy many enemies, we couldn't do that in one stroke, but must beat them one by one. This means that we should launch surprise attacks with less endeavor and frontal attacks at opportune times. But even this doesn't mean to carry out a battle of attrition with no result like the one perpetrated by the First Air Fleet in March and April of this year. We should attack in waves with fair strength on appropriate chances. But I regret that now it's like a case of a scalded cat dreading water.

It's also deplorable to see that the replenishment of the Base Air Force is so slow. There has been a whale of a difference between words and deeds since last year. We have always been disappointed with every issue. It's only natural that, under such a circumstance, planning and execution of operations all go wrong. We must plan a steadier build-up of strength.

Friday, 22 September 1944. Rain, later cloudy. An enemy task force attacked the Manila area all day yesterday (total eight hundred planes.) Damages: forty-four planes lost (navy alone), thirteen vessels sunk or damaged, a floating dock sunk, etc. Our base aircraft didn't launch actual attacks, though orders were issued. Since early this morning fighters went out to attack the enemy but they couldn't do more than burn planes on deck. This morning's enemy position of two groups was 162 miles bearing 60° from Manila (six to eight carriers).

As the first wave today, about three hundred came to attack from 0740 to 0950 and their attacks extended as far as to the sea west of Manila.

[*Halsey struck Manila twice on 22 September. He claimed that the two-day operation resulted in 405 aircraft destroyed or damaged, 103 ships sunk or damaged, much damage to airfields and others at a cost of fifteen planes and approximately twelve men. Although his planes launched only forty miles off Luzon, none of his ships was touched.*[12]

[On Saturday, 23 September, Ugaki's ships went to sea for training, en route holding "a ceremony for the autumnal equinox." They found and disposed of four floating mines. "Were it at night, they might have caused great damage, and we might have suffered a great deal from our own mines."]

The enemy task force seems to have withdrawn after the attacks in the morning of the 22nd. But the Second Air Fleet issued an order to retreat and readied itself against tomorrow's raid.

The First Air Fleet seems to have lost most of its available strength after carrying out only some fruitless attacks. (Later it was reported that they made several hits on three carriers and one cruiser.) Thus, the enemy's method of gradually reducing will be intensified, and in the end we shall be made unable to fight a decisive battle.

They are still fighting gallantly at both Peleliu and Angaur. Enemy carriers operating in the Palau area seem to be more than eight and belong to Halsey's Third Fleet.

The enemy announced names of the commanders, etc., as follows (Palau area):

Commander, Task Force	Halsey, 3rd Fleet
Commander, Carrier Force	[Vice Admiral Marc A.] Mitscher (Commander TF 58 at Marianas)
Commander, Invasion Force and Amphibious Force	[Vice Admiral T. S.] Wilkinson
Commander, Amphibious Force	[Rear Admiral W.H.P.] Blandy, [Rear Admiral G. H.] Fort.

Landing forces at Peleliu and Angaur were the First Marine Division and Eighty-first Infantry Division.

The enemy seems to have estimated our forces at Palau to be three divisions and eight thousand including construction corps at Peleliu. Apparently they have reserved a powerful force for an invasion of Palau. (According to radio intelligence, they appear to be at sea already.) [*Wilkinson and a regimental combat team of the Eighty-first Division landed on Ulithi, where a large lagoon was a desirable anchorage. He encountered no opposition.*][13]

Sunday, 24 September 1944. Stormy, later cloudy. The enemy task force, which we thought had withdrawn, raided the Tacloban and Cebu area since early this morning, and a carrier was seen from San Bernardino Strait. [*Halsey's carriers hit Coron Bay, sinking several Japanese vessels and destroying thirty-six aircraft.*][14]

Finland signed an armistice with the Soviet Union and severed relations with Japan. On the other hand, the Philippine government declared war against the United States and the United Kingdom. That would be fine if it were the free will of all the people of the Philippines, but apart from Laurel and his party, it's apparently a result of persuasion by our forces. Submission to a stronger one—the stronger one isn't always the same and, therefore, it will be the stronger who suffers indignity while those who submit may be all right as they change according to the time.

[Ugaki went ashore on Monday, 25 September, to hunt. "There was not a pigeon to be seen and I only perspired." Then he visited the local headquarters garrison, which was under his command. Of the 250 personnel, sixty had malaria. Ugaki tried his luck again at Tempa, but saw nothing. "What a day!" That evening he held a party for five of his classmates. "Who can guarantee this will not be the last reunion at the battle front?"

[Tuesday, 26 September, was spent in various types of training. "The Combined Fleet informed us in advance of a good deal of changes to be made in the fleet organization."

[The morning of 27 September was devoted to studying the last maneuvers and gunnery training. Ugaki was pleased to note an improvement. "Effort has its reward and I am very grateful for the pains of my subordinates and men."]

Though there was little particular change in the battle situation, I was glad to notice that medium bombers of the base air force, though in small numbers, came to launch surprise attacks on Peleliu and Morotai at night or dusk. Also an army plan of having about one hundred men sneak into Morotai every night from the main island of Halmahera to attack an enemy in hand-to-hand fighting is a good omen. Everything must be done in this spirit. Even if damage to the enemy is small, the psychological effects will be great. We ourselves can gain by these deeds in uplifting the morale of the whole forces, in consequence increasing our fighting power.

[A war college classmate of Ugaki's, Rear Admiral Namizo Sato, attached to Marine Escort Headquarters, visited *Yamato* to lecture on antisubmarine attack methodology. "His point was to carry out an effective depth-charge attack by means of electronic and acoustic detections, instead of the conventional attack with high speed." So far nothing had been settled about methods of night antiaircraft firing. "I wonder where the leading spirit of the fleet headquarters has gone?" Sato stayed aboard for the night and talked with Ugaki. He agreed with the latter's operational ideas, but Ugaki knew that "this man's agreement will not be enough to change the operational policy of the Combined Fleet."]

Friday, 29 September 1944. Fair. A conference was held on board *Yamato* in the morning to study the battle practice. After the conference, I told the following views to Captain Yamamoto, senior staff officer of the Second Fleet, at his request. He was leaving here for Manila today to see the commander in chief, Combined Fleet, and his staff. So I let him have my views for material for the conference:

1. It is necessary to follow past combat lessons, but to apply them under different circumstances after a long time has elapsed is just like a scalded cat dreading cold water.

2. I absolutely disagree with the conduct of the base air forces at the times of the first and second enemy attacks on the Philippines. That was only a result of the preservation policy to evade the initial action. Unless we adopt an active policy of taking the offensive, we will only end in self-destruction.

3. My component-destruction policy which I have advocated has become more necessary than ever.

   a. Enemy invasions of Peleliu and Morotai are being delayed by our gallant land fighting and defense on both islands. We could hold there considerably longer if we put the enemy in confusion by proper use of aircraft and submarines.

   b. The above disturbance will increase the probability of the enemy task force's making another attack on the Philippines. Our vessels sunk by the second enemy attack were: *Katsuriki, Yaeyama, Aotaka, Kamoi, Matsukaze,* transports, and destroyers totaling fourteen (including victims by submarines while taking refuge), and fourteen sunken merchantmen. (Total loss of merchant ships, 120,000 tons sunk and 40,000 tons damaged.) The damages were so great that we could not think of any progress in strengthening the defense. Unless something is done, our losses will add up, together with those of aircraft. We must destroy the enemy first.

Method: Reinforce air strength in the Philippines and order "Alert for Operation Sho No. 1" with much ease while maintaining a strict patrol. The attack force will advance to Brunei or Coron to stand by while a voyage there is still safe. The Third Carrier Division need not come down to this area, but must stand by at the Southwestern Islands. In case an enemy task force comes, the above three big forces cooperate with each other and attack it. Thus, an enemy invasion of the Philippines would be further delayed and made much more difficult. In the meantime, we could gain time so as to be ready for another enemy attack. Only in this way could we have a hope of winning.

I was glad to see that Captain Yamamoto has shared my views as a result of an extensive study after hearing my talks. However, I question how far he can convince the Combined Fleet.

Saturday, 30 September 1944. Partly fair. A division table maneuver was held in the morning but nothing much was gained. The commander in chief, Combined Fleet, issued a citation for the gallant fighting at Peleliu. But it's regrettable to see that twenty enemy small aircraft are already there.

[On Sunday, 1 October, beginning at midnight, Ugaki's forces sailed out to practice "formation changes and antiair and antisubmarine training." They moved to "the third anchorage," which had the advantage of bearing nearer to Singapore. Fleet Headquarters had decided to send the fleet to Singapore "in three groups for recreation by about the 10th." Ugaki was still dubious about the wisdom of this, but he felt sorry for the men and allowed them to go in increments for a brief morale leave, provided they did not enter the city itself. [*He forbade them the city for security reasons. Their destination was the former British naval base at Seleter port, which had excellent recreational facilities.*][15] The next day, *Musashi* almost had a bad accident when entering the anchorage. "She picked up sand and pebbles in the tube of the bottom log, which was put out of order." Soundings discovered that a spot supposed to be 16 fathoms deep was only 11.5 meters. A few inches had saved *Musashi* from going aground.]

The Combined Fleet finally designated the first and second command post on land. It's no good in the present situation to command at the front line. It has settled where it should be.

Tuesday, 3 October 1944. Partly fair. The fleet carried out antiair warfare practice in the morning. At 1800 *Nagato* returned with sightseers from Singapore on board and I was glad to hear about the great pleasure they expressed.

A summary of the investigation of POWs from *Lexington* which raided the Philippines the other day:

The First Fleet, in Hawaii area; Second Fleet, in Aleutian area; Third Fleet, in the Philippines area; Fourth Fleet, in New Hebrides area: Fifth Fleet, operating in the Marianas area.

Under the Third Fleet (Halsey) there is Task Force 38 (Mitscher), which consists of four groups, each made up of two regular carriers, two converted carriers, sixteen cruisers, and escort destroyers. Besides these, in the first and second groups two or three battleships, three to four cruisers were added, and in the third group four to five battleships and four to five cruisers.

First group: *Wasp, Hornet, Belleau Wood, Cowpens.*

Second group: *Intrepid, Bunker Hill, Cabot, Independence.*

Third group: *Lexington* (Mitscher on board), *Essex, Princeton, Langley.*

Fourth group: *Enterprise, Franklin, San Jacinto, Bataan* (or *Monterey*).

[*Belleau Wood was with Task Group 38.4, not 38.1;* Monterey *with 38.1, not 38.4; in addition,* Hancock *was with 38.2. Total cruiser strength was four heavy cruisers and ten light cruisers. Nevertheless, this was a remarkably accurate estimate of the ship strength.*][16]

Four CVs and four CVLs seem to have been in the area since the beginning of the invasion of Palau, with three to four carriers in the Halmahera area. It isn't clear whether these belong to the said Task Force 38. Anyway, Halsey's forces are powerful indeed.

On Wednesday, 4 October, all except the First Battleship Division carried out antiair training at sea against fighters, and *Nagato* set out for Singapore with the second half of the liberty party. The Second Battleship Division, consisting of *Yamashiro* and *Fuso,* arrived safely. The chief of the Personnel Bureau sent in a list of those "above the rank of commander scheduled to be promoted to higher rank on the 15th." Ugaki presumed this move was in anticipation of "a decisive battle soon," with no transfers to be made until after the battle.]

Thursday, 5 October 1944. Rain, later fair. The Fourth Heavy Cruiser Division sailed out before dawn and carried out practice for assaulting the anchorage. Captain Masami Ban, commander of *Fuso,* came to visit me and we had a good talk about the situation at home, etc. Vice Admiral Nishimura, the newly appointed commander of the Second Battleship Division, came to see me. He told me about the gloomy life in Tokyo, impotence of the Naval General Staff, the circumstance of the cabinet change, and other latest home news, and we exchanged opinions. The Tojo cabinet tried to strengthen itself at the end, but gave up as publicly announced when the attempt failed. Admiral [Keisuke] Okada was said to be in the background all this while. [*Okada was a former premier who had narrowly escaped assassination in the famous "incident" of 26 February 1936.*] Now I could see most of what I couldn't at the time.

Submarine *RO-41* torpedoed an enemy group of three carriers at ninety miles east of Cape Gorango, Morotai Island, on the 30th and reported that she heard four hits as well as one big explosion and separately another big explosion. I'm convinced of her success.

[RO-41 *encountered a task unit or two escort carriers,* Fanshaw Bay *and* Midway *(later renamed* St. Lo*), and four destroyer escorts under Rear Admiral Clifton A. F. Sprague.* RO-41 *hit destroyer escort* Shelton, *killing two officers and eleven men. Later* Shelton *capsized under tow. This incident had a tragic sequel when U.S. forces mistook U.S.S.* Seawolf, *operating in that area, for the Japanese submarine.* Seawolf *was sunk with all hands.*][17]

This is what I have always hoped for, as it's the best chance for us to make surprise attacks upon the enemy fleet while they're operating unmolested either in the Morotai or Palau area as though they had no enemy at all. I'm very glad to see even one succeed. However, a poor *RO*-type with a small radius of action, she was already on her way home under orders to withdraw. It was most regrettable that nothing remained to take her place.

Friday, 6 October 1944. Fair. *Nagato* returned from Singapore at 1800 and dropped anchor in the new anchorage. I was glad that this division's sightseeing tour to Singapore ended without incident. Everybody except the commander and the two captains have had a nice change, and so we feel the same. Now from tomorrow we shall exert renewed efforts to finish our training before the showdown. As there was fear of an enemy task force coming to the north Philippines and Formosa after leaving the Marianas area, those districts were alerted accordingly, but nothing happened. A foreign news report stated that King and Nimitz met at San Francisco and discussed offensives against Japan. A new phenomenon is expected to appear in early November. It's also necessary to guess the enemy's new ideas without being prejudiced by his conventional methods.

[On Saturday, 7 October, *Yamato* and *Musashi* changed anchorage and no longer needed to fear shallows. Reports came in of an enemy task force sighted east of Karenko, Formosa, and also that a surprise enemy landing had been made at Batak Island. "Both may be false reports caused by alarmed imagination."]

While the navy ordered an evacuation of the merchant ships yesterday, the chief of staff of the Southern Army urged the need for continuing to unload within the air defense zone, destroying enemy carriers, and intensifying air defense at strategical points, thus conflicting with the navy's view.

Sunday, 8 October 1944. Fair. The monthly rite for Yamato Shrine was held this morning, as we had been alerted to hold it on the monthly memorial day of the issuance of the Imperial Proclamation of the war. The Fourth Heavy Cruiser Division and half of the Second Destroyer Squadron left for Singapore, leaving me as head of the remaining force. At 1430 *Yamato* sailed out singly for training, having *Musashi* as a target at night, and returned at 0020.

Enemy carrier groups near Palau have disappeared lately. Are they evading attacks by our submarines or are they up to some other attempts?

At 0400 one battleship, two cruisers, and four destroyers appeared near Marcus Island and bombarded it, but neither carrier nor carrier planes were sighted.

[*Rear Admiral Allen E. "Hoke" Smith, with heavy cruisers* Chester, *Pensacola*, Salt Lake City, *and six destroyers, made this diversionary attack on Marcus Island. The intent—unsuccessful—was to deceive the Japanese into believing that the Third Fleet was planning to work its way up through the* Bonins.[18]

[Several key personnel changes were made in the Philippines area, notably Vice Admiral Takijiro Onishi took over as commander in chief, Third Air Fleet, from Vice Admiral Teraoka. Two of the displaced were Ugaki's classmates, and he felt sorry for them but reflected that "it may be for myself tomorrow."

[Monday, 9 October, was uneventful, *Musashi* sailing out for training and "*Yamato* remaining as a target."]

Tuesday, 10 October 1944. Fair. At 0630 the Berbara lookout post reported detecting something like an enemy submarine at seven kilometers bearing 170°, but could not find it after a search. So I ordered antisubmarine patrol in Section W2 with float planes of the Fifth Heavy Cruiser Division and a sweep by two destroyers of the Tenth Destroyer Squadron. *Nagato* went out for her own training, *Yamato* sailed out at 1630 and returned at 2300.

At 0640, about one hundred enemy carrier planes came to Okinawa from the northwest and bombed chiefly the airfield area and shipping and flew away to the south at 0820. Also each of several planes attacked Oshima and Kumejima. Later, enemy attacks continued in several waves.

[*On 10 October, Task Force 38 flew 1,396 sorties, destroying a number of minor Japanese naval vessels, four cargo ships, and approximately 111 aircraft. The United States lost twenty-one planes, five pilots, and four crewmen.*][19]

At 0830 yesterday a patrol plane from the Kanoya Air Group lost contact at a point 440 miles bearing 147° from Toizaki and since then has been missing, giving rise to the suspicion of an enemy air raid. And certainly they came. [*A U.S. patrol plane from Tinian shot down this Japanese reconnaissance plane, but the commandant at Sasebo jumped to the conclusion that a U.S. carrier aircraft was responsible and alerted Kyushu and the Ryukyus to a possible raid.*][20] At 0925 the Combined Fleet ordered the Base Air Forces Alert for Operation *Sho* Nos. 1 & 2 by Combined Fleet Operational Telegram Order No. 331. It also ordered the Second Attack Force to be ready for sortie and the Third and Fourth Carrier Divisions to arrange attacks.

[*Sho-1 postulated a U.S. attack on Leyte, Sho-2 on Formosa. The Third Carrier Division under Vice Admiral Jisaburo Ozawa contained CV Zuikaku—the last survivor of the six which attacked Pearl Harbor—and CVLs Zuiho, Chitose, and Chiyoda. The Fourth Carrier Division under Rear Admiral Chiaki Matsuda contained the two converted battleship-carriers Hyuga and Ise.*][21]

As a result of searches, at 0925 the chief of staff, Second Air Fleet at Kanoya base reported the summing up of the enemy situation as follows:

A task force centering around two carriers (ten cruisers and destroyers) at a point 175 miles southeast of Naha at 1520. Another one with three carriers at a point ninety-five miles east-southeast of Naha at 1533.

Three flying boats (Type 97) equipped with radar carried out the search. The commander in chief, Combined Fleet, was at Shinchiku Air Base (in Formosa) on his way back from the Philippines.

The action of the Combined Fleet this time, taken at the discretion of its chief of staff, was mostly proper and similar to what I envisaged, and it was good that he ordered the base air force and others to attack the enemy task force.

Wednesday, 11 October 1944. Fair. From early this morning, six planes of the First Battleship Division carried out an antisubmarine search in the inland sea but found nothing. According to a destroyer's investigation, a 500-ton tanker passed Berbara Strait around the same time yesterday morning. As it was considered the source of the false report due to the lookout's insufficient vigilance, further search was suspended. Thus the issue was settled, for I as a commander cautioned defense headquarters and the lookout post. The Fourth Heavy Cruiser Division and destroyers of the Second Destroyer Squadron returned in the evening.

A radar-equipped flying boat reported last night the detection of a likely enemy at 310 miles southeast of the Miyakos and also the sighting of a destroyer sailing south. At 1100 a patrol plane from the northern Philippines found an enemy group of three carriers, three battleships and several cruisers at 440 miles bearing 150° from Miyakejima. These seem to be different groups from the one sighted near Minami-Daito Island yesterday, but no other information about the enemy was received today. No enemy raids, either. The enemy seems to be watching for our next move for a while, because I don't think he would withdraw at this stage. Anyhow, the key to any development rests in the hands of the man on the offensive.

(Written later) A few dozen enemy planes raided Engaño airfield near Aparri at 1500 today and strafed the bay.

[*Sixty-one aircraft of Task Group 38.1 and Task Group 38.4 hit Aparri in Luzon, destroying about fifteen planes on the ground, losing seven, all but one due to operational causes.*][22]

Thursday, 12 October 1944. Fair. We spent the whole day studying the last maneuvers. I regretted to see that we could do nothing against the enemy to the east of Formosa. By 0300 last night the 901st Flying Boat group had detected four enemy groups within an area 160 miles bearing 100° to 130° from Cape Garambi. At 0710 enemy planes attacked from Ishigakishima and Karenko to the north and Daito to the south. Takao and Tainan seemed to be the center of the attack.

An enemy force appeared close to Kashoto, while another one seemed to be to the south of Miyako. The enemy apparently came with its whole strength.

[*Task Force 38 flew 1,378 sorties against Formosa on 12 October, inflicting great damage, including the destruction of Fukudome's headquarters and about one-third of his fighters. United States losses were quite heavy—forty-eight planes.*][23]

As late as 1000, the Combined Fleet at last ordered base air forces to "commence Operation *Sho* Nos. 1 & 2." I regretted to see it come so late as usual. T Attack Force deployed in southern Kyushu was scheduled to sortie in the afternoon, attack the enemy at dusk and night, and land on air bases in western Formosa.

Via north Okinawa and Koroku: twenty army heavy bombers, twenty-four torpedo bombers, land bombers, and *Saiuns* totaling sixty-seven.

K501st Squadron: twenty-three *Gingas* (twelve torpedo-equipped, ten bomb-equipped, and one flare-dropping) leaving Kanoya at 1300.

K703rd Squadron: eighteen land torpedo bombers (all torpedo-equipped).

K708th Squadron: seven direct support and torpedo attacks.

[*On the evening of 12 October, Japanese torpedo bombers harassed the U.S. carriers but inflicted no damage, losing forty-two planes, some to Combat Air*

Patrols (CAPs) from CVLs Cabot *and* Independence, *some to Task Group 38.2's antiaircraft.*][24]

Except those needed for patrols, all planes of the Seventh Base Air Force were to concentrate in southern Kyushu, and also planes of the Southwest Forces in the Philippines were ordered to attack. How many will they be able to get? The result of this battle will be of grave importance to our future operations.

Friday, 13 October 1944. Cloudy. Enemy positions as of midnight shown in reports were as follows: 70 miles east of, 125 miles and 175 miles south-east of and 200 miles south-southeast of Karenko. T Attack Force (K501st, K703rd, K708th, and T11th Squadrons)—about one hundred planes in all, of which about seventy were torpedo-equipped—made seven assaults from about 1900 to 2020 and returned in succession from 2000 to bases in Formosa (Shinchiku, Taichu, Tainan, and Takao). Number of returned planes: K501, thirteen; K703, seven; K708, four; T11, seven. Besides, several others appeared to have made emergency landings at army bases. Total results known by 0130: two ships sunk, type unidentified but one of them probably a carrier, and two ships damaged, type unidentified but one of them probably a carrier. [*No ships were sunk or even damaged.*][25]

Previously, I thought enemy carriers could be sunk with nearly one hundred planes even in dusk or night attacks, but the result was unexpectedly small. Moreover, we sustained heavy damage, and only twenty-five planes were able to return. I thought the causes for this failure were as follows:

1. We weren't in a real state of readiness to encounter an enemy. Instead, we made preparations in a hot hurry and sortied as they got ready.

2. The advance distance was long. In addition, we lacked liaison between shadowing planes and the attacking planes.

3. It was cloudy over the battle area, and visibility was poor. Besides, the moon was on her 25th night.

4. Our forces could not be termed sufficiently trained, while the enemy had night fighter escorts.

On the other hand, enemy planes raided the whole island of Formosa continuously from 0700 to 1700 on the 12th. [*On 12 October Halsey's four carrier groups launched 1,378 sorties against Formosa.*][26] About 120 *Ko* and *Otsu* fighters of the Sixth Base Air Force, and army fighters intercepted the enemy and shot down about fifty planes, but we lost forty-nine too. The number of planes available today is only twenty-eight fighters and seven bombers, excluding those of the Eighth Air Division. Other damages sustained included Hozan Radio Station, Toko (seven flying boats burnt up), Takao, and other places. Also ships were sunk and burned. On the whole, it was not favorable to us.

According to POWs, the enemy was Task Force 38 under the command of Mitscher, leaving the Marianas. It was also said to return to the Marianas after three days of air raids on Formosa. Will they withdraw, giving up further raids on account of the damage inflicted last night?

In the meantime, T Force was scheduled to withdraw to Kyushu at 0500 today so no offensive force will be left. Even if the advance of the Third and Fourth carrier divisions was planned and all fighters of the China Area Fleet were concentrated in Formosa by order of the Combined Fleet, it probably would be too late unless the enemy committed some error or was forced to stay to continue attacks.

The Sixth Fleet ordered six type-I submarines to sortie yesterday, but only two sorties today. How could they contribute to developments? Almost everything is done when it is too late.

An enemy broadcast on the morning of the 11th: "A force under the direct command of Mitscher raided the Okinawa area. Thirty-eight vessels sunk and damaged, eighty-nine planes shot down or damaged, U.S. damage slight." The enemy's morale is getting ever higher. Unless we firmly establish a proper encountering plan to meet this occasion and inflict a heavy blow on the enemy, it's feared that we'll lose the chance of victory forever. [Here Ugaki vented his frustration in a brief Chinese poem.] (The above written in the morning.)

The enemy situation:

At 0845, two carriers each at ninety miles bearing 122° and eighty-five miles bearing 131° from Karenko.

At 1620, three carriers at ninety-five miles bearing 135° from Karenko.

At 1722, four carriers, two battleships, and seven others at 125 miles bearing 85° from Takao.

At 1830, 260 miles bearing 90° from Takao.

At 1845, a group of four CVs, four CVLs, three battleships, and more than ten others.

Since early this morning the above enemies raided with ease and grace the Ishigaki, Yonahara, Toko, Heito, and Hozan areas, displaying their ferocity. [*On the morning of 13 October, 974 sorties were launched from a position about seventy miles from Suikoo Roadstead. They found many airfields previously unknown to the Americans.*][27] This certainly proved that the damage inflicted last night was slight. The air units in the Philippines plucked up their courage and left Clark Field at 1315, mobilizing 130 combined fighters of the army and navy, 30 carrier and land bombers, as well as torpedo bombers. T Force was also planning an attack tonight while keeping contact with the enemy. But the weather in the area looked rather bad. I hope they'll succeed somehow.

The chief of the Naval General Staff stated in a telegram that, when he reported the war development to the emperor this morning, His Majesty expressed his satisfaction with last night's results. I didn't know the content of the report, but the emperor's words were much too good for such a result. We who are participating in the war should examine ourselves and be determined to ease His Majesty's anxiety with all our efforts.

Saturday, 14 October 1944. Fair. Notwithstanding the battle to the southeast of Formosa, we sailed out at 1030 and carried out First Battleship Division firing and other training. We returned at 0030.

As I thought, the First Air Fleet's planes (in cooperation with army fighters) which left the Philippines yesterday didn't sight an enemy due to bad weather. And after the force separated, enemy fighters caught and shot down one element while the rest returned to bases in Formosa and the Philippines. By 1200 about half the original strength had been recovered in the Philippines. I felt very sorry that the Philippine force wasn't blessed with luck. I wish them the best of luck tonight, for they plan to launch a surprise fighter attack and torpedo assault at dusk.

At 1620 the T Attack Force found two groups of three and four carriers, respectively, and another one with one carrier at 1720 by two-stage search. Twelve fighters escorted the attacking force as far as the Jiyakojima area and returned there at sunset. Having an excellent chance at dusk, the striking force of thirty-one land torpedo bombers (seventeen torpedo-equipped), six *Gingas* (three torpedo-equipped), (or reportedly twenty-two land torpedo bombers and two land bombers) carried out an effective attack on an enemy carrier group (four regular ones and four others), which was sailing in and out of showers.

[*On 13 October, four bombers attacked* CV Franklin, *one crashing onto the flight deck, doing little damage. Heavy cruiser* Canberra *was torpedoed but not sunk. She was taken under tow.*][28]

After summing up the reports of crews on the 12th and 13th, the commander of T Attack Force at Kanoya Base announced as follows:

12th, six to eight carriers (three to four regular included) sunk.

13th, three to four carriers (two to four regular included) sunk.

Total: nine to thirteen (five to seven)

Besides, other vessels seemed to have been sunk or damaged on both days.

[*This and similar reports, transmuting one slightly damaged CV and one heavily damaged heavy cruiser into some eleven carriers sunk, as well sundry other ships, were widely accepted as accurate in Japan.*][29]

According to the above, the enemy carriers found yesterday ought to have been annihilated, or still not enough to make up the claimed damage. However, according to search of today, the 14th, enemies were found as follows:

At 1710, position of a carrier group, 110 miles bearing 80° from Taito.

At 1750, 160′ east-southeast of Takao.

At 1000, 190′ southeast of Takao.

Summing up to 0900 (according to Kanoya air base): first group, ninety miles bearing 225° from Ishigakishima; second group, seventy miles bearing 90° from Carambi.

At 1300 (army headquarters reconnaissance plane), five carriers 170 miles bearing 73° from Takao, course 160°.

At 1300, five carriers, 220 miles bearing 82° from Takao, course 160°.

At 1715, two carriers, one battleship, 165 miles east-southeast of Takao, course 80°, speed 14 knots.

At 1300 (Eighth Air Division), five carriers, three battleships, 300 miles bearing 110° from Karenko, course 160°.

At 1632, enemy force, 210 miles bearing 90° from Takao.

At 2155, a large enemy force, 260 miles east-southeast of Takao.

At 0030 of the 15th a large enemy force was detected at 360 miles east of Takao. At 0800 of the 14th, fifty fighters and bombers attacked Shinchiku air base. A total of 450 planes in two waves raided all over the island of Formosa, and after 0930 no enemy was sighted. [*On the morning of 14 October, the carriers sent in one strike of 146 fighters and 100 bombers of which seventeen and six, respectively, were lost.*][30] At 1030 the enemy called back their planes by phone. The enemy seemed to commence withdrawing after suspecting our plan. If he had suffered the damage stated previously, he couldn't possibly have carried out attacks like this morning's. We must at least acknowledge, though with regret, the existence of five carriers.

The air groups of the Third Air Fleet and Third Fleet, concentrated in southern Kyushu and placed under the Sixth Base Air Force, were divided into two attacking forces as follows: [*The Third Fleet was the carrier force under Ozawa, but its actual air strength was very minor*][31]

First attacking force, 14 reconnaissances: 98 (80) fighters; 75 (64) bombers (*Suisei, Ginga*); total, 187.

Second attacking force, 20 (12) reconnaissances: 88 fighters; 117 (103) bombers and *Tenzens*; total, 225.

Total: 412 (273)

Note: The number in parenthesis shows planes actually available.

These forces were to sortie from the base early this morning, refuel on the way, except the *Gingas*, and return to bases in Formosa after the attack.

Necessary preparations were made at those bases. If they can reach the enemy, I think they'll be able to inflict considerable damage.

Judging the situation to be developing in our favor, the Combined Fleet again intended to have the Twenty-first Heavy Cruiser Division and First Destroyer Squadron of the Second Attack Force sortie in order to destroy damaged enemy ships and also offer rescue service to wrecked plane crews. So the commander in chief, Combined Fleet, in Shinchiku issued Operational Telegram Order No. 8, by which he ordered the base air forces, Second Attack Force, and submarines at sea of the submarine force to annihilate the remnant of the beaten enemy. The chief of staff, Combined Fleet, also announced the previously stated results of the T Force's attack as they reported.

[*In the evening of the 14th, heavy cruiser* Houston *was torpedoed and taken in tow. Evidently the Combined Fleet believed that* Canberra *and* Houston, *being towed from the battle area, and their destroyer escort, constituted the "remnant" of Halsey's Third Fleet.*][32]

There are occasions when exaggeration may be necessary to uplift morale, but those in a position to direct operations mustn't kid themselves by exaggerating the results achieved.

On the other hand, the Imperial headquarters have announced developments from time to time and made the following announcement at 1730:

(Total of the inflicted damage as previously announced.)

Sunk: three carriers, three ships unidentified.

Damaged: one destroyer, one carrier, one ship unidentified.

I think the above figures are generally right.

An army report from China had warned of enemy planes raiding Formosa from Chengtu. Sure enough, at 1230 a total of one hundred B-29s in formations of a few to over ten entered the Takao, Tainan, area from the west. They bombed mostly the Sixty-first Aircraft Depot and left to the west at 1430. Most of the buildings of the aeronautical depot were destroyed and about fifty killed. More than half of the buildings in Takao and Tainan bases were damaged. We must be fully prepared for a coordinated attack from the China continent from now on. [*The XX Bomber Command sent 115 B-29s from China to bomb targets on Formosa on 14 October.*][33]

Raids on Balikpapan by large enemy planes are becoming more frequent lately. Though many were shot down, our damages have added up, so its refinery capacity must have been badly interrupted.

Half of the Seventh Heavy Cruiser Division and Second Destroyer Squadron returned from Singapore, having finished their rest and recreation. I still can't agree with this sort of idea.

According to statements of POWs, the enemy force operating to the east of Formosa has about nine CVs, twenty-five CVLs, several battle-ships, and twenty cruisers, while tankers are taking separate actions.

(Written later.) The enemy task force reported by an army plane at 1330, bearing 110° from Karenko consists of five carriers with a funnel on the port in the center of a ring formation and sixteen cruisers or destroyers circled outside of it. One battleship takes position at two kilometers out-side rear and three battleships at two kilometers in the center rear. The diameter of the formation was four kilometers.

[On Sunday, 15 October, the promotion list came out, and Ugaki was pleased that Kobe, Inoguchi, and Morishita, respectively skippers of *Nagato, Musashi,* and *Yamato,* became rear admirals, and Yaguchi, the engineer staff officer, made commander. Eight destroyers and two cruisers refueled from *Yamato* "in a busy atmosphere."]

A result of last night's attack reported by crews of the Ninety-fifth Air Regiment, an army air unit operating under the T Force, was as follows:

1. One CV, one CVL, and one heavy cruiser set on fire (certainly sunk). One battleship with lattice mast sunk.

2. One CVL, one battleship, two light cruisers set on fire emitting flame from several places. (Almost certainly sunk).

Enemy situation:

1. At 0750 four carriers and thirteen others at a point 250 miles bearing 66° from Manila, course 240°.

2. At 0920 two carriers as a nucleus at a point 255 miles bearing 90° from Takao.

3. At 0930 one carrier, two battleships, eleven destroyers at a point 240 miles east of Garambi. Carrier and battleships drifting with oil leaking.

4. At 1122 four carriers, seven battleships, and ten others at a point six hundred miles bearing 55° from Manila, course southwest, speed 30 knots.

5. At 0830 unknown (plane of a damaged carrier) at a point 130 miles southeast of Karenko.

At 1015, 150 planes attacked Manila. Fifty of them withdrew without attacks. Our fighters intercepted them and shot down or damaged thirty. [*TG 38.4 hit Luzon while 38.2 and 38.3 stayed near Formosa in the hope Toyoda would commit his surface fleet.*]³⁴

The First Air Fleet launched twenty-six Zeros, of which seven were equipped with bombs. They left Clark Field at 0915 and carried out an attack at 1045, making a hit on one battleship or cruiser and a near miss on a CV. Several planes on her deck fell into the sea due to a sharp turn.

[*The attack of 1045 came from Formosa from which Fukudome sent a small force against Task Group 38.4. The only damage inflicted was a bomb hit on CV*

Franklin, killing three and wounding twelve officers and men. Material damage was slight.][35]

At 1400 the second wave of about ninety combined army and navy fighters and bombers left and carried out attacks at 1600, resulting in one carrier sunk, two carriers set on fire on deck. The first and second waves shot down a total of thirty enemy planes. The third and fourth waves started but both returned without sighting an enemy. Rear Admiral Masafumi Arima, commander, Twenty-sixth Air Flotilla, commenced the attack personally on a medium torpedo bomber and has not returned. I pray for his safe return. [*This attack did no damage. The Japanese Navy later credited Arima with having crashed his bomber into a carrier, but in fact combat air patrol shot him down with some nineteen other aircraft. The rest returned to base.*][36]

At 0955 Force *Otsu* of the Sixth Air Force sent out thirteen fighters and six torpedo bombers from Shinchiku, but several Grumman fighters intercepted them at seventy-five miles south of Ishigakijima. They were forced to disperse with some damage and couldn't find an enemy. [*Fukudome actually sent out three such missions in an attempt to find and destroy "Cripdiv 1"—the damaged heavy cruisers. None succeeded.*][37]

All told, it seems that we failed to attack the enemy east of Formosa today. The commander in chief, Combined Fleet, telegrammed the base air force that, though he appreciated the extreme hardships of the base air force, he still asked them to carry through an immediate chase of the enemy with all-out offensive, thus aiming at ultimate victory.

We celebrated the promotion of the engineer staff officer at dinner and enjoyed a picture show afterward as if there were not a worry in the world.

[Monday, 16 October, began with table maneuvers on board *Yamato*. Senior Staff Officer Yamamoto of the Second Fleet gave Ugaki an account of the Combined Fleet briefing held in Manila. The admiral was pleased to learn that "the general trend" had come close to his ideas.]

Enemy situation:

1. 901st Air Group detected three enemy task forces by 0300.

2. At 0915 two carriers, two battleships, two others, at a point 235 miles or 250 miles bearing 90° from Takao.

3. At 0930 two battleships, two cruisers, several destroyers, at a point 260 miles bearing 90° from Takao, course southeast.

4. At 1130 seven carriers (three CVs and four converted ones), seven battleships, about ten cruisers, 350 miles bearing 97° from Takao.

5. Radio intelligence also hints at the above.

6. The enemy group to the east of Manila disappeared yesterday.

Over twenty torpedo bombers are scheduled to start from Kanoya this evening to attack a large group among the above groups at dusk.

About one hundred planes in the Koroku area were ordered to move to Formosa. I wonder why they didn't attack. [*Ninety-nine carrier-type planes, half fighters and half bombers, left Kyushu to polish off the cripples, but for some unknown reason Toyoda canceled the order.*]³⁸

Commander in chief, Combined Fleet, moved from Shinchiku to Takao Air Base at 1100.

Chief of staff, Combined Fleet, suggested that the Fifth Fleet, which sortied from Okinoshima yesterday morning, sail north of the Southwestern Islands. It was because he took precautions against an enemy.

At 0815 on the 16th chief of staff, Combined Fleet, sent the following telegram to the deputy chief of staff:

> As today's reconnaissance revealed that the enemy's remaining strength is still pretty great, there is a probability of his staying within the striking range of our base air force to rescue damaged ships and also to launch offensive actions. So we can expect our base air force to make attacks for several days to come and also anticipate a chance to add the enemy damaged ships. As a result of study we have reached the conclusion that it is better to dispatch the First Attack Force promptly to wage a decisive battle, thus exploiting the battle results. So I have ordered preparation for sortie. However, sortie would have a grave influence upon future operations as well as on the fuel problem, etc., so, if the sortie is considered necessary after contemplating various matters, you will take steps to have the commander in chief clear and issue the order.

Even if we sortied now, we wouldn't reach the battlefield before the 22nd or 23rd, considering refueling on the way. If and when the enemy withdraws, he'll be out of reach of our air forces by the evening of the 18th. I think, therefore, there will be little possibility that the First Attack Force could accomplish the object of its sortie.

I invited the commanders under my command to dinner to celebrate their promotion.

Tuesday, 17 October 1944. Fair. The Harvest Festival. At 0700 the Suluan lookout post sent in a plain signal reporting the approach of two battleships, two CVLs, and destroyers. Another one followed at 0800, reporting commencement of enemy landing.

At 0810 thirty-eight enemy carrier planes passed over Legazpi to the west. At 0810 about one hundred enemy planes were bombing the Clark Field area. At 1030 an enemy force including three carriers was 275 miles bearing 70° from Clark Field.

At 0950 an enemy task force was sighted south of the Nicobar Islands. At 1010 three carriers, two battleships, four cruisers, seven destroyers came into sight and maneuvered in the south. (This might be a British fleet including the *Renown* type). [*This was indeed a British force, from the Eastern Fleet under Admiral Sir James Somerville, undertaking diversionary strikes on Cape Nicobar and Nancowry Islands in the Indian Ocean. Admiral King hoped thus to convince the Japanese that the main Allied attack would be against Malaya or Indonesia, and in consequence would keep most of the Combined Fleet at Singapore. This ruse was unsuccessful.*][39] These poured in one after another. At 0830 by Operational Telegram Order the Combined Fleet ordered "Stand by for Operation *Sho* No. 1," and then at 0928 another one called for the prompt sortie of the First Attack Force to advance to Brunei.

No intelligence has been received lately indicating an attempt at a large-scale invasion, but judging from the landing at Suluan and the coordinated attack at Nicobar this can be considered a preliminary attempt at a full-fledged landing on the middle and south Philippines. Also, should the recent task force movements in the Formosan area be considered its prelude?

At 1500 of the 16th Imperial headquarters announced the battle result as follows (including those already announced):

Sunk: ten carriers, two battleships, three cruisers, one destroyer.

Damaged: three carriers, one battleship, four cruisers, eleven unidentified.

At 1630 of the 16th another one announced: On the 15th, one carrier was sunk, three carriers and one battleship or cruiser were damaged to the east of Manila.

[*The publication of this announcement occasioned widespread "victory" celebrations in Japan. The army even estimated that there would be no U.S. invasion.*][40]

Fighters and bombers sortied from Formosa yesterday and attacked an enemy at a point 245 miles bearing 112° from Takao and it seemed that something like a carrier was set on fire while one battleship was damaged. [*Although some 41 of the 107 aircraft from Formosa were shot down, one hit the already stricken* Houston *with another torpedo. Only an amazing job of damage control saved the heavy cruiser.*][41] Although our attacks take effect like this day by day, the remaining enemy strength is still fairly big and a new reinforcement appeared today. I consider it urgent to attack the enemy with a new concept under the circumstance that most of our base air forces have been expended.

Expecting that the attack force would reach the scene before dawn on the 22nd, the Combined Fleet ordered the Main Body of the task force to sortie on about the 18th and advance to the east of Luzon Strait, aiming at a diversion.

The subsequent enemy situation:

1. The Eighth Air Division reported at 1148. A detailed report on the remnant of enemy task force at four hundred kilometers bearing 130° from Nishino-Omoto Island: three carriers, three battleships, and more than twenty destroyers in a ring formation with carriers in the center and one battleship in tow. Six planes as interceptors, course 90°, speed 10 knots. (Note: four carriers and four battleships less than those seen yesterday.) (0915)

2. At 1130 eleven battleships, cruisers and destroyers at Homonhon Island, west of Suluan Island, heading west. At 1600, first group, four carriers; second group, one battleship, two cruisers and three destroyers.

3. At 0820 two carriers and nine others, 245 miles bearing 85° from Manila.

4. On the 16th, six enemy submarines concentrated in the Southwest Islands area.

5. The Nicobar area was air raided and bombarded again.

Wednesday, 18 October 1944. Fair, later cloudy. The attack force which had sufficiently completed preparations began sortie, the Red Force leaving at 0100. The First Battleship Division as the rear sailed out at 0205. We left anchorage No. 3, leaving behind a radio signal notifying the garrison force of cessation of communication.

We came in the early spring and left in mid-fall, but with climate and scenery making no change I had to count the time of the stay by my fingers. We sailed quietly east in the dark of night through Tempa Channel, changed course to 60°, and took alert formation positions one hour before sunrise. Then course was altered to 10° to pass west of Great Natuna.

Enemy situation:

1. Nicobar was bombarded again at 0400. One carrier, one battleship, two transports, and three destroyers came into sight and left at 0530.

2. About fifty planes attacked the Manila area and one hundred the Clark Field area. Thirty planes raided the Aparri area. The Tacloban area also seemed to be raided. One hundred planes came to the Laoag area.

3. At 1020 two carriers and five others, four hundred kilometers bearing 90° from Clark Field, course 270°. [*TG 38.4 attacked Luzon 17–19 October.*][42]

4. At 1130 eighteen carriers, battleships, cruisers, and destroyers sailed south twenty kilometers off Tacloban, and two masts of minesweepers were sighted. Landing is most likely.

5. About forty enemy vessels sighted off Suluan. [*This was Task Group 78.4 Dinagat Attack Group under Rear Admiral Arthur D. Struble, embarking Sixth Ranger Infantry Battalion, USA, plus his support forces. The Japanese on Suluan notified Toyoda, who alerted his command for Sho-1. Task Group 78.4 and the other naval forces in Leyte Gulf were under Rear Admiral Jesse B. Oldendorf, pending the arrival of Vice Admiral Thomas C. Kinkaid, commanding the Seventh Fleet and Task Force 77, Central Philippine Attack Force.*][43]

6. From 1330 the Dulag area was bombed and bombarded.

7. At 1530 an enemy telephone order calling for commencement of landing between Dulag and Jose, south of Tacloban, was intercepted.

8. On the 17th a vessel like a battleship went aground on the reef off Cape Bunga on Samar Island.

9. At 1505 a task force at 110 miles east-southeast of Ishigakijima, intelligence report "im."

The commander in chief, Combined Fleet, who returned today from Shinchiku to the first battle command post at Hiyoshi, south of Tokyo, ordered activation of Operation Sho No. 1 by Operational Telegram Order No. 360 at 1732. Preceding this telegram, Imperial headquarters designated the Philippine area as the area of Operation Sho. Also, the Sixteenth Heavy Cruiser Division was removed from the First Attack Force and placed under the Second Attack Force. The latter, now consisting of the Twenty-first Heavy Cruiser Division, First Destroyer Squadron, and Sixteenth Heavy Cruiser Division in turn was removed from the task fleet and placed under the Southwest Area Force to become the main force for counterlanding operations. [*The Southwest Area Force was under Vice Admiral Gunichi Mikawa, located at Manila.*][44]

The chief of staff, Combined Fleet, made known his idea about guiding future operations by a telegram issued at 1110 after judging that the probability of the enemy landing on the Tacloban area is great. What was learned from it were (1) the date of the First Attack Force passing through San Bernardino Strait was fixed on the 24th, (2) the Main Body of the task force was to sortie to the south as diversion, (3) a counterlanding by the Second Attack Force, (4) concentration of all base air force strength to the Philippines to destroy enemy carriers, and (5) cooperation by the submarine force. The point is to what extent the forces other than the First Attack Force could cooperate. This means that the issue primarily depends on the base air forces.

According to radio activities so far observed, the enemy landing operation in the Surigao area seems to be a minor operation aimed at infiltrating our weak points or capturing air bases, and there is little sign of a full-scale major operation aimed at recapturing the Philippines. [*Surigao Strait separates Dinagat Island from Panaon Island and southeastern Leyte.*]

1. This landing force is a part of the newly organized force which has appeared at Hollandia or eastern New Guinea since the 8th and started movements on about the 14th.

2. There were few indications usually observed in the period preceding this sort of landing operation, and especially the concentration of transports for various kinds of forces was not conspicuous.

3. It is considered that excessive forces in Palau and Halmahera will be used in this operation, but they would be about half of those previously used in the Marshalls and Marianas.

4. Radio activities from the rear area indicative of reinforcements are very few.

The chief of the Radio Intelligence Section of the Naval General Staff sent the above telegram (No. 181605), but the Combined Communication Corps sent in a telegram with the opposite meaning. If the former is true, it will be very advantageous for us to destroy enemy components one after another. Apart from the task force, the surface force in the Suluan area today seemed to be seven battleships, eight cruisers, ten destroyers, and ten transports.

[On Thursday, 19 October, a young hawk perched on "the director control tower of the main batteries" and was caged as a mascot. Later, "a faintly illuminated layer of auspicious air" hung near the sea surface. Both these events satisfied Ugaki's sense of symbolism, and he celebrated with one of his short poems.]

The enemy situation:

1. At 1700 of the 18th groups of aircraft continuously detected at 520 miles bearing 62° of Manila (Sub. I-26)

2. At 0945 of the 19th, three carriers, eight others, at 108 miles bearing 130° of Manila.

3. At 1010, two carriers, three cruisers at seventy miles bearing 75° of Manila, course north, speed 12 knots.

4. At 0812, four carriers at 155 miles bearing 90° of Bataan, course west.

[On 18 October aircraft from CVs Wasp and Hornet from Task Group 38.1 and Franklin and Enterprise from Task Group 38.4 struck airfields and shipping in the Manila area. CVs Hancock, Bunker Hill, and Intrepid from Task Group 38.2 struck airfields and installations at Laoag, Aparri, and Camaguin Island—northern Luzon.]⁴⁵

5. On the 18th, four battleships, six cruisers, ten destroyers, fifteen minesweepers, three submarines and three unidentified in Leyte Gulf Island, and one battleship bombarded the Dulag area and Katomon Hill throughout the night. At 1140 the enemy infantry landed at Tacloban.

6. At 0830, thirty transports, two cruisers, at 180 miles bearing 110° of Tacloban, course northwest, speed 0–15 knots.

7. At 1220, a large group, at 580 miles bearing 130° of Manila, and another at 275 miles bearing 130° of Tacloban.

8. At 0850, one large carrier, three battleships, three destroyers, at 130 miles bearing 94° of Tacloban.

[*The forces at Dulag were from Oldendorf's Fire Support Unit South, the Minesweeping and Hydrographic Group under Commander W. R. Loud, and the Beach Demolition Group under Lieutenant Commander C. C. Morgan. The latter's underwater demolition teams landed at the Dulag beaches and returned to report that the beaches were very suitable for landing. On 19 October the Fire Support Unit North, under Rear Admiral G. L. Weyler, worked over Tacloban, likewise reporting favorably on the beaches.*]⁴⁶

9. At 1625, a ring formation with two battleships in center at 165 miles bearing 197° of Putao [Fort Hertz, Burma], course 290°, speed 20 knots.

10. One battleship, one carrier, and four cruisers at twenty kilometers from Nicobar launching attacks. At 1248 sank one destroyer.

11. Manila, Tacloban, Zamboanga, and Davao air raided.

The Imperial headquarter's battle result announcement of the air battle off Formosa; a total of the battle results off Formosa and east of the Philippines since 12 October are as follows:

Sunk: eleven CVs, two battleships, three cruisers, and one cruiser or destroyer.

Damaged: eight CVs, two battleships, four cruisers, and one cruiser or destroyer. Thirteen unidentified, of which twelve emitted flame or a column of fire.

Shot down: 112 (not including those shot down over bases).

Our losses: 312 planes failed to return.

The chief of staff, First Task Fleet, sent in a telegram advising of the Main Body's movement. In the afternoon of the 20th, it will sortie from Okinoshima and advance to the northeast of the Philippines on X-1 Day or X-2 Day to carry out a diversionary attack. It's regrettable to see that much can't be expected from its air attack as the number of planes carried on board is small.

The army strength to be used in a counterlanding operation was of battalion size and could be transported by the Sixteenth Heavy Cruiser Division. So plans were changed to return the Fifth Fleet, consisting of the Twenty-first Heavy Cruiser Division and First Destroyer Squadron, to the task force to engage in a diversionary movement east off the Philippines as a vanguard of the task force's Main Body.

[Ugaki was so sure of victory in the upcoming battle that he wrote another poem on the subject.

[On Friday, 20 October, Ugaki's battleships arrived at Brunei Bay and refueled to cruisers and destroyers. His group used their own planes to screen, but Ugaki was glad to see land planes cooperating in antisub-marine escort. "We had the usual submarine fuss once each yesterday and the day before." He also had to worry about "large-type planes" raiding the site during their refueling.]

The Combined Fleet issued Operational Telegram Order No. 363 by which is designated the time of the First Attack Force's penetrating into the Tacloban area as dawn of the 25th and also coordinated actions of each unit. With this the die was cast.

In telegram No. 201006 the chief of staff further sent detailed studies of the penetrating operation just for "information." It was quite significant to notice that the commander, First Battleship Division, was included in the list of those to whom a copy of the telegram was sent.

[Little further had been heard about the enemy situation, and searches were not practical "when we realized that the air strength in the Philip-pines, the First Air Fleet and the army combined, was not more than sixty or seventy planes altogether." Ugaki took comfort from an old saying, "If you dare act, the devil may avoid you."]

The task fleet's Main Body left Okinoshima this evening. Its strength: The Third Carrier Division of four carriers, *Hyuga, Ise, Oyodo,* two light cruisers, and eight destroyers. Its air strength: eighty Zero fighters (in-cluding twenty-eight bomb-equipped) and thirty-six carrier torpedo bombers (*Suisei, Tenzan,* and Type 97). It wasn't so bad to see that they had a pretty good strength.

Further it was said that *Ise* and *Hyuga* might come down south sepa-rately, depending on the situation, to destroy the remnant of the enemy. This is good, too.

With its Operational Telegram Order No. 367, Combined Fleet placed the First Attack Force under its direct command.

The enemy situation as subsequently learned:

1. Morning of the 20th, fourteen to fifteen battleships and cruisers, seven large (?) carriers and fifty small craft were along Leyte Island while eighty transports and twenty small craft (about three divisions) were along Samar Island. At 1100 three marine battalions landed ten kilometers south of Tacloban.

2. At 1640, five battleships, ten cruisers, twenty transports maneuvering, no carrier.

3. At 1330, four CVLs, two battleships, two cruisers, six destroyers, at eighty miles bearing 80° of Tacloban, course south, speed 20 knots.

4. From 0726 to 1415, a total of 220 planes attacked Manila with three ships slightly damaged. From 1025 to 1155, fifty B-24s and eleven P-38s raided Davao.

[*On 20 October the U.S. invasion of Leyte began. The count in Ugaki's*

*subparagraph (1) was probably taken before 0645 when Barbey's Northern Attack
Force began to deploy. The action in the Tacloban area was by Barbey's force. No
marine battalions were engaged; the troops landing in the northern section were
U.S. Army infantry and cavalry.]*[47]

The enemy task force which attacked Formosa learned from questioning
POWs (not including those previously stated):

Group I. Four carriers, three cruisers, eleven to twelve destroyers.

Group II. Four carriers, two battleships (*Iowa, New Jersey*) five cruisers,
sixteen destroyers.

Group III. Four carriers, five battleships (two *South Dakota* types, one
Iowa, two *North Carolina*), two cruisers, thirteen destroyers.

Group IV. Three to four carriers, one to two battleships (one *South
Dakota* type, one *North Carolina* type), two to three cruisers, twelve to
thirteen destroyers.

Total strength: sixteen carriers, eight to nine battleships, twelve to thirteen cruisers, forty to forty-five destroyers, and, in addition five supply
carriers. According to a different source, besides the above Task Force 38
there are the following eight battleships under the direct command of the
Third Fleet (Note: This makes up the total battleships): *Colorado, Tennessee, California, Nevada, New Mexico, Pennsylvania, Texas, Arkansas.*

[*The count of Task Force 38 was fairly accurate. Except for destroyers, Groups
I and II were exact. Group III had four, not five, battleships*—Washington,
Massachusetts, South Dakota, *and* Alabama. *Group IV had four carriers, no
battleships, and two cruisers. Of the other battleships which Ugaki lists as "under
the direct command of the Third Fleet," none were under Halsey's command.]*[48]

Saturday, 21 October 1944. Fair. Judging from the fact that at 1100
yesterday an enemy plane issued an urgent signal addressed to Morotai of
sighting an enemy, it was considered that the enemy sighted the attack
force just before its arrival here. We took stricter precautions, ordering
second stations from before dawn.

There are fairly high mountains in Borneo, some of them over 4,000
meters. Due to these mountains, this anchorage has some disadvantage for
the use of radar.

The enemy situation:

1. At 0815 of the 20th, six CVLs, four battleships, at 10° 40′ N. 127° 0′
(three Zero fighters attacked, two sixty-kg bombs hit one carrier and one
sixty-kg bomb hit another).

2. 20th, radio intelligence: two fairly powerful rear forces seem to have
left Admiralty on the 19th and are coming up north.

3. At night of the 20th, reconnaissance by two float planes: bright lights

seen in Tacloban and the south of Dulag, thirty small craft were also sighted. At 1250 of the 21st (report from Thirty-third Naval Base Force): the enemy seems to have landed on Laplap Island according to an army report.

4. Enemy announcement made on the 20th: The landing forces, the mid-Pacific force of the Sixth Army, and the Australian force. MacArthur boarded a warship under his direct command and landed on Leyte Island. Landing points, two on Leyte, Panaon Island, the north point of Dinagat Island, and the southern part of Homonhon Island.

5. Reports of the patrol planes up to 1100: At 0813, six transports, six destroyers, 170 miles bearing 110° of Surigao. At 0840, two carriers, four CVLs, twenty others, 105 miles bearing 70° of Surigao. At 0935, one battleship and twenty-four others, 160 miles bearing 350° of Suluan Island. At 0920, surface vessels, 420 miles bearing 91° of Manila and a task force was estimated to be in San Bernardino Strait.

6. In the central Philippines and south thereof there were a good many air raids by carrier planes.

7. At 1330, four carriers, 400 miles bearing 100° of the north end of Catanduanes Island.

[*The action in the Dulag area was that of the Southern Attack Force under Vice Admiral T. S. "Ping" Wilkinson.*]⁴⁹

In view of the present situation, the First Air Fleet is going to organize a Kamikaze Special Attack Corps with twenty-six carrier fighters of the 201st Air Group, all of its present strength, of which thirteen were suicidal ones. They are divided into four units. They intend to destroy enemy carriers without fail—at least put them out of order for a while—before the thrust of the surface force, when they come to the sea east of the Philippines. Oh, what a noble spirit this is! We are not afraid of a million enemies or a thousand carriers because our whole force shares the same spirit. It was reported that a national rally was held at Hibiya Park yesterday to ensure a victory by consolidating the home front. If the hundred million people set out for production and defense with this spirit now, nobody need worry about the future of the empire.

In the United States they are said to be all crazy about the presidential election and [Thomas E.] Dewey is a little ahead. I dare say they can't match us, as their objective in war or their policy of operations are all based on personal benefit.

At 1700, briefing of the operational orders, the commander in chief's address and a toast were held on board *Atago*. Returned at 2000 and after dinner assembled the skippers under my command for briefing.

A staff officer of the Fourteenth Army came aboard and explained the situation at the Tacloban Area. The Sixteenth Division was concentrated for the defense, so he said they were quite confident for its defense if the enemy's rear connection could be cut off.

Tankers *Hakko Maru* and *Yuho Maru* arrived from Singapore at 1200 ahead of schedule and refueled the big ships.

Sunday, 22 October 1944. Cloudy with squall in the morning and fair in the afternoon. We sortied from Brunei at 0800 in order of the First and Second forces and sailed northward thirty miles off Palawan with 18 knots. An army report was received yesterday telling of an enemy landing at Laplap near Legazpi north of the San Bernardino Strait. I pointed out the necessity of changing the operational plan but it turned out to be a false report. Under such circumstances as this, any false report of this kind has no small consequence.

The Third Force (Second Battleship Division, *Mogami*, and four destroyers) will leave Brunei this afternoon and charge into the anchorage from west of Surigao on X-Day or divert enemy surface forces. [*This was Force C, which the United States called Van of the Southern Force, under Vice Admiral Shoji Nishimura. Nishimura's battleships were* Yamashiro *and* Fuso.][50]

The enemy situation:

1. At 0637, three CVs, two battleships, ten others, 500 miles bearing 95° from Tacloban.

2. At 0810, five carriers, seven others, 160 kilometers bearing 90° of Tacloban, course 300°.

3. At 0810, three carriers, five others, 400 kilometers bearing 90° of Saravia.

4. At 0920, two carriers, two battleships, several others 330 miles bearing 87° of Manila.

5. At 0907, eighty transports in Leyte Gulf but no follow-up force outside the gulf.

6. At 1040, B-24s and others bombed Mactan and Cebu airfields and no raid in the Manila area.

7. At 0000 on the 21st, one hundred vessels of various kinds are between Palo and San José. One division seems to have landed there. There is fear of another landing of about one division strength to be made on the Dulag front too. Fierce fighting is going on in the north. We suffered casualties of about one regiment.

[The emperor issued a rescript commending those concerned for the great destruction they were supposed to have inflicted upon the enemy fleet.]

The Sixth Base Air Force, actually the Second Air Fleet, was scheduled to carry out an attack at dusk today but canceled it due to the uncertainty of the enemy condition. Its headquarters has advanced to Manila.

With regard to the movement of the Fifth Fleet, there have been some arguments but finally it was decided to charge into the anchorage from the west entrance of Surigao Strait following the Second Force in the early morning of the 25th. Sometimes it's better to reserve some strength, too.

Monday, 23 October 1944. Fair. Although I had expected it, could there be any worse day than today? I went up on the bridge as usual with the order "all hands to quarters" one hour before sunrise. We were sailing in an alert formation against submarines, with column abreast with 18 knots on course of 35°. While we were simultaneously turning to port in a zigzag movement, at 0625 all of a sudden I saw port ahead the flame of an explosion and what seemed like a spread water column on the dawn sea. I shouted involuntarily, "Done it!" which proved to be the earliest discovery of it.

Immediately we made a simultaneous 45° turn to starboard with the signal "green green." Soon a second explosion took place in the same direction. The same ship seemed to have induced another explosion. Asked about the situation of the Fourth Heavy Cruiser Division, the lookout replied there were three of them. Then, thinking it might have been a destroyer, I came to the port side where I saw a ship lying dead, emitting white smoke, and another one, damaged and heavily listing, which was approaching us. The former was *Takao*, second ship of the line, and the latter *Atago*, first ship. [*The submarine* Darter *accounted for* Atago, *Kurita's flagship.* Darter *also heavily damaged* Takao, *which had to return to Brunei. The early report by* Darter *and her companion,* Dace, *of sighting Kurita's ships was a significant one, for this force had been lost to the United States since it left Lingga.*][51] One destroyer each from the left wing was standing by the damaged ships, while another was sent to the rescue. The visibility gradually widened.

Since there were many friendly ships in addition to enemy submarines, not only did excessive evasion pose a danger, but as a senior commander I couldn't go too far away because of the prevailing visibility. Therefore, following the turning of the Fifth Heavy Cruiser Division, we turned to port and formed a column. At this moment *Maya*, fourth ship of the Fourth Heavy Cruiser Division, sailing starboard ahead, exploded. Nothing was left after the smoke and spray subsided. The firing position of the torpedo could be seen at about 1500 meters port ahead of her. [Dace *sent four torpedoes into* Maya.][52]

How dangerous it was! Had *Yamato* been situated a little bit either way, she would have taken three to four torpedoes. Evading to starboard and still advancing, we found another periscope to the port ahead, so we went over to the starboard. By this time the First Force was put into great confusion; some advanced while others turned back. It was certain that there were four submarines.

[*This was incorrect. Only two submarines were involved. Following this action,* Darter *ran aground on Bombay Shoal.* Dace *took her officers and men on board and brought all safely to Fremantle, Australia.*]53

The position was 9° 28′ N. 117° 7′ E. We could see mountain tops of the southern part of Palawan far away against the eastern sky. As the navigable channel between the shoals near that island and the dangerous area in Pratas was only twenty-some miles, nothing was available for the fleet's passage but the ordinary shipping lane. To ensure the safe passage of follow-up units, I ordered 24 knots with a makeshift formation we could manage to form. It couldn't be helped, even though I knew that it was a difficult order to follow under preparedness for 18 knots instant and 20 knots at twenty-minute notice.

Prior to this, to my great relief I learned by a signal (since 0700 we took care of communications for the flagship) that the commander in chief came on board destroyer *Kishinami*. At 0830 I was ordered to take command in his behalf until he came on board *Yamato*. [*Kurita and his staff had to swim from* Atago *to* Kishinami.]54 On learning this, I signaled it to the whole fleet at 0915 so as to make clear the existence of the command, and since then I have discharged matters with full responsibility.

As the first thing, I asked the chief of staff, Southwest Area Fleet, to arrange for the rescue of *Takao*. Then I reported this morning's mishap to the chief of the Naval General Staff, commander in chief Combined Fleet, and First Task Fleet, and also [advised] that the fleet was going on the scheduled operation temporarily under my command. Later we dropped speed to 23 knots to economize fuel.

Meanwhile we had detected three submarines (one of them discovered by the bombing of a plane), and successfully avoided them. Finally we got out of the narrow channel and set course to 0° sailing to port of the ordinary course.

At 1540 we had *Kishinami* and *Naganami* come alongside *Yamato* and *Musashi*, respectively, and started to bring the staffs of the Second Fleet headquarters and officers and men of *Atago* on board *Yamato* and *Maya*'s officers and men (47 officers including executive officer and 722 petty officers and men) on *Musashi*.

In the meantime there was some fuss about submarines detected by sound-detecting apparatus or finding a trace of torpedoes. Embarkation was finished by about 1620. Vice Admiral Kurita, commander in chief, his chief of staff, and other staff officers came on board. Changing the flag, I returned my command of the fleet to him. The Second Fleet headquarters' wish to change its flagship to *Yamato* by placing the First Battleship Division under its direct command thus materialized incidentally under unfortunate circumstances. This may be fate. Regarding the division's movements, everything was left to the commander in chief's command, thus making clear the extent of my duty. I also instructed my staffs to assist and cooperate with the fleet headquarters. We changed the schedule a little bit and set course to 90° at 2130.

As they had bad weather in Manila today, search was almost impossible, so enemy conditions were unknown, and consequently the air strike was called off. However, enemy activities were quite noticeable and the battle-field was expected to develop greatly.

While undertaking a transport duty, *Aoba,* flagship of the Sixteenth Heavy Cruiser Division, was torpedoed west of the Philippines this morning and rendered incapable of navigation. A bad day is bad to the end.

[*The submarine* Bream *torpedoed heavy cruiser* Aoba. *She did not sink, and the light cruiser* Kinu *towed her to Manila.*][55]

24, 25, 26 October 1944. Decisive Battle (written later). I am going to write rough entries of the three days' decisive battle before I forget them.

Tuesday, 24 October 1944. Fair. First day of decisive battle. Passing the southern end of Mindoro Island before dawn, we headed for the channel north of Tablas Island on course 35°. At 1040, when I was thinking it was about time for the guests to come, twenty-five of them came in before we reached the channel. We shot down a few SB2Cs, F6Fs, and TBFs and thought nothing much of them. However, *Myoko* dropped behind, having received a torpedo. The Fifth Heavy Cruiser Division changed its flagship to *Haguro* while *Myoko* withdrew to the west escorted by a destroyer. *Musashi* signaled that she got a torpedo on the starboard side but was able to maintain fighting ability. I thought then that this wouldn't be too bad.

[*These initial U.S. aircraft came from the CV* Intrepid *of Task Group 38.2 and CVL* Cabot *of Task Group 38.1.* Myoko *had to return Brunei.*][56]

We passed through the two islands and got out of the channel. After a fuss about a submarine for a while, the second wave of twenty-four planes came at 1207. *Musashi* took three torpedoes on her port side and her speed dropped to 22 knots.

At 1330, twenty-nine planes of the third wave came in. Before this, *Musashi* had been making a huge wave at her bow where her port side plate was torn off. As high speed would impose more difficulties on her, I reduced speed to 22 knots in repeating evasive movements. And yet *Musashi* was apt to drop behind. Then she took another torpedo and *Yamato* also took a bomb and a near miss on the bow, while other near misses and the number of torpedoes eluded were too numerous to count. It was regrettable to see that the number of enemy planes shot down was small. As *Musashi* dropped behind further and there was little hope of taking her with us, we had to send her to Manila escorted by destroyer *Kiyoshimo*.

At 1426 the fourth wave of fifty came in and at 1520 the fifth wave of eighty to one hundred. Two bombs hit *Nagato* amidship. *Musashi* was struggling hard away from the main force, and at the fifth attack she ejected black smoke, listed to port, and finally lay dead. Feeling anxious about her, I asked that another destroyer be sent to her. The Second Force was very active and sent heavy cruiser *Tone* to stand by her.

[*The strike at 1330 came from CVs* Essex *and* Lexington *of Task Group 38.3. The 1520 attack included planes from* Intrepid, Cabot, Essex, Franklin, *and* Enterprise. *All told,* Musashi *took nineteen torpedoes and seventeen bombs.* Nagato *and* Yamato *took two bomb hits each, and five near misses damaged* Haruna. *The Japanese did not have all the day's ill fortune. Japanese naval airmen from Luzon attacked Task Group 38.3 that morning, and one of then scored a hit on CVL* Princeton *which, despite valiant efforts at rescue, had to be sunk by U.S. torpedoes.*][57]

At 1530 the fleet turned about. Later I learned that the fleet headquarters appealed to the higher command that it thought it better to advance to the decisive battle scene after the attacks of the base air forces had made some effect. Certainly it seemed that we would expend all our strength before we got there, if and when we were continuously attacked like this. Still we had no choice but to go ahead. This taught us a lesson that it would be best to take up a case which could be the more easily settled when dealt with case by case. That we could do nothing else but go ahead determined to die was what I thought at the time. However, I noticed that it would be more advantageous for tomorrow's fighting if we could deceive the enemy by turning back once before evening.

As a result of this turning, we passed by our partner *Musashi*, whose miserable position was a sorrowful sight. All available compartments for pumping-in had been filled with water, and she listed about 10° to port. Though the Imperial crest was seen, her bow was already under water, with the lowest part of the weather deck in front of the fore turret barely out of the water. She was struck by eleven torpedoes and several bombs, one of which caused what has been feared most aboard a battleship, that is, an induced explosion, disabling the steering ability and blowing up the first bridge. A bomb hitting the radar frame injured the right shoulder of Rear Admiral Inoguchi, her skipper, who was at the antiaircraft command post, and annihilated all men at the first bridge and the operations room.

I hoped they would do their best to save her. As division commander, I also advised them to ground her bow temporarily on a shoal of a nearby island to repair the damage. At the moment I couldn't even think of words to cheer them up. After passing by her once and turning about again, we passed by her again near sunset before 1900. Little change was noticed in her situation, and she gave us her last signal that a part of her engine and the steering could still be used.

Everybody seemed to be sticking to his station without complaining, and therefore I thought she might stick it out until tomorrow morning. But *Tone* was unable to do anything about her and asked to join the thrust. Her wish was granted and at 1830 she was ordered to return to the original group.

Musashi then transfered the crews of *Maya* on board her to a destroyer which came alongside her. But some of the damage control crews still remained on board her. A little after one hour past sunset, the stand-by destroyer signaled that *Musashi* suddenly heeled over and sank at 1937.

[Ugaki was deeply grieved at the lost of this fine ship and felt that she had "sacrificed herself for *Yamato*." He also received a severe professional jolt, having lost half his command at one blow. He realized that if the same thing happened to *Yamato,* there would be no need for a First Battleship Division. "I therefore finally made up my mind to share the fate of the ship without reservation, having decided to have *Yamato* as my death place."]

At 1951 we changed from a ring formation into a column and kept on sailing east. The fleet headquarters was said to have received a telegram from the Combined Fleet to keep on advancing, convinced of heavenly guidance. Enemy planes attacked us only five or six times today, but neither the base air forces nor our own float planes brought any definite report on enemy conditions. All we got were that there was an enemy task force to the east of Manila and that the fleet at Leyte had gone out, leaving few big ships in the bay.

It was my idea at the time that once we got out of the channel we should search for an area where an enemy would most likely be found and attack it. We had enough confidence to deal with an enemy once we could approach and reach it. But what I feared was that the enemy which detected our movements continuously tonight would concentrate their air attacks upon us at a point over one hundred miles off the coast after dawn came. Unless we get enough cooperation from our base air forces, we can do nothing about it, and all of our fighting strength will be reduced to nothing at the end. In such case we should perish by fighting an air battle, hoping it to be a decisive one.

[*Kurita's force encountered no enemy at this time. Halsey had concentrated Task Force 38 and headed north to attack Ozawa's Main Body Northern Force. This was exactly what the Japanese wanted him to do, for the Japanese carrier force was a decoy. The four carriers had only 116 aircraft among them, and of those, Ozawa had sent seventy-six against Task Group 38.3 late in the morning of the 24th. These planes flew on to Luzon, hence Ozawa had only forty aircraft remaining.*[58]

[Knowing that he might not live through another day, Ugaki pledged himself "to be reborn seven times to serve the country."]

Wednesday, 25 October 1944. (X-Day). Sunrise 0627, sunset 1817. Partial squalls in the morning. Second day of the decisive battle. Taking advantage of the dim moonlight of her seventh lunar night through a cloudy sky, we passed San Bernardino Strait without incident at 0035 and formed Alert Formation No. 19 on an easterly course. At 0400 we sailed south about ten miles off the east side of Samar Island on course 150°. We expected to charge into Leyte Gulf at 1100 via the rendezvous point at ten miles east of the light on Suluan Island with the Third Force at 0900. (We haven't received any reconnaissance report due to faulty communication of the float planes, which have been deployed to the bases since the 24th.)

It happens to be the rainy season in this area, and especially on the east coast the weather was bad. Even though dawn had broken, visibility was poor with dark clouds accompanied by squalls hanging low here and there. At 0644, just before an order to form a ring formation was to be issued, all of a sudden we discovered four masts of what seemed to be destroyers at thirty-seven kilometers 60° to port of *Yamato* (position: sixty miles bearing 357° of the light on Suluan). Then, three carriers, three cruisers, and two destroyers having been sighted, an order was issued to deploy to the direction of 110° and we headed for the enemy.

It was an unexpected encounter with the enemy. [*This was indeed an "unexpected encounter," and it is a question whose surprise was the greater, the Japanese or the Americans. The Japanese had sighted CVs with destroyer screen from Rear Admiral C.A.F. "Ziggy" Sprague's Taffy 3.*][59] We hadn't received any information on the enemy since last night. By about 0200 the search by flying boats had detected by radar four enemy groups and issued a summarizing report at 0400. However, this very report was retransmitted from the Thirty-first Communications Corps as late as 1700, only after the actual event. Although the enemy situation was included in the base air force attack order issued early in the morning, it didn't reach us before we met the enemy. We had always thought about how to cope with such an occasion as this, but each unit seemed very slow in starting actions due to uncertainty about the enemy condition. Actions of the fleet headquarters were also apt to lack promptness.

Anyhow, at 0658 the First Battleship Division commenced firing with the fore turrets at the range of thirty-one kilometers. Destroying a ship with two or three salvos, the target was changed to another one. The enemy turned back spreading a smokescreen and began retreating to the east, taking advantage of a squall.

Though its reasoning was unknown, the fleet order called for battleship divisions and heavy cruiser divisions to attack and the destroyer squadron to follow. The fleet's attacking directions were also conflicting and I feared the spirit of all-out attack at short range was lacking. I so advised the chief of staff. The commander in chief ordered me to command the First Division's battle since his chief of staff wasn't familiar with the gunfire command. Since then I commanded both the movements and gunfire of the First Battleship Division.

It was said that they observed the enemy carriers to be six at about 0700. From 0706 we proceeded on an easterly course and bombarded the enemy coming out of the smokescreen together with the secondary batteries. It was about this time that one carrier was sunk, another set on fire, and one cruiser sunk.

[*The Japanese sank no ships at this time, although near misses shook and slightly damaged CVE* White Plains. *As Ugaki indicated, Kurita's orders were confusing and did not make proper use of his great superiority in fire power.*][60]

The range found by radar was 22,000 meters and was still shortening. As visibility was gradually improving from the east, we expected to destroy them with one salvo as soon as they came in sight. Meanwhile, there was an enemy air raid against us. A few salvos of enemy medium-caliber guns reached near *Yamato,* and two hit the starboard after-galley and the outside boat hangar. Later, the latter was found to be a dud.

At 0754, when we were firing at an enemy destroyer at short distance, we found a torpedo trace to the starboard bow and we evaded it to the nonenemy side, turning to port with a direction of the commander in chief. This caused us a lot of trouble afterward because we were caught between four torpedoes on the starboard and two on the port, and enemy slow-speed torpedoes running parallel to *Yamato* with 26 knots didn't permit her to turn for a pretty long time. It was about ten minutes but it felt like a month to me. After the traces disappeared, we finally could turn to starboard and put all our power into the chase.

In the meantime, the enemy changed course to the south, and accordingly our forces chased it southward. As the enemy conditions weren't clear, we ordered the planes ready to take off and catapulted Plane No. 2 at 0814. The aircraft approached the enemy through bad visibility and reported that the enemy interception was persistent and its course was southeast. (It sighted one large carrier and another with four destroyers behind them spreading a smokescreen.) As our course was south, I thought we could just make them.

From about 0822 we commenced radar firing toward the starboard bow.

At this moment *Haruna,* positioned to the south-southeast of *Yamato,* discovered an enemy carrier group thirty kilometers to the southeast and fired on it. At 0851 we dispatched *Yamato*'s Plane No. 1 to confirm this. (In spite of the obstructions by squalls and enemy planes, it sighted carriers, and four destroyers behind them were retreating to the south-southeast, laying a smokescreen.) Since an enemy telephone in plain language asked for rescue and received a reply that it would take two hours, another enemy must have been nearby. At which should we aim? [*At 0701 Sprague had broadcast in plain language, reporting contact and urgently asking for assistance.*][61]

We decided to cut the enemies in two and finish the enemy on the right first before they joined their forces and set course to south-southwest accordingly. However, after a while the headquarters ordered us to head for the enemy to the east. So we turned south-southeast accordingly, but it was too late and we could not find those carriers. Intercepting the Tenth Destroyer Squadron's order to charge, the fleet headquarters issued an order to assemble gradually to the north. We set course to north. It was then 0924.

At the time of sighting the enemy, our formation was quite irregular. Moreover, an order for a ring formation was issued in preparation against an enemy air raid. So promptness was lacking in the initial stage of the engagement. But all units fought quite well.

The Third Battleship Division left us in the midst of the fighting, and *Kongo* displayed her gunfire fairly well. *Haruna* dropped behind a little, though, due to her inferior speed.

Haguro and *Chokai* of the Fifth Heavy Cruiser Division followed the enemy and maneuvered well. But unfortunately *Chokai* received a hit in the middle part of the rudder at 0850, and it induced the explosion of a shell. As a result, she dropped back and had to be scuttled after transfering her crews. A bomb hit *Haguro* on turret No. 2, but she kept on fighting until the remaining ammunition became scarce.

[Chokai *fell to aircraft from CVE* Kitkun Bay. *The strike on* Haguro *came from an aerial bomb, but it is not clear from which carrier's aircraft.*][62]

The Seventh Heavy Cruiser Division's start was extremely slow, and ten minutes after the commencement of firing it suffered a torpedo attack. As torpedoes were seen passing ahead, it didn't evade them, but a torpedo lagging behind hit *Kumano*'s fore part. When she turned to the opposite side of the enemy, she came close to *Suzuya,* the second ship, and the flag was removed to her. But, alas, she too had already been hit by a bomb and was forced to reduce her speed to 20 knots.

[*The hit on* Kumano *came from destroyer* Johnston, *a vessel that fought so gallantly in this engagement that the captain of the Japanese destroyer which sank* Johnston *at 1010 saluted her as she went down.*][63]

Nevertheless, its second section kept on fighting with gun and torpedo firing, but regrettably, at about 0854, *Chikuma* was damaged—her stern was hit by a bomb that made her unable to operate anymore—and dropped behind. She has never been heard of since, together with *Nowake* standing by her.

[*Heavy cruiser* Chikuma's *guns sank CVE* Gambier Bay *at 0907. Shortly thereafter* Chikuma *was sunk by combined air and surface attacks. At 0110, 26 October, destroyer* Nowake *was sunk by gunfire from Rear Admiral D. C. Badger's Task Group 34.5, which Halsey had formed to attempt to prevent the Center Force's escape.*][64]

The Second Destroyer Squadron took position to the east, and the direction of its advance wasn't adequate. It was regrettable that on the way of advance it turned back twice and consequently was left behind to the enemy's rear most of the time, and carried out neither gun nor torpedo firing.

The Tenth Destroyer Squadron remained passive until about 0800, but since then advanced south-southwest. As the enemy withdrew to the west, taking an opportunity it carried out a charge toward the south or southwest between 0905 and accomplished the great feat of sinking three carriers, one cruiser, and one destroyer.

[*Actually, Rear Admiral Masafuku Kimura's Tenth Destroyer Squadron only sank one destroyer—*Johnston*—which had engaged all five of his destroyers.*][65]

At the time of the encounter, enemy planes on the flying deck seemed to be readied for takeoff and about thirty of them appear to have taken off. They strafed and bombed our ships. As we were engaging in a surface battle, the rate of hits was quite good and most of the damages our cruisers sustained were due to them. Moreover, they strafed courageously and one of our ships got as many as five hundred bullets. They assaulted *Yamato* four times, too, but that was during the surface battle so I didn't pay much attention to them.

While we were thus sailing toward the north, we saw flashes of gunfire in the direction of 280°, so we proceeded toward them, concentrating forces on the way. There were slicks of sea surface colored by markers. Passing a fairly big dark red slick, we came to an area where enemy survivors were clinging to cutters and strewn all over. What did they think of the magnificent sight of our fleet in pursuit? As we were the enemies, they made no signs asking for help, though they must have wanted to.

Soon after, twenty-four SB2Cs and TBFs came to attack at 1014. Bombs hit *Suzuya,* and fire broke out in the torpedo tube compartment in the starboard midship, soon spreading and inducing the explosion of torpedoes. She was rendered unable to sail and sank. [*Hit by aircraft from the Taffies, heavy cruiser* Suzuya *sank at 1322 during the pursuit phase.*][66] The Seventh Heavy Cruiser Division headquarters transferred to *Tone.* A destroyer was also damaged. Those enemy survivors must have cheered at the sight of this from far away.

At about 1120 a signal was issued to set course to 225° to charge into Leyte Gulf, prompted by what I don't know. At 1215, thirty more planes came to attack, but by this time the First and Second forces had joined and formed a single ring formation, so no damage was inflicted.

At about this time, I believe, [the following was written in the margin: "At 1148, forty-seven miles bearing 0° of Suluan Light"] something like a mast was sighted on the horizon port abeam (39 kilometers 173°) of *Yamato.* Soon the top lookout said they were the masts of a battleship (*Pennsylvania* type) and four other ships. I said they might be the Second Battleship Division coming east after having penetrated through Leyte Gulf. The fleet staff said no, so I advised them of the need to confirm. However, they only ordered *Yamato*'s plane, which had been dispatched twenty minutes earlier to reconnoiter north and Leyte Gulf, to investigate them, and never tried to approach them by ourselves, a fact which is still regretted even now. It wasn't hard to imagine they were enemy forces including battleships. As we were in a ring formation, we could have approached easily by simultaneous change of direction and commenced firing.

At 1313 they wavered again and canceled the charge into Leyte Gulf in favor of seeking an enemy task force to the north to wage a decisive battle with it. Then course was set to 0° and we sailed northward off the east coast of Samar. [*This attack came from Task Group 38.1; its only hit was a dud, which struck heavy cruiser* Tone.][67] At 1316 seventy enemy planes came to attack but no damage was sustained. As I thought that when we sailed close along the island there would be patches of clouds and rain, and better visibility, I so advised. My advice was accepted and we proceeded on course 10°.

At this time the direction of the wind was 30°. (At the time of this morning's surface battle, the wind direction varied due to squalls, but, as it was generally northerly, the enemy appeared to take advantage of the smokescreen spread by this wind and withdrew with the squall.) As we sighted takeoffs and landing of planes far over the horizon in the direction of 20°, we knew vaguely of the existence of enemy carriers. So I urged going after the enemy in the direction of the wind in order to get them by evening. But this was turned down on the grounds that we wouldn't be able to catch those who had a superior speed of 32 knots. And we proceeded to the northwest. [The following was written in the margin: "Enemy signal: the Seventh Fleet was ordered to concentrate at three hundred miles southeast of Leyte."]

The reasoning for our withdrawal to the north was explained as follows: Enemy carrier planes were being concentrated at Tacloban base. [*Aircraft from Taffy 3 used Tacloban as a temporary landing field. The army engineers had already readied the field in order to handle these planes well.*][68] The enemy task force seemed to have prepared for our attack into the Leyte anchorage by taking a mobile disposition. As the enemy situation at Leyte was unknown, our attack into Leyte would only make us an easy prey for the enemy. Instead, better turn about and attack an enemy task force, located at 113 miles bearing 5° of Suluan Light at 0945, when it least expected us to come.

There would be no difficulty if a war went on without a hitch as planned, but errors and incidents are unavoidable in a war. And I thought we should have attempted a chase as friendly planes could have attacked. I felt irritated on the same bridge seeing that they lacked fighting spirit and promptitude. When the first consideration was directed to the remaining amount of fuel, it was natural that they were apt to head for San Bernardino. If we could destroy the enemy, it wouldn't be impossible for the battleships to refuel to destroyers at night.

We have been air raided three times since then. But, except fire on *Hayashimo* in the last round of raids, no big damage was sustained. The last one was repelled at 1705. As there was moonlight, we were prepared for enemy attacks at night next to dusk attacks, but they hadn't come after all.

We couldn't discover an enemy task force in the north. It couldn't stay in the same place indefinitely. After checking our position, we turned back once, and, as the visibility grew narrower, we entered San Bernardino Strait. We had a submarine fuss near the strait, but couldn't ascertain whether it was false or not. We hurried for home on the same route we took on the way out, both 22 knots and without zigzagging. A man pursued wants to get away from an enemy as quickly as possible. That is only natural. [Passed the strait at 2130.)

Today, X-Day, there were also the Third Force's attempt into Leyte and the cooperating operation of the Main Body of the task fleet from northeast of the Philippines. Though I haven't enough material about them, I'm going to write down what I have heard about them.

The Third Force, consisting of the Second Battleship Division (*Yamashiro* and *Fuso*), *Mogami,* and four destroyers, left Brunei after our departure and passed Balabac Strait without being harassed by submarines. Then it sailed up north into the Sulu Sea, then down south to the west of

Mindoro. Except for one slight air raid in the meantime, they went on rather smoothly and also sent in that they were going to penetrate into Leyte anchorage at 0300. But when they approached the south entrance of Surigao Strait, they were fiercely attacked by PT boats ambushed at night and an enemy battleship force located in T formation. *Yamashiro* was set on fire first, then *Fuso* and *Mogami* shared the same fate. It was complete defeat with only one destroyer surviving.

[*This was the battle of Surigao Strait, where Nishimura lost every ship of his command except the destroyer* Shigure.]⁶⁹

The Fifth Fleet, consisting of *Nachi, Ashigara, Abukuma,* and the First Destroyer Squadron, undertook almost the same movement a little later, sighted the above mishap and withdrew, making a torpedo attack against a likely enemy within the smokescreen. *Nachi* collided with the damaged *Mogami,* and *Abukuma* was lost by an air attack on the way back. [*This was the Second Striking Force under Vice Admiral Kiyohide Shima.*]⁷⁰ The Third Force's movement was based on information of the previous day, when no powerful units were in Leyte Gulf after enemy battleship divisions had sortied to the east. Being overbold, they rushed right into the enemy's hands.

It was no good at all that two forces having the same objective and moving in the same area acted separately; moreover, their order was reversed. They should have been united under a single command and, provided with enough escort, have attempted a penetration after obtaining information on the enemy situation. However, the Fifth Fleet wanted to join the attack on its own accord and followed the movement of the Third Force, so there was no time to communicate between them to arrange a united command.

I tender my deep condolence to the great sacrifices made by Vice Admiral Nishimura, commander of the force, Rear Admiral Ban, skipper of *Fuso,* both of whom I knew so well, and many other officers and men.

The Main Body of the task force, on the other hand, intending to divert the enemy and attack it at an opportune moment in concert with the thrust of the attack force, sailed south leading the Third and Fourth carrier divisions, *Oyodo,* and destroyers. They attempted to attack the enemy on the 24th, the day before the attack, but couldn't find it and most of the planes landed in the Philippines. Enemy planes attacked them the next morning from a short distance of a hundred-odd miles and they lost *Zuikaku, Zuiho, Chitose,* and *Chiyoda.* The headquarters transfered on board *Oyodo.*

Moreover, enemy surface force gunfire wiped out light cruiser *Isuzu* and two destroyers rescuing survivors, while an enemy submarine attacked light cruiser *Tama,* which had departed for Amami-Oshima because of shortage of fuel, and she has not been heard of since. This was another complete defeat.

[*This was the battle between Ozawa's diversionary Main Body and Mitscher's Task Force 38. Along with the losses Ugaki listed, Ozawa also lost two destroyers and an oiler.*][71]

It was too bold a diversion. They should not have acted so boldly with only one hundred planes, especially when most of them were stationed on shore. I wonder what was wrong with them.

We received a telegram saying that His Majesty expressed his satisfaction with the efforts of our surface forces under difficult circumstances when this morning's battle report was presented to him. Commander in chief, Combined Fleet, also sent encouraging words of praise, but I felt it somehow inappropriate.

In the evening an order came in calling for a night engagement if there was a chance and, if not, withdrawal through San Bernardino; however, by that time we were already on the way back. Prior to this, the Main Body of the task force asked us to send in the situation as they were going to cooperate with our night engagement. They intended to do so only with the Fourth Carrier Division and destroyers, but I got the impression they were more than bold in light of their losses of carriers.

The damages of today's decisive battle were not proportionate to the results achieved. Besides, we failed to drive back the enemy landing after all. So I conclude that this failure has spelled a major [factor] in deciding the fate of this war. Its failure was attributed, though in some respect to its planning, mostly to the extreme inactivity of the base air forces, probably hindered by bad weather.

Thursday, 26 October 1944. Fair. Third day of the decisive battle. Before dawn we passed the day-before-yesterday's battle scene to the north of Tablas Island, and we offered a silent prayer for the brave souls of those who went down with *Musashi*. At 0800, when we approached the northwestern tip of Panay after sailing southward west of Tablas, about thirty enemy planes pursued the fleet by trailing oil and attacked. Then, at 0834, fifty more came with some torpedo bombers included in the last round. *Yamato* marvelously evaded them but *Noshiro* was struck and rendered unnavigable. We had a destroyer take her in tow. *Yamato* took two hits in the bow from dive bombing, which caused fairly big damage. The third attack at 1040 was made by thirty B-24s, the first time for us. They flew fearlessly at high altitude and their one-bomb spread reached between *Haruna* and *Kongo* and another on *Yamato*. Although *Yamato* could evade them skillfully to port, the effect of three five-hundred-kilogram-bomb near misses was terrific. Waterspouts and splinters went over the main battery control tower, and the chief of staff was hurt on his right thigh with a rebounding splinter. At about the same time, approximately sixty carrier aircraft came to attack and *Noshiro* was finally struck by torpedoes and sank.

[*The attack by carrier planes which sank light cruiser* Noshiro *came from Task Group 38.2 and 38.3. The B-24s belonged to the Far Eastern Air Force and flew out of Morotai. They scored no direct hits.*][72]

This was the last of their attack against the Main Force. Surely we have had enough! Altogether *Yamato* sustained the following damages: a bomb pierced the cable deck, went deep inside and exploded, causing the compartment below the windlass to be flooded and two fairly big holes in the side plates. Of armor-piercing bombs which hit the shoulder of the armor plate of turret No. 1, one exploded on the spot, and the other exploded after piercing the weather deck and inflicted great damage to the mess deck and its neighborhood. Another one drilled a big hole on the port bow above the waterline near turret No. 1. The gaping hole swallowed seawater with a terrific splash and noise. This caused the flood water in the fore to reach three thousand tons, and this had to be balanced by flooding the after compartments with two thousand tons of water. With five thousand tons of water altogether flooded in, the fore draft was quite deep.

On board *Nagato,* one pierced the cable deck and went out through it, while another hit a roller and exploded outboard, drilling a hole. Two hits made on the middle radio room and the air intake of a boiler room inflicted fairly big damage. Besides, there were numerous holes both in the fore and aft made by splinters from near misses.

Kumano, which had been damaged but was on her way to Manila under her own power, was attacked again by enemy planes off the west coast of Mindoro and her damage was increased. A destroyer standing by her was sunk together with the survivors of *Chokai* who were on board her. [*Probably* Hayashimo *which was bombed and beached on 26 October.*][73] The enemy cleaned up the sea thoroughly, leaving nothing, with the feeling of a victor disposing of the remnant of the defeated enemy. We also had times like that some time ago.

The fleet passed south of Cuyo Island, sailed to the northwest, and passed the channel at the north tip of Palawan with high speed. Then course was set to the northwest heading to the north of Pratas Island because we had quite enough of enemy submarines on our way out.

We canceled the refueling at Coron [Bay], but it couldn't be applied to the destroyers. So we decided to let them go there for refueling and catch up with us after that. Even some of them nearly got stuck before reaching Coron.

Friday, 27 October 1944. Partly fair. We sailed so as to cut through the Pratas from its north end. We were trailing oil, as the enemy announcement said, so we still had to be alert against possible pursuit by enemy planes and submarines. All of our ships were more or less damaged, and any more damage added would have meant the end. Like last night, this morning, too, an opinion was strongly suggested that we had better refuel and repair at Camranh Bay, bringing tankers up there instead of to Brunei, which was under constant enemy watch.

Nagato and *Haruna* took two accompanying destroyers in tow and refueled them for two hours. I thought the navigation through these islands would be very difficult in case of bad visibility. We turned back for a while in the evening to meet the destroyers coming after us after refueling at Coron, but couldn't find them.

Last night *Yamato* buried at sea twenty-nine killed in action, and I attended on the quarterdeck. Today other ships followed suit.

Saturday, 28 October 1944. Cloudy. We headed for Brunei on a southeast course. It clouded up in the afternoon, so fortunately neither enemy planes nor submarines discovered us. We approached the entrance of the bay through a squall and entered safely at 2030, arriving in Anchorage No. 3. We refueled hurriedly from two tankers. As *Yamato*'s windlass was out of order, she rode on *Yuho Maru*'s anchor. What a strange thing to happen! I felt refreshed taking a bath after a long time.

Kobe, in command of *Nagato,* reported on the battle, while Onoda and [Captain D.] Araki, in command of *Takao* and *Atago,* respectively, came in. But I missed Inoguchi, the skipper of *Musashi,* to my deepest regret.

The Combined Fleet ordered that even those vessels which needed repairs stay here for a while to transport army reinforcements of two and a half divisions to Morotai while the First Attack Force assists it indirectly. Without such determination as that, we could hardly prevent the enemy from obtaining his operational objectives. However, I was afraid that, by the time some of the reinforcements arrived at the destination, the enemy would have landed somewhere else.

[On Sunday, 29 October, Ugaki's ships maintained a strict alert against enemy aircraft, but none appeared, "probably prevented by squall clouds over this area." Refueling went on throughout the afternoon and evening.]

The enemy task force was still operating east of Manila. Manila and Clark Field were air raided today. The special attack corps launched an attack.

[*The attack on airfields in the Manila area came from Task Group 38.2. A kamikaze of the "special attack corps" damaged CV* Intrepid. *Ugaki did not mention it in his diary, but the first kamikaze attack of the war was made on the CVEs of Taffy 1, inflicting considerable damage but sinking no ships. Taffy 3 caught it a few hours later. The kamikazes sank St. Lo, damaged Kitkun Bay and Kalinin Bay. Another kamikaze on 26 October struck Suwanee of Taffy 1, which suffered many casualties.*[74]

[The fleet finished refueling by 0500 on Monday, 30 October. The scheduled sortie to support the transportation of reinforcements to Leyte was called off, so emergency repairs "and fixing up" continued apace. There was no air raid, but "activities of large enemy planes in the Celebes and Sulu seas were pretty frequent." *Myoko*'s temporary repairs completed, she was sent to Singapore with a damaged destroyer. The Fifth Heavy Cruiser Division was the only unit still complete. The Second Destroyer Squadron now came under the Southwest Area Fleet for escort duty. "As Hayakawa, its commander, and his staff officers temporarily had nowhere to stay, they came aboard *Yamato*."]

The fleet headquarters sent a summary report of the battle based on investigations of surface battle, etc., after assembling representatives of each unit yesterday.

[*The following summation of the battle results which the Kurita force inflicted on the United States is exaggerated and minimizes the Japanese losses, which totaled four carriers, three battleships, six heavy cruisers, three light cruisers, and eight destroyers, all sunk.*][75]

1. Air raids by enemy planes

24th	6	times	350 planes
25th	11	"	450 "
26th	2	"	140 " (30 B-24s included)
Total	19	"	940 " " " "

Planes shot down: approximately 100 (4 B-24s included). (This seems to me to be exaggerated.)

2. Enemy forces engaged.

Carriers: nine to eleven. Cruisers and destroyers: ten each.

3. [Japanese ships] sunk: four carriers (two large included), one heavy cruiser, two light cruiser, four destroyers.

4. [U.S. ships] destroyed: two carriers (one large or battleship included), two to three cruisers or destroyers.

Tuesday, 31 October 1944. Enemy planes didn't come today, either. *Yamato*, riding on a kedge anchor, hurried temporary repairs while leaking oil. It was quite reassuring that the quantity of the flood water in the fore compartment decreased day by day. The chief of staff, Combined Fleet informed us as follows: The First Attack Force was to stay here to keep a sharp eye on the enemy and, if enemy fleets attacked the second transportation, would advance to the eastern part of the Sulu Sea in advance to directly support the third transportation. Unless we could drive down the landed enemy, our future would be doomed. Of course, we should cooperate to such an extent. But it was quite discouraging that there would be no way of replenishing fuel in case we used it up.

The Kamikaze Special Attack Corps attacked the enemy task force east of Suluan Island yesterday and inflicted fair damage to three carriers and one battleship, of which one CV was reported surely sunk. [*This kamikaze attack struck Task Group 38.4. It damaged CV* Franklin *and CVL* Belleau Wood *so badly that they had to retire to Ulithi.*][76] Then at Peleliu motor launches and small landing craft equipped with torpedoes attacked an enemy convoy in the east at night, taking advantage of the bad weather, and sank three or four of them. Both were sure-to-kill methods, sacrificing their own lives. I'm glad to see that, as the situation becomes critical, this kind of attack method comes to the fore without compulsion, thus displaying our glorious way of warriors.

The enemy proudly announced that in the sea battle east off the Philippines a total of fifty-eight battleships, carriers, cruisers, and destroyers was sunk or destroyed, two-thirds of Leyte and Samar were recaptured with little resistance from the Japanese forces, and 1,500,000 Filipinos liberated. Apart from the former, I was worried lest the latter be true. However, an army reconnaissance made at 1000 this morning brought splendid news that no enemy plane was sighted either on land or in the air at Tacloban, and there were only one battleship and three cruisers or destroyers in the roads; the rest were sixty to seventy sunken transports reclining in the water. Nothing was known about the Dagut area but it seemed to me that the enemy surely must be weakened to some extent. Convoy *Tama* was leaving Manila today and I hoped they would succeed in landing on this occasion.

Casualties of the First Battleship Division in the current battle:

Yamato: 29 killed, 55 seriously wounded, 69 lightly wounded. (Among the seriously wounded, three died later).

Musashi: 949 killed, 58 seriously wounded (stretcher cases). (Commander and 39 officers included.)

Nagato: 38 killed (4) 105 (5) seriously wounded.

For those killed, reaching 1,029, as a commander I felt heartbroken. I knew the only way to repay the sacrifice made by those brave souls was revenge. Both Inoguchi, skipper of *Musashi,* and [Captain Kimitake] Koshino, her gunnery officer, were the highest authorities on gunnery, and both moralists, too. I had known them for a long time, and now they are both gone, dying for loyalty and patriotism. I couldn't help grieving as I thought Koshino gladly shared the fate of Inoguchi.

Second Destroyer Squadron Commander Hayakawa went on board a destroyer bound for Manila tomorrow, and I sent him some sake and candies, wishing him luck.

Wednesday, 1 November 1944. Fair, cloudy in the evening. According to the Intelligence Department's judgment, carriers operating to the east of the Philippines weren't more than five or six, and have gone further east since last night. I wondered whether it was due to refueling or fear of our kamikaze attacks. Only one battleship was in Leyte and several cruisers and destroyers to the east of Suluan.

[*On 1 November U.S. naval fighting forces at and near Leyte Gulf were greatly depleted. The Taffies had left, reaching Manus for upkeep on 29 October. On 30 October Vice Admiral John S. McCain replaced Mitscher as commander, Task Force 38, while Rear Admiral A. E. Montgomery took over Task Group 38.1. Three groups of Task Force 38 were either at Ulithi or en route there. Kinkaid had left Rear Admiral G. L. Weyler in charge of those ships of the Third Fleet remaining in the Leyte area. These consisted of three battleships—* Mississippi, California, Pennsylvania—*heavy cruiser* H.M.S. Shropshire, *light cruisers* Boise, Nashville, *and* Phoenix, *and thirteen destroyers.*][77]

Though B-24s shadowed convoy *Tama* and it sighted several small planes on its way out, it seems to have arrived safely at Ormoc on the west side of Leyte under the First Destroyer Squadron's escort. I think they'll be able to attain their object of landing, if they can surely get direct air cover.

As it was reported that over thirty B-24s headed west from Menado at 1115, we took precautions from 1430 to 1630, but fortunately they didn't come. Was eight hundred miles the limit of that type's attack range?

[Ugaki learned through the Navy Ministry that vice admirals Denkichi, Okochi and Oka had been appointed, respectively, commander in chief of the Southwest Area Fleet and Ominato Naval Base. Ugaki asked himself whether Mikawa was ill or wounded, and thought uneasily that this seemed a backward step "instead of renovation in personnel administration."]

Kanoya Air Base flashed a signal that two enemy task forces without carriers were sighted at 150 miles west of Chichi Jima and 240 miles west of Iwo Jima, respectively, at 1205 and ordered all available planes to concentrate at Matsuyama Base by the 1st. What's the enemy up to now? Are they trying to threaten our empty nest? If it's not just a threat, we must pay attention to it as a grave problem in conducting the war. (Later, the above two groups were found to be a group of one cruiser and three destroyers.)

A lone B-24 raided the north tip of Borneo yesterday and sank the tanker *Itsukushima Maru,* which was taking refuge at Kudat after being struck by a torpedo at Balabac Strait. Tacloban base today issued a plain language signal saying that two enemy battleships, three cruisers, and eight destroyers were sailing to the southeast of Balabac at 20 knots. It's certain that enemy hands are reaching toward north Borneo every day, and, at the same time, there was fear that this plain signal might be reporting their own force by mistake. (Later it was learned that this was originally a deceiving message sent by the Third Communication Corps which the enemy received and rebroadcast.)

[*This was probably the false report of a large enemy force which caused Halsey to form Task Group 34.5 from Task Group 38.2, ordering the latter to provide combat air patrol for the former. Task Group 38.2, already at Ulithi, was ordered back to the east of Leyte, and Task Group 38.1 at Ulithi was sent to another support post. Task Group 38.4, having two of its carriers badly damaged, remained at Ulithi.*][78]

As B-29s raided Truk from the Marianas, precautions since yesterday have been taken at home. This afternoon several of them came to the Tokyo-Yokohama area and carried out reconnaissance of strategic points. An enemy raid on a large scale against our mainland is expected shortly.

[*Although these two B-29s dropped no bombs, they had slipped unnoticed past the offshore patrol system. They were not sighted until directly over Tokyo, shocking the mainland defense personnel.*][79]

Commander in chief, Combined Fleet, issued a strict order calling for smashing the enemy's first attempt and allowing no plane to return. I think it necessary to carry out a surprise attack against the Marianas base and destroy it before the enemy concentrates.

The present enemy strength in Leyte Gulf:

One to two CVLs, seven to nine battleships or cruisers, over ten destroyers, and over fifty transports.

At 1355, six to seven destroyers, three large transports, and seven to eight small transports at a point seventy miles bearing 90° of Suluan.

One cruiser sunk and minor damage given to the bow of a battleship by an air attack.

A plane of the *Baika* Unit (Plum-blossom Detachment) of the Kamikaze Special Attack Corps sighted a battleship or a cruiser sailing south in Panaola Strait and hit the roof of her foremast, causing a big fire.

Thursday, 2 November 1944. Fair. Air units which attacked the enemy in Leyte Gulf yesterday sank three cruisers and inflicted medium damage to a battleship. [*On 1 November Japanese aircraft penetrated the Leyte Combat Air Patrol. Neither a battleship nor cruisers were involved, but destroyer* Abner

Read *was sunk and three others damaged.*][80] The second reinforcement transportation force which arrived at Ormoc yesterday evening made every effort to hurry disembarkation. But twenty-eight B-24s and over ten P-38s attacked it since this morning while screening planes intercepted and the convoy hid in the smoke screen. They succeeded in landing generally in spite of a near miss sinking *Noto Maru,* which slipped into the water from the stern. The convoy left there this evening for Manila on a reserve course.

[*Operation TA had been landing reinforcements successfully at Ormoc since 23 October. This particular convoy landed some eleven thousand troops and nine thousand tons of supplies despite attacks by B-24s from Morotai and P-38s from Tacloban. Noto Maru had unloaded ninety percent of her cargo when B-24 bombing sank her at anchor. The rest of the convoy reached Manila safely.*][81]

A group of three technicians headed by [Technical] Rear Admiral [Masatsume] Yagasaki of the Technical Department arrived from Manila this afternoon to investigate each ship's damage and to decide where it shall be repaired.

[Friday, 3 November, Ugaki's command celebrated "Memorial Day for the Emperor Meiji," the third such occasion during the war. "What a difference in mind and atmosphere we experience every year!" Under the circumstances, he could not think of a satisfactory poem, but jotted down a few thoughts, one of which was "Day of chrysanthemum brings/Devil's cloud with enemy wings."]

The Ormoc transportation force was on the way back to Manila today without being attacked by enemy planes. An army reconnaissance yesterday reported 180 planes at bases on Leyte, of which about half were large-type. We can't let up our attacks for a moment.

Ten land-based medium bombers of the Seventh Base Air Force attacked faraway air bases at Saipan and Tinian last midnight and caused fires at various places, thus taking effective revenge against the enemy B-29 attacks. While only one of them failed to return, eight army heavy bombers which accompanied them either made emergency landings on the way or did not return. In view of this alone, the degree of their skill was quite apparent. They should be employed according to their capacity.

On her way back from transport duty to the Truk area, submarine *I-362* sighted a vessel like a battleship sailing northward at 0640 this morning at a point 370 miles bearing 116° of Tokyo. Together with an enemy sighted west of Iwo Jima, this seemed very strange.

[Ugaki had been reading with interest a book entitled *Loyal Kikuchia* by Kan Kikuchi. He believed the account was not boasting on the part of the author, but "genuine loyalty inherited by generations."]

Saturday, 4 November 1944. Fair. An enemy task force of over ten vessels, including two CVLs, was east of Suluan Island. Communications intelligence, on the other hand, reported noticeable enemy activities, either due to a reinforcement to Leyte or a new attempt. Leyte isn't the only place, and it's quite apparent that the enemy will come to other places in due course.

[*On 3 November Task Group 34.5 joined and again was absorbed into Task Group 38.2 as Halsey prepared to hit Luzon to regain air superiority. All three carrier groups were moving north when I-41 torpedoed light cruiser* Reno. *Casualties were few but damage heavy; however, she made it back to Ulithi under escort.*[82]

[That evening Ugaki heard the reports from rear admirals Wasaburo Iwasaki and Yagasaki. The damaged destroyers could be repaired at Singapore or Surabaja, but most of the others would have to return to Japan for repairs.

[On Sunday, 5 November, Ugaki assembled his staff officers and delivered a speech, praising the officers and men of *Musashi* and repeating his belief that she sacrificed herself for *Yamato,* which otherwise would have come under heavy attack. "Future movements of the fleet are not yet clear," he told them, "but if we go back to the homeland you should consider holding a memorial service for the dead first, before shore leave is permitted." Later Ugaki wrote a poem to express his feelings and added as an interpolation in his diary that, when on the way home they passed the spot where *Musashi* went down, he closed his eyes "in silent prayer."]

Enemy air raids were intensified today. Starting with 170 planes attacking Manila at 0750, several attacks spread down to the Legazpi area in the morning and afternoon. At 1415, three groups of three, five, and four carriers, respectively, at fifty-mile intervals, in addition to five battleships and forty others, were sighted at a point about 225 miles bearing 65° of Clark Field.

At 1330 *Sakon* Unit of the Special Attack Corps sighted two carriers and ten others at a point 140 miles bearing 90° of Cape Encant. One plane hit a CV with superstructure on her starboard. A few minutes after an induced explosion, her stern began to down. Another hit a CVL and set her on fire.

Nachi, which took refuge in Manila, finally sank, and *Akebono,* in attempting to rescue her, was made unnavigable.

[*Task Force 38 divided its forces to attack three areas—Task Group 38.1 northern Luzon including Clark Field, Aparri, and Lingayen Gulf; Task Group 38.2 the Verde Island Passage, North Sibuyan Sea, and airfields at Mindoro; Task Group 38.3 the area between 14° and 15° north, which included shipping in Manila Bay. In addition to many Japanese aircraft destroyed, heavy cruiser* Nachi *was sunk, as Ugaki states. Four kamikazes attacked CV* Lexington. *Three were shot down but the fourth crashed her. She did not sink, but McCain transfered his flag to* Wasp, *and* Lexington *returned to Ulithi with Task Group 38.2. McCain took* Wasp *to Guam to take on a new air group—Air Group 81. During McCain's absence from 6 to 13 November, Rear Admiral Frederick C. Sherman took command of Task Groups 38.2, 3, and 4.*][83]

This apparently greatly hampered the third reinforcement transport attempt scheduled to leave tomorrow. The Twenty-first Heavy Cruiser Division, the main force of the Fifth Fleet, which was named the Second Attack Force, has been reduced by almost half. This instance should make us cautious, especially when we're suspecting a new enemy move.

More than ten B-29s from India attacked Singapore today for the first time and inflicted fairly big damage to *Notoro* and docks, etc. [*"More than ten" was a vast understatement. Fifty-three B-29s attacked the King George VI Graving Dock at Singapore, one of the best in the world, and put it out of commission for three months. Other B-29s hit secondary targets.*][84] Also, large planes continued their fierce attacks on the Cebu area.

The vice chief of the General Staff and its chief of the Operations Section and vice chief of staff, Combined Fleet, were scheduled to fly over here this afternoon but it was canceled. It was regrettable, as I was looking forward to hearing the future policy from the vice chief of staff, Combined Fleet.

Monday, 6 November 1944. Partially fair, a heavy squall in the evening. At 0915 ashes of thirty-three persons killed in action were taken on board the hospital ship *Hikawa Maru No. 2,* which arrived here yesterday and was going to leave this afternoon.

Junyo and *Kiso* loaded with munitions, etc., arrived from home waters. *Yamato* was also supplied with antiaircraft shells for type 94–40 cm guns.

A total of 190 planes attacked the Manila area and 140 planes the Clark Field area from early morning through the afternoon, but it seemed rather mild considering the number of carriers sighted east of Lamon Bay yesterday.

Of the damaged *Kumano* and *Aoba* which accompanied the convoy *Mata* 31, two torpedoes from an enemy submarine struck *Kumano* at a point five miles southwest of Cape Polinao on the west coast of the Philippines at 1052 today and rendered her unnavigable. She listed 11° to starboard with the engine room flooded. It will be fortunate if she can be towed to a suitable shore nearby and rescued.

[*A submarine pack consisting of* Bream, Guitarro, Raton, *and* Ray *at-*

tacked Kumano. *She was further damaged but the Japanese were able to tow her away and beach her on Luzon. There planes from* Ticonderoga *sank her on 28 November.*][85]

It's good that on both the 2nd and 5th three to nine army heavy bombers made surprise night attacks on Morotai base and inflicted considerable damage. This kind of attack isn't a monopoly of the navy; the army should carry it out, too.

Tuesday, 7 November 1944. Cloudy. The enemy task force strength operating east of Lamon Bay was found to be as follows, according to the questioning of POWs, enemy telephone interceptions, and our reconnaissance:

1. Second Group, Task Force 38: *Intrepid, Hancock, Cabot.*
2. Third Group, Task Force 38: *Ticonderoga, Lexington, Essex, Langley.*
3. 4th Group, Task Force 38: *Hornet* and one CVL.
4. Besides, two groups of five CVLs and one CVL.
5. Total: six regular carriers, two converted carriers, and seven CVLs.

New names were found, but it was regrettable to see the old customers' names repeated.

The central part of the Philippines wasn't attacked today, so it was feared that the enemy advanced further north. Escort forces sailing up north were ordered to take refuge.

Late last night an enemy submarine nearby sent an urgent signal to Perth in a great hurry. She must have seen something.

At 1400 today a lone B-24 approached from the direction of Mili to seventeen kilometers of the anchorage and flew to the east after our fighters chased it. It must have observed the whole of our fleet as it transmitted a telegram soon afterward, which Morotai rebroadcast. Hadn't they known until today that we were here? Anyhow, large planes will surely come here from tomorrow. It's a bad policy just to stay here and be subject to their attacks. By evening the fleet headquarters decided to leave here at 0300, intending to return tomorrow evening after avoiding enemy air raids. That would be less effective. We should hide ourselves for at least two days; otherwise, it will be dangerous.

Incidentally, the Southwest Area Fleet had hoped to see that this fleet would operate in the Balbac Channel area on the 9th and 10th to lure enemy large-type planes on the occasion of a reinforcement transport attempt. If we carried out a deceiving diversion for two or three days, I'm sure it would bother the enemy. As for the fuel problem, one way would be to stay without moving in an area out of the usual lane close to Pratas Island, utilizing underwater submarine detectors and planes.

Ashigara of the Fifth Fleet arrived in the evening from her hideout in the Palawan Islands. Unloading of ammunition from *Junyo* lasted until night. Handling large ammunition is a hard job.

Wednesday, 8 November 1944. Cloudy, squall. We left at 0300 through the west entrance in the dim moonlight (22nd lunar night) and sailed away from the coast of Borneo on course 315° with 20 knots. *Junyo,* light cruiser *Kiso,* and heavy cruiser *Tone* also followed.

At first we intended to stay drifting at night on the sea in the Pratas Island area where there was little fear of enemy submarines, but the plan was changed again in the afternoon. Yesterday the Combined Fleet suggested a plan for carrying out an attack on Leyte Gulf on the 11th with the First Attack Force, supported by the second general air attack, the third and fourth reinforcements to be made at the same time.

Without replying to this, however, the Southwest Area Fleet had the third transportation attempt with high-speed vessels leave Manila today, the 8th. Consequently, the Combined Fleet ordered the First Attack Force to support that attempt indirectly, staying in the Sulu Sea on about the 9th and 10th.

Refueling of four accompanying destroyers and *Yahagi* from the battleships was carried out in two hours from 1800 while drifting. At 2100 we sailed around the position (7°–41′N, 114°–57′E) so as to pass through Balbac Strait tomorrow morning. *Ashigara* followed us, but she reported she would take too much time in refueling, so it was decided to send her back to Brunei. Dark clouds and a squall covered the Pratas area. A periscope was reportedly sighted, but the patroling planes saw nothing unusual.

The enemy task force didn't attack the Philippines today. They seemed to have retired far to the rear, planning some future attempts. A low pressure developed in the sea east of the Philippines which eventually became a help to us. However, T Attack Force, a reinforcement sent from home with all the flourish of banners and trumpets, was being held up on Formosa.

Its actual complements were only fifty planes of all kinds combined, and it was extremely depressing to see them. In order to turn the tide of war at this stage, we need at least a five-hundred-plane reinforcement. In past battles, whenever we were at a crossroad of whether we could prevent an enemy advance at a crucial point, we always felt the same shortage of planes, and, as a matter of fact, we were a loser all the time simply because of this. Of course, I don't mean a reinforcement of five hundred planes at one time, but I mean keeping five hundred additional planes [in reserve] at all times. If we can't maintain this extent of production, it's certain that we'll continue [to suffer] the same fate in the future. Can't we manage it somehow?

The land battle on Leyte was also extremely unfavorable to us and the enemy has established positions almost all over the island. Those reinforcements sent there previously were being held up in their advance. With only one division for reinforcement, there would be little hope of turning the adverse tide of the battle. The Southern Army had good reason to sit on the fence with regard to the fourth reinforcement attempt.

The eagerness of the Combined Fleet can be appreciated, but, after all, it would result in failure to send reinforcements impatiently one after another at a time when it was too late.

Though not confirmed, there was a report that ten B-24s appeared west of Lingayen today, and also another one reporting their appearance over the Southwest Islands area. As it is apparent that should the enemy use Leyte Island's base for large-type planes the situation would become extremely unfavorable to us, we should do our best to prevent it. The most we could do, I think, would be to prevent the enemy from stretching his hands any further.

After refueling at Mili, *Oyodo* and *Kiyoshimo* arrived at Brunei.

[Again Ugaki's thoughts turned to Inoguchi's death aboard *Musashi*, and he penned a four-line poem, ending with the poignant words, "Who knows the heart of an admiral brooding?"]

Tuesday, 9 November 1944. Cloudy, frequent squalls. We changed course gradually to the south after dawn and headed for Balbac Strait at noon. Just then we sighted a B-24 at the edge of a squall cloud, so we turned around, giving him about two salvos, and he flew away to the east. Four interceptors just arrived over our heads, but pointing out the direction to them was very difficult, with the result of permitting the enemy plane to send a report about us. Twice we intercepted the enemy communication of this report, and also tried some deceiving communications with the enemy, but a certain station seemed to have realized this and retransmitted it to Morotai. To be discovered was not bad as a diversion attempt, but it would have been still better if it had taken place after we passed the strait.

[Ugaki's ships turned back and passed the strait for the second time. He remembered the passage early in May, with the "magnificent sight" of the whole task fleet advancing. Now, "only six months later, it was a pitiable sight that met my eyes." But still he hoped that the next time "we will be able to pass here triumphantly, bringing captured enemy ships with us."]

After we passed the strait, night came and we set our course to 70° from 10°, intending to turn back at about 0100. Fortunately we didn't meet submarines.

Two typhoons were hovering to the east of the Philippines, so dark clouds and squalls came in and out continuously.

The reason why the enemy task force has retired to the north or north-northwest of Palau after dividing into three groups might be their refueling, but another reason was considered to avoid these typhoons. The enemy often takes advantage of the weather by foreseeing it, which is one of the benefits of the offensive side. [*Task Group 38.1, 38.2, and 38.4 were en route to a refueling rendezvous.*][86]

This afternoon five large planes and twenty P-38s attacked the fourth high-speed transport force under the command of the commander, Second Destroyer Squadron, but partly thanks to fighter cover it escaped the danger with a small fire on one ship and arrived safely at Ormoc in the evening. The next jobs were disembarkation and departure.

[*According to U.S. records, twenty to thirty B-25s and fifteen P-38s participated. As Ugaki stated, damage was light and by that night most of the troops had landed.*][87]

The third transportation left Manila at 0300 as the army seemed to have given in. However, this low-speed convoy was scheduled to arrive at the destination in daylight on the 11th and leave there on the 13th. So the Southwest Area Fleet requested the First Attack Force's support from the 11th to the 13th. But even if we turned back now, we wouldn't have fuel remaining for more than a twenty-four-hours' run at 20 knots when we got back to Brunei. More movements than this were impossible. There seem to be various problems involved in the departure of the third and fourth transports and they were so confused that I could hardly make them out. Combined Fleet remained silent without changing its order to give support on the 9th and 10th.

While even the wisdom should be questioned of having the attack force, which in general cases should operate under an air cover, operate without it as in the last case, such an idea as going out in order to absorb enemy air attacks instead has been little heard of in all military histories abroad and at home, and deserved to be an example in the future. A desperate attempt to make up the shortage of airplanes with warships by subjecting them to merciless air attacks should in every respect be called a reverse of tactics. Even if asked to destroy enemy planes, sacrificing ourselves, how many planes could a formidable warship shoot down? Airplanes must be dealt with by airplanes. Even a grade school pupil at present knows that quantity over a certain amount cannot be dealt with other than by quantity.

Today a telegram from the chief of the Operations Bureau of the Naval

General Staff informed us that 418 planes (all kinds combined) and 410 planes of replenishment were all the navy could muster by the 8th, 15th, and the end of this month. My God! Eight hundred planes! How can we manage with this strength? We have to ask the army for the rest. And when those reserves are expended, what are we going to do? It must be a reasonable request to ask the monthly production of five thousand planes, army and navy combined, today, three years after the outbreak of war.

Friday, 10 November 1944. Cloudy, frequent squalls. At 0100, just before the turnabout, *Haguro* reported sighting a submarine, then a torpedo trace, so that we were strained for a while. Enemy planes didn't shadow, probably due to bad weather. At dawn we approached the east entrance of the strait. With poor visibility and occasional squalls, we met difficulties before we checked our position. We felt relieved for a while when we got through the strait in a squall at 0945. Squalls often interrupt antisubmarine patrols by float planes and fighter cover.

We crossed over the usual shipping lane as on our way out, then changed course gradually from west to southwest, choosing the round-about course south of the Pratas. Though the Combined Fleet wanted us to remain in the Sulu Sea for another half to one day, if possible, for the sake of the overall operation, we couldn't do so, as the signal was received in the afternoon, and also in view of the remaining amount of fuel.

The current typhoon helped us on the one hand, but on the other it affected us pretty heavily: *Kumano*'s anchor slipped while she was taking refuge at San Bernardino and the voyage of the convoys was delayed.

The fourth reinforcement convoy, which arrived safely at Ormoc yesterday evening, couldn't get on with disembarkation well due to poor landing facilities—they seemed to have cast anchor separated to the north and south as the enemy bombarded the jetty—lack of landing craft—only five motor launches assembled due to poor liaison with the army instead of the originally planned fifty—sailing difficulties of small craft in rough seas. After landing personnel and a part of the materials, they sailed out, and enemy planes attacked them since this morning, with the result that one destroyer, *Kashii Maru, Takatsu Maru,* and Transport No. 11 were sunk.

On the other hand, the third reinforcement convoy led by commander, Second Destroyer Squadron, entered the Sibuyan Sea, but one of the transports went aground and was being contacted by enemy planes. Together with poor landing facilities at Ormoc, its success was doubtful. [*As the convoy of the 9th got under way for its return trip, first thirty B-25s, then thirty-two P-38s attacked. Two transports and a minesweeper were sunk. En route to Manila, another transport was sunk.*][88] Wouldn't it be better to change the plan altogether and land them on some other point on another island? Apparently nothing can be done under the present situation. A reckless push against odds with little hope of success was based on the inexperience of a headlong command. Moreover, we had to be cautioned because most of them were made by our navy side.

[What to do about his damaged ships now became an acute worry for Ugaki. The Combined Fleet had informed him it intended to send the First Attack Force to Lingga or Singapore for temporary repairs. But would this be enough? Unless *Yamato* were docked, "her holes can't be patched up." The last voyage had increased her water intake by three hundred tons. But if they went to Japan, "fuel for operations would have been drained" and repair of battleships would be of low priority. Was there nothing left "but to linger at Lingga, waiting to be bombed by enemy planes?" He decided to think of nothing for a while and let matters take their course.]

Saturday, 11 November 1944. Cloudy. Early this morning, sailing on the course east, we sighted a mountain top of Borneo and reached the entrance of the bay at 0900. And we arrived near the anchorage at 1000. As before, *Yamato* stayed drifting. Every ship refueled from *Hakko Maru*.

The daily production of the refinery at Mili was only one thousand tons, and the army was reluctant to increase the monthly allocation for the navy to more than ten thousand tons. As *Hakko Maru* had only four thousand tons and it had to be divided among all of us, we had to be content with seven hundred tons for *Yamato*.

It was reported that a B-24 closely reconnoitered the anchorage at an altitude of two thousand meters for one and a half hours the night before last. An air raid alert was issued last night, too, but seemed to be a mistake. It has become necessary to take strict precautions day and night here.

When the third reinforcement with the inferior speed of 7.5 knots was about to approach the south of Ormoc before noon, it was subjected to merciless attack of 120 fighters and bombers combined. Likely these weren't carrier planes. Though over a dozen army fighters ought to have been there, the whole force except *Asashimo* was annihilated and Commander Second Destroyer Squadron Hayakawa was killed. In yesterday's entry, I predicted that a reckless attempt would result in disaster. [Ugaki recalled that General Tomoyuki Yamashita, Supreme Army commander in the Philippines, had sounded quite confident at his first press interview, because now the Japanese could "fight freely on wide open areas." If the third reinforcement could have landed somewhere like Legazpi, it could have been so used.] So I couldn't help regretting very much the loss of all forces and ships. *Shimakaze, Hamanami, Naganami, Wakatsuki,* Minesweeper No. 30, and four transports (four hundred men and ammunition on board) were sunk and *Celebes Maru* (2,700 men and ammunition on board) went aground, but most of the personnel were rescued.

[*During the night of 10–11 November, the outgoing convoy passed another incoming one and lent it three destroyers. A search plane reported the convoy to Halsey as it left Manila Bay, and he ordered Task Groups 38.1, 38.3, and 38.4 to cancel the scheduled refueling and hurry to attack the convoy. Three hundred forty-seven aircraft struck it, the first wave giving priority to the* Marus, *and sank both of them. Despite Ugaki's statement that most of the men ware rescued, U.S. records claim that all—some ten thousand men—were drowned except a few who swam the mile or so to shore. The second wave hit the destroyers, sinking* Shimakaze, Hamanami, Naganami, *and* Wakatsuki.][89]

At 0920 an army plane sighted thirty transports and nineteen warships sailing on course 310° at a point two hundred kilometers bearing 130° of Suluan Island. Ten battleships or cruisers and fifty to sixty transports (the number increased) were sighted in Leyte Gulf. A report of a large enemy force sailing fifty-five miles northeast of Legazpi gave quite a shock and an attack order was given accordingly, but the report was later found to be false and the order called off. At a time when a warning of a new enemy landing was issued in the light of radio intelligence reporting that a powerful enemy force had refueled and was standing by to the north of Ulithi, this kind of false report should be strictly guarded against.

But it won't be too long before this false report becomes true. The Mindanao area including Davao is now a useless place, like men castrated, as it no longer can afford bases for planes. The next enemy landing will be directed to the main island of Luzon. Only after recapturing Manila can their propaganda take effect.

By the way, Dewey has already admitted his defeat in the presidential election campaign, and Roosevelt likely will be elected for the fourth time. God seems to be still on the enemy side.

Vice Admiral Torahiko Nakajima, who has endured hardships for a long time as commander, First Escort Division, was transfered, and his successor is still unknown. I felt quite honored to have become a unique grand old division commander under the sun both in name and reality.

[Sunday, 12 November, was a routine day. Ugaki learned that Vice Admiral Kimpei Teraoka had been appointed commander in chief, Third Air Fleet. This pleased Ugaki, for the new assignment seemed to compensate Teraoka for his summary dismissal as commander in chief, First Air Fleet, recently.]

Monday, 13 November 1944. Fair. Though alert should be maintained against enemy air attacks, I also saw the need to inspect the damage and the progress of repairs on *Nagato,* so from 1030 I went aboard her. The damage sustained in her midship was fairly big, but it was good to see everybody trying hard to repair and fix things. After the inspection, I spared a short time to see Petty Officer Second Class Yoichi Sato.

When I returned to my ship at about 1200, a telegram from the chief of the Operations Bureau of the General Staff was awaiting me, which said: "A large-scale change will be made in the fleet organization on the 15th of this month, whereby the First Battleship Division will be disbanded. *Yamato* will be flagship of the Second Fleet and *Nagato* will be organized into the Third Battleship Division." I was glad that I had inspected *Nagato* this morning, having a presentiment. Well, it won't be long before I leave this division. Anyway, believing it essential to prepare for disbanding this division and leaving the command to the fleet headquarters, I ordered my staff officers accordingly.

Mr. Wang Ching Wei, who had been recuperating and receiving treatments in Nagoya since last March, passed away at last. His death was regretted for the sake of newly born China. He was posthumously decorated with the Order of the Chrysanthemum with Grand Cordon. [*Wang Ching Wei was the puppet ruler of occupied China.*]

Since early morning through the afternoon, a total of 356 planes in six waves came to attack Manila. Though forty of them were shot down, *Kiso* and five destroyers, *Ondo* and others suffered heavy losses. A total of 120 planes in five waves also raided the Clark Field district, but the damages sustained weren't heavy.

An enemy task force of five to seven carriers was located at a point 170 miles bearing 70° of Manila, but most of the attack planes that went out failed to find the target. So the result achieved was awfully poor.

The Fourth Carrier Division and the Thirty-first Destroyer Squadron scheduled to reach Manila tomorrow were changed to unload materials at Pratas Island. Such should have been done, of course.

Tuesday, 14 November 1944. Fair. Enemy carrier planes raided the central part of the Philippines today. The enemy task force was at a point two hundred miles bearing 70° of Manila in three groups, each consisting of seven carriers and ten ships. Since yesterday our attack forces have made sorties, but few found the enemy due to inaccurate [information about] the enemy position. The result seems to have been small.

[*The carrier raids of 13–14 November came from Task Group 38.1, 38.3, and 38.4. Principal targets were Japanese ships. They sank destroyers* Akebono, Akishima—*survivors of the action of 11 November—*Okinami *and* Hatsuharu *in addition to seven Marus. Strikes on airfields were secondary, but the United States claimed some eighty-four Japanese aircraft either shot down or destroyed* *on the ground, with twenty-five U.S. planes lost. Following these two-day raids, Task Force 38 retired temporarily. Task Group 38.3 returned to Ulithi and Task Group 38.2 took its place.]⁹⁰*

In the afternoon, there was a fuss, one of our medium bombers being mistaken for an enemy B-24.

Wednesday, 15 November 1944. Fair. Both in the morning and afternoon, two B-24s each came only to reconnoiter this place, a phenomenon that made us feel the time for showdown was close at hand.

The large-scale change of the fleet organization was issued with today's date. The task fleet and the Third Fleet were abolished, while the First and Second battleship divisions, Seventh Heavy Cruiser Division, Tenth Destroyer Squadron, Third Carrier Division, and Twenty-first Heavy Cruiser Division were disbanded. At the same time, *Yamato* was made an independent flagship of the Second Fleet and *Nagato* included in the Third Battleship Division.

Until today, ten months have elapsed since I was appointed commander, First Battleship Division, when it was newly organized as of 25 February. Now it's disbanded and I'm going to be relieved of command. I'm the only commander with no successor, so I'm filled with special feelings.

Following the message, I was relieved of command at 0900, but I'm going to stay on board her as a mere passenger.

[Ugaki delivered a brief, dignified speech of farewell to his command, praising their loyalty, bravery, and endurance. Reminding them that the "present situation is most critical and the fate of the empire is staked on it," he urged them to further sacrifices, that they "make use of your war experience, and further strive to improve fighting strength." He closed by wishing them "further efforts and good luck."

[Then he moved from one farewell party to another: lunch in the ward room, a dinner in his honor given by the commander in chief, then another party with two of his classmates. "Drinking after a long time dry makes a man with no job tight."]

As an order arrived instructing seriously damaged ships to go back to the homeland, *Yamato* is going to leave here as soon as her refueling is finished. So I called off my plan of taking a plane from Singapore and decided instead to stay on board her until she reaches the homeland. Though relieved of my command, so far I've heard nothing about my new assignment.

Saturday, 16 November 1944. Fair. At 1100, when I had scarcely got rid of a hangover from yesterday, an air raid alert was issued. Forty B-24s and fifteen P-38s came to attack. One of them surely was shot down and three caused to emit smoke. Divided into several groups, they went after *Haguro* and destroyers, and attacked our damaged vessels in the vicinity of La- buan, but our damage was almost nil.

Yamato circled within the bay at 24 knots, but they didn't come near as they feared our fierce fire. Our main batteries even gave them ten salvos at more than twenty thousand meters. What should come, came after all, so from now on we will be subjected to their daily visits.

As chief of staff of the Fifth Fleet, Rear Admiral Takeshi Matsumoto came to visit me. He said he escaped from Manila on board a destroyer and got here on board *Ashigara*. He told me indignantly about the assault into Leyte Gulf and Manila under bombings. I could imagine and under- stand everything.

At 1730 I invited two skippers and their staff officers to a small farewell party with sake, presented by His Majesty, and some champagne.

At 1830 *Yahagi,* four destroyers (which were included in the Second Destroyer Squadron), *Kongo, Nagato,* and *Yamato* left Brunei for the homeland in that order. We must be especially careful on our way home. *Haruna, Haguro, Oyodo,* and *Ashigara* of the Fifth Fleet were left behind. They had better be sent to Lingga or Singapore, too.

No war news was sent to me, who had left the post, but there seemed to be no great change today.

In the evening, I received a telegram dated yesterday informing me of my assignment as being attached to the Naval General Staff. The question is the next assignment, but I can't know what it is. Like a floating weed, I have to leave it to the stream.

[Ugaki further expressed this sentiment in a two-line poem.

[On Friday, 17 November, the homeward bound ships sailed north through the Pratas Islands. Brunei had been attacked the previous night, so Ugaki felt that they were fortunate to have left earlier. The remaining ships would leave Brunei at 0400, join the Fourth Carrier Division at the Pratas, then proceed to Lingga. The Southeast Area had warned of an enemy sortie, but nothing happened. "This may be regarded as a quiet moment before an action."

[On Saturday, 18 November, the voyage continued, with little fear of submarines, being "well away from the coast of the Philippines." They had been warned that a U.S. task force might reach the Philippines after the 18th or 19th and Formosa after the 19th or 20th. In view of this, Ugaki thought it would be best to "sail along the west side of Formosa." Ugaki noted that the base air force commander in the Philippines had encour- aged his forces to attack enemy reinforcements in Leyte "even with small strength."

[On Sunday, 19 November, they headed west of the Philippine Strait to pass the west coast of Formosa, running into winds "a bit too strong for a monsoon."]

Monday, 20 November 1944. Partly fair, strong winds. "Ignorance is bliss" is an appropriate saying. As I thought nothing happened yesterday, I slept soundly and got up this morning only to be alarmed to learn that the enemy task force made its appearance east of the Philippines. From early this morning about two hundred planes raided the central part, especially concentrating their attacks on the west coast of the Philippines. No major damage was sustained in Manila Bay, but a convoy off San Fernando received fairly big damage.

Our planes attacked this enemy, flying from the Philippines and Formosa, as a result setting one carrier and one battleship on fire and sinking three cruisers. [*On 19 November, Task Groups 38.1, 38.2, and 38.4 struck harbors on Luzon. Few targets were found, but they destroyed over one hundred Japanese planes on the ground at a loss of thirteen aircraft. The Japanese sent eleven small sorties against Task Force 38, but despite Ugaki's claims they did no damage.*][91] As the flying-boat search with radar carried out from 0200 to 0400 this morning detected three groups, a further search was made again this morning, but no enemy was reported within three hundred miles. Though it was certain that they were Task Force 38's *Intrepid, Cabot,* and *Hancock,* have they retired to the rear because of our attacks, or do they intend to come up north to the Southwest Islands or Formosa to meet us again?

That the Submarine *Kikusui* Corps made a successful surprise attack in Ulithi this morning can be seen from the fact that the enemy issued an alert at 0558. Another surprise air attack is going to be launched shortly. This kind of surprise attack should be carried out more frequently at this stage, based upon the traditional Japanese spirit.

[At noon *Yamato* "passed through the passage between the Pescadores and the Formosan main island." Strong winds continued to blow, but there was no sight of an enemy. Ugaki noted that their submarines seldom showed up in that region and thought that "the swiftness of the current" might be a reason. An aircraft reported on radar turned out to be friendly.]

It's said that large planes arriving in China yesterday reached 129. I think there is a great possibility of their coming to attack soon. After all, we can't be safe even at home.

Tuesday, 21 November 1944. Cloudy, visibility dim. On detecting mysterious waves in the directions of 0° and 70° around midnight, we suspended zigzag movements and decided to break through on course of 50°. Later the wave direction moved to the stern, so we thought they were B-29s shadowing us.

At 0301, after complete silence for a while, a dim light flame, together with a waterspout, suddenly arose from *Kongo* sailing at the head of the line. Then another followed. *Nagato,* the second ship on the line, and *Yamato,* the third ship, immediately made an evasive turn, and great confusion followed for a while. After we settled down again, we found we had lost contact with the destroyer *Urakaze,* then sailing to the starboard side of *Kongo.* As someone saw a circle of light to the port stern of *Yamato,* which evaded to port a little after *Kongo* was struck, it was surmised she was also attacked by another submarine and sunk.

Kongo reported her boiler rooms Nos. 6 and 8 were flooded but she was able to make 16 knots. Later she reported her listing to the port side reached 15°. As it was difficult for her to accompany us and enemy waves were still detected, it was decided to send her to Keelung escorted by *Isokaze* and *Hamakaze.* The position where the tragedy took place was sixty miles north of Keelung. As I thought she might be all right if temporary repairs could be made to her there, I retired from the bridge.

This morning, however, a sad report that she sank at 0530 was received, to extreme regret. Wondering what happened to Vice Admiral Suzuki and others, I tried hard to hear any news about them the whole day long, but no news came in by sunset. At the time of the tragedy the wind weakened a little bit, but the sea was still rough, so rescue work in the dark was considered difficult. So I prayed hard for the safety of Vice Admiral Suzuki, a classmate of mine.

Enemy submarines seemed to have closed in to attack, first employing radar and then by means of acoustic detectors. Though we made depth-charge attacks, we didn't see any of them. Their skillful attack through the dark should be termed excellent, though they were our enemy.

[*Both battleship* Kongo *and destroyer* Urakaze *fell to the U.S. submarine* Sealion II.][92]

On the other hand, there was an indication that the enemy task force, though still in the sea east of the Philippines, had withdrawn a little bit. While radio intelligences indicating the imminence of the enemy's new attempt came in one after another, enemy B-29s carried out a large-scale attack on Kyushu this morning. Omura was included again in the list of their targets.

[*This B-29 attack had only moderate success. Due to bad weather, of 109 planes only 61 reached the primary target, Omura, inflicting no new damage to the factory area. Japanese air opposition was unusually strong, and five B-29s were lost to enemy action. One fell to Lieutenant Mikihiko Sakamoto, who dove his fighter into the bomber.*]93

Taking precautions against enemy submarines, task forces, and B-29s, we set course to about 55° and intended to cross the mine barrier to the east tonight, with the aim of advancing to the east of the island line after confirming the enemy task force situation tomorrow morning. That would take more time than planned, but we should be "safety first" at a moment like this.

Wednesday, 22 November 1944. Fair, weather recovered. At last, reports of rescuing survivors of *Kongo* came in from *Hamakaze* and *Isokaze*. It was learned that altogether both ships rescued 13 officers and 224 men, but the name of the division commander wasn't found on the list. In expectation of his being saved, I had prepared a box of clothing for his use for the time being, intending to send it after arrival in Kure to a destroyer aboard which he was rescued. But now there was no necessity of doing so. We couldn't help concluding that he was now beyond hope.

[Ugaki and Suzuki had enjoyed a particularly close friendship, and Ugaki reminisced in his diary about the many times their paths had crossed since their graduation in the same class at Eta Jima. He also remembered Suzuki as a good father to his "big and cheerful family." A new little Suzuki was such a regular occurrence that it became something of a joke between them. The two admirals "had nothing to hide from each other, so we could understand each other perfectly." Suzuki often gave Ugaki sound professional advice, for which he was grateful. "Alas! I can never see his gentle face again, and I shall be unable to hunt good sake to enjoy with him. . . . His soul may well rest in peace."]

At 1100 we crossed Suwa Channel to the east of the Southwest Islands and sailed north, taking a detour. The Combined Fleet especially sent down two destroyers, *Fumitsuki* and *Suzutsuki*, to escort us, but they were no good at all as they were unable even to zigzag. The half moon of the seventh lunar night hung in the mid-sky and the sea was calm. As the last few miles of a long journey are the most important, I wanted everyone to exert further efforts. Since *Kongo* was gone, the sailing of *Yamato* and *Nagato* in line reminded me of the old First Battleship Division sailing home covered by the direct screen. They weren't under my command any more, but it's hard to cut the spiritual relationship between them and me.

Thursday, 23 November 1944. Despite a fuss about a periscope at dawn, we safely slid into the eastern channel of Okinoshima at 1000. In the Inland

Sea, we drifted while refueling to destroyers, which took until the evening. We heard a report by the secondary battery officer, the senior ranking officer among *Kongo*'s survivors. We resumed the movement at midnight heading for Kure, while *Nagato* departed, heading for Yokosuka.

Friday, 24 November 1944. As scheduled, we arrived in Kure at 0800. At 0915 I left *Yamato* with my former staff officers and visited Admiral [Yorio] Sawamoto, commander in chief of the Naval Base. Then I went to the Kikkawa Hotel where they received me cordially as usual.

[On Saturday, 25 November, Ugaki returned to *Yamato,* then to Iwakuni by boat. He intended to fly to Tokyo with the commander in chief, Second Fleet, and his staff, but weather held the plane up. So Ugaki took a train instead.

[The next day he reached his home and was glad to see his son Hiromitsu in good health; his vegetable garden "was in good shape too. . . . An air raid alert was issued today. They only came to confirm the result of yesterday's bombing of the Nakajima plane factory."

[*Ugaki referred to the 24 November raid by XXI Bomber Command. Thirty-five B-29s struck the primary target, the Musashino Works of the Nakajima Airplane Company, cutting its production by about fifty percent. Other B-29s hit secondary targets.*][94]

Monday, 27 November 1944. From 0930 I went to the Navy Ministry, taking an electric train. I paid visits to those concerned, feeling ashamed of the disproportionately small battle results against the sacrifices we had to make. They all greeted me with appreciation, well realizing the circumstances we had to confront, for which I felt rather embarrassed. I was told to await further orders for the time being, as there was no place for me to go either on shore duty or sea duty. Well then, I'll have a good rest.

At about 1330 an air raid alert was issued, and I went into the Navy Ministry's shelter for the first time and had to put up there for over an hour. All persons in the ministry building from the minister and the chief of staff down to girl workers were wasting their valuable time sitting idle in the air raid shelter almost every day. I think something must be done to enable them to work in the shelter.

[*On 27 November, eighty-one B-29s bombed the Tokyo area. All hit secondary targets or targets of opportunity.*][95]

It was cloudy and drizzling outside. The enemy made blind bombings from an altitude of ten thousand meters on Tokyo and even as far as the Tokaido district. A bomb dropped on the Togo shrine, too. It was really irritating.

[On Tuesday, 28 November, Captain Kenkichi Kato, the former executive officer of *Musashi,* with a member of the Education Bureau, visited Ugaki and told him about the battleship's last hours. His report claimed she had taken twenty torpedoes, seventeen direct bomb hits, and eighteen near misses. At Kato's request, Inoguchi wrote in a notebook his thoughts on this solemn occasion, which Kato submitted to the Personnel Bureau of the Navy Ministry. This letter is of such historical interest that we reproduce it in full, as Ugaki did in his diary.]

24 October: As anticipated, we were shadowed by enemy planes.
As, prior to this, we received an air raid warning in the Luzon area early this morning from the Southwest Area Fleet, I ordered reveille at 0530 and had men take positions and be well prepared.

I can hardly find words to apologize for losing this ship, due to my unworthiness, a ship given great expectations not only by the navy but also the whole nation. Only a little consolation for me is to see that this ship absorbed most of the enemy attacks in this battle, and as a result little damage was inflicted upon the other ships.

Another thing for which I could not be excused in this battle was that the power of antiaircraft firing was not fully displayed. Every ship seemed to be poor, for which I felt myself quite responsible. [Here Ugaki interpolated: "Rear Admiral Inoguchi was an expert on gunnery and also the gunfire supervisor of the fleet."] It seemed that they fired excessively, thus inviting a disadvantage of losing targets. Also, cases of firing at long range and firing at running-away targets were many. When the damage mounted, it could not be helped that it got very noisy, but this of course was my fault, too, and I was ashamed of myself. It was a tremendous blow that the main fire director of the main battery was put out of action at the beginning of the battle. That the main director could easily be put out of order by a slight shock should receive attention in the future planning of structure.

Enemy aerial torpedoes were not so powerful, but they fired them at a point to make sure hits and at a high altitude. At first I thought it was low altitude bombing, but eventually it was a torpedo attack. Today's fatal damages were from torpedo hits, five certain and likely seven. Once the ship started turning, needless to say it was difficult to control her as we wished. Even so, we evaded at least five. Better say that they were evaded unintentionally in the course of action.

I think machine guns must be more powerful. In spite of machine-gun hits, enemy planes did not fall easily. The enemy was very tenacious in their attacks. Under an unfavorable situation, not a few waited until it was improved. But there were also some who attacked too soon. When this ship was made unable to move, they seem to have made attacks in a steadier manner. I want to continue efforts until the last moment, but it seems to be hopeless at this moment. Time: 1855.

Due to the darkness I cannot write what I want to. In the worst case, Their Majesties' portraits must be removed, the ensign lowered, and all hands evacuated. In order to preserve as many men as possible, I wished and intended from the outset of this battle to have all survivors abandon the damaged ship. It is natural that I take all responsibility for anything bad. I cannot be excused.

Even if I die, our conviction of a sure victory will hardly be affected. Our country is destined to prosper forever. I want all of you to make further efforts. I am firmly convinced of your achieving the final victory. A good many men were killed today. I want to console the souls of those brave men.

As the loss of this ship is very great, I am afraid it might result in weakening the fighting spirit, even a little bit.

Herein I express my hearty gratitude for the favors I have received. Thinking that no one could ever be luckier than I, I have always been filled with gratitude.

There were some fusses at first, but later at night they all became calm and composed so that work began to be done smoothly.

At the time of this writing, a report just came in from the engine room stating that all hands were in high spirits. Time: 1905.

[Ugaki was deeply moved by these "noble and invaluable" words.
[The officer from the Education Bureau, under instructions from the chief, War Preparation Bureau, Naval General Staff, asked Ugaki's views "on the use and repair of the surface force in the near future." Ugaki had definite opinions and expressed them freely and promptly. At the moment the surface forces could not "display their full strength," lacking air cover, but Ugaki did not believe that meant the surface force was useless. The enemy had been sufficiently concerned about them to try to destroy them. And didn't that same enemy "always accompany carriers with a powerful surface force in his invasion attempts?" Even if the base air force could sink enemy carriers, the surface forces would have to deliver the *coup de grace*. The ships could be used for transportation and in battles near the homeland. "As a last resort, they could be scuttled and grounded in a possible enemy attack area so as to be used as a powerful battery." Ugaki recommended that new construction be suspended, and while priority should be given aircraft production and repair, it should also be a policy "to repair the damaged ships with materials and labor that could be spared and utilize them for the second time."

[Ugaki made no entry of events beyond the date itself on Wednesday, 29 November.]

[*On the previous day, 28 November, the U.S. submarine* Archerfish *sank CV* Shinano, *a supercarrier converted from a* Yamato-*class battleship hull. She had been commissioned only ten days before. The navy kept this sinking so top secret that even a vice admiral of Ugaki's stature was not advised.*][96]

Thursday, 30 November 1944. Rain, air raid. After midnight, sirens screeched an air raid warning, and the air raid siren soon followed. I got up and went into the garden. I heard the droning of engines to the east and south. Our friendly planes were also in the air to intercept, but they were flying extremely low due to rain clouds which happened to come.

Enemy B-29s, divided into groups of one to several planes, carried out an indiscriminate bombing including incendiaries from high altitude on the Tokyo-Yokohama district. Soon after I got to bed after the all-clear, they came again. All of those hiding in a makeshift bomb shelter in the rain complained of chilliness. As the all-clear sounded at 0530, this deserved to be called a war of nerves lasting the whole night long. [*This was the first B-29 raid on Tokyo proper. Twenty-four B-29s struck the docks and industrial areas, also setting major fires in the Kanda and Nihonbashi districts.*][97] As a result, not only did several million inhabitants of the capital suffer, but production was badly affected, too. It's a matter of more than a small fire on parts, and some countermeasures have to be taken up seriously.

It drizzled all day long and it was very cold for a man who had recently come back from the south, and the movement of my hand got heavier than before. I improvised a small charcoal stove in the room hoping to economize on charcoal, but my legs got paralyzed and my waist hurt.

10
Such a Miserable Situation
December 1944–March 1945

U GAKI'S RETURN *to his native shores was not pleasant. The scarcity of food and its high cost made him realize the hardships of the home front. In talking with General Ugaki and the latter's confidential secretary, Mr. Shu Yabe, he gained the impression that the cabinet would probably fall before March. He met again with Yabe and several of the general's "supporters" late in December. They sounded out the admiral delicately, but his reference to Marshal Badoglio shows that he realized that they would not be averse to a peace settlement. The admiral wanted no part in this, persisting in the belief that the Japanese should continue to fight with all possible strength.*

He had a few happy moments in December—a reunion with his son, an audience with the emperor as one of six division commanders so honored, a little hunting. But as the month ended, his "thoughts ran wild seeking ways to save the empire."

Early in January he had the "painful mission" of informing Mrs. Suzuki of her husband's death. Then, facing the possibility of being unable to keep his home, he gave some items of sentimental value to his brother for safekeeping.

The bombing of Ise Shrine shocked him to the core, but he thought some good might come of it if this action roused the nation to continue fighting. He kept in touch with the top brass and made a few entries about the progress of the war. But not until 9 February did he finally receive his long-awaited assignment. He was to be commander in chief of the newly activated Fifth Air Fleet with headquarters at Kanoya.

February saw the first U.S. carrier strike on the home islands since the Doolittle raid of 1942. Once more it was Task Force 58, Spruance having replaced Halsey on 26 January. The attack on Iwo Jima began. Ugaki vastly underestimated the number of men in the initial landing, which may be why he was unduly severe in his judgment of the Japanese Army defenders, who fought well from their entrenched positions. On 23 February Ugaki could record "a good deal of results" in the Iwo Jima area. For once he did not exaggerate—kamikazes sank CVE Bismarck Sea and knocked CV Saratoga out of the war. That same day, however, saw the dramatic flag raising on Mt. Suribachi, and the island fell in late March.

U.S. carrier plane raids on Okinawa early that month led Ugaki to believe that this would be the next battle area. Learning on 9 March that nineteen U.S. carriers of various types were at Ulithi, Ugaki and Combined Fleet Headquarters independently decided to activate a suicide mission—Operation Tan—against that anchorage. Ugaki was filled with admiration, recording the airmen's "last writings," as he had done for the midget submariners before Pearl Harbor. Tan took place on the 10th and although incoming messages indicated a successful attack, later reconnaissance revealed more instead of fewer ships in Ulithi, and Task Force 58 sortied intact on the 14th. Possibly because Ugaki was absorbed in this operation, he made only cursory mention that B-29s raided Tokyo the night of 9–10 March, "causing considerable fire." Actually, the loss of life and property was worse than the atomic bomb would cause at Hiroshima.

Learning of Task Force 58's sortie of 14 March, Ugaki began to prepare for action and in his eagerness made a serious mistake. Although under orders to conserve his aircraft until it was certain the United States would attack the Southern Islands and not the homeland, Ugaki "couldn't stand to see them destroyed on the ground." On his own initiative, he decided to attack with his "whole strength" and called in his planes from their dispersal bases. The Fifth Air Fleet struck Task Group 58.4, inflicting minor damage on Enterprise and Intrepid, somewhat heavier on Yorktown. In exchange for these small results, he lost fifty of his aircraft. Moreover, having denuded his bases of planes, his command could offer little resistance to U.S. carrier aircraft which blasted hangars, barracks, and inland airfields. Early the next day, the Japanese struck Task Group 58.2 with bombs and kamikazes, seriously damaging Wasp and Franklin.

Ugaki was eager to try out the Okas (Cherry Blossoms)—manned suicide bombs—but an attempt on 21 March resulted in a fiasco. This ended the action of that particular battle. As usual, Ugaki recorded wild claims of results, believing at least eight carriers had been sunk.

Meanwhile, Okinawa was under bombardment, and signs of invasion mounted. In preparation, the Combined Fleet activated Operation Ten, which placed the Third Air Fleet, as well as the Fifth, under Ugaki's command.

[Ugaki noted only the date on Friday, 1 December.]

Saturday, 2 December 1944. It has been six days since I came home. Observing a slice of funny little fish and two leaves of vegetable which constituted a ration per person, I thought of the hardships of those who prepare a daily meal instead of the complaints of those who eat it.

I visited Mr. [Yasuo] Hayashi in Totsuya, looking at streets that have been pretty well evacuated. He asked me to come on the phone yesterday after receiving my postcard. He wanted me to see General Kazunari Ugaki in the morning as he was going to Kunitashi in the afternoon. So I went to see the general.

The reason for his trip to China after the cabinet change this summer was that, as he had been asked to be the ambassador to China, he went there to see the situation beforehand at his own expense. After hearing his views about it and the political situation in general, I left there at 1200. I went back to Hayashi's home and exchanged views with him after a long absence, while eating chicken and drinking sake. I heard a chicken cost sixty yen. I could picture the rest of the situation from this fact alone.

[Ugaki noted only the dates for 3 through 6 December.

[On Thursday, 7 December, Shu Yabe visited him, and they discussed the "general political situation" and the changes which had taken place since their last meeting the previous February. "Anyway, the present cabinet doesn't seem to be very popular, and, it's said, it's doubtful whether it will last until March next year. It's discouraging."]

Friday, 8 December 1944. The Great East Asia War enters its fourth year. Comparing the present situation with that at the outbreak of the war, I was filled with deep emotion. Fearing that the enemy might take revenge on the capital for the event of three years ago, an attack was launched on Saipan bases yesterday, inflicting considerable damage. At the same time, a very strict precaution was maintained as a whole, but they didn't come after all, except that an air raid warning was issued in the afternoon.

Saturday, 9 December 1944. I worked in the flower garden and finished fixing the eastern part of the premises. While I was having a few drinks after that, Hiromitsu came back home. Father and son at last! I was very glad to see he had gown up to be a man, getting to be an officer.

Sunday, 10 December 1944. Suicidal attacks daily carried out on land and in the air in the Leyte district reminded me of a feature of the decisive battle.

[*Ugaki probably referred to the torpedo and kamikaze attacks on 7 December against the U.S. forces which had established a beachhead at Ormoc earlier that morning. Destroyers* Mahan *and* Ward *were damaged so severely they had to be sunk by U.S. torpedoes. kamikazes also were active on 10 December.*[1]

[Ugaki found nothing worth noting for 11 through 15 December. On

Saturday he "consolidated notes and other materials" in a storeroom, burning those he considered confidential. That afternoon former Vice Chief of the Naval General Staff Ito visited him. He was slated to become commander in chief, Second Fleet, in the near future, and Ugaki briefed him "with the last operation as the main subject."]

Battles to cut off the supply line to Leyte were still going on, while the enemy landed on the west coast from transports the other day, and a confused battle is now taking place on the island.

On the other hand, the enemy task force attacked bases in the Philippines on both the 13th and 14th. On the following 15th, a great convoy of eighty transports sailed north in the Sulu Sea under the escort of a supporting fleet, and landed about one division strength at San José on the south coast of Mindoro. The place, situated close to the south of Manila Bay, constitutes a great threat to the defense of Luzon Island and also to the safety of the sea lanes west of the Philippines. We have to annihilate them by all means.

[*"Confused" was the word for the engagement when, around midnight of 11 December, Japanese and U.S. forces attempted landings at the same time and virtually the same location near Ipil.*

[*The Third Fleet sortied from Ulithi on 11 December to support the Mindoro landing scheduled for the 15th. Halsey's carriers struck for three days, and he claimed that when they pulled out on the evening of 16 December, they had destroyed 270 planes and sunk thirty-three ships. As the landing convoy was about to enter the Sulu Sea, a kamikaze crashed light cruiser* Nashville, *inflicting heavy damage and many casualties. A kamikaze also hit destroyer* Haraden, *forcing her to return to Leyte.*][2]

Sunday, 17 December 1944. Our air forces sank twenty-five enemy vessels at San José, and yet the enemy continued landings, and land warfare developed there. As our troops stationed there were not considered to be many, in the end this place will fall into enemy hands. [*Landings on Mindoro in the San José area were uneventful, as no Japanese troops were in that section of the island. But, while Ugaki's claim of twenty-five ships sunk at San José is overdrawn, kamikazes kept pounding the resupply ships over the next three weeks, sinking five LSTs and five Liberty ships.*][3] It's deplorable to see the war situation turning unfavorable. This is considered to be the very time for the surface force to make a successful thrusting attack, but they'll never reach the scene in time as they're now at Lingga or in home waters.

Monday, 18 December 1944. At 0815 I left home by a car sent from the Navy Ministry and went to the official residence of the minister of the navy. Afterwards I went to the Imperial Palace.

At 0930, following reports by Vice Admirals Ozawa and Mikawa, the emperor received in audience six division commanders who had recently returned from the front. This was the second time for me to have the honor of seeing His Majesty. We were given a present of white silk. How can I repay such an honor? After saluting at the Imperial Sanctuary, we received ceremonial cups of sake with the Grand Chamberlain in attendance. We returned to the official residence and attended a luncheon party given by the minister and the chief of staff at 1200. Toward its end an air raid warning was issued.

[Tuesday, 19 December, was evidently an anticlimax, for Ugaki recorded nothing. The next day he went to Hiyoshi to hunt for the first time since his return. He bagged four small birds, and considered the expedition "very good for training body and mind, as it refreshed me a great deal after treading hills and fields."]

The German forces have started an offensive at the western front north of Luxembourg, and all the eyes and ears of the world are concentrated on it. It seems to be the last blitz after the mobilization in summer, and it struck the Americans' weak point. I wish them success. [*This was the onset of the famous Battle of the Bulge.*]

Thursday, 21 December 1944. Rear Admirals Choso Suzuki and Shinzaburo Fukuda came to see me. Both were included in the retired list yesterday, but they were full of spirit as before. I felt quite reassured to see that they seemed to be able to do something big even in communities other than the navy.

[Ugaki noted only the date from 22 through 25 December.]

Tuesday, 26 December 1944. I left home at 1500 and took a tram from which I got off at Akasaka Mitsuke. Then Mr. Yabe took me to a place called Suzuki. There I was received by Lieutenant General [Kiyoshi] Kotsuki, who came from the same prefecture as mine, and asked about the war situation.

He introduced himself, saying that he was in Europe at the time of World War I and also served in the Army War College as an instructor. He also said that he thought in directing the war much importance should be placed on politics, shared views with General Ugaki on dealing with China, and in fact he was one of his supporters.

But I think fear isn't lacking that it would result in betraying a country as did [Marshal Pietro] Badoglio to seek a peace settlement when the war is unfavorable to us. [*Badoglio succeeded Mussolini and made peace between Italy and the Allies.*] The most essential thing under the present circumstances should be to carry out the war with all the strength we can muster.

[Several other individuals attended, "said to be supporters of the general." At least one was an acquaintance of the admiral's but he had "little interest in them. Anyway, I much enjoyed the dinner."]

Wednesday, 27 December 1944. In the afternoon, about fifty B-29s in seven groups came to attack Tokyo. Fourteen were said to be shot down and more than twenty destroyed. One of them, which our fighters attacked over Nakano, lowered its altitude, emitting fire, and finally fell into the sea off Oi. People were extremely pleased to see this, and morale in general was greatly stirred up.

[*On 27 December thirty-nine B-29s bombed the Nakajima and Musashino aircraft factories. Japanese defenders claimed nine destroyed, with five probables, and twenty-seven damaged. United States records claim three were lost, one to fighter aircraft, two because of mechanical reasons.*]+

The Eighty-second session of the Diet is now in session with its opening ceremony being held yesterday. Representatives were pleased to have had something to bring back home to talk about.

[Ugaki noted only the date on Thursday, 28 December.]

Friday, 29 December 1944. In cooperation with the base air forces, our surface force carried out a night assault on Mindoro on the 26th, which resulted in the sinking of four transports and PT boats, and bombarded store dumps and airfields. As San José is best suited for us to make a thrust into it, I have longed for such an attack to be made. Well done, boys! Had I been there, I surely would have participated in it.

[*The Japanese force under Rear Admiral M. Kimura included heavy cruiser* Ashigara, *light cruiser* Oyodo, *and six destroyers. Fighters and bombers of the V AAF and the PT boats protecting the merchant ships fended off the attack successfully. Destroyer* Kiyoshimo *was sunk and so many other ships damaged that Kimura withdrew early on 27 December.*]5

[Ugaki found nothing worth recording on Saturday, 30 December.]

Sunday, 31 December 1944. We sent off the year of the decisive battle, again having failed to turn the tide of war. Not only that, we have been further pressed into a corner, and the rise and fall of the empire is now at stake. Average people have now realized the gravity of the situation, but only too late.

However impatient I might be hoping to save this crisis by all means, I can't do anything now. All I can do is to send off the outgoing year, expecting to exert efforts next year. My thoughts ran wild seeking ways to save the empire.

[On 1 January, the Japanese "welcomed the 2605th year of the Imperial

Dynasty amidst fierce battles." They received certain "necessities" to welcome the new year, including a pint of sake. Therefore, Ugaki noted that "in spite of three air raid warnings last night we could still enjoy an atmosphere of the new year."

[Tuesday, 2 January, and Wednesday, 3 January, passed without comment from Ugaki. On Thursday, 4 January, he attended the funeral of an old navy friend and "went to the Naval General Staff and heard the latest situation from the chief of the Operations Bureau." He had nothing to say about the 5th through the 7th.]

Monday, 8 January 1945. Since about the 3rd, the enemy task force has been attacking Okinawa and Formosa, and finally many warships and transports came to Lingayen Gulf. Though the air forces were announcing considerable achievements, those enemies should be knocked out by any means.

[*The Luzon Attack Force, under Vice Admiral J. B. Oldendorf pending arrival of Admiral Kinkaid with the amphibious forces, was subjected to determined and successful kamikaze attacks. These sank CVE* Ommaney Bay, *minesweeper* Long, *minecraft* Hovey *and* Palmer. *Battleships* New Mexico, California, *heavy cruisers* Louisville *and H.M.A.S.* Australia, *light cruiser* Columbia, *CVE* Manila Bay, *and several other vessels were damaged. Personnel casualties were very heavy.*[6]

[The diary skipped Tuesday, 9 January 1945.]

Wednesday, 10 January 1945. Accompanying my elder brother [*Koichi Ugaki*] and Hiromitsu, I took the Nambu Line and went to Tama Cemetery, hunting on the way there. Deep emotion welled up in me when I saw the new tomb of Fleet Admiral Koga erected next to those of Fleet Admirals Togo and Yamamoto. I could hardly find words to apologize to those three fleet admirals. Then we went to our family's tomb place to clean it and offered a prayer in front of Tomoko's tomb.

Three enemy convoys heading for Lingayen came to attack one after another and finally commenced landings yesterday under air support and bombardment. I think this will be the turning point of the war. Brave and fierce attacks should be launched.

[*Despite the kamikazes, landing at Lingayen Bay took place as scheduled on 9 January 1945.*][7]

Thursday, 11 January 1945. At the request of the chief of the Naval Affairs Bureau, [Vice Admiral Takeo] Tada, who is the honorary secretary of our classmates' association, I called at Vice Admiral Suzuki's home at Midorigaoka at 1000. I told Mrs. Suzuki and his eldest son to be prepared to receive informal notification of the admiral's death in a few days. They received the sad news with calmness, which impressed me deeply. Wishing luck to the remaining family of four sons and three daughters, I accomplished my painful mission.

Friday, 12 January 1945. Five years have elapsed since Tomoko passed away. As our country is now facing the greatest crisis she has ever had, I don't know how long I'll be able to stay in my home. Moreover, after Hiromitsu is given a new assignment soon, it will be difficult for him to come back home. So, taking the opportunity of my brother coming to my home, we held the fifth anniversary of Tomoko's death privately, with only family members. I believe her soul must have prayed for good luck for her husband and son, well realizing our devotion.

Though we have no valuable things, some should be kept safe as good souvenirs, so I entrusted them, together with some clothes, to my brother to keep them safe from air raids. After we had dinner together, I sent off my brother at 1930 as far as Yukigaya station. Having seen him well, I wished him more health and prosperity.

[On Saturday, 13 January, Ugaki saw his son off at the end of his leave. The next day he visited General Ugaki, and Vice Admiral Kanji Ugaki joined them later. "He regretted the lack of measures to gain a sure victory at this stage of the war." That night Hiromitsu returned, as he was to inspect a nearby hospital the next day. He had been told informally that he would be assigned to the Kure Naval Hospital, which pleased his father. On Monday, 15 January, Ugaki visited old friends. "It was a pleasant but rare meeting."]

Tuesday, 16 January 1945. On the 14th enemy planes bombed the Ise Shrine, inflicting some damage. The voices of a hundred million people were raised in anger. Though it was regretted to see that the sacred place was thus spoiled, it may be of some use in continuing the war, too, if it can rouse the anger of the whole nation.

[*Ise is one of Japan's most venerated* Daizingu (*great shrines*). *Every Japanese hoped to visit it at least once in his lifetime. The* Naiku (*inner shrine*) *is dedicated to the Imperial Ancestor. It was customary for the emperor to send a message to Ise to report to his ancestor any event, good or ill, of national importance. This attack was probably by B-29s which, on 14 January, struck the Mitsubishi Aircraft Factory at Nagoya, various secondary targets, and targets of opportunity.*][8]

The enemy which attacked the coast of Indochina entered further into the South China Sea and extended its relentless attacks even on Hong Kong, Canton, and Swatow. They completely ignored us.

[Between 10 and 20 January, Halsey took most of his Third Fleet into the South China Sea. They found no Japanese warships, but sank merchant types. Task Force 38 planes raided Hong Kong on 14 January and the next day struck Formosa on the return voyage. At that time kamikazes hit but did not sink CVLs Langley *and* Ticonderoga.[9]

[17 and 16 January passed with no comment from Ugaki.]

Friday, 19 January 1945. In the eastern front of Europe the Red Army commenced an offensive with 190 divisions deploying on a five-hundred-kilometer-long front. They are now approaching the German frontier. Won't this be fatal to Germany?

[On Saturday, 20 January, Hiromitsu graduated and was appointed surgeon sublieutenant. He left for his new post at 1135 on Sunday, 21 January, and Ugaki saw him off. The admiral noted that the Diet resumed sessions, and hoped it would "function as it should."

[Admiral Shimada retired, and Ugaki reflected that when the war situation worsened, those "who were once prosperous" could not escape accusations. "I must think about my own behavior a great deal, too." On Monday, 22 January, Ugaki went to the Naval War College building to see Vice Admiral Naokuni Nomura and heard from him "the delicate circumstances surrounding his two-days' term as minister, transfer to chief of the General Staff and the resignation of Admiral Shimada." Then Ugaki visited Nagano at his home where they "talked about various matters."]

We had two air raid warnings at night after a long time. The enemy task force raided the Okinawa area yesterday. They acted as if there was no opponent in front of them.

[On Tuesday, 23 January, Ugaki visited Mr. Senzo Higai, a long-time government official, who warned that "too much army and navy interference are blocking activities of the business world." He also thought the cabinet would collapse in a month, and no one but General Ugaki "could take responsibility in the present crisis." Ugaki cautioned Higai "against sponsoring" the general.

[The next day Ugaki visited various officials in the Navy Ministry. "Everyone seemed to have a gloomy air." He made no entry beyond the date for Thursday, 25 January.]

Friday, 26 January 1945. The enemy raided Palembang. Activities of the British Fleet have become positive at last, but they must have been discouraged with eight percent of their planes shot down or destroyed. Enemy reinforcements have arrived in the Akyab area.

[The British Pacific Fleet under its carrier commander, Sir Philip Vian,

conducted two successful strikes in January on the oil refineries at Palembang while en route from Ceylon to Australia. The air defense of Palembang was the responsibility of the Japanese Army, which at this stage of the war was reporting highly exaggerated results.[10]

[Ugaki recorded only the date on 27 January. [*Nevertheless, this was an active day. Sixty-five B-29s of the Seventy-third Bomb Wing came over Japan, but weather prevented their striking the primary targets—Musashino and Nakajima airplane factories. Fifty-six bombed the Ginza and Hibiya districts in Tokyo, others alternate targets and targets of opportunity. Japanese fighter defense was the strongest the B-29s had encountered to date. Fighters and anti-aircraft claimed to have downed twenty-two bombers. Actually, five were lost, while four others either crash landed or ditched.*

[Ugaki noted only the date on Sunday, 28 January.]

Monday, 29 January 1945. The longer I stayed in Tokyo without hot water the worse my piles got, so, thinking that my health must come first, though I worried about air raids, I decided to go to Atami. Leaving home at 1115, I boarded a train from Yokohama with my shotgun slung on my shoulder. As I took the third-class car, it was so crowded that I could hardly move all the way to Atami, standing all the while. I arrived at the Naval Club Villa in Izusan and met Mr. Taro Yasuda, a painter, after a long while.

[Ugaki found nothing to be noteworthy on Tuesday, 30 January.]

Wednesday, 31 January 1945. The enemy at Lingayen has been reinforced and is moving south. [*Fechteler's group of the VII Amphibian Force landed the Eleventh Airborne Division at Nasugbu in Batangas Province on 31 January.*][11] On the other hand, the British task force attacked Palembang again on the day before yesterday with 150 planes.

Thursday, 1 February 1945. Big shots of my native country and the Nishioji area have organized an association with my name because of my connection with them last year and want me to come down there. But how can I face them?

[Ugaki recorded only the date on Friday, 2 February.]

Saturday, 3 February 1945. The enemy is gradually advancing southward, while an element landed on Subic Bay on the 30th. Our side is only carrying out a small-scale attrition operation. Bataan will also fall into enemy hands sooner or later.

[*On 3 February, the First Cavalry Division, under marine air cover, reached the suburbs of Manila.*][12]

The Red Army has already swept through five-sixths of eastern Prussia and approached a point fifteen miles from Berlin. Though Germany is boasting of their will to defend their capital to the last, the prospect is extremely dark.

[Ugaki let 4 through 8 February go by without comment.]

Friday, 9 February 1945. While I was enjoying a bottle of sake, I was called by a police telephone which asked me to come to Tokyo tonight. I was wondering, "what's the matter?" when a telephone call from a member of the Personnel Bureau informed me that a ceremony of my appointment in audience with the emperor was to be held tomorrow. I'm resigned that the time for my last service to the country has come finally.

Saturday, 10 February 1945. At 0500 I got up and took the first train leaving Atami at 0627. At 0930 I returned home and immediately got in touch with the Personnel Bureau.

The ceremony of my appointment in audience with the emperor was to be held at 1530. Before I left my home, an air raid warning was issued and about ninety planes came to attack Ota. All clear was given at 1600. So the ceremony was called off, but my appointment as commander in chief of the newly established Fifth Air Fleet nevertheless became effective.

[*On 10 February eighty-four B-29s bombed the Nakajima aircraft factory at Ota. Twelve were lost.*[13]

I'm now appointed to a very important post, which has the key to determine the fate of the empire, with the pick of the Imperial Navy available at present. I have to break through this crisis with diehard struggles. At 1630 Commander [Ryosuke] Nomura, a staff officer of the new fleet, came to accompany me to a dinner party which the navy minister and the chief of the Naval General Staff jointly gave in my honor. I bade farewell to bureau chiefs of the ministry and the Naval General Staff. After being briefed about the situation of the Fifth Air Fleet and so forth by the chief of the Operations Section of the Naval General Staff at the official residence of the chief of the Naval General Staff, I went back home.

Sunday, 11 February 1945. Fair. At 0900 I called at Combined Fleet Headquarters at Hiyoshidai. After paying a visit to Commander in Chief Toyoda, I attended the combined table maneuvers of the fleets, naval stations, and bases. I was briefed about the general situation, judgment on the enemy situation, and conditions of each unit and returned home at 1830.

Monday, 12 February 1945. Fair. Leaving home at 0900, I went to the Imperial Palace, accompanying Commander Nomura. An enemy plane came and a warning was issued. But I was received in audience in an air raid shelter at Fukiage Imperial Garden. His Majesty honored me with kind words and I was deeply moved. After that, I paid my respects at the Imperial Sanctuary and pledged myself to fulfill my duty. After dropping in for a moment at the Naval General Staff, I went to Hiyoshi and attended the table maneuvers. I came back home at 1730.

Tuesday, 13 February 1945. Fair, later cloudy. I went to Hiyoshi by car with Vice Admiral Teraoka, commander in chief, Third Air Fleet, and attended the table maneuvers. Receiving information of an enemy task force leaving Ulithi, the chief of staff and staff officers hurried back to Kanoya. I also decided to leave here one day earlier and came home in the afternoon.

[*The task force in question was Task Force 58, bent upon the first carrier strike against the Japanese home islands since the Doolittle raid in April 1942. At midnight, 26 January 1945, Admiral Spruance assumed command and the Third Fleet again became the Fifth Fleet. Mitscher took over as carrier commander of Task Force 58.*][14]

Wednesday, 14 February 1945. Cloudy. After bidding farewell to the minister, vice minister, the chief and vice chief of the Naval General Staff, the chief of the Personnel Bureau, and the chief of the Naval Aviation Department, I came home with Captain [Takashi] Miyazaki, the senior staff officer, and we had lunch together. After barely saying good-bye to my neighbors, I left home after 1200. Arriving at Atsugi base at 1330, we took a transport plane at once with the vice chief of staff and others. We flew westward in cloudy weather and landed at Kanoya base at 1750. We entered a makeshift house newly built in an evacuation area and hoisted my flag.

Early that afternoon a search plane covering the Marianas area found seventy to one hundred enemy vessels sailing north on course of 330° with 18 knots west of Saipan. I'm glad to have arrived here just in time.

[*This was Blandy's Task Force 52 Amphibious Support Force, including Task Group 52.1 of escort carriers under Rear Admiral C. T. Durgin, bound for Iwo Jima.*][15]

Thursday, 15 February 1945. Rain, later cloudy. The rain since last night cleared up, but it continued cloudy all day due to a discontinuous line of weather. We endeavored to search for an enemy, taking strict precautions.

A plane of the Third Air Fleet sighted an enemy force of thirty vessels south of Iwo Jima. Carrier groups failed to be located.

While the Combined Fleet and others in general are attaching more importance to the southwest area, the probability of the enemy task force attacking the Tokyo area isn't small either, so I called it to my staff's attention. I inspected the air raid shelter and the naval club.

Rear Admiral Chikao Yamamoto, who took command of the force temporarily before I arrived here, left here at noon.

Friday, 16 February 1945. Cloudy, later partly fair. Since early this morning, the enemy task force, which hadn't been traced though its sortie was almost confirmed, came to attack air bases, military installations, and vessels in the Tokyo area and vast areas, Haramachi to the north, Iwo Jima to the south, and Hamamatsu to the west, with carrier planes in three waves.

In the afternoon, contacts were finally made with two groups of them southeast of Cape Inubo, but we didn't have sufficient strength to attack them. Considering that another one was operating west of the Bonin Island line, this fleet searched east of Kyushu, but we couldn't find any.

The Combined Fleet alerted the base air forces for Operation Sho No. 3, but it also called for transfering the main force of this Fifth Air Fleet to the east, to be done under a special order, while the part of its force which has not yet moved in here after regrouping the last time was placed under the Third Air Fleet.

In spite of repeated warnings that an enemy would come, the Kanto district was subjected at last to the enemy's surprise attack, with the result that army and navy planes destroyed on the ground added up to 150. Other damages inflicted on installations and vessels will be fairly big, too. It's most regrettable to see that little improvements have been made in defective patrols and reconnaissance.

[*These attacks damaged aircraft plants and sank a number of ships in Tokyo Bay, including* Yamashiro Maru. *The United States claimed 341 Japanese aircraft shot down and 190 destroyed on the ground. As noted above, Ugaki wrote that 150 planes were destroyed on the ground but he did not give the Japanese figure of aircraft shot down.*][16]

Since early morning, four battleships, twelve cruisers, twenty destroyers, some transports, and twenty landing craft maneuvered off Iwo Jima and bombarded the island. It seems an enemy invasion of the island has started.

[*The initial force at Iwo Jima consisted of six battleships, four heavy cruisers, one light cruiser, and sixteen destroyers.*][17]

The enemy also landed on Corregidor Island, and our garrison force is fighting back hard. [*This landing was by parachute.*][18]

Saturday, 17 February 1945. Fair. Due to a discontinuous line of weather, there was a rain area east off this base which hampered our sending out search planes, but at last it went away to the east.

As there was fear of the enemy task force advancing westward, we extended our searches to the southeast of Kishu Peninsula. The enemy has been attacking again with carrier planes since this morning.

The Combined Fleet endured its challenge and remained quiet in directing the war. It also returned to this fleet the forces temporarily placed under the Third Fleet. Then it assigned this fleet Operation Tan, which aims at launching a suicide attack upon the enemy after it gets back to Ulithi. It calls for a one-way attack with twenty-four land bombers. Special care should be taken in executing this operation.

After dinner the chief of staff showed me around the underground torpedo storeroom and workroom. These underground projects constructed in one and a half months by sailors' hands, when he was in command of the Twenty-fifth Air Flotilla, were on a fairly large scale and I could appreciate their efforts.

Sunday, 18 February 1945. Fair.
Total number of enemy planes on the 16th: 1,000
Total number of enemy planes on the 17th: 650
Among the above, approximately 200 shot down.
[*As usual, Japanese figures on U.S. aircraft shot down were much exaggerated. The actual figure was sixty, with twenty-eight lost due to operational reasons.*][19]
It seemed that the enemy was organized into five groups with eleven carriers and five converted ones, and except for the one operating near Iwo Jima, they attacked from a point off Boso Peninsula east of the line of the Bonin Islands.

Last night some of the enemy passed our patrol line of 140°, but they could not be definitely located. However, this morning this fleet's searches sighted two groups of two carriers with several others and three carriers with eight others at a point two hundred miles west of Chichi Jima. They were nearly five hundred miles away from here, so we couldn't do anything about them. Preparing measures for their approach, I moved a part of the offensive strength to Kanoya. By the evening contact, we found both of them sailing south. They seemed to aim at flank support of the invasion of Iwo Jima. [*Probably Task Group 58.4 under Rear Admiral A. W. Radford, which attacked Chichi Jima as it passed that island.*][20]
On the other hand, the enemy is said to have attempted landing on Iwo Jima twice yesterday, but has been repulsed each time, with one battleship, two cruisers, and one unidentified ship sunk. Surface forces in addition to five carriers were still cruising at sea today. Our horizontal guns still remain hidden and no shot has been fired yet. Commander in chief, Combined Fleet, greatly praised the calm attitude of the defenders. I couldn't

understand why the enemy convoy strength was too small for their attempt at invasion. Were they waiting for follow-up convoys? How long will the enemy task force operate there?

[*No attempt at landing was made on 17 or 18 February. Those days' activities were preliminary, consisting of softening-up bombardment, minesweeping, and beach reconnaissance. The only ship sunk was an LCI(G). Heavy cruiser* Pensacola, *destroyer* Leutze, *destroyer minelayer* Gamble, *destroyer transport* Blessman, *and eleven LCI(G)s were damaged but not sunk.*][21]

The 762nd Air Group Commander [Captain Shuzo] Kuno, 621st Air Group Commander [Captain Motoharu] Okamura, and 801st Air Group Commander [Captain Eiji] Eguchi came to make arrangements for Operation Tan. I saw them after a long time. They're all dauntless veterans. I have no flotilla commanders under my command and instead have seven air group commanders directly under me, which constitutes a feature of this fleet.

Monday, 19 February 1945. Cloudy. Enemy carrier planes have raided the Chichi Jima area lately. Finally at 0800 they began landing on the south beach of Iwo Jima. As their fighting units were fairly many, their landing craft and others were also many, contrary to yesterday's observation. They landed 1,000 men first and 400 in the afternoon as well as 150 tanks.

The south airfield was captured quite easily, and the enemy is reported to have headed for Mt. Suribachi along the west coast. I knew the army's confidence could not be trusted, but I couldn't help being surprised at the vulnerability of the island strongly defended by the navy itself. One way might be to let them land and come close in order to annihilate them at the main defense line. But so far this plan has never succeeded. It has to be regarded as nothing but an excuse for being unable to beat the enemy at the seashore. If this island, noted for its fortification, should fall into enemy hands, the future of our main islands should be feared indeed.

[*Ugaki's estimate of a total of 1,400 men landed on Iwo Jima on 19 February was a vast underestimation. The number was closer to 30,000. He was unduly severe on the army defenders. Under Lieutenant General Tadamichi Kuribayashi, they put up an excellent defense from their well-entrenched positions. United States casualties the first day totaled 2,420.*][22]

Without reluctance, the Combined Fleet relieved the commander, Seventh Land-based Air Force, from command of the operational forces for Sho No. 3, and ordered the Third and Fifth air fleets to readjust their respective forces after the reorganization. The Third Air Fleet was ordered to carry out attacks with its medium land bombers and also special attacks by small aircraft, beginning tomorrow. This fleet must strive by all means to increase its fighting strength preparing for the next enemy raid, while staying in this area. But I don't know if various circumstances will allow us to do so.

A good many enemy planes coming from the Marianas raided the middle part of Honshu today. [*On 19 February the Twentieth AF sent 150 B-29s to bomb the Musoshino aircraft factory in an attempt to draw Japanese air reinforcements from Iwo Jima. Clouds covered this target, so 119 bombed Tokyo port and urban areas while the rest struck "last resort" targets and targets of opportunity. Six were lost.*][23] Our search planes sighted two groups of enemy forces centering around six carriers at a point about 120 miles southwest of Iwo Jima. To sight an enemy and yet be unable to attack it—what sort of tactics that could be called I don't know!

[The local chief of police brought Ugaki a small wild boar. The admiral hoped this would constitute an advance celebration "for us to shoot great big wild boars."]

Tuesday, 20 February 1945. Fair. From today we have changed our search plan in order to have a daytime and night search alternately every other day. This step was taken because we have already lost three planes, and, moreover, the incidental efforts were too great even when enemies were far away. Two groups of six carriers were also discovered at a point 90 to 120 miles southwest of Iwo Jima today. After resuming the briefing in the afternoon, I went back to the bivouac, where the briefing for Operation Tan was held again.

Wednesday, 21 February 1945. Cloudy, later rain and cold. Again today's search planes sighted no enemy. A small number of enemy carrier-borne planes continued to raid Chichi Jima and Haha Jima as well as Iwo Jima. One battleship, twelve cruisers, forty destroyers, and numerous transports and landing craft were around Iwo Jima. The enemy landed twenty to thirty thousand marines on the island. There was a report that a large enemy force approached the Kita Iwo Jima area. Another report also said that a special attack unit of the Third Air Fleet set heavy fires on an enemy carrier, which was certain to be sunk. [*This was* Saratoga, *not sunk but badly damaged. See entry for 23 February.*][24] Although our garrison force on the island fought back furiously, it's considered very difficult to push this large enemy force back into the sea.

At 1030 officers above the rank of flight commander assembled at Kyushu Air Group for an operational briefing. At lunch a toast was drunk with sake given by His Majesty to celebrate the success of a mission in advance. The briefing continued into the afternoon. After returning to the bivouac, the briefing for Operation Tan was held again.

[On Thursday, 22 February, Ugaki attended a dinner party of his staff at a restaurant in Kanoya.]

Friday, 23 February 1945. Cloudy, later fair. A special attack unit of the Third Air Fleet which carried out its attack on the 21st achieved a good deal of results at the Iwo Jima area. [*This time Ugaki did not exaggerate. Kamikazes sank CVE* Bismarck Sea *and damaged CV* Saratoga *so badly she had to be sent to the West Coast for repairs and was out of the war for three months. Several other ships were slightly damaged.*][25] The enemies staying in the vicinity of that island yesterday were two battleships, ten cruisers, nine destroyers, 82 transports, 167 medium transports, and 300 small craft. The enemy landing forces have already reached 40,000 and our forces there are now having a hard time.

Colonel [Shinsaku] Tanahashi, commander of the Training Corps of the Western Army, came to see me. He told me that he was going to command a mixed brigade and also defend Shibushi Bay. He frankly expressed his view that it would be difficult to defend this area with a mere four thousand and poor equipment and asked for cooperation on the part of the navy.

[Having "a little time to spare" on Saturday, 24 February, Ugaki went for a walk. He took his shotgun, but saw no birds. That night at 2300 Imperial Aide de Camp Commander Akijiro Imai arrived at Ugaki's base.]

Sunday, 25 February 1945. Rain. We have been on the alert since last night, as at 2115 our patrol boat sighted a group of three carriers, five cruisers speeding westward at 20 knots at a point 350 miles bearing 140° of Cape Inubo, and another large group, too. From early this morning a total of over six hundred enemy carrier planes raided the Tokyo area again. [*This strike was not very effective, the weather being so bad most of the aircraft had to content themselves with secondary targets. At 1212 Mitscher canceled further operations for the day.*][26] Besides, 130 B-29s from the Marianas joined the attack in the afternoon.

Monday, 26 February 1945. Partly fair. It became warm since yesterday's rain, and made one feel spring was just around the corner. I inspected the Kanoya Base from 0900 to 1200. There were many units—Kyushu Air Group, Detachment of the 762nd Air Group, 801st Air Group, 1022nd Air Group, etc. The inspection covered quite a big area, including dispersed shelters of the different units. The aide de camp's plane, escorted by sixteen fighters, left here at 0930 and arrived safely at Shanghai.

A *Ginga* bomber crashed after takeoff this morning on its test flight and three were killed. It was doubly regrettable as they were members of the *Azusa* Corps of Operation Tan.

At 0915 a patrol plane in "Q" sector sighted one carrier, two cruisers, and three destroyers sailing southwest at 18 knots at a point three hundred miles bearing 180° of Omaezaki. We intensified the patrol and also carried out night patrol. The enemy task force seems to have sailed southward because of the rain in the Tokyo area today, while its elements were readied for encountering with fighters our night attack in the moonlight.

[*Mitscher had intended to hit the Nagoya area, but heavy winds and seas so delayed Task Force 58 that he canceled the mission and headed for the refueling rendezvous.*][27]

The fierce battle on Iwo Jima is intensifying. Being pressed by the enemy's overwhelming strength and forceful attacks, our forces on that island are gradually being reduced and cornered.

[*On 23 February 1945 the dramatic flag-raising atop Mt. Suribachi had taken place. By the 26th, the defenders were being driven toward the northern part of the island.*][28]

Rear Admiral [Nobumichi] Tsuruoka, Commander of the Thirty-first Destroyer Squadron, returned from Formosa by plane. He's said to be staying in the Inland Sea for the time being.

Tuesday, 27 February 1945. Fair. Leaving the quarters at 0840, I began inspection of the Kushira air base at 0930. Though the executive officer of the 701st Air Group came to attend my inspection, a flight commander with the rank of lieutenant was taking charge of the detachment. Some installations have to be fixed immediately. To that end, a competent supervisor and reinforcement of a construction unit is necessary.

After that, I went to Kushira Air Group, a training corps, and heard a report by Captain [Heizo] Takaoka, its commanding officer, on the progress of extracting fuel oil from pine roots and then was shown around spots where extraction was being done. Getting back to the base on a very bad road, I had lunch together with young officers.

Arriving at Kasanohara Base at 1315, I inspected the 202nd Air Group led by Captain [Ryutaro] Yamamoto. Wherever I went, there were always inspections of underground facilities. Due to the spring warmth, I felt like perspiring, while bush warblers sang in the bush and larks twittered in a pleasant spring day. Whatever the outcome of the war may be, nature comes in and goes out as always.

[As searches found no nearby enemy, Ugaki's forces resumed Third Station. His staff operations officer, Nomura, returned from a trip and reported on the result of a briefing, which left Ugaki feeling the fleet's responsibilities "all the more."]

Before 2000, we heard an unusual noise like thunder high in the sky with the full moon, soon followed by the blast of a bomb. At first, it was thought to be an enemy attack, but then came a crash of a friendly plane after disintegrating in the air. But so far no reports came in of any friendly plane having an accident on its training mission.

Wednesday, 28 February 1945. Fair. After investigating last night's sound, we found splinters of an about eight-hundred-kilogram bomb and a crater from the bomb blast on the other side of the middle of Go-no-hara. Judging from the drone of motors, etc., it was surmised that a B-29 flew in at a high altitude and dropped two bombs, one of which exploded in the air and another on contact with the ground. [*The only U.S. aircraft over Japan the night of 27–28 February were eight B-24s flying out of Guam.*]²⁹ This brought home to all of us that no relaxation should be permitted even for a moment. They have come over here, but this was the first time they actually bombed. They seemed to have aimed at the Go-no-hara aviation beacon, which at that time was lit for night flight training.

At 1000 I inspected a damage-control practice of the Kyushu Air Group. The vice chief of staff and others came back from an inspection of northern air bases and made reports.

We were scheduled to move into underground quarters from today, taking advantage of the overall training starting on the 2nd, but out of consideration for the staff's health we changed to having underground living half the time for the time being. We will shift to full time when necessary.

Thursday, 1 March 1945. Cloudy. The first report of enemy carrier planes raiding Okinawa was received at breakfast, then came in from Oshima, Kikaigashima, Minami-Daitojima, Miyakojima, and Ishigakishima, etc. Dividing into two and three waves, the number of enemy aircraft reached about one thousand. We dispatched search planes immediately upon receipt of the first report, but except for a plane in the second stage sighting four enemy destroyers at a point about seventy miles south of Okinawa, we couldn't find the enemy. Judging from the number of raiding aircraft, it was estimated that at least seven or eight carriers were included.

If they came west from the Iwo Jima area, it would be inconsistent with the fact that a total of thirteen hundred aircraft attacked Iwo Jima yesterday. If they were another force belonging to Task Force 38, their strength was rather too big. Anyway, together with yesterday's persistent photoreconnaissance by two B-29s over the Okinawa area, this must be

considered a preparation for the next offensive combining a forced reconnaissance and an actual strike. We must take ever stricter precautions.
I ordered a night search and also preparation for a surprise attack tomorrow morning.

[*The air strike of 1 March on Okinawa came from Mitscher's Task Group
58.1, 2, and 3. Nine CVs plus four CVLs were involved. Ugaki's reference
to Task Force 38 shows that he was still confused as to the U.S. task force's
organization.*][30]

An enemy Grumman shot down a land-based medium bomber on its
way from Kanoya to Tokushima off Miyazaki, and we brought in the
bodies. We should find out whether it was really shot down by an enemy
or by friendly fire.

[Because of the "imminent situation," Ugaki's fleet postponed indefinitely their training scheduled to begin on the 2nd.]

Friday, 2 March 1945. Rain. The departure of search planes was delayed
because of a light rain. At 0120 a search plane flying on the west side of the
islands line found a destroyer on course 40°, speed unknown, at a point
two hundred miles bearing 230° of Cape Sata, and also a night fighter
chased him. Though there was some doubt, thinking it proper to assume
that an enemy group was nearby, I ordered the increase of contact planes,
night torpedoing by heavy bombers, and a special attack by *Gingas* at
dawn. We haven't received any information since then. However, the
weather worsened, bringing rain, and regrettably some were missed on
their way back.

According to the investigation of the returned crews, it seemed most
likely that an island was mistaken for the said destroyer, while the grounds
for [reporting] the enemy night fighter were indeed very weak. I felt that
causing trouble to the whole fleet on account of inexperienced crews, as
well as the resultant loss, were most important points, against which a
leader should be strictly warned.

It continued to rain all day today and the subsequent search was impossible. In view of the fact that no enemy attack was made in the Southwestern Island area, they seem to have gone south, so I ordered Second
Stations resumed. [Ugaki added the following in the margin: "It was later
learned that *Tomozuru* was mistaken for an enemy destroyer, and her M/G
fire for an enemy night fighter."]

Saturday, 3 March 1945. Cloudy, later fair. As the weather improved, we
searched over a fairly vast area. A *Ginga,* a medium bomber, made a forced
landing at a point 180 miles southwest of Minami-Daitojima, while an-

other searching east of Iwo Jima and Minami-Daitojima lost contact near the end of its advance range.

As radio intelligence suggested the possibility of an enemy task force going down south, there was some fear of they might attack tomorrow, so I had my forces alerted.

[On Sunday, 4 March, Ugaki attended a meeting at Kyushu Air Group to study operations of the 1st and 2nd and later a briefing on overall training. No enemy being sighted, he resumed Third Station at 0830. That afternoon he went hunting, "but did not fire even a shot."]

Monday, 5 March 1945. Cloudy, later rain. As the enemy situation allowed us to do so, the first overall training of the Fifth Air Fleet began. Two destroyers of the Seventeenth Destroyer Division left Oita in the Inland Sea and sailed off Tosa to be the target, to which point aircraft were dispatched to search and shadow. But, fearing the cloudy weather would turn into a gale with rains, training was suspended at 1530.

When I left the shelter to go outside, I felt light rain which had already been dropping. Later, the wind and rain became quite strong, justifying our step taken to cope with a quick change of weather. Then discussions were held about our tactical steps to be taken, including committee members, too.

Tuesday, 6 March 1945. Cloudy, later fair with strong winds. Discussions on tactics continued in the morning. Tactics for a sure victory were in the hands of an enemy who could push in force with quantity.

As the weather improved, and I feared any further suspension of training would cause target ships to run short of fuel, training was resumed at 1200. However, the sea was still rough and the movements of the destroyers difficult. In addition to this, in the judgment of the Combined Fleet there was fear that enemy task forces in the east and west would join together and attack again. So we had to put off the training another day and carry out night searches instead.

But from now on this sort of situation will occur as routine and will involve a great deal of trouble and hardship to carry out searches and be ready for encountering each time. We must wait for the completion of bases, otherwise we can't do anything. We need sixty patrol planes and a large quantity of fuel, and we're stuck in that, too. It's wretched.

[The Fifth Air Fleet conducted searches on Wednesday, 7 March, "but it seemed that the enemy was on his way back to Ulithi." Hoping to economize on fuel for the destroyers, they "shifted to a more restricted movement plan." A bird was singing in a nearby bush, and Ugaki wrote a brief poem in its honor.]

Thursday, 8 March 1945. Fair. Though the sea was still fairly rough, the weather gradually improved, so we carried out training mostly as planned, concluding at 1100. I inspected actual preparations of *Oka* [*(cherry blossom), the manned suicide bomb*] made at night and sortie of the *Shinrai* Corps at dawn, as well as damage-control measures to be taken against an enemy raid.

[On Friday, 9 March, the first training was studied. "It was obvious that this training was a failure." The tactics were difficult, liaison between units was poor and the flying crews' skill was even worse. But Ugaki thought the exercise had been useful "in that various defects were thus revealed." After Ugaki had expressed his views, Commander Tadashi Nakajima, executive officer of the 343rd Air Group at Matsuyama "was called in to hear useful battle lessons concerning special attacks carried out in the Philippines and Formosa."]

In the middle of the meeting a report came in from the Fourth Fleet, from a *Saiun* scout reconnoitering Ulithi. It said that six carriers and nine converted ones were sighted in the atoll in addition to a group including four carriers entering the atoll from the northeast. [*Task Force 58 had returned to Ulithi on 4 March.*][31] Judging that most of the enemy task forces had returned there, I decided to carry out the second Tan operation tomorrow. Seemingly with the same idea, the Combined Fleet ordered X-day, the day of activating the operation, set as 10 March. But a strong wind of about thirty miles per hour began to blow in, due to a high pressure extending from the China continent, so that I worried whether the flying boats in Kagoshima Bay could take off.

Saturday, 10 March 1945. Fair. Last night's gale died late at night, so a weather observation plane left at 0300. Therefore I went to the command post at 0545, where I ordered the *Azusa* Special Attack Unit to carry out the operation today and gave them a message. Then I conveyed an encouraging message from the commander in chief, Combined Fleet, to them and toasted the farewell with sake, a gift from the emperor.

One of the flying boats which were to lead the attack force had trouble in starting an engine, thus delaying the departure a little, when the result of studying photos taken in yesterday's reconnaissance began to come in from the Fourth Fleet. So, suspending the take-off for a while, I waited for the follow-up part of the report, which didn't come in time. Some points in one of the series weren't understandable, which caused us to question if those ships considered in yesterday's reconnaissance to be carriers might be other ships. Considering the necessary time to let the weather observation aircraft put about, I thought no time should be lost in hesitation and ordered today's operation suspended.

Later I returned to quarters where, summing up three parts of the report, it was learned that surely one *Saratoga* type, four *Essex* types, three *Independence* types, and seven converted types were in the atoll in addition to four unidentified ships entering the atoll at that time. So I ordered the weather officer to investigate weather conditions as far as Chushan Island just as was made yesterday, while ordering the operation to be carried out tomorrow.

[At this point Ugaki inserted an address he gave upon the sortie of the *Azusa* Special Attack Unit. He stressed the seriousness of the hour, with "B-29s raiding our homeland every day" and Iwo Jima being doomed.

[*U.S. forces were already beginning to use the airfield on Iwo Jima, and on 9 March the CVEs began to leave the area.*[32]

[Being chosen for the mission was a great honor, nevertheless Ugaki appreciated "the hardship involved. . . . I am now seeing you off with my deepest emotion and gratitude." There were supposed to be nineteen U.S. vessels in Ulithi, and the key to success laid in reaching the target area unsuspected. If the mission commander considered the chance of success small, they should not hesitate to return to base for another try later. Ugaki told them he was sure their loyalty, sincerity, and their long, hard training "must be blessed by God's help."

[The Combined Fleet, too, sent a message extolling this "divine chance. . . . Go forward, all of you, pledging yourself to defend our sacred land by surely destroying the arrogant enemy by ramming yourself into the enemy."]

The weather reconnaissance plane turned back from near Okinoshima and returned at about 1530. It sighted an enemy reconnaissance plane in the Minami-Daitojima area, so hid in the clouds. Dangerous indeed!

[Ugaki had several reasons for believing that canceling the day's operation might be something of a blessing in disguise. It gave the attack crews time to be prepared and calm down; the enemy situation in the atoll had been "clarified"; the weather and especially wind conditions were more favorable. The decision "had to be made in a hot hurry" and Ugaki did not hesitate.]

If tomorrow's attack proves to be successful, I won't be able to help feeling that such an accident was nothing but God's help given to me.

[He took advantage of the extra day to invite all the officers of the *Azusa* unit to dinner. The young men seemed in much their usual frame of mind, and Ugaki was happy "to discover the noble and lofty spirit displayed among our Japanese." As he had with the midget submariners of the Pearl Harbor attack, Ugaki recorded the "last writings" of these young men.]

From 0200 to 0400 this morning, 130 B-29s bombed Tokyo indiscriminately, causing considerable fire. But it was said that fifteen of them were shot down and about fifty damaged.

[*"Considerable fire" was a mild description of the devastation B-29 fire raids inflicted upon Tokyo on the night of 9–10 March. About 250,000 homes were destroyed and 83,793 killed—worse damage than the atomic bomb would send upon Hiroshima.*][33]

[Ugaki noted that French Indochina's "cooperation in the joint defense of that district has been lacking," so the Japanese forces had started to "remove antagonistic elements from the government and give assistance to cooperative elements. But our government announced that it has no territorial ambition."]

In the evening, Chief of Staff [Rear Admiral Takayuki] Ishii of the Sasebo Naval Station came for consultation, and I strongly urged the need to strengthen the defense of this area.

Sunday, 11 March 1945. Fair. At 0800 I went to the Kyushu Air Group. The local weather was very fine. The departure of the weather reconnaissance plane was delayed; it took off barely two hours before that of the attack unit. One of the second lead unit took off at 0800, while one of the first lead unit was delayed about twenty minutes in taking off due to engine trouble.

Taking off at 0900, twenty-four attack aircraft set course due south from Cape Sata at 0920, twenty minutes later than scheduled. Though some radioed back their return due to engine troubles, most of them seemed to go on all right. From about 1745 I went into a shelter to wait for their reports, but no news came in. Time passed notwithstanding until it was thought to be quite dark over there. Yet nothing was heard except reports of making emergency landings. (Sunset time at Ulithi was at 1852.)

At 1858 at last came in "a surprise attack made," which was followed by "the whole force will charge in sure hits, at 1903." Then came in, "I am going to hit a regular carrier, at 1903," "I hit a regular carrier at 1905," "I am going to hit at 1906." "A surprise attack made at 1908," was followed by a long dash at 1910. Upon receipt of these reports, I was finally relieved from anxiety.

The enemy issued an air raid alert at 1907, which was cleared at 1955. [*Of 24* Gingas *from Kanoya, at least six reached Ulithi after dark and tried to attack. They made so little impression that neither Samuel Eliot Morison's* Victory in the Pacific *nor the official biography of Spruance, who was present, mentions Operation Tan.*][34] Reports of making an emergency landing came in one after another. Altogether there seemed to be about nine of them, while those who appeared to have succeeded in ramming were considered to be at most eleven. Nothing was heard from the Fourth Company except from those who made emergency landings. Besides, the first lead plane which took off later than scheduled has not been heard of since. The weather reconnaissance aircraft returned to Kagoshima safely at 2350 after accomplishing its mission. Its flight time was sixteen hours and ten minutes, with fuel remaining for another hour's flight. The second lead plane reached Meleyon Island [Woleai] at 2130.

How much damage they were able to inflict upon the enemy has not been determined, but some seems to have been done. But I couldn't be pleased because of the young boys.

[Ugaki explained to his diary that it not because he was unfeeling that he could send them to die "with a smile in these days. . . . I had made up my mind to follow the example of those young boys some day. I was glad to see that my weak mind, apt to be moved to tears, had reached this stage."]

Assistant chief of staff, Sixth Air Army, Major General [Takashi] Aoki, and Thirty-second air army staff officer [Lieutenant Colonel Naomichi] Jin came for a liaison mission. They were very pleased to listen to the last scene of Operation Tan in the operations room.

[On Monday, 12 March, reports came in of the Tan planes which made forced landings, and Ugaki noted them all. "Due to mist, visibility was so poor that identification of vessels was impossible. It is certain that five to seven columns of flame were sighted at the time of the attack."]

Accompanying a flight commander and a sub-lieutenant in command of the weather reconnaissance aircraft, the 801st Air Group commander came to report. On the other hand, a *Saiun* reconnaissance plane starting from Truk Island reconnoitered Ulithi. It was a great disappointment indeed to learn that the number of carriers in the atoll had rather increased, and there was no busy traffic of small craft or any sign of sunken vessels, while no enemy planes were seen on Flalap Island, with little indication of strict alert being maintained. It turned out to be a complete failure.

[As was his custom after a failure, Ugaki noted what he considered to be the causes. In this case, he concluded (1) the planes were not suited for an attack at such a long distance, (2) they reached the target an hour after sunset, so vision was impaired, and (3) the delay in takeoff of the flying boats helped explain the late arrival; also they had to detour a squall area.]

In general, this plan of covering such a great distance with such a plane itself seemed to be against the odds.

The press immediately reported this attempt, adding that the attack result would be announced later. I regret that its result will be contrary to expectations.

[On Tuesday, 13 March, some of the *Tan* crews returned via transport aircraft. The reconnaissance photo "seemingly showed that no damage was inflicted upon the enemy." Ugaki took consolation from the fact "that a sufficient number of crews for manning about ten *Ginga* land bombers were saved by emergency landings."]

Colonel Takeshi Okuyama, chief of staff, Seki Army Group, which is responsible for the defense of this area, came to see me. He comes from the same native town and grade school as mine. This was a strange coincidence. The chief of staff accompanied by Staff Officer [Commander Yuzuru] Fukuhara and Assistant Chief of Staff Aoki (Sixth Air Army) flew to Tokyo on business.

[On the evening of 14 March, Lieutenant Naota Kuromaru, who headed the Tan flight, and Captain Korokuro Tatsumi, came to report to Ugaki. Kuromaru's report was quite detailed and Ugaki recorded it all. Ugaki's summation agreed substantially with the estimate.]

The greatest cause for the failure lay in that they failed to get there in time, because (1) the time of their departure was put off one hour as a result of the weather reconnaissance made the day before, (2) they were already half an hour late at Cape Sata due to the delay in a lead plane's takeoff, (3) they detoured on the way when they met an enemy convoy, and (4) their speed was only 160 miles. Most of these should be attributed to their leader's poor conduct, for which I should be held responsible.

Thursday, 15 March 1945. Rain, later fair. At 2030 a patrol boat of the south patrol line sighted a large enemy group without carriers heading north to the east of Torishima. Its strength seemed to be two battleships, two cruisers, and two destroyers. There was also a report of being bombarded by flare shells.

Such being the case, we have been alerted on the Second Station from early this morning and six line daytime searches were ordered. But the weather worsened, so they were called off. The Yokosuka Naval Station alerted its district sea area, but nothing happened there either.

Visits of army officers have been frequent of late, due to the general cry for home defense. Colonel [Motoyoshi] Ishii, commander of the Seki 15103 Force (regimental commander), came today and said he was in charge of this area. No matter how many of them come, it's the same thing unless they make some progress. Even if they do make some progress, they can hardly resist an enemy with the poor equipment provided.

[On Friday, 16 March, Ugaki inspected various units under his command. At Hinatayama he slept overnight "in a room for a change." The progress made in training and preparations reassured him, and the morale of the young men so pleased him that in one of his brief poems he likened their spirits to the skylarks soaring high in the sky.

[Ugaki began Saturday, 17 March, with a pheasant hunting expedition with two friends.]

When I got back to the hotel, Staff Officer Nomura had arrived there after flying a plane by himself to show me Tokyo's judgment to the effect that the enemy task force was under way to the north after leaving Ulithi on the 14th. [*This was correct. Task Group 58 sortied from Ulithi on 14 March with Spruance in* Indianapolis *in strategic command, Mitscher in tactical.*]³⁵ As Lieutenant General [Michio] Sugahara, commander, Sixth Air Army, was coming to Kanoya in the afternoon, I called off the inspecting of Kagoshima Base scheduled for the afternoon and flew back to Kanoya right after lunch.

We immediately began to make preparations for operations. Lieutenant General Sugahara flew from Fukuoka to inspect communications facilities under his command, and we had a talk with him as a partner whose close cooperation will be needed in the future.

From about 2230, night search planes detected three enemy groups one after another on the sea southeast of Kyushu. Then I entered an underground operations room to begin battle against an enemy task force.

Upon receipt of radio intelligence that the enemy left Ulithi on the 14th, Q section patrol was ordered carried out tonight. At the same time, disposition for Operation A and stand-by for First Attack Method was ordered. These steps were taken because around the 18th was the most probable date for the enemy to come to attack here, if they should come after all.

According to telephone liaison from Hiyoshi, where the Combined Fleet headquarters is situated, the high command is discussing how to cope with the enemy task force, failing to reach an early conclusion. But the general trend seems to be in favor of preserving our strength against them.

The chief of staff returned in the evening.

Sunday, 18 March 1945. Fair. As I have had little time to write down every day's entry, herein I write down its essential points retrospectively.

At 2300, Q-27 search plane suspected large enemy groups at 29° 40′ N, 133° 25′ E and 29° 21′ N, 133° 35′ E, and began shadowing them.

At the same hour, Q-25 search plane suspected a large group at 30° 10′ N, 133° 30′ E.

The enemy consisted of four groups, and it was pretty certain that they were grouped into a task force. I firmly believed so, especially when they fired on our shadowing plane.

Combined Fleet Telegram Order No. 564-A:

1. According to the analysis of various information, there is a great probability of the enemy attempting a landing on the Southwest Islands area in the near future.

2. In case the enemy invasion force hits the Southwest Islands area, the Combined Fleet, in close cooperation with the army, will destroy it with all its strength and secure the islands.

3. Details of the operation. (Omitted) [*Ugaki's omission.*]

4. This operation is designated Operation *Ten* No. 1 and I will give its warning and activation in accordance with the procedure taken at the time of Operation Sho.

Combined Fleet Telegram Order No. 564-B:

The air operations against the enemy task force for the time being until the coming of the enemy invasion force will be carried out in accordance with the following:

1. In case the enemy task force attacks the Kanto area, positive operations will be avoided to preserve strength.

2. In case of its attack on the Kyushu area, strength will be preserved in accordance with the above. However, when it becomes certain that the enemy will invade the Southwest Islands, positive operations will be adopted to destroy the enemy attempt by all means. (Details of the operations in this case are shown in Combined Fleet Telegram Order No. 564-A.)

3. Each air force commander will promptly make efforts to disperse its whole strength in order to maintain its fighting strength.

However, those strengths of the First Land-based Air Task Force, i.e., Fifth Air Fleet, deployed in the Kyushu area, will continue operations against enemy task forces as before, based upon the said operational policy, until the new deployment is completed.

Decoding the above two operational orders had been completed at about 0355 on the 18th. Until then, our understanding, related by telephone exchanges, was "try to preserve strength, but in case your commander deems it impossible to do so in light of the progress in readying the Fifth Air Fleet's rear bases, act at your discretion."

So I had to put in yesterday's fleet order that "in case of an enemy task force attack not accompanying its invasion force, we may preserve our strength, except for interceptions by a part of the fighter strength." As the high command in Tokyo remained indecisive, I took pains in making preparations and also could not issue a clear order to prepare attacks.

At 1530 I ordered "Stand by for First Attack Method." But the situation of our forces was such that they had almost completely dispersed to rear bases in northern Kyushu and Shikoku, so most of them had to make night flights to advance to their designated operational bases. So, in both skill and readiness they were unfit to encounter an enemy task force.

Moreover, enemy attacks by four groups would be so relentless that we wouldn't be able to preserve our strength even if we tried to do so. I couldn't stand to see them destroyed on the ground. Besides, who could dare say it wasn't a preliminary step for an invasion of the Southwest Islands? After careful contemplation, and taking full responsibility for the outcome, at 0205 I decided to launch an encountering attack with full strength and ordered activation of the First Attack Method.

In compliance with this order, the night attack force, heavy bombers, *Tenzans,* and *Gingas* took off at 0350. After 0600 a daylight special attack force consisting of *Suiseis* and bomb-equipped fighters took off generally as planned.

In the meantime, at 0420 enemy aircraft in small numbers appeared near Toizaki. They seemed to be guiding follow-up planes by dropping parachute flares. So we greatly feared enemy attacks at the time of our planes' early takeoff. But fortunately they didn't come to Kokubu base, so all of them could take off safely except one heavy bomber and three *Tenzans* which were ambushed and shot down. From 0540 to 0950 enemy planes continued to come to attack, and their number counted in Kyushu reached 375. However, their raids appeared to be rather inactive and irregular in the beginning, which made us feel that such was caused by our night attacks.

[*These particular night attacks had been small and unsuccessful.*][36]

Summing up reports of ten *Saiuns* sent out early in the morning, at about 0650 it was learned that the enemy consisted of four groups, each including four, three, three, and five carriers, respectively. A carrier in the fourth group was seen on fire. This apparently pointed to a successful night attack.

[*Ugaki's planes, of which he lost fifty, hit Task Group 58.4 some seventy-five miles south of Shikoku. A dud hit and slightly damaged* Enterprise, *a* kamikaze *damaged* Intrepid *slightly, and a bomb damaged* Yorktown *more seriously.*][37]

As the number of reports of "I am going to ram a carrier" increased in the afternoon, the number of enemy attack planes decreased. So I decided to carry out an attack at dusk and issued an order accordingly. However, as I apprehended, the wiring communication system on the ground had been disrupted since the enemy's first wave attack, so liaison between each base could scarcely be maintained. Moreover, each base was subjected to several enemy attacks, which made it impossible for us to launch a dusk attack. So I shifted to a night attack instead.

Thinking it time for the *Shinrai* Special Attack Unit to be employed, I ordered its preparation. But they couldn't be readied in time since their bases were so dispersed that my order failed to reach those bases in time, and also the enemy commanded the air over our bases.

In preparation for night and dawn attacks, I ordered a night search with five flying boats.

As I heard that some damage had been inflicted on hangars of the Kyushu Air Group and the Aeronautical Depot, I went to the airfield to inspect them in the afternoon, when another air raid alert was given. I went into a shelter of the said air group and experienced an enemy air raid nearly overhead after a long time—since October last. In a shelter on the ground, without fear of sinking, there was nothing to worry about except the damn noise.

[*Because Ugaki had sent his planes out to seek the U.S. carriers, aircraft from the latter encountered little opposition and concentrated on hangars, barracks, and inland airfields.*]³⁸

Monday, 19 March 1945. Cloudy, later rain. From about 2300 our night search plane succeeded in finding an enemy force and saw a column of flame, two ships on fire, and one explosion at 0010 and 0530, but details were unknown as nothing has been heard from the attack force.

[*Early in the morning of 19 March, Japanese attacked Task Group 58.2. Wasp was seriously damaged, with heavy casualties, but continued to operate for several days before retiring for repairs. Two bombs hit* Franklin, *damaging her so badly that she was out of the war for the duration. That same morning Task Force 58 hit shipping in the Inland Sea. An aircraft from* Enterprise *hit* Yamato *with minor results.*]³⁹

As the enemy position gradually moved up north, it was judged that it intended to attack Chugoku and Shikoku.

Though we mostly planned on launching daytime attacks in the face of enemy resistance today, the enemy hadn't come to attack here by 1630, which enabled us to carry out a flank attack in comparative ease. Seeing that the enemy attack strength was greatly reduced in the afternoon, I ordered our forces "to attack with all strength, as the result of the attack is telling." But the weather gradually worsened so that it became impossible to launch either the attack force or the night reconnaissance planes.

It was learned that the enemy, 110 miles southeast of Toizaki early yesterday morning, approached as near as thirty to forty miles south of Ashizuri-Misaki at 1400, then sailed east at night and was located deploying from forty miles south of Muroto-Misaki to 110 miles south-southwest of the said cape on the morning of the 19th, dividing into four groups, each including three, two, two, and four carriers.

Listening to the claims of attacks, it looked like we had inflicted heavy damage on the enemy, but the fact wasn't so. Each time a search was made, I wondered why so many remained if the claimed result of attacks were true.

The situation of our planes hasn't been known since this morning. As they were dispersed at rear bases after the attacks, I felt uneasy about continuing attacks. So I ordered them to get back quickly to their original or operational bases, where every effort would be made to fix planes for the next operation. But their movements were awfully slow, and the number of aircraft available for an immediate operation was greatly reduced.

Although I myself worked hard, even doing the business of the chief of staff and the senior staff officer throughout the night, most of my staff officers appeared to be greatly exhausted. Pointing to the above-mentioned situation of our forces, they asked me to issue an order calling for suspension of offensive attacks and regrouping the strength preparing for the next enemy offensive, while planes were preserved in the second preparatory condition.

We had been reduced to such a miserable situation after only two days of fighting. It was extremely deplorable indeed, but I had no choice but to agree with them, as it would have been asking the impossible if I insisted on fighting when they said they couldn't do so.

After this order was issued at 1820, however, Air Group Commander [Captain Tatsuhiko] Kida at Kokubu base asked me the reason behind the said order, since he was making every possible effort to get about twenty *Suiseis* readied for another attack. Thinking it a very reasonable suggestion, I immediately called off the said order and instead, with a high mood, issued an order to pursue.

My staff officers said they thought this operation would be a failure, according to the common rule of air warfare, as it didn't work out well in its initial state. But I told them that tenacious guerrilla tactics should be repeated when fighting with inferior strength. Wasn't it a common purpose of war to attempt an attack with even one plane, hoping to further the result already achieved?

When the vice chief of staff came here later, it was learned that discussions were held at Tokyo with regard to the wisdom of ordering a suspension of attacks, as the Fifth Air Fleet would do too much and lose lock, stock, and barrel, thus leaving nothing to fight with when an enemy invasion actually began. But he urged them not to interfere with this fleet, telling them an instruction couldn't stop us once we actually started attacks.

I think not only those responsible persons in Tokyo but also in the operational forces should be more thoroughly acquainted with the art of war. When one wavers at a decision, one can't go far wrong if he sticks to the principles of war and acts according to historical lessons.

Tuesday, 20 March 1945. As we couldn't launch night search aircraft, the enemy movement wasn't known, and we feared that they might move east to make further attacks. But a small number of enemy planes appeared on the east coast of Kyushu from 0240 to 0509, indicating that they were still operating in the same place. So we took precautions against another enemy attack.

A dawn search of *Saiun* revealed that an enemy sailing south at a point about 120 miles east of Toizaki at 1030 consisted of three groups, each including six, four, and one carriers. It was also learned through the Combined Fleet that so far no air raids were made today. It seems that the enemy has given up another attack due to foul weather.

An all-out pursuit with the 701st Air Group made up of *Suiseis* as the main force was carried out today.

Special Attack Units approached an enemy from north and south, making detours, and made hits amidship an *Essex* type carrier, causing a big explosion, and set a *Saratoga* type on fire, both of which were considered sunk for certain. Besides, another hit the bridge of a carrier, causing a big fire.

[*On 20 March,* kamikaze *crashes damaged destroyer* Halsey Powell. Enterprise *escaped with two near bomb misses only to suffer severe damage and some casualties from U.S. guns when other ships, trying to knock down one of the bombers, aimed too low. Later in the day a Japanese bomb struck the port bow, inflicting minor damage.*][40]

Some skilled *Suisei* pilots, regretting that the result of their attacks could not be confirmed, made a low altitude bombing and confirmed their attacks amidship of an enemy vessel. After returning to a base, they immediately reloaded bombs and started out on another attack. With skilled pilots, this method is more economical and effective. However, if we applied this in general, we wouldn't be able to expect a sure hit. This is a very difficult point with which to cope. I believe, however, we still must place more importance on the spirit of the special attack.

Seeing the noticeable result being achieved, I encouraged them to repeat more fierce attacks, but only a small number of heavy bombers, *Gingas,* and *Tenzans* were available so achieved few results.

My words of praise for the *Suisei* Unit's deed happened to dissatisfy a certain air group commander who said he would be forced to commit *hara kiri* as he couldn't stand as a commander not to share in [the recognition of] his subordinates' meritorious services. Though I could see he was sincere, I just laughed it off, saying that if he could commit *hara kiri* for such a thing as that, he had better go ahead and do it.

Following three-stage searches, four land-based bombers picked up four enemy groups heading south at night and kept shadowing them. As they were heading southwest, I ordered the Southwest Islands area alerted tomorrow. At the same time, in the light of their speed being 10 to 12 knots, there would be a good chance of launching a *Shinrai* attack using so-called *Oka* bombs, so I ordered preparations for it.

Wednesday, 21 March 1945. Fair. Early in the morning twenty *Tenzans* and *Gingas* carried out a search and attack. In the eastern area they succeeded in torpedoing a cruiser, while two others reported they had charged but the result was unknown.

As a result of the early search, two groups of carriers were sighted at a point 320 miles bearing 145° of Toizaki. They seemed to have received considerable damage, so not many interceptors were over them. Besides, the weather was fine with visibility of thirty miles.

[*Probably* Franklin *and her escorts. Spruance had ordered Task Force 58 to stay near the stricken carrier through the 19th and 20th.*][41]

Though the distance was a little bit far, it couldn't be a big problem to the *Shinrai* Unit. Since the 18th, I have sought a chance to make use of this special attack weapon, intending to prove its usefulness by any means. If we missed a chance which presented itself right before us, we'd be forced to attempt another one-way attack upon Ulithi, which has little prospect of success. Making up my mind that we had better launch a *Shinrai* attack right now, I ordered the *Oka* Unit to wait in readiness to carry out an attack.

I went to the airfield to see them off and cheered up Captain Okamura who naturally looked worried. The *Shinrai* Force consisting of eighteen land-based bombers, of which sixteen carried so-called *Oka* bombs, took to the air at 1135. A white headband worn by an *Oka* Special Attack Unit member in a plane taking off struck my eyes. I prayed for their success.

However, the escort fighters which ought to have been fifty-five couldn't be more than thirty due to incomplete preparedness. On the other hand, the subsequent search revealed that three enemy groups, each including three, two, and two carriers, respectively, had joined and sailed to the southwest. Their strength was more than we thought at first. There was also a report of their attacking Minami-Daitojima.

In the underground operations room, I impatiently waited for news of sighting the enemy and launching *Oka* bombs, but nothing was heard at all. Being afraid of their running short of fuel, I ordered them "to go to Minami-Daitojima if the enemy isn't sighted." And yet no reply was received. In the meantime, some of the escort fighters returned and brought back a tragic report with them.

According to it, at about 1420 some fifty Grummans encountered them at a point fifty to sixty miles short of the estimated enemy position. Though only a few of them were shot down in the ensuing dogfight, they were scattered. The land-based bombers jettisoned *Okas* but all of them were knocked down in only a little over ten minutes. What a tragedy!

[*The weight of the* Okas *slowed down the bombers so that they fell easy prey to U.S. fighters.*]⁴²

With this ended our battle against the enemy task force operating to the east of Kyushu which had lasted for the past few days. Total battle results achieved:

1. Confirmed by the crews: five carriers, two battleships, one heavy cruiser, two cruisers, and one unidentified ship sunk.

2. Remaining enemy strength witnessed by the reconnaissance on 21 March: seven carriers, of which one was a converted one, eight battleships, thirteen cruisers, and thirty-three destroyers, with a total of sixty-one vessels.

In view of the above and also the fact that many reported "I am going to ram a carrier" in the daytime special attack, I little doubted that at least eight enemy carriers were either sunk or dropped out, and, besides, more damage must have been inflicted than what was confirmed.

[*Ugaki's estimate of U.S. losses in this battle was highly exaggerated. Combined Fleet Headquarters cut the estimate to four U.S. ships sunk, while the Naval General Staff was satisfied with a count of two.*]⁴³

The number of planes used in the operation: 193 planes for attacks and 53 planes for reconnaissance.

Our losses: 161 planes.

Summing up the above, I believe we scored a good mark in this operation. Especially, if the enemy did come to attack as a preliminary to an invasion of the Southwest Islands, of course it should be encountered, and I was glad I did my duty. I was grateful for the hardships my subordinates had endured for days of continuous fighting, and I expressed my deep condolence to the many loyal officers and men killed in action.

As I returned to the shack on the hill after four days of hard fighting, spring was everywhere, and fatigue from the battle disappeared immediately. Nature's great progress in a few days' time seemed to laugh pityingly at the silly little human world, where we were making a fuss about war and enemy task forces and so on.

[As usual, the beauties of nature inspired Ugaki to write a few two-lined poems.

[On Thursday, 22 March, eighteen officers from Tokyo arrived to study battle lessons. Ugaki learned nothing new but hoped that the lessons learned would influence future operations. He noted that the end had come at Iwo Jima. "I express my gratitude for the efforts of Lieutenant General [Tadamichi] Kuribayashi and other officers and men."

[Friday, 23 March, saw the continuation of the study session at Kyushu Air Group. This time all expressed their views. Ugaki ended the session with a brief speech in which he outlined the conditions under which the attack was made, with "fairly successful" results. As battle lessons he noted that matters do not turn out as planned in war; they must have a flexible policy. As battles tended to "last longer than expected," he asked for "the completion of ground installation at all bases and making efforts to restrict damage, as well as the maintenance of planes and weapons." Enemy aircraft being "hard to find," he asked for further efforts in search and shadowing as well as particular care in reporting battle results.

[After lunch they retired to "a barracks on a hill" where they discussed "regrouping of the force and other matters." He invited officers of captain and above to a sukiyaki party at the Navy Club, so the conference broke up in "high spirits."]

One B-29 came here twice today to reconnoiter this area while enemy carrier planes attacked Okinawa and Daitojima this morning. Thought the total number of enemy aircraft that attack there in the morning and afternoon was less than one hundred, an enemy group consisting of eight battleships and more than twenty destroyers was sighted at a point fifty miles southeast of Okinawa. [*Eight battleships plus one heavy cruiser (Spruance's flagship* Indianapolis) *and ten destroyers bombed Okinawa's southeast coast to cover minesweeping operations.*]⁴⁴ A *Suisei* sent from Okinawa and a *Saiun* from here sighted another group with two to three carriers at a point about seventy miles farther from the above. Whether it was the same task force as last time still continuing operations or another one which had come up north from the Philippines, we couldn't tell at this stage, but we should pay close attention to its attempt.

[*This second sighting was probably part of Task Group 51.1, Western Islands Attack Group under Rear Admiral I. N. Kiland, headed for Kerama Retto with CVEs* Marcus Island, Savo Island, *and* Anzio.⁴⁵

[On Saturday Vice Chief of the Naval General Staff Ozawa visited Ugaki briefly before leaving for Tokyo by way of a conference at Matsuyama. It having been decided that the post of commander, Kyushu Air

Group, merited a flag officer, Rear Admiral Kamenosuke Yamamori arrived to take over.]

Since early this morning, enemy battleship groups at Okinawa have bombarded the southern tip of the island, and enemy attack planes increased in number from yesterday. With signs of an enemy invasion of that island thus intensified, I ordered the fleet to make thorough preparations.

I also ordered fifteen *Tenzans* to make torpedo attacks with Kikaigashima as a stepping spot. Seven of them seemed to participate, but only two fired torpedoes against a battleship and cruiser with no result.

[Ugaki's command received a citation from the Combined Fleet. Ugaki thought it was rather more than they deserved, but he was pleased for the sake of his subordinates.]

Sunday, 25 March 1945. Fair. Enemy air raids and bombardments in Okinawa were fierce today, too. Moreover, the enemy started minesweeping operations off Naha and other places, while there was also a report of their commencing a landing on Kerama Island fifteen miles off the main island.

[*The Americans wanted Kerama Retto, a small group of islands west of southern Okinawa, as a fuel and ammunition replenishing depot.*]46

The Combined Fleet accordingly alerted its forces for *Ten* No. 1 Operation. With this order, those forces now stationed west of Suzuka in the central part of the homeland and in operational condition were placed under my command, but they couldn't be available for immediate use.

With the forecast that the weather would be fine until tomorrow night, then would worsen, I ordered a general offensive of this force to be carried out tomorrow night. The Combined Fleet also issued a special order for this attempt.

Monday, 26 March 1945. Fair. Enemy bombings and bombardments on the Southwest Islands were intensified, while twelve transports were at Kerama Island. It has become apparent that the enemy is going to use that island at a landing base. Today the Combined Fleet activated *Ten* No. 1 Operation whereby the whole forces were ordered to engage in the decisive battle. With this order, the Third Air Fleet also came under my command, but they, too, weren't well trained, so I wasn't reassured.

Chief of Staff Third Air Fleet Yamazumi and Assistant Chief of Staff Sixth Army Aoki came down here. Engineer Inspector General Major General [Zenshiro] Yoshioka and a few others also came to visit me.

It seemed that the *Tenzan* unit attack of last night succeeded in hitting two enemy battleships. We started operations with the daytime search from today, but only a few *Saiuns* were left for use, so they developed troubles one after another. So things didn't go well.

Some enemies stuck to Kerama, but they were dispersed in various places. The army claimed that their heavy bombers carried out the first night attack, getting three cruisers.

[*Only two U.S. ships were damaged on 26 March 1945. Fire support destroyer* Halligan *struck a mine and had be abandoned. A kamikaze hit destroyer* Kimberly, *killing four men and wounding fifty-seven, but the destroyer continued to operate.*][47]

We were favored by a moon of the 14th lunar night, but the weather will worsen after tonight.

Tuesday, 27 March 1945. Cloudy, later rain. The rain came as I predicted. Though I thought our attack of last night was timely, the selection of targets in the *Gingas* and *Suiseis* attacks wasn't proper due to insufficient daytime searches yesterday and also untimely night searches. Regrettable, on account of this we couldn't gain a big result except hits on a cruiser and battleship. An eight-hundred-kilogram bomb hit on the latter was confirmed, while we lost seventeen planes altogether.

On the other hand, ten army special attack planes of the Eighth Air Division were said to have struck the enemy at Kerama after advancing to Okinawa from Ishigakishima, and confirmed their hits on targets.

[*On 27 March a kamikaze crashed on* Nevada *and another hit light cruiser* Biloxi. *Destroyer* O'Brien *was severely damaged, destroyer minelayer* Dorsey *slightly.*][48]

In spite of that, one regular carrier and eight converted ones most probably sortied from Ulithi on the 24th; we have so far failed to reduce enemy carriers directly and only destroyed minor targets, against which we should be strictly warned.

Forces of the Third Air Fleet joined us, but they couldn't be depended upon. While leaving to army special attack forces and the like such an easy target as fixed enemy strength, we, the pick of our whole forces, should exclusively aim at attacking enemy task force carriers. Consistent guerrilla warfare tactics are still worth advocating, but I think we may have to suspend attacks temporarily since it's awfully difficult to catch enemy carriers when sufficient searches can't be made. As the young men are apt to be impatient, I called their attention to this point as an important matter.

In view of the last attack of the enemy task force and also consistent attacks on the Southwest Islands, we anticipated their B-29 strike on our air bases in Kyushu. At 1100 today they made a large-scale attack on northern Kyushu and inflicted damage to base facilities at Oita and Tachiarai and other places, especially at Tachiarai where fifty fighter trainers and six planes of a torpedo bomber squadron were destroyed. The army seems completely defenseless in protecting aircraft on the ground. In view of the above, I further warned my command.

[*This B-29 raid and another on 31 March resulted in heavy damage to major air bases and industrial installations. The strategically vital Shimonoseki Strait was mined and made dangerous to traffic.*][49]

Based upon a Combined Fleet order, the First Attack Force is going to leave the Inland Sea at noon tomorrow and head for Sasebo. Its object of stimulating the destruction of enemy remnants can be somewhat appreciated, but its favorite trick of trying to lure the enemy task force out by sailing south off the east of Kyushu so as to let the First Attack Force hit the enemy task force is laughable.

[Ugaki reflected that such tactics had failed in the Biak and Leyte campaigns. Now the enemy was far too strong to be "tempted or lured by our tricks. When we thought they bit the bait, it was only a coincidence." Therefore, and in view of the scarcity of fuel, Ugaki thought the First Attack Force had better stay where it was. But the order had been issued, so he had to make the best of it.

[That night the vice chief of staff, Combined Fleet, stayed with Ugaki, and a number of officers came to report.]

Wednesday, 28 March 1945. Fair. Hoping to destroy the enemy task force by a night attack following tomorrow's overall search, I issued the necessary orders. From about 1630, however, enemy carrier planes came to attack here and the Amakusa district. Altogether there were 120 Grummans equipped with additional fuel tanks. They strafed base installations but inflicted little damage. Though a way to attack them following a night search was not lacking, we overlooked it, hoping for tomorrow's full-fledged activities. They withdrew in the direction of south to south-southwest.

Commander in Chief Third Air Fleet Vice Admiral Teraoka came here accompanying his staff officers. We two classmates will fight hand in hand.

Thursday, 29 March 1945. Fair. We were prepared for enemy attacks in the early morning, and as expected their fighters came to strike various places at 0630. This time they weren't equipped with additional tanks, but some of them were equipped with bombs. Altogether there were about 150 each in the morning and afternoon. A lookout at Tanegashima sighted two carriers. Those staff officers who since yesterday had advocated the wisdom of attacking an enemy at a long distance now faced the real fact.

And yet some tended to stick to tonight's original plan. The nearest enemy was the very cream of his carrier strength. What else should we go far to get? What the enemy intended would be to command the air over us, thus preventing our attacks against the Southwest Islands. Because of their strikes, forces of the Third Air Fleet stationed in Kyushu were greatly scattered and our subsequent attacks disturbed. Stressing the need of destroying the enemy first, I asked them to change their thinking.

As a *Saiun* search discovered an enemy group including more than one carrier and another one with two carriers to the south of Tanegashima, a daytime special attack force composed of four *Suiseis* was dispatched. Two of them sent back word of ramming enemy carriers. In view of the fact that two or three slicks of oil were sighted by subsequent reconnaissance, apparently they inflicted pretty heavy damage to the enemy, though details of the attack couldn't be confirmed.

[*The kamikaze attacks of 28 March were ineffective. The only ship casualty that day was the minesweeper* Skylark, *which struck two mines and sank.*]⁵⁰

After 1430 we broke off contact with the enemy, so no enemy information has been available since then. Then a flying boat sent from Takumi base on a night search mission picked up an enemy group at a point eighty miles south of Ashizuri-Misaki and since then has kept contact with it. As the enemy gradually came up north, our night torpedo bombers were sent out. No enemy was picked up in searching the southern part, so our forces concentrated to destroy this enemy.

An element of the enemy task force came up north of its own accord, not being lured by a movement of the First Attack Force. So the Combined Fleet suspended movement of the First Attack Force until further orders. This was a reasonable step.

A destroyer accompanying the First Attack Force hit a magnetic mine (?) supposed to have been laid by B-29s the day before yesterday at a point near Himejima and became unable to maneuver. Moreover, the same force erroneously shot down two fighters of the 343rd Air Group at Matsuyama which were flying on the interception mission. Strict caution should be maintained.

[*The 343rd Air Corps, located at Matsuyama air base in Shikoku, was considered the Japanese Navy's crack fighter plane unit. Its commander was Captain Minoru Genda, who had formulated the tactical plan for the Pearl Harbor attack.*]⁵¹

An enemy invasion convoy bound northward entered Kerama last night. It consisted of forty transports and more than thirty landing craft. Several converted carriers with battleships and others were still operating in the vicinity of Okinawa Island and repeating bombardments, but they were engaging in preliminary movements without a landing on the main island yet. The reason why they made no all-out air raid today was believed to be that enemy carriers couldn't operate fully as desired.

A confirmed information sent from the Intelligence Bureau of the General Staff informed that those enemy forces which attacked the Kyushu area last time consisted of ten CVs and six CVLs converted from cruisers in addition to two 27,000-ton supercruisers, *Alaska* and *Guam*. If so, it seems that we sank nine of them after all.

Upon discovery of the enemy invasion convoy, the Combined Fleet ordered the Sixth Air Army to attack it with all its strength, and at last that army's activity seems to have gotten on the right track.

["Being furious at the enemy's insulting attitude," Ugaki spent all night Friday, 30 March, in the underground operations room, "hoping this time to destroy all of the enemy by all means." For the guidance of his staff, he wrote a notice to be hung on the wall of the operations room: "Foresight and close inspection; careful and minute planning and daring decision." These, he thought, were the essentials in directing operations. He noted that the younger staff officers tended to "judge things hastily to their own advantage" and had been trying to correct this fault.]

As enemy fighters attacked a shadowing flying boat in visual contact with the enemy, I hoped for success in our attack, fully relying on it. But God seemingly blessed the enemy. It grew foggy after midnight and only two units ordering "Charge" were heard over the radio.

Fog developed to the north from Kanoya and finally covered half of Kyushu, so my staff officers took pains in giving instruction to the returning planes. Even what might be supposed to be an enemy deceiving track was picked up on radar, but in view of the fact that a torpedo bomber unit sighted two carriers with no bridge and ten cruisers and destroyers at a point seventy miles bearing 90° of Miyazaki at 0200 with the help of flares dropped by army heavy bombers, it wasn't necessarily a mere illusion.

Though our early morning search failed to locate any enemy, it was certain that two or three enemy fighter groups approached Tanegashima and the south coast of Kyushu, and they seem to have failed to close in further on account of fog. I couldn't help but conclude that they gave up their attempt because of our daytime special attacks and torpedoing at night and withdrew taking advantage of fog. A regret at missing the enemy still remained in my mind when the fog cleared up at about 0700.

> Heavy fog clears up at last, revealing nothing.
> Regret still remains for the daydream in the spring.

The Combined Fleet's judgment of the current situation was telephoned to us, saying that our special attacks had stalemated the situation, but the enemy would launch its landing attempt in two or three days.

[Ugaki emerged from his dugout to find spring "in full swing outside."

After supper he took a walk, and a petty officer proudly showed him evidence of enemy attack and told him he and his machine-gun crew had shot down two U.S. aircraft.]

Saturday, 31 March 1945. Fair. As there was fear of the enemy coming up north, searches were ordered. But nothing was found, as I thought. A reconnaissance plane to cover Okinawa failed to return. They must have learned the necessity of hurrying up fixing *Saiuns* and carrying out reconnaissance with the backing of an attack. The enemy captured Tamiyama-jima today and landed tanks there. Our garrison is going to charge into the enemy tonight.

As many enemy transports swarmed in the sea around the main island of Okinawa and it became apparent that the enemy would attempt a landing tonight, I ordered an all-out attack with the whole strength except those saved for the enemy task force.

In the morning several formations of B-29s approached here from the south and went up to northern Kyushu. So a tête-à-tête with Vice Admiral Teraoka was interrupted and we had to go into the shelter. Staff officers of the Fifth and Third air fleets held a good talk on coming operations today and decided to merge into one body so as to carry out operations forcefully. We had a sukiyaki dinner together and were all in high spirits. I sent off March, regretting the speedy process of spring.

II

Pressed Beneath the Pole Star

April–May 1945

IF ONE WORD *could summarize
these months of Ugaki's life, that word would be "frustration." Here was an
intelligent, aggressive admiral, sparked by a burning love of country, entrusted
with the major remaining force of the Japanese Navy, and it was not enough.*

The last voyage of Yamato *typified the desperation of the period.* Yamato,
along with light cruiser Yahagi *and six destroyers, was formed into a Surface
Special Attack (i.e., suicide) Force and sent to Okinawa with the purpose of
running the battleship aground to turn herself into a fortress, her huge guns
sinking American troopships. But this force had scarcely put to sea when two U.S.
submarines spotted it and reported the sortie. Almost all of Task Force 58
"swooped down on them." Two destroyers were all that remained usable. Ugaki
grieved for* Yamato, *on which he had served so long.*

*The usual exaggerated claims of sinkings and damages buoyed him up
throughout much of this period. His kamikazes, in fact, did inflict considerable
damage and loss of life, but most of it was concentrated on destroyers and smaller
craft. Possibly the prime exploit of the period was the crashing of CVs* Bunker
Hill *and* Enterprise. *They did not sink, but were out of the war.*

*Political developments perforce attracted Ugaki's attention. The Koiso cabinet
resigned, and the premiership fell to Admiral Kantaro Suzuki, president of the
Privy Council, who enjoyed the emperor's trust and confidence. The Suzuki
cabinet was top-heavy with admirals, and Ugaki observed sardonically that the
navy, being without ships, was going to fight by means of the cabinet.*

*President Roosevelt died, and Ugaki fancifully attributed his death to Japan's
No. 1 Ten Operation. Mussolini was captured and killed; the Red Army entered
Berlin; the USSR announced that it would abrogate the Japanese-Soviet Neu-
trality Treaty; Hitler met his end and Germany surrendered.*

*An extremely inaccurate report from the Thirty-second Army on Okinawa
sent Ugaki's spirits bounding upward and caused Combined Fleet Headquarters to estimate Japan's chances of victory as fifty-fifty. This euphoria did not last
long. "Every day we try to finish the enemy task force, and yet they can't be
finished." By 22 April, Combined Fleet orders made clear that only guerrilla air*

567

warfare would be possible. As April blended into May, Ugaki noted wistfully that spring would come again, but he feared the same could not be said for "a chance to recover the war situation."

B-29 and/or B-25 raids were almost continuous, while a combination of bad weather and poor reconnaissance hampered Ugaki's Fifth Air Fleet and caused the admiral increasing impatience. One pleasure came to him in May: The army provided his headquarters with three horses. Ugaki became very attached to his mount, and henceforth horseback rides gave him the exercise and relaxation he had formerly found in hunting.

Sunday, 1 April 1945. Fair. At 0700 this morning the enemy started landing on the west coast south of the north and central airfields. By evening the whole beach area had fallen with amazing swiftness. The airfields will soon be in use. The defending army might say that it had an original plan to draw the enemy nearer but, even so, it was too vulnerable. [*The Americans were astounded at the lack of opposition. As Ugaki hinted, the army commander at Okinawa, Lieutenant General M. Ushijima, had moved most of his some 100,000 troops inland with the purpose of "luring" the invaders into positions beyond air and naval cover where they could be "wiped out."*][1] The enemy also made a simultaneous landing at Minatogawa on the southeast coast and brought up fairly big invasion forces off the coast, but this must have been a diversion as they withdrew later. A small party also landed at Kumejima. It is getting quite busy. The whole strength of the enemy seems to be three divisions.

The number of *Saiuns* available for immediate use was only one-third of the original strength. On this pitiable occasion, the Western Army sent in word that at 1000 an Army Headquarters liaison plane sighted an enemy task force including carriers at a point fifty miles southeast of Okinawa. Based on this information, I ordered it attacked from daylight to dusk. But the report turned out to be false, so I suspended the attack at 1500 because I thought our target should be enemy task forces.

However, a *Saiun* that left late sighted an enemy task force including four CVs and four CVLs at a point about fifty miles south of Amamio-shima, but couldn't keep contact with it due to engine trouble, and put about. As the distance was about 250 miles, I thought an attack quite possible even if they stayed in the area and ordered "Stand by for First Attack Method" at about 1700.

The night search planes couldn't depart as usual before 2200 due to the difficult balance between the preservation policy and the necessity for quick dispatch and also to a fear that their departure in daytime would subject them to enemy fighter attacks. Some were delayed further, and several hours passed between sighting the enemy to the time of the second search. Because of this, we couldn't learn at all whether the enemy still stayed there or advanced and withdrew. So we could only await the search planes' reports. Depending on the enemy movements, we could expect some hopeful results, taking advantage of the moon of the 18th lunar night. We're eagerly looking forward to a report of finding the enemy.

Though we carried out attacks with torpedo bombers and six *Oka* special attack planes last night, no news has been learned about them. So I was all the more pleased when reports of their fair success started to come in during the evening. Nothing is more unpleasant and more uneasy for directing operations than having no knowledge of what happened.

[*On neither 31 March nor 1 April did Ugaki mention what was almost a prime kamikaze feat. At 0710 on 31 March one crashed* Indianapolis, *Spruance's flagship, causing considerable damage, killing nine men and wounding twenty. The admiral and his staff were unharmed, but when by 5 April it became apparent that* Indianapolis *would require further repairs, he transfered his flag to battleship* New Mexico.

[*In addition, on 1 April kamikazes damaged* West Virginia *slightly and transport* Hinsdale *so badly that she was out of the war. Another crashed* LST 884, *killing twenty-four and wounding twenty-one sailors and marines. At 1910, at dusk, a kamikaze struck transport* Alpine, *damaging her and inflicting forty-three casualties. Around midnight both a kamikaze and bombs struck transport* Achernar, *with forty-five casualties.*]²

Monday, 2 April 1945. Fair, foggy in the morning. A flying boat of the night search planes sent to the east of Toizaki reported sighting an enemy nearby at about 2300. As its position was almost the same spot where the radar at Toizaki had detected a mysterious reflection since about 2100, this was considered to be an enemy submarine's deception. Furthermore, a land-based bomber reported detection of a large enemy force at a point about 150 miles to the southeast of the cape at 0100. There was a good possibility of the enemy reaching that position if it sailed north from the point it was discovered in the daytime. So, though it involved a good deal of uncertainty, I ordered First Attack Method activated, taking the time element into consideration.

But we didn't catch the enemy after that. In the meantime, another search plane seemingly with confidence reported sighting a carrier and a battleship very near to the south of Kikaigashima, so I sent torpedo bombers against them. But when it became foggy again, the planes returned without finding the enemy. It was most unpleasant to be fooled all through the night. Enemy deception might be its cause, but the cases were too many for that. Some of them might be traced to defects in using the plane's radar.

On top of this, reports of being pursued by enemy fighters aways save us cause to suspect the existence of carriers nearby. There was a great need to study these points. From the standpoint of common sense, I thought it improbable to see an enemy to the south of Kikaigashima, and it was later found to be another case of mistaking an island for an enemy. I felt quite irritable in the morning after all these things. We held a conference in the morning and decided to carry out night torpedo attacks and special attacks against the enemy around Okinawa in order to induce the enemy task force to come up north so that we may damage it.

Judging from communications exchanged, the special attack carried out in the evening with fighter bombers seemed to be mostly successful.

[*At 1836 on 2 April transports which had reembarked soldiers of the Seventy-seventh Division at Kerama Retto were heading south when about ten ka-mikazes attacked. Destroyer transport* Dickerson *had to be scuttled. Transports* Goodhue *and* Telfair *were damaged with combined casualties of 25 killed and 135 wounded.* Henrico, *flagship of Transdiv 50, was knocked out of the war. Among those killed aboard her were Captain Elmer Kiehl, in command of Transdiv 50, and Colonel Vincent Tanzola, commanding officer, 305th Infantry Regiment.*][3]

Chief of Staff Combined Fleet Kusaka came down here with Major General [Kazuo] Tanikawa, its vice chief of staff. [*In the later stages of the war, it was not unknown for army officers to serve with the navy.*] Commander in Chief Tenth Air Fleet Vice Admiral [Minoru] Maeda, who had been placed under my command from 1 April, came here accompanying his chief of staff, [Rear Admiral Chikao] Yamamoto and other staff officers. Heads were well arrayed but planes and skilled fliers weren't.

Tuesday, 3 April 1945. Fair, later cloudy. The result of last night's attack was fairly good, and I think we should adopt this method from now on. In the morning we had a conference including staff officers of the Combined Fleet and Naval General Staff mostly on the land warfare at Okinawa.

Incidentally, a request to intensify air attacks was sent in from the Naval General Staff. The Thirty-second Army's operational policy has been to construct strongholds in the southern part of the island, abandoning the north and central airstrips, and in fact this resulted in the enemy occupying those areas within a day. And now they want to issue a Naval General Staff instruction or order calling for a vigorous counterattack by the Thirty-second Army to nullify the enemy's use of those airstrips. But shifting troops isn't so simple, and I'm afraid it most probably will result in failure. It has become more essential then before to reduce the enemy by air attacks within a week from now. The enemy reinforcement convoy coming from Leyte has already arrived in the vicinity of Okinawa, while it's said more reinforcements will come from the south.

Today's reconnaissance sighted an enemy force including four CVs at a point eighty miles south of Okinawa, while another one, seemingly including carriers, was seen at a point forty miles south of Amamioshima. So we had eight *Gingas* separately attack this force while sending thirty fighters south as a diversion movement. Half of them succeeded in ramming enemies, while the fighters fought dogfights with twenty-seven enemy fighters in the air over Kikaigashima, suffering some losses. They returned to bases after sunset.

[*In the kamikaze attacks of 3 April, LST 599 was knocked out of the war. Destroyer* Prichett, *on radar picket duty, was slightly damaged. CVE* Wake Island *had a hole blown in her side and had to retire to Guam for repairs.*]+

The outline order of the *Kikusui* No. 1 Operation aiming to attack enemy convoys and task forces with all strength was issued. [Kikusui *(floating chrysanthemums) was the crest of a famous samurai, Kusunoke Masashige.*]

[Ugaki rose early on Wednesday, 4 April, and went hunting, bagging a pigeon. Table maneuvers for *Kikusui* No. 1 were held later. Ugaki noted that this operation would require "the utmost care," as it was an all-out gamble and could not be repeated.]

The Combined Fleet ordered attacks on enemy convoys by carrying out a great air battle. Its content was identical with that of our planning, but it was said that its real aim was to spur the Sixth Air Army and Tenth Air Fleet into more activity. As a matter of fact, the attitude of the Sixth Air Army, which has been under the command of the Combined Fleet, has been passive and quite disagreeable toward others. Being informally advised of the said order yesterday, they were said to be quite surprised.

In the meantime, the enemy advanced two or three small-type planes to the north strip and Kamiyamashima. Such being the case, commander of the Okinawa Special Base Force, Rear Admiral Ota, strongly requested as a top priority the destruction of enemy task forces, in the light of past battle lessons.

Then chief of staff, Combined Fleet, sent a long telegram to chief of staff, Thirty-second Army, at Okinawa, in which he requested the army to pour its main force into the north and central strip districts so as to nullify the enemy's use of them. Anyway, each made his point. When a war goes wrong, this sort of argument is apt to take place and become a sign of defeat. The most essential thing, I consider, is for everyone to complete his duty for the common objective and not to depend on others to do things for him.

Due to foul weather at Okinawa, a night attack wasn't carried out today.

Thursday, 5 April 1945. Fair. A briefing of *Kikusui* No. 1 Operation was held in the morning with all commanders concerned present. As we commanders in chief were denied attendance at this, we held talks on various subjects.

The telephone exchange advised that the commander in chief, Combined Fleet, would come down here tomorrow evening to hoist his flag. It's a step that he should take at this most critical stage of the war.

The chief of staff, Thirty-second Army, whose stubborn character is well known, finally gave in, and it was decided to take an offensive to the north on the 7th. He also sent a request to call off an air attack on the same day, but later he withdrew this request, too. His mind was well changed!

The Combined Fleet issued an order to send *Yamato* with *Yahagi* and six destroyers as a surface special attack unit to the west of Okinawa on the 8th, leaving Bungo Strait on the 6th, with the mission of wiping out enemies there. It may be good, too, as this is the decisive battle.

[*The idea was that* Yamato *should run herself aground at Okinawa and turn herself into a fortress, her huge guns and those of her escort vessels sinking U.S. troop ships. The plan was not accepted without bitter opposition.*][5]

While taking a walk in the evening, I shot a jock-snipe with the fourth shot. I was glad, thinking it a good omen for our forces' hunting tomorrow.

The Koiso Cabinet resigned en bloc today after eight months of unpopular regime. Following a conference of important statesmen, an Imperial order to form a new cabinet fell on Admiral Kantaro Suzuki, president of the Privy Council.

[*Admiral Baron Suzuki had served several years as grand chamberlain, and had the emperor's trust and confidence.*][6]

Friday, 6 April 1945. Partly fair. *Kikusui* No. 1 Operation. We carried out a night attack against the enemy around Okinawa and an extensive search in the early morning. Sighting two groups (six carriers) to the south of Amamioshima, we directed the reserve attack strength to them. We found two more groups (six carriers) in the afternoon. This meant that they still had twelve carriers altogether, showing no loss at all.

[*These were Task Group 58.1 and Task Group 58.3, each with three CVs and two CVLs.*][7]

We didn't know the result of our attack except the reports of "I am crashing on a carrier," but judging from the enemy telephones in hurried confusion and requests for help it was almost certain that we destroyed four carriers.

[*No carriers were destroyed in this action, although three CVs, one heavy cruiser, and two destroyers were near-missed. Some thirty Japanese planes were shot down.*][8]

Visibility on the sea wasn't good, clouds fully covering the sky. But there was no waste of our attacks, as those who couldn't find enemies carried out special attacks against enemies around Okinawa. In the meantime, the first wave of our fighter force, twenty-seven planes, lured enemy fighters high up in the sky, while the second, third, and fourth (each wave had the same number of planes as the first) took command of the air over Okinawa and army fighters (approximately forty) flew back and forth on the line of Amamioshima, thus facilitating the advance of special attack planes. Besides, Army Headquarters reconnaissance aircraft dropped radar-deceiving tapes to the east.

The attack against the enemy task force resulted in rounding up the enemy from the south while at the same time we managed to have the large enemy force come toward Minami-Daitojima. Taking advantage of this opportunity, over 110 naval special attack planes, those belonging to the Tenth Air Fleet, detoured to the west and hurled themselves against the enemy fleet at Okinawa. Ninety army special attack aircraft of the Sixth Air Army charged in at about the same time, and those of the Eighth Air Division and First Air Fleet also made coordinated attacks.

The sea around Okinawa thus turned into a scene of carnage, and a reconnaissance plane reported that as many as 150 columns of black smoke were observed, while others described it as difficult to observe them. Judging from the radio-equipped planes' reports of their reaching the objectives without enemy fighter interference, most of them seem to have succeeded. The army should have attacked in response to this result, but they didn't move at all, saying that the general attack was to start in the night of the 8th.

[*The United States suffered severe losses on 6 April, although far short of later Japanese claims. Three destroyer types, two ammunition ships, and an LST were sunk, nine destroyer-types and a minelayer badly damaged; about twelve more had minor damage. Personnel casualties were heavy. The score might have been higher had the U.S. forces not been alerted. United States fighters shot down many Japanese planes before they reached the battle area. Many others were downed during the action either by ships' fire or combat air patrol.*][9]

Commander in Chief Combined Fleet Admiral Toyoda arrived here at 1630 and hoisted his flag temporarily. The flags raised were now increased to four, and the shack became too small. Chief of Staff Kusaka hurried to Tokuyama, where he gave the necessary instructions to the surface special attack force that was going to charge into Okinawa at dawn of the 8th. After seeing them off at their sortie, he returned here in the evening, having finished his sorrowful mission.

The atmosphere in the Second Fleet was gloomy at first, but they were said to have become quite determined after Commander in Chief Ito delivered his address to them. The force sortied from Bungo Strait at 1800 and sailed south along the east coast of Kyushu. Combined Fleet staff said the movement of the special attack force wouldn't affect this fleet, but I couldn't stay aloof. It was only natural to support and cooperate with the friendly force as much as possible to obtain the objective in a related operation.

[*Ugaki could provide only token fighter cover for* Yamato *and her escorts. They had scarcely put to sea when U.S. submarines* Threadfin *and* Hackleback *sighted them and reported the contact.*][10]

Saturday, 7 April 1945. Cloudy. The enemy task force sighted yesterday, including twelve carriers, received considerable damage, but there is still a possibility of its coming up north if it made an active attempt. So night searches covering 250 miles were made last night preparing for an encounter today, but we didn't see any enemy today.

By today's early morning search, two *Essex*-type carriers and one CVL were discovered trailing a great amount of oil and zigzagging to the southwest at 4 to 6 knots near yesterday's battlefield, eighty miles due east of the northern tip of Okinawa. They were seemingly those enemy vessels damaged by yesterday's attack, so a further attack was immediately directed against them as the best prey.

In the meantime, other search planes flew further south and sighted an enemy force including two carriers and a battleship to the southeast of Okinawa, and also four CVLs nearer Okinawa. In the afternoon a *Saiun*, which was dispatched to make contact with the discovered enemy, also sighted a new group of two carriers to the east of the damaged ship group.

[*Mitscher had instructed all of his groups to attack the* Yamato *"Surface Special Attack Force." Only Task Group 58.2, which was refueling, could not participate.*][11]

The attack force, now designated as the Surface Special Attack Force, sailed through Osumi Strait to the west last night when an enemy submarine sighted it and sent an urgent telegram to the enemy. From 0600 to 1000, fighters of this fleet provided a direct screen to the force, preparing for enemy shadowing planes, but an enemy flying boat shadowed the force after our fighters left the scene. So I feared it might be attacked later today. The only consolation was that the weather was gradually worsening from the west, so I thought it might be able to evade enemy attacks due to foul weather.

But many fighters and bombers thought to be coming from those newly discovered enemy carriers passed near Kikaigashima and headed for *Yamato*'s force. From noon, two to three hundred enemy planes repeatedly attacked the force for about two hours. A telegram sent from destroyer *Hatsushimo*, with the First Attack Force commander as its initiator, stated that *Yamato* had been hit by many bombs, *Yahagi* by two torpedoes with other damages to destroyers. The next telegram from the same destroyer related the alarming news that *Yamato* has been further hit by more torpedoes, with the result that she exploded and sank instantly.

Only two destroyers and two others no longer usable remained. The Second Destroyer Squadron commander shifted his flag to a destroyer to continue his command while the Combined Fleet ordered them to go to Sasebo after rescuing survivors.

[*CV* Bennington *claimed the first hits on* Yamato, *but as she took nine torpedoes and five one-thousand-pound bombs before sinking, one cannot credit any one carrier with her destruction. The cost to the United States was ten aircraft and twelve men.*][12]

The Surface Special Attack Force thus met a tragic end before reaching its destination. While *Yamato* was Fleet Admiral Yamamoto's flagship, I was on board her for one full year as his chief of staff. Later, she served as my flagship of the First Battleship Division from May 1944 and participated in the Biak campaign, the battle off the Philippine Sea, and also in the battle of Leyte Gulf, before I was ordered home in late November last year. My dear *Yamato* finally went down in the China Sea with Commander in Chief Ito, Chief of Staff Morishita, her skipper [Rear Admiral Kosaku] Ariga, and many fine officers and men. Alas! [*Morishita did not go down with* Yamato. *See entry for 14 April 1945.*]

[Ugaki noted that he had opposed the idea from the beginning, but the decision came so suddenly nothing could be done except provide such cooperation as he could. He considered it "superficial" to regard battleships as useless because of the scarcity of fuel. "Once offensives are resumed, they will become necessary, as shown by the fact that the enemy is now using many of them right under our noses." Ugaki recorded what he had heard was the rationale for the tactic.]

The main reason for that operation was said to be that when the chief of the Naval General Staff reported the battle situation to the emperor, the emperor asked him if it was a general attack employing only air power, and he replied to the throne that the whole strength of the navy was employed. The responsibility of the chief of the Naval General Staff, who is solely responsible for planning and assisting the emperor in operational matters, should be called great.

About thirty various kinds of special attack planes were directed to the enemy task forces, and unexpectedly they were well distributed among enemy carriers, including the newly discovered one, not to speak of those damaged ones. Six *Suiseis* and eleven *Gingas,* all radio-equipped, reported ramming enemy vessels, while fighter-bombers, together with two army reconnaissance aircraft converted into bombers, rammed enemy ships without any words. The interception of enemy radio exchanges also indicated that two ships were sunk and two others damaged, so I believe that today's attacks either sank or destroyed several enemy vessels. The souls of those who went down with *Yamato* should rest in peace.

[*Battleship* Maryland *was damaged but not disabled by an aerial bomb; CV* Hancock *was bombed and crashed, damaging planes and the flight and hangar decks; destroyer* Bennett, *on radar picket duty, was severely damaged; destroyer escort* Wesson *was crashed but limped into Kerama. The only sinkings were a PGM and a motor minesweeper.*][13]

The result of yesterday's attacks on the invasion force at Okinawa was radioed back by the Thirty-second Army as follows:

A total of the damage inflicted on the enemy since this morning at the west of Katena, southwest of Itoman and south of Okinawa:
Sunk: two battleships, two unidentified ships, three large types, two small types, five transports, and one unidentified vessel.
Damaged: one battleship.
Set on fire: one destroyer, six transports, two small types, and nine unidentified ones.

If most of the special attack planes succeeded in hitting targets, more damage must have been inflicted on the enemy, dealing him a heavy blow. Fifty army *tokko* planes also made suicide attacks today. The morale of the defenders at Okinawa was greatly roused. Tighten your belts and drive the landing enemy into the sea!

[Ugaki was one of the select few notified that the emperor was sending his brother, Prince Takamatsu, to Ise Shrine to pray "as his proxy." Ugaki "was filled with trepidation learning of His Majesty's anxiety," and "firmly determined to relieve His Majesty's anxiety by completing *Ten* No. 1 Operation."]

Two groups of more than one hundred B-29s, each accompanying P-51s, attacked Ogikubo in Tokyo and Nagoya. This was the first time for them to accompany P-51s, which seem to have come from Iwo Jima.

[*One hundred and one B-29s bombed the Nakajima aircraft engine plant near Tokyo, over 150 hit the Mitsubishi aircraft factory at Nagoya, and some thirty others bombarded targets of opportunity. This was the first B-29 raid on Japan to be escorted by P-51s from Iwo Jima, 91 of them, as Ugaki noted.*][14]

Sunday, 8 April 1945. Light rain, later cloudy. After the spring rain moistened the ground, it was cloudy all the rest of the day, so that flights to the Southwest Islands area couldn't be made. I regretted we couldn't carry out either searches or attacks.

However, several enemy groups approached from southeast of Toizaki around 1000 and dropped about thirty small bombs on a village at a little distance from the airfield, killing a farmer in a field and a schoolmaster of a grade school carrying the emperor's portrait. As they weren't seen at all from the ground, they were considered to have bombed from above the clouds without seeing the target. They seemed to be large-type planes coming from the Marianas. It was a coordinated attack of enemy large-type aircraft, an attack which should have been expected, as our air power here was inflicting damage to the enemy invasion attempt of the Southwest Islands.

[*On 8 April forty-eight B-29s hit two airfields at Kanoya and one at Kokubu.*][15]

The 343rd Air Group led by Captain Genda arrived here from Matsuyama today. They said they would display the fine skill of *Shiden* fighters, overcoming the poor condition of the airfield. I hope they will shoot down [enemy aircraft] no matter whether carrier planes or B-29s.

[Ugaki noted that enemy carrier plane activity in the Okinawa region was "extremely low." Only two U.S. carrier groups were estimated to remain, and Ugaki thought they could destroy the task force with sufficient fighter strength. But this they did not have. That afternoon he assembled his commanders for "a briefing of an attack against the task force to be made tomorrow and also of *Kikusui* No. 2 Operation scheduled on the 10th."]

The Thirty-second Army at Okinawa has promised to start its offensive from tonight. We shall have to watch closely how well they can succeed in this counteroffensive since they used to depend on others, while always boasting on the one hand.

Admiral Kantaro Suzuki completed his cabinet by order of the emperor last night. Admiral Yonai remained as navy minister while Admiral Teijiro Toyoda became minister of munitions, transportation, and communications, and Vice Admiral Seizo Sakonji minister without portfolio. It could be called a Naval Cabinet. When the Koiso Cabinet was formed, there was talk among elder statesmen that they would ask the navy next time, and now it has come to pass. There must be men who are disappointed with their prospects snatched away. They shouldn't ask for it themselves, but wait until others ask them.

Now that the good-natured navy is going to take charge of the state at this time of agony, I hope they'll govern forcefully, because it was the unanimous voice of the people at present. The navy, now without ships, is going to fight at the critical time by forming a cabinet with its predecessors. Ha! Ha!

Monday, 9 April 1945. Rain. It poured all day, too heavily for a spring rain. The planes were all soaked. We can't fight a war without umbrellas, like those Chinese soldiers. We shall have to think up something to make blind flying possible in fog and rain, overcoming bad visibility.

The Thirty-second Army at Okinawa could send in pleasant news. The following was an example:

> The following is to be added to the result of the special attacks carried out on the 6th. Groups of naval vessels, each with destroyers and cruisers as the main force, while engaged in reconnaissance and minesweeping the mouth of the bay of Nago, Sebu Shima, and Ie Shima, were attacked by what seemed to be special attacks at 1530. Most of them were sunk as listed below:
>
> 1. Sunk instantly: three cruisers, five destroyers, three minesweepers, one unidentified ship.
>
> 2. Sunk: three destroyers, seven unidentified ships.
>
> 3. Damaged and set on fire: two battleships, six cruisers, two destroyers, two minesweepers, one unidentified ship.
>
> Total: thirty-five ships. Besides, many burning transports were sighted on the sea west of Cape Zaha.

[*This report was wildly inaccurate. No U.S. ships were sunk on 9 April. That morning a suicide boat hit destroyer* Charles J. Badger, *temporarily stopping her engines but inflicting no casualties. That evening, destroyer* Sterett, *patroling No. 4 radar picket station off Okinawa, was attacked by five aircraft, one of which crashed her. She had to be sent to the rear for repairs, but suffered no casualties.*][16]

Together with those previously stated, these add up to sixty-nine ships, in addition to many losses of transports. The great success of *Kikusui* No. 1 Operation was thus clarified.

The Thirty-second Army also started its offensive last night and repulsed the enemy within its defense perimeter. On the other, they also made a charge at Kamiyamashima and destroyed two heavy artillery guns. [*By this time, U.S. forces on Okinawa were encountering extremely strong opposition.*][17] If they can resist as well as they can land at this critical moment, while we continue our efforts at air operations, I have little doubt of *Ten* No. 1 Operation's success. In the morning I chatted with Commander in Chief Toyoda and told the same thing to his chief of staff, Kusaka.

[The overblown battle figures inspired the Naval General Staff to decide "to shift to a general chase . . . overcoming all difficulties." It so informed the Combined Fleet, adding that efforts were under way to replenish planes and fit them for "special attacks." As a result, the Combined Fleet issued an operational order announcing that the enemy was in "an unstable condition and the chance of winning now stands fifty-fifty." So the Combined Fleet would "launch a general chase" to complete *Ten* No. 1

Operation. It followed this with brief general instructions to the major units involved.]

Both telegrams were what I wanted to have. If I could have more planes, the battle would be more profitable. The morale of the whole force is further stirred up.

The brief battle report of the Surface Special Attack Force was received as follows:

> Confirmed number of enemy planes shot down: 10.
> Losses: *Yamato, Yahagi, Hamakaze, Isokaze,* and *Kasumi.*
> *Asashimo* was attacked by enemy planes while moving separately, having engine trouble, and considered most probably sunk. *Suzutsuki* seriously damaged.
> Rescued personnel, Second Fleet headquarters: chief of staff, staff officer in charge of gunnery, adjutant and one other, three petty officers and men.
> *Yamato:* executive officer, 23 officers, and 246 petty officers and men.
> *Yahagi:* skipper, 37 officers, and 465 petty officers and men.
> Second Destroyer Squadron headquarters: All rescued.
> *Isokaze:* All officers and 326 petty officers and men.
> *Hamakaze:* Skipper, twelve officers, and 244 petty officers and men.
> *Kasumi:* Skipper, 15 officers, and 305 petty officers and men.

[On Tuesday, 10 April, Ugaki had to postpone *Kikusui* No. 2 to the 12th because of bad weather, so bad that Ugaki wrote two of his two-line poems about the rain. That evening the Combined Fleet held "a briefing on air operations."]

An old naval battery at Chujo Bay fired on an incoming enemy fleet under air attacks and sank a destroyer and damaged a minesweeper. It was interesting to see that an old installation was utilized.

[Ugaki fretted about the situation in Europe, where Germany's western front had been "penetrated conspicuously." Then, too, the Soviet government had abrogated the Japanese-Soviet Neutrality Treaty. "Naturally, this has been expected." The Soviet Union would thus participate in an anti-Axis conference in San Francisco on 25 April. Ugaki felt Japan should pay "close attention" to these developments.]

Wednesday, 11 April 1945. Fair. The sun is shining brightly, and the weather improved in most of the operational area. Well, let's go out to hunt the enemy task force!

From early morning searches were made to the east of Kyushu and southeast of the Southwest Islands line, and a group including two CVs and one CVL was sighted at a point seventy miles south of Kikaigashima at 0930. So about sixty fighters were sent to it first, then about forty of them as a daytime attack force.

Fighters engaged eight F6Fs in the air over Kakaigashima, while the attack force mostly carried out attacks from 1350 to 1700. Seven fighter bombers equipped with fifty-kilogram bombs and four *Suiseis* reported their ramming carriers, while three fighter bombers reported their crashing on other ships. Hearing their attack reports, we felt that most of the enemy carriers were crashed. Our shadowing planes also noticed their charge on the enemy, but due to fierce antiaircraft fire like pouring rain and also interception by enemy fighters the attack result couldn't be confirmed except for two columns of smoke going up into the sky.

The afternoon search found another group including two carriers at a point fifty miles bearing 100° of Kikaigashima, and also one more group including three carriers thirty miles south of Kikaigashima at 1630. Though it had cleared up, visibility was so bad that *Saiuns* had to fly at the low altitude of fifty meters, thus making thorough searches impossible. Nevertheless, it was certain that three enemy groups were still operating.

In the light of so many reports of crashing on enemy carriers, there can't be so many undamaged carriers still operating, even if they were decoys. From 1530 to 1800 a total of thirty-eight heavy bombers, *Gingas,* and *Tenzans* took to the air for a dusk attack and made torpedo attacks and bombings from 1850 to 1920. Three cruisers were sunk and one battleship or a large cruiser set on fire while torpedo hits were made on another cruiser and two destroyers, in addition to three ships set on fire.

[*Again, Ugaki's estimates were far wide of the mark. A kamikaze crashed* Missouri *but only scorched her paint. Two crashed* Enterprise. *Her fires were quickly brought under control but she had to curtail flight operations for forty-eight hours. The picket destroyers were targeted again. A fighter—not a kamikaze—crashed destroyer* Kidd, *causing damage, killing thirty-eight men and wounding fifty-five, including the skipper. A near-miss damaged CV* Essex, *with sixty-six total casualties. Destroyers* Hale *and* Hank *were slightly damaged by a near-miss bomb and a kamikaze, respectively.*][18]

Every day we try to finish the enemy task force, and yet they can't be finished.

Sixth Air Army Commander Sugahara came down here for liaison with the Combined Fleet and left for Hakata at about 1300.

The enemy made landings on Nago Bay and Unten port in addition to Tsugenjima, and started to capture our battery which commanded Ie Jima under its fire.

Thursday, 12 April 1945. Fair. *Kikusui* No. 2 Operation.

1. An extensive search was carried out last night. I stayed in the underground operations room but, except that something like an enemy was detected off Daitojima, no trace was found of the enemy, which should have been somewhere. I wondered if we had committed the folly of "a scalded cat dreading cold water" after being excessively warned against the folly of radar the other night.

2. Early morning searches were chiefly made to the southeast of the island line with *Saiuns,* and an enemy group including carriers (number unknown) was sighted at a point sixty miles east of Yoron-to at 0830, but shadowing it couldn't be maintained. The whole picture of the enemy couldn't be made available before about 1500, when the afternoon reconnaissance returned to base. It's regrettable that a faulty transmitter made a daylight attack impossible.

At about 1330 three groups of enemy carriers, consisting of six regular ones and two converted ones, were at a point sixty to eighty miles east of the northern tip of Okinawa. They seem to be still powerful, but they'll be all their remaining forces. I want to wipe them out by any means.

3. Seeing that enemy forces frequently enter Chujo Bay, we attempted to lay mines there by dawn with nine land-based medium bombers. Though five of them reported accomplishing their mission, the remaining four failed to return. A factor attributable for their losses was considered to be that they had to go down as low as two hundred meters altitude carrying four mines. Having learned the disadvantage of laying mines near an enemy with effective defense fire, we decided to stop this operation in the future.

4. One hundred and thirty enemy planes have already gathered in the north and central airstrips on the main island of Okinawa. Unless their activities are nullified, special attacks, brought about through painstaking efforts, won't have a chance of success. So their destruction should be given top priority.

It was said that two six-inch cannon prepared to attack the airfield, commencing firing from dawn, while army heavy bombers bombed the airfield, setting a great column of fire there. I'll be glad if those reports are not another case of exaggeration. Besides these, nine night fighters strafed and bombed.

5. To gain command of the air, the fighter forces divided into four waves, the first consisting of fifteen fighters (army fighters stationed at Miyakonojo), and the rest consisting of twenty-four fighters each, left the base at 0700, 1100, 1130, and 1200, respectively. They fought enemy fighters on the islands line and near Okinawa anchorage, and generally attained the object of gaining command of the air. Thirty-four *Shiden* fighters of the 343rd Air Group under their spirited Commander Genda

went down near Amamioshima and Kikaigashima and engaged in dog-fights with about seventy enemy fighters in the air over Kikaigashima and shot down or damaged more than twenty enemy planes for almost certain. But about twelve of them failed to get back.

6. The *Oka* attack force consisting of about forty carrier torpedo bomb-ers and dive bombers (mainly special attack force of the Tenth Air Fleet) left the base between 1100 and 1230 and made daring attacks against enemy vessels around Okinawa from 1445 to 1600.

In concert with this attack, about sixty army special attack planes dashed on enemy vessels. Though some of them reported their charges, most of them weren't equipped with radio, but it was certain that they succeeded in their charge-in.

Yokels of the Tenth Air Fleet's bombers sent in plain-language tele-grams on their way, against which they should be strictly warned.

As enemy land planes are now operating there, I seriously contemplated the use of a so-called *Oka* bomb unit against Okinawa. Finally I decided to use them as the weather was good, too. Those in the operations room were thrilled as reports of "Stand by for release of *Oka*," "Release—hit a battleship," and "One battleship sunk" came in.

It was the third success of an *Oka* attack, and they had barely proved useful when the cherry blossoms were falling. A report by returned crews of mother bombers was no good at all, as they barely confirmed the result of attacks. Out of six planes which sortied, three got back, one of which made an emergency landing on Okierabujima. Most of the others seem to have succeeded.

7. Twenty fighter bombers and two headquarters reconnaissance planes which sortied to attack the enemy task force apparently succeeded in charging in from 1500 to 1600. A night attack force consisting of about thirty heavy bombers and *Gingas* also struck them from 1940 to 2145, and results so far confirmed were one CVL and two unidentified vessels sunk.

8. Fourteen land bombers made a dusk attack against the enemy around Okinawa from 1915 to 1940. The confirmed results were two cruisers sunk, one battleship set on fire, and another battleship torpedoed.

[*While the results were by no means as horrendous as Ugaki wrote, 12 April was a bad day for the United States. On the radar picket line, the follow-ing suffered damages in varying degrees:* destroyers Cassin Young, Purdy, Stanly, *and* Hall, *destroyer minelayer* Lindsey, LCS(L)57, LSM(R)-189. LCS(L)33 *was hit so badly she had to be abandoned. The first* Oka *the U.S. forces had seen in action sank destroyer* Mannert L. Abele.

[*Deyo's Task Force 54 also suffered, with destroyer* Zellers *so severely damaged she had to return to the West Coast. A kamikaze struck battleship* Tennessee, *inflicting minor material damage but killing 23 and wounding 106. Destroyer escorts* Whitehurst, Riddle, *and* Walter C. Wann *were slightly damaged.*

[*Out of 185 kamikazes, 150 fighters, and 45 torpedo planes, Task Force 51 and combat air patrol claimed some 147; Task Force 58 claimed 151.*][19]

The general offensive of today also was successful. We must further attack the enemy task force so as to wipe it out, taking this chance.

Friday, 13 April 1945. Partly fair. A night search was made to contact the enemy task force discovered yesterday, and it was decided to continue the general offensive until today. The night torpedo attack force caught an enemy by its own search and struck it, while its element went to the west of Okinawa and inflicted fairly big damage to enemy battleships and cruisers.

At 0430 the enemy task force was sighted at a point sixty to ninety miles east of the southern tip of Okinawa. Then the daylight search planes left after 0600, and one of them discovered an enemy group including three carriers further south of the position where it had been sighted at night. Soon two enemy fighters chased it, and it has never been heard of since it transmitted "Banzai." Another one made a forced landing due to low oil pressure. As substitute planes couldn't be available soon enough, we were forced to give up today's offensive.

A night search plane sighted five unidentified ships burning near our attack position, so there was a good possibility of most of the enemy attempting to withdraw to the south. Though the number of enemy aircraft attacking Kikaigashima and Okinawa have decreased a great deal, the British task force has been attacking Formosa lately, though in small numbers. They were indeed impertinent.

[*Task Force 57, British Carrier Force, with four carriers and support ships, hit northern Formosa on 12 and 13 April.*][20]

At midnight our search plane twice detected a mysterious radio wave at a point fifty miles north of Kikaigashima, and a reconnaissance float aircraft sighted a carrier with her lights on engaging in plane takeoffs and landings on the same spot. It was none other than a night-fighter carrier. It was a night hawk intending to intercept our attack planes on their way, besides commanding the sky over Kikaigashima almost all night. Now we can see the reason enemy night fighters have appeared of late. I decided to carry out a hunt for enemy night fighters tonight.

When the battle situation was not against odds, various information and radio intelligence came in, and I'm writing down some of them herewith:

1. Our naval attaché in Portugal sent in a cable indicating that losses the United States sustained in Kyushu and the Southwest Islands up to March 31 were about the same as or more than we had estimated.

2. According to observations of military experts, the United States Navy's losses were extremely heavy, so if it continues like this it will result in a tragic end within two weeks.

3. The flagship of [Vice Admiral Richmond Kelly] Turner, commander, Invasion Force, was attacked on the 6th and 12th but was still operating.

4. Fifth Fleet Commander Spruance's flagship sent the highest grade urgent telegram this morning, and Nimitz requested that it be retransmitted with more power as its sensitivity was bad. But the former replied that he couldn't comply with the request, which made us feel the former sustained considerable damage.

[*A shell fell on* New Mexico *on 12 April but failed to explode. Damage was minimal.*][21]

5. By the 10th, the enemy had finished landing 100,000 men, two marine divisions, and three divisions, and still possessed a reserve force of 30,000 men. But so far there is no indication of the next step to be taken shortly. If they make the next invasion following this, the likely target is said to be either South China or Borneo in late April.

6. Anti-Axis countries think Germany will fall soon, as she is being attacked from the east and west.

7. There are four hundred B-29s based at Guam and Saipan.

8. It was officially announced that Roosevelt fell at Hot Springs yesterday and died at 1640. Vice President [Harry S.] Truman succeeded him and the San Francisco Conference will be held as originally planned. We should send a cable of condolence for the death of Roosevelt promptly! *Ten* No. 1 Operation thus overthrew the cabinet and killed Roosevelt, creating various reactions. [*Of course,* Ten-go *had nothing to do with Roosevelt's death.*] I hope for further changes.

[Ugaki took advantage of a few spare moments to go for a drive and tried his luck at a few birds, but got nothing. He noted the wheat was "pretty high" and the trees "vividly green. Maybe it is time for me to give up shooting."]

Saturday, 14 April 1965. Fair. Operation against the enemy task force:

Last night's nighthawk hunt was a failure, as we couldn't find any of them. We couldn't expect to get them with only one try. Well, better hunt them in the daytime.

Strenuous efforts have been made to ready *Saiuns;* even the chief of staff, Combined Fleet, inspected a plane where the work is being done. But, after all, the basic problem is materials; an improvement of the present organization is the next one. Troubles kept on popping up today, too, and we could only carry out some searches.

At 0943 an army reconnaissance plane sighted an enemy group of eight vessels including a CV at a point 75 miles bearing 125° of Tokunoshima, so seven *Okas* and 21 fighter bombers under the escort of 125 fighters including *Shidens* were sent out to attack them.

But the *Shidens* took an erroneous movement toward Zero fighter units near Kikaigashima, so the latter jettisoned detachable tanks and couldn't reach the originally planned point. Together with the fact that the commander's plane put about on its way to attack due to trouble, an attempt to take command of the air came to a regrettable end. More attention should be paid to a combined command of fighter squadrons. Through radio we learned that one *Oka* had been released, but nothing was heard about the rest. There was a great possibility of their being shot down. Only two fighter bombers reported their charges, but nothing was learned about the situation of enemy carriers.

According to information on the enemy sent from the First Air Fleet, two CVLs were in Kerama at 1000. So a surprise attack was attempted on them with eight fighter bombers, but nothing was heard from them. This was largely attributed to the enemy's jamming the radio.

One *Shiden* was sent out to supplement the shortage of *Saiuns*. At 1336 markings, oil slicks, and layers of black smoke that seemed to be signs of a sunken vessel were sighted at a point forty miles northeast of Kikaigashima. I optimistically thought that it might be a result of strikes by our special attack force.

Furthermore, a *Saiun* dispatched later sighted at a point sixty miles east of Kikaigashima a ship so covered with black smoke that she couldn't be identified. It was very hard to tell its relation to our special attacks. As she was burning, there could be little doubt that she was a ship. Though for the sake of my subordinates I would like to know who hit it, from a higher standpoint it doesn't matter at all who did it. What we ultimately aim for is to reduce the enemy strength by any means.

This very *Saiun* flew further south and discovered an enemy group of fifteen ships including more than one CV and one CVL at a point sixty miles northwest of Minami-Daitojima. It also saw two black smoke [columns] arising among them. What else can this be but a result of our special attack?

A total of eighteen heavy bombers and *Gingas* were directed against this enemy group. At about 2030, both the 762nd Air Group and the army's Ninety-eighth Air Regiment converged on the enemy, and five of them torpedoed under sufficient illumination. They claimed that one battleship was attacked from both sides and sunk, together with an unidentified ship sunk, while a large ship, most probably a carrier, was seen burning for over an hour.

Four *Tenzans* were sent to Okinawa via Kikaigashima, but only one reported a charge-in. Though we could not confirm the result of today's attacks, it is judged that they had considerable success.

[*Some fifteen Japanese aircraft attacked Task Force 58's radar picket line on 14*

April, slightly damaging destroyer Hunt *and crashing destroyer* Sigsbee, *which had to be towed to Guam.*[22]

[Rear Admiral Morishita, chief of staff, Second Fleet, came to report to the Combined Fleet. That evening he visited Ugaki in the latter's shelter. They "had lots to talk about," but it all came down to the *Yamato* force's last sortie. Ugaki decided that, in addition to the chief of the Naval General Staff's responsibility, upon which he had already commented, events revealed "a wrong judgment on the current situation made by the commander in chief, Combined Fleet." Ugaki tried to cheer up Morishita and sent him on his way.]

The Second Fleet so dear in my memory is said to be disbanded on the 20th. Now the naval tradition only lives in spirit, having no ships at hand. What shall we do? When we think of the painstaking efforts our predecessors made around 1887 and our tradition against the army's challenge for a unified command system and a unification of the armed forces, I can't help contemplating this and that.

[Ugaki was preparing for bed at a few minutes after midnight when the operations room reported sighting of an "enemy fleet . . . of thirty vessels." So Ugaki climbed back into his uniform and returned to the shelter. "Thinking that we might be fooled again, but with no other choice," he ordered a thorough search and preparation for an early morning attack. But the dawn search found no enemy. Ugaki "later learned that from an altitude of one thousand meters a lower layer of clouds was mistaken for the wake of ships, and it led to a false report that some of the crews had even seen ships." By this time the date was Saturday, 15 April.

[After breakfast he took a walk and felt reassured by seeing the progress of food plants growing "in spare lots."

[That afternoon commanders attended a briefing for *Kikusui* No. 3 Operation. Later Ugaki visited Teraoka.] Receiving a report of enemy planes approaching from the south, I came back to my own shack on the hill. An air raid alert soon followed. Due to ignorance of how to switch the circuit, the air raid siren wasn't sounded.

No sooner had I reached the operations room than the bang of bombings sounded. The air defense staff officer had taken it a little bit too easy. Including those which attacked Kagoshima, about eighty enemy carrier planes came to attack this district. Where did they come from? It's most likely that they came from carriers, but, as they're said to have attacked with their tanks still on, they might have come from Okinawa bases. About ten planes parked outside of shelters were set on fire. It was nothing much, but still we must be wary of such a waste for nothing.

[*These planes came from Task Force 58, whose pilots claimed to have destroyed fifty-one aircraft on the ground and to have shot down twenty-nine.*][23]

With our fighters being sent to chase those returning enemy planes, *Kikusui* No. 3 Operation was started. How much damage can we inflict upon the enemy by strafing Okinawa bases, dusk attacks by heavy bombers, and naval land bombers or fighter attacks tomorrow morning?

[Ugaki received word that those in his home in Tokyo seemed frightened by the recent air raids. He reflected that they would "have to expect occasional enemy air raids on the capital in the future." He hesitated to have them evacuate, noting, "When a man having responsibility for this war evacuates his house, the mental influence would affect other persons much more greatly." The house itself was of no concern to him, for he had "determined not to live long."]

Sunday, 16 April 1945. Fair, a long spell of fine weather.

Kikusui No. 3 Operation. In this operation, the Sixth Air Army was placed under my command by Combined Fleet order.

1. In cooperation with the army's Dauntless Fighter Unit, ten special attack fighters strafed and bombed the north and central airstrips from dusk yesterday and succeeded in a surprise attack.

2. Night search detected an enemy group at a point sixty miles southwest of Kikaigashima, while the daytime search discovered three groups. Enemy carriers seem to consist of six regular ones and three converted ones. A good prey always seems to be somewhere around this point. Well, let's go and get them!

3. Then attacks were carried out from 1200 to 1400 with about fifty fighters to control the air, and a total of sixty fighter bombers, *Suiseis,* and *Gingas.* Eight of them reported ramming on carriers, five on vessels, while four crashed on targets which couldn't be identified.

From 2100 to 2130, a total of twenty-two *Gingas,* torpedo bombers, and heavy bombers attacked, sinking one unidentified ship or a cruiser and also setting a battleship on fire.

4. At dawn a total of eight *Suiseis,* night fighters, and Zero night fighters struck the north and central airstrips, inflicting considerable damage.

Fifty-two Zero fighters with the mission of challenging the air supremacy left the base early this morning and exchanged air duels over the island line and the northern tip of Okinawa from 0840 to 0900, thus achieving their mission.

On the other hand, the *Shiden* fighter unit fought enemy fighters over the air between Amamioshima and Kikaigashima. As enemy fighters pursued them on their way back, they sustained some loss.

From 0600 to 0700, about forty dive bombers and fighter bombers, twelve *Gingas,* and six *Okas* left the base and attacked between 0830 to

1000. Besides, fifteen army fighters and fifty special attack planes cooperated in the above attack. One reported ramming on a carrier, five on a battleship, three on enemy vessels, and two on transports, while the release of one *Oka* was reported. All considered, two battleships or cruisers seem to have been almost surely sunk.

According to a reconnaissance report, one battleship, one cruiser, and four transports were seen sunk off Kadena in the initial stage of the attack, but most regrettably the result of attacks in other districts was not confirmed.

[*Again Ugaki overestimated his fliers' success. No battleship or cruiser was sunk. Nevertheless, U.S. forces suffered considerably on 16 April. In Task Force 58, a kamikaze crashed the flight deck of CV* Intrepid, *sending her to a navy yard for repairs and inflicting ninety-seven casualties. Another Task Force 58 ship, destroyer* McDermott, *was damaged by "friendly" fire.*

[*Instead of Ugaki's "four transports . . . sunk," LCS 51 was damaged when a downed plane smashed against her; LCS 116 suffered severe damage and twenty-four casualties from a kamikaze. As usual, the radar picket line took the brunt of the attack. Destroyer* Laffey *experienced twenty-two attacks from all quarters in some eighty minutes. She was hit by six kamikazes, four bombs, and was strafed. Her casualties totaled 103. Superb handling saved her so that she could be towed to safety. Her guns shot down eight Japanese aircraft. Destroyer* Bryant, *hurrying to aid* Laffey, *took a kamikaze strike which killed thirty-four men and wounded thirty-three. She made it safely to Kerama Retto. Destroyer* Pringle *broke in two and sank after a kamikaze crash. Minesweeper* Hobson *shot down a plane which fell near enough to damage her but was able to recover survivors from* Pringle *before retiring to anchorage. Destroyer* Bowers, *off Ie Shima, also was crashed but reached harbor. She suffered forty-eight killed and fifty-six wounded, including her skipper. A kamikaze near miss damaged minesweeper* Harding, *killing twenty-two and wounding ten. This ship retired to Kerama.*][24]

6. From about 1030 to 1130, some one hundred enemy carrier planes attacked the southern Kyushu area, strafing and bombing mostly with fighters. Several planes were set on fire. Now they came to attack us while we were attacking them over there. This was fun, too.

[*These aircraft were from Task Force 58.*][25]

In the afternoon, five B-25s accompanying more than ten P-51s further raided the Kushira area and one Kanoya base. This was the first time for this type of plane to come from Iwo Jima. [*As Ugaki wrote, this was the first VLR fighter operation from Iwo Jima. P-51s of the VII Fighter Command (FC), escorted by B-29s, hit targets at Kanoya. Thereafter B-25s escorted the fighters.*][26] From now on, we have to expect enemy raids both from Iwo Jima and Okinawa. We'll get busier.

Night and day fighting, together with lack of sleep, made us feel languid, so I took a walk, bringing a stick with me. Not only did it serve as exercise, it taught me things. When I noticed something, I could tell it to my staff.

Tuesday, 17 April 1945. Fair. The weather continues to be fine. We mustn't slacken our attacks. As we picked up an enemy at almost the same position as yesterday by the night search, we sent out three *Suiseis* and three Zero night fighters at 0300 in preparation for an enemy's dawn attacks. And one of them sighted an enemy.

Further *Suiseis* and *Gingas* sortied from 0640 to 0720 and charged an enemy group of two regular carriers and one converted one from 0920 to 0940. Besides, sixty-two fighters challenged to command the air, and its elements engaged in an air fight over the Kikaigashima district.

Today's attack was made without waiting for the result of the *Saiuns'* daytime searches and launched in the usual territory of enemy carriers while attempting to challenge command of the air on the one hand. Reports of "enemy surface force sighted," "carrier sighted," and "I am ramming an enemy carrier" came in one after another, which made us think that they might have charged in without being intercepted by enemy fighters. I was pleased to learn that.

According to yesterday's overall reconnaissance, there existed three groups of the enemy, one of which included three regular ones [carriers] and the remaining two, two regular ones and one converted one. And an aerial photo taken by an army headquarters reconnaissance plane this afternoon confirmed the existence of (1) seven vessels without carrier, (2) twenty-three vessels including three regular carriers, and (3) thirteen vessels including one converted one at a point thirty miles southwest of Kikaigashima.

When considering that eight reported their charges on carriers on the 16th and not less than seven today, it should be concluded that three regular carriers and two converted ones were surely sunk or destroyed. I think we need one more push to wipe out the enemy task force, but I regret that our fighting strength can't be maintained any longer. Key officers and others are exhausted, so readjustments and rearrangements have to be made.

Ten No. 1 Operation is developing extremely in favor of our side. The enemy received a heavy blow this time, and odds are apparently leaning to our side. Some even think that victory will be ours with one more push.

[But Ugaki took "a somewhat different view." While the primary objective was destruction of the U.S. invasion force, the Japanese were concentrating on wiping out the U.S. task force. On the other hand, "the enemy is securing Okinawa at the sacrifice of their task force." Therefore, he considered it necessary "to concentrate all our strength at one time to attack Okinawa bases and convoys." Moreover, Sixth Air Army headquarters was complaining that the navy was only hitting the task force and was "not enthusiastic about attacking enemy convoys which constitute the basic element of land warfare." Ugaki admitted that it would be "extremely hard" to drive the United States off Okinawa. The Japanese might try a counterlanding or paratroops, but not unless they were sure of success. In the past "unreasonable sacrifices were made too late." He wanted the Combined Fleet and the high command in Tokyo to think about these things seriously.]

But, unlike past operations, *Ten* No. 1 Operation is closely connected with the forthcoming *Ketsu* Operation, which means "Final." [Ketsu *Operation had been on the planning boards since 8 April and was divided into several parts, depending upon which landing areas the United States chose. Emphasis was on* Ketsu 6 (Kyushu) *and* Ketsu 3 *(the Kanto plain around Tokyo). Certain navy men, entertaining a dim view of* Ketsu's *chances for success, dubbed the plan* Okatonbo Sakusen *after a slow-crawling red insect.*][27] Even if we can't succeed in driving the enemy down from Okinawa, it's absolutely necessary to keep on pressing the enemy all the time. So I think it inevitable that we continue this operation, replenishing our strength in the future. (I explained this to the chief of staff, Combined Fleet, on the 18th and 19th, and I also had my Chief of Staff Yokoi understand this.) [*Ugaki added the parenthetical sentence later.*]

Wednesday, 18 April 1945. Cloudy, later rain. Today was a bad day for me with many unpleasant memories.

[*18 April 1945 brought a special sorrow to many in the United States. The beloved and trusted war correspondent Ernie Pyle was killed instantly during the invasion of Ie Shima.*][28]

On this day when we would have liked a day's cease-fire in order to repair our planes, between 0730 end 0830 about sixty B-29s came and bombed strategical points in Kyushu and Shikoku. At Kanoya, Kasanohara, Kushira, and Kokubu, more or less damage was inflicted. [*Over one hundred B-29s struck airfields on Kyushu and Shikoku—Tachiarai, Izumi, Kokubu, Nittagahara, and Kanoya.*][29]

By the recent air raid from the enemy task force, Marianas, and Iwo Jima, more than twenty aircraft were burnt up and fifty damaged. Although those damages were classified as slight in reporting them, I think something must be done about it. I would like to see a terrible blow given to the enemy by our *Shiden* fighters, which perform remarkably at high altitude. What did the enemy's concentrated attacks on southern Kyushu mean? We may be satisfied, if we consider it as their support of their current operation in the Southwest Islands, where they feel the brunt of our fierce attacks.

Enemy air raids on the Kikaigashima district have somewhat slackened recently. Since the Combined Fleet relieved me of operational command of the 10th Air Fleet yesterday, Commander in Chief Maeda and his staff officers are to return to Kasumigaura, leaving his forces which have already been concentrated or are being concentrated here as they were. They left this morning, planning to inspect various bases on their way back to their original headquarters. I thanked them for their cooperation so far even to us, while hoping they would strive to improve their strength in preparation for *Ketsu* Operation.

A result of reconnaissance of Ulithi dispatched from Truk on the 17th revealed as follows: three *Essex*-type CVs, four battleships (*Washington* types and *Idaho* types), seven cruisers, thirty destroyers, ten destroyer tenders, seventy-five large, forty medium, and fifty-five small transports and others. That is enough strength to make up a fleet, while the number of transports corresponds to one invasion strength. We can see how heavy our future task will be.

Total Operational Sorties Since 16 March

From 16 March to 5 April
  Against Task Forces
        Sortie of attacks: 291
        Special Attacks: 152
        Fighters: 75
        Reconnaissance: 138
From 6 April to date (including *Kikusui* Nos. 1, 2, and 3)
  Against Task Forces
        Attacks: 116
        Special Attacks: 284
        Fighters: 300
        Total: 730
  Okinawa
        Attacks: 52
        Special Attacks: 227
        Fighters: 239
        Attacks on bases: 32
        Minelaying: 13
        Total: 563
  Reconnaissance: 137

[Ugaki sent his chief of staff to Sixth Army headquarters "to promote mutual understanding." He himself went for a walk that afternoon and in the evening dined with members of Combined Fleet headquarters.

[He reported that the emperor had reacted to news of the battle situation by remarking that while the navy had been doing very well, the enemy also was "fighting tenaciously with its abundant materials, so we must be resolved to carry on by all means."

[Ugaki also noted that the Allies had reached within twenty kilometers of Berlin, "and Hitler issued a strict order to defend positions to the last." Ugaki reflected that if the German army needed such an order, its end was not far off. "Sad indeed!"]

Thursday, 19 April 1945. Rain, later fair. The rain hampered both sides' battle activities. The enemy at Okinawa commenced its general offensive from the north front yesterday, but enemy air activities were rather dull today. Also, very few planes raided Oshima and Kikaigashima.

[A briefing for the next operation was held that afternoon. Combined Fleet headquarters had been scheduled to return to Hiyoshi in Tokyo that day but at the request of the Naval General Staff postponed the move until the 23rd. Having a little spare time, Ugaki wrote home with instructions on how to dispose of his house.]

Number of Planes Used (approximate number)

Since Enemy Invasion of Southwest Islands on 23rd [of March]
Number of planes used: 1,406
Number of planes possessed: 598
Number of planes lost: 600
Destroyed on ground: 50
Number of planes Fifth Air Fleet possessed: 668
Number of planes sent from Third Air Fleet: 420
Number of planes sent from Tenth Air Fleet: 317

Friday, 20 April 1945. Fair, dust storm. The weather improved, but a dust storm was worse than a fog. Hoping to launch the second general offensive against the enemy task force tomorrow, a daytime search was made, but found no enemy. We're going to find them by a night search. To think that they'll always be on the same spot is the guess of a green young man. They might need refueling, and they also might change their positions due to our attacks. The press is headlining that the Okinawa campaign is turning out in our favor, and with one more push victory will be ours.

[Braving the dust storm, Yokoi returned, and Ugaki was glad to learn that he would be promoted to rear admiral effective 1 May. That night an unnamed staff officer awoke Ugaki to lecture him "on how to utilize fighters." Leaving the shelter, this officer fell down and broke two bones and dislocated an ankle. If Ugaki felt any satisfaction, he did not confide it to his diary, merely remarking that an accident to "an important staff officer" would have no slight influence. Ugaki went for a walk that afternoon and made himself "a whip and a fishing rod."]

Saturday, 21 April 1945. Fair. Except for a group of several vessels including battleships being sighted about fifty miles east of Okinawa, no enemy task force was found to the north of that island. So we had to put off today's general attack until tomorrow. However, a flying boat which returned to a base at dawn reported detection of a large enemy group at a point one hundred miles east of Kikaigashima at about 0200. It couldn't send a telegram due to trouble with its transmitter. Too late to do anything! [The following was written in the margin: "A staff officer, who was disappointed on hearing that six regular and two converted carriers still remained, was pleased to learn that his estimate was correct when an aerial photo revealed that they were four regular and three converted carriers."]

While we were alerted after being informed at about 0600 of the approach of an enemy plane formation, some 280 B-29s came to attack naval air bases in Kyushu from 0630 to 0830 and inflicted considerable damage. Especially, runways at Kasanohara, Usa, and Izumi were holed and made unusable. It was quite troublesome that time-fused bombs were included.

[*Two hundred and nineteen B-29s struck naval air bases at Kanoya, Kokubu, Kushira, Izumi, Nittagahara, Oita, and Tachiarai. Others bombed targets of opportunity, including Kagoshima. This was one of a series of raids on naval air bases in support of the Okinawa campaign.*][30]

Zero fighters which took off to intercept them couldn't return to Kasanohara base and had to land elsewhere. What else could it be but the fighter unit's lack of fighting spirit and inadequate intercepting tactics that they failed to attain as good results as *Shidens*? I had been expressing my dissatisfaction with the fighter unit, and now I felt the time had come when something must be done about them.

Scattered children are difficult to assemble. They have to be returned to their own bases for refueling before they are made ready for another attack, so the general attack slated for this morning had to be postponed until the afternoon. Those fighters used in interceptions can't be employed in offensive attacks. It has become absolutely necessary to station intercepting fighters on each base.

Rear Admiral Takeji Ohno, who has been designated for the post of chief of the Personnel Bureau, came here to sound out our views. A classmate of mine, [Vice Admiral] Gisaburo Yamaguchi, was appointed commander in chief, Chinkai Naval Base, yesterday. His predecessor, Vice Admiral Takasumi Oka, is being regarded as the man who should accept the responsibility of the chief of the Naval Affairs Bureau at the time Shimada was navy minister in the Tojo Cabinet. When a military officer becomes too much of a politician, he no longer can be evaluated as a military man.

[The shooting season being over, Ugaki turned in his hunting license. His experience in that line "will be one of the nice memories I have in this world, as I don't know whether I will be alive when the shooting season comes again in the fall."]

Sunday, 22 April 1945. Cloudy. What happened to them I don't know, but last night's search planes failed to pick up the enemy. Neither did the night and dawn attack forces. I was worried until we learned that they had radio trouble again. In fact, the enemy seems to be in the usual place.

From early morning, after I spent the night in the underground operations room, B-29s raided this area for an hour and a half. There were only thirty of them, but as the runway was damaged the daylight search couldn't take off before 1100. [*Over eighty B-29s struck Izumi, Kanoya, Kushira, Miyazaki, and Tomitaka airfields.*][31]

Unless interceptors are provided here, it will be difficult to continue operations in the future. At the same time, from the standpoint of restricting damage, a great deal of consideration should be given to the disposition of forces under the command. Anyway, a troublesome time has come. In view of this situation, the Combined Fleet ordered three *Raiden* interceptor units which have been attached to each naval station to come to southern Kyushu to be placed under my command.

Two of our search planes sighted two enemy surface forces each ninety miles south and southeast of Oshima respectively at about 1345. But both seem to have been shot down since then. Though nothing was heard about details, some forty fighters were dispatched first, then five *Suiseis* and eight fighter bombers. Due to delay and faulty communications after bombing, the main attack force, *Oka* unit, and fighter bombers couldn't be dispatched. Therefore we couldn't expect much from today's attack.

Fighter units engaged in an air fight with enemy fighters over Oshima and gained a considerable result. Judging from an unidentified ship being sighted set on fire and sinking east and southeast of Oshima as well as large oil slicks and bubbles, it seems certain that those of the attack force which failed to return succeeded in making charge-ins. So one or two enemy vessels seem to have been destroyed.

[*This was a solid estimate. On 22 April kamikazes sank minesweeper* Swallow *and* LCL(L)15, *and badly damaged destroyer* Isherwood, *with about eighty-four casualties; however, she reached Kerama Retto safely.*]32

The Combined Fleet issued its policy for subsequent air operations. In the end, it means that from now on our strength doesn't permit us to carry out more than air guerrilla warfare in both name and reality. Now we have come to the stage that we have expected to reach for some time. We can't do anything at all, with little money remaining in our pocket when it's most needed. Most regrettably, our past operations have always taken the same course. And that's the very reason why we have been following the road to defeat.

As bad weather was anticipated, our attack tonight was somewhat eased, but it didn't rain even after night came. We lost in weather forecasting, too. It was very good to see that more than thirty army special attack planes have already charged in today's attack, and some more are participating in the night attack.

Monday, 23 April 1945. Cloudy. I was surprised to see the growth of wheat after the battle against the enemy task force last month, and now it has grown to full length with its ears all pointing upward like spearheads, as if calling the whole nation to arms.

[Predictably, this thought inspired Ugaki to one of his two-line poems. There was no B-29 raid that night. Ugaki noted that some forty *Raiden* interceptors were concentrated in Kanoya, while the remaining large planes "were dispersed in northern bases. This step will be effective in preventing our damage from enemy attacks, but at the same time it is also apparent that some inconvenience will be brought about in inter-unit communications." The Combined Fleet had sent some instructions about future air operations, and Ugaki found them in accordance with what he had expected.]

Tuesday, 24 April 1945. Partly fair. We have refrained from making attacks for two days anticipating rain, but it didn't rain in this district after all. This morning it drizzled in the Okinawa area, and a *Saiun* reconnaissance plane put about without seeing an enemy after insufficient reconnaissance.

We were alerted against B-29s which sortied from the Marianas, but they didn't come where we were ready. One hundred twenty of them attacked the Tokyo area instead. Tokyo will be ruined in the end. I hope reconstruction will be made afresh.

[*Because of weather forecasts, the B-29s struck in the Tokyo area instead of against the Kyushu bases. They hit the Tachikawa factory of the Mitachi Aircraft Corporation located at Yamato. They wrecked the plant, which manufactured radial engines for army aircraft, and production stopped. They encountered unusually strong opposition, with four bombers shot down and sixty-eight damaged.*][33]

In the meantime, I paid a visit to Commander in Chief Combined Fleet Toyoda, together with Commander in Chief Teraoka. Admiral Toyoda left here for Hiyoshi in Tokyo at 1215. That reduced the admiral flags raised here to two.

Chief of the Naval Medical Bureau [Surgeon Vice Admiral Nobuaki] Hori came here to inspect welfare conditions in the Kyushu district, and I had a talk with him. The digging of shelters and dugouts all over the place has progressed well, but unless, along with their progress, other facilities are made, the welfare condition and how to prevent epidemics in the coming rainy season and summer will be my special concern.

Rough calculations of the loss of aircraft, etc., since 25 March were as follows: 620 missing and 80 destroyed on the ground. The total number of planes under my command at present amount to 620, of which 370 are in operational condition.

When we learned that the monthly outputs this month were six hundred navy planes and four hundred army planes, we couldn't expect to get more replenishment. Even if aircraft are produced, the result will be the same without fuel.

The Red Army finally entered Berlin. Hitler still remained in the city to encourage defenders, but their fate is now sealed. He who attempted to wipe out the Bolsheviks is now going to be destroyed by them.

Wednesday, 25 April 1945. Cloudy. An anti-Axis countries conference is being held in San Francisco today. What are they going to discuss? It's most mortifying to learn that they're going to discuss how to govern Germany and Japan after the war. We must let it be a case of counting chickens before they're hatched. The Soviets' attitude toward Japan has gradually worsened, and it's said Stalin intends to join the war so as to have a lion's share, if and when our Okinawa campaign fails. How is he going to deal between the east and west?

The Western Army and the Sasebo Naval Station issued an air raid warning against B-29s, and we followed suit, too. This was like one dog setting the whole town abarking. I pitied ourselves for the weakness of being passive. Searches by *Saiuns* only discovered a cruiser and several destroyers. The weather has not yet settled. So considerable doubt was entertained as to whether *Kikusui* No. 4 Operation, slated to be activated from today to the 29th, will be started as planned.

The Combined Fleet as well as the Naval General Staff strongly desire another *Tan* Operation employing special attack *Gingas*. But the skill of crews to be used in such a mission is lower than that of the last time while, on the other hand, the difficulties involved are estimated to have increased. Finally, however, a settlement was made by picking twelve planes each from the Third and Fifth air fleets to be placed under command of the Fourth Fleet at Truk, in order to let them sortie from there. This is considered a good solution.

Effective today, the Grand Naval Command was established with Combined Fleet, Grand Escort Command, naval stations, and naval bases under it, and it's to be operated concurrently by the present Combined Fleet. Such had already existed in the operational chain, so I didn't see any need for such a change.

It was only a while ago that we laughed at the army's establishing so many command posts, so I wondered if the navy was now trying to compete with it by this new establishment. However, learning that it was established in order to alleviate public criticism of the Combined Fleet for staying ashore instead of being on board a ship, I was simply astonished. Trapped by such a silly idea, they made administration more complicated. I think this is far from being the way to win the war. Those responsible persons in Tokyo who are particularly fond of making changes and revisions should restrain themselves a great deal.

A weather reconnaissance plane was dispatched to observe the weather conditions in the sea east of here and found a rain area due to a discontinuous line of weather. Efforts were made to carry out a night attack but in vain.

A special rite enshrining the souls of more than 41,000 persons killed in action was held at Yasukuni Shrine. That of the late Fleet Admiral Yamamoto was included among them. Two years have elapsed since his death. For his sake, I was truly ashamed of the present war situation.

Thursday, 26 April 1945. Rain. Today was the fifth anniversary of Tomoko's death. A private memorial service for her was held last January on the occasion of my brother's coming to Tokyo. But today I'm here engaging in the present decisive battle, while Hiromitsu is elsewhere on duty. So we couldn't do anything today.

When B-29s left a short while past 1100 after persistently attacking here since early morning, I came out of the shelter and picked a wild rose to dedicate to her memory.

Wild rose, dewy and fresh, pretty and sweet,
Beautiful and attractive to the eyes you greet.

In the morning about thirty enemy planes raided southern Kyushu persistently, flying in small numbers over thick clouds. Even with the help of pathfinders, targets must have been very hard to find. So they mostly attacked such radar stations as those at Cape Sata and Toizaki, with most of the bombs only hitting the sea. But some damage was inflicted on Tomitaka, Miyazaki, and others. In spite of bad weather with occasional rains, the enemy came to attack us. On the other hand, we've been unable to attack for the past four days. It's regrettable indeed.

[A certain civilian wrote to Ugaki that a victory in the Okinawa campaign was needed to better the domestic situation, so he hoped. Ugaki would do his best "with the firmest determination." Ugaki found the request natural, but added that the man with responsibility was "more determined than you suppose. And all that I wanted to have were more planes and nothing else."]

Friday, 27 April 1945. Fair. While I was taking a walk on a fine morning after so many bad days, a report came in of two groups of scores of large enemy planes approaching on course of 280° to the west of Haha Jima. A warning was issued after breakfast, and I went into the shelter. Until after 0900, about seventy planes attacked southern Kyushu. It was troublesome as they used time-fused bombs again. Interceptor fighters joined by *Raiden* interceptors took off. I thought they did fairly well. It's said three enemy planes were shot down.

The moon is going to be past the full. Taking advantage of the improved weather, we're attempting to launch a continuous night attack from tonight and the general offensive tomorrow. In cooperation with the Sixth Air Army, we plan to attack air bases at Okinawa and enemy vessels staying around Okinawa. A night attack force from Miyazaki base suffered some loss in personnel and materials due to time-fused bombs before they took off. Those reaching their destination couldn't produce sufficient results, as a smoke screen covered the anchorage.

[*On 27 April, a suicide boat damaged destroyer* Hutchins, *but she suffered no casualties. Destroyers* Ralph Talbot *and* Rathburne *were each hit by a kamikaze but damage and casualties were light. Both reached Kerama Retto safely. A kamikaze crashed* Canada Victory, *a converted merchant ship hauling ammunition, and she sank, but with surprisingly few casualties—thirty-nine.*[34]

[Ugaki received a letter from home; his house so far had escaped with only three broken glasses, but his relatives would be relieved when his "uniforms, decorations, etc." had been moved to a place of safety arranged by a friend on the Naval General Staff.]

Tuesday, 28 April 1945. Fair. Night searches failed to discover the enemy. At 0300 when the attack was over, I came out of the shelter and slept in the shack. At 0545 I got up after receiving a report of enemy planes coming up to the north. After breakfast, seventy B-29s came to attack as expected, and this time our interceptors fought back well, shooting down seven of them and damaging twenty others. We're inflicting some damage to their daily flight sortie to here.

Sighting an enemy task force including four carriers at a point seventy miles south of Oshima by the daylight search, an attack was ordered, but it was later called off as the afternoon search found them going down to the southeast. The enemy seems to have started to withdraw, fearing our attack, after seeing our search plane. It was a natural step.

Chief of Staff Combined Fleet Kusaka left here for Tokyo.

The entire fighter strength was sent over Okinawa, and they fought Sikorski fighters in the air over Ie Shima and surely shot down three of them.

From 1830 to 1900, twenty-eight naval special attack planes consisting of torpedo bombers and fighter bombers charged in at almost the same time as the army's special attacks. In light of the enemy telephone exchange showing considerable confusion, it's certain that three enemy vessels were either sunk or damaged. As enemy radars detected about forty of our aircraft, it was apparent that our planes could close in the enemy anchorage.

[*On 28 April near misses slightly damaged destroyers* Daly *and* Twiggs. *LCI 580 was hit with minor damage. That night, some fifty miles southeast of Okinawa, a kamikaze crashed the fully lighted, readily identifiable hospital ship* Comfort, *destroying the surgery and the entire medical corps tending the wounded therein. But she was able to continue on her own power.*][35]

The special attacks seem to have become less effective lately. The cause for that lays in their unsystematized strikes. Enemy interceptors and anti-aircraft fire are shooting down a good many of them before they can ram on targets. In addition to this, I'm afraid that the explosive power of our planes might not be big enough.

At Miyazaki base more than a dozen large planes were lost this morning on account of time-fused bombs that hit near the shelter, so a night attack tonight was made impossible. Only two type Zero reconnaissance seaplanes and *Zuiuns* could sortie from Ibusuki in southern Kyushu. It's regrettable that much damage can't be inflicted on the enemy accordingly.

Sunday, 29 April 1945. Fair. I wished His Majesty long life, welcoming his birthday in the midst of the decisive battle. Thinking of his anxiety, I trembled with trepidation.

It was very cold at night in the underground operations room and even with an overcoat on I still felt cold in my legs. I made an inspection of radiomen who have been working night and day. In spite of brisk activities observed in the evening, no news of charge-in came in all through the night.

Information sent from Tokyo after midnight hinted at indications of an enemy sortie at midnight, and about one hundred planes came to attack southern Kyushu from 0700 to 0930. Fifty of them dropped bombs in this area.

Several *Raidens,* which were sent down here after all our troubles, were set on fire and destroyed on the ground. As they can't fly more than one hour, they're apt to be caught on the ground when forced to land during a long air raid. This point should be taken into consideration in bringing out the newly designed rocket-equipped interceptor, the debut of which is being awaited a great deal.

An effective way of disposing of time-fused bombs has not yet been found. Airfields are said to be covered with small red flags indicating the existence of these bombs. They can't be disposed of as duds too soon, for some are timed with as long as a seventy-two-hours' fuse. Seven of them were shot down and more than twenty were damaged in this attack.

A *Saiun* plane which left the base at 0600 sighted two enemy groups, each including three and two carriers, respectively, sailing north at a point seventy miles east of the northern tip of Okinawa at 0830, so an order to attack it was issued. Because this was an offensive attack after the interception operation, we couldn't mobilize more than thirteen fighters for the mission. So army fighters cooperated with us.

Thirty-five fighter bombers, those from the Tenth Air Fleet equipped with 250-kilogram bombs and those from the *Shinrai* Unit with 500-kilogram bombs, were divided into three groups to search and attack. From 1630 to 1745, only two reported sighting enemy fighters while eight reported their ramming on carriers and eleven on other vessels. It was quite a success, and I felt keen delight after a long time. [*Ugaki's "keen delight" was unjustified. His fliers scored only two destroyers. Kamikazes crashed and near-missed* Haggard *of Task Group 58.4. She retired to Kerama Retto with fifty-one casualties.* Hazelwood, *coming to* Haggard's *aid, was also damaged by a crash and a near miss. She was taken under tow with heavy damage, twenty-six wounded and forty-six killed, including her skipper* LCS(L)37 *was damaged by a suicide boat.*][36] The army is going to send more than twenty special attack planes tonight. We're also launching a night attack. The First Air Fleet sighted south of Miyakojima an enemy task force which consisted of five transport carriers.

A telegram from Tokyo stated that there is a report that Germany surrendered unconditionally, though its authenticity is not yet confirmed. There would be no need to surrender if guerrilla warfare was continued.

Monday, 30 April 1945. Fair. The night search failed to pick up an enemy. There must be some reason for not being able to find an enemy recently, when he should be there.

A torpedo bomber reported torpedoing a battleship which stopped on the sea to east-northeast of the northern tip of Okinawa, while another plane reported sighting a ship on fire at the same place. [*The only notable casualty of 30 April was* Terror, *flagship of Task Group 52.2 Mine Flotilla, which was slightly damaged.*][37] Special attack seaplanes didn't take off tonight again. I wonder why they came here? A series of enemy attacks rendered an airstrip at Kikaigashima unfit for landing and take-off of planes, while many materials had been sent there in haste. Machine-gun ammunition was air shipped there by a medium bomber last night. Transportation difficulties are keenly felt.

The routine flight of B-29s came a little late this morning. About thirty of them came to this district while the rest seemed to go east of Bungo Strait. I wondered whether the fact that they came from southwest of the mouth of Kagoshima Bay might be because they changed their advance course due to our interception.

At my breakfast time, a telephone call from Sasebo Naval Station reported that a land bomber sent from Omura sighted an enemy force including a carrier at a point one hundred miles west-northwest of Oshima at 0445. At last they have entered the east China Sea. It might be a night fighter carrier. Immediately a reconnaissance plane was sent out, but it had to put about due to engine trouble.

Enemies chased two search lines [of aircraft] extending east of the island line, so they failed to find out what they were. In the afternoon an army headquarters reconnaissance plane discovered an enemy task force consisting of five carriers at a point one hundred miles south of Kikaigashima. Did this mean that all of yesterday's attacks accounted for only two carriers? So I questioned the authenticity of that report.

Only a few planes are left for use among the fighter group, crews of which are so exhausted that they said they just didn't care about anything. Employing even those few planes and army fighters as a fighter cover, I promptly decided to launch a special fighter bomber attack upon the newly sighted enemy.

As it turned out, however, army fighters couldn't be sent out, while it was learned that only a few fighters of ours would be available for an immediate sortie. Moreover, it was awfully difficult to pull fighter bombers out from shelters and prepare them. There being little hope of making a daytime attack, I called it off. And the weather was no good, with a rainy zone approaching, so we couldn't carry out a night attack either.

As the Vice chief of the Naval General Staff sent in a telegram that the army was going to launch a general offensive on the 4th with the aim of destroying the enemy main force in the south, I issued an order calling for our air forces to carry out *Kikusui* No. 5 Operation on the same day.

The enemy has been less active these days, indicating that he's planning something. He seldom sets out on an attack unless everything is made ready. I think the best course to take, under the present situation, is to give him a heavy blow now. Moreover, we could get materials from the enemy after destroying him.

[Ugaki recorded that the emperor had expressed satisfaction with the "gradual success" of *Ten* Operation and hoped the navy would "make further efforts in the future, too." Ugaki was glad to see that "those responsible men in the central authorities were now concentrating on *Ten* Operation," realizing how closely it was connected with defense of the homeland.]

I learned from the *Official Gazette* that I was promoted to the senior grade of fourth court rank. Though it's far from the top, it's still an honor worthy to be cherished in a family.

In the midst of the decisive battle, April thus is going to pass away. I don't regret the passing of the spring. Spring will come again, but what I fear is that a chance to recover the war situation won't come again.

Tuesday, 1 May 1945. Rain. Rain has come from early morning, since then becoming quite heavy. We had to suspend air activities on account of it; nevertheless, several enemy B-29s flew overhead from around lunch time.

We were informed that yesterday, too, His Majesty gave a word of praise for the fighting of our air forces, for which I'm extremely grateful. We have to exert ourselves more to develop the results already achieved.

Today, Admiral Toyoda was appointed supreme commander in chief of the navy, concurrently occupying the posts of commander in chief, Combined Fleet and Grand Escort Command. Nomura, Sawamoto, and Tsukahara were shoved up as members of the Council of War, while Kanazawa, [Vice Admiral Dotaro] Totsuka, and Daigo were appointed commanders in chief of Kure and Yokosuka Naval Stations and the Sixth Fleet, respectively. [Rear Admiral Tomoyuki] Senoo was made chief of the Kure Naval Arsenal. All of these posts are occupied by younger men now. Does this mean that with this reshuffle a large-scale renovation of personnel has been made, thus paving the way for an all-out decisive naval battle?

[On Wednesday, 2 May 1945, Ugaki was confined to his quarters with "fairly heavy diarrhea," an affliction he accepted in good part as "it served to clean up my insides." He noted that Mussolini had been captured and executed. "The fate of a defeated man is almost like this." That night his forces attacked in the Okinawa area. "A cruiser and transports were sunk."

[He was still ill the next morning. He recorded that "about sixty B-29s came and bombed Kasanohara, Kanoya, and Kokubu from about 1330." He thought one was shot down.]

Immediately after an air raid alert was issued all of a sudden in the evening, we heard the drone of planes nearby followed by sounds of strafing and blasts of bombs shaking our shack. Three of what seemed to be B-25s penetrated into Shibushi Bay at an awfully low altitude and made a surprise assault with their navigation lights on following the landing of our land-based bombers. As a result, several planes were destroyed and some twenty killed and wounded.

Our army forces at Okinawa are going to start their general offensive from dawn tomorrow, hoping to destroy the enemy Twenty-fourth Army in the south. This attempt does not have much prospect of success, but better to be venturesome, hoping to put up a fight while they have enough guts, than to be knocked out while idle. Anyway, it's good to make a positive fight, and we're going to concentrate all available army and navy planes there from this district and also from Formosa from this evening through tomorrow.

[*The exploits of Ugaki's kamikazes on the afternoon and evening of 3 May were part of* Kikusui No. 5, *which he recorded on 4 May. Radar Station No. 10 took the brunt. Destroyer* Aaron Ward, *hit by a bomb and four kamikazes, was so badly damaged that repairs would have been impractical. She was decommissioned. Another four kamikazes crashed destroyer* Little, *which sank within twelve minutes of the first strike.* LSM(R)-195, *going to the aid of the two stricken destroyers, was hit and sank.* LCS(L)-25 *was damaged by a near miss but rescued many survivors of the two destroyers. On No. 9 Station, a kamikaze hit destroyer* Macomb. *Damage was not serious, but she lost seven killed and fourteen wounded.*[38]

[Ugaki recorded formation of the Maritime Transport Command to handle all shipping of the army, navy, and civil agencies. He had recommended this during his hospitalization. "Only when shipping itself became scarce has such materialized. This, too, is another major cause for our losing the war."

[With sorrow, Ugaki recorded the death of Hitler. "But his spirit will remain long with the German nation, while the United States and Britain will suffer from communism some day and regret that their powerful supporter, Hitler, was killed." He hoped Hitler's successor, Grand Admiral Karl Doenetz, would hold the German nation together "and continue fighting as our partner."]

Friday, 4 May 1945. Fair. *Kikusui* No. 5 Operation. An air raid warning was issued at midnight and several B-29s passed over. At 0540 a few more approached. The enemy has now come to attack us from night to dawn to prevent our attack attempts. As a result, how to take off and land during the alert, which has been maintained almost all day recently, has had an important bearing on the conduct of operations. In *Kikusui* No. 5 Operation we planned our sortie for before the enemies came in the early morning, and yet preparing runways and planes can't escape being affected somehow.

    1. Night attacks:

        a. A total of forty land-based bombers, *Suiseis,* Zeros, and seaplane bombers, besides nineteen planes from the Sixth Air Army, bombed stockpiles at bases from midnight to 0400.

        b. A total of thirty-seven *Gingas,* army heavy bombers, and *Tenzans* attacked vessels in port from midnight to 0400.

    2. From 0730 to 0900, ten fighters of the Sixth Air Army in the first wave, forty-eight in the second wave, and twenty of the Sixth Air Army in the third wave advanced to the enemy anchorage to control the air.

    3. From 0645 to 0800, fifteen fighters of the Sixth Air Army and twenty-four *Shiden* fighters advanced to Kikaigashima and Amamioshima to control the air.

    4. From 0830 to 0900, a total of sixty-four torpedo bombers, dive bombers, fighter bombers, and seaplane bombers, together with seven *Okas,* made special attacks.

    5. From 0630 to 0715 an attempt to deceive enemy radar was made near the enemy anchorage.

Except that the number of participating planes was reduced and the time of the special attack delayed, this time the operation was carried out mostly according to schedule.

Our fighters engaged in air fighting over Kikaigashima and other places and shot down about twenty enemy planes. Special attack forces were able to charge in an enemy group sailing south at a point twenty miles southwest of Okierabujima. Explosions and the burning of two battleships, three cruisers, and five unidentified ships were seen from shore. Besides, the sinking of several cruisers or destroyers and the burning of a battleship were also seen off Kadena. Thus we achieved a great deal of success.

[*As usual, Ugaki's claim of sinking three battleships and several heavy cruisers was grossly exaggerated. Nevertheless, Kikusui No. 5 greatly damaged lesser shipping. On Radar Station No. 12, destroyer* Luce *sank with 149 killed and 57 wounded including her skipper.* LSM-190 *also sank in the same attack with 13 killed and 18 wounded. On Station No. 1, four planes crashed destroyer* Morison *which sank with 153 killed and 108 wounded. A kamikaze sank* LSM(R)-194, *while destroyer* Ingraham *was put out of the war by two near misses and a crash. On Station No. 2, destroyers* Lowry, Massey, *and* Gwin *were damaged by near misses. Destroyer* Shea *took a kamikaze at Station No. 14, with 27 killed and 91 wounded.* Shea *made Hagushi anchorage but was out of the war. Elsewhere, heavy cruiser* Birmingham, *anchored off Hagushi, took a kamikaze hit which killed 51 and wounded 81. She had to retire to Guam for repairs.*

[*On this day, while its battleships and heavy cruisers were bombarding Miyako airfields, British Task Force 57's carriers were attacked. A kamikaze crashed* H.M.S. Formidable, *killing eight and wounding 47. Another kamikaze near-missed* H.M.S. Indomitable. *The British carriers had steel flight decks and thus were able to take more punishment than the U.S. flattops with their wooden flight decks.*[39]

[Ugaki was under the impression that the land offensive on Okinawa was progressing in Japan's favor. In fact, "the Thirty-second Army sent in its appreciation" for the navy's efforts. Ugaki saw the need for further cooperation and ordered attacks that night "to further the achieved battle result." He was sure that "when our troops can see enemy vessels sunk and set on fire in front of their very eyes and observe planes with the Rising Sun mark fly overhead, their morale surely will soar."]

Saturday, 5 May 1945. Fair. Yesterday's pursuit turned out to be a failure. The weather was attributable to some extent, but it has to be admitted that the number of our planes was extremely small. If I ordered the whole schedule of attacks at the beginning, my subordinates would tend to economize strength to be used in the initial stage. Anyway, the failure has to be traced to the shortage of our fighting strength.

Responsible army staff officers in Tokyo have gradually come to recognize the urgency of *Ten* Operation, together with the smooth progress of the present situation. I was glad to hear that they're now considering concentrating its whole fighter strength in this area, except for a small number which have to be reserved at key points for interception. Seventy enemy planes came in the morning and attacked the naval arsenal at Hiro, while about thirty others bombed air bases in a vast area of Kyushu in the afternoon. At Gonohara slight damage was inflicted on shelters. Five of them were shot down.

[*On 5 May a major raid on Hiro Naval Aircraft Factory at Kure was coordinated with other missions against Kyushu airfields—Oita, Tachiarai, Kanoya, and Chiran. At Kure the Seventy-third and Fifty-eighth Bomb*

*Wings—the latter flying the first mission against Japan from Tinian—reduced
production at the Hiro plant by almost 50 percent. Other B-29s mined Tokyo and
Ise bays and points in the Inland Sea.*]⁴⁰

It was decided to carry out the third *Ten* Operation on the 7th, the day
after tomorrow.

[Imperial Aide-de-Camp Captain Rokuro Noda visited Ugaki's headquarters, and the admiral was rather worried about his safety. It was the
occasion of Boy's Festival, but this passed with no celebration "except that
my stomach at last improved."

[On Sunday, 6 May, Noda gave presents from the emperor to Ugaki and
"all members of the fleet and all the wounded." He and his chief of staff
briefed the aide who then inspected various installations. Noda was an old
acquaintance of Ugaki's, having been his student at the Naval War College
and having served with him as senior staff officer of the First Battleship
Division.]

Several enemy planes approached southern Kyushu in the morning, but
didn't attack. Pretty many enemy carrier planes attacked Kikaigashima
yesterday. In spite of the fact that the enemy task force exists somewhere for
sure, our search planes came back from the halfway point today, having
failed to accomplish their mission.

On the other hand, a search extended along the course of tomorrow's *Ten*
Operation saw enemy planes twice and a submarine once. Compared with
the previous attempt, we'll have to pass south through an area more closely
patrolled and more jammed with traffic.

Colonel Arao, chief of the Military Affairs Section of the War Ministry,
and four others came here. I had a talk with him for about one hour
expressing my views on various matters, as we have known each other for a
long time.

Monday, 7 May 1945. Fair, later cloudy. Third *Tan* Operation. At 0410 I
left the office and went to the airfield together with Commander in Chief
Teraoka to say farewell to the members of the Fourth *Mitate* Unit of the
kamikaze special attack force. In the eastern sky dawn was breaking. Lieutenant Katsumi Noguchi, its commander, and all other members of the unit
were picked up from the Third Air Fleet, so I let the Third Air Fleet mostly
take care of the third *Tan* Operation.

As in the past, departure was delayed, and takeoff was finished at 0645.
One of them crashed on the ground right after takeoff. Out of twenty-four
Gingas which had been prepared, twenty-one planes took to the air, thus
ominously casting a dark cloud over the outcome of the operation.

A weather observation flying boat reported a squall area extending for
scores of miles south of Okinotoroishima, but failed to make a preattack

reconnaissance of Ulithi and also a weather observation. Planes that put about from the way due to engine troubles gradually increased, and those still flying toward the destination at last were reduced to only nine. Though the scheduled time of "charge in" set as 1530 to 1600 passed, no news came in, and no change was observed in enemy radio activities. As sunset time at Ulithi was 1754 and they still had some time to fly, I suppressed my impatience to wait for further news when the report of the *Gingas*'s return to the base came in. And, alas, they were reduced to six now.

A great many clouds hovered near Okinotorishima. Though the lead land-based bomber managed to find the island after combing through thick clouds, the attack force failed to follow it. As those which followed the commander's plane were reduced to only four, and in addition met enemy planes on the way two or three times, he gave up the attack and returned to base.

Much fuss and little result! It only ended in another case of reducing our own strength by our own hands. Nothing but a complete failure! The *Gingas* have a long radius of action, but their "Homare"-type engines have many defects. In the previous attempt, one-third of the participating *Gingas* were forced to drop out, while in this attempt more than that dropped out.

Moreover, we should realize the foolishness of attempting to forecast weather conditions along a fourteen-hundred-mile course from here with little data. An area supposed to be having the best weather actually turned out to be covered with clouds and squalls. It was very difficult to determine their position on the way, thus piling up tremendous obstacles before them. I knew that it wasn't proper to order the execution of this operation without realizing the extreme difficulty involved in it, after only dreaming of the thrill of launching a long surprise attack. That's why I have a different view on the use of *Gingas* in special attacks and am opposed to *Tan* Operation.

In the morning about thirty enemy large planes came, but they didn't bomb this area.

[A retired admiral visited Ugaki, who showed him around "as a courtesy." The old sailor was "in great spirits," but regretted that people in that location, "who were supposed to be brave, were afraid of air raids."]

Tuesday, 8 May 1945. Cloudy, later light rain. It has been fifty days since the enemy landed on the main island of Okinawa. Despite losses of vessels, he has consolidated himself on the land. Already three B-29s and nearly two hundred small planes are stationed at the north and south airfields, while a runway at Ie Shima has been completed.

On the other hand, we no longer find the enemy task force, and enemy vessels around the island have decreased, too. Our army troops' offensive also ended in a failure, while our air strength had been reduced, troubles increased, and the third *Tan* Operation had to be given up. How to cope with this crisis is a very important matter. So I ordered my staffs to study it.

Today's B-29s bombed an area north of Miyakonojo from above the clouds and did us no harm. Scores of P-51s attacked air bases in the Kanto district, inflicting small damage.

[*Forty B-29s struck the airfields at Kanoya, Matsuyama, Miyakonojo, and Oita. P-51s of the VII Fighter Command from Iwo Jima flew ninety-four sorties against Kisarazu airfield.*[41]

[Toyoda came to Ugaki's headquarters and hoisted his flag. At a dinner party that night, they discussed "a forthcoming reshuffle of high-ranking officers." Ugaki was somewhat skeptical: "It's all very well to see that younger officers are going to be appointed, but I can't help wondering if we can eventually win the war this way."

[Wednesday, 9 May, was devoted to studying future operations. They decided to carry out *Kikusui* No. 6 on 11 May and to resume the third *Tan* Operation on the 12th. Ugaki noted that Germany had signed the unconditional surrender terms on the 7th.]

Thursday, 10 May 1945. Fair. Again we had guests—large enemy planes from early this morning until 1000. About ten of them bombed Kanoya with little damage. It was said 280 of them altogether raided the Kure and Tokuyama areas. They were pretty many.

[*They were indeed "pretty many." In addition to forty-two B-29s bombing the usual Kyushu airfields, 302 others hit fuel installations at Tokuyama, Otake, and Amamioshima.*][42]

The number of available *Saiuns* for operations having reached ten, we carried out searches after some time. In the morning, two enemy groups, including two to four carriers, respectively, were sighted at a point about sixty miles south of the southern tip of Okinawa. Many other ships such as ferry carriers accompanied them.

Another group of one regular carrier, one converted one, and four battleships was further to the east of Okinawa and at the same distance from there. If they're too strong, it will be too difficult to initiate *Kikusui* No. 6 Operation and also *Tan* Operation, so in the afternoon further searches were made to confirm them.

A report of sinking a battleship off Chujo Bay yesterday evening came in from Okinawa. There was another report of torpedo attacks setting a great fire on a carrier at today's dawn. Eight guerrilla attacks have been carried out achieving some results each time.

[*On 9 May, British Task Force 57 attacked Sakishima Gunto. Two kamikazes crashed H.M.S.* Victorious, *leaving three killed and nineteen wounded but little material damage. Another destroyed seven aircraft aboard* Formidable. *Although not badly damaged,* Formidable *had only fifteen available planes and had to retire temporarily with* Victorious.

[*The U.S. destroyer escort* Oberrender, *in antisubmarine screen off Okinawa, shot down a plane which crashed her, killing and wounding fifty-three. Her damage was so heavy she had to be decommissioned. Destroyer escort* England, *in antisubmarine screen off Kerama Retto, was crashed, with thirty-five killed and twenty-seven wounded. She was sent to the rear for repairs.*][43]

Friday, 11 May 1945. Cloudy, later rain. *Kikusui* No. 6 Operation.

With the aim of preventing the enemy from consolidating their bases, navy and army planes attacked them continuously from last night until this morning. Two *Oka* planes were also used, hoping to make a large hole in them, but eventually they failed. Some of the *Oka* crews were said to reset our interception of enemy fighters and want to be allowed to ram an enemy base. We decided to let them await another chance.

As a night search discovered an enemy task force near yesterday's position, we sent part of the attack force to it. Otherwise [the operation] was carried out just the same as in the past case.

At Kokubu No. 2 base, a Zero fighter deviated from the runway in takeoff, crashed into planes lined up ready to attack, and exploded. Fires broke out one after another and more than ten planes were destroyed. It's regrettable indeed. There were some casualties, too.

The number of planes employed in today's attack:

Attack on base: ten night fighters, two *Okas*, six *Zuiuns*, and two heavy bombers. (Army, about thirty planes).

Attack on vessels in port: eight *Kyokukkos*, five carrier bombers, six seaplanes, four *Okas*, fifteen fighter bombers, and ten *Tenzans*. (Army, fifty special attack planes).

Results achieved: four charged on carriers (two *Kyokukkos*, two fighter bombers), two more charged on vessels. One *Oka* released and two *Tenzans* torpedoed.

Fighters employed in air cover: sixty-five Zero fighters.

Attack against enemy task forces: twenty-six fighter bombers, while sixteen *Suiseis* did not take off.

Results achieved: four charged on carriers, and another four on vessels. At 1020 planes entered the radio insensitive zone, so they could not be heard from since, though much was expected from them.

[*Early action by* Kikusui *No. 6 centered around Picket Station No. 15 where destroyers* Hugh W. Hadley *and* Evans *were attacked by some fifty aircraft that broke through combat air patrol. Four planes and parts of others crashed* Evans, *killing thirty and wounding twenty-nine. She was towed first to Ie*

Shima, then to Kerama. Hadley *took a bomb, an* Oka, *and a kamikaze, with twenty-eight killed and sixty-seven wounded, including her skipper. She too was towed to Ie Shima and from there to Kerama.*

[*Shortly after 1000, two kamikazes crashed Mitscher's flagship, CV Bunker Hill. One dropped its bomb before striking. These attacks set fierce fires and killed 396, with 264 wounded. At 1630 Mitscher transferred his flag to Enterprise. Bunker Hill had to go to Bremerton for repairs and was out of the war.*][44]

Army special attack planes flew south along the west of Okinawa where enemy interceptors attacked them. Generally, enemy interception today was fierce, as expected. But it seems that today's general offensive inflicted considerable damage on the enemy. Those special attack planes that were reinforced by the Tenth Air Fleet have been almost expended in today's attack.

> Flowers of the special attack are falling,
> When the spring is leaving.
> Gone with the spring
> Are young boys like cherry blossoms.
> Gone are the blossoms,
> Leaving cherry trees only with leaves.

In the morning about three hundred B-29s raided chiefly the Chugoku district. Army and navy fuel installations at Tokuyama and Iwakuni were attacked and a good many killed. At about 2200 one or two enemy planes which seemed to be B-25s surprised the Kanoya district and dropped bombs and incendiary bombs. Unless we sleep in shelters, we no longer can sleep soundly. We shall have to revert to the primitive life of cavemen.

[*On this date some fifty B-29s flew their last mission against the Kyushu airfields in support of the Okinawa invasion. Others hit the Konan plant of the Kawanishi Aircraft Company at Kobe so heavily that the company removed most of the remaining machine tools.*][45]

Saturday, 12 May 1945. Fair. Effective midnight of today, the Combined Air Force is to be set up with this air fleet and the Third Air Fleet. It was designated as the *Ten* Air Force. I was assigned to command the new force to continue the current operation. With this it's made clear that the Third Air Fleet will be our partner. The work of staff officers will also become easier, and it's also said that those units of the Third Air Fleet now under training will be placed under my command. But how much we can increase our fighting strength and how far we can take advantage of this new setup has to be seen.

It was rather quiet today except for the enemy's routine visit, so I went out to a vegetable garden. We had a sukiyaki party as a farewell for the outgoing paymaster. When I got back after a walk, which I took for exercise, an alert was sounded again. More than ten enemy small planes were very stubborn in their attacks.

[*This was part of a "night heckler" attack from* Enterprise *on various Japanese installations.*

[*Curiously, Ugaki did not record the attack of 12 May on* New Mexico. *A kamikaze inflicted heavy damage, killed 54, and wounded 119. The battleship continued operations until 28 May when she sailed for Guam for repairs.*]⁴⁶

A report of a *Saiun* reconnaissance aircraft, which reconnoitered Ulithi from Truk today, stated that nothing was in the atoll except two *Casablanca*-type carriers. Well, they must have sortied again. Moreover, in view of their night fighter attacks of late, it's judged that they must be close to Kyushu, so I ordered strict precautions taken. However, our strength to encounter it was extremely small, and neither have we any wonderful ideas. Although we have a good number of planes, there's a great difference in all aspects compared with the time of the encountering operation in the middle of March.

Sunday, 13 May 1945. Fair. At 0450 a *Suisei* night-fighter sighted four carriers and five destroyers at a point 130 miles bearing 140° of Cape Sata. A seaplane found two other groups sixty miles to the east of the above, but didn't report before dropping its report-ball to the base at dawn.

Enemy air raids, which of course we expected, started with the first wave of 300 planes from 0622 to 0800. Its second wave of 220 aircraft came from 1120 to 1300. After an interval, during which about 20 planes came to attack, some 300 aircraft came here by the evening. At night they also came to attack occasionally, but not so frequently as last night.

Due to damage or troubles, *Saiuns* couldn't be used fully for reconnaissance, and with only *Shiden* fighters two enemy groups of twenty-two vessels, including three carriers, two battleships, and two battleships or cruisers were discovered. They seem to be all of the enemy strength at present. [*Ugaki probably referred to raids by and sightings of Task Groups 58.1 and 58.3 which moved northward to attack installations on Kyushu and Shikoku. Japanese aircraft damaged destroyer* Bache *badly, killing forty-one and wounding thirty-two. She had to be towed to Kerama.*]⁴⁷ So I activated First Attack Method and also ordered attacks from tonight to early tomorrow morning.

A night search flying boat picked up an enemy group at 120 miles south of Cape Ashizuri. An attack force consisting of 16 heavy bombers and *Gingas* sortied accordingly. I hope they'll succeed in their torpedoing in the face of fierce enemy antiaircraft fire.

Monday, 14 May 1945. Fair, later cloudy. The night search went on quite well and discovered an enemy force. More than ten night-attack planes torpedoed enemy battleships and others, but their attack result couldn't be confirmed. They didn't seem to have made hits.

At dawn twenty-eight fighter bombers, with escort of forty fighters, sortied to get the enemy. Six of them deported ramming on carriers and two on other vessels. [*Early in the morning of 14 May, a kamikaze crashed CV* Enterprise, *inflicting major damage. Casualties were surprisingly light— thirteen killed, sixty-eight wounded—considering the damage.* Enterprise *was out of the war, and Mitscher transfered his flag the next day to CV* Randolph.]⁴⁸ A search plane which left the base at dawn couldn't make clear the whole picture of the enemy except for sighting an enemy group at a point sixty miles east of Toizaki. Another one was sent out to confirm attack results, but its departure was delayed because it developed troubles. As late as 1520 it finally discovered a group at a point 140 miles bearing 120° of Toizaki and another one at 1650. Escort fighters sent out in the morning only sighted a converted CVL burning, but they failed to ascertain any other results.

Tan Operation wouldn't make any sense at all if enemy carriers weren't in Ulithi. Aiming to take this opportunity, we planned to launch a special attack with fifteen *Gingas* and twelve *Suiseis* in the evening, while keeping command of the air in our hands with fighters.

As today's intercepted enemy radio exchange directed its attacks north of Miyakonojo, a small number of enemy planes came to this district while the rest of them went up to northern Kyushu. Fighters first took off from Kasanohara, but when a *Ginga* was about to take off at Kanoya, forty to fifty Grumman fighters dove in from above and frustrated the takeoff. Their approach had been known through radar, but the departure of *Gingas* was delayed until after those fighters covering the air were all gone.

It's rather fortunate that we lost only one *Ginga* due to a fire and two land-based bombers [were] damaged, but we had to give up their attacks. Moreover, as rain was anticipated at night, both night search and attack had to be suspended. Thus we missed the enemy except for the early morning attack on it.

Though we must admit that we weren't blessed, factors contributing to our permitting the enemy's rampant activities were (1) we failed to get definite information of the enemy's sortie from its base, so that our search had to be made too late, and (2) our attacking force was small.

[On Tuesday, 15 May, reports of U.S. planes approaching sent Ugaki somewhat reluctantly to the shelter, but nothing happened. That day a staff conference was held to study regrouping of strength and future tactics. "It is most discouraging to see that our fighting strength is gradually dwindling."

[Toyoda left for Sasebo, intending to return to Kiyoshi on the 18th. Clearing weather permitted a search of the sea to the southeast, but no enemy was found within 250 miles except for a surfaced submarine. "The enemy task force has gone!" Ugaki was very disgruntled that, "instead of giving them a fatal blow," they had seen Japan's weakness. So he anticipated an increase in "the enemy task forces' arrogant activities," as well as an advance in the U.S. time to invade the homeland.]

Wednesday, 16 May 1945. Fair. In the morning and also in the afternoon, searches were extended to the sea east of the Southwest Islands to seek enemy task forces. But again we couldn't attain our objective due to *Saiuns'* troubles. It was decided to employ the *Gingas* unit saved from the Third *Tan* operation in torpedo and bombing attacks against Okinawa from tomorrow.

[On the 15th, there had been a large "reshuffle of high-ranking position of the navy." He thought this might presage a major change in the chief of the Naval General Staff and the supreme commander. But Ugaki knew that a war could not be won with personnel reorganizations. Germany had made just such a change the previous summer, "but after all it was nothing but the last struggle for life."]

Early yesterday morning, four hundred B-29s passed over Kii Channel separating the homeland and Shikoku and bombed Nagoya. The famous castle of gold dolphins was reduced to ashes. I regretted that a 306-year-old historic treasure was destroyed.

[*Completed in 1612, Nagoya castle featured a copper roof with gold dolphins at each end of the ridge, the male pointing north, the female south. The castle and other structures on the grounds and the works of art within them were listed as national treasures.*]⁴⁹

Recently the enemy commenced laying magnetic mines in various shipping lanes in the Inland Sea, and our shipping loss has been so great that our transportation is becoming ever more difficult. The enemy is employing various sorts of attacks, and the defender has little time to deal with them.

The army has provided three horses for our use, and we built a stable near the quarters. We take care of them with love. Recently officers' saddles arrived here at our request, so I tried a ride today. My bad right hand didn't seem to bother my riding.

[On Thursday, 17 May, Captain Kida, who had been commanding the naval detachment at Kikaigashima, gave Ugaki's headquarters "a clear picture" of the situation there. Ugaki believed that "what the front line force wants done should be done before it is asked for" and hoped the top brass in Tokyo kept this in mind.]

The enemy issued an order to minesweeping forces to load materials. It became necessary to be thoroughly prepared for the next enemy move and also for the task force, thus endorsing my warning issued this morning.

While we were enjoying a movie at a garden in the evening for the first time since we have been here, a twin-motored enemy plane came to attack and dropped a flare and some rockets, spoiling the show. Compared with seeing movies at Lingga anchorage last year, I can see how the war has deteriorated since then. We saw the Southern Cross overhead then, and now we are pressed beneath the Pole Star. We have now been deprived of ships and most of the naval forces now are stationed on land. How can we not regret this?

[Ugaki received a letter from the vice chief of staff, Grand Naval Command, Rear Admiral Shinkazo Yano. Yano was to move up to chief of staff and wanted Yokoi to become vice chief. Ugaki took a dim view of losing his chief of staff while they were "in the middle of an important operation," and replied accordingly.

[Friday, 18 May, was Army Day, and a number of top-ranking army officers, including War Minister General Korechika Anami, came to Ugaki's headquarters to express thanks to the navy for its cooperation, for discussions, and to be shown "around the neighborhood."

[Saturday, 19 May, was a rather frustrating day for Ugaki. Worsening weather forced cancelation of an attack by the Sixth Air Army. There were many signs that the United States was planning "some new attempt," but searches failed to discover any enemy. A talk with the chief of the First Section, Naval General Staff, revealed that Tokyo "still entertained a hope of driving the enemy off Okinawa and hope to intensify air activities." But they could not provide any new equipment and could only suggest using "medium-class training planes and seaplanes in special attacks and also to fix damaged planes for further use."]

Sunday, 20 May 1945. Rain, later fair. We had pouring rain late at night. The thunder sounded like bomb blasts and woke me up.

After 0900 I took a horseback ride for two hours and went around the valley and the airfield. I noticed some damage done by rainfall and also some shelters flooded. Strict precautions should be taken in advance against a summer with a lot of rainfall.

Since yesterday important communications have been exchanged frequently between the Fifth Fleet, the Task Force, and Okinawa, surely indicating that they're planning something. As soon as the weather cleared, searches were made while preparations were made against the enemy coming up north.

Several enemy groups, each consisting of two regular carriers and four converted ones, were discovered at a point 110 miles bearing 100° of the southern tip of Okinawa at 1420. But they were so far away that we couldn't do anything about them. Though the number of enemy carriers was the same as before, the content was different.

[Rain continued for all of Monday, 21 May, and most of Tuesday, 22 May, forcing Ugaki to forego a ride and also postponing *Kikusui* No. 7 Operation for twenty-four hours.]

Wednesday, 23 May 1945. Fair. As the weather on the mainland has almost cleared up and that in the operations area has also improved, it was decided to carry out *Kikusui* No. 7 Operation tomorrow. Its preparations were started beginning today, and today's fairly extensive search sighted the following:

At 1309, one carrier, two converted ones, two battleships, and more than ten others at a point sixty miles southwest of Minami-Daitojima.

At 1335, two super-cruisers, two cruisers, and others at a point twenty miles north of Kumejima.

At 1350, two battleships and ten others at a point twenty miles south of Kumejima.

At 1430, one carrier and four others at a point thirty miles southeast of the southern tip of Okinawa.

After supper, I went to the airfield on horseback to see off the sortie of medium-class training planes for *tokko* attacks. As it was raining at Okinawa and an attack from Formosa was called off, we too postponed the commencement of *Kikusui* Operation by another one day.

A telephone exchange with the Naval General Staff informed me that His Majesty is placing great expectations upon the forthcoming operation. So we're hoping for its success.

Rear Admiral Shinkazo Yano came down here for liaison and inspection as the newly appointed vice chief of staff, Grand Naval Command. Chief of Staff Third Air Fleet Yamazumi also came here.

Thursday, 24 May 1945. Fair. At 0045 a *Zuiun* seaplane sent from Koniya on Oshima sighted a convoy of about fifty ships under escort of eight destroyers sailing at 15 knots on course of 40° at a point fifteen miles northwest of Ie Jima. But, due to a hitch in communication routes, this important news failed to reach here before this morning. Accordingly, I sent out a *Shiden* fighter to confirm; it found nothing strange on various islands. However, this information seemed to be true, and there might be some error in the reported position. Together with a report of sighting several enemy vessels to the west of Tokunoshima last night, it made us suspect that the enemy is planning something positive.

The overall search sighted two groups with two regular carriers and six converted ones to the south of Oshima and two other groups of two regular carriers and four converted ones to the east of the southern tip of Okinawa. Together with a good deal of positive activities mentioned above, does this mean that the enemy is now planning an infiltration operation to the north? Taking this opportunity, we should destroy them by all means. Accordingly, *Kikusui* No. 7 Operation Method A was activated. [The following was written in the margin later: "As a result of further investigation, it was learned that they were two regular carriers and ten ferry carriers."]

While we were guessing the enemy situation, enemy carrier planes came up and attacked southern Kyushu. Altogether there were 120 Sikorski fighters and carrier bombers, but our losses were slight except for five *Gingas* destroyed at Miyazaki base. Anyway, they were easier to handle than Those B-29s which flew up north near Haha Jima late last night totaled four hundred, half of which bombed and burned Shinagawa, Ebara, Maguro, Denenchofu, and even Hiyoshi of Tokyo. They were pretty many and powerful.

[*The B-29s which attacked on 23–24 May totaled 562—the largest number on a single mission during World War II. The primary target was an urban area of Tokyo stretching along the harbor south of the Imperial Palace. There was the usual scattering of "aborts and strays," but 520 made it over the target and burned out over five square miles. Fighter opposition was relatively light but antiaircraft was deadly. Seventeen were lost, four of them to operational causes, and 69 were damaged.*][50]

The enemy now is attempting to reduce our fighting strength and also frustrate our fighting spirit by launching coordinated attacks against us from the east and west. But we can't be beaten in this way. We shall take revenge upon them for this from tonight until tomorrow.

In the evening, Western Army Commander Lieutenant General [Isamu] Yokoyama came to visit me on his tour of inspection. He stayed here tonight, but I couldn't entertain him as we were executing operations.

In the evening a shadowing plane was sent out, but couldn't find any enemy. Why was that?

Friday, 25 May 1945. Cloudy. Night attack planes didn't find the enemy task force either, and they only torpedoed a battleship and a cruiser near Okinawa. A night search plane reported two enemy task forces to the north of Oshima, but it was learned later that they were only several ships, maybe submarines, sending blinker signals.

Even after 0245 *Suisei* night fighters failed to find an enemy, so we gave up an attack against the enemy task force and switched over to Method B.

Prior to this, eleven army heavy bombers, each boarding about ten commandos, left Kumamoto in the evening. Five of them successfully landed on the north field of Okinawa, two of them on the central field. Together with flying crews, those commandos set fire to enemy planes. Operation *Giretsu* [faith] thus succeeded.

[*Only one* Giretsu *aircraft succeeded in landing. Its ten men hurled hand grenades and phosphorus bombs, destroying seven U.S. planes and damaging twenty-six others. These men also blew up two fuel tanks, killed two Americans, and wounded eighteen others. All ten* Giretsu *men were killed.*][51]

Jointly concentrating army and navy planes, night attacks were also made on Ie Jima, mixing time-fused bombs. Enemy radio banned the use of the north field and then also the central field and issued an instruction to land on carriers at a point fifty miles bearing 90° of Cape Zaha. We were very pleased to hear that. Taking advantage of this, I had our night attack unit informed that an enemy night fighter carrier would be in that position.

Attacks were also directed to vessels around Okinawa, and medium-class trainers were among them. An intercepted enemy telephone said that their destroyers, with a speed of 85 to 90 knots, were pursuing Japanese planes. Some staff officers laughed, saying that the reverse would be true. Planes to be employed in *tokko* attacks are gradually getting scarce, and it has become necessary to employ some trainers. Apart from their use at night, they couldn't stand even one second against enemy fighter attacks. Therefore, when they have to be used, we should provide them with thorough command of the air. Though they are many in number, we can't expect much from them.

Almost simultaneously with the sortie of the early morning *Saiuns* search, fighter units and special attack planes took off successively. But most regrettably it started to rain both in the eastern sea of Kyushu and in the Okinawa district, so visibility became very poor. Some of the fighters engaged in aerial combat with enemy fighters.

Four special attack *Gingas* finally found an enemy group consisting of battleships and carriers and charged in upon them. Except for them, all others, including the *Shinrai* unit bringing *Okas* with them, came back without attacking.

More than one hundred army special attack planes also sortied, out of which about thirty returned, while the rest either charged the enemy or made forced landings elsewhere.

It's regrettable indeed that *Kikusui* No. 7 Operation ended in failure in spite of the success of *Giretsu* Operation's dauntless attempt, mostly due to interference by the enemy task force and also quicker deterioration of the weather than expected. Our losses were rather small, so I hope to carry out No. 8 Operation to make up for it as soon as the weather improves.

From 1430 I inspected Nozato and Kanoya No. 2 field on horseback for about two hours. Bomb craters in air bases and wheat fields are constantly increasing, leaving the look of devastation.

Saturday, 26 May 1945. Fair. In yesterday's attacks, not many naval special attack planes participated while about seventy aircraft from the army sortied, out of which more than twenty charged successfully and about thirty returned without attacking. Thus they achieved a good deal of success, competing with that of *Giretsu* Operation.

[*On 25 May destroyer* Stormes *was knocked out of the war with twenty-one killed and six wounded. Two kamikazes crashed destroyer transport* Bates *which was towed to Hagushi where she capsized and sank the same day. Destroyer transport* Barry *was crashed so badly she had to be decommissioned and her hull used as a decoy. Her wounded totaled thirty but no one was killed. Minesweeper* Spectacle *was crashed with twenty-nine casualties and towed to Kerama.* LSM-135, *carrying survivors from* Spectacle, *was set on fire and had to be abandoned after beaching.*][52]

Though the weather in this district cleared, it was still unsettled in the south of Kikaigashima. We're impatient to attack but can do nothing at all. As our attacks are completely up to the weather condition, such can't be helped, to my regret.

More than one hundred B-29s bombed the Tokyo district this morning. The Navy Ministry seems to have been bombed, too, for telephone communication couldn't be maintained. In the air raid on the 24th, the inner garden of the Imperial Palace was damaged. I was filled with trepidation.

[*Ugaki's "more than one hundred" was an understatement. Five hundred and two B-29s struck the area just north of the one bombed on May 23–24. This target took in sections of the commercial, financial, and government districts. A combination of smoke and clouds forced bombing by radar, which probably accounts for the palace grounds being struck. B-29 crews were instructed to avoid the palace. On this day defense was unusually strong, and twenty-six B-29s were lost from all causes and one hundred damaged—the highest B-29 loss of the war. Ugaki had more to say about this raid in his entry of 28 May.*][53]

[Later that day, 26 May, Ugaki recorded that communications had evidently been restored, for he received a few letters. He was grateful for the goodwill they expressed and pledged "to continue fighting with never-tiring efforts."]

Mr. Kobayashi, an adviser to the cabinet, sent me his first letter after his appointment to the post from the official residence of the premier. In it he said that the domestic political situation was so hopeless that he wondered whether he should tell the poor old premier or not. Realizing that everywhere is the same with no sunshine at this moment, we should only aim to break through this national crisis, arousing our utmost courage.

Since 23 March stricter alerts than Second Station have been maintained at all times, suspending all liberty and recreation. As no lull is foreseen in the near future however long we wait, I'm afraid that any more suspension will result in lowered morale. Therefore, yesterday I issued an order permitting liberty within a short distance twice a month. Hardships that my men are enduring in these days deserve appreciation.

[Sunday, 27 May, was Navy Day, and Ugaki indulged in some dismal reflections. "I don't think we have lost any of our naval traditions, but why have we been pressed into such a tragic plight?" He reviewed the war situation, from the first wartime Navy Day when the Indian Ocean and South Pacific rang with "song of victory" to the present, when Japan was fighting "alone with the whole world as our enemy." For himself, all he wanted to do was fight "even after death takes me away, hoping to add more glory to our naval traditional spirit."]

In concert with the ninth general offensive against Okinawa by the Sixth Air Army, *Kikusui* No. 8 was ordered carried out. In addition to twenty medium-class trainers which will sortie at dusk as the spearhead, fifteen seaplanes will be sent as special attack aircraft. Besides them, six *Gingas,* eleven heavy bombers, four *Tenzans,* and four land-based bombers will attack enemy vessels while six land bombers and eleven night fighters will be used to take command of the air over the north airfield.

[*Several U.S. ships were damaged on 27 May, including destroyer* Braine, *which was crashed twice, with sixty-six killed and seventy-nine wounded. She was towed to Kerama.*

[*On 27 May, Halsey relieved Spruance, McCain replaced Mitscher, and Task Force 58 again became Task Force 38. Halsey's new flagship was the battleship* Missouri.]⁵⁴

The Sixth Air Army is going to attack enemy bases late tonight, with the aim of launching special attacks tomorrow morning. I regret that we're unable to send fighters over Okinawa tomorrow morning, as we're going to be prepared for the enemy task force.

Leaving the billet at 1400, I went to Kasanohara base on horseback. After looking around the underground living quarters, I entered a command post where I listened to reports by the air officer and maintenance officer. Fighter units should make progress in their activity, mobility, and maneuverability. Damage sustained on airfields and local people's houses there was worse than I had heard about. Almost nothing original is left, and bomb craters, big and small, are dangerous to the horse's legs. We returned at 1700, man and horse both sweating.

Monday, 28 May 1945. Fair. In spite of the small number of attack planes, the following results were confirmed in last night's attacks: three cruisers, one destroyer, and one big transport sunk; one cruiser and two unidentified ships torpedoed and set on fire, while one cruiser and one transport were also torpedoed but the result is unknown. As no news was received from the special attack planes, the result of their attacks couldn't be clarified. But enemy radio communications arising from our last night's attack showed that altogether eleven vessels were either sunk or destroyed.

[*No cruisers were sunk or damaged. On 28 May destroyer* Drexler *was crashed twice. One of the Japanese planes carried two bombs, and the resultant explosions sank* Drexler *immediately with 158 killed and 51 wounded, including her skipper. In addition, three merchant ships and transport* Sandoval *were damaged. Ugaki's further comments reveal that he overestimated the success of this day's work.*][55]

As it was raining near Ishigaki Island, before the sortie my staff officers had feared the feasibility of the attack. Nevertheless, I ordered it executed; therefore, I was glad to have achieved such a result. I thought its success could be attributed to the full moon and to the divine help of our predecessors on the occasion of Navy Day.

Since early morning a few small enemy planes continuously appeared in southern Kyushu, preventing our liaison flights and aircraft maintenance. Whether it was a revenge for our yesterday's attack or a preliminary step toward a new attempt we don't know, it was quite a nuisance. No actual loss was sustained.

[*These were fighters from the VII Fighter Command on Iwo Jima. They hit Kasumigaura and conducted heckler raids against Kyushu.*][56]

As a result of the B-29s' night air raid [of 25–26 May] upon Tokyo, though about fifty of them were shot down, a part of the Imperial Palace, the Empress Dowager's Palace, and most of the princes' palaces were burned down, and the Navy Ministry building was heavily damaged, but the function of the Naval General Staff was little affected. Furthermore, 130,000 houses were destroyed and 500,000 persons rendered homeless, with 700 killed and 2,000 wounded. Enemy news from Guam stated that many incendiary bombs hit the palace, and this statement was considered to indicate a change in attack policy. I felt relieved on hearing that Their Majesties and the Imperial Sanctuary were safe.

Taking the opportunity of his flying over Chiran, General [Shozo] Kawabe, commanding the General Air Army, dispatched his senior staff officer to my headquarters to ask for further cooperation with the Sixth Air Army. He seems to have taken this step because effective today the Sixth Air Army was released from the operational command of the Grand Naval Command, a fact which everyone is worrying about. However, I have never worried over this point from the outset, and I don't see any objection to an early change of the commander in chief, Grand Naval Command.

Any act of betrayal among the army and navy, and also among the people, at a time when nothing should stand in the way of attaining the command objective under the present circumstances, should be regarded as treason to the country. This is especially so, under the circumstances, whereby the loss of strength will make it impossible to continue future operations unless mutual assistance be given within the armed forces. Yesterday, I received a cordial telegram from Sugahara, Sixth Air Army commander, to whom I sent a return message. So please refrain from worries about this! Future deeds will prove our cooperation and connections.

With the weather forecast making tonight's strike possible, attack forces prepared for sortie but were called off in view of intercepted enemy communications. Communications hitches due to a reduction and a shifting of the land front line at Okinawa Island immediately affected the accuracy of the weather forecast, thus increasing the difficulties of attacks.

After supper I rode a horse to the foot of a hill. Now I have come to feel unwell when I don't take a ride.

Tuesday, 29 May 1945. Rain, later cloudy. Since dawn it started to rain in this area, pretty heavily later in the morning. It's difficult to forecast May rains, and it's a nuisance that we're going to have a lot of them soon.

This morning more than one hundred B-29s flew up north to the west of Haha Jima. Were they heading for Tokyo again?

[*Four hundred and fifty four B-29s, accompanied by 101 P-51s, fire-bombed Yokohama, destroying the main business district. One hundred and fifty fighters rose in defense and seven B-29s and three P-51s were lost.*[57]]

[Ugaki noted various changes in the high command but was pessimistic about such measures. "A renovation in personnel is all very well, but what can be accomplished by it? I hope we won't follow Germany's suit."]

Wednesday, 30 May 1945. Cloudy, later occasionally fair. Bad weather. An attack couldn't be made today. I ordered my staff to prepare an address to be delivered for the purpose of uplifting morale, innovation of thought, clarification of the guiding policy, unification of concepts, and rousing attention.

When operations are prolonged and there's no strong spiritual stimulation, the general morale tends to be stagnant and dull. Especially, it was feared, the resumption of liberty after more than two months might cause them to misunderstand the battle situation. Even among my staff officers, who are very close to me, how many can really understand my mind?

Thursday, 31 May 1945. Cloudy. A search plane lost contact near Okinawa; moreover, the weather reconnaissance aircraft reported bad weather, so today's attack was called off. As the moon was on her 19th lunar night and rose as late as 2300, special attacks employing medium-class trainers can't be launched from tomorrow, to my regret.

Notwithstanding the development of the war situation, the seasons go and come, and now the Southwest Islands area entered the rainy season. After two months of hard fighting, the ground force at Okinawa had to reduce its battle line and yielded the enemy entrance into Naha and Shiri palace. But the enemy losses on land and at sea were extremely heavy, and enemy communications indicating its hardship were seen occasionally. This can be said to have shown the necessity for a decisive battle. We should attack the enemy more consistently and tenaciously.

A continuous decisive air battle seems to be endless as the month of May departs.

12

To Die as a Samurai

1 June–15 August 1945

AN INEXORABLY *deteriorating military situation marked these last months of Ugaki's life. Even the weather was miserable—"Rain, rain, rain!"—and added to his operational problems. Raids by B-29s and other U.S. aircraft were almost daily occurrences. Ugaki admitted that a day without U.S. planes overhead was "quite unusual." One incident symbolized Japan's essential helplessness—a U.S. pilot coolly set his flying boat down on Kagoshima Bay and rescued some crewmen who had been shot down. With the fall of Okinawa, Ugaki began to worry about a possible U.S. landing on the Japanese home islands; hence, it was "absolutely necessary to destroy the enemy at sea."*

That was easier written than done. Most of his personnel were inexperienced and badly needed the training that lack of fuel and ammunition precluded. These same shortages curtailed Japan's fighter plane activity to the point where U.S. air raids encountered virtually no opposition, greatly to Ugaki's chagrin. The naval air arm was not the only sufferer—Japan's few remaining ships were equally hamstrung for want of fuel.

More and more Ugaki had to record heavy damage to the home cities. Yet he could still bluster. He dared Halsey's task force to come north where Ugaki's men could "get" it. And when the Potsdam Declaration called upon Japan to surrender unconditionally, Ugaki angrily wrote that, on the contrary, Japan should be demanding the unconditional surrender of the Allies!

Early in August Ugaki transfered his headquarters from Kanoya to Oita and received word that he was to become commander in chief, Combined Air Fleet and the Third Fleet, concurrently. But before this could take place events moved to a rapid climax.

When the Hiroshima bomb struck, Ugaki was immediately sure of its nature, conceded that it was "a real wonder" that would make "the outcome of the war more gloomy." However, he gave no hint that this development might make peace necessary or even desirable. He wished that Japan had the same weapon and meanwhile the nation must devise some countermeasure.

The Nagasaki bomb followed the USSR's declaration of war. Japan was conducting peace negotiations in the utmost secrecy. Since the government-controlled media had consistently deceived the public, many Japanese yet believed that Japan was winning. So, when on 10 August Ugaki's chief intelligence officer, with "a look of horror on his face," brought the admiral the "most hateful news" that Japan had applied for acceptance of the Potsdam Declaration, Ugaki was truly staggered. He wanted to continue fighting—large army forces remained intact, and the Japanese could conduct guerilla warfare until the enemy gave up. Many shared this unrealistic attitude and it required the emperor's personal assurance that he wanted peace to bring about cabinet capitulation.

On 15 August, Ugaki learned that Japan had indeed surrendered and that the emperor would broadcast at noon. It was all too much for the admiral. He ordered five Suisei aircraft prepared so that he could lead a last "special attack" against Okinawa. He listened to the Imperial broadcast but could make little of it due to static. Perhaps that is why he was able to ignore the emperors' touching appeal to "bear the unbearable." Instead, Ugaki hoped the Japanese would overcome the anticipated hardships so that they could "finally revenge this defeat in the future."

Nothing was heard of Ugaki's last protected kamikaze action, and the general assumption is that they crashed at sea.

Friday, 1 June 1945. [Watching fireflies and hearing a cuckoo during an outdoor movie, Ugaki welcomed June with several couplets in their praise.]

Upon receipt of an army information to the effect that twenty enemy vessels sailed north near Tokunoshima yesterday afternoon, we were alerted and also carried out an early morning search, but it turned out to be another false report.

Saiuns could make only half of the scheduled search. It was really typical rainy weather, and nothing could be done today. About 350 B-29s raided Osaka today, inflicting considerable damage.

[*The 458 B-29s that attacked Osaka concentrated on districts along the Yodo River where a mixture of heavy and light industries, warehouses, yards, etc., were located. One hundred forty eight P-51s started as escorts but ran into such bad weather that many collided, costing twenty-seven planes and twenty-four pilots. Another twenty-seven succeeded in their mission. Opposition was heavy, and ten B-29s were lost. A little over three square miles were burnt out, with 4,222 factories and many more houses destroyed.*][1]

Saturday, 2 June 1945. Cloudy, light rain. While the weather was bad due to the passing of the discontinuous weather line, about 150 F6Fs and P-51s, numbers uncertain since they flew over clouds, came to attack. Except that a part of them strafed, they weren't active. While taking precautions against an enemy task force's approach, a search was made with two *Saiuns*. They turned back as the weather on the island line was bad, but saw no enemy east of the island line. Did they come from Okinawa?

[*On 2 June fighters from Task Group 38.4 attacked airfields on Kyushu, and P-47s of the VII AF conducted heckler strikes, also against Kyushu.*][2]

Though it was planned to send most of the fighter strength to cooperate with the Sixth Air Army's nineteenth daytime special attack today, it was called off because of foul weather. But the enemy actually came to attack, while we had to sit idle. Nothing is more deplorable. We shouldn't remain satisfied with a result of twenty-seven *Shidens* shooting down thirteen out of twenty Sikorski fighters near Cape Sata.

Furthermore, at about 1500, when I was inspecting a dugout of the weather observation unit, an alert was sounded, and more than ten Grummans, followed by a Martin flying boat, came over Kagoshima Bay. After circling, the flying boat alighted on the bay and picked up crewmen of a plane shot down that morning, then flew away. I can't stand even to see an enemy submarine picking up survivors off shore, much less this arrogant behavior right in the middle of Kagoshima Bay. Prior to this, a telephone call from Ibusuki base reported that a Grumman was circling over a plane forced to ditch in the bay. Unless we prevent this kind of action with a prompt report and swift dispatch of a small plane, the enemy will become more arrogant.

An attempt to withdraw Lieutenant Colonel Jin, staff officer of the Thirty-second Army, from Okinawa to the homeland by seaplane has been tried several times, but so far in vain. It's regrettable indeed when compared with the splendid feat of the Germans in rescuing Mussolini from a lonely castle two years ago.

The weather cleared up in the evening at last, and *Tenzans* and land-based bombers sortied for night attacks, but regrettably they had to put about due to a thunderstorm over the anchorage.

Through the good offices of the Naval General Staff I have sent my war diary and uniforms to my native town to be kept there safely, and I received a letter from my brother informing me of their safe arrival. As I wrote it in the course of the war development so far as I knew it, keeping it confidential, I sincerely hope that it will be kept safely.

Sunday, 3 June 1945. Fair. Everyone became lively with the clearing of the weather. The Sixth Air Army's tenth attack began, while *Kikusui* No. 9 was also activated.

Soon after breakfast about eighty enemy small-type planes consisting of

F4Us and F6Fs—the army said there were 170 altogether—came in from the direction of Tanegashima and attacked southern Kyushu. [*Like that of 2 June, this group also came from Task Group 38.4.*][3] On account of this strike, the departure of about thirty army special attack planes, timed to be made at the enemy's lunchtime, was delayed for forty-five minutes. Notwithstanding, I had nine dive bomber special attacks escorted by sixty Zero fighters strike in coordination with the above army attack.

At 0955 a *Saiun* search plane sighted an enemy group of two rear carriers, one converted one, one battleship, two cruisers, and several others at a point sixty miles west of Minami-Daitojima, while another one saw another group of three regular carriers, two battleships, and more than ten others at a point fifty-five miles northwest of the above force sailing west at 16 knots at 0926. It isn't clear whether or not these two are the same.

On the other hand, an ensign captured at Chiran said that he took off at 0700 from *Shangri-La* [*Task Force 38's flagship*] sailing north and was shot down at 0930. It's certain, therefore, that those small planes came from a task force. Come on up north! We'll get you by Attack Method No. 2 Alternative. We fear that the weather won't last long. So I hope the enemy will come near tomorrow.

Of seven carrier dive bombers participating in the daytime attack, five put about on the way while more than ten army special attack planes succeeded in making charge-ins. Except that some fighters engaged in an air dogfight, all the rest turned back without seeing an enemy as it was raining in the Ie Jima district. According to the intercepted enemy telephone, seventeen were said to have been shot down. In view of the weather in the Southwest Island district gradually deteriorating, we were forced to give up *Kikusui* No. 9 Operation, on which we had placed such expectation. We can't regret too much an air operation that the weather hampered so easily.

[*The only U.S. ship damaged on 3 June was* LCT(L)-90.][4]

Monday, 4 June 1945. Cloudy. It is said that yesterday twenty enemy vessels bombarded Ihiraya Jima. Though searches were attempted with much effort, foul weather forced reconnaissance planes to put about just after their departure, so we couldn't do anything at all again today. On the other hand, the enemy around Okinawa gradually moved south, while fierce bombardments and bombings were repeated on the land. Enemy troops now have approached Koroku airfield and the Naval Base Force position. Five mortars with primers scheduled to be sent to that island by plane couldn't be sent.

Reshuffles were made among enemy commanders, Spruance with Halsey and Turner with [Vice Admiral Harry W.] Hill, and others. Though such a change seems to have been made because of the prolongation of operations, we should be prepared for a new enemy attempt, too.

No enemy aircraft came to attack the whole day.

[Attempting to avoid a typhoon, Halsey ordered Task Group 38.4 to break off air operations and join Task Group 38.1. Both flagships, Halsey's Missouri *and McCain's* Shangri-La, *were with Task Group 38.4.]*[5]

Commander in Chief Third Air Fleet Teraoka arrived here in the evening and hoisted his flag at this base.

Tuesday, 5 June 1945. Occasionally fair. B-29s attacked the Kobe-Osaka area this morning.

[Kobe was the primary target of this 473-plane raid, which destroyed over 51,000 buildings and burned out over four square miles. Fighter opposition was determined; eleven B-29s were lost—two from operational causes—and 176 damaged.][6]

The enemy weather forecast said yesterday that there was a depression of typhoon nature to the south of Okinawa and it was moving north. In the meantime, however, winds have become pretty strong, and it seems to have changed its course to northwest. But the weather reconnaissance to the sea east of Kyushu reported that the weather there was good. So at 1400 I activated *Kikusui* No. 9 Operation.

[The typhoon of 5 June inflicted considerable damage on U.S. forces. Nearly every ship in Task Group 38.1 was damaged, as were four ships of the fueling group. None were sunk, but heavy cruiser Pittsburgh *lost over one hundred feet off her bow and was taken under tow. She reached Guam on 10 June, and the next day her recovered bow was towed in to join her. Aircraft losses were heavy—thirty-three swept overboard, thirty-six jettisoned, seven damaged beyond economical repair, and sixteen others badly damaged but repairable. Personnel losses were surprisingly light—one officer and five men killed, four men injured.]*[7]

However, attack planes that sortied in the evening put about after 2000 from their way to attack due to foul weather. This surely showed that either a depression or a line of discontinuous weather existed there. Thereupon I had to order the operation postponed again.

At 0700 submarine *Ha-363* picked up a group sound at a point one hundred miles north of Okinotorishima, but couldn't see them due to the rough sea and reported that their course was 350° and their speed 16 knots. They couldn't be determined to be a task force, but I decided to take precautions against them for safety's sake.

A briefing on ground defense was held in the morning and another one on the use of fighters at night including representatives from the Sixth Air Army. We were concerned with how to use a small number of fighters for both interception and attack.

Wednesday, 6 June 1945. Cloudy. Night searches were extended to the southeast direction with seaplanes, *Suisei* night fighters, and land-based bombers as a precaution against the enemy task force. But all of them put about from points near this base due either to rain or poor visibility. *Saiuns* dispatched early this morning couldn't reach the end of the search line either, so no information came in on the enemy situation. Neither was any news received from radio intelligence. So the precaution was restored to the original station.

After 1400, about fifty small planes and more than ten large aircraft came to attack southern Kyushu, inflicting little damage.

[*These were thirty-six P-47s from Ie Shima which hit various targets of opportunity in southern Kyushu.*][8]

At 1515, a reconnaissance from the First Air Fleet reported an enemy group of several ships including carriers at a point eighty miles south-southwest of the southern tip of Okinawa. Night attacks were called off. Two large enemy planes came to Shibushi Bay at night.

[*Although Ugaki had canceled his night attacks, at 1713 approximately eight Japanese aircraft attacked two light minelayers,* J. William Ditter *and* Harry F. Bauer, *off Nakagusuku Wan. Two of them hit* Ditter, *killing ten and wounding seventeen. She had to be towed to Kerama Retto.*][9]

The Okinawa base commander, Rear Admiral Ota, has been in the Koroku airfield district together with the 951st Air Group and finally sent in his farewell message when he lost contact with the army. The latter withdrew to the southern part of Okinawa Island because of an enemy landing and penetration close to the airfield. Four battalions and most of the cannon under his command had been expended, having been sent into the front-line battle. As a naval landing force commander since the China Incident in 1937, Rear Admiral Ota participated in the Midway invasion, the defense of the Solomon Islands, and finally perished at Okinawa. We, the air forces, are also responsible for his death. His last poem left behind said:

> Though I may rot in far Okinawa
> Japan's mainland will be defended forever.

Thursday, 7 June 1945. Fair. The depression and discontinuous line of weather are all gone and a high pressure area is covering us with fine weather. Searches with *Saiuns* early this morning failed to locate any enemy. A plane that the First Air Fleet sent from Formosa sighted four carriers, four cruisers, and several destroyers at a point one hundred miles east of Miyako Jima. They're really in a bad spot.

Nothing was heard about the fate of the Southwest Air Group commander, Commander [Takashi] Kawamura, but he was supposed to be in the vicinity of Koroku airfield. On the other hand, Captain [Sei] Tana-machi, a staff officer of the Combined Fleet, was still at the Okinawa Base Force command post and yesterday advised that he was going to put a full stop to his communications. So I sent a message to both of them in which I expressed my appreciation for their loyal efforts and hoped for their further efforts in fighting.

But the Okinawa Base Force was said to have lost communications since 0230, so I doubted if that message actually reached either of them. I would like to see this kind of telegram handled more swiftly, so that I could say more to them before they were killed, though we'll meet together in the next world.

In the morning, a small number of enemy planes came to attack.

[*Twenty P-47s from Ie Shima struck various targets such as radio stations, warehouses, etc., on Kyushu. This was possibly of more immediate interest to Ugaki than that day's raid of 409 B-29s on Osaka against such targets as Japan's largest army arsenal. None were lost to Japanese action, but antiaircraft damaged four.*][10]

Kikusui No. 9 Operation was activated. Though it sounded like a big operation, only forty-six planes participated altogether, including fighters, air transports, and attack planes against enemy vessels, and only ten of them actually struck enemy ships.

[*Actually, the only U.S. ship to suffer at all from* Kikusui *No. 9 on 7 June was destroyer* Anthony, *slightly damaged by debris from a shot-down plane.*][11]

The combined number of planes belonging to the Fifth Air Fleet and those of the Third Air Fleet stationed in this district reached a few thousand on paper, of which about 700 were available, and of which, in turn, 570 planes were in operational condition. In reply to my request that they should be more active, it was explained that, while we saved some strength for the enemy task force, most of the rest were unable to fly at night due to their poor skill. It's very distressing.

Certain responsible persons in the central authorities haven't been doing more than sitting on the fence, watching the current battle developments in the present circumstances under which land warfare at Okinawa has followed the natural course of events under unfavorable air and sea operations. At last they have begun to show many signs of concentrating their energy into the decisive homeland battle. This is what they should do.

The Grand Naval Command directly ordered the Third Air Fleet to launch an attack against enemy large-type planes at the Marianas with forty *Gingas* and also attempt to slash the enemy's carrier strength at the Marianas, Carolines, and Leyte. Many difficulties are expected in these attempts. It also notified the Third and Tenth air fleets of its decision to separate the airborne force and air-ground service force to be applied to those fleets.

Apart from a question of its being advisable or not, the personnel reshuffle resulted in a temporary animation. I think that the enemy will follow this trend, too, in changing their operational force commanders.

Friday, 8 June 1945. Fair. Two of our night search planes were missing because of enemy night fighter attacks, but no enemy was sighted. We succeeded in dropping materials and foodstuffs on Okinawa and Kikaigashima, as our fighter cover over enemy airfields proved effective. At Okinawa, however, our friendly forces failed to receive them.

Torpedo attacks without flares succeeded in sinking two large-type ships.

As the weather continued fine, and also in view of the battle situation at Okinawa, I ordered night attacks continued by all means.

In the morning a small number of enemy planes came to attack. This morning we sent out most of our fighters to Kikaigashima for the purpose of challenging enemy fighters flying over there to keep command of the air, but they came back empty-handed, having seen no enemies. Not only was it just a waste of gasoline, but we couldn't intercept seventy to eighty enemy carrier planes which came to attack in three groups soon after lunch. An alert was sounded while we were still eating lunch, and before we reached the entrance to the shelters there came enemy strafings and bombings. All of them concentrated on Kanoya and attacked planes in shelters. Several aircraft were burnt up, and more than forty were holed. We can't underestimate them at all.

Enemy telephone disclosed that those enemy planes were directed by *Yorktown, Ticonderoga,* and others. They belonged to the fourth group of Task Force 38, which also includes *Shangri-La* and *Independence.* [*This was correct. Fighters of Task Group 38.4 attacked airfields in southern Kyushu, using variable time fuses for the first time.*][12] Suspecting that they were operating quite nearby, I ordered a search made to the south of Amamioshima, but none of them were found. It seems after all that they came from a position east of the southern tip of Okinawa with additional fuel tanks attached. I regretted that the only course left for us was to ambush them from Kikaigashima and Minami-Daitojima. They came at night, too, though in small numbers, and we had to go into shelters three times today.

The Okinawa Base Force is still in contact and sent in reports on the battle situation. An assault squad of fourteen men laid land mines and blew up an M-4 tank and damaged another. They also found seventy enemies fast asleep in a dugout and finished them off with twenty-five hand grenades.

When the chief of the Naval General Staff reported the battle situation to the throne, he received a word of praise from the emperor for the gallant fighting of the Okinawa Base Force. A telegram also said that His Majesty expressed his anxiety over the battle situation. What shall we do to relieve his anxiety?

The extraordinary session of the Diet confronting the decisive battle was opened today.

Saturday, 9 June 1945. Fair. No results were confirmed in last night's attack. Some planes failed to return.

The morning search sighted a group of three regular carriers and three converted ones at a point ninety miles southeast of the southern tip of Okinawa. Thinking that it might come up north in case it attempted an attack like yesterday's, we searched an area south of Okinawa and three hundred miles from here, but found no enemy. Neither did any enemy carrier planes attack today. From about 1630 several P-47s came to attack.

[During a ride after supper Ugaki spotted white buckwheat flowers and composed a couplet in their honor. He also noted that Supreme Commander Ozawa and his staff had changed plans and left for Sasebo and Omura, Vice Chief of Staff Yano arriving alone at Ugaki's headquarters.]

As a result of the interpretation of aerial photos, we learned that those carriers of the newly found task force were all light converted ones. Judging from an enemy attack on Daitojima and also the detection of a large force last night, another powerful task force seems to be to the southeast of the same island.

[*Task Force 38 refueled on 9 June; however, Cruiser Division 16—heavy cruisers* Guam *and* Alaska *and five destroyers—bombarded Okino Daito.*][13]

Sunday, 10 June 1945. Fair. Last night's attack had to put about en route due to foul weather, of course without any results. However, night fighters flew to Oshima and they seem to have shot down an enemy fighter.

[*On 10 June a lone Japanese aircraft sank destroyer* William D. Porter *on Radar Station 15 at 0825. The plane near-missed, but its bomb exploded so close that it acted as a mine, and the destroyer sank at 1119. She had sixty wounded but no dead.*][14]

A small number of P-47s came to attack in both the morning and afternoon, while a few F4Fs attacked Kokubu. Supreme Commander Ozawa and others arrived here in the evening and I visited him at his quarters.

Monday, 11 June 1945. Occasionally fair. In the morning eleven B-24s and thirty P-47s came to attack here. Forty Zero fighters intercepted them with no results at all. On the contrary, we lost four planes. In view of this rotten result the need for further training is obvious. But fuel stocked in southern Kyushu is running so low that little will be spared for training. We are now getting stuck for fuel. In the morning I reported to Supreme Commander Ozawa on my force's current situation.

Lieutenant Colonel Jin, an air staff officer of the Thirty-second Army, managed to get out of Okinawa by canoe and returned to Kushira early this morning after flying from Tokunoshima. Then he came straight here. I was glad to see that he was all right. Thus I was able to hear the first-hand report of the doomed battle on Okinawa Island.

[Ugaki admitted that the main cause for the defeat was the withdrawal of the Ninth Army, but noted that much in their preparations, planning, training, and command had been "left unfinished." But he paid tribute to their "gallant efforts" against a superior enemy. They had withdrawn to hills in southern Okinawa, and Ugaki had heard that it would be a miracle if they could hold out another ten days. Despite the commander's thanks which he sent Ugaki, the admiral felt that he, too, had a responsibility for the defeat. Jin also brought a letter from Tanamachi to Ugaki's chief of staff which described the situation and battle lessons in detail. "This might become his last words," Ugaki noted.

[Later that day Ugaki took a gallop, then attended a sukiyaki party which Ozawa gave, noting, "Sake is very effective on an empty stomach."]

Tuesday, 12 June 1945. Cloudy with noisy winds. Seemingly with the purpose of attacking at lunchtime, about thirty P-47s and F4Us came and bombed.

I ordered preparations for *Kikusui* No. 10 Operation carried out on or about the 14th in concert with a general attack by the Sixth Air Army.

It was quite hot in the shack but nice and cool in the underground shelters.

At 1600, we lost contact with the Okinawa Base Force, which has continued its last fight at Koroku. The chief of the Naval General Staff again sent in that he had received a word of praise from the throne for the gallant fighting of the Okinawa Base Force when he reported to the throne on the battle situation. The souls of Rear Admiral Ota, Captain Tanamachi, Southwest air group commanders, and others may repose in peace.

[Ugaki's area was rainy on Wednesday, 13 June, although fairly good weather prevailed in the Okinawa district. That morning, a few U.S. planes "came to south Kyushu but did no harm." The day was spent in discussion and briefing for *Kikusui* No. 10 Operation, deciding upon a different method. "Expecting to make sure hits with *Okas* this time, it was decided to provide direct fighter support to the attack force."

[But on 14 June they had to call off the attack because of "Rain, rain, rain!" Ozawa was confined to his quarters with diarrhea, so Ugaki visited him there for a talk about various subjects, even "personal matters" concerning Ugaki's staff. His chief of staff, Yokoi, had been in poor health, and Captain Chihaya Takahashi would be assigned as his vice chief of staff. Ugaki considered it urgent to strengthen his staff, with *Ten* and *Ketsu* operations coming up. But Ugaki always had time to notice the aspects of nature as he rode about the countryside, and he jotted down three couplets about wheat harvesting, which was already in progress in southern Kyushu.]

Friday, 15 June 1945. Rain. Supreme Commander Ozawa left here by car at 0500 to take a train from Miyakonojo. Commander in Chief Sasebo Naval Station Vice Admiral Sugiyama came here at 1140 on his inspection tour, and we had lunch together.

B-29s air raided the Osaka district on a large scale, inflicting fairly heavy damage.

[*This was a "mop-up" raid by 444 B-29s against Osaka and Amagasaki. While the area that was burned out was not as extensive as on previous raids, the area was more highly industrialized. No B-29s were lost, and only one was damaged.*][15]

Saturday, 16 June 1945. Rain. Pretty many enemy planes came up north from Okinawa in the morning and afternoon but failed to attack on account of rain. We heard only one or two planes overhead. They sortied from Okinawa, where the weather was good, and to their surprise found this rain. I wondered if they hadn't yet decoded our weather report signals. This country's rainy season must surprise them. When we fought overseas, we had no need to worry about this country's rainy season. But after being forced to fight near our homeland, both we and the enemy were affected by it, and we're now looking at the sky more frequently.

[Ugaki briefly turned his attention to Europe, remarking that the Allies had not yet recognized Doenetz's government and were having difficulties establishing their zones and policies. Some believed that the USSR was bound to go to war with Japan, but the government had tried to "seek peace through Soviet Russia." Ugaki had no faith that "such a trick" would work out. "The eagle eye of Stalin will discover everything, and he will try to profit by it."

[The next day, 17 June, the rain finally stopped, so Ugaki and his horse caught "a breath of fresh air." He spent the night chatting with Teraoka, commander in chief, Third Air Fleet. They had been friends since Eta Jima days, and, according to Ugaki, Teraoka's "noble personality is enhanced by skilled calligraphy and poems." That night "scores of enemy B-29s came to southern Kyushu, attacking mainly the eastern part of the Japanese homeland.]

Monday, 18 June 1945. Rain. Last night's enemy planes were so persistent that the All Clear wasn't given before 0230. They came in from the southeast direction and attacked Kagoshima city with incendiary bombs, inflicting heavy damage to buildings and houses there. Altogether eighty-thousand houses were reduced to ashes and eighty thousand persons made homeless. Before dawn, the western sky looked like the evening glow.

[*On the night of 17–18 June, over 450 B-29s fire-bombed the secondary cities of Hamamatsu, Kagoshima, Omuta, and Yokkaichi. Estimated square mileage destroyed ranged from 4.1 percent of total for Omuta to 7 percent for Hamamatsu.*][16]

Seventy-second Air Flotilla Staff Officer [Lieutenant Jyoji] Norichika came back from his trip and told us about the devastations of Tokyo, Yokohama, Osaka, and Kobe. Does the enemy intend to destroy all the cities in this country?

Mr. Kobayashi at the official residence of the premier wrote me that its Japanese-style room was burnt out and he lost all his possessions. I regret-ted that the room was burnt out by the enemy before my suggestion of destroying the room by our own hands was adopted.

They came to attack again in the afternoon, and I went into the shelter through the rain. While almost everywhere the shelters suffered from leakage of water, here we were lucky in having no leakage of water at all. A Douglas plane which Commander in Chief Teraoka boarded left here at 0700.

Today, a plane of the First Air Fleet sighted five converted carriers, two battleships, and several others between the main island of Okinawa and Ishigaki Jima.

Tuesday, 19 June 1945. Cloudy, later occasionally fair. As a discontinuous line of weather moved south, intermittent showers came unexpectedly one after another before it gradually cleared and finally the sun came out. In the afternoon I heard opinions of the Kyushu Air Group commander and staff officer [Commander Hijiri] Urabe on the ground defense in this area, and I decided to take necessary measures as this is a pressing problem. Many problems are involved in preparing for land warfare while on the other hand carrying out air operations.

We received a report of sighting two enemy groups consisting of five converted carriers, four battleships, and others at almost the same spot as sighted yesterday.

According to an enemy announcement, the supreme commander, ground forces at Okinawa, Lieutenant General [Simon Bolivar] Buckner, was killed by our bombardment on the 18th. It won't only be the Thirty-second Army that rejoices to hear that. [*Tragically, Buckner was killed just four days before Okinawa was officially announced as taken. After a five-day interim command by Marine Major General Geiger, Lieutenant General Joseph C. "Vinegar Joe" Stilwell assumed command.*][17] It's said that some urge the need for an "on-the-spot investigation" in view of the heavy casualties at Okinawa, thus quarreling with Admiral [Chester W.] Nimitz.

[*Certain newsmen and "Monday morning quarterbacks" criticized the army's tactics at Okinawa. Statements by Secretary of the Navy James V. Forrestal, Turner, and Mitscher failed to stop the carping, so Nimitz held a press conference on Guam with seventy-six correspondents, pointed out the facts of life in regard to Okinawa's terrain, and warmly praised the army for its conduct of the campaign.*][18]

Twelfth Air Flotilla Commander Jyojima arrived here in the evening and hoisted his flag here for the time being. Soon after we had talked together, an air raid alert was issued. About one hundred enemy large-type planes in several groups seemed to be attacking northern Kyushu, but details couldn't be learned because telephone communications were disrupted.

Maybe due to bombing damage, the *Kagoshima Daily Press*, the only newspaper in this district, failed to come since yesterday.

Wednesday, 20 June 1945. Rain, later partly fair with winds. In the morning about thirty enemy small-type planes came to the Omura district, braving bad weather on the way.

Last night's B-29s bombed Fukuoka for the first time with incendiary bombs (time-fused ones mixed) and burnt out some eight thousand houses. [*Not only Fukuoka but Shizuoka and Toyohashi were fire-bombed by about 480 B-29s on 19–20 June. Percentages of area destroyed were high. Evidently Ugaki saw some good in this.*][19] It's fortunate that with this air raid the Western army and the Sixth Air Army opened their eyes. There have been no air raids on cities in northern Kyushu, so the army and the civilians as well have been completely unaware of the urgent need for air defense.

Thursday, 21 June 1945. Fair. In these days, we have been finding no need to worry about on what day of the week the date fell, so I won't write it down in my diary from now on. [*Ugaki must have changed his mind, for he continued the practice.*] The weather was fine since morning. A weather reconnaissance plane also reported favorable conditions. So I activated *Kikusui* No. 10 Operation.

Telephone communications with Tokyo, Sasebo, the Sixth Air Army in Fukuoka were all out of order due to cut-off of the main cable above ground at the Kagoshima telephone office. We don't know how far the Sixth Air Army will rouse its forces and cooperate with us.

Today, two enemy groups of five carriers and one carrier as hitherto seen were also sighted to the southwest of Okinawa. All of them were light converted carriers. The main force of regular carriers seems to be in Leyte making preparations for the next move. [*This estimate was correct. Task Force 38 anchored at Leyte on 14 June.*][20]

Six army special attack planes carried out dusk assaults, and four of them succeeded, gaining some success. (It's claimed that they inflicted minor damage to a cruiser, set a destroyer on fire, and sank one unidentified ship and a transport.)

[*At 1830 on 21 June kamikazes penetrated Kerama Retto. Seaplane tender* Kenneth Whiting *was slightly damaged by a plane she had shot down. Seaplane tender* Curtiss *was more seriously damaged, with forty-one killed and twenty-eight wounded, and was out of the war. LSM-59 was towing destroyer* Barry's *hull for use as a decoy when both were attacked and sunk. LSM-59's casualties were light—two killed and eight wounded.*][21]

The Sixth Air Army is adopting a method of making small-scale attacks, while the navy prefers to attack with all its strength after announcing its attempt from the night before, placing much emphasis on keeping command of the air in our hands while attacking. Which is better? It's a matter that should be well studied under the present circumstances. My staff officers have no definite ideas about it.

Friday, 22 June 1945. Occasionally fair. *Kikusui* No. 10 Operation.

Four *Gingas*, five heavy bombers, five *Tenzans*, eight *Zuiuns*, ten *Shiragikus*, six Zero-type observation seaplanes, nine land-based bombers (all of which were equipped for special attacks), eight *Suisei* night fighters (not including those which put about on their way to attack) sortied from 1900 to 2330. They attacked from 2300 to 0130 and torpedoed three of what seem to be carriers. One hit was confirmed, while they also torpedoed one destroyer and one unidentified ship with unconfirmed results.

[*Actual results were nowhere near this estimate. The only ships hit were LSM-213 and LST-534. Neither sank, but both were out of the war. Station No. 15 was attacked again but this time combat air patrol shot down twenty-nine of an estimated forty and drove off the rest.*][22]

Six *Okas* and eight fighter bombers left from 0520 to 0530 and attacked from 0845 to 0930. One *Oka* was released over the Naha district and another failed to be released over Ie Jima. Two of them put about on the way due to engine trouble.

Fifty *Shiden* fighters attempted to receive the returning attack force near Oshima and engaged in an air fight in which they shot down seven enemy fighters.

I spent the whole night at the underground shelter. At 0330 I left the quarters and went to the *Shinrai* unit to encourage crews of *Okas* and fighter bombers who were going to ram the enemy. Then I saw them off. This is the first time for us to give direct fighter cover to an *Oka* force and have them attack Okinawa, so I hoped for their success.

But a great many fighters put about on the way, so that the number of escorting fighters was reduced to half of the original strength. Moreover, some *Okas* failed to join the strike force, to my great regret. At the time of attack, a good deal of jamming of communications occurred so that the result couldn't be guessed. That eleven planes out of twelve army special attack aircraft made successful charge-ins should be attributed to our co-operative attack. As a whole, this time *Kikusui* No. 10 Operation, made at a break in the rainy season, is considered to have achieved a considerable result.

Both in the morning and afternoon a small number of enemy planes came as usual.

[Ugaki recorded with bitter regret that the last signal from the Thirty-second Army on Okinawa had been received on the 19th. As usual, he felt "greatly responsible for the calamity," although he could not see what other course he could have followed.

[That afternoon he made a long inspection trip. He was most dissatis-fied with the state of the airfields, and looking at the extensive beach he thought that "a mere division couldn't defend it." He found it "regrettable indeed to see the situation in such a state after I had been urging the need to defend this district since February last. It's absolutely essential to de-stroy the enemy on the sea, going back to the basic principle of national defense."]

Saturday, 23 June 1945. Cloudy. By a night attack of six heavy bombers last night, an unidentified ship was sunk and another hit confirmed on another ship. In the morning about forty enemy small planes came but they did no harm to this base.

[He noted that rice seemed to be growing nicely, and hoped for a satisfactory harvest in the fall.

[Sunday, 24 June, brought a report from Formosa of a large U.S. fleet and a task force 260 kilometers of Taipei. Ugaki took it with a pinch of salt, although it was "generally believed the next U.S. offensive would be directed "toward the China coast." To his irritation if not surprise, the report turned out to be false.

[Telephone connections with Tokyo were restored that afternoon. With their being broken "at every bombing, urgent communications often won't be able to be made in time."

[On Monday, 25 June, the rain finally let up, and Ugaki had a visit from some top army brass, including Field Marshal Shinroku Hata, commander of the Second General Army and the vice chief of the Naval General Staff. He hosted them at a dinner party at the Navy Club. Hata "was in great spirits" and stayed overnight.]

Tuesday, 26 June 1945. Heavy rain. Except those which put about on the way, more than ten medium-class planes and type Zero seaplanes seem to have made charge-ins last night.

Preparing for an enemy task force, extensive night searches were made over a vast area, including the sea east of Kyushu, after a long time. A flying boat reported an engagement with enemy night fighters and sighting a large formation, a ship, and a light at a point 200 miles bearing 150° of Toizaki at the end of its search line at 0200. Later, a seaplane that made a forced landing at Shibushi reported by telephone that it sighted a dozen lights in the east of the above position.

I ordered all hands on the First Station after 0400 and also had them stand by for an attack against the enemy task force. However, the weather, supposed to have been through with the rainy season, turned worse from about 0200, and pouring rain continued all through the morning. So a daytime search was impossible. As no enemy air raids were reported in the Kikaigashima area, the alert was accordingly relaxed. It's not clear at all whether there is really something or if it's just an erroneous identification.

The enemy started landing on Kumejima this morning. The garrison unit on the island were only sixty-eight army and navy combined. After trying to resist, they ceased their communication at 1250. The enemy has shown signs of landing there several times, and they did it at last. This might be considered a proof that the enemy's next offensive will be directed to the China continent. [*There had been some discussion along those lines. In fact, in the autumn of 1944, Spruance had recommended a landing on the China coast at some point north of Formosa.*][23]

At 1640 a report came in that eighty large and small vessels were sailing north at Leyte. Though not a large force, where are they heading? It might tell us the direction of the next enemy offensive.

A comfort unit of several men and women dispatched by the Osaka *Mainichi Press* came to visit us and performed some variety acts of accordion playing, jokes, and singing.

Wednesday, 27 June 1945. Rain. The new Vice Chief of Staff Takahashi, Senior Staff Officer Miyazaki, and others made a forced landing at Kagoshima yesterday evening and after a difficult automobile trip finally arrived here early this morning. In the morning I received their report on the briefing held at the Grand Naval Command Headquarters. Everything is now connected to Operation *Ketsu,* the decisive homeland defense. Now at last we have been pressed into the final decisive battle. We must be more determined and do our best so as to leave no stone unturned.

Twelfth Air Flotilla Commander Jyojima has been here to see his subordinates off for a special attack mission but left today to return to Oita, as moonlight attacks couldn't be made as desired because of foul weather.

Though the weather chart was not of a rainy season type, heavy rains have continued to fall since the night of the day before last and extended all over the Kyushu area today. Damage to river banks and shelters due to rainfall increased greatly.

Of late I've been regarding nihilism as the first requisite for building up my personality, not as an ideology or a principle, but to clear me of selfishness after emptying my mind. Thus, keeping peace of mind at all times, I hope to make myself worthy to be a commander.

[On Thursday, 28 June, Ugaki again entertained army brass, including Lieutenant General Kanji Nishihara, commander, Fifty-seventh Army. They had dinner with Major General Gennosuke Kurosu, a brigade commander, and Colonel Takeshi Okuyama, chief of staff, Seki Army Corps. The latter had attended the same school as Ugaki, and he had met the others on various occasions. "They were all in great spirits and couldn't leave early. So I got a little bit drunk. At long last, the rain ceased."

[A briefing on *Ketsu* was held on Friday, 29 June, but Ugaki did not attend. His chief of staff went to Oita to negotiate concerning fleet installations to be built there, while his operations staff officer, Lieutenant Commander Masaomi Tanaka, had to go to Beppu Hospital, suffering from a stomach ulcer. Meanwhile, as Ugaki recorded, the war continued.]

From 0030 to 0210 about forty enemy planes raided Sasebo and dropped incendiary bombs from above the clouds. The naval station headquarters, the communications center, the naval barracks the garrison unit, the naval hospital, the Welfare Association Hospital, and the Navy Club were all burned, together with the whole city north of the railway station. While Yokosuka and Kure still remain unscathed, the farthest, Sasebo, was destroyed first. Moji and Shimonoseki are said to have been attacked simultaneously with Sasebo.

[*On 28–29 June, 487 B-29s fire-bombed Moji, Nobeoka, Okayama, and Sasebo. As Ugaki indicated, damage was heavy.*][24]

On the occasion of the end of the Okinawa campaign, the government issued an announcement requesting the nation to be conscious of the grave situation and rouse themselves to action. The navy minister also issued a message to the navy.

At 1600 about forty enemy planes came from Okinawa, and eighteen P-47s attacked Kanoya, causing ten casualties. This was due to a delay in the alert. [*On 29 June, thirty-four P-47s from Ie Shima struck airfields at Kanoya and Kushira with rockets and "machine guns."*]²⁵

Saturday, 30 June 1945. Cloudy. In the morning small planes came to attack.

After supper, I took a ride after a pretty long time and saw a number of people working at an alcohol distillery, now converted into a munitions factory.

This unpleasant June is about to pass.

Sunday, 1 July 1945. Cloudy, later fair. Since breakfast time small planes came to attack, and they were a real nuisance. Their attacks lasted until evening.

[*The "nuisances" were eighty-four fighters from Iwo Jima that struck Hamamatsu, Itami, Kasumigaura, and Nagano. In addition, thirty-three B-25s from Okinawa bombed Chiran Airfield.*]²⁶

The United States made public that two of our special attack planes hit *Bunker Hill* on 11 May in the Okinawa campaign. She sustained heavy damage and is now in Bremerton Naval Yard. It also said that Commander Task Force 58 Mitscher, who was on board her, narrowly escaped death by an explosion. This was a result of our attacks in *Kikusui* No. 6 Operation, in which two enemy groups were sighted to the east-southeast of Okinawa the night before, and four fighter bombers rammed carriers at 0900 and four others on vessels. The fact that even two hits from five-hundred-kilogram-bomb-equipped suicidal planes couldn't sink the enemy carrier taught us the need to concentrate more special attack planes in future strikes.

Under the guidance of Staff Officer [Lieutenant Commander Masami] Imamura, I left the quarters at 1430 and inspected from Takasu to Furue Beach. I don't think that the enemy will land in this district.

While I was waiting for the arrival of my horse after coming back to Takahashi on the Furue highway, I saw ten enemy F4Fs circling over the base. After making a large circle three times in a loose formation, two of them charged into Kasanohara base. There was neither filter interception nor antiaircraft fire against them. I hated to see their arrogant behavior displayed in front of me. If and when fighter interceptions against enemy small planes can't be permitted due to the shortage of fuel, and antiaircraft fire is also restricted because of the shortage of ammunition, the enemy will act with complete freedom, and the consequences can't be overlooked.

Monday, 2 July 1945. Cloudy, later fair. Staff officers held a table maneuver of *Ketsu* Operation. Chief of Staff Yokoi returned from Oita in the evening.

Kure city was air raided last night. Twenty-six thousand houses were burnt out and about 180,000 persons made homeless, of which about 600 were killed, including 20 naval personnel. Damage sustained outside of the city was slight.

[*On 1–2 July, over 530 B-29s simultaneously fire-bombed Kumamoto, Kure, Shimonoseki, and Ube. As Ugaki indicated, Kure was the hardest hit.*][27]

Tuesday, 3 July 1945. Fair. We studied the staff table maneuvers of the other day. From morning enemy planes appeared in small numbers and from about lunch time scores of B-25s and P-47s came to attack.

[*On 3 July, thirty-six B-25s from Okinawa hit Chiran Airfield. P-51s from the Fifth Air Force struck Japan for the first time, shooting up float aircraft in the Fukuoka harbor area. In addition, over 560 B-29s fire-bombed Himeji, Kochi, Takamatsu, and Tokushima. Damage was severe at all these sites, especially Takamatsu.*][28]

Wednesday, 4 July 1945. Fair. A good many enemy planes flew up north from about 1100 into the afternoon.

[*Probably these were the 161 fighters from Iwo Jima that attacked Omba, Kasumigaura, Tsukuba, and Yokosuka Naval Base on 4 July. Also, P-51s struck the west coast of Kyushu.*][29]

As an Army Headquarters reconnaissance aircraft sighted a convoy and vessels going up north both sides of Okinawa, we decided to carry out a night search tonight.

With the rainy zone gradually moving to the east, the heat under the July sun rose as it cleared up. Voices of cicadas resounded in the woods. It was pleasant, too, to avoid the heat in the underground shelter occasionally. In the evening, I rode a horse past the airfield and the third section of plane embankments, which were pretty deserted after most of the planes were withdrawn to northern bases. As most buildings and installations worth destroying have actually been leveled, it's no wonder that enemy planes haven't come here recently.

Thursday, 5 July 1945. Partly fair. At almost lunchtime, enemy planes came to attack. [*Forty-six B-24s and twenty-five B-25s from Okinawa bombed the Omura-Nagasaki area.*][30]

Vice Chief of Staff Sasebo Naval Station Ishiwara came down here and told me about the other day's air raid damage. A saying goes that a nation perishes but mountains and rivers remain. It might be better if the nation remains even if mountains and rivers are burned.

In yesterday's search, *Saiuns'* engines developed troubles as usual, so that the number of available planes for operational uses couldn't be increased at all. Searches from night until dawn failed to sight an enemy sailing north.

The enemy seems to be very cautious about the next offensive. Thus we can gain time, but I wonder if we can roughly complete preparations for encountering the enemy by the coming 15th.

I'd like to hear an expression of confidence from the higher army commands regarding ground defense. I was pleased to see that they're getting on well in rice planting.

Friday, 6 July 1945. Cloudy, later rain. I received a report on a table maneuver, jointly presided over by the Air General Army and the Grand Naval Command, held at Fukuoka on both the 4th and 5th. We're still far from being ready, and we need much more effort.

Scarcely had I thought they [enemy aircraft] wouldn't come today before they came after lunch as usual. They flew north to the west of Oita and attacked northern Kyushu.

The flat part of Kure city was completely burnt out and so were Kochi, Tokushima, and Takamatsu. Scores of B-24s and P-47s also attacked Omura, with the result that many *Shiden* fighters and even special attack planes were set on fire and damaged on the ground. [*Ugaki referred to the raids of 3 and 5 July. On 6 July 517 B-29s fire-bombed Akashi, Chiba, Kofu, and Shimizu while 59 others hit the Maruzen Oil Refinery at Osaka. Also, fighters from Iwo Jima struck airfields at Chiba, Kumagaya, and Yamagata.*][31] When we withdrew our planes to the north from southern Kyushu, the enemy got wise and came up there too. It would be better to intercept them in the air than be destroyed sitting idle on the ground, but the shortage of fuel prevented us from doing so. We had a sukiyaki party at Amiya to cheer up my staff officers.

Saturday, 7 July 1945. Intermittent rain. A discontinuous line of weather moved to the east so that we have had intermittent rains since yesterday. At lunchtime, as usual, several enemy groups approached but flew away to the south due to a heavy rain which happened to come. In the afternoon, many of them were flying north to the west.

There are signs of a powerful enemy force coming out from Ulithi and Leyte. [*This was Task Force 38, which sortied from Leyte Gulf on 1 July to operate in waters near Japan. It comprised Task Group 38.1 under Rear Admiral T. L. Sprague, Task Group 38.3 under Rear Admiral G. F. Blogan, and Task Group 38.4 under Rear Admiral A. W. Radford. Each group had three CVs and two CVLs as well as a screen of battleships, cruisers, and destroyers.*][32] The next enemy offensive seems to be close at hand and is considered to be directed toward the China coast and the Southwest Islands district, trying to infiltrate there. In case of an enemy task force attack being made upon us while we're transfering planes, fuel, and ammunition in preparation for *Ketsu* Operation, a great deal of confusion can be foreseen. So I issued a warning against this.

Sunday, 8 July 1945. Cloudy. A discontinuous line of weather running from east to west stood still over Kyushu, so after a light rain in the morning it was cloudy all day long.

Last night's search of the sea east of Kyushu turned back from the halfway point, but others dispatched elsewhere were able to complete their mission without sighting any enemy. It has become certain from radio intelligence that the enemy task force left Leyte yesterday. If they come to attack here, it will be the day after tomorrow.

[*Task Force 38 was refueling east of Iwo Jima on 8 July.*][33]

Probably because of the discontinuous line of weather hovering near Tanegashima, no enemy planes came up today. This was quite unusual.

Monday, 9 July 1945. Cloudy. Information from the Naval General Staff said that quite probably the enemy hasn't gone to sea yet. In the morning twenty to thirty enemy planes flew up north to the west.

[*This was a very small sample of U.S. air activity over Japan on 9–10 July. Four hundred seventy-five B-25s fire-bombed Gifu, Sakai, Sendai, and Wakayama; sixty-one attacked the Yokkaichi oil refinery; forty-three B-24s bombed Omura airfield, and over one hundred fighters from Iwo Jima struck in the Aichi, Hamamatsu, Itami, and Washinomiya areas.*][34]

The new Assistant Chief of Staff Grand Naval Command [Rear Admiral Tomoza] Kikuchi came down here. He came back home at the end of last month when the First Air Fleet was disbanded and now is assigned to this new post. I appreciated his hardships.

While I was returning on horseback after inspecting the wreck of No. 2 Kanoya base this evening, the horse in a bad temper threw me off. But I was very lucky, as I leaped over the horse's head, turning a somersault in the air, and landed on both feet without a scratch.

Tuesday, 10 July 1945. Shower. A telephone call from Tokyo at breakfast time said that there was an air raid by an enemy task force. The enemy task force whose sortie from base had been reported once but soon called off really came at last. From 0510 to 1700 a total of twelve hundred carrier planes raided bases in the Kanto area, but damage was slight. [*On 10 July aircraft from Task Force 38 attacked airfields in the Tokyo area. Planes on the ground had been carefully camouflaged, but Halsey's men hunted out many. The admiral claimed 109 destroyed and 231 damaged. There was no aerial interception and antiaircraft fire was surprisingly light. After this raid, Task Force 38 retired to refuel.*]35 As if in response to this attack, pretty many enemy planes came to Kyushu bases from Okinawa.

From 0900 officers above commanding officer and representatives of all forces assembled for a briefing on the forthcoming *Ketsu* Operation and for table maneuvers in the afternoon. The shelter was crowded and became terribly hot.

I ordered searches over the whole area, but owing to foul weather only a part of the reconnaissance planes were able to take off. An army daytime reconnaissance reported sighting three groups, including twelve carriers, at a point 250 kilometers bearing 130° of Nojimasaki. At noon the enemy broadcasted to the states from on board ship that they were attacking the Tokyo district with one thousand planes. They even mentioned the names of some ships. What insolence!

Wednesday, 11 July 1945. Occasional showers. Intercepting an enemy telephone that enemy planes launched from their carriers put about at 0900 due to foul weather, the enemy position is supposed to be three hundred miles southeast of Shiono-Misaki heading west. A discontinuous line of weather prevented their attacks.

We finished the table maneuver in the morning and studied it in the afternoon. Ending it at 1800, I addressed all commanders, requesting their further efforts before the deployment of strength for *Ketsu* Operation. Regarding my speech as if expressing the will of their father, all present were very impressed and pledged themselves to do as I asked. When a man is thoroughly determined to devote himself to his country, there will be nothing to worry about or to fear.

At night, I invited officers from above captain to Amiya and the rest to the Navy Club to lift their morale.

Thursday, 12 July. Same bad weather as yesterday. Owing to bad weather, we could only partially complete the search last night. So the enemy position couldn't be determined. We had visitors from Okinawa both in the morning and afternoon, and they were pretty many.

[*The "visitors from Okinawa" were B-25s and A-26s of the VII AF, the latter flying their first mission against Japan.*]36

In the morning, I attended a lecture on U.S. tactics by Captain [Yuzuru] Sanematsu held at Kyushu Air Group.

[On Friday, 13 July, the U.S. force had changed its course eastward. Ugaki learned through the *Naval Gazette* that on 15 August 1944 he had been decorated with the First Order of the Sacred Treasure, based on his "long service to the country," and he considered this a great honor.]

Saturday, 14 July 1945. Continuous worse weather than the rainy season. The enemy task force, which had been considered to be in the southeast direction, appeared off Tsugaru Strait early this morning and attacked Hokkaido and the northern part of Honshu with more than one hundred planes. Simultaneously more than ten battleships, cruisers, and destroyers bombarded Kamaishi city. There was some loss of ships. They maneuvered as if nobody was standing in their way after making a thorough, precise reconnaissance. Was their attack against that area merely a task movement, or was it a diversionary attack with the additional mission of an actual result? We shall have to determine this point.

[*Hokkaido and northern Honshu had thus far escaped bombing, being beyond the range of the B-29s. Task Force 38 sent off 1,391 sorties and encountered no air opposition, but claimed 25 planes destroyed. They struck shipping in Muroran and Hakodate harbors in southern Hokkaido. Destroyer* Tachibana, *two destroyer escorts, and eight auxiliaries were sunk; destroyer* Yanagi *and seven other craft were damaged. Twenty merchant ships were sunk and 21 damaged. The force attacking Kamaishi was under Rear Admiral John F. Shafroth and comprised battleships* South Dakota, Indiana, *and* Massachusetts, *heavy cruisers* Quincy *and* Chicago, *and nine destroyers. They bombarded the Kamaishi Ironworks, which were already working at less than capacity. After Shafroth's bombardment, production halted. In the course of the two-hour attack, no Japanese opposition was encountered.*][37]

Sunday, 15 July 1945. Cloudy with high ceiling and the sun peering out occasionally. The task force attacked the Akkeshi area since this morning, and Muroran was said to have been bombarded, too.

[*The attacks of 15 July disrupted the Aomori-Hakodate car ferry. Eight of twelve ferries were sunk, two beached, and two damaged. Seventy auxiliary sailing colliers were sunk, eleven damaged, ten steel freighters sunk, and seven damaged. About 30 percent of Japan's coal traffic between Hokkaido and Honshu went by this route. The raid reduced the capacity by an estimated 50 percent. Also on 15 July a task force under Rear Admiral Oscar C. Badger— battleships* Iowa, Missouri, *and* Wisconsin, *light cruisers* Dayton, Atlanta, *and eight destroyers—bombed the Nihon Steel Company and Wanishi Ironworks and damaged the city of Muroran. It is estimated this unopposed bom-*

bardment cost the Japanese two and a half months of coke production and almost as much of pig iron.][38]

With the recovery of the weather, about one hundred enemy bombers and fighters flew up north, and thirty to forty of them raided Kasanohara.

Enemy forces in the southwest area are still pretty active, but their recent aim isn't clear. The enemy broadcast said that the purpose of their task force movement was to lure out and destroy Japanese planes. That might be so. A letter from Mr. Kobayashi was entirely pessimistic. He should be encouraged.

Monday, 16 July 1945. Rain and cloudy. More than one hundred large and small planes came from Okinawa in the morning. [*These were A-26s, B-24s, B-25s, P-47s, and P-51s that struck targets on Kyushu.*][39] I went into a shelter although we weren't attacked. Until one is killed in action or acknowledges responsibility by committing suicide, it is the rule of a samurai and a man of responsibility not to become sick or to be hurt by trifles.

A small number of carrier planes came to the northern part of Honshu, and the task force shows of coming south gradually. [*After the raids of 14–15 July, Task Force 38 again retired to refuel. On 16 July CVE* Anzio *and escorts were hunting submarines off the east coast of Honshu. Destroyer escorts* Lawrence C. Taylor *and* Robert F. Keller *sank* I-13, *flagship of Submarine Division.*][40] Forty B-29s attacked Oita city tonight. It would be better if all inflammable things were burnt out before this headquarters moves up there.

Tuesday, 17 July 1945. Cloudy, occasionally light rain. Leaving at 0800, I went to the 634th Air Group's seaplane base at Sakurajima accompanying three staff officers. It took one hour fifty minutes. Just when we got out of a car, we saw eight small-type planes, then heard twenty to thirty aircraft bomb Kagoshima.

[*These were P-47s dive-bombing railroad tunnels near Kagoshima.*][41]

[Ugaki found the 634th in a valley overlooking Sakurajima. A few aircraft were concealed in trees. These came out at night to scout the nearby sea. As Ugaki and his party moved westward on Sakurajima, he saw "several villages all covered with fruit trees." At Hakamagoshi they visited the Fifth Special Attack Squadron headquarters. Living quarters had been completed, but no "special attack midget submarines" had arrived, and a ramp was still under construction. The activity at this location struck Ugaki as "slow and leisurely." On the way back, they visited Tarumizu Air Group, which had not yet been air raided. Eight torpedo workshops had been constructed underground. Then, at Shinjo, they "saw underground hangars of special attack boats constructed underneath a cliff. Ugaki feared that the hangars were too near the beach, which could be dangerous in the typhoon season. The party returned to headquarters at 1630.]

A small number of enemy carrier planes appeared in the Kanto district today. According to an intelligence report, they were said to be from a British task force.

[*British Task Force 37 had rejoined Task Force 38 from Sydney. Heavy raids had been planned for 17 July but bad weather kept all but the first two strikes away from their targets.*]⁺²

Aerial photos of Okinawa have been taken at long last. Though pretty many activities were observed, enemy convoys and vessels didn't seem to have especially increased.

Wednesday, 18 July 1945. Heavy rain in the morning, later cloudy and fair. A discontinuous line of weather lying from east to west moved up and down, connected with low pressure zones. No wonder it rained so much!

A small number of enemy planes came both in the morning and afternoon. Okayama and Himeji were also said to have been bombed.

[*On 18 July, P-47s and P-51s hit targets of opportunity on Kyushu. Nor was that all, as Ugaki reported.*]⁺³

It is said that 180 carrier planes attacked the navy yard and the ammunition depot at Yokosuka in the afternoon. The enemy is still operating from a point 110 miles east of Inubosaki and Nojimasaki.

[*In these raids on Yokosuka, battleship* Nagato *was damaged, submarine I-372, destroyer* Yaezakura, *and three other craft were sunk and five damaged. The attackers encountered heavy antiaircraft, and combined U.S. and British losses were fourteen aircraft and sixteen men. After this raid, Task Force 38 retired to replenish.*]⁺⁺

Thursday, 19 July 1945. Fair. The enemy task force to the east is divided into two groups, one of which is especially connected with Okinawa. On the other hand, according to a reconnaissance report from the Ninth Air Division in Formosa, eight light converted carriers, eight battleships, ten cruisers, and a total of 307 transports are at Okinawa. Besides, small craft were active, indicating signs of a new movement of about two division-strength troops.

Come on, whether it's a task force or an invasion force! I don't care about them at all. We'll only show them that we're quite different from those stationed in the Kanto district.

[After lunch Ugaki asked his operations staff officers to study *Ketsu* Operation, particularly to consider how much confidence could they have in the operation's success "with 5,300 navy planes and more than 4,000 army planes?" Assuming success, they should consider methods to adopt in future attacks on enemy convoys and supporting forces.

[There was no air raid that morning, and the United States had issued a typhoon warning. Ugaki devoutly hoped that this kamikaze (divine wind) would "blow away enemy planes and sink enemy vessels."]

At supper time, an army reconnaissance report was brought in which said that one carrier, one cruiser, and one destroyer were sailing on 250° at 15 knots at a point 200 kilometers bearing 160° of Shiono-Misaki, and, besides, more than ten wakes of ships were seen to the west of the above position and eight fighters were flying over there. So we attempted a night search, but due to foul weather they turned back from a point about ninety miles from here without seeing an enemy.

[That evening the Seventy-second Air Flotilla commander advanced to Oita.

[No attack came on Friday, 20 July. The typhoon had passed west of Kyushu, bringing only "occasional light rain." Ugaki decided to hold a routine staff meeting every morning at 1130.

[Saturday, 21 July, passed with no attack, and Ugaki thought the typhoon might have "inflicted a fair amount of damage on the enemy."

[On Sunday, 22 July, the East China Sea south of Korea was searched following a report of U.S. bombardments in that area, but the report turned out to be false. He recorded that the previous night four *Tenzans* attacked ships in Chujo Bay, with claims to have damaged a battleship, a cruiser, and a transport.

[Due to weather conditions, Ugaki called off a "general night attack against Okinawa." Nor did the United States attack. Ugaki took the opportunity to inspect Iwakawa Air Base. He flew there with the Sixth Air Army Assistant Chief of Staff Aoki and his own Staff Officer Imamura. There the Fuyo Force commander, Lieutenant Commander Tadashi Minobe and the Saijo Air Group commander, Captain Shinji Doi, briefed them. Ugaki was quite satisfied with concealment measures; weeds almost covered the airstrip and small planes were hidden amid trees. He thought Minobe had done a fine job and agreed with his suggestion to utilize night fighters further, as they could "hardly maintain command of the air in the daytime." After being hospitably entertained by the Seki Corps Commander, Lieutenant General Wataro Yoshinaka, Ugaki flew back to Kanoya.]

Tuesday, 24 July 1945. Fair. An air-raid warning was sounded at 0630. Starting with carrier plane attacks on Takumi at 0600, the first wave of fourteen formations raided Shikoku, the western part of Chugoku, and central and northern Kyushu. Also, enemy radio activities were picked up to the east, making me realize that the long-awaited enemy task force had come again. As its bearing was considered to be generally 135° of Ashizuri-zaki, two *Saiuns* were sent out to search, but both of them seem to have been shot down, for they failed to respond to calls. In the afternoon two more were dispatched. Though an order calling for "Stand by for Attack Method No. 3" was issued, no enemy was found, so the order was lifted.

In the first attack wave, about one hundred planes raided Kyushu and another one hundred Chugoku and Shikoku, while in the second wave attack four hundred planes struck Chugoku and its coast facing the Japan Sea, and about seventy planes came to attack Shikoku in the third wave. As a result, considerable damage seems to have been inflicted.

[*In raids of 24 and 29 July, battleships* Haruna, Ise, *and* Hyuga, *as well as heavy cruisers* Tone *and* Aoba, *were badly damaged, settled on the bottom, and had to be abandoned. Another cruiser, five destroyers, and many small craft were damaged. CV* Amagai *was damaged, CV* Katsuragi *and CVL* Ryuho *knocked out of action. Again, the Japanese put up no defense, in line with their policy of saving aircraft for the anticipated invasion. The United States suffered a loss on 24 July when submarine I-53 blew up destroyer escort* Underhill *with heavy personnel losses, including her captain.*][45]

A *Saiun* reconnaissance plane dispatched in the afternoon reported after returning to its base to the effect that it had sighted a group of two carriers, two battleships or cruisers, and more than ten others at a point one hundred miles bearing 160° of Muroto-zaki. It failed to transmit its report due to trouble with a transmitter.

So an order calling for "Stand by for Attack Method No. 1" was issued while night searches were made. The full moon hung in the middle sky. And I placed great expectations on tonight's attack.

Wednesday, 25 July 1945. Fair, later cloudy. Four land-based bombers which left at about 2200 couldn't carry out night searches due to some radar troubles. Therefore, placing expectations on the results of early morning reconnaissance, the order was changed to "Attack Method No. 2 Alternative."

In the meantime, there was a report of enemy battleships and cruisers bombarding Kushira. Since this morning a good many enemy planes came to attack the eastern part of Chugoku, its coast facing the Japan Sea, and the Oita district. Yesterday's attack more or less damaged those vessels laid up in Kure.

One of the morning reconnaissance aircraft failed to return, so no information came in on the enemy situation. After 1500, a *Saiun* dispatched from Kisarazu sighted a group at a point sixty miles bearing 145° of Shiono-Misaki and four more groups at a point sixty miles farther than the above position. Altogether there were fifteen carriers, thus making the whole picture of enemy Task Force 38. Its position was three hundred miles from here, a little bit too far to do anything about it.

About ten *Ryuseis* of the Third Air Fleet closed in the enemy in the evening, but most of them seem to have been discovered and shot down.

Land-based bombers attempted to shadow the enemy at night, but couldn't find it. Eight *Gingas* which sortied from Taisha accordingly couldn't meet the enemy, thus ending in a complete failure.

A good many large enemy planes have come in these days to the Chugoku and Kanto districts from the Marianas in a concerted attack with the task force.

Thursday, 26 July 1945. Fair, later light rain. No news of carrier attacks was received this morning. It has become certain that the enemy task force has withdrawn south since yesterday evening. I regretted that after all we failed to take revenge upon the enemy task force with even one strike.

An opportunity with one hundred percent chance of success isn't easily obtained. Even when the chance is considered good, no attack can be made unless all the conditions are met.

Friday, 27 July 1945. Fairly fair with northwest wind and cool. With the clearing of weather in the south, enemy air raids from that district increased remarkably.

[*On 27 July, over sixty B-24s struck Kagoshima, while their escort of fifty P-51s hit targets of opportunity. Also, over 150 P-47s struck commercial and industrial targets on Kyushu.*]⁴⁶

A temporary farewell party was held at the Navy Club inviting staff officers of the Kyushu Air Group, Aeronautical Depot, and Construction Depot.

Saturday, 28 July 1945. Partly fair. The enemy telephone made clear that torpedo attacks by four *Tenzans* last night either sank or destroyed three cruisers and others at Okinawa. As the enemy telephone was picked up in the direction of 92° since last night, we have been alerted accordingly. As expected, since early this morning carrier planes came to attack Shikoku, the western part of Chugoku, and the northern part of Kyushu, while planes from Okinawa attacked the southern part of Kyushu and those coming from the Marianas struck the Kanto district, thus covering almost the whole country.

Kanoya and Kasanohara were also attacked but with no serious damage. I sensed that 170 B-25s and 110 P-47s hovered over the Kanoya district all day long. It's apparent that small planes are cooperating with large aircraft which play the main role. A loss of several planes couldn't be avoided at Kanoya, while Kasanohara was holed at fifty places, and more than 100,000 rounds of machine-gun ammunition were lost in an induced explosion. Considering that this kind of loss will add up almost every day from now on, some countermeasures should be taken.

[*28 July was indeed an active day over Japan. Four hundred seventy-one B-29s fire-bombed secondary cities; 137 P-47s rocketed and strafed targets on Kyushu; A-26s and B-25s struck airfields at Kaoya; 70 B-24s hit shipping at Kure; and B-25s and P-51s attacked shipping in the Inland Sea.*]⁴⁷

The enemy task force is said to be at a point about one hundred miles bearing 110° to 135° of Ashizuri-zaki, but searches both from the east and west by *Saiuns* actually failed to locate it. We planned tomorrow morning's attack after night searches.

Sunday, 29 July 1945. Fair. Six land-based bombers searched until 0200, but couldn't locate the enemy. Also, the search and attack by *Suisei* night fighters dispatched to the eastern direction failed. Most of them turned back due to foul weather.

[*The kamikazes scored one success on 29 July when an ancient fabric-and-wood two-float biplane crashed destroyer* Callahan *on Radar Station 9A. She sank with 120 total casualties. A worse U.S. loss, which Ugaki did not mention, was that of heavy cruiser* Indianapolis, *sunk later that night by submarine I-58.* Indianapolis *was on her way to Leyte Gulf from Guam after having delivered elements of the atomic bomb to Tinian. Losses were heavy, and many were not rescued until 2–3 August. A total of 883 perished.*]⁴⁸

Six hundred fifty carrier planes and 110 B-25s divided into waves attacked Kure yesterday. Vessels and its west coast were bombed. As a result, *Ise, Hyuga, Oyodo, Katsuragi,* and most of the others were either sunk or destroyed. Casualties were considered many, too. [*See comment on entry for 24 July 1945.*] Enemy planes came from Okinawa occasionally but didn't attack this base. A fire was sighted near the mouth of Kagoshima Bay. Enemy position is unknown.

As a result of the general election in Britain, the Labor party got the majority and [Clement] Attlee formed the cabinet, while Churchill resigned.

Though its details are not known, the United States, United Kingdom, and China seem to have issued an announcement asking this country's unconditional surrender. The navy minister issued a statement in which he urged the whole navy to do its best without being bothered by such a thing. He had better not issue such a weak instruction, but instead send a recommendation asking those three countries to surrender unconditionally. [*This was the Potsdam Declaration of 27 July 1945. The Japanese government decided to disregard it at this time.*][49]

Monday, 30 July 1945. Partly fair, later cloudy. Enemy air raids were frequent as before. [*There was no B-29 action over Japan, but other bombers and fighters hit targets in the Izumi and Sendai areas and southern Kyushu.*][50] A depression zone which has hovered for a while developed into a typhoon and is now in the south of Okinawa. Winds with center velocity of fifty meters per second might rage over the whole area.

The whereabouts of the enemy task force are unknown. Since last night there have been reports of its bombarding Omae-zaki or its position being one hundred miles south of Iro-zaki and so on, but its true character is completely unknown. [The following was written in the margin later: "The Hamamatsu and Shimizu districts were bombarded, while fifteen hundred carrier planes attacked bases in the Kanto area."]

[*Destroyer Squadron 25, flagship* John Rodges, *bombarded an aluminum plant at Shimizu but the plant was almost inoperable by that time. Carrier raids of 30 July were against Tokyo and Nagoya.*][51]

[Ugaki had planned a dinner at the Navy Club for various local functionaries, but liaison was poor and neither the mayor nor his deputy showed up. Although the Navy Club suggested that Ugaki spend the night there, he returned to his "shack."]

Tuesday, 31 July 1945. Cloudy, later rain. At about 1500 about forty B-25s came from Okinawa and bombed the first, second, and fifth sectors from above clouds.

[*A-26s, B-24s, and B-25s struck, among other places, Kagoshima, Nagasaki, Kanoya, Myazaki, and Sasebo, while fighters hit other targets on Kyushu.*][52]

I was to leave Kanoya at about 1800 to move my flag to Oita, but because of the typhoon the weather turned worse from about 1700 and finally became a gale with rain. So I called off my departure.

As I had finished my packing and my room had been cleared, I went to the Navy Club to spend the night there. Both were satisfied accordingly.

This month is also going to pass without achieving much battle results, in busy preparation for *Ketsu* Operation.

Wednesday, 1 August 1945. Rain with typhoon approaching. We couldn't leave here by plane early this morning either. As train conditions are unknown, I regret that we'll have to await clearing of the weather after all.

I went to the Navy Club and executed some calligraphy, but the results weren't satisfactory. I sweated in calligraphy after a long time.

After a bath, I had a small party with the remaining staff officers to forget unpleasant things in the past. While we were relaxing, an urgent telegram came in, so we went back to the underground quarters. The telegram sent at about 2230 said that "an enemy convoy of thirty vessels in three columns was sighted sailing northeast in the east of Izu-Oshima."

Based upon this report from a lookout post, the Grand Naval Command issued an order calling for "Section No. 3 Alert for *Ketsu* Operation." The Yokosuka Naval Station was also upset and issued an attack order, thus the whole navy was taken by surprise. As to ourselves, we should move to the new position as soon as possible to take the necessary steps for the decisive homeland battle. But a night search plane soon discovered that phosphorescent microbes had been mistaken for an enemy convoy, and everything was restored to the former condition.

Just as in the case of Davao last year, this sort of thing took place when men were pressed by the constant fear of an enemy attack as the time of a decisive battle approached, and they weren't blessed by good confidence in the defense. We should be more cautious and act more calmly.

[*It was ironic that the navy was "upset" over a mistaken report, when on 1–2 August 894 B-29s—the largest one-day mission of the Twentieth Air Force in World War II—fire-bombed cities, hit the Kawasaki petroleum installations, and continued sowing mines in Shimonoseki Strait. Some thirty P-51s hit targets in the Osaka-Nagoya area.*[53]

[On Thursday, 2 August, Ugaki and his staff officers decided to go to their new location by train since the rain continued with "little prospect" of let-up. They stopped at Ninatayama Hot Springs and visited Kirishima Hospital, "where most of the patients had been removed into shelters and its office into a bamboo bush." After a bath and supper, they entrained again at 1850, reaching their destination at Oita at 0740 on Friday, 3 August, three and a half hours late. They raised Ugaki's flag at an underground location. His quarters were in a four-room house belonging to a farmer, and the area was infested with mosquitos and fleas. The commanders of the Seventy-second and Twelfth air flotillas visited Ugaki to talk "about pertinent matters."]

At about 1730 Chief of Staff Grand Naval Command Yano phoned me to say that the Combined Air Fleet would be established soon, and I would be its commander in chief, concurrently [with] that of Third Air Fleet, and asked my views on selecting its staff officers. This organization setup had been advocated, but had been shelved for a while. Now it seems to be revived all of a sudden. I felt rather reluctant to leave the Fifth Air Fleet to go to the Third Air Fleet, but it couldn't be helped from the standpoint of the overall command. I consulted with Rear Admiral Yamamoto, designated its chief of staff; Captain Takahashi, designated its assistant chief of staff; and Rear Admiral Yokoi on selecting its staff officers.

[On Saturday, 4 August, the weather improved, and Ugaki inspected the Seikai Air Group. With Takahashi, Ugaki flew to Tomitaka on Sunday, 5 August, to inspect the base there.]

From about 1100 enemy planes kept on coming to southern Kyushu and attacked some air bases and iron works. [*These were some one hundred P-51s which attacked airfields and other military installations over a widespread area.*][54]

We took off at 1600 and landed at Saeki base after twenty minutes. This base had been attacked only twice and all the buildings except that of the garrison force remained intact. It was an extraordinary case in these days to see that they were still using regular buildings. The fact that there were no M/G installed in this base, coupled with the bad air currents over here, was considered the reason for this. I inspected the status of concealing medium trainers for special attack purposes in the Kakizaki district.

Tenth Special Attack Squadron Commander [Rear Admiral Noboru] Owada accommodated his headquarters here, and I saw him after a long time. He arranged especially to bring one of the *Koryu* midget submarines alongside a wharf to show it to me. *Koryu* midget submarines are expected to be underwater special attack weapons. I wished him further efforts and success.

We took off from Saeki at 1845 and returned to the base in ten minutes. While in the air, even as mere passengers, we couldn't relax at all and I acted as a lookout.

At 1425, a *Ginga* on its way to Formosa reported the sighting of three carriers, three battleships, and others at a point 200 miles bearing 220° of Saishu Island, south of Korea. So I ordered a night search which picked up three groups farther south of that position.

Monday, 6 August 1945. Fair. *Saiuns* searched the suspected area but located no enemy. A search plane sent from Formosa sighted three light converted carriers with battleships and cruisers bearing 30° of the northern tip of Formosa. The enemy bombarded Chushan Island desultorily yesterday.

As I thought I had better have my tooth attended to on this occasion, I went to Beppu Naval Hospital by car. Thanks to my staff officers' arrangements, I stayed the night at Suginoi Hotel. The quiet, the view of Beppu Bay, the cool breeze, and also the hospitalities which the hotel rendered me as a temporary Navy Club were surely enough to refresh me after six months of bitter life at the battle front.

Tuesday, 7 August 1945. Fair. After a sound sleep last night, I took a bath and then wrote some calligraphy for the host.

After a day of peace without being bothered by the war, I was going down a hill at 0915 when an air raid alert sounded. I went to the hospital nevertheless to have my tooth attended to while hearing occasional drones of enemy planes. I left there at 1115 and returned to the base in forty-five minutes.

At about 0825 yesterday two or three B-29s came over Hiroshima and dropped two or tree large-type bombs with parachutes attached. They exploded about fifty meters above ground with a terrific flash and explosion, with a result that about 80 percent of the houses in the city were leveled and burnt out. Casualties suffered reached over 100,000.

A radio broadcast from San Francisco this afternoon said that seventeen hours before an atomic bomb had been dropped for the first time in history, on Hiroshima, an army base. Though its result wasn't confirmed due to thick clouds over thirty thousand feet high, this bomb was twenty thousand times more powerful than the "Grand Slam" bomb of the B-29s and its effect was equivalent to that of two thousand kilograms of TNT. In the experimental explosion made in New Mexico on 16 July, a steel tower on which the bomb was placed evaporated and window panes 250 miles away from the spot shook, while men staying six miles away were knocked to the ground.

According to the above, it is clear that this was a uranium atom bomb, and it deserves to be regarded as a real wonder, making the outcome of the war more gloomy.

We must think of some countermeasures against it immediately, and at the same time I wish we could create the same bomb.

[*The Japanese had long been working toward an atomic bomb, but having no success abandoned the project in favor of what seemed to be more urgent needs. Many Japanese were reluctant to concede that the United States had succeeded where they had failed, hence did not admit for days that this was truly the atomic bomb. Three planes took part in the mission, but only one, the B-29* Enola Gay, *dropped a bomb.*][55]

Wednesday, 8 August 1945. Fair. The second table maneuver of the *Ten* Air Force was held, mostly to train lower-rank key members engaging in reconnaissance.

Pretty many planes came to attack various places, inflicting some damage at Tsuiki and Usa bases. Some fighters attempted interceptions but without much result.

[*B-24s, B-25s, A-26s, P-51s, and P-47s struck many targets on Kyushu includ-*

ing, as Ugaki noted, Usa and Tsuiki airfields. Fighters also hit airfields and industrial targets in the Osaka area, and B-29s fire-bombed Yawata.[56]

[Ugaki went fishing that evening. He broke two rods and took in only one prawn.]

Thursday, 9 August 1945. Fair. Leaving the base early in the morning, I went to Beppu Hospital. While I was chatting in the chief surgeon's room as they told me that my crown would be finished today if I waited for an hour and a half, a telephone call from Oita informed me that a broadcast from New Delhi reported the Soviets going to war with us. So I hurried back to the base.

Various reports successively received made it clear that the Soviets declared war against us at midnight today, and their warships bombarded Rashin, while their troops entered northern Korea. Air attacks made, too. Though the Potsdam Declaration didn't mention this point, Stalin's realism finally made him declare war against us.

Since before the Tripartite Alliance was signed, I had some idea about keeping peace with Soviet Russia. Though a nonaggression pact couldn't be concluded, I was very pleased to see a peace treaty concluded between the Soviets and this country. But in June 1941, when the Germans declared war against the Soviet Union, my hope was shattered. Since then I hoped to see the Germans make a separate peace with the Soviets, and especially in these days I hoped for better relations between the Soviet Union and Japan. But now every hope is completely ruined.

Now this country is going to fight alone against the whole world. This is fate indeed! I won't grumble about anything at this moment. I only hope we do our best in the last battle so that we'll have nothing to regret even if destroyed.

By detecting enemy telephone bearings since this morning, it was learned that the enemy task force was going up north, and at 1200 an enemy force including four carriers was sighted at a point 180 miles bearing 45° of Inubosaki. Their carrier planes came to attack the northern part of Honshu. It was considered to be an attempt connected with the Soviet's joining the war.

[*Nimitz, having intelligence of a large air concentration in northern Honshu, ordered Task Force 38 to destroy it. These aircraft were some two hundred bombers scheduled to crash-land on B-29 bases in the Marianas. As a result of this raid, some 251 aircraft were claimed destroyed, 141 damaged, and the Japanese plan was ruined. During this raid, a kamikaze crashed destroyer Borie, heavily damaging her and inflicting 114 casualties.*][57]

Pretty many enemy planes came to attack this area today, too, and a railway bridge at Tsurusaki was destroyed. Last night sixty B-29s bombed

Fukuyama with incendiary bombs and 80 percent of the city was said to be burnt out. Many relatives and friends of my deceased wife were there, so I wondered what happened to them.

[*B-25s hit the Tsurusaki area. B-29s fire-bombed Fukuyama the night of 8–9 August. According to U.S. records, over 73 percent of the city was destroyed.*]⁵⁸

An urgent confidential telegram came in from the chief of the Personnel Bureau. It said: "Dated 10th Kusaka attached to the Grand Naval Command headquarters. After his arrival there, Ugaki will be assigned as commander in chief, Third Air Fleet, Teraoka to be attached to the Naval General Staff and Kusaka to be commander in chief, Fifth Air Fleet."

As of yesterday, Takahashi was also assigned to be assistant chief of staff, Third Air Fleet, and Yamazumi attached to the Fifth Air Fleet. Thus everything was progressing toward strengthening the Third Air Fleet, but I heard some opposed the idea of a Combined Air Fleet. I don't care what happens, however.

A table maneuver to study *Ketsu* Operation was suspended today and a study of it was made.

Friday, 10 August 1945. Fair. I heard a report from Staff Officer Imamura, who incidentally encountered the atomic bomb attack while staying in Hiroshima on official business. He came back here by plane this morning with a slight wound after making an on-the-spot investigation.

According to Captain Genda who arrived here from Omura, the explosion of the same kind of bomb, which was dropped on Nagasaki yesterday, could be seen from Omura. The Mitsubishi shipbuilding yard, together with its branch yard, was seriously destroyed, while the city was partly leveled and set on fire.

The Grand Naval Command issued its operational policy against Soviet Russia. But it contained nothing positive. The Red Army invaded various places in Manchuria and north Korea, while their planes made mild attacks. This might be called the Soviet way, but they'll gradually increase their power of attack. Rear Admiral [Gobei] Namba, head of the Twelfth Aeronautical Depot, came over and expressed his views on our policy toward the Soviets, but it's too late to do anything. The new Thirty-second Air Flotilla commander, Taguchi, arrived here to assume his duty.

Balloon barrages in the city of Oita and this base were attacked yesterday and four were downed. Stray bullets hit living quarters of this headquarters.

Saturday, 11 August 1945. Fair. After breakfast an air-raid warning was sounded which kept on all day long, causing a nuisance. Some enemy planes attacked the east district. They attacked the Kanto district yesterday.

Though no information on the enemy task force that attacked the Kanto district yesterday has been received so far, their radio exchanges show a good deal of activity. These indicate a considerable probability that they have avoided a typhoon of 720 millimeters that was moving north-northeast after passing near Okinotorishima. Will they come to this area soon?

[*On 10 August Task Force 38 again struck northern Honshu, this time against two previously unknown fields. The fleet received word that Japan had accepted the Potsdam Declaration in principle, but were discussing terms, so Halsey decided to keep up the pressure after refueling on the 11th. A threat of the typhoon canceled an attack planned for the 12th.*][59]

I've been writing calligraphies in these days, hoping to give them to each of my staff officers as a remembrance and have just finished them at last in spite of frequent interruptions by air raids during which we had to withdraw into shelters.

In the afternoon the chief intelligence officer, a look of horror on his face, brought me the most hateful news which said:

> Radio broadcast from San Francisco: Japan applied for acceptance of the Potsdam Declaration on condition that Emperor Hirohito be left as he was; otherwise, unconditional surrender. A few hours later, the Strategical Bombing Force commander at the Marianas announced that atomic bomb attacks would be suspended until Japan replied concerning the Potsdam Declaration.

My God! What's the matter? Yet there can be no smoke without fire. An order from the Grand Naval Command received early this morning called for taking positive action against enemy task forces regardless of the progress of preparations for *Ketsu* Operation, while strengthening our attacks on Okinawa at the same time. Considering this to be a sign that they were forced to lift the ban on taking positive actions in light of *Ketsu* Operation, as we had advocated, the morale of the men rose temporarily.

After receiving the above news, however, my staff learned through telephone liaisons to the Grand Naval Command headquarters at Hiyoshi that they had noted comments somewhat confirming the news, which had been considered enemy propaganda. Why wasn't the commander in chief, having the full responsibility, consulted in such an important matters? The above incredible broadcast, while hiding [the decision] from us, gave me a shock.

[*Japan's peace negotiations were being conducted in the utmost secrecy, and many more highly placed than Ugaki did not realize just what was going on, hence his shocked reaction.*]⁶⁰

While we were completely absorbed in preparing for the last stand after being pressed to the homeland, the atomic bomb attacks and the Soviet's joining the war, thus deteriorating our position, shocked us. But we can take some countermeasures against them. We still have enough fighting strength remaining, which was saved just because of restrictions.

Furthermore, don't we have large army forces still intact on the China continent and in our homeland? It might be the view of some clever fellows to surrender with some strength left, instead of being completely destroyed, if and when we can't avoid defeat anyway. But those fellows advocating that idea are nothing but selfish weaklings who don't think seriously about the future of the nation and only seek immediate benefits.

Even if we dared to commit ourselves now, it's apparent that the enemy, notwithstanding, will follow the original policy, paying little consideration to us, and we would be completely destroyed. Moreover, it's clear, too, that the whole nation wouldn't be pressed to taste the bitterness of war, and some cunning fellows would take advantage of a defeat so that the traditional Japanese spirit would be basically destroyed and even the noble spirit of revenge be lost, making the prospect of the empire extremely dark. In the end, the future of this empire will be completely ruined.

Even though it becomes impossible for us to continue organized resistance after expending our strength, we must continue guerrilla warfare under the emperor and never give up the war. When this resolution is brought home, we can't be defeated. Instead, we can make the enemy finally give up the war after making it taste the bitterness of a prolonged conflict.

[*Ugaki was by no means alone in this opinion. War Minister Anami, Chief of the Army General Staff Umezu, and Chief of the Naval General Staff Toyoda espoused this line of thought. They required the emperor's personal word that he desired peace before they agreed. Even then, some hotheads in both services tried to circumvent the emperor's orders. Ugaki mused about the problem he faced.*]⁶¹

This is a great problem for me, too, as commander in chief. Though an emperor's order must be followed, I can hardly stand to see us suspending attacks while still having this fighting strength. I think many things remain to be done after consulting with those brave men willing to die. When and how to die as a samurai, an admiral, or a supreme commander, a subject I have long resolved in my mind, should be seriously studied for the sake of the future of the Japanese nation. I renewed a resolution today of entrusting my body to the throne and defending the empire until death takes me away.

A confidential telegram sent from the chief of the Naval General Staff at 0900 warned us to devote ourselves to fighting our main enemy, the United States, while encountering Soviet Russia on the one hand, and not to be bothered by the current rumor. At night I learned that there was some little doubt involved in other related Imperial orders also, which relieved me a great deal.

However, the special intelligence unit still reported broadcasts on the scene of victory celebrations in London and blowing of car horns in joy at Pearl Harbor after hearing of Japan's applying for surrender. We should consider them as propaganda on the joyous occasion of the atomic bomb attacks and Soviet Russia's joining the war and proceed to fight without being bothered by them at all.

Sunday, 12 August 1945. Fair. A message jointly signed by the navy minister and the chief of the Naval General Staff was sent to all commanders in chief. It said:

> With the participation of the Soviet into the war, the crisis of the empire is more pressed, so that we should fight until the last man. However, the government has started peace negotiations with the Allied powers, so we are requested to follow the national policy in a well-organized manner without being bothered by public opinion.

Judging from this, it's now evident that this kind of negotiation is going on, and this made me feel awfully unpleasant. But I felt refreshed later when a foreign broadcast reportedly said that the enemy refused our request because they wouldn't recognize the continuation of the present position of Hirohito and his descendants.

On the other hand, the grand naval commander sent in a confidential telegram calling for continuing the current operations by all means with firm determination. This gave me the impression that some discrepancy exists in the upper echelon, and the high command seems to suggest that the government's action of seeking negotiations should be regarded as a separate one.

The enemy task force is still operating east of the Japanese homeland.

The Soviet army surrounded Hailar city and penetrated into north Korea. It was also reported that they made a landing on Rashin.

Upon receipt of information that an enemy fleet centering around three cruisers seemed to be going either south or southwest, night searches were made.

After the enemy air raids were over, I left the base at 1545 for Beppu Hospital and had my tooth crown finished, to be ready for any emergency.

Surgeon Rear Admiral [Zumi] Kanai, the president of Totsuka Medical School, and two others came to explain how to reduce the mens's rations by 10 percent.

An operations conference was held at night to hear the report of a staff officer who has come back from his liaison trip to the Sixth Air Army. He was indignant because preparations for *Ketsu* Operation had made little progress at all.

Monday, 13 August 1945. Fair. Leaving the quarters at 0630, I went to inspect the underground site of the new fleet headquarters at Otachi, accompanying my assistant chief of staff. It's a fairly big one, having been previously prepared by the Twelfth Aeronautical Depot, and preparations are being made also to accommodate headquarters of both the Thirty-fourth Air Fleet and Sixth Air Army.

We received an operational order of the Grand Naval Command alerting the third, fourth, fifth, sixth, and seventh sections for *Ketsu* Operation. This is because the enemy task force attacked the Kanto district down to Numazu from 0630 this morning, and four groups were one hundred miles off the shore of Inubosaki. Considerably strong forces were also detected to its east and south. [*On 13 August Task Force 38 destroyed 254 planes on the ground and damaged 149, while combat air patrol shot down eighteen in the air.*][62] This order is also thought to have been given because a concentration of enemy transports was seen in the Okinawa district.

I, who am commanding *Ten* Air Force, received an order to concentrate our reserved strength for enemy task forces and also an instruction on future air operations in general. There was also an order calling for moving a part of the underwater special attack force to the Tokai district. All these orders were given because there is an increased probability of the enemy landing on the east and west with the Soviets participating in the war.

Though the Combined Air fleet hasn't been established, the Tenth Air Fleet was placed under the command of *Ten* Air Force yesterday and the 723rd Air Group today. Things in general are moving in along this line.

A foreign radio broadcast intercepted since this morning said that they were studying Japan's request for an amendment and a reply would be given within twenty-four hours. Nimitz at Guam also called up Tokyo by the international call signal and said that, as it took time to communicate via Switzerland, communication should be made in plain English, and he also instructed what wave channel to use. What an insult! [The following was written in the margin: "It seems to be true that Japan hasn't made a reply in the past twenty-four hours to the amendment placing the emperor under the control of the president of the United States, which was made at Japan's request to continue the position of the emperor."]

At night a lookout post at Okinoerabushima reported sixty-five enemy sailing north to the west of the island, while an Army Headquarters reconnaissance plane dispatched in the morning also sighted a considerable number of enemy vessels farther south. So I ordered night searches, judging that they were heading toward Oshima.

Last night's attack on Okinawa with *Tenzans* sank two enemy vessels, and it's almost certain that two of those fighter-bombers which sortied from Kikaigashima after dusk today rammed a carrier and another ship. Daytime attacks by the Third Air Fleet against the enemy task force seem to have set two enemy ships on fire. So I gave an order to finish the damaged ships with four *Tenzans* tonight.

[Ugaki's successor, Kusaka, postponed his arrival. In view of the alert for *Ketsu* and "insufficient communications facilities at Yamato and Kisarazu bases," Ugaki considered it best that he remain in position to command the *Ten* Air Force. He notified the chief of the Personnel Bureau accordingly, asking that the changes be held off until further advice from Ugaki. "A reshuffle of commanders in chief under a crucial situation needs a good deal of consideration."]

Tuesday, 14 August 1945. Fair. Though I spent the night in the shelter waiting, no enemy information could be obtained. An Army Headquarters reconnaissance plane dispatched in the morning sighted one cruiser, several destroyers, and thirty transports sailing south at a point 180 miles bearing 240° of Bonomisaki. As its report reached us at 1400, I hurriedly ordered searches.

As usual, *Saiun* planes couldn't take off in sufficient number, and we couldn't locate an enemy. Three *Suiseis* were sent from Kokubu for a search and attack mission, but they also ended in failure. Night searches by seaplanes didn't find any enemy either. But it was generally considered certain that some enemy force has been operating in the East China Sea of late for decoy purposes.

The enemy task force is still operating off the Kanto district, but its count couldn't be made available in spite of the Third Air Fleet's arduous efforts. [*Task Force 38 was refueling on 14 August.*] On the other hand, we received a request from the Grand Naval Command to destroy a Soviet fleet upon its sortie from a port. How to catch it is a prerequisite, and we can't do it alone under the current circumstances unless we receive cooperation from other forces.

A discontinuous line of weather moved south, so the weather in the Kanto district was not good. Two hundred B-29s, which flew up north passing east of this base, attacked the Iwakune district.

[*Three hundred and two B-29s bombed the naval arsenal at Hikari and the army arsenal at Osaka. One hundred and eight others struck railyards at Marifu. That night—14–15 August—another group of over 160 fire-bombed Kunagaya and Iseraki. Another 132 bombed the Nippon Oil Company at Tsuchizakimimato. Another 39 laid mines. These were the last B-29 missions over Japan.]*[63]

I waited until night, but Vice Admiral Kusaka failed to arrive here after all.

Foreign broadcasts are reporting various things about Japan's decisions, but, summing them up, it seems that this country is inclined to accept the surrender terms. They also report that the use of atomic bombs will be suspended until Japan's reply is received, and MacArthur is preparing to move to Tokyo. I can't help feeling gloomy even though I tried to get rid of it.

[That evening Ugaki entertained the mayor of Oita, who hoped they might speak together again, but Ugaki was sure that "such a chance will never come to me."]

Wednesday, 15 August 1945. Late at night, the Grand Naval Command alerted *Ketsu* Nos. 1, 2, 11, 12, and 13, too. With this order, the whole country has been alerted. Its chief of staff especially warned this fleet that an enemy landing on our homeland would be near at hand. We could see persistent movements of the enemy task force and also what seemed to be activities of enemy invasion forces following the task force, but all these were not considered to be enemy attempts to land on our homeland. I rather considered them, stepped up as they were by strength in all directions, to be maneuvers aimed at hastening our subjugation, taking advantage of our proposing surrender.

[*At 0415 on 15 August the last air strike on Tokyo began. These aircraft were over Tokyo when Halsey received orders to cease air operations, as Japan had surrendered. The last air battle occurred when six F6Fs from Yorktown engaged fifteen to twenty Japanese aircraft at Tokurozama airfield just as they received the word to break off. The F6Fs shot down nine Japanese but lost four of their own. While the U.S. Fleet celebrated Japan's surrender, several Japanese planes approached Task Force 38. All were shot down or driven off.*]*[64]

Shortly afterward the Grand Naval Command, through the Kure Naval Station, ordered the suspension of any positive attack on Okinawa and against Soviet Russia. This seems to be endorsing our surrender. I completely disagreed with the order, as I believe that we should fight until the last moment.

Broadcasts from abroad said that Japan had surrendered unconditionally, and that the emperor himself would broadcast at noon today. So I made up my mind to ram enemy vessels at Okinawa, directly leading special attack aircraft, and gave an order to prepare *Suisei* planes at this base immediately.

At noon, following the national anthem, His Majesty himself made a broadcast. What he said wasn't very clear because of the poor radio conditions, but I could guess most of it. I've never been filled with so much trepidation. As one of the officers the throne trusted, I met this sad day. I've never been so ashamed of myself. Alas!

Following the chief of staff, Twelfth Air Flotilla Commander Jyojima came over to ask me to reconsider, but there will be no command difficulties at all after my committing a suicide attack, as my successor is expected to arrive here this evening.

We haven't yet received the cease-fire order, so there is no room for me to reconsider. I'm going to follow in the footsteps of those many loyal officers and men who devoted themselves to the country, and I want to live in the noble spirit of the special attack.

I've been in this post for six months since I received His Majesty's order. As to the brave, hard fighting of those forces my direct command or my operational command, I need add no more here. As their commander, I'm deeply grateful. I'm also glad to see that our cooperation with the army air forces and also with the naval air forces in Formosa were beyond criticism.

There were various causes for today's tragedy, and I feel that my own responsibility was not light. But, more fundamentally, it was due to the great difference in national resources between both countries. I hope from the bottom of my heart that not only military men but all the Japanese people will overcome all hardships expected to come in the future, display the traditional spirit of this nation more than ever, do their best to rehabilitate this country, and finally revenge this defeat in the future. I myself have made up my mind to serve this country even after death takes my body from this earth.

Now at 1600 my staff officers are waiting for me to drink the farewell cup, so I'm going to end this war diary. This *Sensoroku* covers from an era preceding the outbreak of the war up to date and is divided into fifteen volumes. Those things mentioned in various entries contain personal and confidential matters, some of which might be top secret. So I entrust the case of this to the secretary of my classmate association. This diary must never be placed in enemy hands.

[*There is no record of Ugaki's suicide squad crashing any U.S. ship at Okinawa. Apparently they went down at sea.*]

EPILOGUE
The Last Scene: Ugaki's Departure

AFTER DRINKING *a last farewell cup of sake with his staff at Fifth Air Fleet Headquarters, Commander in Chief Ugaki headed for Oita airfield by car, accompanied by his staff. He held in his hand a short sword given him by the late Fleet Admiral Yamamoto. At the airfield, eleven Suisei dive bombers were warming up, their roaring engines blowing the summer grass. In front of the command pit, twenty-two flying crewmen lined up. On each man's forehead was a tightly bound white headband; in each center a red disk of the sun shone.*

Lieutenant Tatsuo Nakatsuru, commander of the 701st Air Group's detachment at Oita, stood in front of the lined-up flying crews. No sooner did Ugaki say to him, "Commander, the order must be given for five planes," than Nakatsuru shouted back, his cheeks flaming with excitement: "Although our commander in chief is going to launch a special attack by himself, we can't stand by and see only five planes dispatched. My unit is going to accompany him with full strength!"

Hearing this, Ugaki climbed onto a stand placed in front of them and asked: "Will all of you go with me?"

Instantly, the flying crews shouted, "Yes, sir!" and raised their right hands high in the air.

"Many thanks to all of you." The determined admiral stepped down from the stand calmly but solemnly. He then bade farewell to each of his staff, firmly shaking their hands. His usually impassive face seemed to brighten at the prospect of fulfilling his duty.

Ugaki boarded his plane and was seen waving his hand as his aircraft taxied. With accelerated roars, the attack group took off one by one into the sky while the staff and others shed tears. The attack group soon disappeared into the southern sky.

On his way to the destination, Ugaki sent in the following message:

> *Despite brave fighting by each unit under my command for the past six months, we have failed to destroy the arrogant enemy in order to protect our divine empire, a failure which should be attributed to my lack of capabilities. And yet, believing that our empire will last forever and the*

665

special attack spirit of the Ten *Air Force will never perish, I am going to proceed to Okinawa, where our men lost their lives like cherry blossoms, and ram into the arrogant American ships, displaying the real spirit of a Japanese warrior. All units under my command shall keep my will in mind, overcome every conceivable difficulty, rebuild a strong armed force, and make our empire last forever. The emperor* Banzai! *Time: 1924, 15 August 1945. From on board plane.*

Ugaki's adjutant later found the commander in chief's belongings neatly in order. Among them was Ugaki's last note, left to one of his staff. It read: "Having a dream, I will go up into the sky."

Appendices

Notes

Bibliography

Index

Appendix 1

CAREER BRIEF, VICE ADMIRAL MATOME UGAKI, IJN

15 February 1890	Born in Okayama prefecture
11 September 1909	Entered Naval Academy at Etajima
17 July 1912	Graduated from Naval Academy. Midshipman on board *Azuma* on training cruise to Australia.
1 May 1913	Light cruiser *Hirado*
1 December 1913	Promoted to ensign
27 May 1914	Cruiser *Ibuki*
1 December 1915	Promoted to sublieutenant
1 December 1916	Battleship *Kongo*
10 September 1917	Training aboard cruiser *Iwate;* training cruise to North America
3 August 1918	Destroyer *Nara*
1 December 1918	Promoted to lieutenant; entered Naval Gunnery School to become a gunnery officer
1 December 1919	Gunnery officer of destroyer *Minekaze*
1 December 1921	Secondary gunnery officer of battleship *Kongo*
1 December 1922	Entered Naval War College
1 December 1924	Promoted to lieutenant commander; gunnery officer of light cruiser *Oi.*
1 December 1925	Staff officer, Naval General Staff
15 November 1928	Dispatched to Germany
10 December 1928	Promoted to commander
1 November 1930	Ordered back to Japan
1 December 1930	Staff Officer, 5th Cruiser Division
1 December 1931	Staff Officer, 2nd Fleet
15 November 1932	Instructor, Naval War College
1 December 1932	Promoted to captain
30 October 1935	Senior Staff Officer, Combined Fleet
1 December 1936	Commanding officer, training cruiser *Yagumo*
1 December 1937	Commanding officer, battleship *Hyuga*
15 November 1938	Promoted to rear admiral
15 December 1938	Director, 1st Bureau (Operations), Naval General Staff

10 April 1941	Commanding Officer, 8th CA Div. (*Tone* and *Chikuma*)
10 April 1941	Chief of Staff, Combined Fleet
1 November 1942	Promoted to vice admiral
18 April 1943	Wounded en route from Rabaul to Bougainville
22 May 1942	Attached to Naval General Staff for hospitalization
25 February 1944	Commanding officer, 1st Battleship Division (*Yamato* and *Musashi;* took part in Mariana and Leyte campaigns
15 November 1944	Ordered to report to Naval General Staff
10 February 1945	Commanding officer, 5th Air Fleet; took part in Okinawa campaign
15 August 1945	Flew final mission

Appendix 2

NAMES CITED IN TEXT

Name and Rank	Position
Abe, RADM Hiroshi	Cmdr. 8th CA Div.; later as VADM Cmdr. 11th BB Div.
Abe, VADM Katsuo	Naval Attaché in Berlin
Abe, Capt. Toshio	Cmdr. 10th DD Div.
Adachi, Lt. Gen. Hatazo	Cmdr. 18th Army
Ainsworth, RADM W. L. "Pug"	Task Force Cmdr.
Akiyama, VADM Seneyuki	as a Cmdr., Senior Staff Officer of the Combined Fleet under Admiral Heihachiro Togo
Anami, Gen. Korechika	War Minister
Aoki, Lt. Gen. Shigemasa	ACS, General Affairs, Southern Army
Aoki, Maj. Gen. Takashi	ACS, 6th Air Army
Aoki, Lt. Cmdr. Tatano	logistics staff officer, Combined Fleet
Araki, Capt. D.	skipper, *Atago*
Araki, Capt. Tamotsu	skipper, *Furutaka*
Arao, Col. Okikatsu	Chief, Military Affairs Section, War Ministry
Ariga, RADM Kosaku	skipper, *Yamato*
Arima, Capt. Kaoru	skipper, *Musashi*
Arima, Capt. Masafumi	skipper, *Shokaku;* later as RADM, cmdr. 26th Air Flotilla
Arima, Capt. Seiho	with 2nd Escort Force
Arima, Cmdr. Takayasu	torpedo staff officer, Combined Fleet
Arisue, Col. Suguru	staff officer, 17th Army
Asada, Cmdr. Masahiko	staff officer, 11th Fleet
Asakura, RADM Bunji	skipper, *Musashi;* later C/S, 1st Southern Expeditionary Fleet
Attlee, Clement	Prime Minister, Great Britain

671

Badger, RADM D. C.	Cmdr., TG 34.5
Bagdolio, Marshal Pietro	Italian leader
Ban, Capt. Masami	skipper, *Fuso*
Barber, Lt. Rex T.	fighter pilot
Barbey, VADM Daniel E.	Cmdr., VII Amphibian Force
Beppu, Capt. Akitomo	skipper, *Hiyo*
Blandy, RADM W.H.P.	Cmdr., Amphibious Force
Bogan, RADM G. F.	Cmdr., TG 38.3
Brown, VADM Wilson	U.S. Carrier Cmdr.
Buckner, Lt. Gen. Simon B.	Cmdr. Ground Forces, Okinawa
Callahan, RADM Daniel J.	Cmdr. TG 67.4
Carlson, Lt. Col. Evans F.,	USMC CO, 2nd Rangers
Chiang Kai-shek	Chinese Generalissimo
Chihaya, Masataka	former Cmdr. IJN; translator of diary
Chudo, Capt. Kanei	chief, Intelligence Section, NGS
Churchill, Winston	Prime Minister, Great Britain
Clark, RADM J. J.	U.S. Carrier Cmdr.
Conolly, RADM Richard L.	Cmdr. TF 53
Crutchley, RADM V.A.C.	cruiser force Cmdr.
Daigo, RADM Tadashige	Cmdr. 5th Submarine Sqdn.; to NGS; later Cmdr. 6th Fleet
Dewey, Thomas E.	Republican presidential candidate
Deyo, RADM M. L.	Cmdr. TF 54
Doenetz, Grand Admiral Karl	Hitler's successor
Doi, Capt. Shinji	CO, Saijo Air Group
Doolittle, Lt. Col. James H.	heads first U.S. air raid on Japan
Doorman, RADM K.W.E.M.	Dutch admiral
Durgin, RADM C. T.	Cmdr. TG 52.1
Eaton, Ens. Charles R.	sights minesweeper group (Midway)
Ebima, Ens. Kenzo	took dictation from Ugaki
Eguchi, Capt. Eiji	Cmdr. 801st Air Group
Eisenhower, Gen. Dwight D.	CinC European forces

Emura, Lt. Cmdr. Kusao	staff officer on Guadalcanal
Ezaki, RADM (Shipbuilding) Iwakichi	member, NGS
Fechteler, RADM W. M.	Cmdr. VII Amphibian Force
Fitch, RADM Aubrey W.	U.S. carrier Cmdr.
Fletcher, RADM Frank J.	U.S. carrier Cmdr.
Forrestal, James V.	Secretary of the Navy
Fort, RADM G. H.	U.S. amphibian force Cmdr.
Fujii, Cmdr. Shigeru	staff officer, Military Policy, Combined Fleet
Fujita, RADM Ruitaru	Cmdr. 11th (float plane) Div.
Fukuda, RADM Shinzaburo	on retired list
Fukudome, VADM Shigeru	Chief, 1st Bureau, NGS; later C/S combined Fleet; CinC 2nd Air Fleet
Fukuhara, Cmdr. Yuzuru	staff officer, 5th Air Fleet
Fukuzaki, Cmdr. Noboru	Adjutant, Combined Fleet
Fuller, Maj. Gen. Horace A., USA	Cmdr. at Biak
Funahashi, Lt. Masatoshi	spotting officer on Guadalcanal
Fushimi, Admiral Prince Hiroyasu	former chief, NGS
Futami, Maj. Gen. Akisaburo	C/S 17th Army
Gandhi, Mohandas K.	Indian leader
Geiger, Maj. Gen. Roy S., USMC	Cmdr., landing force Guam
Genda, Cmdr. Minoru	air staff officer, 1st Air Fleet; later as Capt., Cmdr. 343rd Air Group
Goto, RADM Aritomo	Cmdr. 6th CA Div.
Grace, RADM J. G., RN	Cmdr. Support Group
Halsey, Admiral William F.	CinC 3rd Fleet
Hara, RADM Chuichi	CinC 5th Cardiv; later Cmdr. 8th CA Div.
Harada, Capt. Kaku	skipper, *Chiyoda*
Harrill, RADM W. K.	Cmdr. TF 58.5

Hart, Admiral Thomas C.	CinC Asiatic Fleet
Hasegawa, Admiral Kiyoshi	Governor General, Formosa
Hashida, Kunihiko	Secretary of Education, Tojo Cabinet
Hashimoto, RADM Shintaro	Cmdr. 3rd DD Div. later as VADM Cmdr. Crudiv 5
Hata, Field Marshal Shinroku	Cmdr. 2nd General Army
Hatta, Yoshiaka	Minister of Railroads
Hattori, Col. Takushiro	chief, 2nd Section, Army GS
Hayakawa, Capt. Mikio	skipper, *Chokai;* later as RADM, Cmdr. 2nd DD Sqdn.
Hayashi, Maj. Tadahiko	staff officer, 17th Army
Hayashi, Mr. Yasuo	friend of Admiral Ugaki
Helfrich, VADM C.E.L.	Cmdr. Allied Naval Forces
Higai, Mr. Senzo	long-time government official
Higashi, Shinobu	translated portion of diary
Hill, VADM Harry W.	U.S. amphibious Cmdr.
Hiranuma, Baron Kiichiro	former premier
Hirata, VADM Noboru	CinC Yokosuka Naval Station
Hirohito, His Imperial Majesty	Emperor of Japan
Hisamune, Capt. Yonajiro	skipper, *Aoba*
Hitler, Adolf	leader of Germany
Hori, Surgeonobuaki	chief, Naval Medical Bureau
Hull, Cordell	U.S. Secretary of State
Hu Shih, Dr.	Chinese ambassador to U.S.
Hyakutake, Lt. Gen. Harukichi	Cmdr. 17th Army
Ichiki, Col. Kiyonao	Cmdr. Midway Landing Force; later Cmdr. Guadalcanal Landing Force
Ichimaru, RADM Rinosuke	Cmdr. 21st Air Flotilla
Imada, Surgeon RADM Ibuo	chief surgeon, Combined Fleet; later superintendent, Kaijinkai Hospital
Imai, Cmdr. Akijiro	Imperial aide-de-camp
Imamura, Lt. Gen. Hitoshi	Cmdr. 8th Area Army

Imamura, Lt. Cmdr. Masami — defense staff officer, 5th Air Fleet

Imamura, RADM Susumu — Cmdr. 10th Base Force; later Cmdr. Base Force

Imanaka, Cmdr. Kaoru — staff officer, Combined Fleet

Ino, Sekiya — minister of agriculture, Tojo Cabinet with additional duty as minister of colonization

Inoguchi, Capt. Binpei — dean, Naval Gunnery School; later skipper, *Musashi;* RADM

Inouye, VADM Shigeyoshi — CinC 4th Fleet; later commandant, Naval Academy

Inouye, VADM Yasuo — Cmdr. 1st Escort Force

Irifune, RADM Naosaburo — returned from Germany

Ishii, Col. Motoyoshi — senior staff officer, Southern Area Army

Ishii, RADM Takayuki — C/S, Sasebo Naval Station

Ishiwara, Capt. Itsu — senior staff officer, Southwest Area Fleet; later vice C/S, Sasebo Naval Station

Ishizaki, RADM Noboru — Cmdr. 8th Submarine Sqdn.

Itagaki, Capt. Akira — Cmdr. Base Battalion, Ballale

Ito, VADM Seiichi — vice chief NGS; later Cmdr. 2nd Fleet

Ito, Cmdr. Seiroku — senior staff officer, 2nd Cardiv

Iwabuchi, Capt. — Cmdr. at Munda

Iwamura, Michimori — Minister of Justice, Tojo Cabinet

Iwamura, Seiichi — Chief, Naval Ship Administration Department

Iwasaki, Technical RADM Wasaburo — Technical Department at Manila

Jin, Lt. Col. Naomichi — air staff officer, 32nd Army

Joshima, RADM Takaji — Cmdr. 11th Cardiv

Jyojima, RADM Takatsugu — Cmdr. 2nd Cardiv, later Cmdr. 12th Air Flotilla

Kakimoto, RADM Gonichiro — Cmdr. Combined Communications Corps

Kaku, Capt. Tomeo — skipper, *Hiryu*

Kakuta, RADM Kakuji — Cmdr. 4th Cardiv; later as VADM Cmdr. 2nd Naval Base Force; later CinC 1st Air Fleet

Kameda, RADM — CinC 1st Fleet

Kami, Capt. Shigenori — staff officer, NGS

Kanai, Surgeon RADM Zumi — president, Totsuka Medical School

Kanazawa, VADM Masao — Cmdr. Hq. 8th Naval Base; CinC Kure Naval Base

Kanda, Lt. Akira	midget submariner
Kaneko, RADM Shigeharu	chief, Communications Bureau, NGS
Kanome, Capt. Zensuke	adjutant, NGS
Katagiri, VADM Eikichi	chief, Air Administration Department, NGS
Kato, Capt. Kenkichi	former executive officer, *Musashi*
Kato, Lt. Gen. Rimpei	C/S 8th Area Army
Kawabe, Gen. Shozo	Cmdr. General Air Army
Kawaguchi, Maj. Gen. Kiyotake	detachment Cmdr., Guadalcanal
Kawamura, Cmdr. Takashi	Cmdr. Southwestern Air Group
Kaya, Okinobu	Finance Minister, Tojo Cabinet
Kelly, Capt. Colin P.	U.S. pilot
Kida, Capt. Tatsuhiko	Air Group Cmdr. Kokubu; later Cmdr. Naval Detachment, Kakaigashima
Kiehl, Capt. Elmer	Cmdr. Transdiv 50
Kijima, Capt. Kikunori	senior staff officer, 6th CA Div.
Kikuchi, Kan	author
Kikuchi, RADM Tomoza	ACS, Grand Naval Command
Kiland, RADM I. N.	Cmdr. TG 51.1
Kimmel, Admiral Husband E.	CinC U.S. Pacific Fleet
Kimura, RADM Masafuku	Cmdr. 10th DD Sqdn.
King, Admiral Ernest J.	CinC U.S. Fleet
Kinkaid, RADM Thomas C.	Cmdr. TF 16
Kira, VADM Shunichi	CinC 3rd Air Fleet
Kishi, RADM Fukuji	Cmdr. 9th CL Div.
Kishi, Nobusuke	secretary, Communications and Information, Tojo Cabinet
Kitamura, Paymaster Capt. Gen.	Paymaster, Combined Fleet
Kiyama, Capt. Tatsuo	Cmdr. 81st Garrison Headquarters
Knox, Frank	secretary of the navy
Kobayashi, RADM Kenzo	C/S 1st Fleet
Kobayashi, Mr.	cabinet adviser
Kobe, Capt. Yuji	skipper, *Nagato;* later RADM

Koga, Admiral Mineichi	CinC Combined Fleet
Koiso, Gen. Kuniaki	Premier
Koizumi, Chikahiko	welfare minister, Tojo Cabinet
Komatsu, VADM Teruhisa	Cmdr. 6th Fleet
Komura, Capt. Keizo	skipper, *Chikuma;* later C/S aboard *Zuikaku*
Kondo, VADM Nobutake	vice chief NGS 1940; later CinC 2nd Fleet
Konishi, Capt. Yukie	Cmdr. 705th Air Group
Konoye, Prince Fumimaro	premier until 15 October 1941
Konuma, Col. Haruo	C/S 17th Army
Kosaka	Cmdr. 26th Air Flotilla

[*This may be an error of Ugaki's. He mentions two other officers as commanding the 26th Air Flotilla.*]

Koshino, Capt. Kimitake	gunnery officer, *Musashi*
Kotsuki, Lt. Gen. Kiyoshi	supporter of Gen. Ugaki
Koyanagi, RADM Tomiji	C/S 2nd Fleet
Kuno, Capt. Shuzo	Cmdr. 762nd Air Group
Kuribayashi, Lt. Gen. Tadamichi	Commanding on Iwo Jima
Kurita, RADM Takeo	Cmdr. 7th Crudiv; later as VADM Cmdr. 3rd BB Div.; CinC 2nd Fleet
Kuromaru, Lt. Naota	Cmdr. and 1st Sqdn. leader, *Azusa*
Kuroshima, Capt. Kameto	senior staff officer, Combined Fleet
Kurosu, Maj. Gen. Gennosuke	brigade Cmdr.
Kurusu, Saburo	special envoy to Washington
Kusaka, VADM Jinichi	CinC 11th Air Fleet; later CinC Southern Area
Kusaka, RADM Ryunosuke	C/S 1st Air Fleet; later as VADM C/S 3rd Fleet; C/S Combined Fleet
Kuwabara, RADM Torao	Cmdr. 3rd Cardiv
Kuzume, Col. Naoyuke	Cmdr. at Biak
Lanphier, Lt. Thomas G., Jr.	fighter pilot
Laurel, José	President, Philippines
Laval, Pierre	French Premier
Lee, RADM Willis A. "Ching"	Cmdr. TF 64

Loud, Cmdr. W. R.	Cmdr. Minesweeper and Hydrographic Group
MacArthur, Gen. Douglas	Cmdr. Allied forces
McCain, VADM John S.	Cmdr. 81st Inf. Div.
Maeda, Maj. Gen. Masami	C/S 24th Army, Southwest Asia
Maeda, VADM Minoru	CinC 10th Air Fleet
Martin, Maj. Gen. Frederick L.	Cmdr. Hawaiian Air Force
Masukata, Capt. (Shipbuilding) Naosaburo	attached to Combined Fleet
Matsuda, Capt. Chiaki	skipper, *Yamato;* later as RADM, Cmdr. 4th Cardiv
Matsuki, RADM Masakichi	chief 1st Bureau, Naval Ships Administration
Matsumoto	staff officer, 17th Army
Matsumoto, RADM Takeshi	C/S 5th Fleet
Matsumura, Cmdr. Medori	senior staff officer, 6th Fleet
Matsuo, Sublt. Keiu	midget submariner
Matsuoka, Yosuke	Foreign Minister, 2nd Konoye Cabinet
Matsuyama, RADM Mitsuharu	Cmdr. Kure Naval Base; later Cmdr. 18th CL Div.; Commandant, Tateyama Gunnery School
Mifu, Sublt.	midget submariner
Mikasa, Major Prince	brother of H.I.M. Hirohito
Mikawa, VADM Gunichi	Cmdr. 3rd BB Div.; later CinC 8th Fleet; CinC Southern Area Fleet; CinC 3rd Southern Expeditionary Fleet
Minobe, Lt. Cmdr. Tadashi	Cmdr. Fuyo Force, Iwakawa
Mito, RADM Hisashi	C/S 6th Fleet
Mitscher, VADM Marc A.	Cmdr. TF 58
Miwa, RADM Shigeyoshi	Cmdr. 3rd Submarine Sqdn.
Miwa, Capt. Yoshitake	operational staff officer, Combined Fleet
Miyake, Kaoru	with Combined Fleet
Miyazaki, Maj. Gen. Shuichi	C/S 17th Army; later as Lt. Gen. Chief, 1st Bureau, Army General Staff
Miyazaki, Capt. Takashi	senior staff officer, 5th Air Fleet
Miyazato, Capt. Hidenori	skipper, *Yamato*

Miyo, Cmdr. Tatsukichi	staff officer, Operations Section, NGS
Montgomery, RADM A. E.	Cmdr. TG 58.2, later TG 38.1
Monzen, Capt. Kanae	leader, Construction Unit, Midway Invasion Force; later Cmdr. Guadalcanal garrison
Morgan, Lt. Cmdr. C. C.	Cdg. Beach Demolition Group
Morishita, Capt. Nobue	skipper, *Oi;* later as RADM skipper, *Yamato;* C/S 2nd Fleet
Mueller, Maj. Gen. Paul J.	Cmdr. 81st Inf. Div.
Murata, Cmdr. Shigeharu	torpedo ace
Muroi, Lt. Cmdr. Suteji	staff officer, Combined Fleet
Murray, RADM George D.	Cmdr. TF 17
Mussolini, Benito	"Duce" of Italy
Nabeshima, RADM Shunsaku	C/S 4th Fleet
Nagano, Admiral Osami	chief NGS
Nagata, Cmdr. Shigeru	navigation officer, Combined Fleet
Nagumo, VADM Chuichi	CinC 1st Air Fleet; later CinC 3rd Fleet; CinC Sasebo Naval Station
Naito, Cmdr. Takeshi	returned from Germany
Nakahara, RADM Giichi	director, Personnel Bureau, NGS; later C/S Southeast Asia Fleet
Nakajima, Cmdr. Chikataka	staff officer, Combined Fleet
Nakajima, Cmdr. Tadashi	executive, 343rd Air Group
Nakajima, RADM Torahiko	C/S Kure; later Cmdr. 1st Escort Div. VADM
Nakamura, VADM Toshibejin	Imperial aide de camp
Nakane, Mr.	secretary to Prince Fushimi
Nakao, Cmdr. Kumataro	Military Education Bureau
Nakase, Capt. Wataru	Chief 1st Section, NGS
Nakatsuru, Lt. Tatsuo	Cmdr. 701st Air Group, Oita Detachment
Nakazawa, Capt. Tasuku	chief Operations Bureau, NGS; C/S 5th Fleet; later as RADM chief, Personnel Bureau, NGS
Namba, RADM Gobei	Chief, 12th Aeronautical Dept.

Nasu, Maj. Gen. Yumio	Cmdr. Aoba Detachment
Niimi, Capt. Kazuki	tanker *Toho Maru* liaison officer
Nikaido, RADM Yukitake	Director, Technical Research Institute
Nimitz, Admiral Chester	CinC Pacific Fleet
Nishida, Capt. Masao	skipper, *Hiei*
Nishihara, Lt. Gen. Kanji	Cmdr. 57th Army
Nishimura, RADM Shoji	Cmdr. 4th DD Sqdn.; later Cmdr. 7th CA Div.; later as VADM Cmdr. 2nd BB Div.
Nishimura, 1st Lt. Teiji	son of above
Noda, Capt. Rokuro	Imperial aide de camp
Noguchi, Lt. Cmdr. Hoichi	skipper, *Kenko Maru*
Noguchi, Lt. Katsumi	Cmdr. 4th Mitate unit
Nomura, Admiral Kichisaburo	Ambassador to U.S.
Nomura, VADM Naokuni	CinC Kure Naval Station; later navy minister; CinC Yokosuka, concurrently Cmdr. Maritime Escort Force
Nomura, Cmdr. Ryosuke	operations officer, 5th Air Fleet
Nomura, Capt. Tomekichi	skipper, *Hyuga*
Norichika, Lt. Jyoji	staff officer, 72nd Air Flotilla
Norimitsu, Capt. Saiji	Cmdr. 61st DD Div.
Noyes, RADM Leigh	Cmdr. TF 18
Obata, Maj. Gen. Hideyoshi	Cmdr. on Guam
Obayashi, Capt. Sueo	skipper, *Zuiho*
Odajima, Surgeon Capt. Shokichi	chief, 2nd Section, Medical Affairs Board
Ohmae, Cmdr. Toshikazu	staff officer, 11th Air Fleet
Ohno, Capt. Takeji	chief, Personnel Bureau, NGS; later RADM
Oikawa, Admiral Koishiro	navy minister in 1940
Oishi, Capt. Tamotsu	senior staff officer, 1st Air Fleet
Oka, RADM Takasumi	director, Naval Affairs Bureau, NGS
Okada, Capt. Jisaku	skipper, *Kaga*
Okada, Admiral Keisuke	former premier

Okamura, Capt. Motoharu	Cmdr. 621st Group
Okochi, VADM Denkichi	CinC Southwest Area Fleet
Okuyama, Col. Takeshi	C/S Seki Army Corps
Oldendorf, RADM Jesse B.	Cmdr. TG 78.4
Onishi, RADM Shinzo	C/S 8th Fleet
Onishi, RADM Takijiro	Cmdr. 11th AF; later chief, General Affairs Bureau, Naval Aeronautical Department; as VADM CinC 3rd Air Fleet
Onoda, Capt. Sutejiro	staff officer, NGS; later skipper, *Takao*
Oogi, Cmdr. Kazuta	a Japanese representative in Berlin
Ota, Capt. Minoru	designated Cmdr. Midway Landing Force; later as RADM Okinawa Base Cmdr.
Otani, Capt. Inako	staff officer, Southwest Area Fleet
Owada, RADM Noboru	Cmdr. 10th Special Attack Sqdn.
Ozawa, VADM Jisaburo	Cmdr. Southern Expeditionary Fleets; later CinC 3rd Fleet
Patch, Maj. Gen. Alexander M., USA	Cmdr. on Guadalcanal
Percival, Lt. Gen. Arthur E.	Cmdr. Singapore
Phillips, Admiral Sir Tom	Cmdr. Far East Asia Fleet
Pownall, Lt. Gen. Sir Henry	C/S Malay Force
Pyle, Ernie	U.S. correspondent
Quezon, Manuel	President, Philippines
Radford, RADM A. W.	Cmdr. TG 58.4
Reeves, RADM John W.	Cmdr. Cardiv 3
Reid, Ens. Jack	sighted Midway Invasion Force
Roberts, Owen J.	associate justice, U.S. Supreme Court
Roosevelt, Franklin D.	President, United States
Rupertus, Maj. Gen. W. H., USMC	Cmdr. 1st Marine Div.
Saigo, Nansha	Japanese hero
Saito, Lt. Gen. Yoshitsugu	army Cmdr. on Saipan
Sakaguchi, Maj. Gen.	Cmdr. Southern Area Army
Sakamaki, Ens. Kazuo	midget submariner

Sakamaki, RADM Mumetaka — C/S 11th Area Fleet

Sakamoto, Lt. Mikihiko — fighter pilot

Sakonji, VADM Seizo — minister without portfolio

Sakonju, RADM Naomasa — Cmdr. 16th CA Div.

Samejima, VADM Tomoshige — naval aide to H.I.M.; later CinC 1st Fleet; CinC 4th Fleet; CinC 8th Fleet

Sanada, Col. Jyoichiro — chief, Operations Section, Army General Staff

Sanagi, Cmdr. Sadamu — staff officer, NGS; later Capt.

Sanematsu, Capt. Yuzuru — with Kyushu Air Group

Sasaki, Cmdr. Akira — air staff officer, Combined Fleet

Sasaki, Capt. Hanku — Cmdr. 9th Submarine Div.

Sato, RADM Namizo — attached to Marine Escort Hq.

Sato, Petty Officer 2/C1 Yoichi — on *Musashi*

Saunders, Brig. Gen. Laverne G. "Blondie" — Cmdr. B-29 Wing

Sawamoto, Admiral Yorio — CinC Kure Naval Base

Scott, RADM Norman — Cmdr. TF 64

Sejima, Maj. Ryuzu — staff officer, Army General Staff

Senoo, RADM Tomoyuki — Chief, Kure Naval Arsenal

Shafroth, RADM John F. — BB Force Cmdr.

Sherman, RADM Frederick G. — Cmdr. TG 38.2, 3, and 4

Shigenada, Capt. Kazutake — skipper, *Haruna*

Shiki, Capt. Tsuneo — Personnel Bureau, NGS; later senior staff officer, 2nd Fleet

Shima, RADM Kiyohide — Cmdr. 19th Div.; later as VADM Cmdr. 5th Fleet

Shimada, Admiral Shigetaro — Navy Minister, Tojo Cabinet

Shimada, Capt. Tojiro — chief, Munitions Bureau

Shimizu, VADM Mitsumi — CinC 6th Fleet, later CinC 1st Fleet

Shintani, Capt. Kiichi — senior staff officer, 24th Div.

Shiraishi, RADM Kazutaka — C/S 2nd Fleet, later Cmdr. 7th CA Div.

Shiraishi, Warrant Officer	midget submariner
Short, Lt. Gen. Walter C.	CG Hawaiian Dept.
Simiyoshi, Maj. Gen. Tadashi	CG 17th Army Artillery
Smith, RADM Allen E. "Hoke"	Cruiser Group Cmdr.
Somerville, Admiral Sir James	Eastern Fleet force Cmdr.
Sprague, RADM C.A.F. "Ziggy"	CVE group Cmdr.
Sprague, RADM T. L.	CVE group Cmdr.
Spruance, Admiral Raymond A.	Cmdr. TF 16; later Cmdr. 5th Fleet
Stahmer, Heinrich	German diplomat
Stalin, Josef	USSR dictator
Stark, Admiral Harold R.	CNO
Stilwell, Lt. Gen. Joseph	Cmdr. U.S. forces in China; later Cmdr. on Okinawa
Struble, RADM Arthur D.	Cmdr. TG 78.4, Dinagat attack group
Suematsu, Lt. Cmdr. Torao	communications staff officer, 1st BB Div.
Sugahara, Lt. Gen. Michio	Cmdr. 5th Army Air Corps; later Cmdr. 6th Air Army
Sugiura, Capt. Norio	chief, 2nd Section, NGS
Sugiyama, Gen. Gen	chief, Army General Staff; later as field marshal, Inspector General
Sugiyama, VADM Rokuzo	CinC 3rd Expeditionary Fleet; later CinC Sasebo Naval Station
Sumiyoshi, Maj. Gen. Tadashi	Cmdr. 17th Army artillery
Suzuki, RADM Choso	chief, Gunnery Experimental Station (ret. 21 December 1944)
Suzuki, Admiral Kantaro	Japanese Premier in April 1945
Suzuki, Lt. Cmdr. Suguru	intelligence officer
Suzuki, Lt. Gen. Teiichi	member, Planning Board (Tojo Cabinet)
Suzuki, Mrs. Yoshio	widow of Yoshio Suzuki
Suzuki, RADM Yoshio	chief, 2nd Bureau, NGS; Cmdr. 3rd BB Div.; later as VADM died aboard *Kongo*

Sweeney, Lt. Col. Walter C.	B-17 pilot, attacks Tanaka Force at Midway
Tada, VADM Takeo	chief, Naval Affairs Bureau, NGS
Taguchi, Capt. Taro	chief, 2nd Section, NGS; later chief, 1st Section, NGS; later Cmdr. 32nd Air Flotilla
Takada, Capt. Toshitane	senior staff officer, 3rd Fleet
Takagi, RADM Takeo	Cmdr. 5th CA Div.
Takagi, Miss Yuri	Fiancée of Prince Mikasa
Takahashi, Capt. Chihaya	VCS, 5th Air Fleet
Takamatsu, Cmdr. Prince	brother of H.I.M.; member NGS; later RADM
Takaoka, Capt. Heizo	Cmdr. Kushira Air Corps
Takasaki, Lt. Cmdr. (Baron) Masamitsu	original translator of diary
Takasu, VADM Shira	CinC 1st Fleet; later NGS
Takata, Surgeon RADM Rokuro	surgeon, Combined Fleet
Takata, Capt. Sakae	Military Affairs Bureau
Takayanagi, Capt. Gihachi	skipper, *Yamato;* later RADM
Takeda, RADM Moriji	CinC 24th Sqdn. (Raider)
Takeda, Major Prince Tsunenori	member, Army General Staff
Takeshita, Capt. Yoshiyuke	executive officer, *Myoka*
Tamura, Cmdr. Reizo	member, Communications Section, NGS
Tanahashi, Col. Shinsaku	Cmdr. Western Army Training Corps
Tanaka, Maj. Koji	army pilot
Tanaka, Lt. Cmdr. Masaomi	operations staff officer, 5th Air Fleet
Tanaka, RADM Raizo	Cmdr. 2nd DD Sqdn.
Tanaka, Maj. Gen. Shinichi	chief, Operations Bureau, Army General Staff
Tanaki, Capt. Ryujiro	Ugaki classmate
Tanamachi, Capt. Sei	staff officer, Combined Fleet, on Okinawa
Tanii, Col.	air operations officer, Southern Area Army
Tanikawa, Maj. Gen. Kazuo	Vice C/S Combined Fleet
Tanzola, Col, Vincent	Cmdr. 305th Inf. Rgt.
Tatsumi, Capt. Korokuro	*Tan* officer

Tayui, VADM Jo — C/S China Area Fleet; later CinC 1st Southern Expeditionary Fleet

Teraoka, VADM Kimpei — CinC 1st Air Fleet; later CinC 3rd Air Fleet

Terashima, VADM Ken — minister of communications and railway, Tojo Cabinet

Terauchi, Gen. Hisaichi — CinC Southen Army; later field marshal

Togo, Admiral Heihachiro — hero of Russo-Japanese war

Togo, Capt. Minoru — skipper, *Shiriya*

Togo, Shigenori — Foreign Minister, Tojo Cabinet

Toibana, Cmdr. Kurio — staff officer, Combined Fleet

Tojo, Gen. Hideki — Premier

Tokunaga, RADM Sakae — chief, Education Bureau, Navy Ministry

Tomioka, Capt. (Baron) Sadatoshi — chief, 1st Section, NGS

Tonaki, Capt. Morisada — member, NGS

Totsuka, VADM Dotaro — Cmdr. Yokosuka Naval Station

Toyoda, Admiral Soemu — CinC Combined Fleet

Toyoda, VADM Teijiro — vice navy minister; later minister of munitions, transportation,& communications

Truman, Harry S — President, United States

Tsuji, Col. Masanobu — chief, Operations Section, Army General Staff

Tsukahara, VADM Nishizo — CinC 11th Air Fleet

Tsuruoka, RADM Nobumichi — Cmdr. 31st DD Sqdn.

Turner, VADM Richmond Kelly — Cmdr. TF 51 Joint Expeditionary Force

Uchida, Cmdr. Shigeshi — Staff officer, Operations Section, NGS

Ugaki, Chiku — Admiral Ugaki's mother

Ugaki, Hiromitsu — Admiral Ugaki's son

Ugaki, VADM Kanji — C/S China Fleet

Ugaki, Gen. Kazunari "Issei" — influential general

Ugaki, Koichi — Admiral Ugaki's brother

Ugaki, RADM Matome — C/S Combined Fleet; later as VADM CinC 1st BB Div.; CinC 5th Air Fleet

Ugaki, Tomoko — deceased wife of Admiral Ugaki

Ugaki, Zengo — Admiral Ugaki's father

Umezu, Gen. Yoshijira	Cmdr. Kwantung Army; later chief, Army General Staff
Unno, Cmdr. Jyunji	weather officer, Combined Fleet
Urabe, Cmdr. Hijiri	staff officer, Kyushu Air Group
Ushijima, Lt. Gen. M.	army Cmdr. on Okinawa
Vandegrift, Maj. Gen. Alexander A., USMC	Cmdr. on Guadalcanal
Vian, VADM Sir Philip	Carrier Cmdr., British Pacific Fleet
Wada, Cmdr. Yujiro	communications staff officer, Combined Fleet
Wang Ching Wei	China puppet ruler
Watanabe, Capt. Yasuji	plans officer, Combined Fleet
Wavell, Field Marshal Sir A. P.	Cmdr. Allied forces in Western Pacific
Welles, Sumner	U.S. under-secretary of state
Weyler, RADM G. L.	Cmdr. Fire Support Unit North
Wilkinson, VADM T. S.	Cmdr. of Amphibians
Wright, RADM Carleton H. "Bosco"	Cmdr. TF 67
Yabe, Shu	confidential secretary to Gen. Ugaki
Yagasaki, Technical RADM Masatsume	Technical Department, Manila
Yaguchi, Lt. Cmdr. Yoshio	engineering staff officer, 1st BB Div. later Cmdr.
Yakamura, Capt. Goro	chief engineer, Combined Fleet
Yamada, Gen. Otozo	Cmdr. Kwantung Army
Yamagata, Maj. Gen.	Cmdr. 3 companies at Giruwa
Yamagata, RADM Masanori	Cmdr. 26th Air Flotilla; CinC 4th Southern Expeditionary Fleet; VADM
Yamaguchi, VADM Gisaburo	CinC Chinkai Naval Base
Yamaguchi, RADM Tamon	Cmdr. 2nd Cardiv
Yamamori, RADM Kamenosuke	Cmdr. Kyushu Air Group
Yamamoto, Capt. Chikao	member, 1st Section, Naval Ships Administration Hq.; later as RADM Temporary Cmdr. 5th Air Fleet and C/S 10th Air Fleet
Yamamoto, Admiral Isoroku	CinC Combined Fleet
Yamamoto, Capt. Ryutaro	Cdg. 202nd Air Group

Yamamoto, Capt. Yoshio — Chief 1st Section, Naval Affairs Bureau

Yamamoto, Capt. Yugi — staff officer, 1st Bureau, NGS; later senior staff officer, 2nd Fleet

Yamashita, Gen. Tomoyuki — General Army Cmdr. in Philippines

Yamazaki, RADM Shigeaki — Cmdr. 1st Submarine Sqdn.

Yamazumi, Capt. Chusaburo — C/S 8th Fleet, later C/S 3rd Air Fleet

Yanagimoto, Capt. Ryusaku — skipper, *Soryu*

Yano, Capt. Minoru — Cmdr. relief force, Milne Bay

Yano, RADM Shinkazo — Vice C/S Grand Naval Command

Yashiro, RADM Yukichi — Cmdr. 6th Naval Base

Yasuba, RADM Yasuo — torpedo expert

Yasuda, Mr. Taro — painter

Yasuda, Capt. Yoshitatsu — Cmdr. at Buna

Yokoi, RADM Toshiyuki — C/S 5th Air Fleet

Yokoyama, Lt. Gen. Isamu — Cmdr. Western Army

Yonai, Admiral Mitsumasa — ex-premier; later navy minister

Yoshida, Admiral Zengo — member, War Council

Yoshihara, Maj. Gen. Kane — C/S 8th Army

Yoshii, Capt. Michinori — senior staff officer, 4th Cardiv

Yoshimura, Capt. Shiku — Ugaki classmate

Yoshinaka, Lt. Gen. Wataro — Cmdr. Seki Force

Yoshioka, Maj. Gen. Zenshiro — engineering inspector general

Yoshitomi, RADM Setsuzo — Cmdr. 4th Submarine Sqdn.; later Cmdr. 7th Submarine Sqdn.

Young, Capt. Cassin — skipper, *San Francisco*

Yuzawa, Michio — Home Minister

NOTES

1. Now Our Combined Fleet Forces Are Deploying

1. The "Chinese Incident" is considered to have formally begun on 7 July 1937 at the Marco Polo Bridge.

2. The First Bureau was in many ways the key section of the Naval General Staff, being occupied with operational plans.

3. The pact was signed on 27 September 1940. By its provisions Japan, Germany, and Italy agreed to "assist one another with all political, economic, and military means when one of the three contracting parties is attacked by a power at present not involved in the European War or in the Sino-Japanese conflict." (United States Department of State, *Papers Relating to the Foreign Relations of the United States: Japan, 1931–1941,* vol. 2, Washington, D.C., 1943.) The pact was obviously aimed at the United States.

4. For an excellent account of the Japanese background leading up to Japan's participation in World War II, see Robert J. C. Butow, *Tojo and the Coming of the War* (Princeton, N.J., 1961).

5. The "uncanny complication" that brought down the Hiranuma Cabinet was the Russo-German Nonaggression Pact of 24 August 1939.

6. The United States froze Japanese assets on 24 July 1941 and embargoed oil on 1 August. For a discussion of these actions and their meanings, see Gordon W. Prange, *At Dawn We Slept* (New York, 1981), chap. 20.

7. Roosevelt's decision not to meet with Konoye has been controversial. Some believe the experiment should have been tried. See, for example, Dexter Perkins, "Was Roosevelt Wrong?" *Virginia Quarterly Review* (Summer 1954), 368–70. Others, however, believe no good could have come of it. See, for example, Gordon W. Prange, *Pearl Harbor: Verdict of History* (New York, 1986), pp. 169–76.

8. Ugaki probably referred to the Imperial Conference of 6 September to ratify the "Minimum Demands" and "Maximum Concessions" the cabinet had approved on 4 September. See *Japan's Decision for War: Records of the 1941 Policy Conferences,* ed. and trans. Nobutake Ike (Stanford, Calif., 1967), pp. 135–36.

9. Tojo was war minister when he became premier and retained that position.

10. Yonai had been premier from 14 January to 22 July 1940. He was a friend and patron of Yamamoto, who had served as his vice minister when Yonai was navy minister, 1937–39. See, for example, John Deane Potter, *Yamamoto: The Man Who Menaced America* (New York, 1965), chap. 4.

11. Hugh Byas, *Government by Assassination* (New York, 1942), pp. 138–40.

12. Interview by Gordon W. Prange with Capt. Kameto Kuroshima, 10 May 1948.

13. Ibid., 12 May 1948.

14. Prange interviews with VADM Ryunosuke Kusaka, 24 April, 23 August, 24 June, and 2 December 1947. In fact, all the members of the First Air Fleet whom Prange consulted concerning Pearl Harbor agreed that Nagumo "had a negative attitude" toward the Pearl Harbor operation.

15. See, for example, Prange, *At Dawn We Slept,* p. 143n.

16. Saigo had assembled an army of some 30,000 to invade Korea. He committed suicide when the government put down his rebellion.

17. Prange interview with VADM Zenshiro Hoshina, 7 June 1951: Takushiro Hattori, *Daitoa senso zen-shi ("The Complete History of the Great East Asia War")* (Toyko, 1953), p. 206.

18. Ugaki was correct. The cabinet and General Staffs had decided on war. Unpublished notes of Cmdr. Shigeshi Uchida, 2 November 1941; unpublished diary of RADM Giichi Nakahara, 2 November 1941. Both in Prange files.

19. Despite Ugaki's words of praise, key operational officers of the First Air Fleet were unsatisfied. Capt. Minoru Genda, unpublished report on the Pearl Harbor operation prepared for Prange, May 1947; Prange interview with Capt. Mitsuo Fuchida, 26 July 1947. Both in Prange files. See also Minoru Genda, *Shinjuwan Sakusen Kaikoroku* (Tokyo, 1972), p. 214.

20. This was the final rehearsal for Pearl Harbor. *Nagato* blinked congratulations to the task force, but Genda considered the bombing test "disheartening." Prange interview with Fuchida, 24 July 1947, and Genda report. Both in Prange files.

21. See, for example, *Shinjuwan Sakusen Kaikoroku,* p. 170; Mitsuo Fuchida, *Shinjuwan Sakusen No Shinso: Watakushi Wa Shinjuwan Juko No Ita,* (Japan, 1949), p. 83.

22. For an inside story of the midget submarine operation against Pearl Harbor, see Kazuo Sakamaki, *I Attacked Pearl Harbor* (New York, 1949). Prange had several interviews with Sakamaki.

23. The task force had already reached its rendezvous point—Hitokappu Bay on Etorofu Island in the Kuriles. For an account of activities there, see Prange, *At Dawn We Slept,* chaps. 45–47.

24. This note was not an ultimatum, as the Japanese and later some Americans contended. For an analysis, see Prange, *Pearl Harbor: Verdict of History,* pp. 182–92.

25. State Department Memorandum of Conversation, 14 and 16 April 1961, Papers of Cordell Hull, Library of Congress, Box 60; Cordell Hull, *The Memoirs of Cordell Hull,* vol. 2 (New York, 1948), pp. 995–96.

26. Ike, *Japan's Decision,* p. 283; Hattori, *Complete History,* pp. 231–34.

27. Prange interview with Capt. Yasuji Watanabe, 15 September 1949; Notes by Chihaya on draft manuscript.

28. The Second Fleet under VADM Nobutake Kondo was charged with naval and amphibious operations against the Philippines, Malaya, and the Netherlands East Indies. For details of the organization, see Samuel Eliot Morison, *The Rising Sun in the Pacific* (Boston, 1950), pp. 273–76.

29. The Southern Expeditionary Fleet (Malaya Force) was under the command of VADM Jisaburo Ozawa. It had been under way in small increments to avoid detection since 20 November. Prange interview with Ozawa, 22 December 1948.

30. Prange, *At Dawn We Slept,* pp. 366–68.

31. On 6 December 1941 a British reconnaissance plane discovered the Malaya

Force off the southeast coast of Indochina, and the Japanese fired at the aircraft. This may be considered the first actual shot of the Pacific war. The Malaya Force sent a message to *Nagato:* "Have been discovered by a British plane. Opened fire against it." As Ugaki makes clear, this gave Yamamato and his staff "no little concern" about a possible premature opening of hostilities. Prange interview with Watanabe, January 1948 (no day given).

2. No Greater Victory

1. Many incidents of this confusion are related in Gordon W. Prange, *Dec. 7, 1941: The Day the Japanese Attacked Pearl Harbor* (New York, 1987).

2. For concise coverage of the second wave action, see Prange, *At Dawn We Slept,* pp. 530–39. A more detailed account is contained in Prange, *Dec. 7, 1941,* chaps. 23–27.

3. The Eleventh Air Fleet, commanded by Adm. Nishizo Tsukahara, was land-based on Formosa. Its mission was to support the Philippines and Malaya invasions. Prange interviews with Tsukahara, 6 and 14 May 1949.

4. Three Japanese ships attacking Kota Bharu were driven off, but troops landed the next day. See Morison, *Rising Sun in the Pacific,* p. 188.

5. The Seventh CA Division under VADM I. Takahashi consisted of *Nachi, Haguro,* and *Myoko.* Prange interview with Watanabe, January 1948.

6. Prange interviews with Watanabe, 7 and 14 November 1949; Kuroshima, 14 June 1948.

7. Morison, *Rising Sun in the Pacific,* p. 180n.

8. The Japanese aircraft that sunk *Prince of Wales* and *Repulse* were landbased in Indochina at Saigon and Soktran. Prange interview with Watanabe, January 1948. For a concise account of this action, see Morison, *Rising Sun in the Pacific,* pp. 188–90.

9. On 5–18 January 1942 a war patrol took several U.S. submarines as far as the Japanese coast. See Morison, *Rising Sun in the Pacific,* p. 258.

10. There is no way of knowing how this was picked up, unless at a considerable distance by a "freak" radio wave.

11. The sunken Japanese DDs were *Kisaragi* and *Hayate.* Morison, *Rising Sun in the Pacific,* p. 231n.

12. Mili Island is in the southern Marshalls.

13. Yamaguchi ardently favored a second major strike on Pearl Harbor. Prange interview with Capt. Eijiro Suzuki (Yamaguchi's air officer), 12 June 1948.

14. Fleet Admiral William F. Halsey, USN and Lt. Cmdr. J. Bryan III, USNR, *Admiral Halsey's Story* (New York, 1947), p. 84.

15. Prange interview with Capt. Itaru Tachibana, 9 August 1950; Shigeru Fukudome, *Shikan: Shinjuwan Kogeki* (Tokyo, 1955), p. 230.

16. According to U.S. records, B-17s raided shipping in Davao Bay on 5 January 1942. *The Army Air Forces in World War II: Combat Chronology, 1941–45,* comp. Kit C. Carter and Robert Mueller, (Washington, D.C., 1974), p. 5.

17. Morison, *Rising Sun in the Pacific,* pp. 361–63.

18. Ibid., p. 304.

19. Ibid., p. 260.

20. A concise account of *Lexington*'s sinking is contained in Gordan W. Prange, *Miracle at Midway* (New York, 1982), pp. 41–42.

21. Morison, *Rising Sun in the Pacific*, pp. 285–90.

22. For an account of the Roberts Commission, see Prange, *At Dawn We Slept*, chap. 70.

23. For a characteristically colorful account of this action, see Halsey and Bryan, *Admiral Halsey's Story*, pp. 89–95.

24. Morison, *Rising Sun in the Pacific*, pp. 261–63.

25. Ibid., pp. 299–303.

26. Ibid., p. 304.

27. Ibid., p. 309.

28. Ibid., pp. 309–10.

29. Ibid., pp. 316–20.

30. Ibid., pp. 321–30.

31. Prange, *Miracle at Midway*, p. 16; Prange interviews with Watanabe, 25 September 1964 and 7 January 1965. Ultimately, Premier Tojo vetoed the Indian Ocean project, principally for political reasons.

32. Morison, *Rising Sun in the Pacific*, pp. 266–68.

33. Ibid., p. 268; Halsey and Bryan, *Admiral Halsey's Story*, pp. 98–99.

34. Morison, *Rising Sun in the Pacific*, pp. 359–63.

35. Ibid., p. 364.

3. A Second Victory Celebration

1. Morison, *Rising Sun in the Pacific*, pp. 363–70.

2. Prange interview with Watanabe, 6 October 1964; Prange, *Miracle at Midway*, p. 143.

3. Halsey and Bryan, *Admiral Halsey's Story*, p. 100.

4. Morison, *Rising Sun in the Pacific*, pp. 387–89.

5. Prange, *Miracle at Midway*, p. 32.

6. These staff meetings were concerned with the projected Midway Operation. Prange interviews with Watanabe, 25 September 1964 and 7 January 1965.

7. Samuel Eliot Morison, *Coral Sea, Midway and Submarine Actions* (Boston, 1949), p. 220.

8. See, for example, Potter, *Yamamoto*, p. 31; Joseph C. Grew, *Ten Years in Japan* (New York, 1944), pp. 232–42.

9. Prange, *Miracle at Midway*, pp. 22–23.

10. Morison, *Rising Sun in the Pacific*, pp. 382–83.

11. Ibid., pp. 384–85.

12. Many accounts exist of the Doolittle Raid. See, for example, Morison, *Rising Sun in the Pacific*, pp. 389–98; Halsey and Bryan, *Admiral Halsey's Story*, pp. 101–04. Prange, *Miracle at Midway*, pp. 24–27, stresses the psychological effect upon Japanese thinking and planning.

13. Prange, *Miracle at Midway*, pp. 28–29; unpublished diary of Capt. Yoshitake Miwa, 29 April 1942.

14. For accounts of these four-day war games, see Prange, *Miracle at Midway*,

pp. 30–37; Mitsuo Fuchida and Masatake Okumiya, *Midway: The Battle That Doomed Japan* (Annapolis, 1955), pp. 93–99.

15. Morison, *Coral Sea, Midway and Submarine Actions,* pp. 14–16.

16. *Combat Chronology,* p. 14.

17. Morison, *Coral Sea, Midway and Submarine Actions,* pp. 25–27.

18. Ibid., pp. 39–42.

19. Ibid., pp. 33–37.

20. Ibid., pp. 37–39.

21. Ibid., pp. 43–62.

22. Ibid., pp. 224–25.

23. Halsey and Bryan, *Admiral Halsey's Story,* pp. 105–06.

24. Prange interviews with Capt. Mitsuo Fuchida, 14 February and 27 November 1964.

25. Prange, *Miracle at Midway,* p. 87.

26. Masataka Chihaya, "Midget sub attack on Madagascar Island," unpublished study.

4. Don't Let Another Day Like This Come

1. Morison, *Coral Sea, Midway, and Submarine Actions,* pp. 65–68.

2. Chihaya, "Midget sub attack on Madagascar Island."

3. Prange interview with RADM Kameto Kuroshima, 28 November 1964; Prange, *Miracle at Midway,* pp. 23–24.

4. Prange, *Miracle at Midway,* pp, 160–66; letter, Capt. Jack Reid to Prange, 10 December 1966; diary of U.S. Naval Air Station, Midway Island; "The Battle of Midway, including the Aleutian Phase, June 3 to June 14, 1942, Strategical and Tactical Analysis," U.S. Naval War College, 1948.

5. Prange, *Miracle at Midway,* pp. 172–73; NAS diary; Midway Analysis; Enc. B, Contact Reports for Period May 30–June 6, 1942, to letter, CO, U.S. Naval Air Station, Midway Island, to CinCPAC, 18 June 1942, Subject: Report of Engagement with Enemy, Battle of Midway, May 30–June 7, 1942.

6. Prange, *Miracle at Midway,* pp. 19–20.

7. Ibid., pp. 31–32, 122–23; interview conducted by Robert E. Barde with Capt. Tatsukichi Miyo, 6 May 1966. (Prange files.)

8. Prange, *Miracle at Midway,* p. 123.

9. Ibid., pp. 181–82; Ryunosuke Kusaka, *Rengo Kantai* (Tokyo, 1952), p. 82.

10. Kusaka, *Rengo Kantai,* p. 10.

11. For an analysis of Japanese errors contributing to their defeat at Midway, see Prange, *Miracle at Midway,* chap. 40.

12. See, for example, ibid., chaps. 23–28, 32.

13. Prange interview with Admiral Raymond A. Spruance, 5 September 1964.

14. Prange, *Miracle at Midway,* pp. 319–20.

15. Ibid., pp. 30–31.

16. See listing, ibid., pp. 431–35; Morison, *Coral Sea, Midway, and Submarine Actions,* pp. 173–74.

17. U.S. Office of Naval Intelligence, *The Japanese Story of the Battle of Midway (A Translation) OPNAV P32–1002* (Washington, D.C., June 1947), p. 39.

18. Prange interview with Spruance, 5 September 1964.

19. Prange, *Miracle at Midway*, pp. 70, 147–48; material furnished Prange by Captain Sakamoto of the Japanese Self-Defense Agency's historical department, through Masataka Chihaya; Office of Naval Intelligence, *Japanese Story*, p. 6.

20. Prange, *Dec. 7, 1941*, pp. 375–77.

21. Morison, *Coral Sea, Midway and Submarine Actions*, pp. 215–16.

22. Samuel Eliot Morison, *Breaking the Bismarcks Barrier* (Boston, 1950), pp. 33–34.

23. Prange, *Miracle at Midway*, p. 367.

5. The Scene of a Fierce Battle

1. Morison, *Coral Sea, Midway, and Submarine Actions*, pp. 283–92.

2. Ibid., p. 293.

3. Ibid., pp. 294–95.

4. Samuel Eliot Morison, *The Struggle for Guadalcanal* (Boston, 1949), pp. 17–64. See also Potter, *Yamamoto*, pp. 272–75.

5. Morison, *Struggle for Guadalcanal*, p. 61.

6. Morison, *Coral Sea, Midway, and Submarine Actions*, p. 235.

7. Ibid., pp. 235–40.

8. Morison, *Struggle for Guadalcanal*, p. 67.

9. Ibid., p. 70; Prange, *Miracle at Midway*, p. 60.

10. Morison, *Struggle for Guadalcanal*, p. 70.

11. Ibid., p. 87.

12. Ibid., pp. 73–74.

13. Morison, *Coral Sea, Midway, and Submarine Actions*, pp. 240–41.

14. Morison, *Struggle for Guadalcanal*, pp. 69–73.

15. Ibid., pp. 80–81.

16. Ibid., p. 81.

17. Ibid., p. 83.

18. Ibid., pp. 97–102.

19. Ibid., p. 103.

20. Ibid., p. 88.

21. Ibid., pp. 104–05.

22. Ibid., p. 81.

23. Allied Translation and Interpreter Section Documents, Military Intelligence Section, Headquarters, Far East Command, ATIS Document No. 57582, statement of former Capt. Chiyosaburo Urayana, IJR, 15 April 1950.

24. Morison, *Struggle for Guadalcanal*, p. 106.

25. Morison, *Coral Sea, Midway and Submarine Actions*, p. 212.

26. Morison, *Struggle for Guadalcanal*, p. 109.

27. Ibid., p. 109.

28. Ibid., pp. 110–12.

29. Morison, *Breaking the Bismarcks Barrier*, p. 38.

30. Ibid., p. 38

31. Morison, *Struggle for Guadalcanal*, pp. 118–21.

32. Morison, *Breaking the Bismarcks Barrier*, p. 39.

33. In corrections and comments Chihaya forwarded to Goldstein on 7 May 1985, he advised, "We could not ascertain whether a torpedo or torpedoes hit an enemy carrier, but it was a fact that such a message was received." In his exhaustive account of the actions of 7 to 8 September 1942, Admiral Morison made no mention of such an incident. See Morison, *Struggle for Guadalcanal*, pp. 123–25.

34. Morison, *Struggle for Guadalcanal*, pp. 124–25.

35. Ibid., p. 125.

36. *Combat Chronology*, p. 40.

37. Morison, *Struggle for Guadalcanal*, p. 126.

38. Ibid., p. 127.

39. Ibid., p. 129.

40. Ibid., pp. 130–31.

41. Ibid., pp. 131–37.

42. Ibid., pp. 137–38.

43. Ibid., p. 138.

44. Ibid., p. 138.

45. Ibid., pp. 138–39.

6. The Chief of Staff Must Never Relax

1. Morison, *Coral Sea, Midway and Submarine Actions*, p. 227.

2. Ibid., p. 226.

3. ATIS Doc. No. 48740, Statement by Capt. Toshikazu Ohmae concerning Solomons Area Operations.

4. Morison, *Struggle for Guadalcanal*, pp. 142–46.

5. Ibid., p. 161.

6. Ibid., pp. 148–71.

7. Ibid., p. 148.

8. Ibid., p. 172; *The Army Air Forces in World War II*, vol. 4, *The Pacific: Guadalcanal to Saipan*, ed. W. F. Craven and J. L. Cate (Chicago 1950), p. 55.

9. Morison, *Struggle for Guadalcanal*, pp. 173–75; *Guadalcanal to Saipan*, pp. 55–56.

10. Morison, *Struggle for Guadalcanal*, p. 174.

11. Ibid., p. 176.

12. Ibid., p. 177.

13. Ibid., p. 182.

14. Ibid., p. 182n.

15. Ibid., pp. 190–91.

16. Ibid., p. 192.

17. Ibid., pp. 194–96.

18. Ibid., pp. 196–97.

19. Ibid., p. 198.

20. *Guadalcanal to Saipan*, p. 430.

21. Morison, *Struggle for Guadalcanal*, p. 205.

22. Ibid.

23. Ibid., pp. 204–14; Halsey and Bryan, *Admiral Halsey's Story*, pp. 121–22.

24. Morison, *Struggle for Guadalcanal,* pp. 199–224; *Combat Chronology,* p. 53; Halsey and Bryan, *Admiral Halsey's Story,* p. 122; Murata career brief.

25. Morison, *Struggle for Guadalcanal,* pp. 221–22

26. Morison, *Struggle for Guadalcanal,* p. 226.

27. Ibid., p. 226.

28. Ibid., p. 227.

29. Ibid.; Halsey and Bryan, *Admiral Halsey's Story,* pp. 124–25.

30. Morison, *Struggle for Guadalcanal,* p. 229.

31. Ibid., pp. 229–31; Halsey and Bryan, *Admiral Halsey's Story,* p. 125.

32. Morison, *Struggle for Guadalcanal,* pp. 233–58; Halsey and Bryan, *Admiral Halsey's Story,* pp. 126–27.

33. Morison, *Struggle for Guadalcanal,* pp. 244–48, 251, 259–61.

34. Ibid., pp. 233, 236, 260–61.

35. Ibid., pp. 262–63.

36. Ibid., p. 264.

37. Ibid., p. 261.

38. Ibid., pp. 266–69; Halsey and Bryan, *Admiral Halsey's Story,* p. 130.

39. Morison, *Struggle for Guadalcanal,* p. 234.

40. Ibid., p. 271.

41. Ibid., pp. 270–71.

42. Ibid., pp. 279–82.

43. Ibid., pp. 283–84.

44. Ibid., pp. 285–87; Halsey and Bryan, *Admiral Halsey's Story,* p. 131.

45. Morison, *Breaking the Bismarcks Barrier,* pp. 42–43.

46. Ibid., p. 44.

47. Ibid., p. 49.

48. Morison, *Struggle for Guadalcanal,* p. 293.

49. Ibid., pp. 295–315; Halsey and Bryan, *Admiral Halsey's Story,* pp. 132–35.

50. Morison, *Breaking the Bismarcks Barrier,* p. 49; *Reports of General MacArthur: The Campaigns of MacArthur in the Pacific,* vol. 1 (Washington, 1966), pp. 89–93.

51. Morison, *Struggle for Guadalcanal,* p. 318.

52. Ibid.

53. Ibid., p. 319.

54. *Combat Chronology,* p. 67.

55. Ibid., p. 67; Morison, *Struggle for Guadalcanal,* p. 334.

56. Morison, *Struggle for Guadalcanal,* p. 319.

57. Halsey and Bryan, *Admiral Halsey's Story,* pp. 140–41; Morison, *Breaking the Bismarcks Barrier,* pp. 90–91; Morison, *Struggle for Guadalcanal,* p. 322.

58. Morison, *Struggle for Guadalcanal,* pp. 319–20.

59. Ibid., p. 324.

60. Morison, *Breaking the Bismarcks Barrier,* p. 48.

61. Ibid., p. 49.

62. Prange interview with Watanabe, 25 May 1947.

63. Morison, *Breaking the Bismarcks Barrier,* p. 117.

64. Ibid., p. 125.

65. Ibid., p. 120.

66. Ibid., pp. 121–24.

67. Ibid., p. 125.

68. Ibid., pp. 125–26.

69. Ibid., pp. 126–27.

70. See entry for 18 April 1944.

71. Prange interview with Watanabe, 25 February 1949.

72. For an interesting account of the American preparations for and execution of this ambush, see Burke Davis, *Get Yamamoto* (New York, 1969).

73. Chihaya corrections and comments; Prange interview with Watanabe, 24 October 1949.

74. Potter, *Yamamoto*, p. 315.

75. Ugaki and Fukudome career briefs.

76. Prange interview with Watanabe, 25 November 1947.

7. Time Is Running Out

1. Samuel Eliot Morison, *Aleutians, Gilberts and Marshalls* (Boston, 1950), pp. 115–78, 201–78; Samuel Eliot Morison, *The Two-Ocean War* (Boston, 1963), pp. 313–14; VADM E. P. Forrestel, USN (Ret.), *Admiral Raymond A. Spruance, USN: A Study in Command* (Washington, 1966), pp. 113–17; Butow, *Tojo and the Coming of the War*, pp. 427–28.

2. Gordon W. Prange, *Target Tokyo* (New York, 1984), p. 130.

3. Butow, *Tojo and the Coming of the War*, p. 428.

4. Morison, *Breaking the Bismarcks Barrier*, pp. 410–11.

5. Butow, *Tojo and the Coming of the War*, p. 428; Leonard Mosley, *Hirohito: Emperor of Japan* (Englewood Cliffs, N.J., 1966), p. 273.

6. Samuel Eliot Morison, *New Guinea and the Marianas* (Boston, 1953), pp. 12–13.

7. *Combat Chronology*, pp. 289–94; Morison, *Breaking the Bismarcks Barrier*, pp. 444–46.

8. Morison, *New Guinea and the Marianas*, p. 10.

9. Morison, *Breaking the Bismarcks Barrier*, pp. 425–30.

10. Morison, *New Guinea and the Marianas*, p. 31.

11. *Combat Chronology*, p. 305.

12. Forrestel, *Admiral Raymond A. Spruance*, pp. 119–20; Morison, *New Guinea and the Marianas*, p. 31.

13. Morison, *New Guinea and the Marianas*, pp. 32–33.

14. Ibid., p. 13.

15. Ibid., p. 33.

16. Ibid., pp. 33–34.

17. Prange interviews with Capt. Mitsuo Fuchida, 18, 20, and 22 February 1964; Morison, *New Guinea and the Marianas*, pp. 54–55.

18. Morison, *New Guinea and the Marianas*, pp. 32–33.

19. For details of the ambush, see Davis, *Get Yamamoto!*, pp. 3–20, 109–74.

20. Morison, *New Guinea and the Marianas*, p. 9.

21. Forrestel, *Admiral Raymond A. Spruance*, p. 121.

22. Morison, *New Guinea and the Marianas*, pp. 36–37.

23. Ibid., p. 38.

24. Ibid., pp. 8, 38–41.

25. Ibid., p. 39.

26. Morison, *Two-Ocean War,* pp. 330–31.

27. Morison, *New Guinea and the Marianas,* p. 217.

28. *Guadalcanal to Saipan,* p. 626.

29. Ibid., pp. 628–29; *Campaigns of MacArthur in the Pacific,* vol. 1, pp. 150–51.

30. Morison, *New Guinea and the Marianas,* p. 220.

31. Ibid., p. 220.

32. Ibid., pp. 103–07; Morison, *Two-Ocean War,* p. 320.

33. Morison, *New Guinea and the Marianas,* pp. 117–18.

8. Awakened from a Dream of Victory

1. Morison, *New Guinea and the Marianas,* p. 119.

2. Ibid., p. 120.

3. Ibid., p. 120.

4. Ibid., pp. 123–24.

5. Ibid., pp. 120–24.

6. Ibid., p. 220.

7. Forrestel, *Admiral Raymond A. Spruance,* p. 126.

8. Morison, *New Guinea and the Marianas,* pp. 227–28.

9. Chihaya comments and corrections.

10. *Guadalcanal to Saipan,* p. 638.

11. Morison, *New Guinea and the Marianas,* p. 220.

12. Ibid., p. 125.

13. Ibid., p. 120.

14. *Guadalcanal to Saipan,* p. 638.

15. Morison, *New Guinea and the Marianas,* p. 126.

16. Ibid., p. 127.

17. Ibid., p. 220.

18. Ibid., pp. 174–75.

19. Ibid., pp. 174–75.

20. Ibid., p. 175.

21. Ibid., p. 407.

22. Ibid., p. 179.

23. Ibid., pp. 180–81.

24. Ibid., pp. 182, 407.

25. Ibid., pp. 174–75.

26. *The Army Air Forces in World War II,* vol. 5, *The Pacific: Matterhorn to Nagasaki,* ed. W. F. Craven and J. L. Cate (Chicago, 1953), pp. 99–101; *Combat Chronology,* p. 372.

27. Morison, *New Guinea and the Marianas,* p. 182.

28. Ibid., pp. 237–40.

29. Ibid., p. 241; Forrestel, *Admiral Raymond A. Spruance,* p. 135.

30. Morison, *New Guinea and the Marianas,* p. 207.

31. Ibid., pp. 216–17.

32. Ibid., pp. 269–71.

33. Ibid., pp. 268–71; Forrestel, *Admiral Raymond A. Spruance,* p. 139.

34. Morison, *New Guinea and the Marianas,* pp. 271–72.

35. Ibid., pp. 278–82; Forrestel, *Admiral Raymond A. Spruance,* p. 140; Masatake Okumiya and Jiro Horikoshi, with Martin Caidin, *Zero!,* (New York, 1956), pp. 235–36.

36. Morison, *New Guinea and the Marianas,* pp. 320–21.

37. Forrestel, *Admiral Raymond A. Spruance,* p. 142.

38. Ibid., p. 143.

39. Morison, *New Guinea and the Marianas,* p. 295.

40. Ibid., p. 321.

41. Ibid., pp. 295–96; Forrestel, *Admiral Raymond A. Spruance,* p. 143.

42. Morison, *New Guinea and the Marianas,* pp. 311–13.

43. Ibid., pp. 312–13.

44. Ibid., pp. 335–37.

45. Ibid., p. 337.

46. *Matterhorn to Nagasaki,* pp. 104–05.

47. Morison, *New Guinea and the Marianas,* p. 353.

48. Ibid., pp. 381–82.

49. See, for example, Hull, *Memoirs of Cordell Hull,* p. 1328.

50. Morison, *New Guinea and the Marianas,* pp. 323–24; Butow, *Tojo and the Coming of the War,* pp. 432–33; statement by ex-General Shigeru Hasanuma (ADC to Emperor Hirohito), 30 March 1950, ATIS Document No. 58225.

51. Morison, *New Guinea and the Marianas,* p. 374.

52. Statement of Marquis Yasumasa Matsudaira, 5 August 1949, ATIS Document No. 61636.

53. Morison, *New Guinea and the Marianas,* pp. 361–62.

54. Chihaya comments and corrections.

55. Morison, *New Guinea and the Marianas,* p. 367.

56. Ibid., pp. 338, 369.

57. *Matterhorn to Nagasaki,* pp. 107–10.

58. Morison, *New Guinea and the Marianas,* pp. 400–01.

59. Samuel Eliot Morison, *Leyte* (Boston, 1970), pp. 70, 160–61; statement by ex-Col. Takushiro Hattori, 1 June 1948, ATIS Document No. 50735; Prange interviews with Fuchida, 24 and 25 February 1964. At the time of *Sho,* Captain Fuchida was air staff officer of the Combined Fleet and actively engaged in the project.

60. *Matterhorn to Nagasaki,* p. 114.

9. Another Complete Defeat

1. Cmdr. Edward P. Stafford, USN, *The Big E: The Story of the U.S.S. Enterprise* (New York, 1962), pp. 364–66.

2. Ibid., p. 365.

3. *Combat Chronology,* p. 443.

4. Stafford, *The Big E,* pp. 366–67.

5. Ibid., pp. 369–70; Halsey and Bryan, *Admiral Halsey's Story,* p. 198.

6. Halsey and Bryan, *Admiral Halsey's Story,* pp. 197–99.

7. *Combat Chronology,* pp. 449–51.

8. Halsey and Bryan, *Admiral Halsey's Story,* pp. 199–200.

9. Morison, *Leyte,* pp. 19–29, 34–36.

10. Ibid., pp. 44–45.

11. Halsey and Bryan, *Admiral Halsey's Story,* p. 202.

12. Ibid., p. 202.

13. Morison, *Leyte,* pp. 47–49.

14. Admiral Frederick C. Sherman, USN, *Combat Command* (New York, 1950), pp. 274–75.

15. Chihaya comments and corrections.

16. Morison, *Leyte,* pp. 424–28.

17. Ibid., pp. 27–28.

18. Ibid., p. 87.

19. Ibid., pp. 90–91.

20. Ibid., p. 90.

21. Ibid., p. 430.

22. Ibid., p. 92.

23. Ibid., p. 93.

24. Ibid., p. 93

25. Ibid., p. 93

26. Ibid., p. 93

27. Ibid., p. 93

28. Ibid., pp. 94–96; Sherman, *Combat Command,* pp. 276–77; Stafford, *The Big E,* p. 385; Halsey and Bryan, *Admiral Halsey's Story,* pp. 205–06.

29. Morison, *Two-Ocean War,* p. 429; Statement by ex-Col. Takushiro Hattori, 6 October 1948, ATIS Document No. 56425.

30. Morison, *Leyte,* p. 94.

31. Chihaya comments and corrections.

32. Morison, *Leyte,* pp. 98–99; Halsey and Bryan, *Admiral Halsey's Story,* pp. 206–07.

33. *Matterhorn to Nagasaki,* pp. 137–38; *Combat Chronology,* p. 474.

34. Stafford, *The Big E,* pp. 385–89; Morison, *Leyte,* p. 100.

35. Morison, *Leyte,* p. 101.

36. Ibid., p. 101.

37. Ibid., p. 101.

38. Ibid., pp. 101–02; Halsey and Bryan, *Admiral Halsey's Story,* pp. 207–08.

39. Morison, *Leyte,* p. 61.

40. Morison, *Two-Ocean War,* p. 429; Halsey and Bryan, *Admiral Halsey's Story,* p. 206.

41. Morison, *Leyte,* pp. 102–04; Halsey and Bryan, *Admiral Halsey's Story,* pp. 206–09.

42. Stafford, *The Big E,* pp. 389–96.

43. Morison, *Leyte,* pp. 118–19.

44. Ibid., p. 431.

45. Ibid., p. 106; Stafford, *The Big E,* pp. 390–95.

46. Morison, *Leyte,* pp. 123–27.

47. Ibid., pp. 130–31; *Reports of General MacArthur,* vol. 1, pp. 181–82.

48. Morison, *Leyte,* pp. 424–28.

49. Ibid., pp. 140–41.

50. Ibid., p. 431.

51. Ibid., pp. 170–72; Sherman, *Combat Command,* pp. 287–90.

52. Morison, *Leyte,* p. 172.

53. Ibid., pp. 173–74.

54. Ibid., p. 172.

55. Morison, *Two-Ocean War,* pp. 470–71.

56. Morison, *Leyte,* p. 186.

57. Ibid., pp. 176–86; Morison, *Two-Ocean War,* pp. 439–41; Sherman, *Combat Command,* pp. 290–96.

58. Morison, *Leyte,* pp. 193–97, 319, 322–28; Halsey and Bryan, *Admiral Halsey's Story,* pp. 216–22; Morison, *Two-Ocean War,* pp. 463–70; Sherman, *Combat Command,* pp. 309–11.

59. Morison, *Leyte,* pp. 245–48.

60. Ibid., pp. 252–53.

61. Ibid., p. 250.

62. Ibid., pp. 284–85, 267.

63. Ibid., pp. 274–75.

64. Ibid., pp. 284, 288, 330.

65. Ibid., pp. 272–74.

66. Ibid., pp. 279, 308.

67. Ibid., p. 309.

68. Ibid., p. 281.

69. Ibid., pp. 198–241.

70. Ibid., p. 230.

71. Ibid., pp. 317–38.

72. Ibid., p. 311; *Combat Chronology,* p. 482.

73. Morison, *Leyte,* pp. 311–12.

74. Ibid., pp. 300–03.

75. Ibid., pp. 430–32.

76. Ibid., pp. 341–42.

77. Morison, *Leyte,* pp. 342–44.

78. Ibid., pp. 345–46.

79. Okumiya et al., *Zero!,* pp. 271–72.

80. Morison, *Leyte,* p. 344.

81. Ibid., pp. 351–52.

82. Ibid., pp, 347–48; Sherman, *Combat Command,* p. 317.

83. Morison, *Leyte,* pp. 348–39; Halsey and Bryan, *Admiral Halsey's Story,* p. 230; Sherman, *Combat Command,* pp. 317–18.

84. *Combat Chronology,* p. 489.

85. Morison, *Leyte,* pp. 408–09.

86. Ibid., p. 353.

87. Ibid., p. 352.

88. Ibid., p. 352.

89. Ibid., p. 353.

90. Ibid., pp. 355–56.

91. Ibid., p. 356.

92. Ibid., p. 410.

93. *Matterhorn to Nagasaki,* p. 141; Okumiya et al., *Zero!,* p. 272.

94. *Matterhorn to Nagasaki,* pp. 558–59; *Combat Chronology,* p. 505; Okumiya et al., *Zero!,* p. 272.

95. *Combat Chronology,* p. 508.

96. Morison, *Leyte,* pp. 410–11; Chihaya comments and corrections.

97. Okumiya et al., *Zero!,* p. 272.

10. Such a Miserable Situation

1. Morison, *Leyte,* pp. 380–88.

2. Ibid., p. 390; Halsey and Bryan, *Admiral Halsey's Story,* pp. 235–36; Morison, *Two-Ocean War,* p. 477.

3. Morison, *Two-Ocean War,* pp. 477–78.

4. *Combat Chronology,* p. 532; Okumiya et al., *Zero!* p. 274.

5. Morison, *Two-Ocean War,* p. 478.

6. Ibid., pp. 480–84.

7. Ibid., p. 484.

8. *Japan: The Official Guide,* ed. Nobutake Ike (Tokyo, 1941), p. 137; *Combat Chronology,* p. 546.

9. Halsey and Bryan, *Admiral Halsey's Story,* pp. 244–45; Morison, *Two-Ocean War,* p. 486; Sherman, *Combat Command,* pp. 326–29.

10. Samuel Eliot Morison, *Victory in the Pacific* (Boston, 1960), pp. 103–04; Chihaya comments and corrections.

11. Morison, *Two-Ocean War,* p. 488.

12. Ibid., p. 488.

13. *Combat Chronology,* p. 568.

14. Morison, *Victory in the Pacific,* pp. 20–21.

15. Ibid., pp. 25–27, 373.

16. Forrestel, *Admiral Raymond A. Spruance,* p. 173; Morison, *Victory in the Pacific,* pp. 22–25; Sherman, *Combat Command,* pp. 336–37.

17. Morison, *Victory in the Pacific,* p. 26.

18. Morison, *Two-Ocean War,* pp. 488–89.

19. Forrestel, *Admiral Raymond A. Spruance,* p. 173.

20. Morison, *Victory in the Pacific,* p. 25.

21. Ibid., pp. 28–32; Forrestel, *Admiral Raymond A. Spruance,* pp. 176–77.

22. Morison, *Victory in the Pacific,* pp. 35–44; Forrestel, *Admiral Raymond A. Spruance,* pp. 177–78; Morison, *Two-Ocean War,* pp. 518–20.

23. *Combat Chronology,* p. 576.

24. Morison, *Victory in the Pacific,* pp. 53–54.

25. Ibid., pp. 54–56; Forrestel, *Admiral Raymond A. Spruance,* p. 178; Sherman, *Combat Command,* p. 341.

26. Morison, *Victory in the Pacific,* p. 57.

27. Ibid., pp. 57–58.

28. Ibid., pp. 61–63.

29. *Combat Chronology,* p. 585.

30. Morison, *Victory in the Pacific,* p. 58; Forrestel, *Admiral Raymond A. Spruance,* p. 183; Sherman, *Combat Command,* p. 342.

31. Forrestel, *Admiral Raymond A. Spruance,* p. 183.

32. Morison, *Victory in the Pacific,* p. 65.

33. *Reports of General MacArthur,* vol. 2, pt. 2, pp. 593–94; Okumiya et al., *Zero!,* pp. 276–77.

34. Chihaya comments and corrections.

35. Forrestel, *Admiral Raymond A. Spruance,* p. 190.

36. Ibid., p. 190; Morison, *Victory in the Pacific,* p. 94.

37. Morison, *Victory in the Pacific,* p. 94; Stafford, *The Big E,* pp. 441–44; Forrestel, *Admiral Raymond A. Spruance,* pp. 190–91.

38. Morison, *Victory in the Pacific,* p. 94.

39. Ibid., pp. 95–97; Forrestel, *Admiral Raymond A. Spruance,* p. 192; Stafford, *The Big E,* pp. 444–45.

40. Stafford, *The Big E,* pp. 446–49; Morison, *Victory in the Pacific,* pp. 99–100.

41. Forrestel, *Admiral Raymond A. Spruance,* p. 192.

42. Morison, *Victory in the Pacific,* p. 100.

43. Interview with four ex-IJN officers (Sadatoshi Tomioka, Toshikazu Ohmae, Mitsuo Fuchida, and Yoshimori Terai), 9 September 1949, ATIS Document No. 50572. Hereafter cited as Joint Interview.

44. Forrestel, *Admiral Raymond A. Spruance,* p. 197.

45. Morison, *Victory in the Pacific,* pp. 119–20.

46. Ibid., p. 117.

47. Ibid., pp. 115–16, 124.

48. Ibid., pp. 133–34.

49. *Combat Chronology,* pp. 610, 614; *Matterhorn to Nagasaki,* pp. 631, 667–68.

50. Morison, *Victory in the Pacific,* p. 134.

51. Okumiya et al., *Zero!,* p. 283.

11. Pressed Beneath the Pole Star

1. Morison, *Victory in the Pacific,* pp. 170–71; Forrestel, *Admiral Raymond A. Spruance,* p. 200.

2. Forrestel, *Admiral Raymond A. Spruance,* pp. 199–200; Morison, *Victory in the Pacific,* pp. 154–55, 175, 390.

3. Morison, *Victory in the Pacific,* pp. 176–77.

4. Ibid., p. 179.

5. Prange interview with Fuchida, 28 February 1944; joint interview.

6. Statement by Matsudaira, 5 August 1949, ATIS Document No. 61636, and by Marquis Koichi Kido, 20 December 1949, ATIS Document No. 62131.

7. Morison, *Victory in the Pacific,* pp. 199, 382–84.

8. Ibid., p. 199.

9. Ibid., pp. 195–97, 390; Forrestel, *Admiral Raymond A. Spruance,* p. 203.

10. Prange interview with Fuchida, 28 February 1964; Morison, *Victory in the Pacific,* p. 200.

11. Morison, *Victory in the Pacific,* p. 203.

12. Ibid., pp. 205–09.

13. Ibid., pp. 197, 209, 390–91.

14. *Combat Chronology,* p. 620.

15. Ibid., p. 621.

16. Morison, *Victory in the Pacific*, pp. 217, 221–22.

17. Ibid., p. 215.

18. Ibid., pp. 210–11; Stafford, *The Big E*, pp. 453–56.

19. Morison, *Victory in the Pacific*, pp. 222–30.

20. Ibid., p. 214.

21. Forrestel, *Admiral Raymond A. Spruance*, p. 206.

22. Morison, *Victory in the Pacific*, pp. 247–48.

23. Ibid., p. 248.

24. Ibid., pp. 235–38, 248.

25. Ibid., p. 248.

26. *Combat Chronology*, p. 630.

27. Statement by Lt. Gen. Torashiro Kawabe, 9 September 1949, ATIS Document No. 50569; Prange interview with Fuchida, 29 February 1949.

28. Morison, *Victory in the Pacific*, p. 241.

29. *Combat Chronology*, p. 632.

30. Ibid., p. 635.

31. Ibid., p. 636.

32. Morison, *Victory in the Pacific*, p. 244.

33. *Matterhorn to Nagasaki*, p. 649.

34. Morison, *Victory in the Pacific*, pp. 238–39, 243.

35. Ibid., pp. 239, 244.

36. Ibid., pp. 247, 391.

37. Ibid., pp. 276, 391.

38. Ibid., pp. 251–53.

39. Ibid., pp. 253–56, 264–65, 267.

40. *Matterhorn to Nagasaki*, p. 649; *Combat Chronology*, p. 646.

41. *Combat Chronology*, pp. 647–48.

42. Ibid., p. 648.

43. Morison, *Victory in the Pacific*, pp. 265, 268–69.

44. Ibid., pp. 256–58, 262–63; Sherman, *Combat Command*, p. 361; Stafford, *The Big E*, pp. 458–59.

45. *Matterhorn to Nagasaki*, pp. 649–50; *Combat Chronology*, p. 649.

46. Stafford, *The Big E*, pp. 460–63; Morison, *Victory in the Pacific*, pp. 269–70; Forrestel, *Admiral Raymond A. Spruance*, p. 210.

47. Morison, *Victory in the Pacific*, p. 258.

48. Ibid., pp. 263–64; Sherman, *Combat Command*, pp. 361–62; Stafford, *The Big E*, pp. 464–67.

49. *Japan: The Official Guide*, pp. 398–99.

50. *Matterhorn to Nagasaki*, p. 638; *Combat Chronology*, p. 654.

51. Morison, *Victory in the Pacific*, pp. 270–71.

52. Ibid., pp. 271–72.

53. *Matterhorn to Nagasaki*, pp. 638–39; *Combat Chronology*, p. 655.

54. Morison, *Victory in the Pacific*, pp. 259–60; Forrestel, *Admiral Raymond A. Spruance*, p. 215; Halsey and Bryan, *Admiral Halsey's Story*, pp. 250–51.

55. Morison, *Victory in the Pacific*, pp. 260–61.

56. *Combat Chronology*, p. 656.

57. Ibid., p. 656.

12. To Die as a Samurai

1. *Matterhorn to Nagasaki*, pp. 640–41; *Combat Chronology*, p. 658.

2. Halsey and Bryan, *Admiral Halsey's Story*, p. 253; Sherman, *Combat Command*, p. 362; Morison, *Victory in the Pacific*, p. 298; *Combat Chronology*, p. 658.

3. Halsey and Bryan, *Admiral Halsey's Story*, p. 253; Morison, *Victory in the Pacific*, p. 298; Sherman, *Combat Command*, p. 362.

4. Morison, *Victory in the Pacific*, p. 392.

5. Ibid., pp. 298–99.

6. *Matterhorn to Nagasaki*, p. 641; *Combat Chronology*, p. 649.

7. Morison, *Victory in the Pacific*, pp. 299, 307; Halsey and Bryan, *Admiral Halsey's Story*, pp. 253–54.

8. *Combat Chronology*, p. 659.

9. Morison, *Victory in the Pacific*, pp. 273–74.

10. *Combat Chronology*, p. 660; *Matterhorn to Nagasaki*, pp. 641–42.

11. Morison, *Victory in the Pacific*, p. 274.

12. Ibid., p. 307.

13. Ibid., p. 307.

14. Ibid., p. 274.

15. *Matterhorn to Nagasaki*, p. 642; *Combat Chronology*, p. 663.

16. *Combat Chronology*, p. 664; *Matterhorn to Nagasaki*, p. 674.

17. Morison, *Victory in the Pacific*, p. 276.

18. Ibid., p. 273.

19. *Combat Chronology*, p. 665; *Matterhorn to Nagasaki*, p. 674.

20. Halsey and Bryan, *Admiral Halsey's Story*, p. 254.

21. Morison, *Victory in the Pacific*, pp. 279, 392.

22. Ibid., pp. 279, 392.

23. Forrestel, *Admiral Raymond A. Spruance*, p. 209.

24. *Combat Chronology*, p. 668; *Matterhorn to Nagasaki*, pp. 674–75.

25. *Combat Chronology*, p. 669.

26. Ibid., p. 670.

27. Ibid., p. 670; *Matterhorn to Nagasaki*, p. 675.

28. *Combat Chronology*, p. 670; *Matterhorn to Nagasaki*, p. 675.

29. *Combat Chronology*, p. 671.

30. Ibid., p. 671.

31. Ibid., p. 671.

32. Halsey and Bryan, *Admiral Halsey's Story*, pp. 255–57; Morison, *Victory in the Pacific*, p. 310.

33. Morison, *Victory in the Pacific*, p. 310.

34. *Combat Chronology*, p. 673.

35. Morison, *Victory in the Pacific*, pp. 310–11; Halsey and Bryan, *Admiral Halsey's Story*, pp. 257–59.

36. *Combat Chronology*, p. 674.

37. Morison, *Victory in the Pacific*, pp. 311–13; Sherman, *Combat Command*, p. 366; Halsey and Bryan, *Admiral Halsey's Story*, pp. 259–60.

38. Morison, *Victory in the Pacific*, pp. 312–13.

39. *Combat Chronology*, p. 676.

40. Morison, *Victory in the Pacific*, p. 314.

41. *Combat Chronology,* p. 676.

42. Morison, *Victory in the Pacific,* p. 314.

43. *Combat Chronology,* p. 677.

44. Morison, *Victory in the Pacific,* p. 316; Halsey and Bryan, *Admiral Halsey's Story,* pp. 262–63; Sherman, *Combat Command,* p. 367.

45. Morison, *Victory in the Pacific,* pp. 318, 331; Halsey and Bryan, *Admiral Halsey's Story,* p. 264; Sherman, *Combat Command,* p. 367.

46. *Combat Chronology,* p. 680.

47. Ibid., p. 681.

48. Morison, *Victory in the Pacific,* pp. 280, 319–24.

49. See *Reports of General MacArthur,* vol. 2, pt. 2, pp. 703–04, for full text of the Potsdam Declaration; Toshikazu Kase, *Journey to the Missouri* (New Haven, 1950), pp. 207–10.

50. *Combat Chronology,* p. 682.

51. Morison, *Victory in the Pacific,* p. 332; Sherman, *Combat Command,* p. 368.

52. *Combat Chronology,* p. 682.

53. Ibid., p. 683.

54. Ibid., p. 684.

55. Statement by ex-Lt. Gen. Torashiro Kawabe, 23 August 1948, ATIS Document No. 61539; Okumiya et al., *Zero!,* p. 288; *Matterhorn to Nagasaki,* p. 716.

56. *Combat Chronology,* p. 686.

57. Morison, *Victory in the Pacific,* pp. 332–33.

58. *Combat Chronology,* p. 686; *Matterhorn to Nagasaki,* p. 675.

59. Morison, *Victory in the Pacific,* p. 333; Halsey and Bryan, *Admiral Halsey's Story,* p. 268.

60. For an excellent account of these negotiations, see Kase, *Journey to the Missouri,* pp. 198–265.

61. Statements by Shigenori Togo, 17 May 1949, ATIS Document No. 50304 and 28 November 1949, ATIS Document No. 54562; Sumihasa Ikeda, 27 December 1949, ATIS Document No. 54483; *Reports of General MacArthur,* vol. 2, pt. 2, pp. 716–17.

62. Morison, *Victory in the Pacific,* p. 334.

63. *Combat Chronology,* p. 688.

64. Morison, *Victory in the Pacific,* pp. 334–35.

SELECTED BIBLIOGRAPHY

Unpublished Sources

(The following unpublished sources are located in the files of Gordon W. Prange.)

Allied Translation and Interpreter Section Documents, Military Intelligence Section, Headquarters, Far East Command. Statements by:

Former General Shigeru Hasanuma, 30 March 1950, Doc. No. 58225

Former Col. Takushiro Hattori, 1 June 1948, Doc. No. 50735

Sumihasa Ideda, 27 December 1949, Doc. No. 54483

Former Lt. Gen. Torashiro Kawabe, 9 September 1949, Doc. No. 50569

Former Lt. Gen. Torashiro Kawabe, 23 August 1948, Doc. No. 61539

Former Marquis Koichi Kido, 20 December 1949, Doc. No. 62131

Former Marquis Yasumasa Matsudaira, 5 August 1949, Doc. No. 61636

Former Capt. Toshikazu Ohmae, 20 December 1948, Doc. No. 48740

Shigenori Togo, 17 May 1949, Doc. No. 50304

Shigenori Togo, 28 May 1949, Doc. No. 54562

Former Capt. Chiyosaburo Urayana, 15 April 1950, Doc. No. 57582

Interview with four ex-IJN officers (Sadatoshi Tomioka, Toshikazu Ohmae, Mitsuo Fuchida and Yoshimori Terai, 9 September 1949, Doc. No. 50572

Chihaya, Masataka, "Midget Sub Attack on Madagascar Island."

Diary of Capt. Yoshitake Miwa, 29 April 1942.

Diary of RADM Giichi Nakahara, 2 November 1941

Encl. B. Contact Reports for period 30 May to 6 June 1942 to letter, U.S. Naval Air Station, Midway Island, to CinCPAC, 18 June 1942, Subject: Report on Engagement with Enemy, Battle of Midway, 30 May to 7 June 1942.

Letter, Capt. Jack Reid to Gordon W. Prange, 10 December 1966. Material furnished Prange by Capt. Sakamoto of the Japanese Self-Defense Agency's Historical Department, through Masataka Chihaya.

707

Notes and Comments by Masataka Chihaya concerning the manuscript of *Fading Victory*.

Report on the Pearl Harbor operation which Capt. Minoru Genda prepared for Prange, May 1947.

State Department Memorandum of Conversations, 14 and 16 April 1941, Papers of Cordell Hull, Library of Congress, Box 60.

Interviews

(With one exception, asterisked, these interviews were conducted by Gordon W. Prange. All are in his files.)

Capt. Mitsuo Fuchida: 24 and 27 July 1947, 29 February 1949, 14, 18, 20, 22, 24, 25, 28 February 1964, 27 November 1964.

VADM Zenshiro Hoshina, 7 June 1951.

RADM Kameto Kuroshima: 10 and 12 May 1948, 14 June 1948, 28 November 1964.

VADM Ryunosuke Kusaka: 24 April 1947, 24 June 1947, 23 August 1947, 2 December 1964.

*Capt. Tatsukichi Miyo, 6 May 1966. (Conducted by Robert W. Barde.)

VADM Jisaburo Ozawa, 22 December 1948.

Admiral Raymond A. Spruance, 5 September 1964.

Capt. Eijiro Suzuki, 12 June 1948.

Capt. Itaru Tachibana, 9 August 1950.

Admiral Nishizo Tsukahara: 6 and 14 May 1949.

Capt. Yasuji Watanabe: 25 May 1947, 25 November 1947, January 1948 (no day given), 25 February 1949, 15 September 1949, 24 October 1949, 7 and 14 November 1949, 25 September 1964, 7 January 1965.

Published Sources

The Army Air Forces in World War II: Combat Chronology, 1941–45. Comp. Kit C. Carter and Robert Mueller. Washington, D.C.: U.S. Government Printing Office, 1974.

The Army Air Forces in World War II. Vol. 4, *The Pacific: Guadalcanal to Saipan.* Ed. W. F. Craven and J. L. Cate. Chicago: University of Chicago Press, 1950.

The Army Air Forces in World War II. Vol. 5, *The Pacific: Matterhorn to Nagasaki.* Ed. W. F. Craven and J. L. Cate. Chicago: University of Chicago Press, 1953.

Butow, Robert J. C. *Tojo and the Coming of the War*. Princeton, N.J.: Princeton University Press, 1961.

Byas, Hugh. *Government by Assassination*. New York: Alfred A. Knopf, 1942.

Coffey, Thomas M. *Imperial Tragedy*. New York: World Publishing Co., 1974.

Craig, William. *The Fall of Japan*. New York: Dell Publishing Co., 1967.

Davis, Burke. *Get Yamamoto*. New York: Random House, 1969.

————. Diary of U.S. Naval Air Station, Midway Island: "The Battle of Midway, including the Aleutian Phase, June 3 to June 14, 1942, Strategical and Tactical Analysis." U.S. Naval War College, 1948.

Forrestel, VADM E. P., USN (Ret.). *Admiral Raymond A. Spruance, USN: A Study in Command*. Washington, D.C.: U.S. Government Printing Office, 1966.

Fuchida, Mitsuo. *Shinjuwan Sakusen No Shinso: Watakushi Wa Shinjuwan Juko No Ita*. Nara, Japan: Yamato Taimusa Sha, 1949.

Fuchida, Mitsuo and Masatake Okumiya. *Midway: The Battle That Doomed Japan*. Annapolis: U.S. Naval Institute, 1955.

Fukudome, Shigeru. *Shikan: Shinjuwan Kogeki*. Tokyo: Jiyu Ajiya-sha, 1955.

Genda, Minoru. *Shinjuwan Sakusen Kaikoroku*. Tokyo: Yomiuri Shimbun, 1972.

Grew, Joseph C. *Ten Years in Japan*. New York: Simon & Schuster, 1944.

Halsey, Fleet Admiral William F., USN and Lt. Cmdr. J. Bryan III, USNR, *Admiral Halsey's Story*. New York: McGraw-Hill Book Co., 1947.

Hattori, Takushiro. *Daitoa senso zen-shi ("The Complete History of the Great East Asia War")*. Tokyo: Hara Shobo, 1953.

Hull, Cordell. *The Memoirs of Cordell Hull*, vol. 2. New York: Macmillan Co., 1948.

Ike, Nobutake, ed. and trans. *Japan's Decision for War: Records of the 1941 Policy Conferences*. Stanford, Calif.: Stanford University Press, 1967.

————. *Japan: The Official Guide*. Tokyo: Bureau of Tourist Industry, 1941.

Kase, Toshikazu. *Journey to the Missouri*. New Haven, Conn.: Yale University Press, 1950.

Kusaka, Ryunosuke. *Rengo Kantai*. Tokyo: Mainichi Shimbun, 1952.

Morison, Samuel Eliot. *Aleutians, Gilberts and Marshalls*. Boston: Little, Brown & Co., 1950.

————. *Breaking the Bismarcks Barrier*. Boston: Little, Brown & Co., 1950.

————. *Coral Sea, Midway and Submarine Actions*. Boston: Little, Brown & Co., 1949.

————. *Leyte*. Boston: Little, Brown & Co., 1970.

————. *New Guinea and the Marianas*. Boston: Little, Brown & Co., 1953.

————. *The Rising Sun in the Pacific*. Boston: Little, Brown & Co., 1950.

————. *The Struggle for Guadalcanal*. Boston: Little, Brown & Co., 1949.

————. *The Two-Ocean War*. Boston: Little, Brown & Co., 1963.

————. *Victory in the Pacific*. Boston: Little, Brown & Co., 1960.

Mosley, Leonard. *Hirohito: Emperor of Japan*. Englewood Cliffs, N.J.: Prentice-Hall, Inc., 1966.

Okumiya, Masatake and Jiro Horikoshi, with Martin Caiden. *Zero!*. New York: E. P. Dutton & Co. Inc., 1956.

Perkins, Dexter, "Was Roosevelt Wrong?" *Virginia Quarterly Review*, Summer 1954, pp. 355–72.

Potter, John Deane. *Yamamoto: The Man Who Menaced America*. New York: Viking Press, 1965.

Prange, Gordon W. *At Dawn We Slept*. New York: McGraw-Hill Book Co., 1981.

————. *Dec. 7, 1941: The Day the Japanese Attacked Pearl Harbor*. New York: McGraw-Hill Book Co., 1987.

————. *Miracle at Midway*. New York: McGraw-Hill Book Co., 1982.

————. *Pearl Harbor: Verdict of History*. New York: McGraw-Hill Book Co., 1986.

————. *Target Toyko*. New York: McGraw-Hill Book Co., 1984.

Reports of General MacArthur: The Campaigns of MacArthur in the Pacific, vol. 1. Washington, D.C.: U.S. Government Printing Office, 1966.

Reports of General MacArthur: Japanese Operations in the Southwest Pacific Area, vol. 2, pt. 2. Washington, D.C.: U.S. Government Printing Office, 1966.

Sakamaki, Kazu. *I Attacked Pearl Harbor*. New York: Association Press, 1949.

Sherman, Admiral Frederick C., USN. *Combat Command*. New York: E. P. Dutton & Co., Inc., 1950.

Stafford, Cmdr. Edward P., USN. *The Big E: The Story of the U.S.S. Enterprise*. New York: Random House, 1962.

Toland, John. *The Rising Sun*. New York: Random House, 1970.

United States Department of State. *Papers Relating to the Foreign Relations of the United States: Japan, 1931–1941*, vol. 2. Washington, D.C., 1943.

U.S. Office of Naval Intelligence, *The Japanese Story of the Battle of Midway (A Translation)*, OPNAV P32-100, Washington, D.C.: U.S. Government Printing Office, 1947.

United States Strategic Bombing Survey (Pacific). *The Campaigns of the Pacific War*. Washington, D.C.: U.S. Government Printing Office, 1946.

Watts, A. J. and B. G. Gordon. *The Imperial Japanese Navy*. New York: Doubleday & Co., 1971.

INDEX

711